appeared around 1800 in Paris. Early "velos" were powered by pushing on the ground with the feet and were not steerable until 1818. Velos were powered using treadles and rods by 1840 and by foot pedals in 1861. Finally, in approximately 1869, a chain was used to transmit power, creating a machine that is recognizable as a modern bicycle.

In other situations, an invention's date was established by determining when the device or process was first depicted in illustrations or mentioned in writings. In yet other cases, the date a patent was issued for the process or device is indicated. Obviously, the dates of recent discoveries are accurate as a result of better record keeping and documentation.

In some cases, two dates are shown matching the two places that those events/discoveries (or variations of the technology) took place. This may be useful in understanding the time that elapsed for a given technology in moving from one locale to another (technology diffusion) or in evolving separately in two different societies.

Event	Date
Chronometer	1735
Circumnavigation of globe	1589
Cities	8000 BCE
Clock (mechanical)	1300
Clock (pendulum)	1656
Clock (water)	1400 BCE
Cloning (fish)	1981
Coca-Cola	1866
Codes/ciphers	2000 BCE
Coffee	1400
Coins	700 BCE
Compact discs	1982
Compass	300 BCE
Computer (mechanical)	1832
Computer (electromechanical)	1942
Computer (electronic)	1946
Computer (digital/binary)	1938
Computer (personal)	1975
Computer (programmable)	1941
Concrete	200 BCE
Contact lens	1887
Container shipping (ships/trucks)	1954
Contraception	2000 BCE
Contraceptive pill	1956
Contracts (written)	2700 BCE
Copper	6400 BCE
Copying (Xerography)	1937
Crank handle	100 BCE
Crayons (Crayola)	1902

Event	Date
Crop rotation (theory)	1804
Crossbow	200 BCE
Crystal radio	1901
Diaper (disposable)	1951
Dinosaurs (era)	245 to 65 MYA
DNA discovered	1953
DNA evolves	1.8 BYA
Drill (bow)	20,000 BCE
Drill (dental)	1790
DVD	1995
Dynamite	1867
Earth Day	1970
Electrocardiogram (EKG)	1924
Electroencephalogram (EEG)	1929
Elevator (electric)	1887
E-mail	1987
Embryo transplant (cattle/human)	1950/1983
Erector set	1901
Escalator	1911
Fastener (Velcro)	1948
Fastener (zipper)	1923
Fax machine	1902
Fetal surgery	1984
Fiber optics	1955
Fire (human made)	1.5 MYA
First mammals	65 MYA
Fork	600
Formation of Earth	5 BYA

(continued at back of book)

UPDATED FOURTH EDITION

Society, Ethics, and Technology

MORTON E. WINSTON
The College of New Jersey

RALPH D. EDELBACH
The College of New Jersey

WADSWORTH
CENGAGE Learning™

Australia • Brazil • Japan • Korea • Mexico • Singapore • Spain • United Kingdom • United States

WADSWORTH
CENGAGE Learning™

Society, Ethics, and Technology, Updated Fourth Edition

Morton E. Winston, Ralph D. Edelbach

Publisher: Clark Baxter

Sr. Sponsoring Editor: Joann Kozyrev

Assistant Editor: Joshua Duncan

Editorial Assistant: Marri Straton

Media Editor: Kimberly Apfelbaum

Marketing Manager: Mark T. Haynes

Marketing Coordinator: Josh Hendrick

Marketing Communications Manager: Laura Localio

Content Project Manager: PreMediaGlobal

Art Director: Jennifer Wahi

Sr. Print buyer: Diane Gibbons

Senior Rights Acquisition Specialist, Text: Katie Huha

Production Service: PreMediaGlobal

Cover Designer: Michelle DiMercurio

Cover Image: © Jupiter Images

© 2012, 2009, 2007 Wadsworth, Cengage Learning

ALL RIGHTS RESERVED. No part of this work covered by the copyright herein may be reproduced, transmitted, stored, or used in any form or by any means graphic, electronic, or mechanical, including but not limited to photocopying, recording, scanning, digitizing, taping, Web distribution, information networks, or information storage and retrieval systems, except as permitted under Section 107 or 108 of the 1976 United States Copyright Act, without the prior written permission of the publisher.

For product information and technology assistance, contact us at
Cengage Learning Customer & Sales Support, 1-800-354-9706

For permission to use material from this text or product, submit all requests online at **www.cengage.com/permissions.**
Further permissions questions can be emailed to
permissionrequest@cengage.com.

Library of Congress Control Number: 2010941446

ISBN-13: 978-0-8400-3380-2

ISBN-10: 0-8400-3380-X

Wadsworth
20 Channel Center Street
Boston, MA 02210
USA

Cengage Learning products are represented in Canada by Nelson Education, Ltd.

Cengage Learning is a leading provider of customized learning solutions with office locations around the globe, including Singapore, the United Kingdom, Australia, Mexico, Brazil and Japan. Locate your local office at **international.cengage.com/region.**

For your course and learning solutions, visit **www.cengage.com**.

Purchase any of our products at your local college store or at our preferred online store **www.cengagebrain.com**.

Instructors: Please visit **login.cengage.com** and log in to access instructor-specific resources.

Printed in the United States of America
1 2 3 4 5 6 7 14 13 12 11 10

For our children and grandchildren

CONTENTS

PREFACE

THE IDEA FOR THIS BOOK began at The College of New Jersey in 1993 with the decision to introduce a new general education core course entitled "Society, Ethics, and Technology" (SET). Among the ideas that influenced the development of this course were the discussions of the "New Liberal Learning," the development of a vigorous "Science, Technology, and Society" (STS) movement under the auspices of the National Association for Science, Technology, and Society (NASTS), and the New Liberal Arts (NLA) program that was sponsored during the 1980s through grants made by the Sloan Foundation.

These trends made it clear that general education at the undergraduate level should include courses and curricula that help students understand the profound role that science and technology play in shaping modern society and that provide them with a method for evaluating the benefits and risks associated with technological change. This new edition of the reader was developed under the assumption that scientific and technological literacy remains an essential aspect of what it means to be an educated person in the twenty-first century.

The editors wish to thank James S. Taylor for his help with Appendix A. We are also grateful to our reviewers for their comments on earlier editions, and to our editor at Cengage, Joann Kozyrev, for her encouragement and support. Finally, we thank Biswa Jyoti Sur and his team at PreMediaGlobal for their thorough copyediting.

M.W. & R.E.
November 2010

HOW TO USE THIS BOOK

THIS BOOK IS DESIGNED for use in standard 15-week undergraduate Science, Technology, and Society (STS) courses. Courses of that type are intended to provide an interdisciplinary bridge between the humanities, particularly ethics, the social sciences, and the natural sciences and engineering by developing a framework for analyzing the social, environmental, and ethical implications of contemporary science and technology. A principal goal of these courses is to empower students to think critically about contemporary technological issues, such as privacy on the Internet, genetic engineering, and global warming, and to learn to accept the social responsibilities of educated citizens in a global technological society.

The key bridge idea that links science and technology with ethics and social science is the dictum "ought implies can, but can does not imply ought." The first half of this statement asserts that one cannot be obliged to do something that one cannot do; the second half says that just because one can do something does not mean that one ought to do it. Science and technology, by enlarging the domain of what we humans know how to do, are continually enlarging the class of actions that we can perform. As a consequence of this expansion of our power to do more things, we are obliged to ask ourselves whether we ought to be doing all the things that science and technology now allow us to do. "Ought questions" are ethical questions, and to answer these sorts of questions, one needs to understand how ethical values and traditional moral standards can be applied to evaluating past and present scientific and technological innovations.

The introductory essay, "Children of Invention Revisited," provides students with a conceptual framework for thinking about the relationship between scientific and technological innovation and the social and ethical issues that such innovations can raise when new technologies are deployed and diffused in society. All too often, new technologies are developed and deployed without proper reflection on their likely consequences for society. One reason for this is ignorance about the nature of technology and the processes by which new technologies are developed and deployed. Addressing the need for students to be scientifically and technologically literate has long been a primary goal of the STS movement, and it is also a primary goal of this book.

However, another reason for the failure to evaluate technology ethically is that traditional ethical theories were primarily intended to evaluate persons and their actions rather than socio-technical practices. To correct this, students need a little understanding of ethics and to be familiar with the essential features of the major traditional ethical theories, such as ethical egoism, utilitarianism, natural law, and Kantian deontological ethics. Explaining how these theories can be adapted to the evaluation of technology is also necessary so that methods are provided for applying familiar ethical principles to particular controversial issues surrounding contemporary science and technology. Finding books that serve these multiple purposes is unusual.

The introductory essay attempts to provide an ethical framework through which students can approach the evaluation of technology. We advise that the introductory essay be assigned early in the course because it provides students who are new to STS with a comprehensive overview of the subject matter as well as a concise introduction to the ethical and social aspects of technology.

The selections in Part 1 convey general perspectives on the historical, social, and philosophical aspects of technology, and those in Part 2 deal with several issues in specific fields of contemporary technology.

In selecting readings for this text, we have tried to provide current selections on a number of standard STS topics, such as computers, automation, robotics, the Internet, genetic engineering, artificial reproduction, population, energy, and environmental policy issues. We have departed slightly from the standard set of topics by also including several readings dealing with the phenomenon of globalization.

Each selection is preceded by a brief introduction describing the topic and major themes of the reading, mentioning something about its author, and providing several focus questions for students to keep in mind while reading the essay. Usually, at least one of these focus questions asks the reader to compare the view in the present reading with that found in another selection that presents a competing or complementary perspective. This allows instructors to design their syllabus using such topical links instead of the standard organization.

What is new in this edition is the addition of two appendices: Appendix A contains a selection of news articles that highlight current social and ethical issues related to technology. Each of these short readings is accompanied by questions for discussion and links for further study. Appendix B contains a set of ethical codes and normative standards that can be used as references and can also be applied to the ethical issues raised by the reading selections.

However, as we noted in the preface to the earlier editions, the range of topics and issues related to the social and ethical implications of technological change is so broad and is changing so quickly that no printed anthology can possibly do justice to all the topics that might be covered in courses dealing with these issues. Instructors using this text for courses should feel free to supplement it with their own readings on topics of interest.

Morton Winston
Ralph Edelbach

INTRODUCTION

Children of Invention Revisited

Morton Winston

IF NECESSITY IS THE MOTHER of invention, who is the father, and who, or what, are invention's children? Necessity, of course, is a matter of degree: We actually only *need* air, water, and food to survive. Shelter, clothing, and a few material possessions are also nice, as are companionship, affection, security, and several other psychological goods that we crave as social animals. But we humans learned how to satisfy these basic biological needs millions of years ago. Why then did we embark on the long journey that transformed us from cavemen into cosmonauts? What was it that made possible the ascent from the Stone Age to our present global technological civilization?

Clearly, the leading answer to these questions is superior intelligence. But in what specific respects is human intelligence superior to that found in other species? Is it our capacity to learn from observation and experience and to transmit what we learn to others? Is it our ability to create and use language? Or might it be these two general cognitive capacities for culture and language, together with our unique ability to discover new solutions to old problems, better ways of making and doing things? In short, is it our unique capacity as a species to form science and technology? Coupled with our needs and desires, which provide the motives that propel us to discover and invent, our scientific and technological creativity has guided the development of civilization through the development of theories, tools, inventions, and technologies that have transformed the ways that we live and work.[1]

For most of us, a world without technology is inconceivable. The inventions that it has given us are all around us. In fact, most of us spend most of our lives in completely artificial environments, wrapped in a technological cocoon that provides us with much more than merely food and protection from the elements. We are so wrapped up in our technological culture, in fact, that it takes an effort to distance ourselves from it in order to understand how technology has transformed human existence from its natural state. Such a historical perspective also helps us see how contemporary technologies, such as genetic engineering and the Internet, are now changing us in even more dramatic ways, creating new opportunities for humans to flourish, new ways of life, and also, in some cases, new social and ethical problems. These social and ethical issues arising from technological innovation are the "children of invention" that this book is about. To understand these issues, however, it is first necessary to get a clear view of their source—*technology.*

THE SCOPE OF TECHNOLOGY

The word *technology* is itself of fairly recent coinage; Johann Beckman of Gottingen first used it in 1789. Its root, *techne,* is the ancient Greek word for "art," "craft," or "skill," which itself is derived from an earlier Indo-European root, *teks,* which means "to weave" or "to fabricate" (*teks* is also the root of the word *textile*). Recent archeological evidence suggests that the weaving of cloth predates the birth of agriculture and the dawn of civilization, going back to about 35,000 BCE, making it one of the first technologies. As the etymology suggests, a *techne* is a method, craft, or skill used in making things, not the things themselves, which are called *artifacts.* For instance, a woven object made from animal hairs that have been twisted together into long strands, dyed with vegetable colors, and interlaced by a weaver is an artifact. Let's say that this object functions primarily as a blanket; a person wraps her- or himself in it to stay warm. A typical use, or function, of an artifact is called its purpose or end, and the knowledge of how to gather the fibers, twist them, dye them, and weave them are the individual *techniques* that comprise this particular technology. Thus, the core meaning of the word *technology* refers to the ensembles of techniques by which humans make artifacts that serve certain useful ends. However, this original meaning is too restrictive for the contemporary context in which we think about the relationship between technology and modern society.

As Rosalind Williams (Selection 1.1.4) notes, in recent years there has been an unfortunate tendency to narrow the definition of technology to contemporary information-communications technologies (ICTs) such as personal computers, the Internet, and the digital gadgets advertised in *Wired.* This way of thinking about technology is clearly too restrictive; it ignores other areas of contemporary technological innovation, such as biotechnology and nanotechnology, as well as the technologies of earlier periods, such as the automobile, the steam engine, or the water wheel. When one ordinarily thinks of technology, what most likely comes to mind are technological *artifacts*—the objects, machines, structures, and devices that are the useful end products of technological design. Then, perhaps, one thinks of the less familiar but potentially more impressive machines and industrial processes tucked away in the factories that manufacture the various gadgets and widgets that we use. Finally, one might visualize the scientists, engineers, and technicians in white laboratory coats, hard at work in the laboratories of the Research and Development Division, designing the next generation of technological devices and processes.

Although it is true that each context through which artifacts come into being—design, manufacturing, and end use—is a technological context, it is still too narrow a view to identify technology with only the material culture of designed or manufactured physical objects. We take an even broader view: Technology consists of not only useful artifacts and the tools and processes needed to produce them but also the entire social organization of people and materials that permits the acquisition of the knowledge and skills needed to design, manufacture, distribute, use, repair, and eventually dispose of these artifacts. Technology is not a collection of things but is a systematic and rational way of doing things; it is, in general, *the organization of knowledge, people, and things to accomplish specific practical goals.*[2]

Technology includes not only the obvious candidates—the mechanical, structural, and electronic know-how that directs the purposeful organization of materials—but also the less obvious *invisible technologies* that control the purposeful organization of people and their labor. The mechanical clocks described by David Landes (Selection 1.1.1), for instance, enabled people to coordinate their activities and thus made possible a more productive use of human labor. But clocks and calendars are useful as ways of measuring units of time—the minutes, days, weeks, months, and the like—that comprise the invisible technology of time. The monetary system, the banks, and the stock and commodity markets are technologies for the distribution of economic value that was once associated with gold coins, then with pieces of paper, currency notes, or stock certificates, and is nowadays represented by encrypted bits of digital data. The ideologies of free-market capitalism and centralized planned economies are competing economic theories about how best to organize social production. Even governmental systems, ranging from varieties of representative democracy to theocracy and dictatorship, are competing political technologies for managing concerted societal action and resolving political conflicts. People ask, "Is there a better way to run the government?" no less frequently than "Is there a better way to design a mousetrap?" Both questions are requests to find a better technology—that is, to acquire knowledge that enables one to solve a practical problem.

Contemporary writers often speak of technology as consisting of systems; for instance, Ruth Schwartz Cowan (Selection 1.1.2) describes the telegraph and telephone, the railroad, the petroleum, and the electrical systems that came about in the later half of the nineteenth century. Large-scale technological systems are linked with one another, often in relationships of mutual interdependence; for instance, telegraph wires were strung along railroad rights of way, and railroads came to depend on the telegraph for scheduling and signaling. Similarly, contemporary ICT systems, such as the Internet, depend on a great many other technological systems for their creation and use but then are used by them, creating a matrix of complex interdependencies. One might think of the entire *technosphere*—that is, the sum total of all human-created artifacts together with the enabling knowledge that created it and sustains it—as constituting one giant technological system. However, this definition of the scope of technology is too broad to be of much practical use. Instead, we will think of technologies as consisting of several distinguishable but interacting aspects: (1) skills, techniques, human activity-forms, or sociotechnical practices; (2) resources, tools, and materials; (3) technological products, or artifacts; (4) ends, intentions, or functions; (5) background knowledge; and (6) the social contexts in which the technology is designed, developed, used, and disposed of. These six aspects are present in every technology.

The first aspect of technology is the *human activity-form*—that is, the particular skills, techniques, methods, practices, or ways of doing things. We know that animals other than humans can make and use tools; for instance, chimpanzees strip branches off tree limbs to make sticks that can be used for gathering insects. For the purposes of our characterization of the technological system, we restrict activity-forms or techniques to those employed by human beings. Some human activity-forms employ natural objects rather than tools to achieve ends; for instance, if one throws a spear in order to try to kill an animal for food, one is employing a particular technique. But throwing spears is a primitive and not very useful hunting technique; our technologies for providing our food have improved considerably. Today, there are complex ensembles of techniques for doing just about everything from planting and harvesting crops to figuring out the orbit of a moon of Jupiter, from designing a house to conducting a leveraged hostile takeover, from cooking lasagna to programming a computer to sort sales data. Such complex techniques represent what is called *procedural knowledge,* or more commonly "know-how," and is contrasted with *propositional knowledge,* or "know-that." Both of these types of knowledge are necessary aspects of technological systems, but techniques are its essence. Procedural knowledge forms the basis of technology because it provides the patterns for the sociotechnical practices or human activity-forms that we use to create artifacts of all kinds and to build and maintain our complex technological systems.

One of the main consequences of technology is to increase our capacity to do things. Technologies, techniques, and tools extend, enhance, and sometimes even replace our natural powers such as sight, hearing, muscle, and even memory and thought. By using tools, we can accomplish things that we could not otherwise achieve and to do things that we could not otherwise do, thus increasing our repertoire of human activity-forms. Tools are artifacts at our disposal that can be used to make other artifacts, but tools, even the dawn stones used by our distant ancestors, are themselves artifacts that have been transformed from their natural states in some way by means of human action.

Earth itself is of course not an artifact but has for many centuries been viewed as a *resource well* into which we can dip at will in order to satisfy our needs and desires. Technology requires resources of various kinds as inputs to technological processes, and by employing specific techniques or human activity-forms, we act on and transform these resources from their original or natural states. Once a *built environment* has been created, however, everything in it can serve as a resource to further technological development. The term *infrastructure* describes elements of the built environment that are available to be used to create or apply new technologies. We live on an increasingly anthropogenic planet, one in which the evidence of the built environment can be seen from outer space in the form of clusters of light emanating from our major cities. In fact, if we include the unintended effects on Earth's atmosphere and climate caused by anthropogenic global warming, there are very few things on Earth that are unaffected by human activity.

By acting on either natural or artificial resources, through techniques, we alter them in various ways and thus create *artifacts,* which form the third aspect of technologies. A clay pot is an example of a material artifact, which, although transformed by human activity, is not all that far removed from its natural state. A plastic cup, a contact lens, and a computer chip, on the other hand, are examples of artifacts that are far removed from the original states of the natural resources needed to create them. Artifacts can serve as resources in other technological processes. This is one of the important interaction effects within the technological system: Each new technology increases the stock of available tools and resources that can be employed by other technologies to produce new artifacts, forming what Deborah Johnson and Thomas Powers (Selection 1.3.4) call the *artifactual platform.*

The fourth aspect concerns the ends or functions of an artifact or technique. Most artifacts have typical or intended uses, but artifacts can in fact be embedded in multiple contexts of use or can serve multiple ends, a property that Richard Sclove (Selection 1.2.1) calls *polypotency.* However, most artifacts have an intended use, or *focal function;* a toaster, for instance, is designed to lightly burn slices of bread, but it is also polypotent and can be used as hand warmer or as a murder weapon. There is a double ambiguity in the relations between artifacts and practices and between ends and practices; the same artifacts can be used to achieve different ends, and different practices and their associated artifacts can be used to accomplish the same ends. For instance, I could have written this sentence with a quill pen, a pencil, a ballpoint pen, a typewriter, or a personal computer (PC) running text-editing software (although I used the last). And I could have used my PC to play an adventure game or calculate my income tax instead of writing this sentence. Because artifacts are designed and created to serve certain functions, it is possible to talk about the ends of these objects—that is, their intended purposes or focal functions even though the objects themselves may often also be used in ways that were not intended. The term *valence* is sometimes used to refer to the typical or conventional uses of artifacts, which may or may not match their intended purposes.[3]

The fifth aspect of technological systems is *knowledge-that*, or factual knowledge about what the universe consists of and how it operates. To employ our technologies, we need background knowledge of various kinds: what resources to use and where to find them, what techniques to employ to fabricate various artifacts, the ends and purposes that are typically served by various techniques and objects, and how all these elements fit together in a systematic way. Both knowledge-how and knowledge-that have always been an important aspect of technologies. However, since the scientific revolution of the seventeenth century, scientific knowledge—that is, both factual and theoretical knowledge about the universe and the way it works—has come to play an increasingly important role in technological development.

The sixth aspect of technology is the *social context or* organization in which technologies are developed, distributed, and employed. A division of labor in which different individuals perform different tasks or occupy different roles to accomplish common or coordinated ends characterizes technological societies. The schemes that we use for organizing human labor represent a kind of technology that can be applied to the most important resource of all—ourselves. Complex schemes for organizing human activities that have become more or less institutionalized can be called *social artifacts.* Examples of social artifacts include the stock market, battalions or divisions in an army, baseball teams, hospitals, schools, and corporations. In each case, human resources are organized in a particular way according to a plan or technique involving a division of labor in which different persons occupy different roles, and their labor is coordinated to accomplish specific sorts of goals. It is important to understand that technology encompasses not only material artifacts but also social and organizational forms and even the cognitive techniques that produce the material and social infrastructure of human civilization. These *invisible technologies* frequently consist of formal, mathematical, or analytical techniques—for instance, the scientific method, statistical analysis, or procedures for creating a balance sheet—and many other specific, high-order thinking skills, which are the content of higher education. Becoming a scientifically or technologically educated person consists mainly in the acquisition of a fairly extensive repertoire of such cognitive techniques.

The social and psychological aspects of technological systems are the least obvious but also the most important. Technology is a human social construction. This is true in an obvious and straightforward sense when we speak of large technological structures—such as bridges, buildings, or dams, which obviously came into existence only by the coordination of the activities of numerous individuals—but it is equally true in the case of the lonely amateur inventor toiling in the attic. Inventions today are rarely the result of such solitary creativity, but even when they are, the resources and techniques employed and the knowledge by which they are put to use by the inventor are themselves the products of prior social processes. Even the inventor's own knowledge and abilities have been shaped by her education and by the repertoire of cognitive techniques that she has acquired through education. So, there is really very little, only the raw materials and the laws of nature, that has not in some way resulted from a process of social production. Even when an inventor succeeds in inventing something new, it is still unlikely to be brought into production and placed on the market unless it has some social value or is of use to other people. So, all technologies must be seen as embedded in social contexts of development, deployment, and use.

To summarize this discussion, we can define technological systems as the *complex of techniques, knowledge, and resources that are employed by human beings in the creation of material and social artifacts that typically serve certain functions perceived as useful or desirable in relation to human interests in various social contexts.*

TECHNOLOGICAL REVOLUTIONS

The use of technologies to satisfy our needs is a fundamental feature of human nature. All human societies we know of, both those presently existing and those that existed hundreds of thousands of years before the dawn of civilization, were technological to some degree. For almost all of our species' evolution, we lived in small, nomadic bands whose main means of livelihood were hunting, gathering, and scavenging. But we were also toolmakers and tool-users during this long period of human evolution, and tools were the principal means by which we satisfied our physiological needs for food, warmth, and shelter. Our hominid ancestors first began chipping stones to make simple hand tools about 2.5 million years ago. Fire was used as early as 1.5 million years ago. If *Homo sapiens* (literally, "man the wise") is now the dominant species on the planet, it is in large part because he is also *Homo faber* ("man the maker").

Early human societies were organized as hunter-gatherer groups, gathering edible plants in season and supplementing their diet with the meat or marrow of hunted animals. Quite likely, these bands of hunter-gatherers were nomadic, following animal migrations and seasonal food-plant distributions. As with present-day hunter-gatherers, ancient nomadic societies were severely limited to only those objects that they could take with them; thus, they tended to develop simple portable technologies for hunting, gathering, cooking, transportation, and defense. Perhaps surprisingly, life does not seem to have been especially hard for hunter-gatherers. The secrets of their success seem to have been populations that did not exceed the food supply, simple and limited material needs, and the ability to move to another area when the local food supply ran out. Nomadic hunter-gatherer societies have persisted into the twentieth century in such diverse environments as the African desert, the tropical rain forest, and the Arctic tundra. Remoteness might be the key to avoiding conversion to more technologically intensive ways of life. For the rest of us, our lives now deeply depend on far-flung and complex technological systems.

About 10,000 years ago, the first great technological revolution occurred in several fertile river valleys of Asia Minor and North Africa. During the *agricultural revolution,* humans learned how to domesticate animals and to plant, grow, and harvest crops to sustain their existence. This enabled humans to give up the nomadic lifestyle and to build permanent cities. *Civilization,* which means the building of cities, originates at this time, as do morality, law, religion, record keeping, mathematics, astronomy, class structures, patriarchy, and other social institutions that have since come to characterize the human condition. With the adoption of settled agriculture in the fertile river valleys, the history of humankind begins. Permanent houses could be built, tools and objects could be accumulated from year to year, and so humanity began the long climb toward the collections of miscellany and junk that now clutter people's closets, attics, and garages.

Settled agriculture had many advantages and a few disadvantages. The quantity of food that could be produced per acre was much higher, so population densities could also be much greater. With permanent dwellings, creature comforts could be made that did not have to be portable. With larger numbers of people living together, specialization of activities could take place, and specialists were more likely to find better ways to do things. Larger concentrations of people could better share and perpetuate knowledge and band together to cooperate on projects that smaller groups could not attempt. Thus, we see that even at this early stage of technological development, the organization of people, information, and accumulated resources were essential aspects of emerging technological societies.

In regions with insufficient rainfall to sustain many crops, it was necessary to design, construct, and maintain either irrigation canals or aqueducts. There is evidence of canal irrigation in both Mesopotamia and Egypt as early as the sixth millennium BCE, and in areas where the topography posed challenges various devices were developed to raise water above its natural level. Some of these devices, such as the noria used with flowing water, were sophisticated; others, such as the chain-pump used with still water, were simple, being powered either by animals or humans. Devices of the latter type are still being used today in some parts of the world. Even with the Nile River's normally adequate supply of water for irrigation in Egypt, it was usually necessary to employ technology to direct and control its distribution, making agriculture a more complex undertaking than originally might be thought.

The disadvantages of settled agriculture sprang from the fact that society had "put all its eggs in one basket" and had committed itself to living in one place. A settled society is prey to flood, drought, and insects. Persistent weeds must be removed from fields before they displace crops. Houses and farm implements must be maintained. Crop seeds must be gathered and sown. The final product, food, must be harvested, stored, and distributed. In short, the settled farmer has more but must work harder to maintain his or her improved standard of living. Irrigated agriculture is even more technologically intensive and requires more complex social organization. Large irrigation projects demand larger groups to support them and must be maintained throughout the year, not just during the growing season. Irrigated farms produce more food per acre, more reliably than dry farms that rely on uncertain rainfall, but they also require more work per person fed. At the extreme are rice paddies in the river deltas of southeast China where three crops are grown each year. They are the most productive farmlands but also the most labor intensive. Today, most agricultural production in industrialized countries occurs on large farms where energy-intensive farm machinery substitutes for human labor and chemical fertilizers maintain soil fertility.

The second great technological revolution took place many centuries later, during the eighteenth century in Europe about 250 years ago. The *Industrial Revolution* replaced the muscle power of animals with coal-fired steam energy and then later, about 100 years ago, with gasoline-driven internal combustion engines. The first steam engines, patented in 1698, were designed to pump water from coal mines in England, but before long they were improved and used to power looms and other machines in factories. The machine age caused profound changes in economic and social relations. The number of people needed to produce food declined as the number of people engaged in factory work increased. People migrated from rural areas to cities in search of higher-paying factory jobs, and new inventions such as the cotton gin, the locomotive, and the telegraph laid the groundwork for the emergence of the complex technological society that we live in today.

The methods that a society uses to produce goods have a profound effect on what life is like in that society, for both producers and consumers of goods. Prior to the industrial age, production was organized by crafts. Individual artisans both designed and produced each individual product, usually guided by traditional techniques that were occasionally modified by creative innovations. The relative value of the product was largely determined by the artisan's skill. As a result, artisans were relatively autonomous, and production units often consisted of a single artisan and several apprentices in cottage industries.

When the invention of the steam engine made power available on a scale never previously possible, it became feasible to concentrate larger numbers of workers in one place, and to have each worker perform only a small part of the production process. This resulted in a much more specialized division of labor, and the factory system was born. The factory system required far greater concentrations of power, labor, and raw materials than either agriculture or cottage industries. It also required the development of infrastructure for transportation of raw materials to the factory site and finished products from the site. Railroads and canals were thus as essential a part of the Industrial Revolution as the factories themselves. The industrial system also required a large labor force near the factory, so society's living patterns were reorganized to include factory towns where workers lived and the means to supply them with food and other necessities. Factories were often located near sources of power or raw materials, resulting in net population shifts away from agricultural lands.

In the early twentieth century, technological experts working under the banner of "scientific management," developed by F. W. Taylor in 1911, studied the production process and learned what each worker knew about making the product. They then ordained the perfect way to produce a given product using standardized parts, the division of labor, and mass-production techniques, what each worker would do, and at what pace he or she would do it. Each worker needed fewer skills and could be paid less per item. Cheaper workers making larger numbers of products using specialized machinery resulted in less expensive goods. Lower prices resulted in increased standard of living for consumers. Factory work may have become onerous, but a salary could buy more than it could previously. In recent decades, much of the world's production has moved to low-wage countries such as China and India where workers are paid far less for their work than workers in developed countries would be paid for comparable labor; workers in these countries usually do not have the right to form unions and bargain collectively with their employers. But jobs with low wages and limited rights, many claim, are often better than no jobs at all or trying to scrape out a subsistence living on small farms.

In the search for increased productivity, working conditions in early factories were often harsh and dangerous. In response to the many abuses that existed, employees often battled tyrannical bosses for the right to form unions and bargain collectively, many times suffering injuries or even death for their actions. The sacrifices made by such organizing drives secured improved working conditions and raised the standard of living of millions of workers and their families. A similar process of humanizing conditions of factory workers is now taking place in the developing countries where most current production is located. Despite the dominance of the factory system, crafts did not vanish entirely. They survived in niches where no one could think of an economical way of applying mass-production techniques or as a way to produce distinctive, high-quality goods. In some cases, they survived because traditional cultural values prevailed over the lure of newer technologies. As David Edgerton (Selection 1.1.3) notes, in many countries sewing machines continued to be used in homes to make clothes for the family, and in India, Mohandas Gandhi revived the spinning wheel as an alternative to mass-produced thread. But the dominant trend throughout the latter half of twentieth century was toward mass-produced, globally distributed consumer goods produced by workers in low-wage countries.

The technologies of power production were driving forces of the industrial system, and each new source of power required industrialized society to provide an accompanying infrastructure to make the system work. Water power, an ancient technology, was limited in availability and location prior to the building of aqueducts and required relatively little additional infrastructure beyond that already available in an agricultural and craft society. Coal could be more widely distributed, but coal-powered factories were large because efficient steam engines were large. Railroads and canals began to crisscross the countryside from mine to factory to market. Monetary supply and financial services had to expand to serve a system with increasing separation between producer and consumer. Electricity is a more flexible source of power, capable of efficiently driving both large and small machines. As Ruth Schwartz Cowan (Selection 1.1.2) observes, electricity permitted greater decentralization of industry supported by a network of power grids that eventually reached nearly every house and factory in the country. Oil and gasoline revolutionized transportation and distribution of goods. Internal combustion engines fueled by gasoline and diesel oil made it possible to have smaller vehicles, and smaller vehicles continued the trend toward decentralization. However, gas- and oil-powered vehicles required more and better roads. The U.S. interstate highway system, built in the 1960s–1980s (and similar systems in other industrialized countries) are society's most recent contributions to an industrial technology system based on oil, a system that may now be reaching its final phrase, perhaps to be replaced during the twenty-first century by a "greener" energy system that uses renewable forms of energy.

Many people believe that since the mid-1970s we have been going through a third great technological transformation—from the machine age to the *information age* (also called the "third wave" and the "knowledge revolution"). Computers, communications satellites, fiber-optic cable, and other developments—which make possible global, high-capacity, high-speed communications technologies such as the Internet—are already profoundly changing the way that we live, work, and play.

Revolutionary developments in computing and communications technology have transformed the workplace, faster than some would like but slower than its visionaries had hoped for. The earliest successes of computers in industry were in payroll, inventory, and similar routine and repetitive kinds of record keeping. The automated processes were well understood, straightforward, and implemented exactly as they had been done before the advent of computers. In some cases, they didn't even save time or work, but they were the wave of the future.

The next stage gave decision makers more and better information to enhance efficiency, competitiveness, and other factors reflected in the bottom line. Computers made it possible to gather and organize data on an unprecedented scale. Also successful were the attempts to use computers to improve scheduling and reduce inventory in the production process. Goods stored in inventory cost money to store and contribute nothing to profit until they are used or sold. Predicting exactly how much of which raw materials and parts are needed at which steps of the manufacturing process and scheduling their arrival in the factory at precisely the right place at precisely the right time was the just-in-time manufacturing technique developed in Japan that led to real gains in productivity that drove the global economy in the 1990s.

As computers and computer programmers got better, computers became capable of doing jobs that were formerly thought to require human intelligence. Typically, computers proved capable of doing far more than most people would have predicted in advance and far less than their most vocal proponents claimed was possible. Although the conceptually most impressive achievements were in areas like expert systems for medical diagnosis, the biggest successes of computer technology were in the simpler applications now so common that we take them for granted: automatic pilot, antilocking brakes, electronic fuel injection, and most important, in more flexible, general-purpose tools and machines for making other products.

With flexible, modifiable, reprogrammable tools, it was no longer necessary to have long production runs to amortize the setup time of the machinery. Computer-controlled machinery could switch quickly from one task to another, and customized production runs became in some cases economically viable. Supply could now more accurately follow demand, and both idle machinery and unproductive inventory were virtually eliminated in those industries adopting the new technology.

The synergies created by computers, user-friendly software applications, satellite-mediated communications, the Internet, containerization, and rapid and relatively inexpensive air freight made possible the kind of geographically distributed production systems that are characteristic of the contemporary era *of globalization*. One can now order a computer to one's precise specifications on the Internet, have it custom built in a Chinese factory, and delivered by an air freight carrier to your door in a matter of days. In fact, without computers and rapid worldwide communications, our present-day global marketplace would not be possible. Some authors, such as Thomas Friedman (Selection 2.1.1) believe that around the year 2000 we entered a new phase of this information-revolution form of globalization, what he calls "Globalization 3.0." This new phase springs from a Web-based global platform that enables multiple forms of knowledge sharing and collaboration irrespective of distance; this in turn creates a "flatter" world in which the economic playing field is getting more level between people in the developed and the developing countries. Cass Sunstein (Selection 2.2.1) explores how Web-enabled collaboration using wikis, open-source software, and blogs is changing the way in which knowledge is assembled, transformed, and disseminated in the information age. But ICT is not only changing commerce and industry but also transforming the power of government and big corporations to collect and assemble data on individuals, as described by Jay Stanley and Barry Steinhardt (Selection 2.2.3). It is also altering the way in which soldiers operate on the battlefield, as described by Max Boot (Selection 2.2.2). Futurists such as Rodney Brooks (Selection 2.3.1) and Ray Kurzweil (Selection 2.3.4) predict that by the middle of the twenty-first century synergies created by the convergence of ICTs, artificial intelligence, robotics, biotechnology, and nanotechnology will create another technoscientific revolution, what Kurzweil calls a "singularity," in which the intellectual capabilities of our machines will exceed that of human intelligence. While some, like Kurzweil, welcome such developments, others, such as Bill Joy (Selection 2.3.3), fear that we may not be able to control the technological genies once they are out of the bottle. Still other authors, such as William Clocksin (Selection 2.3.2), doubt that artificially intelligent machines will ever be able to master the complexities of human narrative communication. Whichever of these future projections turn out to be correct, it is certain that we will have to grapple with the social impacts and ethical challenges of twenty-first-century technologies.

SCIENCE, TECHNOLOGY, AND SOCIETY

In the modern world, technology and science often go together, with science supporting technology and technology supporting science. Although they now share a great deal in common, their goals have been historically different. In the ancient world, science, then known as natural philosophy, was viewed as an elevated activity involving pure contemplation and the value-free pursuit of knowledge, whereas technology was associated with more practical concerns and with the arts. It was not until the beginning of the modern period in the seventeenth century that there was a decisive shift to the view that scientific knowledge was valuable because it was useful to us in gaining mastery over nature. This shift was largely due to the writings of several influential philosophers such as Rene Descartes and Francis Bacon. Bacon's works, particularly *Novum Organon* (1620) and *New Atlantis* (1624), are notable for their contempt of traditional speculative philosophy and their emphasis on the importance of empirical methods of investigation through which the secrets of nature could be revealed by means of judicious experiments. In 1637 Descartes wrote the *Discourse on Method* in which he proclaimed that

> It is possible to attain knowledge which is very useful in life; and that, instead of speculative philosophy which is taught in the Schools, we may find a practical philosophy by means of which, knowing the force and the action of fire, water, air, stars, the heavens, and all other bodies that environ us, as distinctly as we know the different crafts of our artisans, we can in the same way employ them in all those uses to which they are adapted, and thus render ourselves masters and possessors of nature.[4]

This change in the dominant view of the nature and bases of human knowledge set the stage for the modern belief in progress, which was expressed by Bacon as the belief that "the improvement of man's mind and the improvement of his lot are one and the same thing."[5]

Despite the marriage of science and technology in the modern period, some significant differences remain between the two enterprises. Technologists primarily seek to answer the question "How?" ("How can we keep warm in the winter?" or "How can we see distant objects that are invisible to the naked eye?") Engineers seek to design and produce useful material objects and systems that will function under all expected circumstances for the planned lifetime of the product. Science, on the other hand, may be considered as a form of systematic empirical inquiry, which seeks to describe the underlying laws governing the behavior of natural objects. Scientists primarily try to answer the questions "What?" and "Why?" ("What kind of thing is this?"

and "Why does it behave the way it does?"). In the early stages of science when little was known, the immediate goal of the science was to describe and classify the phenomena of the natural world. As more things became known, the sciences began asking, "How do these things change over time and interact with each other?" Scientists sought laws and principles that would enable them to predict and explain why things in nature behave as they do. This search produced the scientific revolution in the seventeenth and eighteenth centuries, culminating in the work of Sir Issac Newton. But Newton's universe has been superceded by Einstein's, and his by quantum mechanics and string theory. Despite the abstract nature of contemporary physical theory, natural science continues to provide the intellectual basis for technology.

Technology needs science to predict how its objects and systems will function so that it can tell if they will work, and science supplies the predictive laws that apply to these objects and systems. However, although the laws of science are often simple to state, applying them to the complex objects of technology is often anything but simple. Sometimes the engineer must experiment with the complex objects that are the building blocks of a technology to find out what will happen. At the same time, technology makes direct and obvious contributions to the progress of science. The laboratory equipment that the scientist uses is the product of technology. The biologist would discover little without a microscope and the particle physicist even less without an accelerator. In recent years, the lines between the role of the scientist and that of the engineer or technologist have become increasingly blurred. Much of the current research agenda is dictated by the possible practical applications of new scientific knowledge, and most research is carried out by multidisciplinary teams. This merging of science and technology has led some writers, such as Bruno Latour, to speak of contemporary research as *technoscience,* a term used to draw attention to the interdisciplinary character of most contemporary research as well as the social and historical contexts in which innovation takes place.[6]

The conventional linear understanding of the relationship between science and technology holds that science discovers natural laws, technology applies scientific knowledge to practical problems, and the market selects which technologies are destined for widespread diffusion and use by society. However, this simplistic model has been replaced in recent years by a more sophisticated understanding known as the social construction of technology (SCOT) model. According to SCOT, science and technology have a symbiotic relationship, each one helping the other, while social values shape the precise forms that technological artifacts take. As Judy Wajcman (Selection 1.2.3) points out, the new sociology of technology supports the view that "technological artifacts are socially shaped, not just in their usage, but especially with respect to their design and technical content."

Social values play a crucial role in shaping technologies and in determining which of several technological options gain widespread acceptance in society. The use context of technology ultimately determines the meaning and deployment of technological innovations. Consider the Amish religious sect of central Pennsylvania and Ohio who shun the use of many modern conveniences such as the radio, televisions, video recorders, and telephones in the home because they fear that their use would destroy the rhythm of family life and cause separation to develop among members of the community. However, the Amish make compromises with modern technology, allowing flashlights, hearing aids, and electric welders for what they collectively decide to be legitimate reasons.[7] But if society's values and attitudes toward technology play a central role in determining the course that technological change takes, what attitudes should we have toward technology? What kinds of moral values should guide the future development of technology in the twenty-first century?

TECHNO-OPTIMISM VERSUS TECHNO-PESSIMISM

Our attitudes toward technology are complex and often ambivalent. We cannot but acknowledge and credit science and technology with delivering many wonders that have improved and extended our lives, and many people believe that improved technologies hold the solution to our problems in the twenty-first century. But many people are also disturbed by what they view as technology being out of control and see technology as a threat to our traditional ways of life, to our environment, and even to our survival as a species. These contrasting attitudes toward technology are often referred to as *techno-optimism* and *techno-pessimism*.

Techno-optimists tend to emphasize technology's benefits; they believe that science and technology are not the cause of society's current ills; they do not believe that technology needs to be controlled or regulated; and they have faith in "technological fixes" that will solve outstanding social problems. Techno-pessimists, by contrast, tend to emphasize the risks and costs of technological changes; believe that many social ills are attributable to technology; and think that technology needs to be controlled or is incapable of being controlled. They do not have faith in "technological fixes" to solve social problems, instead emphasizing moral or political solutions.[8]

While there are some extreme Luddites (those who are opposed to technological changes) and antitechnologists, the dominant view of contemporary society still seems to be a cautious form of techno-optimism. The modern idea of scientific and technological progress continues to hold sway not only for people in the developed countries but also increasingly for those in the less developed nations of the world who tend to see development largely in terms of access to more sophisticated forms of technology. However, although technological development can raise the standard of living, rapid technological and social change also brings with it social dislocation, identity confusion, and a sense of disappointment and social alienation. Part of the problem is that technology has been allowed to assume a greater and greater role in human affairs without anyone in particular being responsible for this change. Some writers see this as a problem, and others see free technological innovation as the source of prosperity and human progress.

Among the ideas that critics of technology question is the concept of progress. Throughout most of history, most societies believed strongly in tradition, and changes were presumed to be unwelcome and probably harmful. Kings sat comfortably (or uncomfortably) on their thrones, and when they were replaced through succession or conquest by other kings, quality of life changed little for the general populace. As late as 1800, life was relatively little different than what it had been in prehistoric times—most people lived in extreme poverty. Then came the steam engine, the railroad, and the automobile.

Productivity exploded in the factory and on the farm as new crop varieties and chemical fertilizers enabled fewer farmers to produce more food than ever before. As gains in productivity outstripped population growth, the industrial societies of England, Germany, and the United States grew wealthier faster than any societies in history. Telephones and railroads shrank time and space, and the factory system mass-produced goods that offered unimagined comfort and convenience to the bulk of society. Improvements in agriculture, medical advances, and improvements in public health and hygiene increased life span. In the industrialized world, progress was more than an idea; it was an everyday fact of life, and the cornerstone of progress was seen to be scientific discovery and technological innovation.

In the industrialized world, however, over a century of unchallenged belief in progress was disturbed by several rude surprises. World Wars I and II demonstrated that human cruelty and brutality were still with us, only magnified by weapons capable of producing mass death. Although science and technology could put a man on the moon, the Cuban missile crisis in 1962 reminded the world that we were only a button's push away from a global nuclear war that could destroy humankind. That same year, Rachel Carson published *Silent Spring* in which she warned that pesticides such as DDT were accumulating in ever-larger amounts in species that progressed up the food chain until eagles and peregrine falcons could no longer reproduce. DDT was making their eggshells too thin to keep from cracking. It did not take a genius to realize that humans are also high on the food chain, and DDT was eventually banned. But more bad news was to follow. Mountain lakes in the northeastern United States and Europe were found to be too acidic to support fish, and the problem was traced back to acid rain, automobile emissions, and the exhaust of coal-burning electric power plants. Asbestos, our modern weapon against the age-old danger of fire, turned out to cause the lung disease mesothelioma in asbestos workers and in people living and working in asbestos-lined buildings. Radioactive by-products of nuclear power plants piled up, and no one could think of a foolproof way to keep them isolated and sealed for the thousands of years that they would be a hazard. In 1986 the Chernobyl nuclear disaster spread radioactive contamination as far away as Sweden, and the world became even more worried about the dangers of nuclear power.

Once the myth of technology as unmitigated blessing was destroyed, some people began looking for hazards posed by technology with as much fervor as had previously accompanied the search for benefits. They were not disappointed; there were heavy metals in the rivers and fish, farmland soil erosion and salinization, lead paint in pipes, houses built on industrial waste dumps, health problems of people processing radioactive materials, smog, ozone holes, radon, and global climate warming. Technology helped in the search for its own defects by supplying satellite photographs and instruments that could detect trace chemicals in parts per billion.

Many potential threats to human well-being have been identified, and others no doubt soon will be. Some may be false alarms that are best ignored; some may be early warnings for which action will someday have to be taken; and some may be urgent last calls for which the optimum time to respond has already passed. If technology is responsible for many of our present problems, it will likely be technology that will enable us to overcome them, sometimes in the narrow sense of finding a technological fix but more often in the wider sense that the processes of democratic decision making and economic restructuring are social technologies that we use to address and resolve social problems. As Sheila Jasanoff (Selection 1.2.4) urges, the issue is "no longer whether the public should have a say in technical decisions, but how to promote more meaningful interaction among policy-makers, scientific experts, corporate producers, and the informed public." Taking part in these decisions in a democratic society, however, depends on informed "technological citizens" who have attained a degree of scientific and technological literacy.

Technological citizenship is a modern moral virtue. Being a good technological citizen implies an understanding of mutual rights and responsibilities between oneself and other citizens and between citizens and the government. Among our rights as citizens are the right to receive knowledge and information about technologies and how they might affect our lives, the right to express views and opinions about the development and use of technologies, and the right to participate in decisions concerning the development and deployment of technologies that are potentially harmful to us. To exercise any of these rights, however, citizens must first accept the responsibility to educate and inform themselves about the nature of the technologies that are changing their lives and to understand the ethical and public policy dimensions of the decisions in which they claim the right to participate.

As Langdon Winner (Selection 1.2.2) emphasizes, technologies are not value neutral. In each case, there are human ends and values that stand behind and direct the technological processes. Technology itself is perceived by most people as of positive value because they understand that through technology we can increase our powers and capabilities and are therefore better able to satisfy our needs and desires. But most people also realize that technological innovations are seldom all for the good, and almost inevitably trade-offs need to be considered. A new drug may help cure a disease but may also produce undesirable side effects in some patients and may in the long run promote the spread of new and more drug-resistant forms of the disease. Car ownership may enable one to move about freely and comfortably, but it also entails loan payments, insurance payments, repairs, gasoline, smog, car accidents, global warming, and other downside effects.

Predicting how inventions and technological innovations will be used and how they will ultimately affect society is often very difficult. The history of technology is full of stories of inventors and innovators who had no idea of how their inventions and innovations would ultimately be used or the far-reaching effects that they would have on society. Johannes Gutenberg, inventor of the printing press and movable metal type, was a devout Catholic who would have been horrified to know that his invention enabled the Bible to be widely printed and so helped stimulate the Protestant Reformation. Thomas Edison apparently believed that the phonograph would be mainly used for recording people's last wills and testaments and would undoubtedly be amazed by today's tapes, CDs, and MP3 players, all of which are descended from his invention for recording sound. And who, until recently, would have thought that chlorofluorocarbons, which have been used for decades as refrigerants, would be eating away the ozone layer in the upper atmosphere? Given enough experiences of this kind, one gets the idea that every new technology has not only known and expected benefits and costs but also unknown and unforeseen benefits and costs. New technologies sometime even produce consequences exactly the opposite of what they were intended to produce, what the author Edward Tenner calls "revenge effects."[9] Powerful new technologies alter the social context in which they arise; they change the structure of our interests and values; they change the ways in which we think and work, and they may even change the nature of the communities in which we live.

Another feature of technological change is the way in which it produces winners and losers in society. If technology is a source of power over nature, it is also a means by which some people gain advantage over others. Every technological revolution has witnessed the competition among technologies and the eventual replacement of one technology or technological system by another. Think of what happened to blacksmiths when the automobile came along, or what happened to watchmakers when the quartz-electric digital watch came along, or what is today happening to bank tellers with the introduction of ATMs. In such processes of technological change, groups and individuals whose interests and livelihoods are connected to the older technology are usually the losers, and those whose interests are connected to the "next wave" of technological innovation are the winners. However, because the directions and effects of technological change are often unpredictable, it's difficult to tell in all cases whether any particular individual or group will come out as a winner or a loser.

Similar social phenomena are occurring today in the midst of the information and biotechnology revolutions and the economic phenomenon known as *globalization*. By and large, the wealthier and better-educated people in society remain largely favorably disposed toward new technologies such as computers, the Internet, gene splicing, and robots and toward the globalization of production and distribution that these technologies have made possible. Many others, however, see these developments as threatening their jobs and livelihoods, their religious beliefs, and their traditional ways of life. New technological elites are being created in each of these fields while other people are becoming newly unemployed. Such social effects of technological change bring into sharp relief the need to consider the ethical and moral dimensions of technology.

TECHNOLOGY AND ETHICS

In considering the ethical issues arising from technology, it is important to distinguish clearly between the specific products of technological development, artifacts (for example, clocks, internal combustion engines, digital computers, respirators, and nuclear bombs), and the typical uses to which people put them, or what might be termed their associated *sociotechnological practices*. The fact that a particular device or technology is available for human use does not by itself imply that we ought to adopt and use that technology, nor does it tell us how the technology should or should not be used. A gun, for instance, can be used in many ways: as a paperweight, for recreational target practice, for hunting, for personal protection, or for the commission of a crime. Although a gun has many uses, its valence lies in the social practices of use typically associated with it, which may or may not match its intended purpose. We can and do make moral judgments concerning the various sociotechnological practices associated with different products of technology. We accept some uses as morally legitimate, find others to be morally questionable or problematic, and take steps to restrict or outlaw certain other uses to which these devices may be put. In some cases, such as chemical or biological weapons whose only purpose is to produce mass death and destruction, we attempt to outlaw them entirely rather than to regulate their use. The war in Iraq that began with the U.S. invasion in March 2003 was premised on the notion that such weapons of mass destruction were present in Iraq and that, if not found and destroyed or allowed to fall into the wrong hands, could produce catastrophic results.

When we consider these sorts of questions about how the products of technology ought to be used, we are really asking questions about how people ought to behave or act. Questions about whether to use products of technology or how such products should be used are ethical questions; that is, they are questions concerning what we *ought* to do rather than about what we *can* do. Ethical questions related to technology are basically no different from other ethical questions that we ask about human conduct: In each case, we must attempt to determine which action or policy, from a range of alternative possible actions or policies that we might follow, is the one that we morally or ethically ought to choose. Viewed from the standpoint of technology, broadly defined, morality, ethics, and their cousin, law, are social techniques for regulating human behavior in society. They arose in human history at about the same time when most humans gave up the nomadic lifestyle and began building the permanent settlements that we call cities. Cities require the maintenance of high levels of social cooperation based on reliable expectations that others will act as they are required to do. For instance, a simple commercial transaction in which one person buys something from someone else at a mutually agreed-on price presupposes that the buyer and seller cooperate in settling on a price and, once a price has been agreed on, in actually exchanging the goods and money that the deal requires. Such economic exchanges are regulated by social custom and, in modern societies, by a complex system of laws permitting the drawing up of contracts that legally bind individuals to the performance of the agreement terms. Other laws, such as those that prohibit theft of private property or forbid others from assault, rape, and murder, are part of a social contract that we make with one another that allows us to live together in mass societies with a reasonable degree of freedom and security.

Many people are skeptical about whether there is single, universal correct moral viewpoint. However, almost everyone believes that there is a difference between right and wrong and that most people understand that difference and can use that understanding to guide their behavior. Ethical decision making, like most other things in the modern age, is something that can be rationalized and practiced in accordance with a technique. The technique of ethical decision making consists in a conscious attempt to get a clear view of the issues, options, and arguments that present themselves in any situation that calls for ethical judgment or decision. The technique is basically this:

1. Identify all *stakeholders*—that is, all individuals whose interests might be affected by a decision.
2. Identify all possible courses of action that one might follow.
3. Review all arguments for each option, developing pros and cons in terms of their potential risks and rewards for all stakeholders.
4. Then, after having carefully worked through such deliberations, make a rational choice about which of the available options has the strongest set of moral reasons behind it.[10]

Moral reasons are those that involve ethical principles governing such notions as fairness, justice, equality, duty, obligation, responsibility, and various kinds of rights. In most ethical decisions, such reasons contend with other, nonmoral reasons for actions based on prudence or self-interest, efficiency, and economy. From the moral point of view, ethical reasons ought always override nonmoral reasons for action when the two kinds of reasons conflict, although people do not always do what they ought to. Ethical decisions concerning the use of technologies involving judgments of value and obligation, responsibility and liability, and assessments of risk and benefit can arise at various levels: the personal level of individual behavior, the level of institutional or organizational policy, and the social level of public policy. As individuals, we are the consumers and users of the products of technology in our everyday lives; as workers or students, we belong to and participate in institutions or organizations whose policies and practices can affect our health and well-being; and as citizens, we all must be concerned about the ethical issues that we face because of modern technology.

Ethical concerns arising from technology can be divided into four kinds. The first and most basic address questions about whether and how traditional ethical values and norms apply in new technological contexts. Technological innovations enlarge the scope of possible human action by allowing us to do some things that we could not do before (for example, liver transplants) and to do things we could do before in different ways (for example, reheat food in microwave ovens). Each new technology thus raises the implicit ethical questions: "Should we employ this new technique/technology?" and if so, "How should we employ this new technique/technology?" In many cases, such questions are answered easily. However, in many other cases, decisions about whether, how, and when to use particular technologies can raise difficult and troubling ethical issues about how our traditional ethical values and rules apply in new technological contexts.

To illustrate this kind of issue, consider how our traditional notion of privacy is being altered by modern computer and communications technologies that make it much easier to collect and analyze information about individuals. In this arena, people are asking how the traditional value that we place on privacy can be protected in the digital age. Jay Stanley and Barry Steinhardt (Selection 2.2.3) raise the alarm concerning the increasing use of electronic-surveillance technologies by the government and giant corporations, and James Stacey Taylor (Selection 2.2.4) argues that on balance the use of these types of technologies will make us more rather than less secure, assuming that their use is properly regulated and controlled. But as even Taylor admits, how the calculation of risks and benefits turns out will depend to a great extent on the social and political contexts in which these technologies are employed and by whom.

Traditional approaches to ethics are basically two kinds: *utilitarian* (consequentialist) and *deontological* (Kantian). Consequentialist reasoning in ethics involves evaluating the rightness or wrongness of actions or policies in terms of the goodness or badness of the consequences that they produce. Ian Barbour (Selection 1.3.1) points out that it is often impossible to apply utilitarian, or consequentialist, reasoning to ethical problems involving technologies because it is difficult to quantify and compare the expected benefits, harms, and risks that they may produce when placed in use. One main theme of this book is that when we evaluate which new technologies to develop, which to deploy, and how to deploy them, we need to consider carefully both the benefits and costs and the opportunities and risks that the technologies entail—to the extent that we are capable of making such judgments. Often doing this sort of *cost-benefit analysis* is very difficult or extremely inaccurate because (1) manifold aspects need to be considered, (2) costs and benefits often have no common measurement scale (if they can be measured at all), and (3) we are uncertain in predicting future or long-term consequences of introducing a new technology into society. A second problem with the consequentialist approach is that it does not take into account the way in which benefits and harms are distributed and thus may give rise to allocations of social costs and benefits that are unjust. Despite these problems, consequentialist reasoning remains the dominant approach in the moral evaluation of technology.

Deontological theories in ethics emphasize not only justice but also rights and duties, which in some cases will lead to ethical judgments that would require us to follow a moral rule, honor a right, or discharge a moral duty even if doing so does not produce the greatest good. The theory of John Rawls may provide a way of combining the best elements of each approach by suggesting a way in which we can balance freedom and equality that allows each person the maximal liberty to pursue his or her own self-interest, compatible with an equal liberty on the part of others, while also requiring that deviations from equality be arranged so that they benefit the least advantaged.[11] Under this sort of view, for instance, everyone would have an equal liberty to benefit from new pharmaceutical treatments for disease, but the poorest and sickest among us would be entitled to social support to ensure that they can access these lifesaving technologies. Generally speaking, deonotological considerations set limits on the possible uses of technologies and counsel us to employ our technologies only within the limits of what is ethically permissible. So, for instance, although supercomputers operated by the National Security Agency make it technologically possible for the government to monitor the billions of e-mail messages that fly around the planet each day, ethical considerations concerning civil liberties such as freedom of speech and privacy should determine what forms of electronic surveillance should be allowed.

A second kind of ethical problem arises concerning some sociotechnological practices that, although innocuous in themselves, when employed by individuals, raise serious concerns when their effects are aggregated across millions of users. There is, for instance, nothing intrinsically wrong with throwing empty bottles and cans into the trash to be carted off to the nearest landfill. But when millions of American households engage in this practice on a regular basis, we find that we are wasting recyclable resources and running rapidly out of space for new landfills. Similar sorts of *aggregation problems* arise with respect to air and water pollution, overfishing, suburban development, and many other cases in which the aggregate and cumulative effects of individual sociotechnological choices threaten the long-term well-being of all.

The current debate over global climate change due to the accumulation of greenhouse gases in Earth's atmosphere exemplifies this kind of ethical issue. The 2007 report of the Intergovernmental Panel on Climate Change (IPCC) documents the fact that "the atmospheric concentrations of carbon dioxide, methane, and nitrous oxide have increased markedly as a result of human activities since 1750 and now far exceed pre-industrial values."[12] The changes are mainly due to the burning of fossil fuels and agriculture and are thus anthropogenic—that is, caused by human activity. We are already seeing the effects of this global warming in phenomena such as the shrinking of glaciers, the defrosting of the tundra, and the reduction in Arctic ice in the summer. The IPCC predicts that unless we do something to stabilize the atmosphere, Earth may reach a "tipping point" later in this century that will dramatically alter Earth's climate and produce a significant rise in the ocean levels that will inundate many coastal areas and cause other significant environmental damage. In his popular documentary film, *An Inconvenient Truth,* former vice president Al Gore states his view that global climate change "is not a political issue; it is a moral issue, one that affects the survival of human civilization."[13] (Gore and the IPCC were awarded the 2007 Nobel Peace Prize for their work on the issue of global climate change.)

Garrett Hardin (Selection 2.5.1) analyzed similar moral problems in his famous essay "The Tragedy of the Commons," using as his example herdsmen overgrazing common lands. In such cases, each herdsman treats the common pasture as an inexhaustible resource and seeks to maximize his own self-interest. But if every herdsman does this, the result is that the pastureland soon becomes overgrazed so that nobody can use it. Earth's atmosphere has been treated in this way by humankind throughout most all of our history, but especially since the beginning of the industrial age. We are rapidly reaching the limits of how much carbon the atmosphere can absorb without altering its geochemistry. Hardin argues that voluntary measures to limit this kind of

sited 19

succeed and that the only solution available to us is greater responsibility is based not on individual acts of conscience but on "definite ...ts" under which we mutually agree to coerce ourselves into reducing of greenhouse gases into the atmosphere.

...phen Gardiner (Selection 2.5.2) points out, we use the term *responsibility* in ... backward-looking, or retrospective, and a forward-looking, or prospective, ...se. In the retrospective sense, we think of responsibility primarily as liability for causing past harms, particularly in order to allocate blame and determine who should make amends. If we adopt this view of responsibility for global climate change, then clearly the older industrialized nations—such as England, Germany, and the United States—are responsible for the greater proportion of the greenhouse gases that have accumulated in the atmosphere and thus should bear the primary responsibility for cleaning up the mess. A second reason for allocating responsibility primarily to the older industrialized nations is that they are richer than other nations and can more easily bear the burden. On the other hand, from the prospective point of view, we still need to determine how to control future emissions of greenhouse gases, and in this case, various proposals have been made about how to allocate this responsibility for the present and future. One proposal that Gardiner discusses suggests that we determine the current acceptable level of anthropogenic greenhouse gas emissions necessary to safeguard the health of the planet and then allocate shares of that amount to each country based on its population. Under this scenario, however, the older industrialized countries would still bear the greatest burden of reduction. The United States with roughly 5 percent of the world's population is responsible for emitting roughly 25 percent of the greenhouse gases, while India and China, although they are both rapidly industrializing, still are below their per capita allocations. Under most all of these scenarios, it is becomingly increasingly clear that continued delay in addressing this global problem is not an acceptable option.

A third class of ethical problems associated with technology concerns questions of *distributive justice* and social equality. New technologies generally benefit or advantage certain groups or members of society over others—namely, those who have mastery over or access to the technology first. In many cases, we think that because such advantages are earned through hard work or special knowledge they are therefore deserved. However, in other cases, we may feel that such restricted access to some technologies gives certain individuals or groups unfair advantages over others, and we seek to extend access to everyone in the society. Public libraries, for instance, were built to ensure that everyone could obtain access to books and learning. Today, we are putting computers and Internet connections into public schools for the same reason. Questions of social justice and equality of opportunity thus can be occasioned by technological innovation. Freeman Dyson (Selection 1.3.3) discusses several historical examples of this phenomenon and goes on to propose some technologies of the future that may increase social justice.

Questions of social justice are also at the heart of the debate over the current wave of globalization. Some authors, such as Thomas Friedman (Selection 2.1.1) and Jagdish Bagwati (Selection 2.1.2), believe that globalization, as it has developed over the past several decades since the advent of the information age, is a net benefit to everyone on the planet and has the potential to alleviate poverty and create prosperity worldwide. Others, such as Joseph Stiglitz (Selection 2.1.3) and the International Forum on Globalization (IFG) (Selection 2.1.4), believe that the rules under which globalization has been conducted thus far are inherently unfair and are designed to allocate the benefits primarily to the already-rich countries and corporations at the expense of the poor and vulnerable. They argue that considerations of social justice demand that the global economic system be reformed to produce greater fairness and justice for all citizens of Earth. And in the spirit of Hans Jonas's notion of long-range responsibility (Selection 1.3.2), the IFG proposes that certain critical resources, such as freshwater, be placed off-limits to the market.

A fourth and final kind of ethical question raised by technology concerns the scope of modern technology's power to alter the world. In earlier and simpler times, we humans did not have the power to disturb very much the balance of nature or affect the life prospects of other species or future generations of human beings. But when we entered the *nuclear age*, all that changed. With nuclear weapons, we now have the power to destroy virtually all life on Earth. Nuclear waste material from our reactors will last 10,000 years, posing a potential threat to generations as yet unborn. Issues and concerns of this type raise what are perhaps the most profound ethical questions about humankind's relationship to nature through technology. Should we continue down the course set for us by Bacon and Descartes, who advised us to seek knowledge so that we could become the masters of nature, or should we change this course toward stewardship and long-term sustainability?

As Hans Jonas (Selection 1.3.2) argues, some contemporary technologies seem to open new and deeply troubling ethical issues, issues of a kind that humankind has never had to address before. The existence of nuclear weapons, for instance, forces us to "consider the global condition of human life, and the far-off future, even, the existence of the human race." The emerging technology of genetic engineering creates the prospect of our designing our own children and turning humanity itself into a kind of artifact. Some authors, such as Lee Silver (Selection 2.4.1), seem to welcome this prospect, but others, such as Leon Kass (Selection 2.4.2), believe that we are at a crossroads that requires that we relinquish the opportunity to acquire the knowledge that would enable us to create such a brave new world. Others, such as Michael Sandel (Selection 2.4.3), believe that we can place reasonable limits on how biotechnology and genetic engineering will be employed on human beings that will allow some uses but prohibit others. Genetic engineering of plants and some animal species is already in widespread use, as pointed out by Claire Hope Cummings (Selection 2.4.4), and it may already be impossible to put this particular genie back in the bottle. Jonas, for his part, believes that technologies such as these that give us the capability to alter nature in fundamental ways should be approached with a sense of "long-range responsibility" and, above all, a sense of humility.

ENERGY, ENVIRONMENT, AND A SUSTAINABLE FUTURE

Increasing evidence shows that our current technological society is rapidly transforming Earth's environment and probably not for the better. Hardly a day goes by that we do not hear of global environmental problems such as deforestation, species extinction, depletion of nonrenewable resources, desertification, acid rain, water pollution, ozone destruction, and atmospheric warming. In part, these problems represent the long-term and largely unforeseen effects of the Industrial Revolution, but they are also caused by the sheer weight of human population growth and the increasing demands that it places on Earth's ecosystem.

As Robert Kates (Selection 2.5.4) points out, there has been much discussion of the idea of a transition to systems of sustainable development, and many organizations and institutions now say they are committed to helping to bring about a more sustainable future. However, until recently the concept of sustainable development was ambiguous and ill defined, and discussions often tended to sidestep difficult questions about the real trade-offs between economic growth and environmental protection, and between the interests of the present and future generations. But a study group of the National Academy of Sciences in 1999 helped clarify the matter by defining a sustainability transition as one "that would meet the human needs for food, nurture, housing, education, and employment" for what is now predicted to be a maximum human population of about 10 billion people around the midpoint of the twenty-first century. Meeting this goal will require significantly reducing current levels of hunger and poverty while maintaining the essential life-support systems of the planet.

In 2000 the United Nations adopted the Millennium Development Goals (MDGs) in which the nations of the world committed themselves to the goals of eradicating extreme hunger and poverty; achieving universal primary education; promoting gender equality and empowering women; reducing child mortality; improving maternal health; combating HIV/AIDS, malaria, and other infectious diseases; and ensuring environmental sustainability.[14] According to the most recent MDG progress report, some progress has been made in some regions in meeting these goals by the target date of 2015, but much more still needs to be done. In particular, it is crucial that the richest countries honor their commitments to provide development assistance to the poor countries of the world. Particularly troubling is the continued increase of climate-warming carbon dioxide in Earth's atmosphere and the continuing migration of poor people from rural areas into already overcrowded cities. However, there are some hopeful signs even here as Janet Sawin and Kristen Hughes (Selection 2.5.3) report in their analysis of the ways in which improved building design, construction techniques, and energy-saving technologies can help us to create "greener" cities. The seeds of a future sustainable society are already present, but we need to nurture them so that they continue to grow.

The global threats of the twenty-first century require social solidarity and technological innovation for their solution. These threats are different in several important ways from the threats that we faced throughout most of our previous history. First, these threats arise not mainly from the consequences of individual acts or omissions or from forces beyond humankind's control but from our own collective action. Second, they do not involve direct harms, for the most part, but rather increased risks of harm that are distributed very broadly across individuals, often without their active participation or knowledge. Third, the threats affect not only the present but also the future—often the distant, incalculable future. Fourth, they threaten not only humans but also other animals, the natural environment, and life itself. Fifth, they are also to one degree or another the result of technology; they are problems that have arisen in part because of new powers given to us by technological progress, powers that we have not always learned to use wisely and responsibly. Sixth, they not only affect single communities or even single nations but also the whole of humankind.

Our previous ethics has not prepared us to cope with such global threats. Traditional ethics has focused primarily on the moral requirements concerning individual action, on the direct dealings between persons, rather than on the remote effects of our collective action. This problem is particularly important with respect to widely distributed technologies, such as the internal combustion engine, whereby the cumulative effects of individual decisions can have a major impact on air quality even though no single individual is responsible for the smog. By and large, traditional moral norms deal with the present and near-future effects of actions of individual human beings and do not prepare us to deal with cumulative effects and statistical deaths. Traditional ethics, above all, has been anthropocentric—the entire nonhuman world has been viewed as a thing devoid of moral standing or significance except insofar as it could be bent to satisfy human purposes. We have assumed that the natural world was our enemy and that it did not require our care (for what could we possibly do to harm it really?), and nature was not regarded as an object of human responsibility.

In the past, we have attempted to fashion our ethical theories in terms of these assumptions. The traditional maxims of ethics—for example, "Love thy neighbor as thyself," "Do unto others as you would have them do unto you," and "Never treat your fellow man as a means only but always also as an end in himself"—are in keeping with the individualistic, present-oriented, and anthropocentric assumptions of our ethical traditions. Even the Christian ethic of universal love does not transcend the barriers of time, community, and species. Even more modern ethical theories such as utilitarianism and Kantian ethics do not provide particularly good guidance when it comes to the sorts of ethical concerns raised by technology. In part this is because they were designed to be used to evaluate individual actions of particular moral agents. But the sociotechnological practices that comprise our collective action are not only made up of many individual choices—such as the choice to have a child, to eat a hamburger, or to invest in a mining stock—but also the aggregation of these individual choices, plus those of organized collectivities such as corporations and governments. In most cases, the individuals, business executives, or politicians who are making the choices that add up to our collective insecurity do not intend these threats to result, and neither they nor we consequently feel any sense of responsibility for them.

Although individuals view themselves as moral agents and consider themselves bearers of responsibility in all the roles in which they participate, the collectivities to which we belong do not. All the threats that we face are in part the result of this diffusion of responsibility. How then should we, the citizens of Earth, be responding to these environmental questions? Do people in richer countries have any responsibility to help those in poorer ones? Do we, in general, have any responsibilities to future generations concerning the long-term social and environmental effects of our present economic, lifestyle, and political choices? The notion of responsibility that we need to cultivate is not the backward-looking notion of responsibility as liability, which seeks to allocate blame for past harms, but the forward-looking sense of responsibility in which each of us and every organization and institution "takes responsibility" for doing our part to combat social injustice and to protect environmental quality for future generations of humans and the nonhuman species with whom we share this planet. This notion of social responsibility, although it is voluntary and discretionary, places real demands on us as individuals and members of communities and requires that we think carefully about the decisions and choices that we make.

All too often, decisions that involve complex political choices involving technologies are left to the discretion of elites (for example, scientists, engineers, policy "wonks," and corporate and government officials) even though the consequences of their decisions will usually affect the interests of others who are not elites. The other interested but often silent parties are sometime called *stakeholders*. We are all stakeholders in decisions concerning technology, but not infrequently the scientific, political, or corporate elites make decisions about these questions in ways that primarily benefit themselves at the expense of other stakeholders. It is often relatively easy for elites to "manufacture consent" for policies that they prefer by selectively sharing information about the possible risks and benefits of a particular technology policy with other stakeholders whose interests might be adversely affected by it.[15] For instance, in the 1950s U.S. soldiers were ordered to witness nuclear explosions and were told that there was no risk of harm due to radiation. In fact, there was a risk, and years later many of the soldiers who participated in these tests began developing lethal cancers. More recently, automobile companies, such as General Motors, conspired with giant oil companies and corrupt officials to "kill" a prototype electric car, the EV-1, despite consumer interest in an economical and nonpolluting alternative to petroleum-based personal transportation.[16]

To protect citizens against such unscrupulous practices, the government has established various special agencies, such as the Food and Drug Administration (FDA), the Environmental Protection Agency (EPA), and the Occupational Safety and Health Administration (OSHA), which are mandated to act as watchdogs and look out for the interests of the public and to prevent people from being exposed to unnecessary or unreasonable risks without their consent. However, the operations of these very governmental agencies have often become politicized, and key officials appointed to run these agencies sometimes represent corporate interests rather than the public interest.

Given the phenomena of regulatory capture by corporate interests, a more reliable line of defense is the hundreds of nongovernmental organizations (NGOs), such as Common Cause, Greenpeace, or the International Center for Technology Assessment, who conduct independent research, educate the public, and lobby decision makers to enforce and protect the stakeholder interests that they are supposed to represent. Such public-interest groups and the social movements that they represent play an important role in politics and provide a means, in addition to the ballot, by which ordinary citizens can participate in large-scale decisions that many affect their lives for good or for ill.

However, none of these advocacy groups can be effective without the support of an informed and attentive citizenry. In democratic societies, individuals and groups are given the right to inform themselves on the issues, associate with others having similar or common interests, and participate in the political discussions that will determine which laws and policies will be enacted. If we fail as individuals to exercise these rights—that is, if we shirk our responsibilities as technological citizens—it is likely that others will end up making these decisions for us, and when they do, they may not always have our best interests at heart or in mind. If we accept the responsibility to educate ourselves about the issues and to participate in the public conversations about them, then we will have some voice in how things will be decided and some control over the future directions that our technological society will take. In the last analysis, there is no way for us to escape this responsibility, living as we do at the cusp of the Third Millennium, for we are now all the children of invention.

Morton Winston
August 2007

NOTES

1. For a rather long but still incomplete list of some of humankind's most significant inventions, see the Time Line of Significant Technological Innovations on the inside front and back covers.
2. Compare this definition to that found in Rudi Volti, *Society and Technological Change*, 2nd ed. (New York: St. Martin's Press, 1992), in which technology is defined as "a system based on the application of knowledge, manifested in physical objects and organizational forms, for the attainment of specific goals" (p. 6).
3. The term *valence* is also used to describe the way in which tools and technological systems have "a tendency to interaction in similar situations in identifiable and predictable ways." The terms *end* and *focal function* refer to the purpose in the mind of the designer of the artifact. See Corlann Gee Bush, "Women and the Assessment of Technology: To Think, to Be; to Unthink, to Free," in *Machina ex Dea*, Joan Rothschild (Editor) (New York: Teachers College Press, 1983), 151.
4. Rene Descartes, "Discourse on the Method of Rightly Conducting the Reason and Seeking for Truth in the Sciences" (1637), *The Philosophical Works of Descartes*, Vol. I, trans. E. S. Haldane and G. R. T. Ross (Cambridge, England: Cambridge University Press, 1970), 119.
5. Francis Bacon, "Thoughts and Conclusions," in *The Philosophy of Francis Bacon*, ed. B. Famington (Chicago: University of Chicago Press, 1964), 93.
6. See Bruno Latour, *Science in Action* (Cambridge, MA: Harvard University Press, 1987).
7. See Donald B. Kraybill, *The Riddle of Amish Culture* (Baltimore: Johns Hopkins University Press, 1989), especially Chapter 7.
8. The terms *techno-optimism* and *techno-pessimism* were suggested by the discussion of pessimism and optimism about technology found in Mary Tiles and Hans Oberdiek, *Living in a Technological Culture: Human Tools and Human Values* (New York: Routledge, 1995), 14–31.
9. See Edward Tenner, *Why Things Bite Back: Technology and the Revenge of Unintended Consequences* (New York: Random House, 1996).
10. For more on ethical decision making, see C. E. Harris, Jr., *Applying Moral Theories*, 3rd ed. (Belmont CA: Wadsworth, 1997).
11. John Pauls, *A Theory of Justice* (Cambridge, MA: Harvard University Press, 1971).
12. Intergovernmental Panel on Climate Change, "Contribution of Working Group I to the Fourth Assessment Report," February 5, 2007; available online at http://www.ipcc.ch. Accessed July 7, 2007.
13. Davis Guggenhein, *An Inconvenient Truth*, Paramount Pictures, 2006.
14. United Nations, "Millennium Development Goals"; available online at http://www.un.org/millenniumgoals. Accessed July 9, 2007.
15. The idea of manufacturing consent is based on the work of Noam Chomsky, See especially, Noam Chomsky, "The Manufacture of Consent," in *The Chomsky Reader*, ed. J. Peck (New York: Pantheon Books, 1987), 121–136.
16. Chris Paine, *Who Killed the Electric Car?* Sony Pictures, 2006.

PART ONE

Perspectives on Technology

1.1 Historical Perspectives

1.2 Social/Political Perspectives

1.3 Ethical Perspectives

1.1 HISTORICAL PERSPECTIVES

1.1.1 The Invention of Invention

DAVID LANDES

In his book *The Wealth and Poverty of Nations,* David Landes, Coolidge Professor of History and Professor of Economics Emeritus at Harvard University, explores the role of technology in determining the economic status of three major world regions, Europe, the Middle East, and the Orient, during the second millennium.

From his perspective as both a historian and an economist, he identifies five major technologies that were highly developed and refined during the Middle Ages although their beginnings predate this era. Landes proposes that various social and cultural conditions in those three societies encouraged the refinement of these and other technologies. In turn, these technologies had major impacts on the lives of citizens and also prompted subsequent technological advances.

As the title of this selection suggests, Landes believes that how a society encourages and supports the development of technology determines the power and influence it achieves as well as its sustainability. Although technological innovation is not the only driver of social and economic change, its importance cannot be discounted.

FOCUS QUESTIONS

1. Discuss ways in which this article suggests that technology challenges authority and aids in the redistribution of the power held by a few to a greater number of individuals. What long-range impacts did these technologies have, and what might have happened if such changes did not occur?
2. What factors not related to technology were at work in the societies examined in this article? Discuss how they either facilitated further technological development or were an impediment to it.
3. How does the focus of this article on five unique technological innovations compare with Cowan's view of technological systems in Section 1.1.2? Explain the differences and similarities in their perspectives by examining selected technologies from each historical period.
4. In what ways do the points made by Landes in this article compare with issues presented in the Globalization and Economic Development section? Do the cultural factors discussed by Landes still operate in our present globalized world? Explain.

KEYWORDS

division of labor, ecclesiastical authority, free market, institutionalized property rights, inventive society, key-machine, productivity, religious zealot, replication, secular authority, theocracy

---

Source: From *The Wealth and Poverty of Nations: Why Some Are So Rich and Some Are So Poor* by David S. Landes, pp. 45–49. Copyright © 1998 by David S. Landes. Reprinted by permission of W.W. Norton & Company, Inc.

When Adam Smith came to write about these things in the eighteenth century, he pointed out that division of labor and widening of the market encourage technological innovation. This in fact is exactly what happened in the Europe of the Middle Ages—one of the most inventive societies that history had known. Some may be surprised: for a long time one saw these centuries as a dark interlude between the grandeur of Rome and the brilliance of the Renaissance. That cliché no longer holds in matters technological.[1] A few examples:

1. *The water wheel.* It had been known to the Romans, who began to do interesting things with it during the last century of the empire, when the conquests were over and the supply of slaves had shrunk almost to nothing. By then it was too late; order and trade were breaking down. The device may well have survived on Church estates, where it freed clerics for prayer. In any event, it was revived in the tenth and eleventh centuries, multiplying easily in a region of wide rainfall and ubiquitous watercourses. In England, that peripheral, backward island, the Domesday census of 1086 showed some 5,600 of these mills; the Continent had many more.

Even more impressive is the way waterpower technique advanced. Millwrights increased pressure and efficiency by building dams and ponds and by lining the wheels up to utilize the diminishing energy for a variety of tasks, beginning with those that needed the most power, and descending. At the same time, the invention or improvement of accessory devices—cranks, toothed gears—made it possible to use the power at a distance, change its direction, convert it from rotary to reciprocating motion, and apply it to an increasing variety of tasks, hence not only grinding grain, but fulling (pounding) cloth, thereby transforming the woolen manufacture; hammering metal; rolling and drawing sheet metal and wire; mashing hops for beer; pulping rags for paper. "Paper, which was manufactured by hand and foot for a thousand years or so following its invention by the Chinese and adoption by the Arabs, was manufactured mechanically as soon as it reached medieval Europe in the thirteenth century.... Paper had traveled nearly halfway around the world, but no culture or civilization on its route had tried to mechanize its manufacture."[2] Europe, as nowhere else, was a power-based civilization.

2. *Eyeglasses.* A seemingly banal affair, the kind of thing that appears so commonplace as to be trivial. And yet the invention of spectacles more than doubled the working life of skilled craftsmen, especially those who did fine jobs: scribes (crucial before the invention of printing) and readers, instrument and toolmakers, close weavers, metal workers.

The problem is biological: because the crystalline lens of the human eye hardens around the age of forty, it produces a condition similar to farsightedness (actually presbyopia). The eye can no longer focus on close objects. But around the age of forty, a medieval craftsman could reasonably expect to live and work another twenty years, the best years of his working life ... if he could see well enough. Eyeglasses solved the problem.

We think we know where and when the first spectacles appeared. Crude magnifying glasses and crystals (*lapides ad legendum*) had been found earlier and used for reading.[3] The trick was to improve them so as to reduce distortion and connect a pair into a wearable device, thus leaving the hands free. This apparently first happened in Pisa toward the end of the thirteenth century. We have a contemporary witness (1306) who says he knew the inventor:

> Not all the arts [in the sense of arts and crafts] have been found; we shall never see an end of finding them. Every day one could discover a new art.... It is not twenty years since there was discovered the art of making spectacles that help one to see well, an art that is one of the best and most necessary in the world. And that is such a short time ago that a new art that never before existed was invented.... I myself saw the man who discovered and practiced it and I talked with him.[4]

These convex lenses were obviously not uniform or of what we would call prescription quality. But here medieval optical technology, however primitive, was saved by the nature of the difficulty: the lenses to correct presbyopia do not have to be extremely accurate. Their function is primarily to magnify, and although some magnify more than others, just about any and all will help the user. This is why people will occasionally borrow glasses in a restaurant to read the menu, and why five-and-dime stores can put out boxes of such spectacles for sale. The buyer simply tries a few and picks the most suitable. Myopes (short-sighted people) cannot do that.

That was the beginning. By the middle of the fifteenth century, Italy, particularly Florence and Venice, was making thousands of spectacles, fitted with concave as well as convex lenses, for myopes as well as presbyopes. Also, the Florentines at least (and presumably others) understood that visual acuity declines with age and so made the convex lenses in five-year strengths and the concave in two, enabling users to buy in batches and change with time.

Eyeglasses made it possible to do fine work and use fine instruments. But also the converse: eyeglasses encouraged the invention of fine instruments, indeed pushed Europe in a direction found nowhere else. The Muslims knew the astrolabe, but that was it. The Europeans went on to invent gauges, micrometers, fine wheel cutters—a battery of tools linked to precision measurement and control. They thereby laid the basis for articulated machines with fitted parts.

Close work: when other civilizations did it, they did it by long habituation. The skill was in the hand, not the eye-and-tool. They achieved remarkable results, but no piece was like any other; whereas Europe was already moving toward replication—batch and then mass production. This knowledge of lenses, moreover, was a school for further optical advances, and not only in Italy. Both telescope and microscope were invented in the Low Countries around 1600 and spread quickly from there.

Europe enjoyed a monopoly of corrective lenses for three to four hundred years. In effect they doubled the skilled craft workforce, and more than doubled it if one takes into account the value of experience.[5]

3. *The mechanical clock.* Another banality, so commonplace that we take it for granted. Yet Lewis Mumford quite correctly called it "the key-machine."[6]

Before the invention of this machine, people told time by sun (shadow sticks or dials) and water clocks. Sun clocks worked of course only on clear days; water clocks misbehaved when the temperature fell toward freezing, to say nothing of long-run drift as a result of sedimentation and clogging. Both of these devices served reasonably well in sunny climes; but north of the Alps one can go weeks without seeing the sun, while temperatures vary not only seasonally but from day to night.

Medieval Europe gave new importance to reliable time. The Church first, with its seven daily prayer offices, one of which, matins, was in spite of its name a nocturnal rite and required an alarm arrangement to wake clerics before dawn. (Hence our children's round, *Frére Jacques:* Brother Jacques has overslept and failed to sound the bells for matins.)* And then the new cities and towns had their temporal servitudes. Squeezed by their walls, they had to know and order time in order to organize collective activity and ration space. They set a time to wake, to go to work, to open the market, close the market, leave work, and finally a time to put out fires (*couvre-feu* gives us our word "curfew") and go to sleep.

All of this was compatible with the older devices so long as there was only one authoritative timekeeper; but with urban growth and the multiplication of time signals, discrepancy brought discord and strife. Society needed a more dependable instrument of time measurement and found it in the mechanical clock.

We do not know who invented this machine or where. It seems to have appeared in Italy and England (perhaps simultaneous invention) in the last quarter of the thirteenth century. Once known, it spread rapidly, driving out the water clocks; but not solar dials, which were needed to check the new machines against the timekeeper of last resort. These early versions were rudimentary, inaccurate, and prone to breakdown—so much so

*The English and German versions of the verse (and maybe others) traduce the meaning by saying that "morning bells are ringing." The point is, they are not ringing.

that it paid to buy a clockmaker along with the clock.

Ironically, the new machine tended to undermine ecclesiastical authority. Although Church ritual had sustained an interest in timekeeping throughout the centuries of urban collapse that followed the fall of Rome, Church time was nature's time. Day and night were divided into the same number of parts, so that except at the equinoxes, day and night hours were unequal; and then of course the length of these hours varied with the seasons. But the mechanical clock kept equal hours, and this implied a new time reckoning. The Church resisted, not coming over to the new hours for about a century. From the start, however, the towns and cities took equal hours as their standard, and the public clocks installed in the towers and belfries of town halls and market squares became the very symbol of a new, secular municipal authority. Every town wanted one; conquerors seized them as specially precious spoils of war; tourists came to see and hear these machines the way they made pilgrimages to sacred relics. New times, new customs.

The clock was the greatest achievement of medieval mechanical ingenuity. Revolutionary in conception, it was more radically new than its makers knew. This was the first example of a digital as opposed to an analog device: it counted a regular, repeating sequence of discrete actions (the swings of an oscillating controller) rather than tracked continuous, regular motion such as the moving shadow of a sundial or the flow of water. Today we know that such a repeating frequency can be more regular than any continuous phenomenon, and just about all high-precision devices are now based on the digital principle. But no one could have known that in the thirteenth century, which thought that because time was continuous, it ought to be tracked and measured by some other continuity.

The mechanical clock had to meet the unsparing standards of earth and sun, no blinking or hiding its failures. The result was relentless pressure to improve technique and design. At every stage, clockmakers led the way to accuracy and precision: masters of miniaturization, detectors and correctors of error, searchers for new and better. They remain the pioneers of mechanical engineering—examples and teachers to other branches.

Finally, the clock brought order and control, both collective and personal. Its public display and private possession laid the basis for temporal autonomy: people could now coordinate comings and goings without dictation from above. (Contrast the military, where only officers need know the time.) The clock provided the punctuation marks for group activity, while enabling individuals to order their own work (and that of others) so as to enhance productivity. Indeed, the very notion of productivity is a by-product of the clock: once one can relate performance to uniform time units, work is never the same. One moves from the task-oriented time consciousness of the peasant (one job after another, as time and light permit) and the time-filling busyness of the domestic servant (always something to do) to an effort to maximize product per unit of time (time is money). The invention of the mechanical clock anticipates in its effects the economic analysis of Adam Smith: increase in the wealth of nations derives directly from improvement of the productive powers of labor.

The mechanical clock remained a European (Western) monopoly for some three hundred years; in its higher forms, right into the twentieth century. Other civilizations admired and coveted clocks, or more accurately, their rulers and elites did; but none could make them to European standard.

The Chinese built a few astronomical water clocks in the Tang and Sung eras—complicated and artful pieces that may have kept excellent time in the short run, before they started clogging. (Owing to sediment, water clocks keep a poor rate over time.) These monumental machines were imperial projects, done and reserved for the emperor and his astrologers. The Chinese treated time and knowledge of time as a confidential aspect of sovereignty, not to be shared with the people. This monopoly touched both daily and year-round time. In the cities, drums and other noisemakers signaled the hours (equal to two of our hours), and everywhere the imperial calendar defined the seasons and their activities. Nor was this calendar a uniform, objectively determinable datum. Each emperor in turn had his own calendar, placed his own seal on the passage of time. Private calendrical calculation would have been pointless.

These interval hour signals in large cities were no substitute for continuing knowledge and awareness. In particular, the noises were not numerical signifiers. The hours had names rather than numbers, and that in itself testifies to the absence of a temporal calculus. Without a basis in popular consumption, without a clock trade, Chinese horology regressed and stagnated. It never got beyond water clocks, and by the time China came to know the Western mechanical clock, it was badly placed to understand and copy it. Not for want of interest: the Chinese imperial court and wealthy elites were wild about these machines; but because they were reluctant to acknowledge European technological superiority, they sought to trivialize them as toys. Big mistake.

Islam might also have sought to possess and copy the clock, if only to fix prayers. And as in China, Muslim horologers made water clocks well in advance of anything known in Europe. Such was the legendary clock that Haroun-al-Raschid sent as a gift to Charlemagne around the year 800: no one at the Frankish court could do much with it, and it disappeared to ignorance and neglect. Like the Chinese, the Muslims were much taken with Western clocks and watches, doing their best to acquire them by purchase or tribute. But they never used them to create a public sense of time other than as a call to prayer. We have the testimony here of Ghiselin de Busbecq, ambassador from the Holy Roman Empire to the Sublime Porte in Constantinople, in a letter of 1560: "...if they established public clocks, they think that the authority of their muezzins and their ancient rites would suffer diminution."[7] Sacrilege.

4. *Printing.* Printing was invented in China (which also invented paper) in the ninth century and found general use by the tenth. This achievement is the more impressive, in that the Chinese language, which is written in ideographs (no alphabet), does not lend itself easily to movable type. That explains why Chinese printing consisted primarily of full-page block impressions; also why so much of the old Chinese texts consists of drawings. If one is going to cut a block, it is easier to draw than to carve a multitude of characters. Also, ideographic writing works against literacy: one may learn the characters as a child, but if one does not keep using them, one forgets how to read. Pictures helped.

Block printing limits the range and diffusion of publication. It is well suited to the spread of classic and sacred texts, Buddhist mantras, and the like, but it increases the cost and risk of publishing newer work and tends to small printings. Some Chinese printers did use movable type, but given the character of the written language and the investment required, the technique never caught on as in the West. Indeed, like other Chinese inventions, it may well have been abandoned for a time, to be reintroduced later.[8]

In general, for all that printing did for the preservation and diffusion of knowledge in China, it never "exploded" as in Europe. Much publication depended on government initiative, and the Confucian mandarinate discouraged dissent and new ideas. Even evidence of the falsity of conventional knowledge could be dismissed as appearance.[9] As a result, intellectual activity segmented along personal and regional lines, and scientific achievement shows surprising discontinuities. "The great mathematician Chu Shih-chieh, trained in the northern school, migrated south to Yang-chou, where his books were printed but he could find no disciples. In consequence, the more sophisticated of his achievements became incomprehensible to following generations. But the basic scientific texts were common property everywhere."[10] Basic texts, a kind of canonical writ, are not enough; worse, they may even chill thought.

Europe came to printing centuries after China. It should not be thought, however, that printing made the book and invented reading. On the contrary, the interest in the written word grew rapidly in the Middle Ages, especially after bureaucracy and the rise of towns increased demand for records and documents. Government rests on paper. Much of this verbiage, moreover, was written in the vernacular, shattering the hieratic monopoly of a dead but sacred tongue (Latin) and opening the way to wider readership and a literature of dissent.

As a result, scribes could not keep up with demand. All manner of arrangements were conceived to increase reading material. Manuscripts were prepared and bound in separable fascicles; that divided the labor of writing while enabling several people to read the book at the same time. And as in China, block printing came in before movable type, yielding flysheets more than books and once again copiously illustrated. So when Gutenberg published his Bible in 1452–55, the first Western book printed by movable type (and arguably the most beautiful book ever printed), he brought the new technique to a society that had already vastly increased its output of writing and was fairly panting after it. Within the next half century, printing spread from the Rhineland throughout western Europe. The estimated output of incunabula (books published before 1501) came to millions—2 million in Italy alone.

In spite of printing's manifest advantages, it was not accepted everywhere. The Muslim countries long remained opposed, largely on religious grounds: the idea of a printed Koran was unacceptable. Jews and Christians had presses in Istanbul but not Muslims. The same in India: not until the early nineteenth century was the first press installed. In Europe, on the other hand, no one could put a lid on the new technology. Political authority was too fragmented. The Church had tried to curb vernacular translations of sacred writ and to forbid dissemination of both canonical and noncanonical texts. Now it was overwhelmed. The demons of heresy were out long before Luther, and printing made it impossible to get them back in the box.

5. *Gunpowder.* Europeans probably got this from the Chinese in the early fourteenth, possibly the late thirteenth century. The Chinese knew gunpowder by the eleventh century and used it at first as an incendiary device, both in fireworks and in war, often in the form of tubed flame lances. Its use as a propellant came later, starting with inefficient bombards and arrow launchers and moving on to cannon (late thirteenth century). The efficiency and rationality of some of these devices may be inferred from their names: "the eight-sided magical awe-inspiring wind-and-fire cannon" or the "nine-arrows, heart-penetrating, magically-poisonous fire-thunderer."[11] They were apparently valued as much for their noise as for their killing power. The pragmatic mind finds this metaphorical, rhetorical vision of technology disconcerting.

The Chinese continued to rely on incendiaries rather than explosives, perhaps because of their superior numbers, perhaps because fighting against nomadic adversaries did not call for siege warfare.* Military treatises of the sixteenth century describe hundreds of variations: "sky-flying tubes," apparently descended from the fire lances of five hundred years earlier, used to spray gunpowder and flaming bits of paper on the enemy's sails; "gunpowder buckets" and "fire bricks"—grenades of powder and paper soaked in poison; other devices packed with chemicals and human excrement, intended to frighten, blind, and presumably disgust the enemy; finally, more lethal grenades filled with metal pellets and explosives.[12] Some of these were thrown; others shot from bows. One wonders at this delight in variety, as though war were a display of recipes.

The Chinese used gunpowder in powder form, as the name indicates, and got a weak reaction precisely because the fine-grain mass slowed ignition. The Europeans, on the other hand, learned in the sixteenth century to "corn" their powder, making it in the form of small kernels or pebbles. They got more rapid ignition, and by mixing the ingredients more thoroughly, a more complete and powerful explosion. With that, one could concentrate on range and weight of projectile; no messing around with noise and smell and visual effects.

This focus on delivery, when combined with experience in bell founding (bell metal was

*The Chinese would seem to have been more afraid of rebellion from within than invasion from without. More modern armaments might fall into the wrong hands, and these included those of the generals. Cf. Hall, *Powers and Liberties,* pp. 46–47.

convertible into gun metal, and the techniques of casting were interchangeable), gave Europe the world's best cannon and military supremacy.[13]

As these cases make clear, other societies were falling behind Europe even before the opening of the world (fifteenth century on) and the great confrontation.* Why this should have been so is an important historical question—one learns as much from failure as from success. One cannot look here at every non-European society or civilization, but two deserve a moment's scrutiny.

The first, Islam, initially absorbed and developed the knowledge and ways of conquered peoples. By our period (roughly 1000 to 1500), Muslim rule went from the western end of the Mediterranean to the Indies. Before this, from about 750 to 1100, Islamic science and technology far surpassed those of Europe, which needed to recover its heritage and did so to some extent through contacts with Muslims in such frontier areas as Spain. Islam was Europe's teacher.

Then something went wrong. Islamic science, denounced as heresy by religious zealots, bent under theological pressures for spiritual conformity. (For thinkers and searchers, this could be a matter of life and death.) For militant Islam, the truth had already been revealed. What led *back* to the truth was useful and permissible; all the rest was error and deceit.[14] The historian Ibn Khalduun, conservative in religious matters, was nonetheless dismayed by Muslim hostility to learning:

> When the Muslims conquered Persia (637–642) and came upon an indescribably large number of books and scientific papers, Sa'd bin Abi Waqqas wrote to Umar bin al-Khattab asking him for permission to take them and distribute them as booty among the Muslims. On that occasion, Umar wrote him: "Throw them in the water. If what they contain is right guidance, God has given us better guidance. If it is error, God has protected us against it."[15]

Remember here that Islam does not, as Christianity does, separate the religious from the secular. The two constitute an integrated whole. The ideal state would be a theocracy; and in the absence of such fulfillment, a good ruler leaves matters of the spirit and mind (in the widest sense) to the doctors of the faith. This can be hard on scientists.

As for technology, Islam knew areas of change and advance: one thinks of the adoption of paper; or the introduction and diffusion of new crops such as coffee and sugar; or the Ottoman Turkish readiness to learn the use (but not the making) of cannon and clocks. But most of this came from outside and continued to depend on outside support. Native springs of invention seem to have dried up. Even in the golden age (750–1100), speculation disconnected from practice: "For nearly five hundred years the world's greatest scientists wrote in Arabic, yet a flourishing science contributed nothing to the slow advance of technology in Islam."[16]

The one civilization that might have surpassed the European achievement was China. At least that is what the record seems to show. Witness the long list of Chinese inventions: the wheelbarrow, the stirrup, the rigid horse collar (to prevent choking), the compass, paper, printing, gunpowder, porcelain. And yet in matters of science and technology, China remains a mystery—and this in spite of a monumental effort by the late Joseph Need-ham and others to collect the facts and clarify the issues. The specialists tell us, for example, that Chinese industry long anticipated European: in textiles, where the Chinese had a water-driven machine for spinning hemp in the twelfth century, some five hundred years before the England of the Industrial Revolution knew water frames and mules[17]; or in iron manufacture, where the Chinese early learned to use coal and coke in blast furnaces for smelting iron (or so we are told) and were turning out as many as 125,000 tons of pig iron by the later eleventh century—a figure reached by Britain seven hundred years later.[18]

The mystery lies in China's failure to realize its potential. One generally assumes that knowledge and know-how are cumulative; surely a superior technique, once known, will replace older methods. But Chinese industrial history offers examples of technological oblivion and regression. We saw

*For reasons well worth exploring in the context of the history of ideas and the invention of folklore, a number of scholars have recently tried to propagate the notion that European technology did not catch up to that of Asia until the late eighteenth century. The most active source at the moment is the H-World site on the Internet—a magnet for fallacies and fantasies.

that horology went backward. Similarly, the machine to spin hemp was never adapted to the manufacture of cotton, and cotton spinning was never mechanized. And coal/coke smelting was allowed to fall into disuse, along with the iron industry as a whole. Why?

> It would seem that none of the conventional explanations tells us in convincing fashion why technical progress was absent in the Chinese economy during a period that was, on the whole, one of prosperity and expansion. Almost every element usually regarded by historians as a major contributory cause to the industrial revolution in northwestern Europe was also present in China. There had even been a revolution in the relations between social classes, at least in the countryside; but this had had no important effect on the techniques of production. Only Galilean-Newtonian science was missing; but in the short run this was not important. Had the Chinese possessed, or developed, the seventeenth-century European mania for tinkering and improving, they could easily have made an efficient spinning machine out of the primitive model described by Wang Chen.... A steam engine would have been more difficult; but it should not have posed insuperable difficulties to a people who had been building double-acting piston flame-throwers in the Sung dynasty. The crucial point is that nobody tried. In most fields, agriculture being the chief exception, Chinese technology stopped progressing well before the point at which a lack of scientific knowledge had become a serious obstacle.[19]

Why indeed? Sinologists have put forward several partial explanations. The most persuasive are of a piece:

• The absence of a free market and institutionalized property rights. The Chinese state was always interfering with private enterprise—taking over lucrative activities, prohibiting others, manipulating prices, exacting bribes, curtailing private enrichment. A favorite target was maritime trade, which the Heavenly Kingdom saw as a diversion from imperial concerns, as a divisive force and source of income inequality, worse yet, as an invitation to exit. Matters reached a climax under the Ming dynasty (1368–1644), when the state attempted to prohibit all trade overseas. Such interdictions led to evasion and smuggling, and smuggling brought corruption (protection money), confiscations, violence, and punishment. Bad government strangled initiative, increased the cost of transactions, diverted talent from commerce and industry.

• The larger values of the society. A leading sociological historian (historical sociologist) sees gender relations as a major obstacle: the quasi-confinement of women to the home made it impossible, for example, to exploit textile machinery profitably in a factory setting. Here China differed sharply from Europe or Japan, where women had free access to public space and were often expected to work outside the home to accumulate a dowry or contribute resources to the family.[20]

• The great Hungarian-German-French sinologist, Etienne Balazs, would stress the larger context. He sees China's abortive technology as part of a larger pattern of totalitarian control. He does not explain this by hydraulic centralism, but he does recognize the absence of freedom, the weight of custom, consensus, what passed for higher wisdom. His analysis is worth repeating:

> ...if one understands by totalitarianism the complete hold of the State and its executive organs and functionaries over all the activities of social life, without exception, Chinese society was highly totalitarian.... No private initiative, no expression of public life that can escape official control. There is to begin with a whole array of state monopolies, which comprise the great consumption staples: salt, iron, tea, alcohol, foreign trade. There is a monopoly of education, jealously guarded. There is practically a monopoly of letters (I was about to say, of the press): anything written unofficially, that escapes the censorship, has little hope of reaching the public. But the reach of the Moloch-State, the omnipotence of the bureaucracy, goes much farther. There are clothing regulations, a regulation of public and private construction (dimensions of houses), the colors one wears, the music one hears, the festivals—all are regulated. There are rules for birth and rules for death; the providential State watches minutely over every step of its subjects, from cradle to grave. It is a regime of paper work and harassment [*paperasseries et tracasseries*], endless paper work and endless harassment.
>
> The ingenuity and inventiveness of the Chinese, which have given so much to mankind—silk,

> tea, porcelain, paper, printing, and more—would no doubt have enriched China further and probably brought it to the threshold of modern industry, had it not been for this stifling state control. It is the State that kills technological progress in China. Not only in the sense that it nips in the bud anything that goes against or seems to go against its interests, but also by the customs implanted inexorably by the raison d'Etat. The atmosphere of routine, of traditionalism, and of immobility, which makes any innovation suspect, any initiative that is not commanded and sanctioned in advance, is unfavorable to the spirit of free inquiry.[21]

In short, no one was trying. Why try?

Whatever the mix of factors, the result was a weird pattern of isolated initiatives and Sisyphean discontinuities—up, up, up, and then down again—almost as though the society were held down by a silk ceiling. The result, if not the aim, was change-in-immobility, or maybe immobility-in-change. Innovation was allowed to go (was able to go) so far and no farther.

The Europeans knew much less of these interferences. Instead, they entered during these centuries into an exciting world of innovation and emulation that challenged vested interests and rattled the forces of conservatism. Changes were cumulative; novelty spread fast. A new sense of progress replaced an older, effete reverence for authority. This intoxicating sense of freedom touched (infected) all domains. These were years of heresies in the Church, of popular initiatives that, we can see now, anticipated the rupture of the Reformation; of new forms of expression and collective action that challenged the older art forms, questioned social structures, and posed a threat to other polities; of new ways of doing and making things that made newness a virtue and a source of delight; of Utopias that fantasized better futures rather than recalled paradises lost.

Important in all this was the Church as custodian of knowledge and school for technicians. One might have expected otherwise: that organized spirituality, with its emphasis on prayer and contemplation, would have had little interest in technology. Surely the Church, with its view of labor as penalty for original sin, would not seek to ease the judgment. And yet everything worked in the opposite direction: the desire to free clerics from time-consuming earthly tasks led to the introduction and diffusion of power machinery and, beginning with the Cistercians, to the hiring of lay brothers (*conversi*) to do the dirty work. Employment fostered in turn attention to time and productivity. All of this gave rise on monastic estates to remarkable assemblages of powered machinery—complex sequences designed to make the most of the waterpower available and distribute it through a series of industrial operations. A description of work in the abbey of Clair-vaux in the mid-twelfth century exults in this versatility: "cooking, straining, mixing, rubbing [polishing], transmitting [the energy], washing, milling, bending." The author, clearly proud of these achievements, further tells his readers that he will take the liberty of joking: the fulling hammers, he says, seem to have dispensed the fullers of the penalty for their sins; and he thanks God that such devices can mitigate the oppressive labor of men and spare the backs of their horses.[22]

Why this peculiarly European *joie de trouver*? This pleasure in new and better? This cultivation of invention—or what some have called "the invention of invention"? Different scholars have suggested a variety of reasons, typically related to religious values:

1. The Judeo-Christian respect for manual labor, summed up in a number of biblical injunctions. One example: When God warns Noah of the coming flood and tells him he will be saved, it is not God who saves him. "Build thee an ark of gopher wood," he says, and Noah builds an ark to divine specifications.

2. The Judeo-Christian subordination of nature to man. This is a sharp departure from widespread animistic beliefs and practices that saw something of the divine in every tree and stream (hence naiads and dryads). Ecologists today might think these animistic beliefs preferable to what replaced them, but no one was listening to pagan nature worshippers in Christian Europe.

3. The Judeo-Christian sense of linear time. Other societies thought of time as cyclical, returning to earlier stages and starting over again. Linear time is progressive or regressive,

moving on to better things or declining from some earlier, happier state. For Europeans in our period, the progressive view prevailed.

4. In the last analysis, however, I would stress the market. Enterprise was free in Europe. Innovation worked and paid, and rulers and vested interests were limited in their ability to prevent or discourage innovation. Success bred imitation and emulation, also a sense of power that would in the long run raise men almost to the level of gods. The old legends remained—the expulsion from the Garden, Icarus who flew too high, Prometheus in chains—to warn against hubris. (The very notion of hubris—cosmic insolence—is testimony to some men's pretensions and the efforts of others to curb them.)

But the doers were not paying attention.

NOTES

1. The key piece is the seminal article of Lynn White, Jr., "Technology and Invention in the Middle Ages," *Speculum*, 15 (1940): 141–59.
2. Jean Gimpel, *The Medieval Machine*, p. 14. Cf. White, *Medieval Religion and Technology*, pp. 226–27. White also points out that whereas paper from Muslim lands (not mechanically produced) never shows watermarks, such trademarks appear in Italian paper by the 1280s, a sign of commercial enterprise.
3. On these glasses before eyeglasses, see the work of Zecchin, *Vetro e vetrai di Murano* (Venice, 1989), cited by Ilardi, "Renaissance Florence," p. 510.
4. The speaker is the Dominican Fra Giordano of Pisa, in a sermon at Santa Maria Novella in Florence in 1306. Quoted in White, "Cultural Climates," p. 174; also in reprint, 1978, p. 221. White cites the Italian original. I have made small stylistic changes in the translation. See also Rosen, "Invention of Eyeglasses"; and Ilardi, *Occhiali* and "Renaissance Florence."
5. Moses Abramovitz argues that a longer life span encourages investment in human capital and makes people readier to move to new places and occupations. How much more when the extra years can be the best—"Manpower, Capital, and Technology," p. 55.
6. "The clock is not merely a means of keeping track of the hours, but of synchronizing the actions of men. The clock, not the steam-engine, is the key-machine of the modern industrial age ... at the very beginning of modern technics appeared prophetically the accurate automatic machine.... In its relationship to determinable quantities of energy, to standardization, to automatic action, and finally to its own special product, accurate timing, the clock has been the foremost machine in modern technics; and at each period it has remained in the lead; it marks a perfection toward which other machines aspire"—Mumford, *Technics and Civilization*, pp. 14–15.
7. Cited in Lewis, *The Muslim Discovery of Europe*, p. 233.
8. Sivin, "Science and Medicine," p. 165, says that printing with movable type did not replace the older method until the twentieth century.
9. Cf. Hall, *Powers and Liberties*, p. 49.
10. Elvin, *Pattern of the Chinese Past*, p. 180.
11. Needham, "The Guns of Khaifeng-fu," p. 40.
12. Levathes, *When China Ruled the Seas*, p. 102.
13. On this point, note the development, as early as the sixteenth century, of a formal claim by victorious armies to all bells, or to the best bell, in and around a conquered place: "the right to the bells." Cipolla, *Guns, Sails, and Empires*, p. 30, n. 1.
14. In 885, all professional copyists in Baghdad were required to swear an oath not to copy books of philosophy. On the conflicts of Muslim science and Islamic doctrine, see Hoodbhoy, *Islam and Science*, especially chapters 9 and 10.
15. Ibn Khaldūn, *The Muqaddima: An Introduction to History* (London: Routledge and Kegan Paul, 1978), p. 373, cited in Hoodbhoy, *Islam and Science*, pp. 103–04. We have an analogous example of arrant cynicism and zealotry in Christian annals: when the French "crusader" army sent to repress the Cathar heresy broke into Béziers and was permitted (ordered) to put its inhabitants to the sword, the commander was asked how they might distinguish the good Christians from the heretics: to which he replied: "God will know his own."
16. White, *Medieval Religion and Technology*, p. 227.
17. Elvin, *Pattern of the Chinese Past*, p. 184.
18. *Ibid.*, p. 85. Elvin gives the figure as "between 35,000 to 40,000 tons and 125,000 tons," but says he prefers the higher estimate. He relies here on Yoshida Mitsukuni, a Japanese specialist writing in 1967. Subsequent work by Robert Hartwell, "Markets, Technology, and the Structure of Enterprise," p. 34, also advances the higher figure. In Hall, *Powers and Liberties*, p. 46, this becomes

"at least 125,000 tons." That's the way of historical numbers—they grow.
19. Elvin, *Pattern of the Chinese Past*, pp. 297–98.
20. Cf. Goldstone, "Gender, Work, and Culture."
21. Balazs, *La bureaucratie céleste*, pp. 22–23.
22. Cited in White, *Medieval Religion and Technology*, pp. 245–46.

1.1.2 Industrial Society and Technological Systems

RUTH SCHWARTZ COWAN

As the Civil War came to an end, America began the transition from a preindustrial society into the industrial age. The period from 1870 to 1920 saw many changes in America, and at the end of that era, it had become the largest economy in the world—one that was far less dependent on nature than it once had been.

While we currently use many different technological systems, Ruth Schwartz Cowan, professor emeritus of history at the State University of New York, Stony Brook, discusses five developed during that fifty-year period to demonstrate the increasing complexity of life and the development of infrastructure we now largely take for granted. Eventually, this increasing complexity spread across the world. The characteristics of an industrialized society can now be found in even the most remote corners of the globe.

The increased levels of productivity in manufacturing, including agriculture, had economic as well as political ramifications. As these changes occurred, few thought about what was happening or what the long-range implications would be. Today's globalized world is vastly different from what it once was, with many people more reliant and interdependent on one another. Our lives are increasingly more intertwined than ever before.

FOCUS QUESTIONS

1. Explain the rationale behind Cowan's assertion that industrialization has made us less independent and more closely connected to many other people than ever before.
2. Consider the key points of this article in relation to the ethical issues raised in the Jonas piece (Selection 1.3.2). What new individual responsibilities might arise from the new networks extending far beyond the nuclear family?
3. If technology continues to improve the quality of life for many more people in the world, what might our future look like if the networks discussed by Cowan become larger and more common, linking even greater numbers of people throughout the world?

KEYWORDS

balance of trade, entrepreneurs, hunter-gatherers, industrialization, infrastructure, international trade, investment banking, manufacturing, productivity, transportation

---

Source: From *Social History of American Technology* by Ruth Schwartz Cowan, pp. 149–172. Copyright © 1997 by Oxford University Press, Inc. Used by permission of Oxford University Press, Inc. Notes omitted; interested readers should consult the original.

Between 1870 and 1920, the United States changed in ways that its founders could never have dreamed possible. Although American industrialization began in the 1780s, the nation did not become an industrialized society until after the Civil War had ended. The armistice agreed to at Appomattox signaled, although the participants probably did not realize it, the beginning of the take-off phase of American industrialization. Having begun as a nation of farmers, the United States became a nation of industrial workers. Having begun as a financial weakling among the nations, by 1920 the United States had become the world's largest industrial economy.

What did this transformation mean to the people who lived through it? When a society passes from preindustrial to industrial conditions, which is what happened in the United States in the years between 1870 and 1920, people become less dependent on nature and more dependent on each other. This is one of history's little ironies. In a preindustrial society, when life is unstable, the whims of the weather and the perils of natural cycles are most often to blame. In an industrial society, when life is unstable, the whims of the market and the perils of social forces are most often to blame. Put another way, this means that in the process of industrialization individuals become more dependent on one another because they are linked together in large, complex networks that are, at one and the same time, both physical and social: technological systems.

INDUSTRIALIZATION, DEPENDENCY, AND TECHNOLOGICAL SYSTEMS

Many Americans learned what it means to become embedded in a set of technological systems in the years between 1870 and 1920. Today we have become so accustomed to these systems that we hardly ever stop to think about them; although they sustain our lives, they nonetheless remain mysterious. In the late twentieth century, people have tended to think that, if anything, industrialization has liberated them from dependency, not encased them in it, but that is not the case. We can see this clearly by imagining how a woman might provide food for a two-year-old child in a nonindustrialized society.

In a hunter-gatherer economy, she might simply go into the woods and collect nuts or walk to the waterside and dig for shellfish. In a premodern agricultural community (such as the one that some of the native peoples of the eastern seaboard had created), she might work with a small group of other people to plant corn, tend it, harvest it, and shuck it. Then she herself might dry it, grind it into meal, mix it with water, and bake it into bread for the child to eat. In such a community, a woman would be dependent on the cooperation of several other people in order to provide enough food for her child, but all of those people would be known to her and none of them would be involved in an activity in which she could not have participated if necessity had demanded.

In an industrialized economy (our own, for example), an average woman's situation is wholly different. In order to get bread for a child, an average American woman is dependent on thousands of other people, virtually all of them totally unknown to her, many of them living and working at a considerable distance, employing equipment that she could not begin to operate, even if her life (quite literally) depended on it and even if she had the money (which isn't likely) to purchase it. A farmer grew the wheat using internal combustion engines and petroleum-derivative fertilizers. Then the wheat was harvested and transported to an organization that stored it under stable conditions, perhaps for several years. Then a milling company may have purchased it and transported it (over thousands of miles of roads or even ocean) to a mill, where it was ground by huge rollers powered by electricity (which itself may have been generated thousands of miles away). Then more transportation (all of this transportation required petroleum, which itself had to be processed and transported) was required: to a baking factory, where dozens of people (and millions of dollars of machinery) were used to turn the flour into bread. Then transportation again: to a market, where the woman could purchase it (having gotten herself there in an automobile, which itself had to be manufactured somewhere else, purchased at considerable expense, and supplied with fuel)—all of this before a slice of it could be spread with peanut butter to the delight of a two-year-old.

The point should, by now, be clear. People who live in agricultural societies are dependent on natural processes: they worry, with good reason, about whether and when there will be a drought or a flood, a plague of insects or of fungi, good weather or bad. People who live in industrial societies are not completely independent of such natural processes, but are more so than their predecessors (many floodplains have been controlled; some droughts can be offset by irrigation). At the same time, they are much more dependent on other people and on the technological systems that other people have designed and constructed. The physical parts of these systems are networks of connected objects: tractors, freight cars, pipelines, automobiles, display cases. The social parts are networks of people and organizations that make the connections between objects possible: farmers, bakers, and truck drivers; grain elevators, refineries, and supermarkets.

Preindustrialized societies had such networks of course, but in industrialized societies, the networks are more complex and much denser—all of which makes it much harder for individuals to extricate themselves. A small change very far away can have enormous effects very quickly. Daily life can be easily disrupted for reasons that ordinary people can find hard to understand, and even experts can have difficulty comprehending.

People live longer and at a higher standard of living in industrial societies than in preindustrial ones, but they are not thereby rendered more independent (although advertising writers and politicians would like them to think they are) because, in the process of industrialization, one kind of dependency is traded for another: nature for technology. Americans learned what it meant to make that trade in the years between 1870 and 1920. We can begin understanding what they experienced if we look at some of the technological systems that were created or enlarged during those years.

THE TELEGRAPH SYSTEM

The very first network that Americans experienced really looked like a network: the elongated spider's web of electric wires that carried telegraph signals. The fact that electricity could be transmitted long distances through wires had been discovered in the middle of the eighteenth century. Once a simple way to generate electric currents had been developed (a battery, or voltaic pile, named after the man who invented it, Alessandro Volta), many people began experimenting with various ways to send messages along the wires. An American portrait painter, Samuel F. B. Morse, came up with a practicable solution. Morse developed a transmitter that emitted a burst of electric current of either short or long duration (dots and dashes). His receiver, at the other end of the wire, was an electromagnet, which, when it moved, pushed a pencil against a moving paper tape (thus recording the pattern of dots and dashes). The most creative aspect of Morse's invention was his code, which enabled trained operators to make sense out of the patterns of dots and dashes.

In 1843, after Morse had obtained a government subvention, he and his partners built the nation's first telegraph line between Baltimore and Washington. By 1845, Morse had organized his own company to build additional lines and to license other telegraph companies so that they could build even more lines, using the instruments he had patented. In a very short time, however, dozens of competing companies had entered the telegraph business, and Morse had all he could do to try to collect the licensing fees to which he was entitled. By 1849, almost every state east of the Mississippi had telegraph service, much of it provided by companies that were exploiting Morse's patents without compensating him.

Beginning around 1850, one of these companies, the New York and Mississippi Valley Printing Telegraph Company, began buying up or merging with all the others; in 1866, it changed its name to the Western Union Telegraph Company. In the decades after the Civil War, Western Union had an almost complete monopoly on telegraph service in the United States; a message brought to one of its offices could be transmitted to any of its other offices in almost all fairly large communities in the United States. Once the message was delivered, recipients could pick it up at a Western Union office. During these decades, only one company of any note succeeded in challenging Western Union's almost complete monopoly on telegraph service. The Postal Telegraph Company specialized in providing pick-up and delivery services for telegrams; yet even at the height of its success, it never managed to corner more than 25 percent of the country's telegraph business.

In 1866, when Western Union was incorporated, it already controlled almost 22,000 telegraph offices around the country. These were connected by 827,000 miles of wire (all of it strung from a virtual forest of telegraph poles, many of them running along railroad rights of way), and its operators were handling something on the order of 58 million messages annually. By 1920, the two companies (Western and Postal) between them were managing more than a million miles of wire and 155 million messages. Yet other companies (many of the railroads, for example, several investment banking houses, several wire news services) were using Western Union and Postal Telegraph lines on a contractual basis to provide in-house communication services (the famous Wall Street stock ticker was one of them).

As a result, as early as 1860, and certainly by 1880, the telegraph had become crucial to the political and economic life of the nation. Newspapers had become dependent on the telegraph for quick transmission of important information. The 1847 war with Mexico was the first war to have rapid news coverage, and the Civil War was the first in which military strategy depended on the quick flow of battle information over telegraph lines. During the Gilded Age (1880–1900), the nation's burgeoning financial markets were dependent on the telegraph for quick transmission of prices and orders. Railroad companies used the telegraph for scheduling and signaling purposes since information about deviations in train times could be quickly transmitted along the lines. The central offices of the railroads utilized telegraph communication to control the financial affairs of their widely dispersed branches. When the Atlantic cable was completed in 1866, the speed and frequency of communication between nations increased, thereby permanently changing the character of diplomatic negotiations. The cable also laid the groundwork for the growth of international trade (particularly the growth of multinational corporations) in the later decades of the century.

In short, by 1880, if by some weird accident all the batteries that generated electricity for telegraph lines had suddenly run out, the economic and social life of the nation would have faltered. Trains would have stopped running; businesses with branch offices would have stopped functioning; newspapers could not have covered distant events; the president could not have communicated with his European ambassadors; the stock market would have had to close; family members separated by long distances could not have relayed important news—births, deaths, illnesses—to each other. By the turn of the century, the telegraph system was both literally and figuratively a network, linking together various aspects of national life—making people increasingly dependent on it and on one another.

THE RAILROAD SYSTEM

Another system that linked geographic regions, diverse businesses, and millions of individuals was the railroad. We have already learned about the technical developments (the high-pressure steam engine, the swivel truck, the T-rail) that were crucial to the development of the first operating rail lines in the United States in the 1830s. Once the technical feasibility of the railroad became obvious, its commercial potential also became clear. The railroad, unlike canals and steamboats, was not dependent on proximity to waterways and was not (as boats were) disabled when rivers flooded or canals froze.

During the 1840s, American entrepreneurs had began to realize the financial benefits that railroading might produce and railroad-building schemes were being concocted in parlors and banks, state houses, and farm houses all across the country. By the 1850s, a good many of those schemes had come to fruition. With 9,000 miles of railroad track in operation, the United States had more railroad mileage than all other western nations combined; by 1860, mileage had more than trebled, to 30,000 miles.

The pre-Civil War railroad system was not yet quite a technological system because, large as it was, it still was not integrated as a network. Most of the existing roads were short-haul lines, connecting such major cities as New York, Chicago, and Baltimore with their immediate hinterlands. Each road was owned by a different company, each company owned its own cars, and each built its tracks at the gauge (width) that seemed best for the cars it was going to attempt to run and the terrain over which the running had to be done. This lack of integration created numerous delays and additional expenses. In 1849, it took nine transshipments between nine unconnected railroads (and nine weeks of travel) to get freight from Philadelphia to Chicago. In 1861, the trip between Charleston and Philadelphia required eight car changes because of different gauges. During and immediately after the Civil War, not a single rail line entering either Philadelphia or Richmond made a direct connection with any other, much to the delight of the local teamsters, porters, and tavern keepers.

The multifaceted processes summed up under the word "integration" began in the years just after the Civil War and accelerated in the decades that followed. The rail system grew ever larger, stretching from coast to coast (with the completion of the Union Pacific Railroad in 1869), penetrating into parts of the country where settlement did not yet even exist. There were roughly 53,000 miles of track in 1870, but there were 93,000 miles by the time the next decade turned, and 254,000—the all-time high—by 1920. In that half century, the nation's population tripled, but its rail system grew sevenfold; the forty-eight states of the mainland United States became physically integrated, one with the other.

The form of the rail system was just as significant as its size. By 1920, what had once been a disjointed collection of short (usually north–south) lines had been transformed into a network of much longer trunk lines (running from coast to coast, east–west), each served by a network of shorter roads that connected localities (the limbs) with the trunks. Passengers could now travel from New York to San Francisco with only an occasional change of train and freight traveled without the necessity of transshipments. What had made this kind of integration possible was not a technological change, but a change in the pattern of railroad ownership and management.

From the very beginning of railroading, railroad companies had been joint-stock ventures. Huge amounts of capital had been required to build a railroad: rights of way had to be purchased, land cleared, bridges built, locomotives ordered, passenger cars constructed, freight cars bought. Once built, railroads were very expensive to run and to maintain: engines had to be repaired, passengers serviced, freight loaded, tickets sold, stations cleaned. Such a venture could not be financed by individuals, or even by partnerships. Money had to be raised both by selling shares of ownership in the company to large numbers of people and by borrowing large sums of money by issuing bonds.

As a result, both American stockbroking and American investment banking were twin products of the railroad age. Some of America's largest nineteenth-century fortunes were made by people who knew not how to build railroads, but how to finance them: J. P. Morgan, Leland Stanford, Jay Gould, Cornelius Vanderbilt, and George Crocker. These businessmen consolidated the railroads. They bought up competing feeder lines; they sought control of the boards of directors of trunk lines; they invested heavily in the stock of feeder roads until the feeders were forced to merge with the trunks. When they were finished, the railroads had become an integrated network, a technological system. In 1870, there had been several hundred railroads, many of which were in direct competition with each other. By 1900, virtually all the railroad mileage in the United States was either owned or controlled by just seven (often mutually cooperative) railroad combinations, all of which owed their existence to the machinations of a few very wealthy investment bankers.

As railroad ownership became consolidated, the railroad system became physically integrated. The most obvious indicator of this integration was the adoption of a standard gauge, which made it unnecessary to run different cars on different sets of tracks. By the end of the 1880s, virtually every railroad in the country had voluntarily converted to a gauge of 4 feet, 8½ inches in order to minimize both the expense and the delays of long-distance travel. On this new integrated system, the need for freight and passengers to make repeated transfers was eliminated; as a result, costs fell while transportation speed increased.

The railroad system had a profound impact on the way in which Americans lived. By 1900, the sound of the train whistle could be heard in almost every corner of the land. Virtually everything Americans needed to maintain and sustain their lives was being transported by train. As much as they may have grumbled about freight rates on the railroads (and there was much injustice, particularly to farmers, to grumble about) and as much as they may have abhorred the techniques that the railroad barons had used to achieve integration, most Americans benefited from the increased operational efficiency that resulted.

In the years in which population tripled and rail mileage increased seven times, freight tonnage on the railroads went up elevenfold. Cattle were going by train from the ranches of Texas to the slaughter houses of Chicago; butchered beef was leaving Chicago in refrigerated railroad cars destined for urban and suburban kitchens. Lumber traveled from forests to sawmills by train; two-by-four beams to build houses on the treeless plains left the sawmills of the Pacific Northwest on flat-cars. Some petroleum went from the well to the refinery by train; most kerosene and gasoline went from the refinery to the retailer by train. Virtually all the country's mail traveled by train, including cotton cloth and saddles, frying pans and furniture ordered from the mail-order companies that had begun to flourish in the 1880s.

Even as fundamental and apparently untransportable a commodity as time was affected by the integration of the rail system, for scheduling was an important facet of integration. People who were going to travel by train had to know what time their trains would leave, and if connections had to be made, trains had to be scheduled so as to make the connections possible. Schedules also had to be constructed, especially on heavily trafficked lines, to ensure that trains did not collide. But scheduling was exceedingly difficult across the long distances of the United States because communities each established their own time on the basis of the position of the sun. When it was noon in Chicago, it was 12:30 in Pittsburgh (which is to the east of Chicago) and 11:30 in Omaha (to the west). The train schedules printed in Pittsburgh in the early 1880s listed six different times for the arrival and departure of each train. The station in Buffalo had three different clocks.

Sometime in the early 1880s, some professional railroad managers and the editors of several railroad publications agreed to the idea, first proposed by some astronomers, that the nation should be divided into four uniform time zones. By common agreement among the managers of the country's railroads, at noon (in New York) on Sunday, November 18, 1883, railroad signalmen across the country reset their watches. The zones were demarcated by the 75th, 90th, 105th, and 120th meridians. People living in the eastern sections of each zone experienced, on that otherwise uneventful Sunday, two noons, and people living in the western sections, skipped time. Virtually everyone in the country accepted the new time that had been established by the railroads, although Congress did not actually confirm the arrangement by legislation for another thirty-five years. Such was the pervasive impact of the integrated rail network.

THE PETROLEUM SYSTEM

In 1859, a group of prospectors dug a well in a farmyard in Titusville, Pennsylvania. Although they appeared to be looking for water, the prospectors were in fact searching for an underground reservoir of a peculiar oily substance that had been bubbling to the surface of nearby land and streams. Native Americans had used this combustible substance as a lubricant for centuries. The prospectors were hoping that if they could find a way to tap into an underground reservoir of this material, they could go into the business of selling it to machine shops and factories (as a machine lubricant, an alternative to animal fat) and to households and businesses (as an illuminant, an alternative to whale oil and candles).

The prospectors struck oil—and the American petroleum industry was born. Within weeks the news had spread, and hundreds of eager profiteers rushed into western Pennsylvania, hoping to purchase land, drill for oil, or find work around the wells. The Pennsylvania oil rush was as massive a phenomenon as the California gold rush a decade earlier.

The drillers soon discovered that crude petroleum is a mixture of oils of varying weights and characteristics. These oils, they learned, could be easily separated from one another by distillation, an ancient and fairly well-known craft. All that was needed was a fairly large closed vat with a long outlet tube (called a still) and a fire. The oil was heated in the still and the volatile gases produced would condense in the outlet tube. A clever distiller (later called a refiner) could distinguish different portions (fractions) of the distillate from each other, and then only the economically useful ones needed to be bottled and sent to market.

The market for petroleum products boomed during the Civil War: northern factories were expanding to meet government contracts; the whaling industry was seriously hampered by naval operations; railroads were working overtime to transport men and material to battlefronts. By 1862, some 3 million barrels of crude oil were being processed every year. Under peacetime conditions the industry continued to expand; by 1872, the number of processed barrels had trebled.

Transportation of petroleum remained a problem, however. The wells were located in the rural, underpopulated Appalachian highlands of Pennsylvania, not only many miles away from the cities in which the ultimate consumers lived, but also many miles away from railroad lines that served those cities. Initially crude oil had been collected in barrels and had been moved (by horse and cart or by river barges) to railroad-loading points. There the barrels were loaded into freight cars for the trip to the cities (such as Cleveland and Pittsburgh) in which the crude was being refined and sold. The transportation process was cumbersome, time-consuming, and wasteful; the barrels leaked, the barges sometimes capsized, the wagons—operating on dirt roads—sometimes sank to their axles in mud.

Pipelines were an obvious solution, but a difficult one to put into practice, given that no one had ever before contemplated building and then maintaining a continuous pipeline over the mountainous terrain and the long distances that had to be traversed. The first pipeline to operate successfully was built in 1865. Made of lap-welded cast-iron pipes, two inches in diameter, it ran for six miles from an oil field to a railroad loading point and had three pumping stations along the way. This first pipeline carried eighty barrels of oil an hour and had demonstrated its economic benefits within a year. Pipeline mileage continued to increase during the 1870s and 1880s (putting thousands of teamsters out of business), but virtually all of the lines were relatively short hauls, taking oil from the fields to the railroads. Throughout the nineteenth century and well into the twentieth, the railroads were still the principal long-distance transporters of both crude and refined oil. After the 1870s, the drillers, refiners, and railroads gradually dispensed with barrels (thus putting thousands of coopers out of business) and replaced them with specially built tank cars, which could be emptied into and loaded from specially built holding tanks. As it was being constructed, the network of petroleum pipelines was thus integrated into the network of railroad lines. It was also integrated into the telegraph network. Oil refineries used the telegraph system partly to keep tabs on prices for oil in various localities and partly to report on the flow of oil through the lines.

The most successful petroleum entrepreneurs were the ones who realized that control of petroleum transportation was the key ingredient in control of the entire industry. The major actor in this particular economic drama was John D. Rockefeller. Rockefeller had been born in upstate

New York, the son of a talented patent medicine salesman, but he had grown up in Cleveland, Ohio, a growing commercial center (it was a Great Lake port and both a canal and railroad terminus), and had learned accountancy in a local commercial college. His first job was as a bookkeeper for what was then called a commission agent, a business that collected commissions for arranging the shipment of bulk orders of farm products. A commission agent's success depended on getting preferential treatment from railroads and shipping companies. Rockefeller carried this insight with him, first when he went into a partnership as his own commission agent and then, in 1865, when he became the co-owner of an oil refinery in Cleveland.

Rockefeller and his associates were determined to control the then chaotic business of oil refining. They began by arranging for a secret rebate of oil shipments from one of the two railroads then serving Cleveland. Then in the space of less than a month, using the rebate as an incentive, they managed to coerce other Cleveland refiners into selling out and obtained control of the city's refining. Within a year or two, Rockefeller was buying up refineries in other cities as well. He had also convinced the railroads that he was using that they should stop carrying oil to refineries owned by others, so that he was in almost complete control of the price offered to drillers. In the early 1870s, a group of drillers banded together to build pipelines that would take their oil to railroads with which Rockefeller wasn't allied. Rockefeller responded to this challenge by assembling a monopoly on the ownership of tank cars (since the pipelines did not go all the way to the refineries and railroad tank cars were still necessary), and by 1879, he had been so successful in squeezing the finances of the pipeline companies that their stockholders were forced to sell out to him. In that year, as a result of their control both of refineries and pipelines, Rockefeller and his associates controlled 90 percent of the refined oil in the United States.

Having bought up the competing pipelines (having let other people take the risks involved in developing new technologies for building and maintaining those lines), Rockefeller was quick to see their economic value. In 1881, one of his companies completed a six-inch line from the Pennsylvania oil fields to his refinery in Bayonne, New Jersey—the first pipeline that functioned independently of the railroads. By 1900, Rockefeller had built pipelines to Cleveland, Philadelphia, and Baltimore, and Standard Oil (Rockefeller's firm) was moving 24,000 barrels of crude a day (he still used the railroads to move the oil after it had been refined).

By that point, hundreds of civil and mechanical engineers were working for Rockefeller's pipeline companies (which held several patents on pipeline improvements), and several dozen chemists and chemical engineers were working in his refineries (and developing new techniques, such as the Frasch process for taking excess sulfur out of petroleum). In addition, Standard Oil was pioneering financial, management, and legal techniques for operating a business that had to control a huge physical network, spread out over several states. Since the laws dealing with corporations differed in each state and since some of them prevented a corporation in one state from owning property in another, one of Rockefeller's attorneys worked out a corporate arrangement so that Standard Oil had a different corporation in each state in which it operated (Standard Oil of New Jersey, Standard Oil of Ohio, and so forth). The stockholders in each corporation turned their stock over to a group of trustees, who managed the whole enterprise from New York—the famous Standard Oil Trust, of which Rockefeller himself was the single largest stockholder and therefore the major trustee. (The trust, as a way to organize a complex business, was soon picked up in tobacco and sugar refining and other industries involved in large-scale chemical processing, leading Congress, worried about the monopolistic possibilities, to pass the Sherman Anti-Trust Act in 1890.)

By 1900, the Standard Oil Trust (which had successfully battled antitrust proceedings in court) controlled most of the oil produced in Pennsylvania, and it owned most of the new oil fields that had been discovered in Ohio and Indiana. Rockefeller's almost complete stranglehold on the industry wasn't broken until oil was discovered early in the twentieth century in Texas,

Oklahoma, Louisiana, and California, outside the reach of the pipelines he controlled and the railroads with which he was associated. Increased competition was accompanied by the continued growth not only of the pipeline network, but also of the industry as a whole: 26 million barrels of petroleum were processed in 1880, 45 million in 1890, 63 million in 1900, 209 million in 1910 (as gasoline was just beginning to edge out kerosene as the most important petroleum product), and 442 million in 1920 (when the Model T had been in production for almost eight years).

Like the telegraph and the railroad (and in combination with the telegraph and the railroad), the oil pipeline network had become a pervasive influence on the American economy and on the daily life of Americans. In the last decades of the nineteenth century, a very large number of Americans, especially those living outside of the major cities, used one of its products, kerosene, for heating and lighting their homes and for cooking. During the same decades, American industry became dependent on other fractions of petroleum to lubricate the machinery with which it was producing everything from luxurious cloth to common nails. Finally, in the early decades of the twentieth century, with the advent first of the internal combustion engine fueled by gasoline and then of automobiles and trucks powered by that engine, Americans discovered that access to petroleum was becoming a necessary condition not only of their working lives but also of their leisure time.

THE TELEPHONE SYSTEM

Technologically the telephone was similar to the telegraph, but socially it was very different. The device patented by Alexander Graham Bell in 1876 was rather like a telegraph line: voices rather than signals could be transmitted by electric current because the transmitter lever and the receiving pencil had been replaced by very sensitive diaphragms. Aware of the difficulties that Morse had encountered in reaping profits from his patents—and aware that he had no head for business—Bell decided to turn over the financial and administrative details of creating a telephone network to someone else.

The businessmen and the attorneys who managed the Bell Telephone Company did their work well. While the railroad, telegraph, and petroleum networks had been integrated by corporate takeovers, the telephone system was integrated, from the very beginning, by corporate design. A crucial decision had been made early on: Bell Telephone would manufacture all the telephone instruments, then lease the instruments to local companies, which would operate telephone exchanges under license to Bell. This meant that for the first sixteen years of telephone network development (sixteen years was then the length of monopoly rights under a patent), the Bell Telephone Company could dictate, under the licensing agreements, common technologies for all the local telephone systems. Bell could also control the costs of telephone services to local consumers.

Because of this close supervision by one company, the telephone system was integrated from the very beginning. Between 1877 and 1893, the Bell Telephone Company, through its affiliated local operating companies, controlled and standardized virtually every telephone, every telephone line, and every telephone exchange in the nation. Indeed in the 1880s, the officers of Bell were confident that they could profitably begin long-distance service (that is, service that would connect one local operating company with another) precisely because all of the operating companies were using its standardized technology. Bell needed to hire physicists and electrical engineers to solve the technical problems involved in maintaining voice clarity over very long wires, but the organizational problems involved in connecting New York with Chicago and Chicago with Cleveland turned out to be minimal.

On the assumption that the telephone system would end up being used very similarly to the telegraph network, the officers of Bell had decided that their most important customers would be other businesses, particularly those in urban areas. They decided, as a marketing strategy, to keep rates fairly high, in return for which they would work to provide the clearest and most reliable service possible. By the end of the company's first year of operation, 3,000 telephones had been leased, 1 for every 10,000 people. By 1880, there were 60,000

(1 per 1,000), and when the Bell patents expired in 1893, there were 260,000 (1 per 250). About two-thirds of these phones were located in businesses. Most of the country's business information was still traveling by mail and by telegraph (because businessmen wanted a written record of their transactions), but certain kinds of businesses were starting to find the telephone very handy: in 1891, the New York and New Jersey Telephone Company served 937 physicians and hospitals, 401 pharmacies, 363 liquor stores, 315 stables, 162 metalworking plants, 146 lawyers, 126 contractors, and 100 printing shops.

After the Bell patents expired, independent telephone companies entered the business despite Bell's concerted effort to keep them out. By 1902, there were almost 9,000 such independent companies, companies not part of the Bell system. When the organizers of the Bell system had analogized the telephone to the telegraph, they had made a crucial sociological mistake. They understood that in technological terms the telephone was similar to the telegraph, but they failed to understand that in social terms it was quite different. The telephone provided user-to-user communication (with the telegraph there were always intermediaries). In addition, the telephone was a form of voice communication; it facilitated emotional communication, something that was impossible with a telegraph. In short, what the organizers of the Bell system had failed to understand was that people would use the telephone to socialize with each other.

The independent companies took advantage of Bell's mistake. Some of them offered services that Bell hadn't thought to provide. Dial telephones were one such service, allowing customers to contact each other without having to rely on an operator (who sat at a switchboard, manually connecting telephone lines, one to another, with plugs). Operators were notorious for relieving the boredom of their jobs by listening in on conversations, something many customers wanted to avoid. Party lines were another such service. Anywhere from two to ten residences could share the same telephone line and telephone number, which drastically lowered the costs of residential services. Many lower-income people turned out to be willing to put up with the inconvenience of having to endure the ringing of telephones on calls meant for other parties in exchange for having telephone service at affordable rates.

Yet other independent companies served geographic locales that the Bell companies had ignored. This was particularly the case in rural areas where there were farm households. Bell managers apparently hadn't thought that farmers would want telephones, but it turned out that they were wrong. Farm managers used telephones to get prompt reports on prices and weather. Farm households used telephones to summon doctors in emergencies and to alleviate the loneliness of lives lived far from neighbors and relatives. In 1902, relatively few farm households had telephones, but as the independent companies grew, so did the number of farm-based customers; by 1920, just under 39 percent of all farm households in the United States had telephone service (while only 34 percent of non-farm households did).

All this competition in telephone service had the net effect that any economist could have predicted: prices for telephone service fell, even in the Bell system. In order to keep the system companies competitive, the central Bell company had to cut the rates that it charged its affiliates for the rental of phones, and these savings were passed on to consumers. In New York City, as just one example, rates fell from $150 for 1,000 calls in 1880 to $51 in 1915 (figures adjusted for inflation).

As a result, in the period between 1894 and 1920, the telephone network expanded profoundly. Middle-class people began to pay for telephone service to their homes. Farm households became part of the telephone network (in record numbers). Retail businesses began to rely on telephones in their relations with their customers. By 1920, there were 13 million telephones in use in the country, 123 for every 1,000 people. Eight million of those 13 million phones belonged to Bell and 4 million to independent companies that connected to Bell lines. In just forty years, the telephone network, which provided point-to-point voice communication, had joined the telegraph, railroad, and petroleum networks as part of the economic and social foundation of industrial society.

THE ELECTRIC SYSTEM

Like the telegraph and telephone systems, the electric system was (and still is) quite literally a network of wires. Physicists, who had been experimenting with electricity since the middle of the eighteenth century, knew that under certain conditions electricity could produce light. Unfortunately, the first devices invented for generating a continuous flow of electricity—batteries—did not create a current strong enough for illumination. However, in 1831 the British experimenter Michael Faraday perfected a device that was based on a set of observations that scientists had made a decade earlier: all electric current will make a magnet move and a moving magnet will create an electric current. Faraday built an electric generator (a rotating magnet with a conducting wire wound around it)—a device that could, unlike the battery, create a continuous flow of current strong enough to be used for lighting.

Within a short time, the generator was being used to power arc lamps in which the light (and a lot of heat) was produced by sparking across a gap in the conducting wires. Arc lamps were first used in British and French lighthouses in the 1860s; the generator that created the electricity was powered by a steam engine. A few years later, arc lamps were also being used for street lighting in some American cities. Unfortunately, arc lamps were dangerous; they had to be placed very far away from people and from anything that might be ignited by the sparks. By the mid-1870s, several people in several different countries were racing with each other to find a safer form of electrical lighting, the incandescent lamp. In such a lamp, light would be derived from a glowing, highly resistant filament and not a spark; but the filament had to be kept in a vacuum so that it wouldn't oxidize (and disappear) too fast.

Thomas Alva Edison won the race. In 1878, when Edison started working on electrical lighting, he already had amassed a considerable reputation (and a moderate fortune) as an inventor. His first profitable invention had been the quadruplex telegraph, which could carry four messages at once, and he had also made successful modifications to the stock ticker, the telegraph system for relaying stock prices from the floor of the stock exchange to the offices of investors and brokers. These inventions had enhanced his reputation with Wall Street financiers and attorneys. In 1876, when he decided to become an independent inventor, building and staffing his own laboratory in Menlo Park, New Jersey, and again in 1878, when he decided that he wanted his laboratory to crack the riddle of electric lighting, he had no trouble borrowing money to invest in the enterprise.

Actually, they were enterprises. From the beginning, Edison understood that he wanted to build a technological system *and* a series of businesses to manage that system. The first of these businesses was the Edison Electric Light Company, incorporated for the purpose of financing research and development of electric lighting. Most of the stock was purchased by a group of New York financiers; Edison received stock in return for the rights to whatever lighting patents he might develop. Once Edison had actually invented a workable lightbulb (it had a carbonized thread as its filament), he proceeded to design other devices, and create other companies, that would all be parts of the system. The Edison Electric Illuminating Company of New York, founded in 1880, was created to build and maintain the very first central generating station providing electric service to customers. When this station opened its doors in 1882 (as its site Edison chose the part of Manhattan with the highest concentration of office buildings), it contained several steam-driven generators (built to Edison's design by the Edison Machine Company) and special cables to carry the electricity underground (made by the Edison Electric Tube Company). Customers who signed up for electric service had their usage measured by meters that Edison had invented; their offices were outfitted with lamp sockets that Edison had designed into which they were to place lightbulbs that another Edison company manufactured.

Information about this new system spread very fast (thanks to publicity generated by the

Edison Electric Light Company), and within a few months (not even years), entrepreneurs were applying to Edison for licenses to build electric generating plants all over the country, indeed all over the world. Having been designed as a system, the electrical network grew very fast. There was only one generating plant in the country in 1882, but by 1902, there were 2,250, and by 1920, almost 4,000. These plants had a total generating capacity of 19 million kilowatts. Just over a third of the nation's homes were wired for electricity by 1920, by which time electricity was being used not only for lighting but also for cooling (electric fans), ironing (the electric iron replaced the so-called sad iron quickly), and vacuuming (the vacuum cleaner was being mass-produced by 1915).

The Edison companies (some of which eventually merged with other companies to become the General Electric Company) were not, however, able to remain in control of the electric system for as long (or as completely) as the Bell companies were able to dominate the telephone business or Standard Oil the petroleum business. Part of the reason for this lay in the principles of electromagnetic induction, which can be used to create electric motors as well as electric generators. The same experimenters who were developing electric generators in the middle years of the nineteenth century were also developing electric motors, and one of the first applications of those motors was in a business very different from the lighting business: electric traction for electric intraurban streetcars, often known as trolley cars. The first of these transportation systems was installed in Richmond, Virginia, in 1888 by a company owned by Frank Sprague, an electrical engineer who had briefly worked for Edison.

Sprague had invented an electric motor that, he thought, would be rugged enough to power carriages running day in and day out on city streets. As it turned out, the motor had to be redesigned, and redesigned again, before it worked very well, and Sprague also had to design trolley poles (for conducting the electricity from the overhead wires to the carriage) and a controlling system (so that the speed of the motor could be varied by the person driving the carriage). In the end, however, the electric streetcar was successful, and the days of the horse-pulled carriage were clearly numbered. Fourteen years after Sprague's first system began operating, the nation had 22,576 miles of track devoted to street railways.

Electric motors were also being used in industry. The earliest motors, like the streetcar motors, had been direct current (D.C.) motors, which needed a special and often fragile device (called a commutator) to transform the alternating current (A.C.) produced by generators. In 1888, an A.C. motor was invented by Nikola Tesla, a Serbian physicist who had emigrated to the United States. Tesla's patents were assigned to the Westinghouse Company, which began both to manufacture and to market them. At that point, the use of electric motors in industry accelerated. The very first factory to be completely electrified was a cotton mill, built in 1894. As electric motors replaced steam engines, factory design and location changed; it was no longer necessary to build factories that were several stories high (to facilitate power transmission from a central engine) or to locate them near water sources (to feed the steam boilers). The first decade of the twentieth century was a turning point in the use of electric power in industry as more and more factories converted; by 1901, almost 400,000 motors had been installed in factories, with a total capacity of almost 5 million horsepower.

In short, the electrical system was more complex than the telephone and petroleum systems because it consisted of several different subsystems (lighting, traction, industrial power) with very different social goals and economic strategies; because of its complexity, no single company could dominate it. By 1895, when the first generating plant intended to transmit electricity over a long distance became operational (it was a hydroelectric plant built to take advantage of Niagara Falls, transmitting electricity twenty miles to the city of Buffalo), there were several hundred companies involved in the electric industry: enormous companies such as Westinghouse and General Electric that made everything from generators to lightbulbs; medium-sized companies, such as the ones that ran streetcar systems or that provided electric service to relatively small geographic areas; and small companies, which made specialized electric motors or parts for electric motors. Despite this diversity, the electric system was unified by the fact that its product, electric energy, had been standardized. By 1910, virtually all the generating companies (which, by now, had come to be called utility companies) were generating alternating current at sixty cycles per second. This meant that all electric appliances were made to uniform specifications and all transmission facilities could potentially be connected to one another. By 1920, electricity had supplanted gas, kerosene, and oils for lighting. In addition, it was being used to power sewing machines in ready-made clothing factories, to separate aluminum from the contaminants in its ores, to run projectors through which motion pictures could be viewed, to carry many thousands of commuters back and forth, and to do dozens of other chores in workplaces and residences. As transmission towers marched across the countryside and yet another set of wire-carrying poles were constructed on every city street, few Americans demonstrated any inclination to decline the conveniences that the youngest technical system—electricity—was carrying in its wake.

THE CHARACTER OF INDUSTRIALIZED SOCIETY

As inventors, entrepreneurs, and engineers were building all these multifarious technological systems, Americans were becoming increasingly dependent on them. Each time a person made a choice—to buy a kerosene lamp or continue to use candles, to take a job in an electric lamp factory or continue to be a farmer, to send a telegraph message instead of relying on the mail, to put a telephone in a shop so that customers could order without visiting—that person, whether knowingly or not, was becoming increasingly enmeshed in a technological system. The net effect of all that construction activity and all those choices was that a wholly new social order, and wholly different set of social and economic relationships between people, emerged: industrial society.

In industrial societies, manufactured products play a more important economic role than agricultural products. More money is invested in factories than in farms; more bolts of cloth are produced than bales of hay; more people work on assembly lines than as farm laborers. Just over half (53 percent) of what was produced in the United States was agricultural in 1869 and only a third (33 percent) was manufactured. In 1899 (just thirty years later), those figures were reversed: half the nation's output was in manufactured goods and only a third was agricultural, despite the fact that the nation's total farm acreage had increased rapidly as a result of westward migration. Manufacturing facilities were turning out products that were becoming increasingly important aspects of everyday life: canned corn and lightbulbs, cigarettes and underwear.

In a preindustrial society, the countryside is the base for economic and political power. In such societies, most people live in rural districts. Most goods that are traded are agricultural products; the price of fertile land is relatively high; and wealth is accumulated by those who are able to control that land. Industrialized societies are dominated by their cities. More people live and work in cities than on farms; most goods are manufactured in cities; most trade is accomplished there; wealth is measured in money and not in land. Furthermore, the institutions that control money—banks—are urban institutions.

As the nineteenth century progressed, more and more Americans began living either in the rural towns in which factories were located (which, as a result, started to become small cities) or in the older cities that had traditionally been the center of artisanal production and of commerce. Native-born Americans began moving from the countryside to the city; many newly arrived Americans (and there were millions of newcomers to America in the nineteenth century) settled in cities. Just over half of all Americans (54 percent) were farmers or farm laborers in 1870, but only one in three was by 1910. Some American families underwent the rural–urban transition slowly: a daughter might move off the farm to a rural town when she married, and then a granddaughter might make her fortune in a big city.

Others had less time: a man might be tending olive groves in Italy one day and working in a shoe factory in Philadelphia two months later.

During the 1840s, the population of the eastern cities nearly doubled, and several mid-western cities (St. Louis, Chicago, Pittsburgh, Cincinnati) began to grow. In 1860, there were nine port cities that had populations over 100,000 (Boston, New York, Brooklyn, Philadelphia, Baltimore, New Orleans, Chicago, Cincinnati, and St. Louis)—by 1910, there were fifty. Just as significantly, the country's largest cities were no longer confined to the eastern seaboard or to the Midwest. There were several large cities in the plains states, and half the population of the far west was living not in its fertile valleys or at the feet of its glorious mountains, but in its cities: Los Angeles, Denver, San Francisco, Portland, and Seattle. By 1920, for the first time in the nation's history, just slightly over half of all Americans lived in communities that had more than 10,000 residents.

Money was flowing in the same direction that people were; by 1900, the nation's wealth was located in its cities, not in its countryside. The nation's largest businesses and its wealthiest individuals were in its cities. J. P. Morgan and Cornelius Vanderbilt controlled their railroad empires from New York; Leland Stanford and Charles Crocker ran theirs from San Francisco; John D. Rockefeller operated from Cleveland and New York; Andrew Carnegie, at least initially, from Pittsburgh. Probably by 1880, and certainly by 1890, stock exchanges and investment bankers had become more important to the nation's economic health than cotton wharves and landed gentry.

This transition to an urban society had political consequences because political power tends to follow the trail marked out by wealth (and, in a democracy, to some extent by population). In the early years of the nineteenth century, when the independent political character of the nation was being formed, most Americans still lived on farms and American politics was largely controlled by people who earned their living directly from the land. After the Civil War, city residents (being both more numerous and more wealthy) began to flex their political muscles and to express their political interests more successfully. The first twelve presidents of the United States had all been born into farming communities, but from 1865 until 1912, the Republican party, then the party that most clearly represented the interests of big business and cities, controlled the White House for all but eight years, and those eight years were the two terms served by Grover Cleveland, who before becoming president had been the mayor of Buffalo, New York.

The transition to an urban society also had economic and technological consequences. In a kind of historical feedback loop, industrialization caused cities to grow and the growth of cities stimulated more industrialization. Nineteenth-century cities were, to use the term favored by urban historians, walking cities. Since most residents could not afford either the cost or the space required to keep a horse and carriage, they had to be able to walk to work or to work in their own homes. Since businesses also had to be within walking distance of each other, this meant that as cities grew they became congested; more and more people had both to live and to work within the same relatively limited space. With congestion came disease; all nineteenth-century American cities were periodically struck by devastating epidemics: cholera, dysentery, typhoid fever.

Even before they understood the causes of these epidemics, city governments became convinced that they had to do something both to relieve the congestion and to control the diseases. Streets had to be paved, running water provided, sewers constructed, new housing encouraged. This meant that reservoirs had to be built, aqueducts and pumping stations constructed, trenches dug, pipes purchased, brickwork laid, new construction techniques explored. All of this municipal activity not only stimulated American industry but also served as a spur to the growth of civil engineering.

In addition, in the years between 1870 and 1920, many American cities actively stimulated industrialization by seeking out manufacturing interests and offering operating incentives to them. Many of the nation's older cities found themselves in economic trouble as railroad depots became more important than ports as nodes in the country's transportation system. In their distress, these cities decided that their futures lay not in commerce but in manufacturing, and they began to seek out manufacturing entrepreneurs to encourage industrial growth. By that time, the steam engine having been perfected and its manufacture made relatively inexpensive, manufacturers had ceased to depend on waterwheels as a power source, which meant that they could easily (and profitably) establish their enterprises in cities rather than in the countryside; the development of the electric motor only served to increase this potential.

Minneapolis became a center of flour milling, Kansas City of meatpacking, Memphis of cotton seed oil production, Rochester of shoe manufacturing, Schenectady of electric equipment, New York of ready-made clothing, Pittsburgh of steel and glass manufacture. Local banks helped manufacturers start up in business and local politicians helped recruit a docile labor force, all in the interests of stabilizing or augmenting a city's economy. Nationwide, the net result was a positive impetus to the growth of industry; the processes of industrialization and urbanization are mutually reinforcing.

If American cities grew prodigiously during the second half of the nineteenth century, so, too, did the American population as a whole: between 1860 and 1920, the population of the United States more than tripled (from 31 million to 106 million). Some of the increase was the result of a high natural birthrate; in general, American families were larger than what is needed to keep a population at a stable size from one generation to the next. In addition, as the result of improvements in public health and improvements in the food supply, the death rate was declining and life expectancy was rising. People were living longer and that meant that in any given year a declining proportion of the total population was dying. On top of this, immigrants were arriving in record numbers. The figures are astounding; the total, between the end of the Civil War and the passage of the Immigration Restriction Acts (1924), came to over 30 million people. Like their native-born contemporaries, immigrants had a high birthrate and a declining death rate and more of their children lived past infancy and then enjoyed a longer life expectancy, all of which further contributed to the mushrooming size of the American population. This startling population increase—almost 20 percent—reflects another crucial difference between societies that have become industrialized and those that have not. In a preindustrialized society, the size of the population changes in a more or less cyclical fashion. If the weather cooperates and the crops are bounteous and peace prevails, people remain reasonably healthy and many children live past infancy; over the course of time the population will grow. But eventually the population will grow too large to be supported by the available land or the land itself will become infertile. Droughts may come or heavy rains; locusts may infest the fields or diseases may strike the cattle. Men will be drawn off to battle just when it is time to plow the fields or soldiers engaged in battles will trample the wheat and burn the barns. Then starvation will ensue. People will succumb to disease; fewer children will be born, and more of them will die in infancy. The population will shrink.

Under preindustrial conditions, such population cycles have been possible. Sometimes the cycle will take two generations to recur, sometimes two centuries, but it has recurred as long as there have been agricultural peoples who have been keeping records of themselves. Industrialization breaks this cyclical population pattern. Once a country has industrialized, natural disasters and wars do not seem to have a long-term effect on the size of its population; the rate of increase may slow for a few years or so, but there is still an increase. And the standard of living keeps rising as well. People stay relatively healthy; they live longer lives. Generally speaking, they can have as many (or as few) children as they want, knowing that, also generally speaking, most of their children will live past infancy. This is the salient characteristic that makes underdeveloped countries long for development: industrialized countries seem able to support extraordinarily large populations without any long-term collapse either in the size of the population or in the standard of living.

Industrialized countries can do this because agriculture industrializes at the same time that manufacturing does. In the transition to industrialization, what is happening on the farm is just as important as what is happening in the factories since, to put it bluntly, people cannot work if they cannot eat. These social processes—sustained growth of the population and the industrialization of agriculture—are interlocked. Both were proceeding rapidly in the United States between the years 1870 and 1920 as American farmers simultaneously pushed west and industrialized, settling new territory and developing more productive farming techniques. As the frontier moved westward, roughly 400 million new acres were put under cultivation: virgin prairies became farms, fertile mountain valleys were planted in orchards, grassy hills became grazing land for sheep and cattle. The total quantity of improved acreage (meaning land that had been cleared or fenced or otherwise made suitable for agricultural use) in the United States multiplied two and a half times between 1860 and 1900.

This alone would have considerably expanded the nation's agricultural output, but newly introduced agricultural implements profoundly altered the work process of farming (particularly grain growing) and increased its productivity. The first of these was the reaper (patented by Cyrus McCormick in 1834 and in limited use even before the Civil War). The reaper, which was pulled by horses, replaced hand labor. Once a reaper had been purchased, a farm owner could quadruple the amount of acreage cut in one day or fire three-day laborers who had previously been employed for the harvest or greatly increase the acreage put to plow (since the number of acres planted had always been limited by what could be reaped in the two prime weeks of harvest).

The reaper was followed by the harvester (which made binding the grain easier), followed by the self-binder (which automatically bound the grain into shocks), and—in the far west—followed by the combine, a steam-driven tractor (which cut a swath of over forty feet, then threshed and bagged the grain automatically, sometimes at the rate of three 150-pound bags a minute). In those same years, haymaking was altered by the introduction of automatic cutting and baling machinery, and plowing was made considerably easier by the invention of the steel plow (John Deere, 1837) and the chilled-iron plow (James Oliver, 1868), both of which had the advantage of being nonstick surfaces for the heavy, wet soils of the prairies.

The net result, by 1900, was that American farmers were vastly more productive than they had been in 1860. Productivity has two facets: it is a measure both of the commodities being produced and of the labor being used to produce them. Statistics on wheat production indicate how radically American agriculture was changing in the second half of the nineteenth century. In 1866, there were roughly 15.5 million acres devoted to wheat production in the United States; farmers achieved average yields of 9.9 bushels per acre, resulting in a total national production of about 152 million bushels. By 1898, acreage had roughly trebled (to 44 million), yields had almost doubled (to 15.3 bushels per acre), and the total production was 675 million bushels.

All this was accomplished with a marked saving of labor. By the hand method, 400 people and 200 oxen had to work ten hours a day to produce 20,000 bushels of wheat; by the machine method, only 6 people (and 36 horses) were required. Farms were getting larger, ownership was being restricted to a smaller and smaller number of people and more machinery was required for profitable farming (between 1860 and 1900, the annual value of farm implements manufactured in the United States went from $21 million to $101 million)—at the same time, the farms were becoming more productive.

What this means, put another way, was that a smaller proportion of the nation's people were needed to produce the food required by its ever larger population. Some people left their farms because they hated the farming life, some because they could not afford to buy land as prices began to rise, some because they were forced off the land by the declining profitability of small farms. The farming population (this includes both owners and laborers) began to shrink in relation to the rest of the population.

New transportation facilities and new food-based industries made it easier and cheaper for the residents of cities and towns to eat a more varied diet. The fledgling canning industry was spurred by the need to supply food for troops during the Civil War. After the war, the canners turned to the civilian market, and by the 1880s, urban Americans had become accustomed to eating canned meat, condensed milk (invented by Gail Borden in 1856), canned peas, and canned corn. The Heinz company was already supplying bottled ketchup and factory pickles to a vast population, and the Campbell's company was just about to start marketing soups. By 1900, cheese and butter making had become largely a factory operation, made easier and cheaper by the invention of the centrifugal cream separator in 1879.

After the Civil War, the railroads replaced steamboats and canal barges as the principal carriers of farm products (from wheat to hogs, from apples to tobacco), thus both shortening the time required to bring goods to market and sharply lowering the cost of transportation. After the 1880s, when refrigerated transport of various kinds was introduced, this trend accelerated: even more products could be brought to market (butchered meat, for example, or fresh fish) in an even shorter time. New refrigeration techniques transformed beer making from a home to a factory operation; by 1873, there were some 4,000 breweries in the United States with an output of 10 million barrels a year. Commercial baking had also expanded and Americans were becoming fond of factory-made crackers and cookies. In the end, then, another historical feedback loop had been established, a loop connecting industrialization with agricultural change. Industrialization made farming more productive, which made it possible for the population to increase, which created a larger market for manufactured goods, which increased the rate of industrialization.

CONCLUSION: INDUSTRIALIZATION AND TECHNOLOGICAL SYSTEMS

By 1920, a majority of Americans had crossed the great divide between preindustrial and industrial societies. The foods they ate, the conditions under which they worked, the places in which they lived—all had been transformed. The majority of Americans were no longer living on farms. They were eating food that had been carried to them by one technological system (the railroad) after having been processed by machines that were powered by a second (electricity) and lubricated by a third (petroleum). If they wanted to light their domiciles at night or heat their dwelling places during cold weather, they could not avoid interacting with one or another technological system for distributing energy—unless they were willing to manufacture their own candles (even then, they might have ended up buying paraffin from Standard Oil). The social ties that bound individuals and communities together—someone has been elected, someone else has died, young men are about to be drafted, a young woman has given birth—were being carried over, communicated through, and to some extent controlled by technological networks that were owned by large, monopolistically inclined corporations. More people were living longer lives; fewer babies were dying in infancy; the standard of living for many Americans (albeit not for all) was rising. And at the very same time, because of the very same processes, people were becoming more dependent on each other.

Early in the nineteenth century the process of industrialization had appeared (to those who were paying attention) as a rather discrete undertaking: a spinning factory in a neighboring town, a merchant miller up the river, a railroad station a few miles distant. By the end of the century, virtually all Americans must have been aware that it had become something vastly different: a systematic undertaking that had created interlocking physical and social networks in which all Americans—rich or poor, young or old, urban or rural—were increasingly enmeshed.

1.1.3 The Shock of the Old: Production

DAVID EDGERTON

Standard accounts of the history of technology tend to emphasize invention and innovation as the key events for understanding the impact of technology on society. Often the history of technology is reduced to a timeline, such as appears on the inside front and back covers of this book, that simply lists the approximate year in which a particular technology was first invented. British historian of technology David Edgerton, however, disagrees with this approach and argues that the way to understand the true impact of technology on society is to look at technology-in-use. Technologies have life cycles of use in which they move from invention, to limited production, to mass production, to widespread adoption and use, and onto eventual obsolescence where selected technological artifacts live on only as exhibits in science and technology museums. But surprisingly, some technological solutions live on existing beside newer alternates—for instance, the humble paper clip or the mechanical clock. If one looks at the history of technology in the twentieth century in this use-centric way, one realizes that "twentieth-century technology is not just a matter of electricity, mass production, aerospace, nuclear power, the Internet and the contraceptive pill. It will involve the rickshaw, the condom, the horse, the sewing machine, the spinning wheel, the Haber–Bosch process, the hydrogenation of coal, cemented carbide tools, bicycles, corrugated iron, cement, asbestos, DDT, the chain saw and the refrigerator" (Edgerton, xii). One important advantage of the use perspective is that it enables us to view technology globally and not just in the countries of origin.

In this selection, taken from his book *The Shock of the Old: Technology and Global History since 1900,* Edgerton illustrates his thesis by discussing global trends in the production of goods and services.

FOCUS QUESTIONS

1. What are some examples of twentieth-century technologies that fostered greater productivity in the household worldwide?
2. How did changes in the dominant agricultural technologies affect different countries around the world?
3. What accounts for the emergence of the poor countries as the major centers of manufacturing in the last quarter of the twentieth century?
4. How does Edgerton's account of technological trends in the production of goods and services help us understand the character of the current era of globalization? Why has its effects been different in the rich world and the poor world? Explain.

KEYWORDS

branding, collectivizaton, green revolution, household production, leisure technologies, mass production, service industries, the long boom

---

Source: From David Edgerton, *The Shock of the Old*, pp. 52–74. Copyright © 2007 Oxford University Press. Reprinted by permission of Oxford University Press.

The output of the world economy has increased much faster than a rapidly growing population through most of the twentieth century. One period stands out for particularly rapid growth and change: the three decades after the Second World War. These years saw output increases which were unprecedented in world history and have not been seen since then in the rich countries. As important historical transition periods go, it is rather modestly named. It is called the "long boom," or the "golden age," terms which do not conjure up revolutionary change. In technological history—if considered at all—it tends to be relegated to a third or fourth industrial revolution. But in many parts of the world, including much of Europe, this was the period of the first industrial revolution, as employment shifted decisively from agriculture into industry and services. It was an era when productive processes increased very rapidly in efficiency, turning out long-known products at ever lower prices. That process has continued since, with unprecedented rates of growth, in the poor world.

The usual story of production goes like this: there has been a shift in employment and output from agriculture to industry and then to services. The first is labelled the industrial revolution. The second is called a transition to post-industrial, knowledge or information societies, linked to what many called post-modernism, what some Marxists called "new times," and, what capitalist Wall Street gurus called the "new economy." In one version peddled in the 1990s, modern economies are becoming "weightless" and "dematerialised." Such accounts resurrect an old argument, as if it had never been made before, that in future it will not be land or capital which will have power, but knowledge. They promise, again, a world where "intellectual property" and "human capital" rule.

Yet this stage theory of history, focusing on *shares* of employment, easily misrepresents the whole. In the twentieth century the output of agriculture expanded enormously and it continues to do so. The long boom saw the most radical revolution in the history of rich-country agriculture: productivity increase was so rapid that employment decreased even as output increased. Industrial output expanded enormously and continues to do so, even as employment in industry started to fall in the rich countries in the 1970s. Services too have long been growing. The expansion of employment in services is in part the extension of services that can be provided only by employing more people. To a very crude and counter-intuitive first approximation, falling employment is not necessarily a measure of failure or backwardness, but of rapid technical change. We should recognize too that the boundaries between these artificial categories are not as clear-cut or revealing of underlying trends as they are made to seem. The killing of animals is usually classified under manufacturing industry, not agriculture; publishing as well as printing are manufacturing industries; some maintenance activities come under services, together with transport.

The tripartite division into agriculture, industry and services also misses a vitally important dimension—the non-market productive activities of households, a fundamental part of total production, whether in agriculture, industry or services. It has long been recognized that the standard national income (GDP) data in use since the 1950s has not included non-traded goods and services. Because there are no wages for most housework, it does not figure in most national accounts. Most unpaid work in the rich world is done by women, though by no means all. The one area where men do more than women is maintenance and repair. We know this from use-of-time studies and the "satellite" national accounts including household work created in recent years. For the rich countries the figures vary between 30 and more than 100 per cent of the conventionally measured GDP. In many parts of the world the household remains a key economic unit, both for subsistence and for production for the market, particularly in agriculture, as in the "peasant" household, that great neglected economic and cultural unit of the twentieth century. The household is a good place to start.

HOUSEHOLD PRODUCTION

The 1922 *Encyclopaedia Britannica* entry on "mass production" noted of the "factory system" that its first effect was "to emancipate the home from being a mere adjunct to the loom or bench, and its later effect was to provide the home with means to develop the dignified status which it has now attained." Siegfried Giedion, a pioneer of the study of the mechanization of the rich household, wrote in 1948 that "One can hardly speak of household 'production.'" There is much to be said for the rich household as a place where machines are used for consumption rather than production.

Indeed domestic technologies of leisure deserve more serious consideration than they usually get in the history of technology. In the rich world the household was to take up technologies of leisure such as the radio, TV and video recorders much faster than washing machines or vacuum cleaners. The car and the telephone have behaved more like radio and television than washing machines and both were, at least at first, primarily leisure technologies. Cars were for visiting and going on trips rather than travelling to work. The telephone, though first sold as a business tool, was very quickly taken up by women, for what telephone engineers saw as frivolous—socializing and gossiping. In largely family-run US farms in the 1920s, the motor car diffused much faster than the truck or tractor. By 1920 there was the extraordinary total of 2 million cars on US farms, compared with 250,000 tractors and 150,000 trucks; by 1930 the number of cars reached about 4 million, where it stayed into the late 1950s. In 1920 roughly half of all midwestern farms had cars, well over that had telephones, while less than 10 per cent had tractors, running water or electric lights; in 1930 80 per cent had cars, 60 per cent had telephones, 30 per cent had tractors, and 15–20 per cent had electric lights and running water. Around 40 per cent had radios in 1930. This pattern of acquisition by households would endure, however much some complained that slum dwellers bought televisions before sewing machines, or Japanese farmers of the 1950s bought gaudy tiles and kimonos rather than washing machines.

Yet production remained a key role of the household. From at least the interwar years the wealthier households of rich countries were seen as places requiring new domestic technologies and a new scientific organization of domestic work, devoted to the production of food, cleanliness, order. The seemingly private world of the domestic kitchen now had its own experts, pioneer social researchers interested in the impact of modernity, students of budgets and of time use, activist promoters of new kinds of hygienic living, and proponents of "home economics," "domestic science" and "household engineering." Many of these studies were promoted by interested parties, for example the Rural Electrification Agency in the USA, the electric appliance manufacturers and industry-funded bodies such as the British Electrical Development Association. They would not have recommended one-woman domestic production for the manufacture of domestic appliances.

One of the hoariest old clichés of the advertisers and the sponsored researchers was that new technologies in the home had relieved rich-world housewives of drudgery and given them leisure. Yet in the United States middle-class women had seen an increase in domestic work earlier in the century, with a decline only in the 1960s, long after the widespread use of new domestic technologies. Machines replaced domestic servants, changing the role of the middle-class housewife from supervisor of workers to machine operator. The labor productivity of domestic work increased, but this led not to a decrease in work, but rather to increased domestic production. By how much domestic productivity and production have increased, and how this compares with large-scale industry or with agriculture is unclear, for the outputs of this sort of domestic production are not measured. Despite its importance in the provision of so many quickly changing outputs from increasingly clean clothes to many new types of domestically prepared food, this vast world of production is hardly charted.

But we can say something about the tools of household production. The machine tools of the rich home were very different, generally, from those of industry, as were the non-machine tools. These tools were called "consumer durables" and not "producer durables"; they were not an "investment" but "consumption." The tools of the household were the product of large-scale industry and scientific investigation, and many were cheapened very considerably by mass production. So dominant did some firms become that trade names were not just familiar, but sometimes became the generic name: we have only to think of Singer or Hoover to make the point.

Even seemingly old-fashioned tools were remade by large corporations. One particularly long-lived, though not widely diffused, type of cooking range which is now associated with nineteenth-century domesticity, provides an interesting case. The AGA range was launched in 1929, the product of a very large and inventive Swedish firm (AGA—or, in English, "gas accumulator company") that in the interwar years made, among other things, cars, radios and film equipment. The president of the company, who oversaw its growth between 1909 and 1937, was Nils Gustav Dalén, winner of the 1912 Nobel Prize in physics, for his work on inventions concerning the storage and use of acetylene, and the related automatic lighthouse, which launched the company on its path to success. Dalén personally developed the AGA range, making it the most fuel efficient ever made, in the sense that it converted a high proportion of fuel into usable heat. By 1934 it was being sold worldwide and was later manufactured in some ten countries. AGA stopped making them in 1957, but production continued in Britain; indeed still does. Another long-lived technology, it acquired the patina of retro-chic in an era when the major expansion was in gas and electric ranges.

Gas and electric ranges, like the AGA, did not change radically from their introduction in the late nineteenth century to the present. The novelties in domestic production technology have been few. Baths, showers, sewing machines, cooking ranges, vacuum cleaners, washing machines, electric irons, refrigerators, freezers and dishwashers were all available in the interwar years, and most long before that. Most have remained much the same for many decades. The extent of use has been a story not of time and innovation, but economics, and the availability of inputs, such as electricity, gas and piped water. As countries became richer they acquired more of them. And they became richer by producing more and more of them. The levels of consumption of motor cars, washing machines, telephones and the like which were seen in the United States in the 1920s were not to be found in the rich parts of Europe until the 1950s and 1960s. They would spread to the rest of the world later still.

THE SEWING MACHINE AND THE SPINNING WHEEL

A particularly good example of the complex history of household technology, not least because of its global diffusion, is provided by the sewing machine. In the rich countries, the watch, bicycle, piano and sewing-machine industries were very much in the vanguard of the new consumer-durable industry in the years before the Great War. The sewing machine was produced on a huge scale by essentially one global enterprise, the Singer Sewing Machine Company, a pioneer not only in mass production but in mass selling through credit. In 1905 Singer had the then very large number of 30,000 workers making sewing machines in eight factories round the world, but they were dwarfed by the global sales force of 61,444 in more than 4,000 branch offices. Singer, with perhaps 90 per cent of world market (outside the USA) was selling around 2.5 million machines before the Great War, with around 1.3 million coming from the Clydebank plant in Scotland.

Through the twentieth century sewing-machine production would increase. In the late 1960s Japan, by then a leading producer, made 4.3 million, mostly for export. Thereafter production was to fall: by the mid-1990s it was down to 4 million worldwide: 2.3 million came from China, followed in order by Taiwan, then Japan, USA and Germany. In China in the 1960s, 1970s and 1980s the sewing machine was one of "four big belongings"; the others were the wristwatch, the radio and the bicycle. In the Chinese countryside in the mid-1980s, each farm family had "1 bicycle, about half had a radio, 43 per cent owned a sewing machine, 12 per cent had a television set, and about half the rural adults owned wristwatches."

Essentially the same sewing machine was employed in various different contexts. Most went to homes, where they were used to make and mend family clothes, and to produce for the market, in vast putting-out systems. They were also installed in small sweatshops and packed into gigantic clothing factories as they developed from the 1930s.

The sewing machine also provides a wonderful example of very long-lived models not only being kept in use, but continuing in production for a long time. Treadle-powered machines, not so different from those made before 1914, were, in the 1960s, "by far the most important modern appliance" in a small town of the district of Huaylas in Andean Peru. In Mae Hong Son, northern Thailand, in April 2002, treadle-operated Singers decorated with a sticker celebrating 150 years of Singer machines were on sale alongside white goods, next to an Internet café. At the other end of the world, an expensive (male) tailor working alone making men's suits in Lecce, Italy, also used a treadle-operated Singer. Treadle-powered sewing machines feature regularly in discussions of micro-credit initiatives supported by international development agencies.

The sewing machine had a very particular place in the thinking of Mahatma Gandhi, as exemplary of an alternative approach to production. Gandhi was a strong opponent of the machine-based industries and famously argued not for mass production, but for production by the masses. Yet, he made what he called "intelligent exceptions" to this hostility to industrially made machines. "Take the case of the Singer Sewing Machine," he said. "It is one of the few useful things ever invented...." His interviewer responded that he could not object to the factories that made them, to which Gandhi replied that he was "Socialist enough to say that such factories should be nationalized, or State-controlled." He claimed that the sewing machine was "but one of the exceptions I have in mind.... I would welcome any day a machine to straighten crooked spindles" so that "when the spindle gets wrong every spinner will have a machine of his own to get it straight." The key machine in Gandhi's ideal world was not the sewing machine, but the spinning wheel, already a defunct technology in India. "The spinning wheel represents to me the hope of the masses," claimed Gandhi. "The masses lost their freedom, such as it was, with the loss of the *charkha* [spinning wheel]. The *charkha* supplemented the agriculture of the villagers and gave it dignity. It was the friend and the solace of the widow. It kept the villagers from idleness. For the *charkha* included all the anterior and posterior industries—ginning, carding, warping, sizing, dyeing and weaving. These in their turn kept the village carpenter and the blacksmith busy." He *reintroduced* the hand spinning wheel or *charkha* to India; and it became part of the Indian National Congress flag.

TOOLS AND SMALL TRADES

Production by the masses characterized a great deal of productive activity by the poor in the twentieth century. It is perhaps not surprising that the symbol of the world Communist movement was not Henry Maudslay's lathe, so celebrated by Marx, nor the spinning mules or the looms of the textile industry, also familiar from Marx, or the Model T. It was instead the hammer and the sickle, the first the key tool of the forge one might find in the countryside, and the second, a key instrument of unmechanized agriculture.

All through the twentieth century small enterprises operated with the simplest of tools. Even in manufacturing trades, between one-quarter and a third of workers in Germany and France around 1900 worked alone. Family-owned and run restaurants were serving 1 million meals a day in Paris in 1939, a figure which fell to 250,000 in 1950, due to the rise of factory and office canteens, though growth then resumed. A Sicilian farming family in 1931 lived in two rooms and a stable—they owned a mule and chickens and few possessions apart from some "rudimentary" agricultural implements. In a proclamation issued in June 1944 a commander of the Greek resistance movement ELAS described the means of production of his community. He spoke of "The butcher with his knife, the grocer with his weights, the café owner with his chairs, the greengrocer with his scales." In the 1980s the country-boats of Bangladesh were made by itinerant boat carpenters, traditionally Hindus (in a Muslim nation), so poor they could not buy the materials to make the boats, or sometimes even their own simple tools.

Traveling through the poor world, it is hard to miss, today, a tiny metal-working shop, in both country and city districts, where the most complex bit of machinery may well be an oxyacetylene, or electric, torch for welding. At dusk bright intermittent light from welding illuminates streets all over the world, issuing from maintenance workshops which might also make simple equipment. Or think of the tiny businesses repairing electronic equipment based on the pavements of Bangkok, or the recyclers of tyres into shoes and many other goods, to be found in many poor cities.

FAMILY FARMS IN THE USA AND THE USSR

The family farms of the North American Midwest were among the richest in the world at the beginning of the twentieth century. These farms were immensely productive, not in terms of land (for here European farmers were well ahead), but in terms of labour. From the 1920s enormous numbers of Fordson tractors appeared: they could replace five horses, and plough three times as fast. A recent large tractor can plough thirty times faster than the horse team. A key effect of the tractor was to reduce the amount of hired help on the Midwestern family-owned farm; this had the consequence too that the farmer's wife was saved the work of feeding large numbers of hired workers, a standard practice, illustrating the blurred line between the home and the farm. Interwar Midwest farm women were very heavily engaged in other non-domestic activities, tending gardens and raising poultry, and smaller but still significant proportions milked cows, did the bookkeeping and worked for a small part of the year in the fields. Even after the Second World War well over 60 per cent of Midwest farms engaged in gardening, dairying and butchering; egg production was also still high. Farm women increasingly had off-farm employment, and worked in the fields, rather in these small-scale enterprises.

How different the conditions in the Soviet Union! Consider the Volga German agricultural settlement of Brunnental in the mid-1920s. The farmers here were much poorer and lived extraordinarily self-sufficient lives. Harvesting was done with the scythe, and for some farmers with reapers and binders; threshing was carried out with horse-powered machines, rarely with a motor-powered one. There was at least one Fordson tractor, but the settlement had to supply much of its own agricultural equipment. Horse-drawn wagons were built by hand, with the help of a lathe, by a cartwright and his two teenage sons. It took four weeks of heavy labor to make; the same process with modern power tools might take twenty hours. Significantly the chronicler who told the above story listed the occupations in the settlement by families, not individuals: there were families of cabinet makers, shoemakers, tailors, plumbers, feltmakers, tanners, blacksmiths and millers. There being no ready-made clothes, farmers' wives and daughters made them at home, often sewed entirely by hand, though the richer farmers' wives had sewing machines. Clothes were made from raw wool; most houses had spinning wheels. Tailors were used only for heavy clothes.

This world was brutally torn apart by collectivisation in 1929. The richer farmers were dispossessed of all their property and sent into internal exile and often death. The rest became semi-employed; some worked for the new central Machine Tractor Stations owned by the state which served three collective farms. Years of famine followed, until recovery came in the late 1930s. In 1941 all these Volga Germans were sent into internal exile in Siberia.

By 1930 the very poor USSR had about a quarter of all Europe's tractors, and two-thirds by 1939. There were many more tractors than cars in the countryside, where there was no electricity and no consumer goods of note. Collectivization was not, however, driven by tractorization, but by a political imperative to change the class structure in the countryside, and to extract grain from farms to feed the cities (and its new factories) and for exports to pay for tractors and other capital goods. Collectivization went much faster than the provision of tractors. In fact, it almost certainly reduced the power available on farms, as farmers killed their animals, including draught animals, which would otherwise have been collectivized. The total number of Soviet agricultural horses collapsed from 33 million at the beginning of 1929 to 15 million at the beginning of 1934. Rural crafts, including clothes making also fell, partly because skilled workers moved to the city, were dekulakized or were too poor. In many villages collectivization brought about a retrogression in living standards and mechanical equipment.

Before the Second World War, collective farms had an average of seventy-five households. After it, Soviet collective and state farms would grow even bigger. These vast farms of thousands of hectares and hundreds of households were stunningly unproductive and failed to increase Soviet agricultural output much at all. Production did increase in the 1960s and 1970s but only at a huge cost in investment and labour. Paradoxically collectivization ensured the continuation of the garden plot that had disappeared from US agriculture. From 1935 collective-farm households could operate a small plot to produce their own food, and could sell the surpluses. These family plots of approximately one acre would be very important indeed in meat, egg, vegetable and fruit production, right up to the present day.

THE AGRICULTURAL REVOLUTION IN THE LONG BOOM

The phrase "green revolution" is applied to the introduction of new varieties, irrigation and fertiliser to agriculture in the poor world in the 1960s. Partly because agriculture is associated with poverty and the past, and because of the focus on novelty, the even more significant agricultural revolution in the rich world was missed.

In the rich world agriculture in the long boom saw much greater rates of labour productivity change than industry or services, and at much greater rates than before. In high land-productivity Britain, yields doubled in the post-war years from a very high base. New regimes of intensive agriculture through irrigation, and addition of artificial fertilizer (especially nitrate, largely produced by the Haber-Bosch process, innovated before the Great War), made plants grow fast and large. Plants were changed too. The introduction of hybrid corn (maize) in the US corn belt in the late 1930s and 1940s was just one example, though an important one, of new varieties being grown.

While traditional rice-production systems in Asia yielded around 1 tonne per hectare, at the beginning of the twentieth century, Japanese farmers were getting 2.5 tonnes; Japanese farmers had doubled yields through irrigation in the nineteenth century, and in its colonies of Korea and Taiwan in the interwar years. Yet in the 1950s, though the Japanese countryside was still routinely regarded as "feudal" and backward, human excrement, night soil, was still used as fertilizer. Very quickly new housing, running water, washing machines, televisions, and then refrigerators were brought in. Agricultural machinery became plentiful on small farms, giving a unique combination of highly mechanized and very intensive output of rice. Japan was to continue to lead the way in Asia in high productivity. By the early 1960s it was getting 5 tonnes per hectare, when the Asian average was around two. Even after the green revolution had long passed, Japan still led. Today it produces 7 tonnes per hectare, compared with half that in Bangladesh.

The green revolution in rich countries made a huge impact on patterns of global trade, belying the standard image of a poor agricultural world exporting food to a rich industrial world. The USA remained, for example, a major wheat exporter, but increasingly to the poor world. It exported wheat to the USSR in the 1970s and 1980s on a huge scale. It remains a major producer of raw cotton, whose principal export market was once Britain, but is now the poor countries of the world where the cotton-spinning industry is concentrated. China imports cotton from the USA, and sells it textiles. Government policy in rich countries protected land and labor-efficient agriculture from the cheaper but less efficiently produced products of the poor world.

The gap in agricultural labor productivity between the rich world and the poor world, already large, widened after the Second World War. The green revolution in the poor countries mitigated a growing divergence between the agriculture of the rich world and that of the poor, but probably at the price of increasing inequalities within the poor world. A short Japanese wheat variety, the Norin No. 10, was the key to making the short wheat plants that could take intensive applications of water and fertilizer. The IR8 rice variety was derived from dwarf strains developed in Taiwan in the interwar years by the Japanese.

In the rich world animal husbandry was industrialized in the long boom, particularly in the case of chickens and pigs. The extreme example is that of chickens. In 1960 there were around 4 billion chickens in the world, whereas at the end of the twentieth century there were 13 billion. But the number killed for meat in a year has increased from 6 billion to 45 billion. Chickens lived much shorter lives. That was just one dimension to the industrialization of the chicken. Since the 1930s the US broiler (eating) chicken has become bigger (nearly twice as heavy), younger (about half the age), and has taken much less feed to bring it to the size needed (less than half). This was done by making significant changes in both the nurture and the nature of chickens. A key series of steps was taken in the 1930s, among them bringing the chickens indoors, which required supplementing their diet with vitamin D, the use of electric lighting and artificial incubation. The intensive study of chicken feed resulted, by the 1950s, in a standard corn-and-soybean-based diet. The 1950s saw the breeding of hybrid chickens adapted to these artificial nurturing regimes. Many had been winners of "The chicken of tomorrow contest."

Pig production too was industrialized. Although the keeping of single pigs had disappeared in Britain by mid-century, even in the early 1960s half of all pigs were in herds with fewer than twenty breeding sows; by the 1990s 95 per cent were in herds of more than 100 breeding sows. Most lived, like broilers, indoors, and were, like the chickens, new sorts of fast-growing hybrids. At the end of the century million-pig installations were being developed. Yet the greatest expansion in the number of pigs since the 1960s was in fact to be in non-industrialized pigs, kept in small numbers by farming households and fed with a variety of foods. In 1960 China had a quarter of the world's pigs, but today it has around half of the world's one billion pigs, not surprisingly because pork remains the staple meat in China, and meat eating has increased markedly. More than 80 per cent are still produced on a small scale, by non-specialist producers.

INDUSTRY AND MASS PRODUCTION

We have told the story of production in terms of household production, agriculture, and small firms. Yet the standard image of twentieth-century production is centered on mass production. The central idea is that the twentieth century, especially during the long boom, saw production dominated by the large-scale production of standard parts. As a result of this mass production, efficiency of production increased dramatically. This led to unprecedented rates of economic growth and material well-being for the working classes now employed in gigantic factories and firms.

Mass production has had extraordinary effects, which are difficult to grasp. At the beginning of the twentieth century one could build a house for the price of a car. Today, in the rich world, one would get little more than a small extension to a house for the price of an immensely more complex motor car. This is despite the decrease in costs of bricks, concrete, doors and windows, and any number of fittings, which are now mass produced. To take a biological example: the price of chicken has fallen much faster than beef. This observation suggests we should not equate mass production with modern production as a whole, even in rich countries since houses and beef are still produced. Even within manufacturing industry mass production accounted for a small proportion of production. In 1969 75 percent of

U.S. industrial production was batch produced, even though in engineering mass-produced components were ten to thirty times cheaper. Yet there were very important increases in efficiency which did not come from the sort of mass production we associate with the car industry, or the making of refrigerators. Across the board productive processes were becoming more efficient.

For example, the scale of Haber-Bosch ammonia plants increased, and the inputs, such as hydrogen, were produced in cheaper ways too. The result was ever larger quantities of cheap nitrogen fertilizer, which had a dramatic effect, combined with other inputs, in increasing the productivity of land. Another powerful example might be the increasing efficiency of the use of fuel, labor and capital in power stations. The key was larger power stations operating at higher temperatures. Another would be the explosion in the efficiency of ships after the Second World War, particularly oil tankers and similar vessels. Growth in the size of ships was crucial to the sustained reduction that took place in freight rates. In the case of crude oil, for example, transport costs decreased rapidly as a proportion of crude-oil prices. World steel production trebled between 1950 and 1970, with plants becoming much larger. In other sectors production increased radically in efficiency, but without necessarily needing increases in scale. Agriculture is a good example.

CARS IN THE LONG BOOM

The mass production of motor cars was pioneered in the United States by one company and one car, Ford and the Model T. At its peak in the 1920s the Model T was produced at an annual rate of 2 million, and by the time production ceased in 1927, 15 million had been built. Ford was at this time easily the largest car manufacturer in the world, and had made America easily the most motorized nation in the world. Even the richest parts of Europe would not reach 1920s' levels of US motorization until the late 1950s, let us recall.

The great boom in car production after the Second World War was largely an American and European affair, with the European makers growing faster, though from a much lower base. In each nation the great car firms were regarded as powerhouses of the booming economies. Even in a poor country such as Italy, car ownership went up more than ten-fold in the fifteen years between 1950 and 1964, from 0.34 million to 4.7 million cars. The number of cars just overtook motorcycle numbers, which increased from 0.7 to 4.3. Between 1955 and 1970, 2.7 million Fiat 500s were made and 3.6 million Fiat 600s between 1957 and 1975. European car workers were not yet able to buy cars themselves, but would be doing so by the late 1960s.

In the long boom the Eastern European economies, like those in the West, grew very fast. Yet, the Soviet Union and its allies, for all the emphasis on standardized production and the possibility at least of plenty for the masses, were places of low consumption. Even in the 1960s the superpower USSR made only 1 per cent of the world's private vehicles, and 12 per cent of commercial ones; in comparison Britain made 10 per cent of the cars, and 9 per cent of the trucks. So committed were the Soviets to mass production that they suffered from "premature mass production," the putting into production of not properly tested goods. But mass consumption in the richest countries was more typically about the extensive multiplication of firms, styles, types, rapid model change, the pursuit of endless novelty.

The mass-producing car industry informed a whole understanding of modern production. It *was* modern industry, the place where the pace was set. The post-war years were labeled with such terms as "Fordism," at least when the mass production of cars in Europe and North America ceased to grow fast from the 1970s. Rapidly expanding Japanese car production became a model for "Post-Fordism." But just as the significance of mass production, or "Fordism," was exaggerated, so were reports of its demise. At the end of the twentieth-century Ford had capacity in Europe to build 2 million cars a year; one factory was making 400,000 Focuses per annum, and another 330,000 Mondeos. In 1996 Volkswagen worldwide turned out over 800,000 Golfs, the car that took over the production record from the Beetle, which itself took over from the

Model T. The world's largest car producers in 2000, still Ford and General Motors, were producing around 8 million vehicles each per annum, many times more than in the interwar years. Even in Britain more cars are produced today than ever before, and at world level production is not only increasing, but is still dominated by North America, Europe and Japan.

SERVICE INDUSTRIES

There is no doubt that the rise of employment in the service industries in the rich countries is one of the major economic changes of the last thirty years. A number of analysts have, perversely, identified this growth in service employment with the rise of an "information society," with connotations of weightlessness, or indeed the "dematerialized" economy. This was a fashionable, and misleading, way of saying little more than that service industries now account for very large proportions of GDP and employment. This is partly the result of mis-specification because services include a vast range of activities, many of them far from weightless or indeed new. Services include transportation, by road, rail, water and air, telecommunications and postal services, the retail sector, as well as banking and finance, and small creative industries. That such a sector is weightless is immediately contradicted by the sheer bulk of the things associated with it, the unprecedented weight of stuff in the shops, the piles of paper in any office, not to mention the proliferation of computers, fax machines and Xeroxes. One need only look at homes in the rich world to see they are crammed with stuff, which is why storage is a growth industry and moving house becomes a bigger and bigger affair. In 2003 research for a British insurance company suggested the existence of £3.2 billion-worth of unused goods, headed by sandwich toasters, electric knives, soda streams, foot spas, and ice-cream makers. There are 3.8 million unused fondue sets. One source of confusion is that vast quantities of stuff used in service industries and in homes are imported, rather than produced domestically, but that is a different issue. The USA and Britain have large trade deficits in manufactured goods, which means that they use more than they produce, that is not to say that manufacturing ceases to be important to them.

The idea that manufacturing is not important, that what really matters is branding and design, is one of those confusions arising from thinking about only part of a story. The idea arises from the observation that *in rich countries* some giant enterprises are in retailing and control brands—the value is added by these activities, not in production. Yet branding and adding value through design are hardly new—they went along with manufacture, often in the same large company, as in the cases of Singer, or Ford or General Electric. We should not confuse the siting of economic activity with its significance. For the concentration of branding, marketing and design in rich countries, and production in poor countries, does not mean that production is no longer important. Indeed it is precisely because of the radical cheapening of manufactures through mass production and the use of very cheap labour that they seem so unimportant to the rich. The point about manufacturing and mass production is that the latter produces goods extraordinarily cheaply, and does so all over the world. Massive economies of scale are exploited as never before on a global level to produce cheap mass-produced goods of great complexity. Think of cheap PCs, mobile phones and IKEA furniture. Mass production is now so common it is invisible.

At the beginning of the twenty-first century Wal-Mart is the largest corporation in the world, by annual sales ($300 billion in 2005/06) and by employee numbers. With nearly 2 million workers it is vastly larger not only than the biggest firms of 1900, but also than the very largest manufacturing employers of the 1960s. But it is a retailer, not a manufacturer. Indeed it indirectly employs many more millions, largely in China, mass producing all sorts of stuff for the American consumer. IKEA, again principally a retailer and designer, controls the mass manufacture of furniture, indirectly employing an estimated 1 million workers. Indeed IKEA provides a wonderful example of the arguments of this book. First, of the continuing significance of what we take to be old, in this case not just furniture, but *wooden* furniture, supplied, obviously, by forests. In terms of industry it exemplifies beautifully the extension rather than the retreat of mass production, and its globalization, producing fantastically cheap outputs. In terms of service industries it is an example of mass retailing and mass consumption of identical goods (it has made 28 million Billy bookcases since launch in 1978); it is also an example of the reduction of transport costs by flat-packing, and an example of the concentration of design and marketing activity in a rich country (Sweden). As a domestic industry it is an example of a family-owned firm, and indeed one which provides goods to be transported home by non-paid domestic workers, and assembled by them too. Such products made its founder and owner, it is alleged, the richest man in the world, richer than Bill Gates of Microsoft, who had briefly taken first place following the death of Walton of Wal-Mart.

One of the great novelties of the last quarter or so of the twentieth century was the emergence of poor countries as suppliers to the world not of food and raw materials, but of manufactures. The case of China is all the more extraordinary, given its history as a Communist nation and one which had had a very particular approach to modern industry. The Chinese had systematically promoted old small-scale technologies in the 1950s. In the Cultural Revolution of the late 1960s and early 1970s, there was a concerted attack on the division between managers and workers—a distinction central to Taylorism and Fordism, and an attack too on the division of labor itself. Small-scale rural industries were promoted, as during the earlier Great Leap Forward. Although the Chinese economy grew, it did so very unstably and relatively slowly. After 1976 the Chinese Communist party changed direction and, with the abolition of collective farming and the move to household farming in the 1980s, presided over a productivity surge in Chinese agriculture. In this same period rural industries grew at a phenomenal rate, many times that of the Chinese economy as a whole. Local "township and village enterprises" were the key to this growth. The transformation of the Chinese countryside in the last twenty years is surely the fastest and deepest in world history, affecting many hundreds of millions of people.

Millions, often women, left the countryside, and, housed in dormitories, toiled for pitiful wages in the factories of the new industrial areas. Chinese growth has been dependent on overseas investment, primarily from Japan, Taiwan and from overseas Chinese elsewhere. Multinational enterprise, Japanese included, has also been important. In these respects the industrialization of China has been very different from that of Japan. Market Stalinism and foreign investment were critical in China's drive to industrialize. Despite its scale and speed and its impact on the global economy, the growth of China is not the product of a profoundly new economy. It has a distinctly old feel to it.

At the beginning of the twenty-first century China was sucking in vast quantities of heavy raw materials, from oil to copper, driving up world prices. It became easily the largest steel producer in the world, with rates of growth comparable to those of steel in the long boom. The "new economy" was being replaced by a very old economy driven by commodity prices. Far from the information superhighway being the conduit for all this new production, it was none other than the ship that carried the great bulk of Chinese production, and indeed world trade as a whole. In the year 2000 the world merchant fleet was rated at 553 million gross registered tonnes (a measure of the carrying capacity of ships), up from 227 million in 1970, 85 million in 1950 and 45 million in 1914. As its scale suggested, it carried more material than ever before in history, and so cheaply that the price of manufactures was hardly affected by freight rates. This industry employed some 1 million seamen, with a majority of officers from rich countries and a majority of ratings from poor countries, largely in Asia.

Most shipping still transports fuel and bulks such as ore and grain, yet manufactures were very important too, largely carried in that great invention of the 1950s, the container. Since then global container traffic, which now dominates all sea traffic excepting bulks, has continued to increase. At the beginning of the twenty-first century the largest container ships, at 90,000 GRT, could carry over 8,000 containers, with a crew of just nineteen. The majority of the vessels were manufactured in the East. Wal-Mart is the largest single importer of containers in the USA, bringing in half a million every year, mostly from China.

The great long boom and the more recent boom in the East, China in particular, far from being primarily cases of successive technological revolutions, are in many ways inflexions of the same technological and industrial revolution happening in succession. Of course it is far from identical, but the similarities are striking: the huge increase in agricultural productivity, the expansion of industry—not least the old classics such as steel making—and the expansion of ship-borne international trade. In both cases the revolutionary nature of each era is masked by a deep political stability in the growing countries. Politics, the nation and borders matter.

1.1.4 History as Technological Change

ROSALIND WILLIAMS

In this selection from her book *Retooling: A Historian Confronts Technological Change,* MIT's dean of undergraduate education and student affairs reflects on how the idea of historical change has become nearly synonymous with technological change and how the term *technology* has been reduced to meaning only information technology. While acknowledging the important role that technological innovation has played in human history, Williams wants to resist the idea that all historical change can be reduced to or explained by technological change. But she also observes that we are now on the verge of another great transformation of the human habitat, comparable in significance to those brought about by the agricultural revolution and the Industrial Revolution. The question is, how will this transformation affect our sense of human identity? Where will we be able to find meaning and purpose in a world that is our own creation?

FOCUS QUESTIONS

1. What does Williams mean when she says that "technological innovation resembles but hollows out the idea of progress"?
2. What are some examples of previous technological revolutions, and how have they transformed the human habitat? According to Williams, what kind of transformation of the human habitat appears to be taking place because of the information revolution?
3. What does she mean when she describes the world of the information age as a reflexive, or "boomerang," world?
4. Discuss and evaluate her claim that "history and nature are weakening as well-defined external frameworks that give meaning to human life."

KEYWORDS

artificial habitats, information technology, innovation, progress, reflexivity, technological revolutions

---

Source: From *Retooling: A Historian Confronts Technological Change* by Rosalind Williams, 2002, pp. 14–26. Reprinted by permission of MIT Press.

One dominant assumption about the information age is that it represents a "new world" of technological change that relentlessly pushes into retreat an "old world" of culturally driven resistance, much as the soldiers of the Roman Empire pushed the Celts back into the western hills of Britain. Today's conflict, we are told, is between the new economy and the old one, between digital and analog, between systems and life-world, between globalization and identity. The human race is split between dynamic "change agents" and the stagnant nonretooled, between neo-nomadic "symbolic analysts" who work with bits and a "disposable labor force that can be automated and/or hired/fired/offshored...."[1]

Such binary thinking is extended to history itself. The information revolution is leading us into a new phase of history, in which technological change will be the major and constant determinant of human life. History becomes the record of a grand struggle between the irresistible force of technology-driven "change" or "innovation" on the one hand and misguided if understandable culturally driven resistance to change on the other, with "change" and "innovation" inevitably winning.

This is supposedly an age without a sense of history, but the view of history as a struggle between technological change and technological resistance is powerful and pervasive today. Implicit rather than explicit, it is less a theory (which would imply some conscious awareness of the issues and some effort at logical consistency) than an ideology (ideologies are not especially logical or consistent).[2] It is an ideology of history in which the very word "history" has been displaced by "technology." Instead of being a figure in the ground of history, technology has become the ground—not an element of historical change, but the thing itself. We have come to assume that where technology is going is where history is going, as if they are now one and the same.

The ideology of technological change has become the dominant, if implicit, theory of history in our time, even for those who never pick up a history book. In Karl Mannheim's famous distinction, ideology is a set of "wish-images" intended to evolve the existing order into a better one, while Utopia represents a wish to break the bonds of the existing order, to overturn it for a new reality. Mannheim adds: "The Utopia of the ascendant bourgeoisie was the idea of 'freedom.' "[3] Innovation has come to define a Utopia of freedom, an ideal place running by market and technological laws, where creative minds and free-flowing capital unite to make a new world abundant in possibilities and energy. This is a much more appealing world than the one we actually live in, where innovations become hardened into bureaucracies, where actions have consequences, and where waves of change wash back on shore. The Utopian "no place" of market-driven innovation presents an agreeable escape from the complexities and consequences of a crowded, risky world. Mannheim emphasizes that ideology and Utopia are ideal types; in practice, it is often difficult to distinguish them within the social order or even within an individual's mind. In the view of history as technological innovation, however, we can often discern a set of "wish-images" that is Utopian without being especially progressive.

As an MIT administrator, I rarely heard anyone talk explicitly about history, but I often heard people express the implicit view of history as technological change. They did this through repeated use of a cluster of deceptively simple words: "technology," "change," "culture," "space," "time," "community." These words are highly interdependent, deriving their meaning from the others and forming a closed world of cross-references. They are also highly reflexive, acquiring meaning from the very changes they are supposed to analyze.[4] They also drain meaning away from other, formerly more significant words, such as "engineering" and "progress."

The sun of this linguistic system is 'technology.' In 1861, when MIT was given its name, the word was novel, even daring, and grandly comprehensive. Proclaimed in chiseled stone below the Great Dome, "technology" still defines, in a lofty way, the Institute's mission. But in everyday meetings below and around the dome "technology" has little grandeur. It has come to mean *information technology*—a recent, drastic, telling reduction. In committee meetings, when we sketched business processes or organizational models on a flip chart, someone would write "technology" with a circle around it. We would talk about designing new learning spaces to accommodate "the technology." We would write and review reports saying things like "The primary motivation to revise the policy [is] the recognition that technology has transformed the means by which we collect, manage, and provide access to student information."

At no time, in any of these contexts, did anyone suggest that "technology" might include more than information technology, nor did anyone challenge its status as an independent entity, "Technology" once was a grand term, though also a dangerous one, because it was so often used as an abstract, independent historical agent.[5] It is still dangerous in this way, but it is no longer grand. It means information technology and it means change.

While "technology" expands its rhetorical reach, that of "engineering" shrinks. Never a glamorous term (though it was a solid one), it is now used more rarely, and mostly in a connection with a specific project or department. Even more conspicuous in its absence is the word "progress." Not long ago, discussions of technology were dominated by "progress talk."[6] At MIT today, people talk a lot about scientific progress, referring to the kind of discovery that would win a Nobel Prize, but little about technological progress, except with irony.

Instead, "technology" is linked with "change." Everyone talks about change as relentless and inevitable but also, almost always, as pointless, in the double sense of lacking a purpose and lacking an end. Progress has a story line; change does not. After one meeting about new software systems, a participant told me that a consultant had advised her to use the concept of a "change journey" to help people overcome their resistance to change. When I inquired what was the destination of such a journey, I was told that it might be thought of as arriving at a point of comfort with change. "Change," like "technology," has been sharply reduced in meaning. Of all the possible types of change—political, intellectual, cultural, social—technological change is all that really matters.[7] The change journey takes us through familiar landscapes of science, engineering, politics, the market, work, family. These too may change, everyone acknowledges, but the assumption is that they will do so only as a consequence of technological change.

Technological innovation resembles but hollows out the idea of progress.[8] Progress is measured in reference to human-defined goals: change and innovation are measured by market success. Market-driven innovation may tend to move in certain directions (Moore's Law, globalism, systems integration), but those directions are defined less by human purposes than by the rules of the market and the inner workings of technology itself. Innovation does not necessarily translate into human progress; any more than biological evolution means progress of the species (as Darwin well understood). Today's ideology of history as technological innovation turns the market, the motor of capitalist acquisition, into the motor of history itself, with technology as its agent.

It is easy to unmask the rhetoric of innovation and change, and to show that it is a cynical management tool justifying any sort of human disruption (moving, working harder or longer, being laid off) as the inevitable downside of the larger good. But then why is this view of history so widely, if semi-consciously, accepted?[9] Management babble is heavily discounted by most of us. In the midst of its ideological torrent, we try to keep living reasonably human lives, trying to figure out who we are, how to connect with others, how to accomplish something meaningful, how to enjoy the time we have. Still, the rhetoric of change management has some ring of truth, because it expresses, however inadequately, everyday experience in a world dominated by technologies we have created.

The rhetoric of change management has the effect, however, of trivializing the whole concept of change. Significant change is much more than a new software system or product. It is historical, in that it involves human relationships, expectations, and meanings. There is no single digital divide that we will step over collectively into the information age, leaving behind the creaky old world of everyday life for a sleek new world of frictionless systems. There are many fault lines in history today, and many of them run right through us.

The change agent and the change re-sister are often the same person.[10] We are living through a transformation of the human habitat that is much more comprehensive than what is usually thought of as "technological change."

THE NEW HUMAN HABITAT

Predictions about the information revolution have become the "airport reading" of the world—a substitute for beach reading in a harried age, just as predictable but a lot less engaging, celebrating not the steamy pleasures of physical reality but the disembodied pleasures of virtual reality. Computing will be ubiquitous, our rooms will read our thoughts, the air will hum with messages, the Internet will become an omninet, we will be lifted out of the mud of localism to digital globalism—all on the other side of the great historical divide. Many historians of technology dismiss most of these predictions as unfounded digital evangelism. Historians are trained to look for continuity, to be wary of revolutionary claims, to spot inconsistencies. On the latter point, Alex Roland, a recent past president of the Society for the History of Technology (SHOT), notes that people who talk about technological revolution are often talking about different things: "Fifteen years ago we were confidently told that we were in a computer revolution. Now it is an information revolution. A more proper label might be a communications revolution. Or it may turn out in hindsight to have been a solid-state-physics revolution, or a digital revolution, or a micro-electronics revolution, or a control revolution. Some people think that the coming revolution in genetic engineering will outweigh all of these."[11]

So what kind of technological change is it that we are living through, and how does it compare with other major transformations in history? Is this another industrial revolution (the productive one of steam engines, cotton mills, and railroads), or is it more like the second industrial revolution (the consumer one of electricity, automobiles, cinema, and chemical industries)? Is the telegraph "the Victorian Internet,"[12] or is the Internet more like electricity? Or should we compare information to energy?

No analogy seems quite right. The industrial revolution of the late eighteenth and the early nineteenth century was defined by an unprecedented leap in human productivity brought about by the exploitation of the vast energy reserves stored in fossil fuels.[13] If you compare the efficiency of the steam-powered thresher in Laurel with the labor of hand threshing, and if you multiply that kind of efficiency millions of times in millions of settings, you begin to grasp the essence of the industrial revolution.

The second industrial revolution (which occurred in the late nineteenth century) also increased productivity, but its distinctive contributions were the distribution of cheap and flexible energy in the form of electricity, the construction of grid upon grid of communication and transportation systems (subways, automobiles, telephone, radio), and what contemporaries called "the democratization of luxury" through the proliferation of cheaper and more varied consumer goods. Collectively these technological innovations made everyday life far more comfortable and interesting than ever before. In the words of another past president of SHOT, Robert Post, "The late nineteenth century was the greatest period of technological change in terms of things that affected huge numbers of people's lives in basic ways—much more so than today."[14]

In all these discussions, historians are trying to develop a sort of historical Richter scale: What are the minor shocks, and what are the major ones? All of us are trying to get a sense of the scale of change in the midst of constant tremors. At one MIT meeting about educational technologies, a participant from the software industry commented: "Education is the building and technology is the earthquake." On the historical Richter scale, however, many historians of technology would say that the so-called information revolution is not so big. They disagree with the hypothesis of fundamental change preached by digital evangelists, in part because historians are used to measuring change by productivity rates and living standards. These measures miss some distinctive features of information technology. At the heart of information technology is the manipulation of symbols, not of matter. It does not simply "impact" culture and society; the technology itself is inherently cultural and social from the start. Directly as well as indirectly, it affects human experiences of space, time, communication, and consciousness.

From this perspective, the most appropriate historical analogy is another communications revolution: the invention of the mass media, or the printing press, or perspective, or numerals and the alphabet, or, behind them all, the invention of language—by far the most complex and sophisticated human invention, and a prerequisite for storing and passing on all other forms of technological knowledge and practice.[15] But this analogy too is inadequate, insofar as information technology has transformed production and consumption as well as consciousness and communications.

If comparisons are hard to find, it is not because technological change is less significant today than in the past but because we are breaking it up into episodes instead of seeing it whole. The digital divide is a major episode, not the whole story. The technological revolution we are living through includes everything Roland names: computers, information, communications, solid-state physics, digital electronics, control, genetics. It also includes the two industrial revolutions, which now may be seen as partial and preparatory. The essential feature of the larger technological revolution is the creation of a new habitat for human existence.[16] On the historical Richter scale, it is The Big One. Elting Morison, a historian who joined the MIT faculty in 1946, described it as follows:

> We are well on the way, in our timeless effort to bring the natural environment under control, to replacing it by an artificial environment of our own contriving. This special environment has a structure, a set of tempos, and a series of dynamic reactions that are not always nicely scaled to human responses. The interesting question seems to be whether man, having succeeded after all these years in bringing so much of the natural environment under his control, can now manage the imposing system he has created for the specific purpose of enabling him to manage his natural environment.[17]

Morison's formulation shows how difficult it is to find adequate and precise (not to mention gender-neutral) language to describe the new human habitat. Calling our environment "artificial" or "special," as Morison does, suggests something unnatural or even abnormal about it. There is nothing more natural, however, than the human creativity and ingenuity that have shaped this new environment. For human beings, the production of technology is as natural as is the production of enzymes for certain bacteria.[18] Nor is an "artificial" environment "replacing" the natural one. Nature has ended not in the sense of going away but only in the sense of being so mixed and mingled with human processes that it can no longer be identified as a separate entity.[19] In the words of the social theorist Ulrich Beck: "Not a hair or a crumb of it is still 'natural,' if 'natural' means nature being left to itself."[20]

Human beings have always tried to control nature so as to make life safer, more predictable, more abundant, and more fulfilling. But since the beginning of recorded history, and back into unrecorded history, non-human nature has been the ground of human life. This relationship between technology and nature, between figure and ground, which had been reversing slowly over centuries, reversed decisively in the past century. The built world has become the ground of human existence, now framing and embedding non-human nature. We have gone from using technology to control and exploit our habitat to using it to detach ourselves from our habitat.[21]

We continue to struggle for words with which to express this new phase of history. As early as the first industrial revolution, Georg W. F. Hegel contrasted "first" or given nature with "second nature" created by humankind. In similar language, the historian of technology Thomas Parke Hughes has referred to the technological world as the "second creation." In the 1960s, Lewis Mumford contrasted "the organic habitat" with "this new megatechnics ... a uniform, all-enveloping structure, designed for automatic operation."[22] I find myself using the verbal shorthand of referring to a technological world, or, more accurately, a *hybrid* world—a world in which technology and nature are inextricably mixed.

There is a convincing historical precedent for the replacement of one human habitat by another: the Neolithic revolution, usually dated around 10,000 BCE and usually defined by the integrated invention of agriculture, of cities, and indeed of history itself, since the concomitant invention of writing permitted, for the first time, a durable collective memory. Left behind, except in specific settings and in deepest memory, was the pastoral life of hunting and gathering, which had been the human, or humanoid, way of life for hundreds of thousands of years.[23] All the transformative events of the Neolithic revolution—writing, agriculture, settlements—were based in material change, but they also redefined what it meant to be human.[24] As the historian of religion Mircea Eliade notes, when most of humankind started raising crops "an ancient world, the world of nomadic hunters, with its religions, its myths, its moral conceptions, was ebbing away." Eliade continues, "Thousands and thousands of years were to elapse before the final lamentations of the old world died away, forever doomed by the advent of agriculture. One must also suppose that the profound spiritual crisis aroused by man's decision to call a halt and bind himself to the soil must have taken many hundreds of years to become completely integrated."[25]

The technological revolution of our times is the "decision"—collective, unconscious, incremental—to unbind ourselves from the soil. Eliade reminds us how far-reaching are the implications of binding ourselves instead to a self-constructed world. For millennia, the fact of settlement—humans living with other humans in a place over time—has shaped our ideas and practices of work, family, time and space, and society. This fact has also shaped our souls: solace, redemption, transcendence, and meaning have been defined by the twin powers of human community and non-human nature. It may be centuries before the lamentations for a lost world fade away and the human imagination can come to terms with its new habitat.

A technological world is partly natural and intensely human. The new fact of history on a material level is that nature is now so thoroughly intermixed with technology. The new fact of history on a social level is that we keep running into ourselves, as it were, as we build our values and our social order into the world. Sociologists describe this as the transition from modern society to something beyond: post-modernism, or (as Anthony Giddens prefers) post-modernity or radical modernity, or (as Ulrich Beck prefers) a risk society. Such thinkers stress the "reflexivity" of our society, meaning that we live in a world of echoes, a "boomerang" world (Beck's term) where everything that goes out comes back, where everything gets sampled and remixed, where everything has consequences, where social relationships co-evolve with material ones, where technology changes the very institutions producing it.[26]

The reflexivity of the world can be read positively (Giddens: "The reflexivity of modern social life consists in the fact that social practices are constantly examined and reformed in the light of incoming information about those very practices, thus constitutively altering their character"[27]) or less positively (Beck: "The gain in power from techno-economic 'progress' is being increasingly overshadowed by the production of risks"[28]). In any case, the process keeps getting more intensely reflexive. Once the marketplace takes the prime role in directing technological change, as it has since the 1970s, the process feeds back into itself.[29] A leading product of information technology is more information technology, all molded by the imperatives of a capitalist economy.

In terms of technological development, this is a virtuous circle—but it is still a circle, which accounts for the cultural paradox that the digital age engenders both a sense of liberating possibilities and a sense of oppression. Because of its socialized nature, information technology enhances social abilities, arguably our most human trait. But as information technology keeps reinforcing its dominance in terms defined by the market, other forms of sociability get selected out. A business-oriented society becomes more and more so as the system responds to its own feedback. In a world we have largely constructed, we keep encountering ourselves—but the projected "selves" we keep running into represent only a part of capacities, and arguably not the finest part.[30]

In the words of the historian Elting Morison, the historical challenge of our time is to build "a technological firmament that will really fit us" and "to organize a technological world we can live in."[31] History has not ended any more than nature is ended. Inevitably history will reveal itself to be much more powerful and unpredictable than the latest software upgrade. Inevitably nature will remind us of the fragility and impermanence of our control of the organic habitat. But history and nature are weakening as well-defined external frameworks that give meaning to human life. For most of human experience they were much more vast than the scale of individual existence, and their vastness provided solace in the case of nature and hope in the case of history. When nature becomes so intermingled with humanity, and when historical change becomes defined as an extension of technological change, neither nature nor history provides a self-evident framework for human meaning and identity. The only larger framework left, it seems, is humanity itself.

NOTES

1. See Nicholas Negroponte, *Being Digital* (Knopf, 1995). (Negroponte, the longtime director of MIT's Media Lab, recently stepped down from that position.) The dichotomy of lifeworld and systems is associated with Jürgen Habermas; see Fred R. Dallmayr, "Life-World: Variations on a Theme," in *Life-World and Politics: Between Modernity and Post-modernity*, ed. S. White (University of Notre Dame Press, 1989), pp. 45–6 and notes. The dialectic of globalization and identity is a major theme of Manuel Castells, whose works are referenced throughout this book. The term "symbolic analyst" comes from Robert Reich, *The Work of Nations: Preparing Ourselves for 21st Century Capitalism* (Knopf, 1991). The quote about the disposable labor force is from Manuel Castells, *The Rise of the Network Society*, second edition (Blackwell, 2000 [1995]), p. 295.
2. This discussion is based on a book by Edward T. Layton Jr.: *The Revolt of the Engineers: Social Responsibility and the American Engineering Profession* (Press of Case Western Reserve University, 1971), p. 53. The historian of technology, Susan Douglas, reminds us that "the study of ideology is essential to the study of technology." She defines it as "the entire constellation of images, myths and ideas through which people come to understand the material world and their place in that world." Social groups are engaged in an ongoing struggle about the myths and meanings that will be accepted as the natural and obvious way to interpret social reality. "This," Douglas claims, "is a struggle invariably won by the dominant classes." (Susan J. Douglas, "Jürgen Habermas Meets Mel Kranzberg What Media Theory Has to Offer the History of Technology and Vice Versa," paper presented at annual meeting of Society of the History of Technology, 1987, p. 2.)
3. Karl Mannheim, *Ideology and Utopia: An Introduction to the Sociology of Knowledge* (Harcourt, Brace, 1936 [1929]), p. 203; see pp. 192–211 passim.
4. In listening for these words, their clustering, and their mutual defining, I am drawing on an honorable tradition in intellectual history—best exemplified by Raymond William's book *Culture and Society, 1780–1950* (Columbia University Press, 1958)—of analyzing the social and cultural implications of the industrial revolution. Williams highlighted the reflexive or circular relationship between key terms of social analysis in the nineteenth century (culture, society, industry, art, etc.) and the changes they supposedly described. In addition, Williams showed how key concepts tended to cluster, so that their meanings shifted in response to alterations in the others. See Marx, "Technology: The Emergence of a Hazardous Concept," *Social Research* 64 (1997), no. 3, p. 967.
5. Leo Marx, who has tracked the use of the word, calls "technology" a "hazardous concept," unstable and reflexive in meaning, and particularly dangerous when used as the subject of a sentence, implying that it is an independent, autonomous historical agent, as in "the archetypal sentence: 'Technology is changing the way we live.'" Marx argues that the word "technology" began to be used in the late nineteenth century to fill a "conceptual void" in explaining how the utilitarian, instrumentalist branch of human activity, directed at controlling the physical world, could so powerfully generate social change. (Marx, "Technology: The Emergence of a Hazardous Concept," pp. 968, 974–975, 977.) The naming of MIT in 1862 was one of the first public uses of the term. (The choice probably was influenced by Jacob Bigelow, a Boston botanist and physician, who had used the term in a Harvard lecture in 1828; he later became an MIT trustee.)

6. John Staudenmaier, "Perils of Progress Talk: Some Historical Considerations," in *Science, Technology, and Social Progress*, ed. S. Goldman (Lehigh University Press, 1989).
7. The process by which technological change began to displace historical change began in the seventeenth century with the controversy of the "ancients" and the "moderns." The "moderns" might concede equality or even superiority to the ancients in arts or philosophy, but they felt they clinched their case in arguing for progress when they emphasized that only the moderns possessed the compass, the printing press, gunpowder, and (most important) the experimental method. These arguments from progress in inventiveness were extrapolated to history as a whole; progress in what we now would call technology was cited as irrefutable evidence for historical progress from antiquity to the modern age. When technology entered the study of history, history itself began to be redefined as the study of the record of human progress. See Richard Foster Jones, *Ancients and Moderns: A Study of the Background of The Battle of the Books* (Washington University Studies, New Series in Language and Literature, no. 6, 1936). See also Hannah Arendt, *The Human Condition* (Doubleday Anchor Books, 1959 [1958]), esp. pp. 119–133.
8. Anthony Giddens, *The Consequences of Modernity* (Stanford University Press, 1990), p. 51. Giddens puts "emptying out" in quotes in the text I am paraphrasing.
9. As Douglas reminds us in "Jürgen Habermas Meets Mel Kranzberg," the "'engineering of consent' is not a one-time event, in which meanings are clamped down and everyone accepts them." Consent is by no means automatic. It is an ongoing process in which people adjust their ideas and beliefs but also protest in a variety of ways. If the ideological framework becomes too much at odds with daily experience and with common sense, then the disparity has to be resolved for the social order to be stable: "The dominant ideology must incorporate certain criticisms and concerns while successfully marginalizing others, and illustrate that such concerns can be resolved best under the existing sociopolitical system."
10. Thomas Friedman makes this point when he uses a Lexus automobile and an olive tree to represent two sides of a technological divide: "Half the world seemed to be emerging from the Cold War intent on building a better Lexus, dedicated to modernizing, stream-lining and privatizing their economies in order to thrive in the system of globalization. And half of the world—sometimes half the same country, sometimes half the same person—was still caught up in the fight over who owns which olive tree." (*The Lexus and the Olive Tree*, Farrar, Straus and Giroux, 1999, p. 27.)
11. Alex Roland, email, March 5, 2000.
12. See Tom Standage, *The Victorian Internet: The Remarkable Story of the Telegraph and the Nineteenth Century's On-Line Pioneers* (Walker, 1998).
13. The concept of revolution migrated from physics (the path of the planets around the sun) to history (the overturning of British rule in America in the 1770s, the end of the monarchy in France in 1789), and then, in the early nineteenth century, in a deliberate analogy with events in France, was applied to machine production in the metaphor of the industrial revolution. When the metaphor of revolution is applied to industry, it implies a suddenness and completeness that might occur in the political arena (the king is executed, Robespierre rules) but does not apply in the arena of production. But to say that the metaphor is misleading is to miss the point. In the words of Leo Marx, "The whole issue becomes irrelevant once we recognize that we are dealing with a metaphor, and that its immense appeal rests, not on its capacity to describe the actual character of industrialization, but rather on its vivid suggestiveness. It evokes the uniqueness of the new way of life, as experienced, and, most important, it is a vivid expression of the affinity between technology and the great political revolution of modern times." (*The Machine in the Garden*, p. 187n.)
14. Steve Lohr, "The Future Came Faster in the Old Days," *New York Times*, October 5, 1997.
15. Lewis Mumford calls the invention of language "infinitely more complex and sophisticated ... than the Egyptian or Mesopotamian kit of tools" ("Technics and the Nature of Man," *Technology and Culture* 7, 1966, no. 3, p. 308).
16. On the term "habitat," see Gayle L. Ormiston, "Introduction," in *From Artifact to Habitat: Studies in the Critical Engagement of Technology*, ed. G. Ormiston (Lehigh University Press, 1990), p. 13.
17. Elting Morison, "Introductory Observations," in Morison, *Men, Machines, and Modern Times* (MIT Press, 1966), p. 16. See my discussion of the language and imagery of the artificial environment in *Notes on the Underground: An Essay on*

Technology, Society, and the Imagination (MIT Press, 1990), pp. 1–8.

18. Manuel Castells (*The Rise of the Network Society*, p. 15) puts it into one long sentence: "Matter includes nature, human-modified nature, human-produced nature, and human nature itself, the labors of history forcing us to move away from the classic distinction between humankind and nature, since millenniums of human action have incorporated the natural environment into society, making us, materially and symbolically, an inseparable part of this environment."
19. Bill McKibben makes this point in *The End of Nature* (Random House, 1989).
20. Ulrich Beck, *Risk Society: Towards a New Modernity* (Sage, 1992 [1986]), p. 81.
21. Here I am paraphrasing Mumford ("Technics and the Nature of Man," p. 303), who writes: "In terms of the currently accepted picture of the relation of man to technics, our age is passing from the primeval state of man, marked by his invention of tools and weapons for the purpose of achieving mastery over the forces of nature, to a radically different condition, in which he will not only have conquered nature but detached himself completely from the organic habitat."
22. Mumford, "Technics and the Nature of Man," p. 303.
23. See Stanley H. Ambrose, "Paleolithic Technology and Human Evolution," *Science* 291 (2001), no. 5509, pp. 1748–1752: "Stone tool technology, robust australopithecines, and the genus *Homo* appeared almost simultaneously 2.5 [million years ago]" (p. 1748). The systematic use of fire evidently began between 1 million and 1.5 million years ago, and around 300,000 years ago "technological and cultural evolution accelerated" in a way that suggests "the emergence of true cultural traditions and cultural areas" (p. 1751). The stone tool technologies between 2.5 and 0.3 million years ago "are remarkable for their slow pace of progress ... and for limited mobility and regional interaction ... with the appearance of near-modern brain size, anatomy, and perhaps of grammatical language ~0.3 [million years ago], the pace quickens exponentially" (p. 1752).
24. See Peter F. Drucker, "The First Technological Revolution and Its Lessons," *Technology and Culture* 7 (1966), no. 2, pp. 143–151. This article is Drucker's presidential address to the Society for the History of Technology, presented on December 29, 1965, in San Francisco. He defines "the first technological revolution" as "the irrigation city, which then rapidly became the irrigation empire" (p. 143).
25. Mircea Eliade, *The Forge and the Crucible*, second edition (University of Chicago Press, 1978 [1956]), pp. 177–178. For a discussion of this passage in a different context, see Williams, *Notes on the Underground*, pp. 1–4.
26. The concept of reflexive modernization was articulated most clearly by Beck in *Risk Society*. See also Anthony Giddens's books *The Consequences of Modernity* (cited above) and *Modernity and Self-Identity in the Late Modern Age* (Stanford University Press, 1992).
27. Giddens, *The Consequences of Modernity*, p. 38.
28. Beck, *Risk Society*, pp. 12–13.
29. Under the governing structures of market relationships, the abiding imperative of capitalist accumulation—to increase profits—is accomplished in a few major ways. The circulation of capital can be maximized through increasing its extension in space (broadening the market) and its intensity over time (accelerating capital turnover). Also, production costs can be lowered, productivity can be raised, and new products can be brought to market. Particularly in the last three decades, all these ways of increasing profit are closely linked to technological innovation, which has become the primary driver of capitalist acquisition. See Castells, *The Rise of the Network Society*, pp. 68–69, 95. Castells comments, "Information processing is focused on improving the technology of information processing as a source of productivity, in a virtuous circle of interaction between the knowledge sources of technology and the application of technology to improve knowledge generation and information processing.... Or, more briefly, a prime characteristic of the information age is its circularity, characterized by the immediate application to its own development of technologies it generates..." (ibid., p. 32).
30. "Meanwhile man ... exalts himself to the posture of lord of the earth. In this way the impression comes to prevail that everything man encounters exists only insofar as it is his construct. This illusion gives rise in turn to one final delusion: It seems as though man everywhere and always encounters only himself. Heisenberg has with complete correctness pointed out that the real must present itself to contemporary man in this way. *In truth, however, precisely nowhere does man today any longer encounter himself, i.e. his essence.*"

(Martin Heidegger, "The Question Concerning Technology," in *The Question Concerning Technology and Other Essays*, Harper & Row, 1977, p. 27.) Hannah Arendt (*The Human Condition*, p. 237) quotes Heisenberg's observation about "man encountering only himself."

31. The first quote (from Morison, *From Know-How to Nowhere)* is cited by Thomas P. Hughes in "Memorials: Elting Morison, 1909–1995," *Technology and Culture* 37 (1996), no. 4, p. 874. The second quote, also from "Memorials," is cited by Leo Marx (ibid., p. 867).

1.2 SOCIAL/POLITICAL PERSPECTIVES

1.2.1 I'd Hammer Out Freedom: Technology as Politics and Culture

RICHARD SCLOVE

Even though technologies are usually developed to meet a particular need or solve a specific problem, they often have secondary functions or unintended effects on our lives. In this article, Richard Sclove is interested in how technologies exist within, are influenced by, and in turn exert influence on society. He claims that they often work in subtle ways to both define and set limits on human interaction.

The view of "technology as society" discussed in this article states that although technology influences the social experience, it is not the sole determinant of how society develops. As a technology goes through various evolutionary stages, it assumes a greater role in our lives, and we become less aware of its influence and less likely to seek alternative ways of doing something. It is important, claims Sclove, for societies to look for alternative technologies more in keeping with humane ideals and aspirations.

FOCUS QUESTIONS

1. Identify one modern technology and discuss its development. In what ways has this technology changed the way you live from both a positive and negative perspective, and what future changes might occur that could have even more impact on your life?
2. Identify one environmental and organizational background imperative of a contemporary technology. How might those conditions have influenced that technology's development and its influence on our lives?

Source: *Democracy and Technology* by Richard E. Sclove. © 1995 The Guilford Press. Reprinted by permission. Notes omitted; interested readers should consult the original.

3. What are some ways in which Sclove's concept of *polypotency* relates to the issues of "freedom, power, authority, community, and justice" raised in the reading by Langdon Winner (Selection 1.2.2)?

KEYWORDS

citizenship, democracy, primary function, social consequences, social structure

Technological innovations are similar to legislative acts or political foundings that establish a framework for public order that will endure over many generations.

LANGDON WINNER

What is technology? People ordinarily think of technology as machinery or gadgetry, as an economic factor of production, as know-how, as what engineers do, or as progress. Often they characterize technologies in terms of a single intended function. What is a hammer? It's what someone uses to pound nails into boards. What is a telephone? It's a device that enables people to converse at a distance. Some technologies, however, have more than one intended function. Hammers, for example, can pound nails into boards but can also extract them. This is the core of the contemporary view of technology. People understand technologies in terms of a primary function—or, occasionally, several functions—that each is intended to accomplish.

Beyond this, our society has in the past few decades come to acknowledge that technologies tend to produce at least two general kinds of "secondary" or "unintended" effects. First, they generate environmental consequences: pollution, resource depletion, and ecosystem modification. Each of these may, in turn, have direct or indirect effects on human life. Second, they promote unintended social consequences—consequences that are generally mediated by economic markets (e.g., the replacement of workers by machines or the emergence of boomtowns). Thus common knowledge has it that technologies perform one or perhaps a few intended functions, while also producing a limited range of unintended social and environmental consequences.

Although this view of technology is straightforward, it is also incomplete and misleading. It diverts attention from many significant aspects of technology, including some of central concern to democracy. By synthesizing recent technological criticism, the alternative view of technology introduced here incorporates the accepted view's sound insights but situates these within a broader perspective that recognizes technologies as a species of social structure.

The phrase "social structure" refers to the background features that help define or regulate patterns of human interaction. Familiar examples include laws, dominant political and economic institutions, and systems of cultural belief. Technologies qualify as social structures because they function politically and culturally in a manner comparable to these other, more commonly recognized kinds of social structures.

TECHNOLOGIES AS SOCIAL STRUCTURES

Ibieca, a Spanish village, found that its indoor plumbing came at the expense of community integration. That is an instance of a technology helping to structure social relations. Upsetting a traditional pattern of water use compromised important means through which the village had previously perpetuated itself as a self-conscious community. In the United States the automobile has played a somewhat similar role in disrupting prior patterns of community life.

These are not isolated cases; technologies designed for such mundane tasks as commuting to work or cooking food also routinely help constitute social systems of cooperation, isolation, or domination.

> Technology often embodies and expresses political value choices that, in their operations and effects, are binding on individuals and groups, whether such choices have been made in political forums or elsewhere.... Technological processes in

contemporary society have become the equivalent of a form of law—that is, an authoritative or binding expression of social norms and values from which the individual or a group may have no immediate recourse.

Coercive Compliance

Technologies help regulate social behavior in part because they are themselves governed by both physical and political laws. For example, the operation of many technologies—such as automobiles, medical X-ray machines, or guns—is legally regulated. Thus their misuse can entail a socially enforced penalty.

However, whether or not they are governed by legal regulations, technologies generally embody a variety of other kinds of coercive mandates. The penalty for resisting these mandates may range from an informal reprimand ("Don't lick the food off your knife!") to economic loss or systemic failure (e.g., the gears in a conveyor belt jam, or a worker's hand is injured). These latter results are akin to the consequences befalling those who ignore physical laws (e.g., when someone literally walks on thin ice). Thus physical constraints, or accompanying legal and social sanctions, are among the obvious means through which technologies help structure human behavior.

Subconscious Compliance

Sometimes technologies shape behavior and relationships less through brute compulsion than via subtle, psychological inducement. For example, social scientists have shown that the physical arrangement of chairs and tables strongly influences the kind of social interaction that occurs in schools, nursing homes, and hospitals. Yet the staff in those institutions had previously attributed behavior (including their own) entirely to the mix of personalities and psychological capabilities. They were surprised to learn that simply shifting the furniture could, for instance, help reanimate a seemingly moribund group of mentally impaired hospital inmates.

Opportunities and Constraints

Social structures are also ambiguous in that while they can restrict opportunities in some respects, they can—when appropriately designed—enhance them in others. For example, well-crafted laws help protect basic civil rights and, by providing a relatively stable and well-ordered social context, make it easier for people to realize their life plans. Besides creating novel opportunities and constraints, technologies also reconfigure prior patterns. For instance, within some offices and factories the proliferation of personal computer networks has enhanced lower level workers' chances to contribute to production decisions while simultaneously challenging midlevel managers' former domains of authority and autonomy. Once deployed, technologies can also aid or hinder the use of other technologies. For instance, telephone systems gradually displaced telegraph services but have more recently facilitated development of computer networks and long-distance data processing.

Background Conditions as Imperatives

In order to function, technologies require various environmental and organizational background conditions. A television set is only useful so long as viewers know how to operate it, it is protected from inclement weather, there is access to electricity, programs are being produced and distributed, and so on.

Frequently when individuals or groups acquire new technologies or technological facilities, they are at best only dimly conscious of the demands that effective operation will impose or require to be developed. Several years ago a town near mine in western Massachusetts approved construction of an industrial research center, hoping thereby to realize tax benefits. But no one asked beforehand the eventual costs (financial, environmental, and emotional) that the town would one day bear in order to accommodate both new research activities and the concomitant growth in commuting, ancillary employment, and residential population. These costs could include hazards associated with toxic waste disposal, future loss of open space to new housing, and the burden of upgrading roads, sewer lines, snowplowing capabilities, schools, and school bus lines.

To the extent that a given technology plays only a small part in one's life, maintaining the conditions needed for its operation may be of no particular concern. But as a person or society grows dependent on a technology, the necessary conditions of its operation loom as practical imperatives. The need to support these conditions represents a way in which technologies exert a profound structural social influence.

Technology As Structural for Nonusers

Often technologies exert comparably significant effects on people who neither operate nor use the technology in question. One clear example involves phenomena that economists label "spill-over effects" or "externalities." Homeowners hear neighbors' radios, lawn mowers, or air conditioners; whole communities breathe noxious fumes from an industrial facility. Each person lives in an aesthetic landscape that reflects the aggregate technological choices made by other people or organizations. The psychological texture of our everyday life reflects the influence of countless technological choices and practices in which we did not participate.

Moreover, often such spillover effects exert a structural influence that is dynamic and transformative. For instance, someone might choose not to purchase a power lawn mower to avoid its noise. However, after a few neighbors have bought theirs, this person may reconsider, thinking, "Since I'm suffering from the noise anyway, why not buy my own power mower and at least benefit from the convenience?" In this way each mower purchased contributes to a cycle that gradually transforms a neighborhood of quiet into one rent by the sound of churning engines.

Next reconsider the background conditions necessary for a technology to operate. Many of those conditions have a tremendous impact on lives even if individuals do not own the technology or use the technological service that establishes their raison d'etre. Suppose, to state the case dramatically, that as a citizen of a modern nation a woman opts for a relatively self-sufficient mode of life: She refuses to own a car, uses solar collectors on the roof of her home, and plants a large vegetable garden in her yard. What has she accomplished? Something, certainly, but the texture of her world still reflects the existence not only of cars and their immediate culture, but of roadways, automobile manufacturing and marketing systems, oil refineries, electric generating facilities, agribusiness, the private or public bureaucracies that manage these things, and their often tumultuous politics. That is part of what it means to say that technologies are social structures. The aggregate result of a society's many technological choices in one way or another affects every member.

Communicative and Cultural Systems

Apart from materially influencing social experience, technologies also exert symbolic and other cultural influences. This is true not only of technologies explicitly called communications devices (e.g., cellular phones, televisions, and radios), but of all technologies.

For example, modern sofas generally have two or three separate seat cushions. There is no compelling technical or economic rationale for this design (an affordable, seamless sofa is an easily conceived alternative—as seamless mattresses and Japanese futon sofa-beds attest). Rather, separate sofa cushions define distinct personal spaces and thus respect—but also help to perpetuate—modern Western culture's emphasis on individuality and privacy.

Technologies even play transformative roles within psychological development. For example, earlier this century Swiss psychologist Jean Piaget determined that young children distinguish living from nonliving things according to whether or not the things move, and—as the children develop psychologically—then according to whether things move by themselves or are moved by an outside force. However, more recently, social psychologist Sherry Turkle found that children who play with computer toys that appear to "talk" and "think" develop different criteria for distinguishing "alive" from "not alive." Instead of relying on physical criteria (such as motion), they invent psychological criteria and hypotheses ("Computers are alive because they cheat" or "Computers are not alive because they don't have feelings"). Children's developmental trajectories, including their conceptions of self and moral reasoning, are transformed as a result of their interactions with these machines.

The process that Turkle described with respect to computer toys is a specific instance of a much more general phenomenon. As they reconfigure opportunities and constraints for action, and function simultaneously as symbols and latent communicative media, technologies also reconfigure opportunities and constraints for psychological development.

Macropolitics: Technology *and* Society Versus Technology *as* Society

Many scholars have described cases in which technologies exert a macrolevel influence on societies. Consider historians who focus on the social role of just one or two important technologies at a time. Large scale dams and irrigation systems may have played a decisive role in the creation and maintenance of states in antiquity. Lynn White, Jr. told a now-famous story of the role of the stirrup in the development of European feudalism: stirrups made possible mounted shock combat, which led in turn to heavy full-body armor, heraldry, chivalry, stronger horse breeds, more efficient plowing methods, and so forth. In America, railroads helped establish national markets; promoted coal mining, steelmaking, and the widespread adoption of steam power; provided an influential model of geographically dispersed, hierarchically managed corporate organization; contributed to the adoption of standardized timekeeping; and served as a dominant metaphor with which Americans interpreted their entire civilization.

More recently in the United States one role of new technologies has been to provide grounds for the growth of the federal government, through the proliferation of such agencies as the Federal Communications Commission for regulating telecommunications, the Federal Aviation Administration for regulating the airline industry, the Nuclear Regulatory Commission and the Department of Energy for administering aspects of national energy production and nuclear weapons development, and the like.

In each of these instances, technological innovation plays a role in establishing, transforming, or maintaining states or societies at the macrolevel. Langdon Winner has explored the further hypothesis that the entire ensemble of modern technological systems—including the background conditions required to keep them operating—tends to promote centrally coordinated, technocratic social administration.

Hence there are numerous examples in which technologies affect societies or states in ways that have macrostructural implications. However, this formulation—while both true and dramatic—nonetheless misses the force of this chapter's earlier analysis. Technologies function politically and culturally as social structures by coercing physical compliance; prompting subconscious compliance; constituting systems of social relations; establishing opportunities and constraints for action and self-realization; promoting the evolution of background conditions; affecting nonusers; shaping communication, psychological development, and culture generally; and constituting much of the world within which lives unfold.

Considering all of the preceding functions and effects together, it would be fairer to say that technologies do not merely *affect* society or states, they also *constitute* a substantial portion of societies and states. That, too, is part of what it means to be a social structure. Recognizing the many respects in which technologies contribute to defining who people are, what they can and cannot do, and how they understand themselves and their world should dispel the common myth that technologies are morally or politically neutral.

Influential, Not Determining

Technologies "structure" social relations in that they shape or help constitute—but do not fully determine—social experience. Water pipes and washing machines did not, for example, literally force Ibiecans to stop gathering at their village's central fountain and washbasin, but instead altered the system of inducements and interdependencies that formerly made such gathering occur naturally.

Aside from the possibility of rejecting or retiring a particular technology, there is always a margin of flexibility in how existing technological artifacts may be used or operated, or in what activities may occur in conjunction with them. This margin is finite, and its extent varies from one technology to the next and over time, but it nevertheless exists. For example, while a conventional assembly line provides only highly restricted opportunities to vary work routines at each station, it does not materially prevent workers from rotating jobs among work stations.

Context-Dependency

Developing a railroad network helped catapult the United States to global economic preeminence, but Britain developed railroads earlier and yet nonetheless gradually lost its world economic predominance. Thus railroads (or other technologies) are socially consequential, but how and why they matter depends on the precise technologies in question in each particular context of use.

Moreover, just as social context—including, among other things, a society's preexisting technological order—regulates each technology's material functions and effects, it also regulates a technology's communicative functions and cultural meanings. A few decades ago a belching smokestack symbolized progress. Today—in a different historical context—the same smokestack is more likely to evoke distress or even outrage.

Finally, one important influence on a technology's functions and effects is the minds and culture of people. Nineteenth-century high-wheeler bicycles were perceived by athletic young men as virile, high-speed devices. But to some women and elderly men the same devices signified personal danger. Indeed, conflicting perceptions of the high-wheeler proved consequential to its subsequent technological development. Its perception as a "macho machine" prompted new bicycle designs with ever higher front wheels. The competing perception of the high-wheeler as an "unsafe machine" prompted designs with smaller front wheels, different seat placement, or higher rear wheels. Thus to understand the social function, meaning, and evolution of the high-wheeler, it is essential to explore its psychological and cultural context.

Public controversies concerning technology offer another occasion for observing the role of culture and cognition in establishing a technology's context, and hence its social role. For example, during the 1970s nuclear engineers and electric utility executives generally viewed centralized production of electricity as a critical social need and essential to the concept of commercial nuclear power. To them an alternative to nuclear power needed to be another means of performing this critical function. But other energy policy analysts saw the expanded production of electricity as so inessential that a perfectly viable alternative could be a panel of foam wall insulation that did not generate any electricity.

In evidence here are fragments of a social process of contesting or negotiating what is or is not to count as an essential function of a technology and hence as an alternative. Thus, when technological consequences or meanings become controversial, processes through which technologies are culturally constituted may emerge openly.

Contingent Social Products

There is residual variability in the structural effects associated with any deployed technology—*within a particular social context and even more so among different contexts.* However, a technology's greatest flexibility exists before its final deployment, when artifacts and their accompanying social organization are being conceived and designed.

Technologies do not just appear or happen; they are contingent social products. Thus it is possible, both before and after the fact, to imagine alternative designs. The process by which one set of designs rather than another comes to fruition is influenced by prevailing social structures and forces, including the preexisting technological order. However, this process also reflects explicit or tacit social choices, including political negotiations or struggles.

For example, it is hard to imagine a modern home without an electric refrigerator, but had the accidents of competing corporate resources played out slightly differently, gas-powered refrigerators that would have run more reliably and quietly could have been the norm. Other feasible alternatives in household technology harbored the potential for even more dramatic social effects. Moreover, although today people think of the guiding impulses behind technological development as necessarily being profit, convenience, or military advantage, throughout history religious or aesthetic motivations have often been just as significant.

Thus there are many potential, competing technological pathways, and each is socially developed. But the flexibility associated with a given technology, or with other social structures, tends to diminish with time. After a society has habituated itself to one technology, alternatives tend to become less accessible. Once designed and deployed, a technology, like a law or a political institution tends—if it is going to endure—gradually to become integrated into larger systems of functionally interdependent artifacts and organizations and then to influence the design of subsequent technologies, laws, and institutions such that the latter all tend to depend on the continued existence of the former. Thus, owing to the accompanying evolution of supporting custom, entrenched interest, and various sunk costs, it is often difficult to achieve radical design alterations once an initial decision has been implemented. A further factor reducing the flexibility of technologies is that they exhibit some of the pure physical recalcitrance that comes with material embodiment. Hence, both technologies and other social structures, once they have come into existence, tend to endure. However, technologies exhibit a remaining characteristic that tends to distinguish them from other social structures and to increase their relative political salience: polypotency.

POLYPOTENCY

Technologies function as social structures, but often independently of their (nominally) intended purposes. This is one of the phenomena that the conventional view of technology obscures. The same obfuscation is reflected in studies that profess a broad interest in the political effects of technology but that discuss only technologies designed explicitly to function politically (such as telecommunications, military and police technologies, voting machines, or computer databases). Such technologies indeed function politically, but everyone knows that. That is these technologies' announced purpose. Harder to grasp is the truth that all technologies are associated with manifold latent social effects and meanings, and that it is largely in virtue of these that technologies come to function as social structures. In other words, technologies exhibit superfluous efficacy or "polypotency" in their functions, effects, and meanings. (The word *polypotency,* meaning "potent in many ways," is introduced here for want of a better existing term. The unfamiliarity wears off quickly if one contrasts it with omnipotence, meaning, literally, "potent in all ways.")

For example, when a man uses an ordinary hammer to pound nails, he also learns about the texture and structural properties of materials, he exercises and develops his muscles, he improves his hand-eye coordination, and he generates noise, all while stressing and wearing the hammer itself. As his competence at hammering grows, he feels his self-respect affirmed and approved. At another level, his activity resonates with half-conscious memories of primeval myths about Vulcan and Thor. He is also reminded of the blacksmith and the mythology of the American frontier. He thinks of a judge's gavel, the hammer as a symbol of justice, and a song popularized by the folksinging trio Peter, Paul, and Mary.

Where did the hammer come from? Somebody chopped down a tree and fashioned the handle. Others located and extracted iron ore. Some of that ore was refashioned into a hammer head. If a man touches his tongue to the hammer, with the taste of oxidized iron he senses fleetingly a former age when once-independent craftsmen and farmers first found themselves working under strict supervision in a factory. When he was a child, an uncle first taught him to use a hammer. Now when he hefts a hammer, he feels embedded in a historical relationship with this and other hammers and with the development of the concept of hammers and technology in general.

The hammer's immediate social context of use can vary. The man may work alone, on a project with others, or in a room where each person pursues a different project. He may or may not choose his task; he may or may not earn a wage. Depending on the precise social context of its use, the hammer means different things to him, he sees it differently, and it helps disclose the world to him in different ways. Likewise, his style of using the hammer discloses to others much about his character, competence, and mood.

The hammer differs from a partially automated assembly line in that the latter requires and helps coordinate the simultaneous efforts of many workers. But a hammer also establishes certain limiting possibilities on the social conditions of its use. Hammers have only one handle. They are not designed to permit the type of close collaboration that is possible through computer networks or necessary when using a long, two-handled saw.

The material result of the man's activity is likely to include some bent nails, scrap wood, a hearty appetite, maybe a bruised thumb, a few sore but marginally strengthened muscles, some excess exhalation of carbon dioxide, perspiration, and a product that becomes part of the humanly shaped world. So, is the nail entering the board necessarily the most important feature of the activity called "hammering"? Hammers, like all technologies, are polypotent in their social functions, effects, and meanings.

Today's accepted view of technology takes a step toward acknowledging polypotency by speaking of technologies' unintended or secondary consequences. However, the term "polypotency" is helpful in not presuming that one knows automatically which of a technology's many functions or meanings are the most important or even which are intended. Many social historians of technology have, for example, argued that a latent but intended function of some innovations in manufacturing technology has been to substitute low-paid unskilled workers for higher-paid skilled workers, discipline the remaining workforce, and weaken unions.

It is furthermore useful to introduce the term "focal function" to refer to a technology's (ostensibly) intended purpose. "Nonfocal" then denotes its accompanying complex of additional—but often recessive—functions, effects, and meanings. Thus, 19th-century New England schoolhouses' focal function was to provide a space for educational instruction, whereas one of their nonfocal functions was to help generate—in part via the symbolism of churchlike architectures—a relatively docile workforce.

Occasionally technologies function as social structures precisely by virtue of their focal purpose. For instance, weapons function coercively because they are designed to do just that. But more often and more subtly, it is technologies' latent polypotency that accounts for their structural performance. This is illustrated by many previous examples, ranging from sofa cushions (which help to latently reproduce our culture's sense of privacy) to computer toys (which unexpectedly alter children's psychological development). Even technologies focally designed to function structurally are apt to structure nonfocally as well.

For instance, nuclear weapons are designed focally to coerce, deter, or destroy other societies, but they contribute nonfocally to legitimating authoritarian government institutions within the societies that possess them. Marshall McLuhan popularized this truth as it applies specifically to technologies focally designated as communications devices: "The medium *is* the message." In other words, the technical means of focally delivering a message can, owing to polypotency, matter more than the message itself.

Moreover, often groups of focally unrelated technologies interact latently to produce a structural effect that no one of them could accomplish alone. Distinct sofa cushions would not help establish cultural norms of privacy and individualism were they not part of a complex of artifacts and ritual behavior that contribute jointly toward that same result. (Other artifacts in the complex with sofa cushions include individual eating utensils, private bedrooms, telephone receivers designed to accommodate one person at a time, and so forth.) In short, to achieve social insight and efficacy, it is essential to consider all the different artifacts and practices that comprise a society's technological order.

There are important functional equivalences between technologies and nontechnological social structures (e.g., legal statutes, government agencies, and large corporations). All represent enduring social products that shape subsequent social experience. However, there are also differences, revolving around contrasting levels of social understanding with respect to each.

First, laws and political and economic institutions are contingent social products, and at some level everyone knows this truth. Societies evolve these things through formal political or juridical processes, and it is commonly understood that alternative choices are possible. In contrast, people are prone to misperceive a society's technologies as inevitable, that is, as naturally determined rather than socially shaped and chosen.

Second, laws and other formally evolved social structures are commonly understood to function as social structures. That is their explicit purpose. Certainly, they can also be implicated in the production of various unintended social consequences. Prohibition-era laws were enacted to stop alcohol production, not to drive it underground and contribute to the expansion of organized crime. However, people at least expect that legal statutes and institutions will—because that is their intent—in some way shape social interaction and history. In contrast, people ordinarily expect most technologies to prove structurally inconsequential, and—because focally most of them do—this expectation appears confirmed. But here is where appearances deceive, insofar as it is frequently a technology's nonfocal aspects alone that conspire to manifest profound structural consequences.

Hence, although technologies are as consequential as other social structures, people tend to be more blind both to the social origins of technologies and to their social effects. This dual blindness is partly due to certain myths or misconceptions, such as the myth that technologies are autonomous self-contained phenomena and the myth that they are morally neutral. It is also inculcated through modern technologies themselves, via both their style and their social process of design.

These dual misperceptions concerning technologies actually enhance their relative structural significance, because they enable technologies to exert their influence with only limited social awareness of how, or even that, they are doing so. This helps explain why people are prone to resign themselves to social circumstances established through technological artifice and practices that they might well reject if the same results were proposed through a formal political process.

So long as their social origin, effects, and dynamics remain so badly misperceived, technologies will not suffer the same liability as would, say, functionally comparable laws or economic institutions, of being challenged on the grounds that they are politically or culturally unacceptable. Furthermore, societies will fail to develop the capacity to seek other technologies more consonant—both focally and nonfocally—with their members' ideals and aspirations.

1.2.2 Artifacts/Ideas and Political Culture

LANGDON WINNER

Although technology usually offers us a bright and rosy future, Langdon Winner suggests that we should be considering what type of technological future we want to build and the extent to which it will be kind to human society. As our modern political culture has evolved, it is important to be aware of the ways in which advancing technology has affected our common experiences of "freedom, power, authority, community, and justice." Even though the artifacts and processes associated with technological systems are taken for granted or thought to be politically neutral, this article examines technology as a major force on our lives, changing relationships between people in subtle but significant ways. This is evident in secondary influences from inventions of the Industrial Revolution, which created an entirely new society

Source: *Whole Earth Review,* No. 73 (Winter 1991), pp. 18–24. *Whole Earth Review,* San Rafael, CA 94901. Subscription available subs@wholeearthmag.com. Reprinted by permission.

that continues to evolve today, even though we might not be conscious of the change. Whether these changes are for the better will be determined by our commitment to building a society in which more people share in the benefits.

FOCUS QUESTIONS

1. Describe the seven concepts mentioned by Winner that are present in the structure of contemporary technology and give an example of two specific technologies utilized today that embody those ideas.
2. Identify a contemporary technology and discuss one probable answer to each of the three questions normally focused on by individuals, groups, and nations. With the benefit of hindsight, how has that particular technology influenced the kind of world that has developed since its inception?
3. Consider the three guiding maxims proposed by Winner to focus discussion about the relationship between technological choice and the future of political culture. How do these concepts relate to the issue of spreading capitalism discussed by Jagdish Bhagwati (Selection 2.1.2)?

KEYWORDS

capitalism, culture, democracy, feudalism, public policy, UTOPIA

This is a time of great excitement about the fruitful possibilities of new technology, but also a time of grave concern about what those possibilities mean for the future of our society. Horizons visible in microelectronics and photonics, biotechnology, composite materials, computing, and other fields hold out prospects of sweeping change in our way of life. How should we regard these prospects?

As individuals, groups, and nations anticipate technological change nowadays, they usually focus upon three questions.

First: How will the technology be used? What are its functions and practical benefits?

Second: How will the technology change the economy? What will it contribute to the production, distribution, and consumption of material wealth?

Third: How will the technology affect the environment? What will its consequences be for global climate change, pollution of the biosphere, and other environmental problems?

While these are important issues, another crucial question is seldom mentioned: What kind of world are we building here? As we develop new devices, techniques and technical systems, what qualities of social, moral, and political life do we create in the process? Will this be a world friendly to human sociability or not?

These are questions about the relationship of technological change to the evolution of modern political culture. In what ways do the development, adoption, and use of instrumental things affect our shared experience of freedom, power, authority, community, and justice? How might we respond creatively to the role technology plays in contemporary political life?

In the titles of a great many books, articles, and conferences these days, the topic is often described as "technology and society" or "technology and culture" or "technology and politics." But if one takes a closer look, such distinctions no longer have much validity. In the late twentieth century, technology and society, technology and culture, technology and politics are by no means separate. They are closely woven together in a multiplicity of settings in which many forms of human living are dependent upon and shaped by technological devices and systems of various kinds. Our useful artifacts reflect who we are, what we aspire to be. At the same time, we ourselves mirror the technologies which surround us; to an increasing extent social activities and human consciousness are technically mediated.

In this light, any attempt to understand the matter might well begin from either of two basic starting points: (1) the technological world seen from the point of view of human beings and (2) the same world seen from the point of view of the artifacts. Although it may seem perverse to do so, I shall begin with the second perspective.

Many of the things that we like to think of as mere tools or instruments now function as virtual members of our society. It makes sense to ask: Which roles, responsibilities, and possibilities for action have been delegated to technological things? Which social features are associated with a particular artifact? For example, does a computer in the workplace function as a servant, slave, controller, guard, supervisor, etc.?

The social roles delegated to the phone answering machine provide a good illustration. It used to be that only executives in business and government could afford to keep a full-time secretary answering the phone, screening calls, and taking messages. Now it is possible to buy a small, inexpensive answering machine that does at least some of that work. An alternative would be to answer the phone yourself, have someone else do it for you, or simply miss some calls. The machine serves as a surrogate, a kind of nonhuman agent that has been given certain kinds of work to do.

An interesting fact about these machines is that their initial use often brings some embarrassment. In the little taped message that precedes the beep, there is often something like an apology. "I'm sorry I can't be here to answer your call..." or "I'm sorry you have to talk to this machine, but...." What one sees in cases like this is, I believe, quite common in modern life: the uneasy feeling that accompanies the renegotiation of social and moral boundaries around a technological change. But what is sometimes at first a source of discomfort eventually becomes a widely accepted pattern—"second nature," if you will.

It is clear that in decades to come a great many things like telephone answering machines and automatic bank tellers will become, in effect, members of our society. As their use spreads, the tone of embarrassment that surrounds their early introduction will gradually vanish. For better or worse, the renegotiation of boundaries will be complete. When I phoned a friend recently, I heard a recorded message that said simply: "It's 1991. You know what to do!"

One can also consider technological innovations from the alternate viewpoint—noticing the roles, responsibilities, and possibilities for action delegated to human beings within and around technological systems of various kinds. Now one can ask: Is a person's guiding hand required for the system to function? Does the human give orders or receive them? Is the person active or acted upon? What social qualities accompany the human presence?

I will offer some illustrations in a moment. But first I want to call attention to the fact that once one has entered the twofold perspective I've suggested, one has the beginning of a social and political vision of technology quite different from the one that economists, engineers, and technology policy makers usually employ. One recognizes, first and foremost, that technologies are not merely tools that one "picks up and uses." They can be seen as "forms of life" in which humans and inanimate objects are linked in various kinds of relationships. The interesting question becomes: How can we describe and evaluate technologies seen as "forms of life"?

By comparison, in the conventional view of things, the story usually goes that people employ technologies as simple tools for rather specific instrumental purposes, attempting to wrest new advantages over nature and to gain various economic benefits. Once these instrumental advantages and economic benefits have been obtained, other things may happen. There are what are called secondary, tertiary, and other distant consequences of our actions, often called the "impacts" or "unintended" consequences, the broader social, cultural, political, and environmental effects of technological applications of various kinds.

For some purposes, it is perfectly acceptable to view technological change in the conventional manner. However, if you take a longer view of history, an interesting fact soon emerges. In the fullness of time, the so-called "secondary" consequences or impacts of technological change are often far more significant than the results thought to be "primary" at the time. This is certainly true, for example, of the kinds of changes we associate with the Industrial Revolution of the eighteenth and nineteenth centuries. One could list the thousands upon thousands of instrumental advantages and economic benefits obtained during that period—techniques for making textiles, extracting coal, making locomotives run, etc. But that is not what is truly important about the Industrial Revolution. What matters is the fact that a whole new kind of society was created. The truly enduring part of that revolution, the truly significant aspect is the multiplicity of relationships between people and between humans and technology we call Industrial Society, results many of which arose largely as so-called "secondary" consequences of technological change.

If one looks carefully at contemporary technological innovations in their broader human context, one often finds emerging forms of political culture. Several years ago Maevon Garrett, a woman who had worked as a telephone operator in Baltimore for 18 years, was called into her supervisor's office and abruptly fired. She was informed that a computer had been installed to monitor the performance of telephone operators and that data gathered by the computer showed that she was less efficient than the average worker in processing phone calls. At that moment Maevon Garrett became the victim of norms of productivity and efficiency embodied in the workings of a new technological system.

What is interesting, however, is not only the fact of Ms. Garrett's firing, but her response to it. She pointed out that some portion of her time each day was spent talking with people who dial a telephone operator because they are lonely or in distress—elderly people who live alone, or "latchkey children," youngsters who come home after school to an empty house because their parents are still at work. Ms. Garrett argued she would not hang up on such people just to meet the phone company's hourly quota.

It is reasonable to conclude that she was behaving responsibly, serving a role in civic culture, but not a role recognized by the norms of efficiency and productivity in the system that employed her. This is a case in which conditions of technical rationality and cultural rationality meet in flagrant conflict.

The good news is that after a union protest Maevon Garrett's job was restored. The bad news, however, is that the system's design, the techno-political regime that caused the problem, still exists and looms before us [as] a rapidly spreading form of life. A study released by the Office of Technology Assessment of the U.S. Congress several years ago noted that approximately seven million American workers now live under rapidly spreading systems of computerized surveillance, an unhappy spin-off of office automation. The title of that report is, appropriately, *The Electronic Supervisor.* To an increasing extent in today's workplaces, computers are delegated the role of supervising; human beings have been assigned roles that involve working faster and faster while ending in less social conversation—all in the name of a system called "communications," but one that drastically limits people's ability to communicate in a human sense.

The term "regime" seems perfectly appropriate in such cases. For once they have been designed, built, and put in operation, sociotechnical systems comprise regimes with features that can be described in a political way. It makes perfect sense to talk about freedom or its absence, equality or inequality, justice or injustice, authoritarianism or democracy, and the kinds of power relationships technological instruments and systems contain.

This is true of extremely simple as well as complex technologies. For example, if one visits the agricultural fields of the southwestern U.S.A., one finds workers using a hoe, "el cortito," a tool with a short handle. There's nothing political about the length of a wooden handle, is there? Well, that depends on the broader social relationships and activities in which it plays a part. To use "el cortito" you must bend over or get down on your knees. A casual observer might say: If you're digging in the ground, isn't it sometimes more comfortable to stand up?

Why, then, has the handle been shortened? The reason is, in large part, that the foremen who manage the work can look across a field, even at a great distance, and tell who is working and who is not. Those who are bending over are the ones working; those standing upright are not and the foreman can apply discipline accordingly. In that light, even the length of the handle of a hoe expresses a regime, a regime of power, authority, and control.

Embodied in the tools and instruments of modern technology is a political world. I am suggesting that we use metaphors and rhetorical devices of political speech to unpack the meaning of various technologies for how we live.

Everyone understands that political ideas can be expressed in language. But ideas of this kind present themselves in material objects as well. In this form they might be called artifact/ideas. In their very silence, artifact/ideas have a great deal to say. They tell us who we are, where we are situated in the social order, what is normal, what is possible, what is excluded. The technological world is filled with artifact/ideas of great consequence for modern political culture. Things often speak louder than words. Among the main ideas present in the structure of contemporary technological devices and systems are the following:

- Power is centralized.
- The few talk and the many listen.
- There are barriers between social classes.
- The world is hierarchically structured.
- The good things are distributed unequally.
- Women and men have different kinds of competence.
- One's life is open to continual inspection.

As they are expressed in the shape of material objects, ideas of this kind are covert. They seldom become topics for discussion in the political sphere as it is usually understood. One reason that artifact/ideas tend to be covert is that most people buy the functional account of the meaning of material things. We are inclined to say: "This is a car which enables us to go from point A to point B." "This is a hoe which helps us to dig in the fields."

Another reason why ideologies in things tend to be covert is that they have been implanted there by those who do not wish those ideas to be known or widely discussed. The apparent solidity of useful things sometimes provides a mask for persons and groups who wish to exercise power while avoiding responsibility. Their alibi is usually something like: "This is the most effective way to do things" or "This is most efficient."

But whatever the source of specific beliefs and instrumental conditions, it is often true that ideas embodied in material things are painful or even dangerous to acknowledge. Artifact/ideas can involve astonishing contradictions. In particular, the mapping of the world encountered in the shape of things frequently contradicts the political ideology to which most people in Western societies claim to be committed.

In particular, many of the artifact/ideas prevalent in our time stand in flagrant contradiction to the ideology of modern democracy. That ideology holds that human beings flourish, achieving what is best in their potential, under conditions of freedom, equality, justice, and self-government. In that light, societies ought to create social conditions and political institutions that make it possible for each human being's potential to develop. Both victories and setbacks in this regard are clearly visible in the laws, constitutions, and political practices that prevail in each historical period.

From this vantage point a technological society is unique only in the sense that it presents new and seemingly unlikely domains—domains of instrumentality—in which the ends of democratic freedom, equality, and justice must somehow be recognized and realized. I take it to be the fundamental failure of modern civilization to have ignored again and again how such questions present themselves in the guise of what appear to be "neutral" technologies. To a considerable extent the ideas embodied in the realm of material things and in opposition to the central ideas that we believe describe and guide our political culture.

There is an important way in which freedom and justice depend in human communities upon the existence of suitable material environments—the creation and maintenance of arrangements in which the goal of becoming free, self-determining individuals is nurtured rather than destroyed. As we look at the kinds of sociotechnical innovations being introduced today, it is often beside the point to ask whether or not they are optimally efficient; by someone's definition they are usually very efficient indeed. Instead the crucial questions concern the kinds of cultural environments such technologies present to us. What one finds are far too many instances of developments of the following kind:

1. communications technologies employed in attempts to control people's thoughts, desires and behaviors;
2. computer technologies used to whittle away people's privacy and erode freedom;
3. information technologies that eliminate what were formerly places of community life;
4. energy systems that make people dependent upon, or even hostage to, sources of fuel over which they exercise no control;
5. systems of manufacturing that seek control by eliminating as much human initiative and creativity as possible.

The appropriate moment to examine and debate conditions such as these is the time during which they are designed and first introduced into the fabric of human activity. At present our society persists in designing a great many technical artifacts in ways that make people feel passive, superfluous, stupid, and incapable of initiating action. Such systems bear the cultural embryos of tomorrow's citizenry. For as we invent new technical systems, we also invent the kinds of people who will use them and be affected by them. The structures and textures of future social and political life can be seen in the blueprints of technologies now on the drawing board.

We often hear these days that the world is engaged in a "technology race" in which nations rise or fall according to their ability to use technologies to competitive advantage. Unfortunately, some of the design strategies that look fabulous from the point of view of efficiency, productivity, and global competitiveness involve what amounts to an ingenious synthesis of oriental feudalism and capitalism. Many people in freedom-loving countries like the United States seem eager to embrace repressive models of social integration expressed in automation, electronic surveillance, and pseudo-democratic "quality circles." But must we embrace these merging patterns of technofeudalism as "the wave of the future"? Would it not be a wiser approach to resist, choosing to explore ways of extending our ideas about freedom and a just society into the realm of technology itself?

In fact, one obvious path that may still be open to us is to cultivate ways of democratizing the process of technology policymaking and, indeed, the process of technological innovation. If this is to be done, both citizens and experts will need to become aware of the social, moral, and political dimensions of choices made in technological policy and technological design. They will need to find ways to act directly and democratically within settings in which the important choices are made.

In that light I would offer three guiding maxims as a way to focus discussion about the relationship between technological choices and the future of political culture. These maxims can be raised at times in which unquestioned assumptions about "productivity," "competitiveness," "the need to innovate," or "technology transfer" seem to provide the only language for talking about the choices at hand.

1. *No innovation without representation.* This suggests that all the groups and social interests likely to be affected by a particular kind of technological change ought to be represented at a very early stage in defining what that technology will be. Yes, let us accept the idea that particular technologies are social creations that arise through a complex, multi-centered process. But let us see to it that all the relevant parties are included rather than kept in the dark in this process. If we find that we do not have the kinds of social institutions that make this possible, then let's change our institutions to create such opportunities.

2. *No engineering without political deliberation.* Proposed technological projects should be closely examined to reveal the covert political conditions and artifact/ideas their making would entail. This ought to become an interpretive skill of people in all modern societies. It is especially important for engineers and technical professionals whose wonderful creativity is often accompanied by an appalling narrow-mindedness. The education of engineers ought to prepare them to evaluate the

kinds of political contexts, political ideas, political arguments, and political consequences involved in their work. Skill in the arts of democratic citizenship ought to become part of the "tool kit" that engineers master in their education.

3. *No means without ends.* Many of the varieties of innovation now pushed on the public these days amount to "tools looking for uses," "means looking for ends." Those who have dealt with the introduction of computers into the schools in recent years can give many colorful examples of this phenomenon. The current promotion of high definition television and renewed efforts to push President Reagan's Star Wars project offer even more stark illustration. For HDTV and SDI bear little relationship to any significant human need. As we study the prospects offered by new technologies, it is always essential to ask: Why? Why are we doing this? What are the ends we have chosen and how well do they fit the pattern of means available? In many cases of high tech planning, suitable background music would be the theme from *The Twilight Zone.*

If you were to look for examples of places in which something similar to these three maxims are actually being put to work, I would begin by pointing to some recent experiments in the Scandinavian democracies where a positive, creative politics of technology has recently become a focus of research and development. In one such project, workers in the Swedish newspaper industry—printers, typographers, lithographers, and the like—joined with representatives from management and with university computer scientists to design a new system of computerized graphics used in newspaper layout and typesetting. The name of the project was UTOPIA, a Swedish acronym that means "training, technology, and products from a skilled worker's perspective."

UTOPIA's goal was to fashion a system that would be highly advanced technically, but also one designed in ways that would take into account the skills, needs, and perspectives of all those who would eventually be using it. Rather than develop a system under management directives and then impose it on workers, the project included representation of the people concerned. UTOPIA became the focus of a rigorous program of research and development at a government-sponsored laboratory: The Center for Working Life in Stockholm. Here was a case in which the purely instrumental and economic thrust of a technological innovation encountered a legitimate set of political ends and enlightened artifact/ideas. The result was democratization expressed in hardware, software, and human relationships.

The technological world of the twenty-first century beckons. Will it be better than the one we now inhabit or worse? Will it realize the promise of human freedom or curtail it? And whose interest will be decisive?

If ordinary citizens are to be empowered in shaping the world to come, we must become very skillful in areas where we are now profoundly ignorant, using ideas and abilities that enable us to define and realize human freedom and social justice within the realm of technology itself: within things like new machines for the workplace, computerized systems of information management, biotechnologies in agriculture and medicine, communications devices introduced into our homes. If we cannot develop these skills or do not care to, if we fail to confront the world-shaping powers that new technologies present, then human freedom and dignity could well become obsolete remnants of a bygone era.

1.2.3 Addressing Technological Change: The Challenge to Social Theory

JUDY WAJCMAN

It is widely believed that technological innovation is the main driver of social change. In this article, Judy Wajcman, professor of sociology at the Australian National University, discusses how contemporary social theory views social change. In an effort to correct this simplistic one-sided "technological determinist" perspective, Wajcman views the relationship between technology and social change as a symbiotic one—technology and society coevolve with each influencing the other. Similarly for the relationship between science and society, recent studies in the history of science confirm that social values and relations are active shapers of scientific inquiry. The many examples provided by Wajcman in this article illustrate how common technological artifacts have evolved as a result of various social factors often in ways not envisioned by their designers. The "use context" of technological artifacts is what gives them their social meaning.

Wajcman explores the contributions of the social studies of science and technology (STS) movement and discusses how it has broadened sociologists' views of the relationship of society and technology from technological determinism to one recognizing that "technological change is shaped by the social circumstances within which it takes place." She provides several examples of how familiar artifacts, such as the microwave oven and the VCR, have been shaped by social values of the users of these devices. But she also argues that social scientists should recognize that technological artifacts are more than just the background context of human action; human sociotechnical practices are forms of power that expand and alter the character of human action itself.

She credits feminist scholars as raising the fundamental question of whether the power of men around the world resulted from their monopolization of technology or because technology is "inscribed with gender power relations." Although there are undoubted gender differences, there is nothing natural or inevitable about the ways in which technologies are defined as "masculine." Citing the increasing number of women in scientific and engineering professions and the writings of feminist authors such as Donna Haraway and Sherry Turkle who embrace technology, Wajcman sees the social shaping of computing and biotechnology as means for women's empowerment.

FOCUS QUESTIONS

1. Discuss the "new technical forces" seen by Wajcman as exerting great influence on society. How might these forces impact your life?
2. What are some of the reasons mentioned by Wajcman for women generally being less involved with the development and adoption of various types of technology?
3. Describe the technologies that some contemporary feminist writers think that women should be more involved with and why they think that is important.

Source: From Judy Wajcman, "Addressing Technological Change," *Current Society*, May 2002, Vol. 50(3), 347–363. Reprinted by permission of Sage Publications, Inc.

4. What role does Wajcman see virtual reality playing in the future, and how might this technology prove to be beneficial?

KEYWORDS

actor-network theory (ANT), cyborg, gender power relations, interpretive flexibility, post-Fordism, postmodernity, STS, technological determinism, technological imperative, techno-science

In their "millennial" reflections on the end of the 20th century and the beginning of the 21st, many sociologists see technology as the impetus for the most fundamental of social trends and transformations. Indeed, understanding the role of technologies in the economy and society is now central to social theory. While there are a variety of social theories that proclaim the radical transformation of society all contain, at their core, claims about technological change and its social impact (Kumar, 1995; Amin, 1994). This is as true of the three paradigmatic theories of the transformation that Western societies are undergoing—the theories of the information society, post-Fordism and postmodernity—as it is of more recent theories of globalization. Much emphasis is placed on major new clusters of scientific and technological innovations, particularly the widespread use of information and communication technologies, and the convergence of ways of life around the globe. The increased automation of production and the intensified use of the computer are said to be revolutionizing the economy and the character of employment. In the "information society" or "knowledge economy," the dominant form of work becomes information and knowledge-based. At the same time leisure, education, family relationships and personal identities are seen as moulded by the pressures exerted and opportunities arising from the new technical forces.

The globalization literature similarly postulates that states and societies across the world are experiencing historically unprecedented change as they try to adapt to a more interconnected but highly uncertain world (Giddens, 1990, 1996; Castells, 1996; Sassen, 1996; Held et al., 1999). Prominence is given to the intensity, extensity and velocity of global flows, interactions and networks embracing all social domains. For example, Manuel Castells (1996) argues that the revolution in information technology is creating a global economy, the product of an interaction between the rise in informational networks and the process of capitalist restructuring. In the "informational mode of development," labour and capital, the central variables of the industrial society, are replaced by information and knowledge. In the resulting "Network Society," the compression of space and time made possible by the new communication technology alters the speed and scope of decisions. Organizations can decentralize and disperse, with high-level decision-making remaining in "world cities" while lower-level operations, linked to the centre by communication networks, can take place virtually anywhere. Information is the key ingredient of social organization, and flows of messages and images between networks constitute the basic thread of social structure (1996: 477). For Castells, the information age, organized around "the space of flows and timeless time," marks a whole new epoch in the human experience.

SOCIAL THEORY AND TECHNOSCIENCE

These ideas—or ideas like them (for example, Urray, 2000)—are now commonplace in sociology and I foreground them here to illustrate the centrality of technology to contemporary theories of social, cultural and economic change. There are strong echoes of the earlier "post-industrial society" thesis in these accounts, and its tendency to adopt a technologically determinist stance. Castells explicitly builds on theories of post-industrialism, moving beyond a teleological model and giving the analysis a global reach (Bell, 1973; Touraine,

1971). However, while he explicitly attempts to distance himself from technological determinism, he does not entirely succeed. The idea that technology, specifically information and communication technology, is the most important cause of social change permeates his analysis of Network Society. The result is a rather simplistic view of the role of technology in society. In this, Castells is typical of most scholars of the information society who fail to engage with the burgeoning literature in the social studies of science and technology that has developed over the last two decades.[1] I will return to this in the next section of my essay.

The consequences of this failure are not confined to the theoretical domain. These metanarratives about the information age can themselves help to constitute that which they purport to describe and analyse. Technologically determinist understandings of the economy play an increasingly important role in political discourse. Governments everywhere legitimate much of their policy in terms of a technological imperative. Thus access to Internet resources and educational training for the information age are promoted as the fundamental equity issues. As if in response to Bill Gates's famous claim that the Internet would be a powerful force for eliminating barriers of prejudice and inequality, the UK government, for example, has undertaken to put a computer in every classroom as a guarantee of equality in education. There can be no clearer example of the belief in simple technological fixes to complex social problems. Rhetoric about the "digital divide," that between the information rich and the information poor, serves to camouflage pre-existing patterns of social and class inequality. Furthermore, much government discourse about the inevitability of globalization also invokes new information technology as an autonomous and largely unassailable force. In this process, technocratic discourse, globalization and free market economics coalesce into an extremely powerful ideological force (Johnson, 2000).

The idea that technological rationality translates into political rationality has a long lineage. Frankfurt School writers such as Marcuse (1968, 1969) and Habermas (1971) were wise to it before the dawn of the computer age. Indeed, Habermas's famous essay, dedicated to Marcuse for his 70th birthday, was entitled. "Technology and Science as 'Ideology.'" Habermas argued that the legitimating role of market liberalism was replaced by a new modernist, technocratic ideology in which economic growth and social development appeared to be determined by scientific-technical progress. His discussion of the "scientization of politics," whereby political problems are seen as technical ones and the "expert" directs the politician, has continuing relevance for the nature of democratic decision-making today.

Key to the conceptualization of technical rationality in that prescient 1968 essay was the question of whether science is neutral or intrinsically about domination. The context was the argument, central to Frankfurt School thinking, that Western science and technology form a project of control or domination over both nature and humanity. In *One Dimensional Man* (1968), Marcuse argued that because domination is intrinsic to capitalist science and technology, a new society would require a new science and a new technology. This would be based not on mastery, but on the liberation of nature. By contrast, Habermas departed from the central Frankfurt School position to defend a positivist conception of science and technology as ideologically pure, value-free, and above all neutral. He disputes Marcuse's claim that a science or technology fundamentally different from the one we presently have is a real possibility for advanced societies.

Although the nuances of this highly abstract exchange have been lost over time, it foreshadowed much of the debate about the relationship between technology and society that is still central to the discipline of sociology. Habermas's separation of two analytically distinct spheres of technical rationality and substantive rationality (or "system" and "lifeworld"), where the former may extend beyond its appropriate sphere and "colonize" the lifeworld, is a form of implicit technological determinism. It is the position that is most evident in abstract discussions of social theory. However, within the social studies of science and technology, Marcuse's argument that science and technology are socially constituted has had more resonance.

The writings of the Frankfurt School were to influence many within the political movements of the late 1960s and early 1970s to develop a radical critique of science. In campaigns against an abused, militarized, and polluting science, it was argued that science was directed towards profit and warfare. Initially science itself was seen as neutral or value-free and potentially useful as long as it was in the hands of those working for a just society. Gradually, however, the radical science movement developed a Marxist analysis of the class character of science and its links with capitalist methods of production. A revived political economy of science began to argue that the growth and nature of modern science were related to the needs of capitalist society. Increasingly tied to the state and industry, science had become directed towards domination. The ideology of science as neutral was seen as formulations of this position, associated with the radical science movement, was that "science is social relations" (Young, 1977). The point was that the distinction between science and ideology could not be sustained because the dominant social relations of society at large are constitutive of science.

During this same period a radical shift took place in the history, philosophy and sociology of science, which added weight to the view that science could no longer be understood as simply the discovery of reality. Kuhn's *The Structure of Scientific Revolutions* (1970) marked the beginning of what was to become a major new field of study known as the sociology of scientific knowledge. Its central premise is that scientific knowledge, like all other forms of knowledge, is affected at the most profound level by the society in which it is conducted. Numerous historical and contemporary studies of science, and the manner in which inquiry proceeds, highlight the social aspects of scientific knowledge. One major strand of research is concerned [with the demonstration of] how social interests construct knowledge, while another has focused on the deconstruction of the language of science.[2]

Despite the advances that were made through the critique of science in the 1970s, gender-conscious accounts were rare. It was to await second-wave feminism, and the growing body of feminist scholarship that flourished with it, to extend the analysis. The women's health, peace and environmental movements all initially saw science and technology as alien and opposed to women's interests. This was particularly a reaction to the way biology and medical science had cast women as different and inferior, and made a case for biologically determined sex roles. Indeed, the continuing fixation in much scientific inquiry with the study of sex difference illustrates the cogency of the feminist critique of biomedicine. Western science was characterized as a masculine project of reason and objectivity, with women relegated to nature rather than culture. Rejecting scientific knowledge as patriarchal knowledge, there were calls for the development of a new science based on women's values.[3]

SOCIAL STUDIES OF TECHNOLOGY

Building on the legacy of this theoretical and political ferment, the social studies of science and technology (STS) developed in the 1970s. Many of us who got involved then had a simple polemical purpose, to shake the stranglehold that a naïve "technological determinism" had on the dominant understanding of the intertwining of society and technology. We were concerned that this view of technology, as an external, autonomous force exerting an influence on society, narrows the possibilities for democratic engagement with technology. It presents a limited set of options: uncritical embracing of technological change, defensive adaptation to it, or simple rejection of it. Against this, STS has its origins in a belief that the content and direction of technological innovation are amenable to sociological analysis and explanation.

Social scientists have increasingly recognized that technological change is itself shaped by the social circumstances within which it takes place. The "new sociology of technology" set out to demonstrate that technological artefacts are socially shaped, not just in their usage, but especially with respect to their design and technical content. Crucially, it rejects the notion that technology is simply the product of rational technical imperatives, that a particular technology will triumph because it is intrinsically the best. Technical reasons are vitally important. But we need to ask why a technical reason was found to be compelling, when it could have been challenged, and what counts as technical superiority in specific circumstances. STS studies show that the generation and implementation of new technologies involve many choices between technical options. A range of social factors affect which of the technical options are selected. These choices shape technologies and, thereby, their social implications. In this way, technology is a socio-technical product, patterned by the conditions of its creation and use.

There is now a vast literature, and a variety of social shaping or constructivist approaches, to the social study of technology.[4] A broad sample of the research can be found in journals such as *Science, Technology, & Human Values; Social Studies of Science; Science as Culture;* and the books series, *Inside Technology,* with MIT Press.[5] As an introduction to the richness of the field, it may be useful at this point to outline the principal concepts that inform it.

The idea of a technological "system" or "network" has been key. Although technological innovation crucially builds on previous technology, it does so not in the form of separate, isolated devices but as part of a whole, as part of a system. An automatic washing machine, say, can work only if integrated into systems of electricity supply, water supply and drainage. A missile, to take another example, is itself part of an ordered system of component parts—warhead, guidance, control, propulsion—and also part of a wider system of launch equipment and command and control networks. The need for a part to integrate into the whole imposes major constraints on how that part should be designed. A technological system is never merely technical: its real-world functioning has technical, economic, organizational, political, and even cultural elements.

Take something you rarely think twice about—the electric refrigerator. We know from historians of technology that once you could choose between an electric refrigerator and a gas refrigerator, both equally effective (Cowan, 1983). General Electric had the financial resources to invest in the development of the electric model, while the manufacturers of gas refrigerators, although they had a product with real advantages from the consumer's point of view, lacked the resources to develop and market their machine. Economic power, not technical superiority, gave the electric refrigerator the edge over its competitor. However, the design of this kitchen "white good" was also shaped by the post-Second World War spread of single-family houses with correspondingly small-scale appliances. This built environment in turn sustains the cultural ideal of the separation of the public and private domestic spheres.[6] Gender roles and sexual divisions are part of the socio-technical system or network.

This example illustrates the way technological decisions are the result of "heterogeneous engineering," engineering "social" as well as "technical" phenomena: constructing an environment in which favoured projects can be seen as viable (Law, 1987). The usual economic explanation, that assumed that firms simply choose technologies that offer the maximum possible rate of profit, has now been the subject of much criticism. In response, some economists utilize the notions of technological trajectory, path-dependence and lock-in to capture the mechanisms through which the evolution of a technology becomes more and more irreversible. The more technologies are adopted and their problems resolved, the better their performance and the greater their adoption. This clearly generates a powerful path-dependence over time, one that marginalizes competing or new technologies.

STS emphasizes, however, that it is not necessarily technical efficiency but rather the contingencies of socio-technical circumstances and the play of institutional interests that favour one technology over another (MacKenzie and Wajcman, 1999: 19–21). Indeed, in situations of technical innovation, costs and profits are inherently uncertain; they cannot be taken as given facts. Economic calculations, such as estimating future costs and profits, are affected by the entire way a society is organized. Even within economics, for example in evolutionary economics, markets are beginning to be understood as embedded in social networks (Granovetter, 1985; Nelson and Winter, 1982).

The general point emerges most sharply when we consider the efficient use of labour, apparently a vital issue in technical change. Noble's (1984) classic study of the development of automatically controlled machine tools in postwar USA shows how production technologies can reflect management's need for control over workers. Noble notes that two options existed: "record playback," whereby the machine merely replicated the manual operations of a skilled machinist; and "numerical control" (NC), in which tool movements were controlled by a mathematical program produced by a technician. He shows how the machine-tool suppliers, technologists, and managers in the aerospace companies deliberately suppressed record playback in favour of NC in order to reduce their reliance on the unionized, craft workers. As it happened, however, management found that it needed to retain skilled machinists to operate the new machines effectively. Thus the intentions underlying the technological design, to shift power from the shop floor to the office, were not fully realized.

Long after artefacts leave the industrial laboratory, the process of technological design is still taking place. Take the example of microwave ovens, a direct descendant of military radar technology, developed for food preparation in US navy submarines. When manufacturers first turned their eyes to the domestic market, they conceived of the microwave as a device to reheat prepared food for use by men, especially single men. As a result, it was marketed as a "brown good" and sold next to hi-fi equipment, televisions, and video recorders—goods for leisure and entertainment. This attempt to frame demand was unsuccessful and subsequently both the product and the consumer were reconstituted as a "white good" for housewives who still want to cook (Cockburn and Ormrod, 1993). The way in which women users appropriated this domestic technology was not foreseen by the male managers and engineers who designed it. The finished form of the microwave, which redefined the gendered character of the user, meant that the microwave literally shifted its place in the department store. It now sits alongside washing machines, fridges and freezers as a humdrum domestic appliance.

These cases highlight the divergent requirements and assumptions of technology developers and users. The making of the microwave is as much a story about the transformation of a quintessentially human activity, cooking, as it is about a technical invention. Technologies are not fixed at the innovation stage but evolve in their implementation and use. The idea of "interpretative flexibility" captures this malleable character of technologies (Pinch and Bijker, 1987). It emphasizes that there is nothing inevitable about the ways technologies evolve. Rather, technological change is a thoroughly contingent and heterogeneous process. Interpretative flexibility refers to the way in which different groups of people involved with a technology can have different understandings of that technology, including different understandings of its technical characteristics. Thus users can radically alter the meanings and deployment of technologies. Pinch and Bijker's focus is not just on the symbolic meaning of technologies but also includes variation in criteria for judging whether a technology "works." For them, machines work because they have been accepted by relevant social groups. As a result, closure or stabilization occurs such that some artefacts become increasingly the dominant forms of the technology. The fact that a machine "works" needs to be explained rather than taken for granted.

This issue goes right to the heart of decisions about the vast techno-science research and development budgets in, for example, military weapons. Think for a moment about the crucial role that testing plays in attempts to justify the Bush administration's missile defence shield. Yet, testing the accuracy of missiles has never been a straightforward empirical matter. MacKenzie's (1990) study of nuclear ballistic missiles reveals the extent to which definitions of accuracy and reliability are constructed rather than being simply factual. For a start, the conditions for peacetime testing are fundamentally different from those under which missiles would have to operate during a war. MacKenzie's point, however, is both more profound and more general than this. He shows that testing inevitably involves a number of differently constructed background assumptions. As a result, no single test is ever accepted by all the parties involved as the ultimate arbiter. Indeed, it is those most closely involved in the scientific work of testing who have the least certainty about their knowledge of missile accuracy figures. The more one looks inside the "black box" of nuclear weapons technology, or any other technological artefact, "the more one realizes that 'the technical' is no clear-cut and simple world of facts insulated from politics" (1990: 381). Whether or not the "Son of Star Wars" works will necessarily be as much a political as a technical judgement.

STS then sees technology and society as bound together inextricably and the traffic between the two as reciprocal. Indeed, since the widespread adoption of "actor-network theory" (ANT), technology and society are no longer seen as separate spheres, influencing each other.[7] Rather, the metaphor of a "heterogeneous network" conveys the view that technology and society are mutually constitutive: both are made of the same stuff—networks linking human beings and non-human entities. The technological, instead of being a sphere separate from society, is part of what makes large-scale society possible. Their most controversial idea, that we cannot deny *a priori* that non-human actors or "actants" can have agency, has helped us to understand the role of technology in producing social life.

In this way, STS has drawn attention to the neglect of technology or materiality in much social theory. Apart from research concerned with the "impact of technology on society," the main focus of sociology has been on *social structure* and *social relations*. Machines, artefacts, things, have generally been treated as background context, rather than dealt with evenhandedly alongside persons, institutions and events.[8] ANT in particular emphasizes the way material resources, artefacts and technology make society possible. As Latour (1991b) expresses it: technology is society made durable. STS approaches contribute to an understanding of social change by exploring how technologies and new forms of social life are co-produced. To talk of "social relations" as if they were independent of technology is therefore incorrect. Indeed, what we call the social is bound together as much by the technical as by the social. "Social classes, occupational groups, organizations, professions—all are held in place by intimately linked social and technical means" (Bijker and Law, 1992: 290). Society itself is built along with objects and artefacts. For this reason, sociology cannot afford to ignore what Latour calls the "missing masses" of "mundane artifacts" (1992).

ANT's conception of the non-human as actant serves as a corrective to a rigid conception of social structure. Its analysis of how socio-technical networks are stabilized or made durable offers new insights into the perennial sociological concern with social order. ANT views society as a *doing* rather than a *being*. The construction of technologies is also a moving relational process achieved in daily social interactions: entities achieve their form as a consequence of their relations with other entities (Law, 1999: 4). This action-orientation is reminiscent of ethnomethodology, and chimes well with the current fascination in sociology with "performativity." While ANT is similarly ill equipped to deal with power as a structural phenomenon, it does sensitize us to the materiality of social relations.

One way of expressing this is in terms of the power of objects. The conceptions of power that prevail in the social sciences tend to neglect this form of power (with the important exception of military technology). Writers such as Lukes (1974) and Held (1995) define power in terms of the capacity of social agents, agencies and social institutions. For example, technology does not figure as one of Held's seven key "sites of power," which he defines as an interaction context or institutional milieu through which power operates to mould people's life-chances and effective participation in public decision-making (1995; 173).[9] Even Foucauldian-influenced writers, leaving aside Foucault's classic metaphor of the "panopticon," limit their discussion of power relations to social technologies.

This neglect is not surprising given that when technical systems are completely integrated into the social fabric, they become "naturalized," disappearing into the landscape. Take for example the way seemingly innocuous technologies such as photography and film assume, privilege and construct whiteness. Dyer (1997) describes how it is extremely difficult to film black and white faces in the same film and do equal justice to both. Each requires a completely different handling of lighting, make-up, and film developing. The variation in filming conditions means that when black and white actors are portrayed together, one group tends to lose out, and systematically it is black actors who are technologically short-changed. Dyer traces this bias in the use of film techniques to the film industry's origins in the USA and Europe. From the mid-19th century, experiments with the chemistry of photographic stock, aperture size, length of development and artificial light all proceeded on the assumption that what had to be got right was the look of the white face. By the time of film (some 60 years after the first photographs), technologies and practices were already well established and shaped subsequent uses.

This idea of the power exercised by objects is generalized in Latour's (1992) concept of "delegation to non-humans." His popular examples of automatic doors and road bumps show how technical objects define actors, the space in which they move and the ways in which they behave and interact. Fittingly called "sleeping policemen," road bumps are delegated the job of reducing motorists' speed where the rule of law does not suffice. In this way, it can be said that the material world itself exercises a kind of agency.

GENDER AND TECHNOLOGY

Much of the most exciting work in STS is being contributed by feminist scholars, reflecting the growing influence of feminist theory on mainstream sociology. Feminists have identified men's monopoly of technology as an important source of their power; women's traditional lack of technological skills is an important element in their dependence on men. A key issue has been whether the problem lies in men's domination of technology, or whether technology itself is inscribed with gender power relations. A long-standing theme has been the impact or effect of technological change on the sexual division of labour in both paid and unpaid work (see, for example, Cowan, 1983; Hartmann et al., 1986, 1987). Consistent with the STS tradition, feminist technology studies conceive of a two-way mutually shaping relationship between gender and technology in which technology is both a source and consequence of gender relations and vice versa (Wajcman, 1991). More recently, this mutual shaping framework has been "recast in a post-structural trope in which gender and technology are seen as *coproduced*" (Faulkner, 2001: 82; see also Berg, 1996). Such feminist perspectives on technology add a new dimension to sociological analyses of gender difference and sexual inequality.

There is nothing natural and inevitable about the ways in which technology is defined as masculine, and masculinity is identified with technical competence. Indeed, it was only with the formation of engineering as a white, male middle-class profession that "male machines rather than female fabrics" became the modern markers of technology (Oldenziel, 1999). During the 19th century mechanical and civil engineering increasingly came to define what technology is, diminishing the significance of both artefacts and forms of knowledge associated with women. At the same time, femininity was being reinterpreted as incompatible with technological pursuits. The continuing under-representation of women in engineering, and indeed, all scientific and technical institutions, is a legacy of this history.

This conventional understanding of technology, with its masculine connotations, has characterized much of the research literature. Within mainstream STS, the ways in which technological objects may be shaped by the operation of gender interests and gender identities have often been overlooked. While innovations are seen as socio-technical networks, it has largely been incumbent on feminists to demonstrate that social relations include gender relations. Despite a burgeoning literature on men and masculinities, the critical role played by technology in hegemonic masculinity has been largely ignored (see, for example, Connell, 1987). This problem was exacerbated in constructivist studies of technology by their concentration on the social groups or networks that directly influence the innovation process. As few women feature among the principal actors, it was commonly assumed that gender interests were not being mobilized. This had the effect of excluding from the picture both the women working further downstream from the design process and those whose primary relation to technology is as users (Star, 1991; Wajcman, 2000).

Indeed, technological systems implicitly place men's experiences and men's investments at the centre, without acknowledging their specificity. The corollary is the simultaneous denial of other realities such as women's. Feminists have demonstrated that the marginalization of women from the technological community has a profound influence on the design, technical content, and use of artefacts (Berg, 1996; Cockburn, 1983, 1985; Grint and Gill, 1995). This is not meant to imply an essentialist or dualistic analysis in which men and women are treated as homogeneous groups. Rather, a gender analysis shows how preferences for different technologies are shaped by a set of social arrangements that reflect men's power and resources in the wider society.

To what extent, for example, are the needs and interests of women as users taken on board in the process of designing ICT's for the home of the future? Anne-Jorunn Berg's (1994) study of the prototypes for "smart" houses reveals a preoccupation with innovations that automate control of leisure technologies and heating, lighting and security. The core aim of automating the smart house turns out to be "integration," that is, centralized control and regulation of all functions in a local network or "house-brain." The designers and producers of the technological home show little interest in housework. It is the technology as such, the way artefacts function in technical terms, that fascinates the designers. The target consumer is the technically interested man, someone in his own image. The neglect of women's knowledge, experience and skills as a resource for technical innovation in the home is evidence of a profoundly gendered innovation process. Berg argues that many innovations that would simplify some tasks, like cleaning and ironing, have not been developed. While there may be limits to the mechanization of household labour, it seems that a labour-saving "self-cleaning" house did not even feature as an objective.

Gender relations then are an integral constituent of the institutions and projects from which technologies emerge. As a result, technological artefacts can be encoded by gender, both materially and symbolically. This is not to imply, however, that gender is a fixed and unitary phenomenon, which exists prior to and independently of technology, and then becomes embedded within it. Contemporary feminist theory stresses that gender is not fixed in advance of social interaction, but is constructed in interaction. Individuals act or perform gender, and demonstrate their gender identity. Gender is a social achievement. This notion of "gender as doing," fits well with the action-orientation of constructivist studies of technology. Both technology and gender are now conceptualized as fluid, relational processes. Thus masculinities and femininities are constituted simultaneously with the production and consumption of technologies. The key argument here is that our relationship to technology is pivotal to the discourse of gender dualisms and gender difference. This issue is explored in the abundant scholarship on how technology as culture is implicated in the construction of subject identity for both sexes.

The most influential feminist commentator writing in this vein is Donna Haraway (1997). She argues that we should embrace the positive potential of technoscience, and is sharply critical of those who reject technology. Famously, she prefers to be a "cyborg"—a hybrid of organism and machine parts—rather than an ecofeminist "goddess." She notes the great power of science and technology to create new meanings and new entities, to make new worlds. Genetic engineering, reproductive technology, and the advent of virtual reality are all seen as fundamentally affecting the basic categories of "self" and "gender." She positively revels in the very difficulty of predicting what technology's effects will be and warns against any purist rejection of the "unnatural," hybrid, entities produced by biotechnology. The cyborg metaphor has been widely adopted, bridging "the language of material feminists working on issues of gender and technoscience, and postmodern feminists working with cultural studies and textual deconstruction" (Kirkup et al., 2000: 4–5). Haraway's work encourages a critical optimism in feminist analyses and politics, exploring the ways in which women's everyday lives are entwined with technologies, albeit in diverse and often complex and contradictory ways.

Although they come from somewhat different intellectual traditions, there is a synchronicity between Haraway's depiction of our cyborg-like existence and STS's emphasis on the seamless web of the socio-technical. This is particularly evident in the increasing preoccupation in sociological theory with the body, sexuality and the role of biomedical technologies—technologies for the body. In studies of childbirth and contraception, in-vitro fertilization, cosmetic surgery and genetic engineering, feminists argue that there is no such thing as the natural, physiological body. One consequence of this work is that the conventional distinction between sex (natural) and gender (social) has been thoroughly contested and deconstructed. Technologies, like science, are now seen as contributing to the stabilization of meanings of the body. With the rise of modern science, bodies have become objects that can be transformed with an increasing number of tools and techniques. Modern bodies are made and remade through science and technology; they too are technological artefacts. Life itself (human, plant, and animal) has been biomedicalized (Clarke, 1998).

These studies illustrate the connection between the gendered discourses of the biomedical sciences and the institutionalization of medical techniques applied to women's bodies. They remind us that the conceptualization of male and female bodies as essentially different, rather than similar, is a modern one, dating only from the 18th century. The identification of the female body as the Other resulted in positioning it as the quintessential medical object. Women were defined in terms of sex and reproduction, and this was reflected in the establishment of gynaecology as a separate branch of medicine. With the emergence of sex endocrinology in the 1920s and 1930s, the essence of femininity came to be located in hormones (Oudshoorn, 1994). The development of a contraceptive pill for women, rather than for men, was the product not of biological necessity but of 20th-century biomedical practices.

In the same way as biomedical technologies are seen as transforming the relations between the self, the body and machines, so too are information and communication technologies. There is a profusion of studies on the Internet, cyberspace and virtual reality. Many authors celebrate the myriad ways modern technology is challenging traditional notions of gender identity and creating new meanings and new entities. In *Life on the Screen: Identity in the Age of the Internet,* for example, Sherry Turkle (1995: 12) enthuses about the potential for people "to express multiple and often unexplored aspects of the self, to play with their identity and to try out new ones." It is the increasingly interactive and creative nature of computing technology that now enables millions of people to live a significant segment of their lives in virtual reality. Moreover, it is in this computer-mediated world that people experience a new sense of self that is decentred, multiple and fluid. In this respect, she argues, the Internet is the material expression of the philosophy of postmodernism.

New communication technologies have certainly opened up novel possibilities for sociality in cyberspace. Excitement has been generated about the capacity they provide to create new communities and the new tools they offer for global information exchange and political organizing, as well as all forms of commerce. Indeed, that communities can exist entirely in cyberspace, without face-to-face interaction, challenges classical sociological theories of "community." Virtual communities reflect the human need for communication and belonging without imposing any of the traditional constraints, duties and responsibilities. Of course the forms they take are not as transcendent as we might imagine—so for example the novel forms of techno-culture articulated in cyberspace are often characterized by violence and pornography. This is a reminder that while the pioneering possibilities of digitalization, the Internet and cyberspace may be thrilling, digital environments largely simulate the mundane outside world. Revolutions in technology do not create new societies, but they do change the terms in which social, political and economic relations are played out.

CONCLUSION

I began this article with a brief discussion of some recent contributions to social theory that claim technological change is shaping new social forms in the late modern social world. For many of these writers, these developments represent significant disruptions of past expectations and herald an increasingly complex and fragmented world that requires new social theories. Yet, I have suggested that these theoretical arguments are much less sophisticated than they initially appear and frequently resort to an implicit technological determinism. In contrast, I have argued that the field of social studies of science and technology provides rich resources for understanding technology as a socio-technical product, patterned by the relations of its production and use.

For many commentators, the present condition of social theory is one of increasingly discordant claims and fragmentation. Yet much of this social theory is disconnected from the social research that would give much greater insight into the nature of technical change and its social character. We do now have a considerable legacy of sophisticated theoretical writing and detailed case studies around which it has been produced. It is work that deserves greater purchase in the public debate. From my review of the field of STS, sociology looks like a healthy collective endeavour, with much evidence of productive convergence where arguments are shaped by their mutual engagement.

NOTES

1. This technological determinism is also evident in Giddens; see, for example, *The Consequences of Modernity* (1990).
2. This project has been particularly associated with the Edinburgh School, and the "strong" programme in the sociology of knowledge. For an introduction to this literature, see Barnes and Edge (1982) and Knorr-Cetina and Mulkay (1983).
3. For an excellent map of the field of gender and science, see Harding (1986).
4. Whereas references to the "new sociology of technology" were common in the 1980s, the term "constructivist studies of technology" is often now used to include the actor-network approach, the social-constructivist approach, the social shaping approach and the systems approach to technology studies. See Bijker (1995), Bijker et al. (1987), Bijker and Law (1992), Callon (1986), Latour (1987, 1991a, 1993), Law and Hassard (1999), and MacKenzie and Wajcman (1999). For a recent overview of the field, see Part One of the revised edition of MacKenzie and Wajcman (1999). See also the Handbook produced by the Society for the Social Studies of Science, Jasanoff et al. (1994).
5. The journal *Technology and Culture* contains some of the best case studies in the social history of technology.
6. See Chapter 5 of Wajcman (1991) for an elaboration of this point.
7. See Callon (1986), Latour (1987, 1991b, 1993), and Law and Hassard (1999).
8. Interestingly, during the same period, the concept of "material culture" has been restored to the core concerns of social anthropology, as illustrated by the 1996 launch of *Journal of Material Culture* (London: Sage).
9. The seven sites are the body, welfare, culture, civic associations, the economy, violence and coercive relations, regulatory and legal institutions.

REFERENCES

Amin, A., ed. (1994) *Post-Fordism: A Reader.* Oxford: Blackwell.

Barnes, B. and Edge, D., eds. (1982) *Science in Context Readings in the Sociology of Science.* Buckingham: Open University Press.

Bell, D. (1973) *The Coming of Post-Industrial Society.* New York: Basic Books.

Berg, A. J. (1994) "A Gendered Socio-technical Construction The Smart House," in C. Cockburn and R. F. Dilic (eds.) *Bringing Technology Home: Gender and Technology in a Changing Europe.* Milton Keynes: Open University Press.

Berg, A. J. (1996) *Digital Feminism,* Report No. 28 Dragvoll, Norway: Senter for Teknologi og Samfunn, Norwegian University of Science and Technology.

Bijker, W. E. (1995) *Of Bicycles, Bakelites, and Bulbs: Toward a Theory of Sociotechnical Change.* Cambridge: MA MIT Press.

Bijker, W. E. and Law, J., eds. (1992) *Shaping Technology/ Building Society Studies in Sociotechnical Change.* Cambridge, MA: MIT Press.

Bijker, W. E., Hughes, T. P., and Pinch, T., eds. (1987) *The Social Construction of Technological Systems.* Cambridge, MA: MIT Press.

Callon, M. (1986) "Some Elements of a Sociology of Translation Domestication of the Scallops and the Fisherman of St Brieue Bay," in J. Law (ed.)

Power, Action and Belief: A New Sociology of Knowledge?, pp. 196–233. London: Routledge.
Castells, M. (1996) *The Rise of the Network Society.* Oxford: Blackwell.
Clarke, A. (1998) *Disciplining Reproduction: Modernity, American Life Sciences, and "the Problems of Sex."* Berkeley: University of California Press.
Cockburn, C. (1983) *Brothers Male Dominance and Technological Change.* London: Pluto Press.
Cockburn, C. (1985) *Machinery of Dominance: Women, Men and Technical Know How.* London: Pluto Press.
Cockburn, C. and Ormrod, S. (1993) *Gender and Technology in the Making.* London: Sage.
Connell, B. (1987) *Gender and Power.* Cambridge: Polity Press.
Cowan, R. S. (1983) *Move Work for Mother: The Ironies of Household Technology from the Open Hearth to the Microwave.* New York: Basic Books.
Dyer, R. (1997) *White.* London: Routledge.
Faulkner, W. (2001) "The Technology Question in Feminism: A View from Feminist Technology Studies," *Women's Studies International Forum* 24(1): 79–95.
Giddens, A. (1990) *The Consequences of Modernity.* Cambridge: Polity Press.
Giddens, A. (1996) "Globalization: A Keynote Address," *UNRISD News* 15.
Granovetter, M. (1985) "Economic Action and Social Structure: The Problem of Embeddedness," *American Journal of Sociology* 91(3): 481–510.
Grint, K. and Gill., R, eds. (1995) *The Gender-Technology Relation: Contemporary Theory and Research.* London: Taylor & Francis.
Habermas, J. (1971) "Technology and Science as 'Idenology,'" in *Toward a Rational Society.* London: Heinemann.
Haraway, D. (1997) *Modest Witness@Second Millennium.* New York: Routledge.
Harding, S. (1986) *The Science Question in Feminism.* New York: Cornell University Press.
Hartmann, H., Kraut, R., and Tilly, L., eds. (1986, 1987) *Computer Chips and Paper Clips: Technology and Women's Employment*, Volumes 1 and 2. Washington, DC: National Academy Press.
Held, D. (1995) *Democracy and the Global Order.* Cambridge: Polity Press.
Held, D., McGrew, A., Goldblatt, D., and Perraton, J. (1999) *Global Transformation: Politics, Economics and Culture.* Cambridge: Polity Press.
Jasanoff, S., Markle, G., Petersen, J., and Pinch, T., eds. (1994) *Handbook of Science and Technology Studies.* Thousand Oaks, CA: Sage.
Johnson, C. (2000) *Governing Change From Keating to Howard.* Brisbane: University of Queensland Press.
Kirkup, G., Janes, L., Woodward, K., and Hovenden, F., eds. (2000) *The Gendered Cyborg: A Reader.* London: Routledge.
Knorr-Cetina, K. and Mulkay, M., eds. (1983) *Science Observed Perspectives in the Social Studies of Science.* London: Sage.
Kuhn, T. S. (1970) *The Structure of Scientific Revolutions.* Chicago, IL: The University of Chicago Press.
Kumar, K. (1995) *From Post-Industrial to Post-Modern Society: New Theories of the Contemporary World.* Oxford: Blackwell.
Latour, B. (1987) *Science in Action.* Buckingham: Open University Press.
Latour, B. (1991a) *The Pasteurization of France.* Cambridge, MA: Harvard University Press.
Latour, B. (1991b) "Technology is Society Made Durable," in J. Law (ed.) *A Sociology of Monsters Essays on Power, Technology and Domination*, pp. 103–31. London: Routledge.
Latour, B. (1992) "Where Are the Missing Masses? The Sociology of a Few Mundane Artifacts," in W. Bijker and J. Law (eds.) *Shaping Technology/Building Society Studies in Sociotechnical Change.* Cambridge, MA: MIT Press.
Latour, B. (1993) *We Have Never Been Modern.* Hemel: Hempstead Harvester.
Law, J. (1987) "Technology and Heterogeneous Engineering: The Case of Portuguese Expansion," in W. E. Bijker, T. P. Hughes, and T. Pinch (eds.) *The Social Construction of Technological Systems.* Cambridge, MA: MIT Press.
Law, J. (1999) "After ANT Complexity, Naming and Topology," in J. Law and J. Hassard (eds.) *Actor Network Theory and After*, pp. 1–14. Oxford: Blackwell.
Law, J. and Hassard, J., eds. (1999) *Actor Network Theory and After.* Oxford: Blackwell.
Lukes, S. (1974) *Power.* London: Macmillan.
MacKenzie, D. (1990) *Inventing Accuracy: A Historical Sociology of Nuclear Missile Guidance.* Cambridge, MA: MIT Press.
MacKenzie, D. (1996a) *Knowing Machines: Essays on Technical Change.* Cambridge, MA: MIT Press.
MacKenzie, D. (1996b) "How Do We Know the Properties of Artefacts' Applying the Sociology of Knowledge to Technology," in R. Fox (ed.) *Technological Change Methods and Themes in the History of Technology.* London: Harwood.
MacKenzie, D. and Wajcman, J., eds. (1999) *The Social Shaping of Technology*, rev and expanded edn.

Buckingham: Open University Press. (Orig. pub. 1985.)
Marcuse, H. (1968) *One Dimensional Man*. London: Sphere.
Marcuse, H. (1969) *An Essay on Liberation*. Boston, MA: Beacon.
Nelson, R. R. and Winter, S. G. (1982) *An Evolutionary Theory of Economic Change*. Cambridge, MA: Harvard University Press.
Noble, D. F. (1984) *Forces of Production. A Social History of Industrial Automation*. New York: Knopf.
Oldenziel, R. (1999) *Making Technology Masculine: Men, Women and Modern Machines in America*. Amsterdam: Amsterdam University Press.
Oudshoorn, N. (1994) *Beyond the Natural Body: An Archaeology of Sex Hormones*. London: Routledge.
Pinch, T. and Bijker, W. (1987) "The Social Construction of Facts and Artefacts: Or How the Sociology of Science and the Sociology of Technology Might Benefit Each Other," in W. E. Bijker, T. P. Hughes and T. Pinch (eds.) *The Social Construction of Technological Systems*. Cambridge, MA: MIT Press.
Sassen, S. (1996) *Losing Control? Sovereignty in an Age of Globalization*. New York: Columbia University Press.
Star, S. L. (1991) "Power, Technologies and the Phenomenology of Conventions: On Being Allergic to Onions," in J. Law (ed.) *A Sociology of Monsters; Essays on Power, Technology and Domination*, pp. 26–56. London: Routledge.
Touraine, A. (1971) *The Post-Industrial Society*. London: Routledge.
Turkle, S. (1995) *Life on the Screen: Identity in the Age of the Internet*. New York: Simon & Schuster.
Urray, J. (2000) "Mobile Sociology," *British Journal of Sociology* 51(1): 185–203.
Wajcman, J. (1991) *Feminism Confronts Technology*. Pennsylvania: Penn State University Press and Cambridge: Polity Press.
Wajcman, J. (2000) "Reflections on Gender and Technology Studies: In What State is the Art?," *Social Studies of Science* 30(3): 447–64.
Young, B. (1977) "Science is Social Relations," *Radical Science Journal* (5): 65–129.

1.2.4 Technologies of Humility: Citizen Participation in Governing Science

SHEILA JASANOFF

What role should citizens have in the formation of science and technology policy? Although technological change carries undoubted benefits for society, it also often imposes significant risks on the citizenry. In light of public concerns about risks such as those associated with global climate change, biotechnology, nanotechnology, genetically modified foods, and a variety of other technological advances that are changing our world, how can citizens play a meaningful role in the evaluation of these technologies? The traditional approach to this problem has delegated the responsibility to evaluate new technologies to expert committees composed of scientists, governmental officials, and corporate experts. But several dramatic failures of adequate oversight suggest that this approach is unsatisfactory and needs to be replaced by one in which citizens play a larger deliberative role. Society's values need to be able to influence the development of new technologies even before their widespread introduction, but how can ordinary citizens make informed judgments about uncertainty and risk in such highly technical issues? The challenge, as Sheila Jasanoff says, is not to replace expertise with citizen participation but to create a culture of technology governance that fosters "more meaningful interaction among policy-makers, scientific experts, corporate producers, and

Source: From Carl Mitcham, Ed., *Technologies of Humility, Encyclopedia of Science*, Vol. a–c, Macmillan Reference, Gale, a part of Cengage Learning.

the informed public." By doing this, we can better ensure that our ethical values are brought to bear in effective ways in the deliberative processes through which new technologies are introduced.

FOCUS QUESTIONS

1. What was the basis of Vannevar Bush's "social contract for science" that has governed American science policy since the end of World War II? What developments since that time have placed this model in question?
2. What does Jasanoff mean by "technologies of hubris" and "technologies of humility"? What factors suggest that we need to bring greater humility to bear in the selection of science and technology policies?
3. What are some examples of the "participatory turn" in the formation of science and technology policy? What are some problems with the way this approach has been applied in the past?
4. What four questions should we ask about any enterprise that intends to alter human society?
5. What are the four key social technologies that Jasanoff believes should be brought to bear to improve the process of civic deliberation about science and technology?

KEYWORDS

deviant science, extended peer review, institutional learning, technology policy, transparency

In his prescient 1984 book, the sociologist Charles Perrow forecast a series of "normal accidents" in high-risk technologies. The term applied with precision to events that were strung like dark beads through the later years of the twentieth century—most notably, the 1984 chemical plant disaster in Bhopal, India; the 1986 loss of the *Challenger* shuttle and, in the same year, the nuclear plant accident in Chernobyl, USSR; the contamination of blood supplies with the AIDS virus in Europe and North America; the prolonged crisis over BSE ("mad cow disease") in the United Kingdom; and the U.S. space program's embarrassing, although not life-threatening, mishaps with the Hubble telescope's blurry lens, and several lost and extremely expensive Mars explores. To these we may add the discovery of the ozone hole, climate change, and other environmental disasters as further signs of disrepair. Occurring at different times and in vastly different political environments, these events nonetheless served collective notice that human pretensions of control over technological systems need serious reexamination.

American theorists like Perrow chalked up these failings of technology to avoidable error, especially on the part of large organizations (Clarke 1989, Short and Clarke 1992, Vaughan 1996), but some European analysts suggested a more troubling scenario. Passionately set forth by the German sociologist Ulrich Beck (1992), the thesis of "reflexive modernization" argued that risks are endemic in the way that contemporary societies conduct their technologically intensive business. Scientific and technical advances bring unquestioned benefits, but they also generate new uncertainties and failures, so that doubt continually undermines knowledge and unforeseen consequences confound faith in progress. The risks of modernity, Beck suggested, cut across social lines and operate as a great equalizer of classes. Wealth may increase longevity and improve the quality of life, but it offers no certain protection against the ambient harms of technological societies. This observation was tragically borne out when the collapse of the World Trade Center on September 11, 2001 ended the lives of some 3,000 persons, not discriminating among corporate executives, stock market analysts, computer programmers, secretaries, firefighters, policemen, janitors, and restaurant workers. In many other contexts, however, vulnerability remains closely tied to socioeconomic circumstances, inequalities persist in the ability of groups and individuals to defend themselves against risk.

"Risk," on this account, is not a matter of simple probabilities, to be rationally calculated by experts and avoided in accordance with the cold arithmetic of cost-benefit analysis (Graham and Wiener 1995). Rather, it is part of the modern human condition, woven into the very fabric of progress. The problem we urgently face is how to live well with the knowledge that our societies are inevitably "at risk." Critically important normative questions of risk management cannot be addressed by technical experts with conventional tools of prediction. Such questions determine not only whether we will get sick or die, and under what conditions, but also who will be affected and how we should respond to uncertainty and ignorance. Is it sufficient, for instance, to assess technology's consequences, or must we also seek to evaluate its aims? How should we choose when the values of science appear to conflict with other fundamental values? Has our ability to innovate in some areas run unacceptably ahead of our powers of control? Will some of our most revolutionary technologies increase inequality, promote violence, threaten cultures or harm the environment? And are our institutions, national or supranational, up to the task of governing our dizzying technological capabilities? (Never far from the minds of philosophers and authors of fiction, some of these concerns were also famously articulated in recent times by Bill Joy, co-founder and chief scientist of Sun Microsystems.)*

To answer these questions, the task of managing technologies has to go far beyond the model of "speaking truth to power" that once was thought to link knowledge to political action (Price 1965). According to this template, technical input to policy problems must be developed independently of political influences; the "truth" so generated adequately constrains subsequent exercises of political power. The accidents and troubles of the late twentieth century, however, have called into question the validity of this model: both as a descriptively accurate rendition of ways in which experts relate to policy-makers (Jasanoff 1990), and as a normatively acceptable formula for deploying specialized knowledge within democratic political systems. There is growing awareness that even technical policy-making needs to get more political—or, more accurately, to recognize its political foundations more explicitly. Across a widening range of policy choices, technological cultures must learn to supplement the expert's narrow preoccupation with measuring the risks and benefits of innovation with greater attentiveness to the politics of science and technology.

But how can this expansion in the expert's role be reconciled with well-entrenched understandings of the relations between knowledge and power or expertise and public policy? How should these understandings be modified in response to three decades of research on the social dimensions of science? Can we imagine new institutions, processes, and methods for restoring to the playing field of governance some of the normative and political questions that were too long side-lined in assessing the risks and benefits of technology? And are there structured means for cultivating the social capacity for deliberation and reflection on technological change, much as expert analysis of risks has been cultivated for many decades?

There is a growing need, to this end, for what we may call "technologies of humility." These are methods, or better yet institutionalized habits of thought, that try to come to grips with the ragged fringes of human understanding—the unknown, the uncertain, the ambiguous, and the uncontrollable. Acknowledging the limits of prediction and control, technologies of humility confront "head-on" the normative implications of our lack of perfect foresight. They call for different expert capabilities and different forms of engagement between experts, decision-makers, and the public than were considered needful in the governance structures of high modernity. They require not only the formal mechanisms of participation but also an intellectual environment in which citizens

*See Selection 2.3.3.

are encouraged to bring their knowledge and critical skills to bear on the resolution of common problems.

THE SOCIAL CONTRACT BETWEEN SCIENCE AND THE STATE

In the United States the need for productive working relations between science and the state was famously articulated not by a social theorist or sociologist of knowledge but by the quintessential technical expert: Vannevar Bush, the distinguished Massachusetts Institute of Technology (MIT) engineer and presidential adviser. Bush foresaw the need for major institutional changes following the intense mobilization of science and technology during the Second World War. In 1945 he produced a report, *Science: The Endless Frontier,* that laid the basis for American policy towards science and technology. Science, in Bush's vision, was to enjoy government patronage in peacetime as in war. Control over the scientific enterprise, however, would be wrested from the military and lodged with the civilian scientific community. Basic research, uncontaminated by industrial application or state ambitions, would thrive in the free air of universities. Scientists would establish the substantive aims as well as the intellectual standards for their research. Bush firmly believed that the bountiful results flowing from scientists' endeavors would be translated into beneficial technologies, contributing to the nation's prosperity and progress. Although his design took years to materialize, and even then was only imperfectly attained, the U.S. National Science Foundation (NSF) eventually emerged as the primary state funder of basic research. (The creation of the National Institutes of Health [NIH] to sponsor biomedical research divided U.S. science policy in a way not contemplated in Bush's original design. In the recent politics of science, NIH budgets have proved consistently easier to justify than appropriations for other branches of science.) The exchange of government funds and autonomy in return for discoveries, technological innovations and trained personnel came to be known as America's "social contract for science."

Signs of wear and tear in the "social contract" appeared in the 1980s. A spate of highly publicized cases of alleged fraud in science challenged the reliability of peer review and, with it, the underlying assumptions concerning the autonomy of science. The idea of science as a unitary practice also broke down as it became clear that research varies from one context to another, not only across disciplines, but—even more important from a policy standpoint—across institutional settings. It was recognized, in particular, that regulatory science, produced to support governmental efforts to manage risk, was fundamentally different from research driven by scientists' curiosity. At the same time, observers of science in society began questioning whether the categories of basic and applied research held meaning in a world where the production and uses of science were densely connected to each other, as well as to larger social and political consequences (Jasanoff, Markle, Petersen, and Pinch 1995).

Rethinking the relations of science with other social institutions generated three major streams of analysis. The first stream takes the "social contract" essentially for granted but points to its failure to work as its proponents had imagined. Many have criticized science, especially university-based science, for deviating from idealized norms of purity and disinterestedness. Despite (or maybe because of) its simplicity, this critique has seriously threatened the credibility of researchers and their claims to autonomy. Others have tried to replace the dichotomous division of *basic* and *applied* science with more differentiated categories, calling attention to the particularities of science done in different settings to meet different objectives. Still others have sought to respecify from the ground up how scientific knowledge is actually produced. This last line of analysis seeks not so much to correct or refine Vannevar Bush's vision of science as to replace it with a more complex account of how knowledge-making fits into the wider functioning of society.

Deviant Science

Scientific fraud and misconduct appeared on the U.S. policy agenda in the 1980s. Political interest reached a climax with the notorious case of alleged misconduct in an MIT laboratory headed by Nobel laureate biologist David Baltimore. He and his colleagues were exonerated after years of inquiry, which included investigations by Congress and the FBI (Kevles 1998). This and other episodes heightened the tendency for policymakers and the public to suspect that all was not in order in the citadels of basic science and greatly increased federal powers for the supervision of research. Some saw the Baltimore affair as a powerful sign that legislators were no longer content with the old social contract's simple *quid pro quo* of money and autonomy in exchange for technological benefits (Guston 2001). Others, like the science journalist Daniel Greenberg (2001), accused scientists of profiting immoderately from their alliance with the state, while failing to exercise moral authority or meaningful influence on policy. American science, at any rate, was asked to justify more explicitly the public money spent on it. A token of the new relationship between science and government came with the reform of NSF's peer review criteria in the 1990s. The Foundation now requires reviewers to assess proposals not only on grounds of technical merit, but also with respect to their wider implications for society—thus according greater prominence to science's social utility. In effect, the fraud investigations of the previous decade opened up other taken-for-granted aspects of scientific autonomy, and forced scientists to account for their objectives as well as their honesty.

To these perturbations may be added a steady stream of challenges to the supposed disinterestedness of academic science. In areas ranging from climate change to biotechnology, critics have charged researchers with having sacrificed their objectivity in exchange for grant money or, worse, equity interests in lucrative start-up companies (Boehmer-Christiansen 1994). These allegations have been especially damaging to biotechnology, because that industry benefits significantly from the rapid transfer of skills and knowledge from universities. Since most western governments are committed to promoting such transfers, biotechnology is caught on the horns of a particular dilemma: how to justify its promises of innovation and progress credibly, when the interests of most scientists are aligned with those of industry, government or, occasionally, public interest advocates.

While financially motivated, pro-industry bias has attracted the most criticism, academic investigators have also come under scrutiny for alleged pro-environment and anti-technology biases. In several cases involving biotechnology—in particular, that of the monarch butterfly study conducted by Cornell University scientist John Losey (1999) in the United States, and Stanley Ewen and Arpad Pusztai's (1999) controversial rat-feeding study in the United Kingdom—industry critics questioned the quality of university-based research and implied that political orientations had prompted premature release or over-interpretation of results. In April 2002 a controversy erupted over an article in *Nature* by a University of California scientist, Ignacio Chapela, who concluded that DNA from genetically modified corn had contaminated native species in Mexico. Philip Campbell, the journal's respected editor, did not retract the paper, but stated that "the evidence available is not sufficient to justify the publication of the original paper," and that readers should "judge the science for themselves" (*Washington Times* 2002). As in the Losey and Ewen and Puzstai cases, critics charged that Chapela's science had been marred by non-scientific considerations. Environmentalists, however, viewed all these episodes as pointing to wholesale deficits in knowledge about the long-term and systemic effects of genetic modification in crop plants.

Context-Specific Science

The second line of attack on the science–society relationship focuses on the basic-applied distinction. One attempt to break out of that dualism was proposed by Donald Stokes (1997), whose quadrant framework, using Louis Pasteur as the prototype, suggested that "basic" science can be done within highly "applied" contexts. Historians and sociologists of science and technology have long observed that foundational work can be done in connection with applied problems, just as applied problem-solving is often required for resolving theoretical issues (for example, in designing new scientific instruments). To date, formulations based on such findings have been slow to take root in policy cultures.

Another example of the contextualing approach can be found in the work of Silvio Funtowicz and Jerome Ravetz (1992). They proposed to divide the world of policy-relevant science into three nested circles, each with its own system of quality control: (1) "normal science" (borrowing the term from Thomas Kuhn), for ordinary scientific research; (2) "consultancy science," for the application of available knowledge to well-characterized problems; and (3) "post-normal science," for the highly uncertain, highly contested knowledge needed for many health, safety, and environmental decisions. These authors noted that, while, traditional peer review may be effective within "normal" and even "consultancy" science, the quality of "post-normal" science cannot be assured by standard review processes. Instead, they proposed that work of this nature be subjected to *extended peer review*, involving not only scientists but also the stakeholders affected by the use of science. Put differently, they saw accountability, rather than mere quality control, as the desired objective when science becomes "post-normal." (A problem with this analysis lies in the very term "post-normal science." When scientific conclusions are so closely intertwined with social and normative considerations as in Funtowicz and Ravetz's outermost circle, one may just as well call the "product" by another name, such as "socially relevant knowledge" or "socio-technical knowledge.")

Sheila Jasanoff's 1990 study of expert advisory committees in the United States provided another perspective on this issue by noting that policy-relevant science (also referred to as "regulatory science")—such as science done for purposes of risk assessment—is often subjected to a special kind of "peer review." Regulatory science is reviewed by multidisciplinary committees rather than by individually selected specialists. The role of such bodies is not only to validate the methods by which risks are identified and investigated, but also to confirm the reliability of the agency's interpretation of the evidence. Frequently, regulatory science confronts the need to set standards for objects or concepts whose very existence was not previously an issue for either science or policy: "fine particulate matter" in air pollution control; the "maximum tolerated dose" (MTD) in bioassays; the "maximally exposed person" in relation to air-borne toxics; or the "best available technology" in programs of environmental regulation. In specifying how such terms should be defined or characterized, advisory committees have to address issues that are technical as well as social, scientific as well as normative, regulatory as well as metaphysical. What *kind* of entity, after all, is a "fine" particulate or a "maximally exposed" person, and by what markers can we recognize them? Studies of regulatory science have shown that the power of advisory bodies to definitively address such issues depends on their probity, representativeness, transparency, and accountability to higher authorities—such as courts and the public. In other words, the credibility of regulatory science rests upon factors that have more to do with democratic accountability than with the quality of science as assessed by peer scientists.

New Modes of Knowledge Production

Going beyond the quality and context-dependency of science, some have argued the need to take a fresh look at the structural characteristics of contemporary science in order to make it more socially responsive. Michael Gibbons and his co-authors (1994) concluded that the traditional disciplinary science of Vannevar Bush's "endless frontier" has been largely supplanted by a new mode of knowledge production. The salient properties of this new mode, in their view, include the following:

- Knowledge is increasingly produced in contexts of application (i.e., *all* science is to some extent "applied" science);
- Science is increasingly transdisciplinary—that is, it draws on and integrates empirical and theoretical elements from a variety of fields;
- Knowledge is generated in a wider variety of sites than ever before, not just universities and industry, but also in research centers, consultancies, and think-tanks;
- Participants in science have grown more aware of the social implications of their work

(i.e., more "reflexive"), just as publics have become more conscious of the ways in which science and technology affect their interests and values.

The growth of this new mode, as Gibbons et al. note, has necessary implications for quality control. Besides old questions about the intellectual merits of their work, scientists are being asked new questions about its marketability, and its capacity to promote social harmony and welfare.

In other work, Helga Nowotny, Peter Scott, and Michael Gibbons (2001) have grappled with the implications of these changes for knowledge production in public domains. Nowotny et al. propose the concept of "socially robust knowledge" as the solution to problems of conflict and uncertainty. Contextualization, in their view, is the key to producing science for public ends. Science that draws strength from its socially detached position is too frail to meet the pressures placed upon it by contemporary societies. Instead, they imagine forms of knowledge that gain robustness from their very embeddedness in society. The problem, of course, is how to institutionalize polycentric, interactive, and multipartite processes of knowledge-making within institutions that have worked for decades at keeping expert knowledge away from populism and politics. The question confronting the governance of science is how to bring knowledgeable publics into the front-end of scientific and technological production—a place from which they have historically been excluded.

THE PARTICIPATORY TURN

Changing modes of scientific research and development provide at least a partial explanation for the current interest in improving public access to expert decision-making. In thinking about research today, policy-makers and the public frequently focus on the accountability of science rather than its quality. As the contexts for science have become more pervasive, dynamic and heterogeneous, concerns about the integrity of peer review have transmuted into demands for greater public involvement in assessing the costs and benefits, as well as the risks and uncertainties, of new technologies. Such demands have arisen with particular urgency in the case of biotechnology, but they are by no means limited to this field.

The pressure for accountability manifests itself in many ways, including demands for greater transparency and participation. One notable example came with U.S. federal legislation in 1998, requiring public access, pursuant to the Freedom of Information Act, to all scientific research generated with public funds (Omnibus Consolidated and Emergency Supplemental Appropriations Act of 1999, P.L. 105-277, 1998). The provision was hastily introduced and scarcely debated. Its sponsor, Senator Richard Shelby (R-Alabama), tacked it on as a last-minute amendment to an omnibus appropriations bill. His immediate objective was to force disclosure of data from a controversial study by the Harvard School of Public Health of the health effects of human exposure to fine particulates. This Six Cities Study provided key justification for the U.S. Environmental Protection Agency's stringent ambient standard for airborne particulate matter, issued in 1997. This sweeping enactment showed that Congress was no longer willing to concede unchecked autonomy to the scientific community in the collection and interpretation of data. Publicly funded science, Congress determined, should be available at all times for public review.

Participatory traditions are less thoroughly institutionalized in European policy-making, but in Europe, too, recent changes in the rules and processes governing expert advice display a growing commitment to involving the public in technically-grounded policy decisions. In announcing the creation of a new Directorate General for Consumer Protection, for example, the European Commission observed in 1997 that, "Consumer confidence in the legislative activities of the EU is conditioned by the *quality and transparency* of the scientific advice and its use on the legislative and control process" (emphasis added). The commitment to greater openness is also evident in the strategies of several new United Kingdom expert bodies, such as the Food Standards Agency, created to restore confidence in the wake of the BSE crisis. Similarly, two major public inquiries—the Phillips Inquiry on BSE and the Smith inquiry on the Harold Shipman murder investigation—set high standards for public access to information through the Internet. All across Europe, opposition to genetically modified foods and crops prompted experiments with diverse forms of public involvement, such as citizen juries, consensus conferences, and referenda (Joss and Durant 1995).

Although admirable, formal participatory opportunities cannot by themselves ensure the democratic and deliberative governance of science. There are, to start with, practical problems. People may not be engaged enough or possess enough specialized knowledge and material resources to take advantage of formal procedures. Participation may occur too late to identify alternatives to dominant or default options; some processes, such as consensus conferences, may be too *ad hoc* or issue-specific to exercise sustained influence on policy. Even timely participation does not necessarily improve decision-making. Empirical research has consistently shown that transparency may exacerbate rather than quell controversy, leading parties to deconstruct each other's positions instead of deliberating effectively. Indeed, the Shelby Amendment reflects one U.S. politician's conviction that compulsory disclosure of data will enable challenges to researchers' own interpretations of their work. It is in this sense an instrument that can be used for formenting scientific dissent. By contrast, participation constrained by established formal discourses, such as risk assessment, may not admit novel viewpoints, radical critique, or considerations lying outside the taken-for-granted framing of a problem.

TECHNOLOGIES OF HUMILITY

Participation alone, then, does not answer the problem of how to democratize technological societies. Opening the doors to previously closed expert forums is a necessary step—indeed, it should be seen by now as a standard operating procedure of democratic politics. But the formal mechanisms adopted by national governments are not enough to engage the public effectively in the management of global science and technology. What has to change is the *culture* of governance, nationally as well as internationally, and for this we need to address not only the mechanics but also the substance of participatory politics. The issue, in other words, is no longer whether the public should have a say in technical decisions, but how to promote more meaningful interaction among policy-makers, scientific experts, corporate producers, and the informed public.

The analytic ingenuity of modern states has been directed for many decades toward refining what we may call the "technologies of hubris." To reassure their publics, as well as to keep the wheels of science and industry turning, national governments have developed a series of predictive methods (e.g., risk assessment, cost-benefit analysis, climate modeling) that are designed, on the whole, to facilitate management and control, even in areas of high uncertainty (e.g. Porter 1995). These methods achieve their power through claims of objectivity and a disciplined approach to analysis, but they suffer from three significant limitations. First, they show a kind of peripheral blindness toward uncertainty and ambiguity. Predictive methods focus on the known at the expense of the unknown, producing overconfidence in the accuracy and completeness of the pictures they produce. Well-defined, short-term risks command more attention than indeterminate, long-term ones. At the same time, technical proficiency conveys the impression that analysis is not only rigorous, but complete—in short, that it has adequately taken account of all possible risks. Predictive methods tend in this way to downplay what falls outside their field of vision, and to overstate whatever falls within (Irwin and Wynne 1996).

Second, the technologies of predictive analysis tend to preempt political discussion. Expert analytic frameworks create high entry barriers against legitimate outsider positions that cannot express themselves in terms of the dominant discourse (Winner 1986). Claims of objectivity hide the exercise of judgment, so that the normative presuppositions of studies and models are not subjected to general debate. The boundary work that demarcates the space of "objective" policy analysis is carried out by experts, so that the politics of making demarcations remains locked away from public review and criticism (Jasanoff 1990).

Third, predictive technologies are limited in their capacity to internalize challenges that come from outside their framing assumptions. Techniques develop and grow more sophisticated, to be sure, but not necessarily in ways that revisit the values on which they were founded. For example, techniques for assessing chemical toxicity have become ever more refined, but they continue to rest on the demonstrably faulty assumption that people are exposed to one chemical at a time. Synergistic effects, long-term exposures, and multiple exposures are common in normal life but have tended to be ignored as too messy for analysis. Even in the aftermath of catastrophic failures, modernity's predictive models are often adjusted only to take on board lessons that are compatible with their initial assumptions. When a U.S.-designed chemical factory in Bhopal released the deadly gas methyl isocyanate, killing thousands, the international chemical industry made many improvements in its internal accounting and risk communication practices. But no new methods were developed to assess the risks of technology transfer between radically different cultures of industrial production.

At the beginning of the twenty-first century, the unknown, unspecified and indeterminate aspects of scientific and technological development remain largely unaccounted for in policy-making; treated as beyond reckoning, they escape the discipline of analysis as well as politics. What is lacking is not just the knowledge to help fill the gaps, but the processes and methods for eliciting what the public wants and for using what is already known. To bring these dimensions out of the shadows and into the dynamics of democratic debate, they must first be made concrete and tangible. Scattered and private knowledge has to be amalgamated, perhaps even disciplined, into a dependable civic epistemology. The human and social sciences of previous centuries undertook just such a task of translation. They made visible the social problems of modernity—poverty, unemployment, crime, illness, disease, and, lately, technological risk—often as a prelude to rendering them more manageable, using what I have termed the "technologies of hubris." Today, there is a need for "technologies of humility" to complement the predictive approaches: to make apparent the possibility of unforeseen consequences; to make explicit the normative that lurks within the technical; and to acknowledge from the start the need for plural viewpoints and collective learning. How can these aims be achieved?

From the abundant literature on technological disasters and failures, as well as from studies of risk analysis and policy-relevant science, we can abstract four focal points around which to develop the new technologies of humility. They are *framing, vulnerability, distribution,* and *learning.* Together, they generate the questions we should ask of almost every human enterprise that intends to alter society: what is the purpose; who will be hurt; who benefits; and how can we know? On all these points, we have good reason to believe that wider public engagement would improve our capacity for analysis and reflection. Participation that pays attention to these four points promises to lead to richer deliberation on the substance of decision-making.

Framing

It is an article of faith in the policy literature that the quality of solutions to perceived social problems depends on the adequacy of their original framing (Schon and Rein 1994). If a problem is framed too narrowly, too broadly, or simply wrongly, then the solution will suffer from the same defects. To take a simple example, a chemical testing policy focused on single chemicals cannot produce knowledge about the environmental health consequences of multiple exposures: the framing of the regulatory issue is more restrictive than the actual distribution of chemical-induced risks, and hence is incapable of delivering the optimal management strategies. Similarly, a belief that violence is genetic may discourage the search for controllable social influences on behavior. A focus on the biology of reproduction may delay or impede effective policies for curbing population growth. When facts are uncertain, disagreements about the appropriate frame are virtually unavoidable and often remain intractable for long periods.

Yet, few policy cultures have adopted systematic methods for revisiting the initial framing of issues, despite calls to do so (Stern and Fineberg 1996). Frame analysis thus remains a critically important, though neglected, tool of policymaking.

Vulnerability

Risk analysis treats the "at-risk" human being as a passive agent in the path of potentially disastrous events. In an effort to produce policy-relevant assessments, human populations are often classified into groups (e.g., most susceptible, maximally exposed, genetically predisposed, children or women) that are thought to be differently affected by the hazard in question. Based on physical and biological indicators, these classifications tend to overlook the social foundations of vulnerability and to subordinate individual experiences of risk to aggregate numerical calculations (e.g. Irwin and Wynne 1996). Recent efforts to analyze vulnerability have begun to recognize the importance of socio-economic factors, but assessment methods still take populations rather than individuals as the unit of analysis. These approaches not only disregard differences within groups but reduce individuals to statistical representations. Such characterizations leave out of the calculus of vulnerability such factors as history, place, and social connectedness, all of which may play crucial roles in determining human resilience. Through participation in the analysis of their vulnerability, ordinary citizens might regain their status as active subjects rather than remain undifferentiated objects in yet another expert discourse.

Distribution

Controversies over such innovations as genetically modified foods and stem cell research have propelled ethics committees to the top of the policy-making ladder in several countries. Frequently, however, these bodies are used as "end-of-pipe" legitimation devices, reassuring the public that normative issues have not been omitted from deliberation. The term "ethics," moreover, does not cover the whole range of social and economic realignments that accompany major technological changes, not their distributive consequences, as technology unfolds across global societies and markets. Attempts to engage systematically with distributive issues in policy processes have not been altogether successful. In Europe, consideration of the "fourth hurdle"—the socio-economic impact of biotechnology—was abandoned after a brief debate. In the United States the congressional Office of Technology Assessment, which arguably had the duty to evaluate socio-economic impacts, was dissolved in 1995 (Bimber 1996). President Clinton's 1994 injunction to federal agencies to develop strategies for achieving environmental justice produced few dramatic results (Executive Order 12298, 1994). At the same time, episodes like the rebellion against Monsanto's "terminator gene" demonstrate a deficit in the capacity for ethical analysis in large corporations, whose technological products can fundamentally alter people's lives. Sustained interactions between decision-makers, experts and citizens, starting at the upstream end of research and development, could do much to expose the distributive consequences of innovation.

Learning

Theorists of social and institutional learning have tended to assume that what is "to be learned" is never a part of the problem. A correct, or at least a better, response exists, and the only issue is whether actors are prepared to internalize it. In the real world, however, learning is complicated by many factors. The capacity to learn is constrained by limiting features of the frame within which institutions act. Institutions see only what their discourses and practices permit them to see. Experience, moreover, is polysemic, or subject to many interpretations, no less in policy-making than in literary texts. Even when the fact of failure in a given case is unambiguous, its causes may be open to many different readings. Just as historians disagree over what caused the rise or fall of particular political regimes, so policy-makers may find it impossible to attribute their failures to specific causes. The origins of a problem may look one way to those in power, and quite another way to the marginal or the excluded. Rather than seeking monocausal explanations, then, it would be fruitful to design more avenues through which societies can collectively reflect on the ambiguity of their experiences and to assess the strengths and weaknesses of alternative explanations. Learning, in this modest sense, is a suitable objective of civic deliberation.

CONCLUSION

The enormous growth and success of science and technology during the last century has created difficult contradictions for institutions of governance. As technical activities have become more pervasive and complex, so too has the demand grown for more complete and multivalent evaluations of the costs and benefits of technological progress. It is widely recognized that increased participation and interactive knowledge-making would improve accountability and lead to more credible assessments of science and technology. Such approaches would also be consistent with changes in the modes of knowledge production, which have made science more socially embedded and more closely tied to contexts of application. Yet, modern institutions still operate with conceptual models that seek to separate science from values and emphasize prediction and control at the expense of reflection and social learning. Not surprisingly, the real world continually produces reminders of the incompleteness of our predictive capacities.

To move public discussion of science and technology in new directions, there is a need for "technologies of humility," complementing the predictive "technologies of hubris" on which we have lavished so much of our past attention. These *social technologies* would give combined attention to substance and process, and stress deliberation as well as well as analysis. Reversing nearly a century of contrary development, these approaches to decision-making would seek to integrate the "can do" orientation of science and engineering with the "should do" questions of ethical and political analysis. They would engage the human subject as an active, imaginative agent in making policy, as well as a source of knowledge, insight, and memory.

BIBLIOGRAPHY

Beck, Ulrich. (1992). *Risk Society Towards a New Modernity.* London: Sage Publications.

Bimber, Bruce. (1996). *The Politics of Expertise in Congress: The Rise and Fall of the Office of Technology Assessment.* Albany: State University of New York Press.

Boehmer-Christiansen, Sonja. 1994. "Global Climate Protection Policy: The Limits of Scientific Advice, Parts 1 and 2." *Global Environmental Change* 4 (2)140–159; 4(3)185–200.

Bush, Vannevar. 1945. *Science: The Endless Frontier.* Washington, DC: U.S. Government Printing Office.

Clarke, Lee. 1989. *Acceptable Risk? Making Decisions in a Toxic Environment.* Berkeley: University of California Press.

Ewen, Stanley W. B., and Arpad Pusztai. 1999. "Effect of Diets Containing Genetically Modified Potatoes Expressing Galanthus Nivalis Lectin on Rat Small Intestine." *Lancet* 354: 1353–1354.

Executive Order 12298. 1994. "Federal Actions to Address Environmental Justice in Minority Populations and Low-Income Populations." Washington, DC: February 11.

Funtowicz, Silvio O., and Jerome R. Ravetz. 1992. "Three Types of Risk Assessment and the Emergence of Post Normal Science." In *Social Theories of Risk*, eds. Sheldon Krimsky and D. Golding. New York: Praeger.

Gibbons, Michael, Carmlle, Limoges, Helga Nowotny, et al. 1994. *The New Production of Knowledge.* London: Sage Publications.

Graham, John D., Jonathan B. Wiener, eds. 1995. *Risk versus Risk Tradeoffs in Protecting Health and the Environment.* Cambridge, MA: Harvard University Press. A preeminent example of the calculative approach.

Greenberg, Daniel S. 2001. *Science, Money, and Politics: Political Triumph and Ethical Erosion.* Chicago: University of Chicago Press.

Guston, David H. 2001. *Between Politics and Science Assuring the Integrity and Productivity of Research.* Cambridge: Cambridge University Press.

Irwin, Alan, and Brian Wynne, eds. 1996. *Misunderstanding Science? The Public Reconstruction of Science and Technology.* Cambridge: Cambridge University Press.

Jasanoff, Sheila. 1990. *The Fifth Branch Science Advisers as Policy-makers* Cambridge, MA: Harvard University Press.

Jasanoff, Sheila, Gerald E. Markle, James C. Petersen, and Trevor Pinch, eds. 1995. *Handbook of Science and Technology Studies.* Thousand Oaks, CA: Sage Publications.

Joss, Simon, and John Durant, eds. 1995. *Public Participation in Science: The Role of Consensus Conferences in Europe.* London: Science Museum.

Kevles, Daniel J. 1998. *The Baltimore Case: A Trial of Politics, Science, and Character.* New York: Norton.

Losey, John E.; L. S. Rayor; and M. E. Carter. 1999. "Transgenic pollen harms monarch larvae" *Nature* 399: 214.

Nowotny, Helga; Peter Scott; and Michael Gibbons. 2001. *Re-Thinking Science: Knowledge and the Public in an Age of Uncertainty.* Cambridge, UK: Polity.

Omnibus Consolidated and Emergency Supplemental Appropriations Act of 1999, P.L. 105-277 (codified at 42 U.S.C. § 1395 et. seq.). 1998. The Office of Management and Budget in the Clinton administration controversially narrowed the scope of the law to apply not to *all* publicly-funded research, but only to research actually relied on in policy-making. The issue was not completely resolved as of May 2005.

Perrow, Charles. 1984. *Normal Accidents: Living with High Risk Technologies.* New York: Basic Books.

Porter, Theodore M. 1995. *Trust in Numbers: The Pursuit of Objectivity in Science and Public Life.* Princeton: Princeton University Press.

Price, Don K. 1965. *The Scientific Estate.* Cambridge, MA: Harvard University Press. The locus classicus of the view of the right relations between knowledge and power.

Schon, Donald A., and Martin Rein. 1994. *Frame/Reflection: Toward the Resolution of Intractable Policy Controversies.* New York: Basic Books.

Short, James F., and Lee Clarke, eds. 1992. *Organizations, Uncertainties, and Risk.* Boulder: Westview Press.

Stern, Paul C., and Harvey V. Fineberg, eds. 1996. *Understanding Risk: Informing Decisions in a Democratic Society.* Washington, DC: National Academy Press.

Stokes, Donald E. 1997. *Pasteur's Quadrant: Basic Science and Technological Innovation.* Washington, DC: Brookings.

Vaughan, Diane. 1996. *The Challenger Launch Decision: Risky Technology, Culture, and Deviance at NASA.* Chicago: University of Chicago Press.

Winner, Langdon. 1986. "On Not Hitting the Tar Baby." In his *The Whale and the Reactor.* Chicago: University of Chicago Press.

INTERNET RESOURCES

European Commission. *1997 Communication of the European Commission on Consumer Health and Safety.* COM (97) 183 fin. Available from http://europa.eu.int/comm/food/fs/sc/index_en.html.

Joy, Bill. 2000. "Why the Future Doesn't Need Us." *Wired,* http://www.wired.com/wired/archive/8.04/joy.html.

Washington Times. "Nature Regrets Publication of Corn Study." April 5, 2002. Available from http://www.washingtontimes.com/national/20020405-9384015.htm.

1.3 ETHICAL PERSPECTIVES

1.3.1 Philosophy and Human Values

IAN BARBOUR

In this selection taken from the author's Gifford Lectures, philosopher Ian Barbour provides a concise primer on modern ethical theory stressing its application to issues involving technology. The two main schools of thought in ethical theory are consequentialist and deontological. He begins by discussing the leading consequentialist theory, utilitarianism, which holds

---

Source: *Ethics in an Age of Technology: The Gifford Lectures 1989–1991,* Vol. 2, pp. 33–41. Copyright © 1993 by Ian G. Barbour. Reprinted by permission of HarperCollins Publishers, Inc.

that the production of "the greatest happiness for the greatest number" is the supreme moral principle. However, Barbour notes several important objections to this theory that undermine its plausibility as a sufficient principle for ethical evaluation and decision making. He goes on to contrast it with the deontological approach that emphasizes rights and obligations, noting that many moral philosophers believe that rights and duties can "trump" a generalized obligation to promote the greatest good. Barbour then explores the ideas of justice, equality, and freedom, briefly explaining how moral philosophers understand each of these important ethical concepts. In particular, he explains the Rawlsian idea of justice and how his concept of the "original position" supports a notion of equality under which inequalities may be allowed if they promote the welfare of the least advantaged members of society. Barbour concludes by identifying the positive and negative senses of freedom and argues that the kinds of freedom that are most important in a technological society are those that enable individuals to participate in decisions affecting their own lives.

FOCUS QUESTIONS

1. How does the concept of cost-benefit analysis relate to utilitarianism? What are the advantages of this approach to economics? What in Barbour's view are the disadvantages of cost-benefit analysis to ethical theory?
2. Is it necessary in Barbour's view for rights and obligations to be "absolute"—that is, allowing no exceptions? How can one understand rights and duties as both binding and flexible?
3. What is Rawls's "original position"? Explain how this idea leads him to propose a theory of justice in which social and economic inequalities should be arranged so as to promote the greatest benefit of the least advantaged.
4. How does Barbour define the ideas of positive and negative freedom? What are some examples of freedoms of each of these kinds that he thinks are critical in a technological society? Explain.
5. How can the ethical principles discussed in this selection help us evaluate technological choices involving issues such as increased surveillance, genetic enhancement, or protecting the global commons? Discuss.

KEYWORDS

consequentialism, cost-benefit analysis, deontology, equality, ethics, freedom, justice, rights, utilitarianism

UTILITARIANISM AND ITS CRITICS

Utilitarianism has been not only an important school of thought among philosophers, but also a major influence among social scientists. Cost-benefit analysis and other formal methods used in environmental and technological decisions share the assumptions of utilitarianism. We can present here only the broad outlines of utilitarian philosophy and some of the issues that it raises for technological policy.

The central principle of utilitarianism is *the greatest good for the greatest number.* That action should be chosen which produces the greatest net balance of good over evil consequences. For Jeremy Bentham, the good was identified with pleasure; one should select the alternative that maximizes the balance of pleasure over pain. John Stuart Mill maintained that happiness is a more inclusive and long-lasting good than pleasure.[1] The utilitarian economists in turn sought to maximize total social welfare, aggregated either from individual welfare or from subjective preferences and perceived satisfactions. There are significant differences among these versions, but some observations can be made about their common assumptions.

Most forms of utilitarianism are *anthropocentric*. "The greatest good for the greatest number" has usually been taken to refer exclusively to human beings. Any harm to other creatures is to be considered only insofar as it affects humanity. We will examine in the next chapter a broader rendition of the principle that includes the good of all sentient beings. Although the principle usually is taken to apply only to presently existing persons, it does not actually distinguish present from future generations. But there are difficulties when future persons are included, since at least in principle the largest total good might be achieved by having an enormous population at a low level of well-being. The question of how much weight to attach to future costs and benefits is also problematic, as we shall see.

Utilitarianism faces serious difficulties in attempting to *quantify* "the greatest good." If the good is identified with happiness, can it be measured on a single numerical scale? Utilitarian economists speak of maximizing satisfactions or preferences. But do people really look on diverse kinds of satisfactions as equivalent and substitutable? Can preferences among persons be compared and then aggregated in order to determine whether the total for society has been maximized? Many economists have concluded that the only practical way to measure people's preferences is by their willingness to pay. But the distribution of purchasing power is very uneven, and it is often misleading to assume that everything that is prized can be priced. The concern for quantification has tended to restrict attention to measurable costs and benefits.

Another criticism is that in utilitarianism only the total good, and not its *distribution* among people, is relevant to moral choice. Suppose the extermination of a small minority would make the majority so happy that the total happiness is increased. Suppose total national income can be increased if we accept great poverty for one segment of society. The utilitarian can object to these actions only if it can be demonstrated that there are indirect repercussions that will harm the total welfare, for utilitarianism finds nothing inherently wrong with injustice or inequality as such. In many cases the long-term social costs of setting a precedent by unjust actions might be so serious that they would outweigh any short-term benefits. But such considerations would not always prevent the sacrifice of some individuals for the social good.

Many contemporary philosophers hold that utilitarian principles must be supplemented by a *principle of justice*. If the total good were the only criterion, we could justify a small social gain even if it entailed a gross injustice. But if justice were the only norm, we would have to correct a small injustice even if it resulted in widespread suffering or social harm. It appears, then, that we need to consider both justice and the total good.[2]

I will suggest later that *cost-benefit* and *risk-benefit* analyses, when supplemented by a principle of justice, are often useful techniques if one is comparing a small number of options and there is a narrow range of very specific objectives. But most policy decisions today involve a large number of options and a broad range of impacts, many of which are difficult or impossible to quantify. The trade-offs are multidimensional and cannot be measured in a single unit or aggregated as a numerical total. They involve highly diverse types of value. I will maintain that environmental impact assessment and technology assessment methods allow a broader range of value considerations and thereby escape some of the limitations of utilitarian calculations. I will also argue that policy choices usually entail value judgments among incommensurables, and therefore the basic decisions must be made through political processes, not by technical experts using formal analytic techniques.

A final objection is a broader one. Utilitarianism judges entirely by consequences. But there are some acts, such as murder or experimentation on human subjects without their voluntary consent, which we do not condone even if they have good consequences. An alternative approach to ethics stresses *duty* and *obligation*, the choice of acts that are right in themselves, apart from the calculation of consequences. Theories based on obligations are called *deontological* (from the Greek *Aeon*, "that which is binding").

Historically there have been many variants of the idea that particular acts can be judged *right* or *wrong* according to universal principles or laws, without attempting to calculate their consequences. The Stoics said that people have a duty to act in accordance with the natural law, the rational and moral order expressed in the structure of the world. Judaism and Christianity stressed obedience to the divine law revealed in scripture. Immanuel Kant held that the right is determined by the unconditional obligation of rational moral law, apart from any consideration of consequences. He maintained that an action is right if the principle it expresses could be universally applied. For Kant, the demand for freedom and justice is based on the equality of persons as autonomous and rational moral agents; individual persons should never be treated merely as means to social ends.[3]

Whereas utilitarianism emphasizes the social good, deontological ethics typically defends *individual rights.* Fundamental rights must not be violated even in the interest of beneficial social consequences. Rights are in general correlated with *duties.* My right to life implies your duty not to violate my life. The language of rights appears to be absolutist and often does lead to inflexible positions. If rights are "inalienable" and "inviolable" and duties are "categorical," there seems to be no room for compromise. However, it is possible to employ a deontological approach with considerable flexibility. For example, one can formulate a universal rule with built-in qualifications that allow for special cases. Moreover, one duty may be outweighed by other duties. When two rights conflict, one of them may be assigned priority. So rights and duties should not be regarded as absolute.[4]

The defense of *individual rights* is indeed important in a technological age in which governments wield vast powers (through electronic surveillance and the control of information, for example), and they frequently defend their actions by pointing to benefits for society. Only a basic respect for persons can lead us to protect a minority from exploitation for the benefit of the majority. But in an ecologically interdependent world, the direct and indirect consequences of our actions are often far-reaching and should not be neglected. Both the protection of the individual and the good of society must be considered in the complex decisions we face today, and there is no simple formula for combining them.

In some cases that we will examine, the social consequences are paramount (for example, nuclear weapons). In other cases individual rights are the main issue (for instance, the confidentiality of computerized personnel records). Sometimes individual rights and the future welfare of society are very difficult to reconcile, as in the debate over population growth. But in general I will use both a broad evaluation of consequences (going beyond utilitarianism and cost-benefit analysis by including non-quantifiable values) and a defense of rights and duties that avoids absolutism.

THE CONCEPT OF JUSTICE

Most ideas of justice start from an assumption of *the fundamental equality of persons.* For some people this may be based on a religious conviction of the equal worth of every individual in God's sight. For others it may derive from a doctrine of equal intrinsic human rights ("natural rights") or the requirements of a harmonious social order. Some philosophers have argued from the common nature of persons as rational beings or the universality of basic human capacities. Others take respect for human beings and belief in their equal dignity to be unanalyzable ultimate attitudes. Distributive justice, then, starts with the idea that people should be treated equally because they are fundamentally equal.[5]

Unequal treatment can be justified on a variety of grounds. Special provisions for people with special needs and disabilities is in itself unequal, but the goal is an equal opportunity for a good life. Individuals are selected for positions of leadership, but such positions should be open to anyone with appropriate qualifications. Some differences in income may be justified as an incentive to productivity, from which everyone supposedly benefits, but inequalities of the magnitude that exists in industrial societies today are hardly justifiable for this purpose.[6] The radical inequalities between nations could never be justified by the need for work incentives.

Unequal treatment is justified, in short, only if it helps to *correct some other form of inequality* or if it is *essential for the good of all.* Inequalities of authority are necessary for maintaining the social order, but there can be equal access to the positions and offices that carry such authority. But are there limits to the degree of inequality that we will tolerate for the sake of other social benefits? Are inequalities in some goods and services more significant than in others? Questions of inequality assume added urgency if technology tends to increase the gap between rich and poor and if global scarcities limit the resources available for distribution.

I would maintain that equality is a more compelling value in the distribution of resources to meet *basic human needs* (such as food, health, and shelter—the lowest levels in Maslow's hierarchy) than in the distribution of other goods and services. Food to meet minimum protein and calorie requirements is necessary for life itself; justice in the production and distribution of food to meet these requirements should have the highest priority. Access to health care also is crucial since it so strongly affects life prospects. But some margin beyond bare survival is a prerequisite for a minimally decent human life. Estimates of the minimal material levels for human dignity and self-respect are of course historically and culturally relative; there is no sharp line between physical needs and psychological desires influenced by changing expectations. In the United States, a poverty line has been established for entitlement to food stamps and health care benefits; unemployment insurance and social security also were instituted in the name of justice rather than charity. A project sponsored by the United Nations has tried to establish quantitative measures for basic needs and standards on which there is an emerging world consensus.[7]

The most influential recent treatment of the relation between justice and equality is John Rawls's *A Theory of Justice*. Rawls asks us to imagine a hypothetical "original position" in which a group of people are formulating the basic principles for a social order. No one knows what his or her status will be in the society that is to be established. In agreeing on a "social contract," each person acts from rational self-interest, but impartiality in formulating the rules is guaranteed because these contracting individuals do not know what their own social positions will be. Such a hypothetical situation can help us establish principles for the fair distribution of scarce resources. It is similar to a situation in which the child who cuts the cake does not know which piece he or she will get.

Rawls maintains that persons in such an "original position" would accept two basic principles for the social order:

1. Each person is to have an equal right to the most extensive total system of equal basic liberties compatible with a similar system of liberty for all.
2. Social and economic inequalities are to be arranged so that they are both: (a) to the greatest benefit of the least advantaged, and (b) attached to offices and positions open to all under conditions of fair equality of opportunity.[8]

As Rawls develops it, the second principle requires equality in the distribution of all the primary social goods (income, wealth, power, and self-respect), with the exception noted. Inequalities are allowed only if they maximize benefits to the least advantaged and are attached to offices open to all. Attention to the impact on *the least advantaged* is a product not of altruism but of the rational self-interest of people in the "original position," any of whom might end up in that worst-off status. Rawls suggests that if the least advantaged benefit, it is likely that most other social groups will benefit also. But he rejects the utilitarian view that a loss to some people can be justified by greater gains to others.

Rawls holds that rational contractors would insist that, once a minimal level of material well-being had been reached, *liberty* should have priority over *equality*. The first principle is thereafter to be fulfilled before and independently of the second. Liberty—especially liberty of conscience and political liberty (equal participation in government-is not to be exchanged for any other benefits, including greater equality. Neither freedom nor justice is subject to trade-offs with other benefits. Political rights should not be sacrificed for the sake of economic gains, except under conditions of extreme scarcity.

Not surprisingly, Rawls has been attacked from the right for being *too egalitarian*. Defenders of free enterprise capitalism say that the degree of equality that Rawls seeks would not provide adequate incentives for the most able persons, and it would protect the indolence of the least able. The enforcement of equality, it is claimed, would require coercive measures and would violate property rights and the acquisition of wealth by legitimate means. If one is really dedicated to freedom, one must set strict limits on the powers of the state, including its power to redistribute legitimately acquired property.[9] But Rawls is attacked from the left for *not being egalitarian enough*. Marxist and socialist critics insist that political equality, which the first principle endorses, is jeopardized by the degree of economic inequality that the second principle allows. For economic power becomes political power in capitalist societies, and inequalities perpetuate themselves.[10]

Rawls's hypothetical "*original position*" has also been criticized. If one starts from separate, autonomous individuals, can an adequate concept of community ever emerge? If one starts by abstracting the individual from all political and historical contexts, can one obtain principles relevant to actual choices in the real world? Despite such limitations, I see the "original position" as a useful analytic device for asking what would be a fair distribution of resources. It is one of the few ways of dealing with justice between generations—simply by asking you to imagine what policies you would recommend if you did not know to which generation you would belong...

FREEDOM AS PARTICIPATION

One consideration in the evaluation of any technological policy is the extent to which it restricts or extends individual freedom. But freedom has many forms, which may be affected in diverse ways by a policy decision. According to the philosopher Joel Feinberg, freedom can be expressed as a relation between *an agent, a constraint, and an activity*. Explicitly or implicitly, it has a general structure: x is free from y to do z. People have particular kinds of constraints and activities in mind when they defend freedom. Sometimes they emphasize the absence of a constraint, and sometimes they emphasize the opportunity for and choice of an activity they deem important.[11]

The negative side of freedom is *the absence of external constraints:* freedom from coercion or direct interference imposed by other persons or institutions. Locke and the early British tradition of libertarian political philosophy interpreted freedom primarily as the absence of interference by other individuals or by the state. They wanted to protect the individual against abuses of the power of government; they sought the maximum scope for individual initiative in economic affairs and in the use of private property. This view was influential among the authors of the U. S. Constitution and was reinforced by the American experience of the frontier, abundant resources, and the vision of a land of unlimited opportunities for everyone. It seemed that a person free of human constraints could pursue the mastery of nature without interfering with other persons.

The positive side of freedom is *the presence of opportunities for choice*. Freedom to choose among genuine alternatives requires a range of real options and the power to act to further the alternative chosen. Even in the absence of external constraints, unequal power results in unequal opportunity for choice. Some degree of personal autonomy is an essential component of freedom. Many of the conditions for the exercise of choice are internal. People vary widely in their awareness of alternatives, ability to make deliberate choices, and personal initiative and self-direction. But in dealing with public policy; we are concerned mainly about the external conditions, the social structures within which people can have some control over their own futures.

The *negative* and *positive* sides of freedom are inescapably related in any social order. If we try to minimize external constraints while there are great inequalities of economic power, the weak will have little protection from domination by the strong. In a complex society, the actions of one person can greatly affect the choices open to other people. Limitations on the actions of some persons are necessary if other persons are to be able to exercise choice. Positive freedom to achieve desired outcomes exists only within an orderly society. The state is an instrument of order and law, but it is also an instrument of freedom when it restricts some actions to make other actions possible. Emphasis on the positive side of freedom is also consistent with the social character of selfhood ... in contrast to the more individualistic view of freedom as absence of interference.

Political freedom too has both negative and positive aspects. On the negative side are limits to the powers of government, such as censorship and arbitrary arrest. I will suggest, for example, that citizens must be protected from invasion of privacy through electronic surveillance and the misuse of personal information in computerized databanks. On the positive side are institutions of political self-determination and democratic forms of government whereby each citizen can have a voice in decision-making processes. Civil liberties, such as freedom of speech, assembly, and the press, can be defended both as basic human rights and as preconditions of democracy. The moves toward democracy around the world in the early 1990s involved the right of dissent and freedom to organize opposition parties.

In technological societies, *the right of governments to intervene* to protect health, safety, and welfare has been expanding to include ever-wider areas, as the uses of private property have had more far-reaching public consequences. Such common resources as air and water can only be protected by collective action through regulations or economic incentives. In other cases, governmental powers were expanded to protect citizens from the growing power of private institutions such as industrial corporations and labor unions.

The forms of freedom that are most relevant to technological policy can thus be understood positively as opportunities to participate in the decisions that affect our lives.

1. *Participation in the Marketplace.* In a free market economy, decisions are decentralized among many producers and consumers. The recent overthrow of communist governments around the world reflects a wide recognition of the economic inefficiencies and bureaucracy of state ownership and central control, as well as a desire for democracy in place of political repression. In a market economy, however, the goals of economic efficiency and social justice are not easily reconciled. Some loss of efficiency accompanies the use of taxes to mitigate extremes of wealth and poverty and to support health and welfare measures designed to ensure that no one lacks the basic necessities of life.

Some types of *government action* entail much greater intervention in the marketplace than others. For example, the individual farmer and the agribusiness corporation make decisions in response to market forces, but some government subsidies and regulations are acceptable in agriculture because it affects so many other areas of public policy: food prices, farm income, foreign trade, soil erosion, water pollution, land use, the quality of rural life, and so forth. Again, a heavy tax on the discharge of industrial pollutants relies on economic incentives and allows a greater variety of responses than strategies that mandate specific abatement technologies or set absolute standards for emissions. Energy conservation proposals range from voluntary restraint, through economic incentives, to mandatory fuel efficiency standards and fuel rationing. In each of these cases the consequences of insufficient regulation must be weighed against the dangers of excessive bureaucracy and the losses in efficiency and private initiative.

2. *Participation in Political Processes.* Democracy requires a free press, the right to dissent, and provisions for the election of representatives at local and national levels. Officials can be held accountable, and citizen input can take place, through legislative and regulatory hearings and court challenges. But citizens often feel incompetent to deal with complex technological decisions. The risks to human health and safety from nuclear reactors and toxic substances, for instance, are very difficult to evaluate. Yet such decisions should not be left to technical experts alone, since they require the comparison of diverse risks and benefits and the assessment of alternative policies, which are not

purely scientific questions. An industry or a government agency that has an interest in promoting a technology usually has far more extensive legal and scientific resources than those opposing it....

3. *Participation in Work-Related Decisions.* The institutions within which work is carried out vary widely, but they should include some provision for the voices of workers to be heard, such as labor unions, labor-management committees, producer cooperatives, small businesses, or owner-operated farms. We will return to these issues in later chapters in discussing particular agricultural and industrial technologies.

All three types of participation are more difficult in *large-scale technologies* than in those of *intermediate scale.* For example, nuclear energy is complex and centralized; it demands huge capital investments and entails unusual risks that require an exceptional degree of government regulation and strict security measures. By contrast, many forms of solar energy are decentralized; equipment can be locally installed and managed. *Decentralization* counteracts the concentration of economic and political power, and it contributes to diversity and local control. Yet in many cases the *centralization* of authority is necessary. Air and water pollution crosses jurisdictional boundaries. Local governments have been ineffective in controlling pollution because they are dependent on industrial growth for new tax revenues. An increasing national role in environmental regulation and resource conservation is unavoidable, but citizen participation is more difficult at the national level.

To sum up: philosophy can help us clarify ethical principles for evaluating technological choices. It can remind us of the importance of taking into account both the good of society and the rights of individuals. It can give more precise meaning to concepts of justice and freedom (and of course many other ethical concepts).

I have defended the idea of justice as the greatest equality compatible with the welfare of the least advantaged. I have suggested that in a technological society the most important form of freedom is participation in the decisions that affect our lives.

NOTES

1. J. S. Mill, *Utilitarianism* (1863; reprint New York E. P. Dutton, 1914); J. J. C. Smart and Bernard Williams, *Utilitarianism For and Against* (New York: Cambridge University Press, 1973); Amartya Sen and Bernard Williams, eds., *Utilitarianism and Beyond* (New York: Cambridge University Press, 1984).
2. William Frankena, *Ethics*, 2d ed. (Englewood Cliffs, NJ: Prentice-Hall, 1971).
3. See Frankena, *Ethics*, chap 2.
4. W. D. Ross, *The Right and the Good* (Oxford: Clarendon Press, 1930).
5. Nicholas Rescher, *Distributive Justice*, (Indianapolis: Bobbs-Merrill, 1966); Hugo Bedau, ed., *Justice and Equality* (Englewood Cliffs, NJ: Prentice-Hall, 1971).
6. Arthur Okun, *Equality and Efficiency* (Washington, DC: Brookings Institute, 1975).
7. John McHale and Magda McHale, *Basic Human Needs* (Houston: University of Houston Press, 1977).
8. John Rawls, *A Theory of Justice* (Cambridge, MA: The Belknap Press of Harvard University Press) p. 83.
9. Robert Nozick, *Anarchy, State, and Utopia* (New York: Basic Books, 1974).
10. Brian Barry, *The Liberal Theory of Justice* (Oxford: Oxford University Press, 1973), Norman Daniels, ed., *Reading Rawls: Critical Studies in a Theory of Justice* (New York: Basic Books, 1974). See also Charles R. Beitz, *Political Theory and International Relations* (Princeton: Princeton University Press, 1979).
11. Joel Feinberg, *Social Philosophy* (Englewood Cliffs, NJ: Prentice-Hall, 1973), chap. 1; P. H. Partridge, "Freedom," *Encyclopedia of Philosophy*, ed. Paul Edwards.

1.3.2 Technology and Responsibility: Reflections on the New Task of Ethics

HANS JONAS

Hans Jonas is one of a relatively small number of twentieth-century philosophers who have reflected carefully on the relationship between technology and ethics. He is also known for his writing on topics in biomedical ethics. He ended his professional career as Alvin Johnson Professor Emeritus of Philosophy at the New School for Social Research.

In this essay that originally appeared in *Social Research* in 1973, Jonas develops the view that traditional ethics is incapable of handling the kinds of ethical problems that are being created by our contemporary global technological civilization. His view is that to adequately evaluate the ethical significance of contemporary science and technology, we need to do so through the lens of a new kind of ethics, what he terms an "ethics of responsibility." He subsequently expanded the ideas presented in this essay in a book published in 1984 entitled *The Imperative of Responsibility: In Search of an Ethics for the Technological Age.*

FOCUS QUESTIONS

1. What are the three characteristics of traditional "neighbor ethics" that Jonas isolates, and in what respects has modern technology made traditional ethics obsolete?
2. How does Jonas's view that "man himself has been added to the objects of technology" compare to the discussion of the ethics of human cloning by Leor Kass (Selection 2.4.2) and Michael Sandel (Selection 2.4.3)?
3. What do you think Jonas means when he says, "We need wisdom the most when we believe in it the least"?

KEYWORDS

behavior control, environmental ethics, genetic engineering, morality, Utopia

All previous ethics—whether in the form of issuing direct enjoinders to do and not to do certain things, or in the form of defining principles for such enjoinders, or in the form of establishing the ground of obligation for obeying such principles—had these interconnected tacit premises in common: that the human condition, determined by the nature of man and the nature of things, was given once for all; that the human good on that basis was readily determinable; and that the range of human action and therefore responsibility was narrowly circumscribed. It will be the burden of my argument to show that these premises no longer hold, and to reflect on the meaning of this fact for our moral condition. More specifically, it will be my contention that with certain developments of our powers the *nature of human action* has changed, and since ethics is concerned with action, it should follow that the changed nature of human action calls for a change in ethics as well: this not merely in the sense that new objects of action have added to the case material on which received rules of conduct are to be applied, but in the more radical sense that the qualitatively novel

---

Source: *Philosophical Essays by* Hans Jonas. Copyright © 1974 by Prentice-Hall. Reprinted by permission of Eleanore Jonas.

nature of certain of our actions has opened up a whole new dimension of ethical relevance for which there is no precedent in the standards and canons of traditional ethics.

I

The novel powers I have in mind are, of course, those of modern *technology*. My first point, accordingly, is to ask how this technology affects the nature of our acting, in what ways it makes acting under its dominion *different* from what it has been through the ages. Since throughout those ages man was never without technology, the question involves the human difference of *modern* from previous technology. Let us start with an ancient voice on man's powers and deeds which in an archetypal sense itself strikes, as it were, a technological note—the famous Chorus from Sophocles' *Antigone*.

> *Many the wonders but nothing more wondrous than man.*
>
> *This thing crosses the sea in the winter's storm, making his path through the roaring waves.*
>
> *And she, the greatest of gods, the Earth—deathless she is, and unwearied—he wears her away as the ploughs go up and down from year to year and his mules turn up the soil.*
>
> *The tribes of the lighthearted birds he ensnares, and the races of all the wild beasts and the salty brood of the sea, with the twisted mesh of his nets, he leads captive, this clever man.*
>
> *He controls with craft the beasts of the open air, who roam the hills. The horse with his shaggy mane he holds and harnesses, yoked about the neck, and the strong bull of the mountain.*
>
> *Speech and thought like the wind and the feelings that make the town, he has taught himself, and shelter against the cold, refuge from rain. Ever resourceful is he.*
>
> *Tie faces no future helpless. Only against death shall he call for aid in vain. But from baffling maladies has he contrived escape.*
>
> *Clever beyond all dreams the inventive craft that he has which may drive him one time or another to well or ill.*
>
> *When he honors the laws of the land the gods' sworn right high indeed in his city; but stateless the man who dares to do what is shameful.*

This awestruck homage to man's powers tells of his violent and violating irruption into the cosmic order, the self-assertive invasion of nature's various domains by his restless cleverness; but also of his building—through the self-taught powers of speech and thought and social sentiment—the home for his very humanity, the artifact of the city. The raping of nature and the civilizing of himself go hand in hand. Both are in defiance of the elements, the one by venturing into them and overpowering their creatures, the other by securing an enclave against them in the shelter of the city and its laws. Man is the maker of his life *qua* human, bending circumstances to his will and needs, and except against death he is never helpless.

Yet there is a subdued and even anxious quality about this appraisal of the marvel that is man, and nobody can mistake it for immodest bragging. With all his boundless resourcefulness, man is still small by the measure of the elements: precisely this makes his sallies into them so daring and allows those elements to tolerate his forwardness. Making free with the denizens of land and sea and air, he yet leaves the encompassing nature of those elements unchanged, and their generative powers undiminished. Them he cannot harm by carving out his little dominion from theirs. They last, while his schemes have their short lived way. Much as he harries Earth, the greatest of gods, year after year with his plough—she is ageless and unwearied; her enduring patience he must and can trust, and he must conform. And just as ageless is the sea. With all his netting of the salty brood, the spawning ocean is inexhaustible. Nor is it hurt by the plying of ships, nor sullied by what is jettisoned into its deeps. And no matter how many illnesses he contrives to cure, mortality does not bow to cunning.

All this holds because man's inroads into nature, as seen by himself, were essentially superficial, and powerless to upset its appointed balance. Nor is there a hint, in the *Antigone* chorus or anywhere else, that this is only a beginning and that greater things of artifice and power are yet to come—that man is embarked on an endless course of conquest. He had gone thus far in reducing necessity, had learned by his wits to wrest that much from it for the humanity of his life, and there he could stop. The room he had thus made was filled by the city of men—meant to enclose and not to expand—and thereby a new balance was struck within the larger balance of the whole. All the well or ill to which man's inventive craft may drive him one time or another is inside the human enclave and does not touch the nature of things.

The immunity of the whole, untroubled in its depth by the importunities of man, that is, the essential immutability of Nature as the cosmic order, was indeed the backdrop to all of mortal man's enterprises, between the abiding and the changing: the abiding was Nature, the changing his own works. The greatest of these works was the city, and on it he could offer some measure of abidingness by the laws he made for it and undertook to honor. But no long-range certainty pertained to this contrived abidingness. As a precarious artifact, it can lapse or go astray. Not even within its artificial space, with all the freedom it gives to man's determination of self, can the arbitrary ever supersede the basic terms of his being. The very inconstancy of human fortunes assures the constancy of the human condition. Chance and luck and folly, the great equalizers in human affairs, act like an entropy of sorts and make all definite designs in the long run revert to the perennial norm. Cities rise and fall, rules come and go, families prosper and decline; no change is there to stay, and in the end, with all the temporary deflections balancing each other out, the state of man is as it always was. So here too, in his very own artifact, man's control is small and his abiding nature prevails.

Still, in this citadel of his own making, clearly set off from the rest of things and entrusted to him, was the whole and sole domain of man's responsible action. Nature was not an object of human responsibility—she taking care of herself and, with some coaxing and worrying, also of man: not ethics, only cleverness applied to her. But in the city, where men deal with men, cleverness must be wedded to morality, for this is the soul of its being. In this intra-human frame dwells all traditional ethics and matches the nature of action delimited by this frame.

II

Let us extract from the preceding those characteristics of human action which are relevant for a comparison with the state of things today.

1. All dealing with the non-human world, i.e., the whole realm of *techne* (with the exception of medicine), was ethically neutral—in respect both of the object and the subject of such action: in respect of the object, because it impinged but little on the self-sustaining nature of things and thus raised no question of permanent injury to the integrity of its object, the natural order as a whole; and in respect of the subject it was ethically neutral because *techne* as an activity conceived itself as a determinate tribute to necessity and not as an indefinite, self-validating advance to mankind's major goal, claiming in its pursuit man's ultimate effort and concern. The real vocation of man lay elsewhere. In brief, action on non-human things did not constitute a sphere of authentic ethical significance.

2. Ethical significance belonged to the direct dealing of man with man, including the dealing with himself: all traditional ethics is *anthropocentric.*

3. For action in this domain, the entity "man" and his basic condition was considered constant in essence and not itself an object of reshaping *techne.*

4. The good and evil about which action had to care lay close to the act, either in the praxis itself or in its immediate reach, and were not a matter for remote planning. This proximity of ends pertained to time as well as space. The effective range of action was small, the time-span of foresight, goal-setting, and accountability was short, control of circumstances limited. Proper conduct had its immediate criteria and almost immediate consummation. The long run of consequences beyond was left to change, fate, or providence. Ethics accordingly was of the here and now, of occasions as they arise between men, of the recurrent, typical situations of private and public life. The good man was he who met these contingencies with virtue and

wisdom, cultivating these powers in himself, and for the rest resigning himself to the unknown.

All enjoinders and maxims of traditional ethics, materially different as they may be, show this confinement to the immediate setting of the action. "Love thy neighbor as thyself"; "Do unto others as you would wish them to do unto you"; "Instruct your child in the way of truth"; "Strive for excellence by developing and actualizing the best potentialities of your being *qua* man"; "Subordinate your individual good to the common good"; "Never treat your fellow man as a means only but always *also* as an end in himself"—and so on. Note that in all those maxims the agent and the "other" of his action are sharers of a common present. It is those alive now and in some commerce with me that have a claim on my conduct as it affects them by deed or omission. The ethical universe is composed of contemporaries, and its horizon to the future is confined by the foreseeable span of their lives. Similarly confined is its horizon of place, within which the agent and the other meet as neighbor, friend or foe, as superior and subordinate, weaker and stronger, and in all the other roles in which humans interact with one another. To this proximate range of action all morality was geared.

III

It follows that the *knowledge* that is required—besides the moral will—to assure the morality of action, fitted these limited terms: it was not the knowledge of the scientist or the expert, but knowledge of a kind readily available to all men of good will. Kant went so far as to say that "human reason can, in matters of morality, be easily brought to a high degree of accuracy and completeness even in the most ordinary intelligence";[1] that "there is no need of science or philosophy for knowing what man has to do in order to be honest and good, and indeed to be wise and virtuous.... [Ordinary intelligence] can have as good a hope of hitting the mark as any philosopher can promise himself";[2] and again: "I need no elaborate acuteness to find out what I have to do so that my willing be morally good. Inexperienced regarding the course of the world, unable to anticipate all the contingencies that happen in it," I can yet know how to act in accordance with the moral law.[3]

Not every thinker in ethics, it is true, went so far in discounting the cognitive side of moral action. But even when it received much greater emphasis, as in Aristotle, where the discernment of the situation and what is fitting for it makes considerable demands on experience and judgment, such knowledge has nothing to do with the science of things. It implies, of course, a general conception of the human good as such, a conception predicated on the presumed invariables of man's nature and condition, which may or may not find expression in a theory of its own. But its translation into practice requires a knowledge of the here and now, and this is entirely non-theoretical. This "knowledge" proper to virtue (of the "where, when, to, whom, and how") stays with the immediate issue, in whose defined context the action *as the agent's own* takes its course and within which it terminates. The good or bad of the action is wholly decided within that short-term context. Its moral quality shines forth from it, visible to its witnesses. No one was held responsible for the unintended later affects of his well-intentioned, well-considered, and well-performed act. The short arm of human power did not call for a long arm of predictive knowledge; the shortness of the one is as little culpable as that of the other. Precisely because the human good, known in its generality, is the same for all time, its relation or violation takes place at each time, and its complete locus is always the present.

IV

All this has decisively changed. Modern technology has introduced actions of such novel scale, objects, and consequences that the framework of former ethics can no longer contain them. The *Antigone* chorus on the *dēinotes*, the wondrous power, of man would have to read differently now; and its admonition to the individual to honor the laws of the land would no longer be enough. To be sure, the old prescriptions of the "neighbor" ethics—of justice, charity, honesty, and so on—still hold in their intimate immediacy of the nearest, day by day sphere of human interaction. But this sphere is overshadowed by a growing realm of collective action where doer, deed, and effect are no longer the same as they were in the proximate sphere, and which by the enormity of its powers forces upon ethics a new dimension of responsibility never dreamt of before.

Take, for instance, as the first major change in the inherited picture, the critical *vulnerability* of nature to man's technological intervention—unsuspected before it began to show itself in damage already done. This discovery, whose shock led to the concept and nascent science of ecology, alters the very concept of ourselves as a causal agency in the larger scheme of things. It brings to light, through the effects, that the nature of human action has *de facto* changed, and that an object of an entirely new order—no less than the whole biosphere of the planet—has been added to what we must be responsible for because of our power over it. And of what surpassing importance an object, dwarfing all previous objects of active man! Nature as a human responsibility is surely a *novum* to be pondered in ethical theory. What kind of obligation is operative in it? Is it more than a utilitarian concern? Is it just prudence that bids us not to kill the goose that lays the golden eggs, or saw off the branch on which we sit? But the "we" that here sits and may fall into the abyss is all future mankind, and the survival of the species is more than a prudential duty of its present members. Insofar as it is the fate of *man*, as affected by the condition of nature, which makes us care about the preservation of nature, such care admittedly still retains the anthropocentric focus of all classical ethics. Even so, the difference is great. The containment of nearness and contemporaneity is gone, swept away by the spatial spread and time-span of the cause-effect trains which technological practice sets afoot, even when undertaken for proximate ends. Their irreversibility conjoined to their aggregate magnitude injects another novel factor into the moral equation. To this take their cumulative character: their effects add themselves to one another, and the situation for later acting and being becomes increasingly different from what it was for the initial agent. The cumulative self-propagation of the technological change of the world thus constantly overtakes the conditions of its contributing acts and moves through none but unprecedented situations, for which the lessons of experience are powerless. And not even content with changing its beginning to the point of unrecognizability, the cumulation as such may consume the basis of the whole series, the very condition of itself. All this would have to be co-intended in the will of the single action if this is to be a morally responsible one. Ignorance no longer provides it with an alibi.

Knowledge, under these circumstances, becomes a prime duty beyond anything claimed for it heretofore, and the knowledge must be commensurate with the causal scale of our action. The fact that it cannot really be thus commensurate, i.e., that the predictive knowledge falls behind the technical knowledge which nourishes our power to act, itself assumes ethical importance. Recognition of ignorance becomes the obverse of the duty to know and thus part of the ethics which must govern the ever more necessary self-policing of our out-sized might. No previous ethics had to consider the global condition of human life and the far-off future, even existence, of the race. There now being an issue demands, in brief, a new concept of duties and rights, for which previous ethics and metaphysics provide not even the principles, let alone a ready doctrine.

And what if the new kind of human action would mean that more than the interest of man alone is to be considered—that our duty extends farther and the anthropocentric confinement of former ethics no longer holds? It is at least not senseless anymore to ask whether the condition of extra-human nature, the biosphere as a whole and in its parts, now subject to our power, has become a human trust and has something of a more claim on us not only for our ulterior sake but for its own and in its own right. If this were the case it would require quite some rethinking in basic principles of ethics. It would mean to seek not only the human good, but also the good of things extra-human, that is, to extend the recognition of "ends in themselves" beyond the sphere of man and make the human good include the care for them. For such a role of stewardship no previous ethics has prepared us—and the dominant, scientific view of *Nature* even less. Indeed, the latter emphatically denies us all conceptual means to think of Nature as something to be honored, having reduced it to the indifference of necessity and accident, and divested it of any dignity of ends. But still, a silent plea for sparing its integrity seems to issue from the threatened plenitude of the living world. Should we heed this plea, should we grant its claim as sanctioned by the nature of things, or dismiss it as a mere sentiment on our part, which we may indulge as fair as we wish and can afford to do? If the former, it would (if taken seriously in its theoretical implications) push the necessary rethinking beyond the doctrine of action, i.e., ethics, into the doctrine of being, i.e., metaphysics, in which all ethics must ultimately be grounded. On this speculative subject I will here say no more than that we should keep ourselves open to the thought that natural science may not tell the whole story about Nature.

V

Returning to strictly intra-human considerations, there is another ethical aspect to the growth of *techne* as a pursuit beyond the pragmatically limited terms of former times. Then, so we found, *techne* was a measured tribute to necessity, not the road to mankind's chosen goal—a means with a finite measure of adequacy to well-defined proximate ends. Now, *techne* in the form of modern technology has turned into an infinite forward-thrust of the race, its most significant enterprise, in whose permanent, self-transcending advance to ever greater things the vocation of man tends to be seen, and whose success of maximal control over things and himself appears as the consummation of his destiny. Thus the triumph of *Homo faber* over his external object means also his triumph in the internal constitution *of Homo sapiens,* of whom he used to be a subsidiary part. In other words, technology, apart from its objective works, assumes ethical significance by the central place it now occupies in human purpose. Its cumulative creation, the expanding artificial environment, continuously reinforces the particular powers in man that created it, by compelling their unceasing inventive employment in its management and further advance, and by rewarding them with additional success—which only adds to the relentless claim. This positive feedback of functional necessity and reward—in whose dynamics pride of achievement must not be forgotten—assures the growing ascendancy of one side of man's nature over all the others, and inevitably at their expense. If nothing succeeds like success, nothing also entraps like success. Outshining in prestige and starving in resources whatever else belongs to the fullness of man, the expansion of his power is accompanied by a contraction of his self-conception and being. In the image he entertains of himself—the potent self-formula which determines his actual being as much as it reflects it—man now is evermore the maker of what he has made and the doer of what he can do, and most of all the preparer of what he will be able to do next. But not you or I: it is the aggregate, not the individual doer or deed that matters here; and the indefinite future, rather than the contemporary context of the action, constitutes the relevant horizon of responsibility. This requires imperatives of a new sort. If the realm of making has invaded the space of essential action, then morality must invade the realm of making, from which it had formerly stayed aloof, and must do so in the form of public policy. With issues of such inclusiveness and such lengths of anticipation public policy has never had to deal before. In fact, the changed nature of human action changes the very nature of politics.

For the boundary between "city" and "nature" has been obliterated: the city of men, once an enclave in the non-human world, spreads over the whole of terrestrial nature and usurps its place. The difference between the artificial and the natural has vanished, the natural is swallowed up in the sphere of the artificial, and at the same time the total artifact, the works of man working on and through himself, generates a "nature" of its own, i.e., a necessity with which human freedom has to cope in an entirely new sense. Once it could be said *Fiat justitia, pereat mundus,* "Let justice be done, and may the world perish"—where "world," of course, meant the renewable enclave in the imperishable whole. Not even rhetorically can the like be said anymore when the perishing of the whole through the doings of man—be they just or unjust—has become a real possibility. Issues never legislated on come into the purview of the laws which the total city must give itself so that there will be a world for the generations of man to come.

That there *ought* to be through all future time such a world fit for human habitation, and that it ought in all future time to be inhabited by a mankind worthy of the human name, will be readily affirmed as a general axiom or a persuasive desirability of speculative imagination (as persuasive and undemonstrable as the proposition that there being a world at all is "better" than there being none): but as a *moral* proposition, namely, a practical *obligation* toward the posterity of a distant future, and a principle of decision in present action, it is quite different from the imperatives of the previous ethics of contemporaneity; and it has entered the moral scene only with our novel powers and range of prescience.

The *presence of man in the world* had been a first and unquestionable given, from which all idea of obligation in human conduct started out. Now it has itself become an *object* of obligation—the obligation namely to ensure the very premise of all obligation, i.e., the *foothold* for a moral universe in the physical world—the existence of mere *candidates* for a moral order. The difference this makes for ethics may be illustrated in one example.

VI

Kant's categorical imperative said: "Act so that you *can* will that the maxim of our action be made the principle of a universal law." The "can" here invoked is that of reason and its consistency with itself: *Given* the existence of a community of human agents (acting rational beings), the action must be such that it can without self-contradiction be imagined as a general practice of that community. Mark that the basic reflection of morals here is not itself a moral but a logical one: The "I *can* will" or "I *cannot* will" expresses logical compatibility or incompatibility, not moral approbation or revulsion. But there is no self-contradiction in the thought that humanity would once come to an end, therefore also none in the thought that the happiness of present and proximate generations would be bought with the unhappiness or even non-existence of later ones—as little as, after all, in the inverse thought that the existence or happiness of later generations would be bought with the unhappiness or even partial extinction of present ones. The sacrifice of the future for the present is *logically* no more open to attack than the sacrifice of the present for the future. The difference is only that in the one case the series goes on, and in the other it does not. But that it *ought to go on,* regardless of the distribution of happiness or unhappiness, even with a persistent preponderance of unhappiness over happiness, nay, even of immorality over morality[4]—this cannot be derived from the rule of self-consistency *within* the series, long or short as it happens to be: it is a commandment of a very different kind, lying outside and "prior" to the series as a whole, and its ultimate grounding can only be metaphysical.

An imperative responding to the new type of human action and addressed to the new type of agency that operates it might run thus: "Act so that the effects of your action are compatible with the permanence of genuine human life"; or expressed negatively: "Act so that the effects of your action are not destructive of the future possibility of such life"; or simply: "Do not compromise the conditions for an indefinite continuation of humanity on earth"; or most generally: "In your present choices, include the future wholeness of Man among the objects of your will."

It is immediately obvious that no rational contradiction is involved in the violation of this kind of imperative. I *can* will the present good with sacrifice of the future good. It is also evident that the new imperative addresses itself to public policy rather than private conduct, which is not in the causal dimension to which that imperative applies. Kant's categorical imperative was addressed to the individual, and its criterion was instantaneous. It enjoined each of us to consider what would happen *if* the *maxim* of my present action were made, or at this moment already were, the principle of a universal legislation; the self-consistency or inconsistency of such a *hypothetical* universalization is made the test for my *private* choice. But it was no part of the reasoning that there is any probability of my private choice *in fact* becoming universal law, or that it might contribute to its becoming that. The universalization is a thought-experiment by the private agent not to test the immanent morality of his action. Indeed, real consequences are not considered at all, and the principle is one not of objective responsibility but of the subjective quality of my self-determination. The new imperative invokes a different consistency: not that of the act with itself, but that of its eventual *effects* with the continuance of human agency in times to come. And the "universalization" it contemplates is by no means hypothetical—i.e., a purely logical transference from the individual "me" to an imaginary, causally unrelated "all" ("*if* everybody acted like that"); on the contrary, the actions subject to the new imperative—actions of the collective whole—have their universal reference in their actual scope of efficacy: they "totalize" themselves in the progress of their momentum and thus are bound to terminate in shaping the universal dispensation of things. This adds a *time* horizon to the moral calculus which is entirely absent from the instantaneous logical operation of the Kantian imperative: whereas the latter extrapolates into an ever-present order of abstract compatibility, our imperative extrapolates into a predictable real *future* as the open-ended dimension of our responsibility.

VII

Similar comparisons could be made with all the other historical forms of the ethics of contemporaneity and immediacy. The new order of human action requires a commensurate ethics of foresight and responsibility, which is as new as are the issues with which it has to deal. We have seen that these are the issues posed by the works of *Homo faber* in the age of technology. But among those novel works we haven't mentioned yet the potentially most ominous class. We have considered *techne* only as applied to the non-human realm. But man himself has been added to the objects of technology. *Homo faber* is turning upon himself and gets ready to make over the maker of all the rest. This consummation of his power, which may well portend the overpowering of man, this final imposition of art on nature, calls upon the utter resources of ethical thought, which never before has been faced with elective alternatives to what were considered the definite terms of the human condition.

a. Take, for instance, the most basic of these "givens," man's mortality. Who ever before had to make up his mind on its desirable and *eligible* measure? There was nothing to choose about the upper limit, the "three score years and ten, or by reason of strength fourscore." Its inexorable rule was the subject of lament, submission, or vain (not to say foolish) wish-dreams about possible exceptions—strangely enough, almost never of affirmation. The intellectual imagination of a George Bernard Shaw and a Jonathan Swift speculated on the privilege of not having to die, or the curse of not being able to die. (Swift with the latter was the more perspicacious of the two.) Myth and legend toyed with such themes against the acknowledged background of the unalterable, which made the earnest man rather pray "teach us to number our days that we may get a heart of wisdom" (Psalm 90). Nothing of this was in the realm of doing, and effective decision. The question was only how to relate to the stubborn fact.

But lately, the dark cloud of inevitability seems to lift. A practical hope is held out by certain advances in cell biology to prolong, perhaps indefinitely extend the span of life by counteracting biochemical processes of aging. Death no longer appears as a necessity belonging to the nature of life, but as an avoidable, at least in principle tractable and long-delayable, organic malfunction. A perennial yearning of mortal man seems to come nearer fulfillment. And for the first time we have in earnest to ask the question "How desirable is this? How desirable for the individual, and how for the species?" These questions involve the very meaning of our finitude, the attitude toward death, and the general biological significance of the balance of death and procreation. Even prior to such ultimate questions are the more pragmatic ones of who should be eligible for the boon: persons of particular quality and merit? of social eminence? those that can pay for it? everybody? The last would seem the only just course. But it would have to be paid for at the opposite end, at the source. For clearly, on a population-wide scale, the price of extended age must be a proportional slowing of replacement, i.e., a diminished access of new life. The result would be a decreasing proportion of youth in an increasingly aged population. How good or bad would that be for the general condition of man? Would the species gain or lose? And how *right* would it be to preempt the place of youth? Having to die is bound up with having been born: mortality is but the other side of the perennial spring of "a natality" (to use Hannah Arendt's term). This had always been ordained; now its meaning has to be pondered in the sphere of decision.

To take the extreme (not that it will ever be obtained): if we abolish death, we must abolish procreation as well, for the latter is life's answer to the former, and so we would have a world of old age with no youth, and of known individuals with no surprises of such that had never been before. But this perhaps is precisely the wisdom in the harsh dispensation of our mortality: that it grants us the eternally renewed promise of the freshness, immediacy, and eagerness of youth, together with the supply of otherness as such. There is no substitute for this in the greater accumulation of prolonged experience: it can never recapture the unique privilege of seeing the world for the first time and with new eyes, never relive the wonder which, according to Plato, is the beginning of philosophy, never the curiosity of the child, which rarely enough lives on as thirst for knowledge in the adult, until it wanes there too. This ever renewed beginning, which is only to be had at the price of ever repeated ending, may well be mankind's hope, its safeguard against lapsing into boredom and routine, its chance of retaining the spontaneity of life. Also, the role of the *memento mori* in the individual's life must be considered, and what its attenuation to indefiniteness may do to it. Perhaps a non-negotiable limit to our expected time is necessary for each of us as the incentive to number our days and make them count.

So it could be that what by intent is a philanthropic gift of science to man, the partial granting of his oldest wish—to escape the curse of mortality—turns out to be to the detriment of man. I am not indulging in prediction and, in spite of my noticeable bias, not even in valuation. My point is that already the promised gift raises questions that had never to be asked before in terms of practical choice, and that no principle of former ethics, which took the human constants for granted, is competent to deal with them. And yet they must be dealt with ethically and by principle and not merely by the pressure of interest.

b. It is similar with all the other, quasi-utopian powers about to be made available by the advances of biomedical science as they are translated into technology. Of these, *behavior control* is much nearer to practical readiness than the still hypothetical prospect I have just been discussing, and the ethical questions it raises are less profound but have a more direct bearing on the moral conception of man. Here again, the new kind of intervention exceeds the old ethical categories. They have not equipped us to rule, for example, on mental control by chemical means or by direct electrical action of the brain via implanted electrodes—undertaken, let us assume, for defensible and even laudable ends. The mixture of beneficial and dangerous potentials is obvious, but the lines are not easy to draw. Relief of mental patients from distressing and disabling symptoms seems unequivocally beneficial. But from the relief of the *patient,* a goal entirely in the tradition of the medical art, there is an easy passage to the relief of *society* from the inconvenience of difficult individual behavior among its members: that is, the passage from medical to social application; and this opens up an indefinite field with grave potentials. The troublesome problems of rule and unruliness in modern mass society make the extension of such control methods to non-medical categories extremely tempting for social management. Numerous questions of human rights and dignity arise. The difficult question of preemption care versus enabling care insists on concrete answers. Shall we induce learning attitudes in school children by the mass administration of drugs, circumventing the appeal to autonomous motivation? Shall we overcome aggression by electronic pacification of brain areas? Shall we generate sensations of happiness or pleasure or at least contentment through independent stimulation (or tranquilizing) of the appropriate centers—independent, that is, of the objects of happiness, pleasure, or content and their attainment in personal living and achieving? Candidacies could be multiplied. Business firms might become interested in some of these techniques for performance-increase among their employees.

Regardless of the question of compulsion or consent, and regardless also of the question of undesirable side-effects, each time we thus bypass the human way of dealing with human problems, short-circuiting it by an impersonal mechanism, we have taken away something from the dignity of personal selfhood and advanced a further step on the road from responsible subjects to programmed behavior systems. Social functionalism, important as it is, is only one side of the question. Decisive is the question of what kind of individuals the society is composed of to make its existence valuable as a whole. Somewhere along the line of increasing social manageability at the price of individual autonomy, the question of the worthwhileness of the human enterprise must pose itself. Answering it involves the image of man we entertain. We must think it anew in light of the things we can do to it now and could never do before.

c. This holds even more with respect to the last object of a technology applied on man himself—the genetic control of future men. This is too wide a subject for cursory treatment. Here I merely point to this most ambitious dream of *Homo faber*, summed up in the phrase that man will take his own evolution in hand, with the aim of not just preserving the integrity of the species but of modifying it by improvements of his own design. Whether we have the right to do it, whether we are qualified for that creative role, is the most serious question that can be posed to man finding himself suddenly in possession of such failed powers. Who will be the imagemakers, by what standards, and on the basis of what knowledge? Also, the question of the moral right to experiment on future human beings must be asked. These and similar questions, which demand an answer before we embark on a journey into the unknown, show most vividly how far our powers to act are pushing us beyond the terms of all former ethics.

VIII

The ethically relevant common feature in all the examples adduced is what I like to call the inherently "utopian" drift of our actions under the conditions of modern technology, whether it works on nonhuman or on human nature, and whether the "utopia" at the end of the road be planned or unplanned. By the kind and size of its snowballing effects, technological power propels us into goals of a type that was formerly the preserve of Utopias. To put it differently, technological power has turned what used and ought to be tentative, perhaps enlightening, plays of speculative reason into competing blueprints for projects, and in choosing between them we have to choose between extremes of remote effects. The one thing we can really know of them is their extremism as such—that they concern the total condition of nature on our globe and the very kind of creatures that shall, or shall not, populate it. In consequence of the inevitably "utopian" scale of modern technology, the salutary gap between everyday and ultimate issues, between occasions, is closing. Living now constantly in the shadow of unwanted, built-in, automatic utopianism, we are constantly confronted with issues whose positive choice requires supreme wisdom—an impossible, and in particular for contemporary man, who denies the very existence of its object: viz., objective value and truth. We need wisdom most when we believe in it least. If the new nature of our acting then calls for a new ethics of long-range responsibility, coextensive with the range of our power, it calls in the name of that very responsibility also for a new kind of humility—a humility not like former humility, i.e., owing to the littleness, but owing to the excessive magnitude of our power, which is the excess of our power to act over our power to foresee and our power to evaluate and to judge. In the face of the quasieschatological potentials of our technological processes, ignorance of the ultimate implications becomes itself a reason for responsible restraint—as the second best to the possession of wisdom itself.

One other aspect of the required new ethics of responsibility for and to a distant future is worth mentioning: the insufficiency of representative government to meet the new demands on its normal principles and by its normal mechanics. For according to these, only *present* interests make themselves heard and felt and enforce their condition. It is to them that public agencies are accountable, and this is the way in which concretely the respecting of rights comes about (as distinct from their abstract acknowledgement). But the *future* is not represented, it is not a force that can throw its weight into the scales. The nonexistent has no lobby, and the unborn are powerless. Thus accountability to them has no political reality behind it yet in present decision-making, and when they can make their complaint, then we, the culprits, will no longer be there.

This raises to an ultimate pitch the old question of the power of the wise, or the force of ideas not allied to self-interest, in the body politic. What *force* shall represent the future in the present? However, before *this* question can become earnest in practical terms, the new ethics must find its theory, on which dos and don'ts can be based. That is: before the question of what *force,* comes the question of what *insight* or value-knowledge shall represent the future in the present.

IX

And here is where I get stuck, and where we all get stuck. For the very same movement which put us in possession of the powers that have now to be regulated by norms—the movement of modern knowledge called science—has by a necessary complementarity eroded the foundations from which norms could be derived; it has destroyed the very idea of norm as such. Not, fortunately, the feeling for norm and even for particular norms. But this feeling became uncertain of itself when contradicted by alleged knowledge or at least denied all sanction by it. Anyway and always does it have a difficult enough time against the loud clamors of greed and fear. Now it must in addition blush before the frown of superior knowledge, as unfounded and incapable of foundation. First, Nature has been "neutralized" with respect to value, then man himself. Now we shiver in the nakedness of a nihilism in which near-omnipotence is paired with near-emptiness, greatest capacity with knowing least what for. With the apocalyptic pregnancy of our actions, that very knowledge which we lack has become more urgently needed than at any other stage in the adventure of mankind. Alas, urgency is no promise of success. On the contrary, it must be avowed that to seek for wisdom today requires a good measure of unwisdom. The very nature of the age which cries out for an ethical theory makes it suspiciously look like a fool's errand. Yet we have no choice in the matter but to try.

It is a question whether without restoring the category of the sacred, the category most thoroughly destroyed by the scientific enlightenment, we can have an ethics able to cope with the extreme powers which we possess today and constantly increase and are almost compelled to use. Regarding those consequences imminent enough still to hit ourselves, fear can do the job—so often the best substitute for genuine virtue or wisdom. But this means fails us towards the more distant prospects, which here matter the most, especially as the beginnings seem mostly innocent in their smallness. Only awe of the sacred with its unqualified veto is independent to fit computations of mundane fear and the solace of uncertainty about distant consequences. But religion as a soul-determining force is no longer there to be summoned to the aid of ethics. The latter must stand on its worldly feet—that is, on reason and its fitness for philosophy. And while of faith it can be said that it either is there or is not, of ethics it holds that it must be there.

It must be there because men act, and ethics is for the reordering of actions and for regulating the power to act. It must be there all the more, then, the greater the powers of acting that are to be regulated; and with their size, the ordering principle must also fit their kind. Thus, novel powers to act require novel ethical rules and perhaps even a new ethics.

"Thou shalt not kill" was enunciated because man has the power to kill and often the occasion and even inclination for it—in short, because killing is actually done. It is only under the *pressure* of real habits of action, and generally of the fact that always action already takes place, without *this* having to be commanded first, that ethics as the ruling of such acting under the standard of the good or the permitted enters the stage. Such a *pressure* emanates from the novel technological powers of man, whose exercise is given with their existence. *If* they really are as novel in kind as here contended, and if by the kind of their potential consequences they really have abolished the moral neutrality which the technical commerce with matter hitherto enjoyed—then their pressure bids to seek for new prescriptions in ethics which are competent to assume their guidance, but which first of all can hold their own theoretically against that very pressure. To the demonstration of those premises this paper was devoted. If they are accepted, then we who make thinking our business have a task to last us for our time. We must do it in time, for since we act anyway we shall have some ethic or other in any case, and without a supreme effort to determine the right one, we may be left with a wrong one by default.

NOTES

1. Immanuel Kant, *Groundwork of the Metaphysics of Morals*, preface.
2. *Op. cit.*, chapter 1.
3. *Ibid.* (I have followed H. J. Paton's translation with some changes.)
4. On this last point, the biblical God changed his mind to an all-encompassing "yes" after the Flood.

1.3.3 Technology and Social Justice

FREEMAN DYSON

Freeman Dyson was born in England and educated at Cambridge University. He served in World War II as an operations research specialist for the Royal Air Force. Following the war, he did graduate training in physics and became professor of physics at Cornell University. In 1953 he joined the faculty at the Institute for Advanced Study in Princeton, New Jersey, where he remains. He is a fellow of the Royal Society of London and a member of the National Academy of Sciences.

The text reprinted here was delivered as the fourth Louis Nizer Lecture on Public Policy for the Carnegie Council on Ethics and International Affairs on November 5, 1997. It relates to themes that he has developed more fully in his book *The Sun, the Genome, and the Internet* (1999). In this lecture, Dyson addresses the issue of whether technological innovation tends to increase or decrease social justice and equality.

There are many who believe that technological innovation is a force for increasing social inequality. New technologies tend to benefit those who are already rich enough to afford them or powerful enough to control them, and because technology is a source of power, its control by elites only serves to enhance their dominance over other members of society. On the other side of this argument, there are those who believe that technological progress is the engine of human progress and that technological innovation acts as a great leveler of society by breaking down the barriers erected by privilege and allowing for a more equitable distribution of knowledge and power.

Source: "Technology and Social Justice," a Carnegie Council on Ethics and International Affairs lecture, delivered November 5, 1997, by Freeman Dyson. Copyright © 1998 Carnegie Council on Ethics and International Affairs. Reprinted by permission.

Dyson examines the evidence for each of these general perspectives and ends up endorsing a qualified "techno-optimist" answer—that "ethics must guide technology toward social justice." Dyson supports his conclusion through a combination of historical reflection, personal anecdotes, and the exercise of technological and moral imagination.

FOCUS QUESTIONS

1. Dyson begins his discussion by giving some historical examples of technological innovations that he claims have increased social justice. What are his examples? Can you think of any others?
2. Why does Dyson believe that "the advent of electrical appliances liberated the servants and shackled their mistresses"?
3. Dyson argues that ethical and religious values can and should influence technological change, and he mentions Max Weber's seminal work *The Protestant Ethic and the Spirit of Capitalism* as providing evidence that this is possible. Do you agree?
4. In the concluding section, Dyson presents a vision in which the nascent technologies of solar energy, genetic engineering, and global Internet communications are combined to help billions of poor people all over Earth to attain a higher standard of living. Do you think this vision is attainable? Why or why not?

KEYWORDS

biomass energy, genetic engineering, high-tech medicine, the Human Genome Project, inequality, the Internet, national health care, social justice, solar energy

It is easy to find historical examples illustrating the thesis that technology may have something to contribute to social justice. In the fourteenth century the new technology of printing changed the face of Europe, bringing books and education out of the monasteries and spreading them far and wide among the people. Printing gave power to the Bible and led directly to the Protestant Reformation in Northern Europe. One may question whether Luther's Germany and Shakespeare's England enjoyed social justice, but they were certainly closer to it than the medieval Germany and England out of which they grew. Luther and Shakespeare brought at least the idea of justice—if not the reality—to ordinary citizens outside the nobility and the priesthood. The Protestant ethic, which took root in Germany, England, Holland, and Scandinavia with the help of printed books, carried with it a perpetual striving for social justice, even if the Utopian visions were seldom achieved.

More recent technologies that contributed in a practical way to social justice were those of public health—clean water supplies, sewage treatment, vaccination, and antibiotics. These technologies could only be effective in protecting the rich from contagion and sickness if they were also available to the poor. Even if the rich and powerful receive preferential treatment, as they usually do, the benefits of public health technology are felt to some extent by everybody. In countries where public health technologies are enforced by law, there is no large gap in life expectancy between rich and poor.

The technology of synthetic materials has also helped to erase differences between rich and poor. Throughout history, until the nineteenth century, only the rich could afford to dress in brilliant colors, furs, and silk. Fine clothes were a badge of privilege and wealth. In the nineteenth century the chemical industry produced artificial dyestuffs. The twentieth century added artificial fur and silk and many other synthetic fabrics cheap enough for working-class women to afford. No longer can one tell a woman's social class by her clothes. It is a measure of social justice in modern societies that the children of the rich now dress down, imitating the style of the majority both in clothes and in behavior.

Household appliances are another technology with a tendency towards social justice. When I was a child in England in the 1920s, my mother employed four full-time servants: a cook, a housemaid, a nursemaid, and a gardener. We didn't consider ourselves rich. My father was a schoolteacher. We were an average middle-class family. In those days an average middle-class family needed four servants to do the hard manual work of cooking, cleaning, child care, and gardening. To do all this work a whole class of people existed who spent their lives as domestic servants. The professional and intellectual classes to which we belonged were riding on the backs of the servant class. Because of the servants, my mother had leisure to organize socially useful projects, such as a club for teenage girls and a birth control clinic. The birth control clinic was undoubtedly a godsend to the women who came to it for instruction in the art of not having unwanted babies. But it did not in any way narrow the gulf between her and them. She always spoke of her birth control clientele like a mistress speaking of servants.

My mother was a kind mistress and treated the servants well, according to the standards of the time, but the servants knew their place. They knew that if they disobeyed orders or answered back, they would be out on the street. Now, like the antebellum South, the servant class in England is gone with the wind, and the wind that blew it away was not the ravaging invasion of Sherman's army, but the peaceful invasion of an army of electric stoves, gas heaters, vacuum cleaners, refrigerators, washing machines, drying machines, garbage disposals, freezers, microwave ovens, juicers, choppers, and disposable diapers. The technology of household appliances made servants unnecessary, and, at the same time, the children of the servant class began to go to college and make the transition to the middle class. The transition was not painless, but it was less painful than a civil war. It was a big step on the road to social justice.

I remember with great fondness the nursemaid, Ethel, who cared for me as a young child. She had left school, as girls of the servant class did in those days, at the age of fourteen. When my sister and I were safely in bed in the night nursery, we sometimes heard the "putt, putt, putt" of a motorbike approaching the house, stopping, and then driving away into the night. That was Ethel's young man taking her out for the evening. The motorbike was the first harbinger of the approaching social revolution. The motorbike was the technology of upward mobility. After Ethel left us and married the young man, she had three daughters of her own, and all of them went to college. One of her grandsons is now a university professor.

Those are enough examples to show that technology can be helpful in the struggle for social justice. But in each case, as Edward Tenner tells us in his book Why Things Bite Back, a step forward in technology tends to bring with it an unexpected step backward. A step forward for some people frequently brings with it a step backward for others. And it often happens that when an old privileged class of people is dispossessed and the blessings of wealth and power are spread more equally, the burdens of equalization fall disproportionately upon women. When the revolutions accompanying the technology of printing destroyed the wealth and power of the monasteries over much of Europe, both male and female orders were dispossessed, but the nuns lost more than the monks. Nuns in the old convents were in many ways more free than wives in the new Protestant communities. The old monastic society provided a refuge where women of outstanding ability—for example, Hildegard of Bingen—had access to higher education. Sheltered and supported by the monastic orders, women could follow their vocations as scholars and artists. When the monasteries were dissolved, nuns had to find shelter in other people's homes, either as wives or as servants. The new secular society replaced the monasteries with colleges and universities. In the universities men scholars could find shelter and security, but there was no place for women.

The technology of household appliances, likewise, brought a step backward to the stratum of society to which my mother belonged, the women of the middle class. My mother would be considered by the standards of today a thoroughly liberated woman. Trained as a lawyer, she helped to write the Act of Parliament that opened the professions in England to women. With the help of her servants, she could take care of her husband and children without being confined to the home. She was free to pursue her interests outside the home—her girls' club and birth control clinic. But she was by no means the most liberated of the women in our family. I had a collection of aunts who were in various ways more liberated than my mother. All of them had husbands and most of them had children, but this did not stop them from being liberated. All of them were more adventurous than their husbands. My Aunt Margaret was trained as a nurse and rose to become a matron, which meant that she was the managing administrator of a large hospital. My Aunt Ruth was a figure skater of international repute who kept an Olympic silver medal among her trophies. My Aunt Dulcibella was the first woman in England to receive an airplane pilot's license. She and her husband had an airplane which they used for traveling around in Africa. They loved Africa, and their lifestyle would have fit in very well with the group of adventurers that Michael Ondaatje describes in his novel *The English Patient.* My Aunt Dulcibella was also a professional actress, and if she had only been eighty years younger, she might have had a starring role in *The English Patient* movie. We did not consider these aunts of ours to be unusual. It was normal at that time for middle-class women to do something spectacular. My mother, with her birth control clinic, was the quiet one, the least daring of the four.

Now, consider what happened to the next generation of middle-class women in England and the United States. Thirty years later, in the 1950s, the servants were gone and the electrical appliances were taking their place. For wives and mothers of the middle class, this was a big step backward. Appliances do not cook the dinner, clean the house, do the shopping, and mind the baby. The middle-class women of the 1950s were far less liberated than their mothers. The liberation that my mother's generation achieved had to be fought for all over again. Even now, in the 1990s, women are only partially liberated. To achieve partial liberation, they have replaced the old domestic servants with day care centers, cleaning ladies, and *au pair* girls imported from overseas. Electrical appliances help, but they only do a small part of the job.

The Institute of Advanced Study, where I have spent my working life, is a peculiar institution with a small permanent faculty. The faculty is supposed to be representative of the most distinguished men and women in academic life. Unfortunately, we have always found it difficult to appoint women to the faculty. The original faculty, appointed in the 1930s, contained one woman, the archaeologist Hetty Goldman. I remember her vividly. She was a formidable lady, small in stature and large in spirit, who led excavations of ancient sites in Turkey, ruling over small armies of Turkish laborers with an iron hand. Her colleagues used to say she was the equal of any two male archaeologists. There was never the slightest doubt that she had the "right stuff" to be an Institute professor. She was a natural leader in her own eyes and in ours. She belonged to my mother's generation of liberated women. She grew up, like my mother, in a society of women with servants. When she retired in 1947, she was not replaced. For almost forty years the Institute faculty was entirely male. In 1985, the sociologist Joan Scott became the second woman to join the faculty. And in 1997 the historian Patricia Crone became the third.

The history of our faculty encapsulates in a nutshell the history of women's liberation: a glorious beginning in the 1920s; a great backsliding in the 1950s; a gradual recovery in the 1980s. It is not altogether fanciful to blame the technology of household appliances for the backsliding. The advent of electrical appliances liberated the servants and shackled their mistresses.

HIGH-TECH MEDICINE AND COMPUTERS

I have discussed four technologies that led to large expansions of social justice. Although each of them had compensating negative effects, especially on women, the overall effects of all of them were predominantly positive. It will be just as easy to find examples of technologies that had negative effects. One could mention the technologies of gas chambers and nuclear weapons, useful for the convenient extermination of people to whom we do not wish to extend the benefits of social justice. But the more troubling examples are two of the technologies that are making the most rapid progress today: high-tech medicine and high-tech communication.

All of us who live in the United States are familiar with the ugly face that high-tech medicine presents to the patient: the initial telephone call answered by a machine rather than a human voice; the filling out of forms in the office; the repetitive answering of questions; the battery of routine chemical and physical tests carried out by technicians wearing rubber gloves; and finally, the abbreviated contact with the physician. It is all very different from the old-fashioned practice of medicine, when doctors were personal friends and advisers to patients and sometimes even made house calls. The face of high-tech medicine is ugly even when the patient is rich, and uglier still when the patient is poor. The ugliness results from many factors working together. First, the prevalence of malpractice litigation, which destroys trust, compelling doctors to conform to rigid rules and surrounding them with layers of bureaucratic documentation. Second, the high cost of the equipment that high-tech medicine demands, forcing medical centers to adopt elaborate cost-accounting systems. Third, the size of the staff needed to operate a high-tech center, with many doctors qualified in narrow specialties so that the patient rarely gets to see the same doctor twice. Fourth, the overwhelming cost of hospitalization, allowing patients a bare minimum of days for rest and recuperation after major illness or surgery. These factors, together, led to the situation that confronts the patient today. What the patient needs most, but finds least, is personal attention.

Since personal attention has become the scarcest resource in high-tech medicine, it is inevitable that it should be distributed unequally. The majority of advanced countries have national health services that attempt, with varying degrees of success, to distribute medical attention fairly. In countries with national health services, medical attention is theoretically available to everybody. This is what the ethic of social justice demands. But the escalating cost of medical attention makes social justice more and more difficult to achieve. One way or another, as personal attention becomes scarcer, people of status tend to receive more of it and people without status to receive less. The national health services in countries where they exist make valiant efforts to preserve the ideal of social justice, but the march of medical technology and the concomitant increase of costs constantly erode the ideal. In the United States, which never had a national health service and does not pretend to distribute medical resources equally, the prospects for social justice are far worse. In the United States a medical system based on the ethic of the free market inevitably favors the rich over the poor, and the inequalities grow sharper as the costs increase.

I have seen in my own family a small example of the dilemma that the growth of high-tech medicine presents to physicians. One of my daughters is a cardiologist. For many years she worked in state-supported hospitals taking care of patients as they flowed through the system, working brutally long hours and still having little time for personal contact with her patients. Her patients in the public hospitals were predominantly poor and uninsured. Many of them had AIDS or gunshot wounds in addition to cardiac problems. The public health system, such as it was, was designed to get these patients out of the hospital and back on the streets as fast as possible. Last year my daughter was offered a job in a private cardiology practice with far shorter hours, better pay and working conditions, and an expectation of long, continued care of her patients. She accepted the offer without much hesitation. She is much happier in her new job. Now, for the first time, she knows her patients as individuals and can tailor their treatments to their individual histories and personalities. She feels that she is a better doctor, and her new job gave her the flexibility to take time off to have her first baby last July. From almost every point of view, her jump into private practice was a wise move. Her only problem was a small twinge of conscience for having abandoned the poor to take care of the rich. In the private practice her patients are not all rich, but they are all paying for the personal attention that she is now able to give them. She was forced to make a choice between social justice and professional satisfaction, and social justice lost. I don't blame her. But in a socially just society, physicians would not be forced to make such choices.

Similar dilemmas, not so stark as the dilemmas of medical practice but equally important, exist in the world of high-tech computing and communications. Here, too, there is a clash between the economic forces driving the technology and the needs of poor people. Access to personal computers and the Internet is like medical insurance: almost everybody needs it, but most poor people don't have it. The people who are wired, the people who browse the World Wide Web and conduct their daily lives and businesses on the Net, have tremendous economic and social advantages. Increasingly, jobs and business opportunities are offered through the Internet. Access to the Internet means access to well-paying jobs. People who are not wired in are in danger of becoming the new servant class. The gulf between the wired and the unwired is wide, and growing wider.

The computer and software industries are driven by two contradictory impulses. On the one hand, they sincerely wish to broaden their market by making computers accessible to everybody. On the other hand, they are forced by competitive pressures to upgrade their products constantly, increasing their power and speed and adding new features and new complications. The top end of the market drives the development of new products, and the new products remain out of the reach of the poor. In the tug of war between broadening the market and pampering the top-end customer, the top-end customer usually wins.

The problem of unequal access to computers is only a small part of the problem of inequality in our society. Until the society is willing to attack the larger problems of inequality in housing, education, and health care, attempts to provide equal access to computers cannot be totally successful. Nevertheless, in attacking the general problems of inequality, computer access might be a good place to start. One of the virtues of the new technology of the Internet is that it has an inherent tendency to become global. The Internet easily infiltrates through barriers of language, custom, and culture. No technical barrier stops it from becoming universally accessible. To provide equality of access to the Internet is technically easier than providing equality of access to housing and health care. Universal access to the Internet would not solve all our social problems, but it would be a big step in the right direction. The Internet could then become an important tool for alleviating other kinds of inequality.

THE PROTESTANT ETHIC AND THE SPIRIT OF CAPITALISM

Up to now I have been talking as if technology came first and ethics second. I have been describing historical events in which technological changes occurred first and then increases or decreases of social justice occurred as a consequence. I depicted technological change as the cause of ethical improvement or deterioration. This view of history is opposed to the view propounded by Max Weber in his seminal book *The Protestant Ethic and the Spirit of Capitalism*. Weber argued that the Protestant ethic came first and the rise of capitalism and the technologies associated with it came second. Weber's view has become the prevailing view of modern historians. Weber said that ethics drove technology. I say that technology drives ethics.

I am not trying to prove Weber wrong. His historical vision remains profoundly true. It is true that the religious revolutions of the sixteenth century engendered an ethic of personal responsibility and restless inquiry, an ethic that encouraged the growth of capitalistic enterprise and technological innovation. It was no accident that Isaac Newton, the preeminent architect of modern science, was also a Protestant theologian. He took his theology as seriously as his science. It was no accident King Henry VIII, the man who brought the Protestant revolution to England, also endowed the college where Newton lived and taught. Henry and Isaac were kindred spirits—both were rebels against authority, enemies of the Pope, tyrants, supreme egoists, suspicious to the point of paranoia, believers in the Protestant ethic, and in love with technology. Henry loved to build ships and Isaac loved to build telescopes. It is true that ethics can drive technology. I am only saying that this is not the whole truth, that technology can also drive ethics, that the chain of causation works in both directions. The technology of printing helped to cause the rise of the Protestant ethic just as much as the Protestant ethic helped to cause the rise of navigation and astronomy.

I am not the first to take issue with Weber on this question. The historian Richard Tawney also studied the interrelationships of religion and capitalism and came to conclusions similar to mine. He held Weber in high esteem and contributed a foreword to the English translation of *The Protestant Ethic and the Spirit of Capitalism.* Here are the concluding sentences of Tawney's foreword: "It is instructive to trace with Weber the influence of religious ideas on economic development. It is not less important to grasp the effect of economic arrangements accepted by an age on the opinion which it holds of the province of religion." Tawney's view is that technology influenced religion as strongly as religion influenced technology. Since my view of history is closer to Tawney's than to Weber's, I now ask the question: How can we push new technologies into directions conducive to social justice? How can we make ethics drive technology in such a way that the evil consequences are minimized and the good maximized? I shall hope to persuade you that the situation we are in is not hopeless, that new technologies offer us real opportunities for making the world a happier place.

THE SUN, THE GENOME, AND THE INTERNET

Finally, I turn to the positive side of my message. Technology guided by ethics has the power to help the billions of poor people all over the earth. My purpose is to help push technology in a new direction, away from toys for the rich and toward necessities for the poor. The time is ripe for this to happen. Three huge revolutionary forces are being harnessed just in time for the new century: the sun, the genome, and the Internet. These three forces are strong enough to reverse some of the worst evils of our time. The evils I am hoping to reverse are well known to you all. All over the earth, and especially in the poor countries to the south of us, millions of desperate people leave their villages and pour into overcrowded cities. There are now ten mega-cities in the world with populations twice as large as New York City. Soon there will be more. We all know that the increase of human population is one of the causes of the migration to cities. The other cause is the poverty and lack of jobs in villages. Both the population explosion and the poverty must be reversed if we are to have a decent future. Many experts on population say that if we can mitigate the poverty, the population will stabilize itself, as it has done in Europe and Japan. I am not an expert on population, so I won't say any more about that. I am saying that poverty can be reduced by a combination of solar energy, genetic engineering, and the Internet. Our task in the next century is to put the new technologies to work in the cause of social justice. Social justice means making the new technologies accessible to everyone, to bring wealth to poor countries and hope to poor people.

I have seen with my own eyes what happens to a village when the economic basis of life collapses, and I have seen how the economic basis of village life can be revived. My wife grew up in Westerhausen, a village in East Germany that was under Communist management. The Communist regime took care of the village economy, selling the output of the farms to Russia at fixed prices, which gave the farmers economic security. The village remained beautiful and, on the whole, pleasant to live in. Nothing much had changed in the village since 1910. One thing the Communist regime did was organize a zoo, with a collection of animals maintained by a few professionals with a lot of help from the local school children. The village was justly proud of its zoo. The zoo was subsidized by the regime so it did not need to worry about being unprofitable. I visited the village under the old regime in 1975 and found it very friendly. Then came 1990 and the unification of Germany. Overnight, the economy of the village was wrecked. The farmers could no longer farm because nobody would buy their products. Russia could not buy because the price had to be paid in West German marks. German consumers would not buy because the local produce was not as good as that available in the supermarkets. The village farmers could not compete with the goods pouring in from France and Denmark. So the farmers were out of work. Most of the younger generation moved out of the village to compete for jobs in the cities, and most of the older generation remained. Many of them, both old and young, are still unemployed. The zoo, deprived of its subsidy, collapsed.

The sad exodus that I saw in the village of Westerhausen when I visited there in 1991 is the same exodus that is happening in villages all over the world. Everywhere the international market devalues the work of the village. Without work, the younger and the more enterprising people move out.

In the seven years since the unification, Westerhausen has slowly been recovering. Recovery is possible because of the process of gentrification. Wealthy people from the local towns move in and modernize the homes abandoned by the farmers. Cottages are demolished to make room for two-car garages. Ancient and narrow roads are widened. The village will survive as a community of nature lovers and commuters. Lying on the northern edge of the Harz Mountains, it is close to the big cities of northern Germany and even closer to unspoiled mountain forests. Its permanent asset is natural beauty.

Two months ago my wife and I were back in the village. The change since we had last visited in 1991 was startling. We stayed in the elegant new home of a friend who had been in my wife's class in the village elementary school fifty years earlier. The village now looks well cared for and prosperous. The recovery from the disaster of 1990 has been slow and difficult, but it has been steady. The government did two things to mitigate the harshness of the free market: it allowed every homeowner to borrow money with almost zero interest from the government to modernize houses, and it allowed every farming cooperative to borrow money with almost zero interest to modernize farms. As a result, the houses that were not bought by outsiders are being modernized, and the few farmers who remained as farmers are flourishing. The zoo has been revived. In addition, there are some new enterprises. A Western immigrant has planted a large vineyard on a south-facing hillside and will soon be producing the first Westerhausen wines. My wife's family and many of her friends still live in the village. They gave us a warm and joyful welcome.

The probable future of Westerhausen can be seen in a thousand villages in England. The typical English village today is not primarily engaged in farming. The typical village remains beautiful and prosperous because of gentrification. Wealthy homeowners pay large sums of money for the privilege of living under a thatched roof. The thatching of roofs is one of the few ancient village crafts that still survives. The thatchers are mostly young, highly skilled, and well paid. The farmers who remain are either gentlemen amateurs, who run small farms as a hobby, or well-educated professionals, who run big farms as a business. The old population of peasant farmers, who used to live in the villages in poverty and squalor, disappeared long ago. Discreetly hidden in many of the villages are offices and factories engaged in high-tech industry. One of the head offices of IBM Europe is in the English village of Hursley not far from where I was born. In the villages of France, at least in the area I know around Paris, the picture is much the same. Wealth came to the villages because they have what wealthy people seek: peace, security, and beauty.

What would it take to reverse the flow of jobs and people from villages to megacities all over the world? I believe the flow can be reversed by the same process of gentrification that is happening in Westerhausen. To make gentrification possible, the villages themselves must become sources of wealth. How can a godforsaken Mexican village become a source of wealth? Three facts can make it possible. First, solar energy is distributed equitably over the earth. Second, genetic engineering can make solar energy usable everywhere for the local creation of wealth. Third, the Internet can provide people in every village with the information and skills they need to develop their talents. The sun, the genome, and the Internet can work together to bring wealth to the villages of Mexico, just as the older technologies—electricity and automobiles—brought wealth to the villages of England. Let me talk briefly about each of the three new technologies, in turn.

Solar energy is most available where it is most needed—in the countryside rather than in cities, and in tropical countries, where most of the world's population lives, rather than in temperate latitudes. The quantity of solar energy is enormous compared with all other energy resources. Each square mile in the tropics receives about 1,000 megawatts averaged over day and night. This quantity of energy would be ample to support a dense population with all modern conveniences. Solar energy has not yet been used on a large scale for one simple reason: it is too expensive. It cannot compete in a free market with imported coal, oil, and natural gas. The country that has used solar energy on the largest scale is Brazil, where sugar was grown as an energy crop to make alcohol as a substitute for gasoline in cars and trucks. Brazil protected and subsidized the local alcohol industry. The experiment was technically successful, but the cost was high. Brazil has now reverted to free-market policies, and the experiment is at an end. What the world needs is not high-cost subsidized solar energy, but solar energy cheap enough to compete with oil.

Solar energy is expensive today because it has to be collected from large areas and there is not yet a technology that covers large areas cheaply. One of the virtues of solar energy is the fact that it can be collected in many ways. It is adaptable to local conditions. The two main tools for collecting it are photoelectric panels, which convert sunlight directly into electricity, and energy crops, like the Brazilian sugar plantations, which convert sunlight into fuel. Roughly speaking, photoelectric collection is the method of choice for deserts, and energy crops are the method of choice for farmland and forests. Each method has its advantages and disadvantages. Photoelectric systems have high efficiency, typically between 10 percent and 15 percent, but are expensive to deploy and maintain. Energy crops have low efficiency, typically around 1 percent, and are expensive and messy to harvest. The electricity produced by photoelectric systems is intermittent and cannot be cheaply converted into storable forms of energy. Fuels produced from energy crops are storable and, therefore, more convenient.

To make solar energy cheap, we need a technology that combines the advantages of photovoltaic and biological systems. Two technical advances would make this possible. First, crop plants could be developed that convert sunlight into fuel with efficiency comparable to photovoltaic collectors, in the range of 10 percent rather than 1 percent. This would reduce the costs of land and harvesting by a large factor. Second, crop plants could be developed that do not need to be harvested at all. An energy crop could be a permanent forest with trees that convert sunlight to liquid fuel and deliver the fuel directly through their roots to a network of underground pipelines. If those two advantages could be combined, we would have a supply of solar energy that was cheap, abundant, ubiquitous, and environmentally benign.

The energy supply system of the future might be a large area of forest with species of trees varying from place to place to suit the local climate and topography. We may hope that substantial parts of the forest would be nature reserves closed to human settlement and populated with wildlife so as to preserve the diversity of the natural ecologies. But the greater part could be open to human settlement, with teeming towns and villages under the trees. Landowners outside the nature reserves would be encouraged, but not compelled, to grow trees for energy. If the trees converted sunlight into fuel with 10 percent efficiency, landowners could sell the fuel for \$10,000 per acre per year and easily undercut the present price of gasoline. Owners of farmland and city lots alike would have a strong economic incentive to grow trees. The future energy plantation need not be a monotonous expanse of identical trees in regular rows. It could be as varied and as spontaneous as a natural woodland, interspersed with open spaces and houses, villages, towns, factories, and lakes.

To make this dream of a future landscape come true, the essential tool is genetic engineering. At present, large sums of money are being spent on sequencing the human genome. The

Human Genome Project is motivated primarily by its medical applications. It will contribute enormously to the understanding and treatment of human diseases. It does not contribute directly to the engineering of trees. But alongside the human genome many other genomes are being sequenced—bacteria, yeast, worms, and fruit flies. For advancing the art of genetic engineering the genomes of simpler organisms are more useful than the human genome. Before long, we shall also have sequenced the genomes of the major crop plants—wheat, maize, and rice—and after that will come trees. Within a few decades, we shall have achieved a deep understanding of the genome, an understanding that will allow us to breed trees that will turn sunlight into fuel and still preserve the diversity that makes natural forests beautiful.

As soon as we can genetically engineer trees to use sunlight efficiently to make fuel, we shall learn to breed trees that convert sunlight into useful chemicals of other kinds, including silicon chips for computers and gasoline for cars. Economic forces will then move industries from cities to the country. Mining and manufacturing could be economically based on locally available solar energy, with genetically engineered creatures consuming and recycling the waste products. It might even become possible to build roads and buildings biologically, breeding little polyps to lay down durable structures on land in the same way as their cousins build coral reefs in the ocean.

But the third, and most important, of the triad of new technologies is the Internet. The Internet is essential to enable businesses and farms in remote places to function as part of the modern global economy. The Internet will allow people in remote places to make business deals, buy and sell, keep in touch with their friends, continue their education, and follow their hobbies and avocations, with full knowledge of what is going on in the rest of the world.

This will not be the Internet of today, accessible only to computer-literate people in rich countries and to the wealthy elite in poor countries. It will be a truly global Internet, using a network of satellites in space for communication with places that fiber optics cannot reach and connected to local networks in every village. The new Internet will end the cultural isolation of poor countries and poor people.

Two technical problems have to be solved to make the Internet accessible to almost everybody on a global scale: large-scale architecture and the problem of the "last mile." Large-scale architecture means choosing the most efficient combination of landlines and satellite links to cover every corner of the globe. The Teledesic system of satellite communication now under development is intended to be a partial answer to this problem. The Teledesic system has 280 satellites in a dense network of low orbits, allowing any two points on the globe to be connected with minimum delay. If the Teledesic system fails, some other system will be designed to do the job. The problem of the "last mile" is more difficult. This is the problem of connecting homes and families, wherever they happen to be, with the nearest Internet terminal. The problem of the last mile has to be solved piecemeal, with methods depending on the local geography and the local culture. An ingenious method of solving the last-mile problem in urban American neighborhoods has been introduced recently by Paul Baran, the original inventor of the Internet. Baran's system is called Ricochet and consists of a multitude of small, wireless transmitters and receivers. Each user has a modem that communicates by radio with a local network. The feature that makes the system practical is that the transmitters constantly switch their frequencies so as not to interfere with one another. The system is flexible and cheap, avoiding the large expense of laying cable from the Internet terminal to every apartment and every house. It works well in the environment of urban America. It remains to be seen whether it is flexible and cheap enough to work well in the environment of a Mexican village or a Peruvian barrio.

Suppose, then, we can solve the technical problems of cheap solar energy, genetic engineering of industrial crop plants, and universal access to the Internet. What will follow? My thesis is that the solution of those three problems will bring about a worldwide social revolution, similar to the revolution we have seen in the villages of England and Germany. Cheap solar energy and genetic engineering will provide the basis for primary industries in the countryside. After that, the vast variety of secondary and tertiary economic activities that use the Internet for their coordination—food processing, publishing, education, entertainment, and health care—will follow the primary industries as they move from overgrown cities to country towns and villages. And as soon as the villages become rich, they will attract people and wealth back from the cities.

I am not suggesting that in the brave new world of the future everyone will be compelled to live in villages. Many of us will always prefer to live in large cities or in towns of moderate size. I am suggesting only that people should be free to choose. When wealth has moved back to villages, people who live there will no longer be forced by economic necessity to move out, and people who live in megacities will no longer be compelled by economic necessity to stay there. Many of us who have the freedom to choose, like the successful stockbrokers and business executives in England and Germany, will choose to live in villages.

So this is my dream: Solar energy, genetic engineering, and the Internet will work together to create a socially just world in which every Mexican village is as wealthy as Princeton. Of course, that is only a dream. Inequalities will persist. Poverty will not disappear. But I see a hope that the world will move far and fast in the directions I have been describing. Ethics must guide technology toward social justice. Let us all help to push the world in that direction as hard as we can. It does no harm to hope.

1.3.4 Ethics and Technology: A Program for Future Research

DEBORAH G. JOHNSON AND THOMAS M. POWERS

The nineteenth-century essayist Thomas Carlyle declared that "man is a Tool-using animal.... Nowhere do you find him without Tools; without Tools he is nothing, with Tools he is all." We typically think of our tools as inert *things* that are only causally active in the world when put to use by human agents who wield them to accomplish specific purposes. Some authors whose work appears in this book—for example, Richard Sclove and Langdon Winner—have claimed that social and political values are embedded in certain technological artifacts that give them a particular kind of valence when deployed in the ways for which they were designed.

Philosophers of technology Deborah Johnson and Thomas Powers, however, take this line of thinking a step further and argue that "artifacts have intentionality, the property of 'aboutness' or directedness toward the actual world and a future designed world" that is distinct from the intentionality of their designers and users. The intentionality of artifacts is, on their view, built into their functions—that is, the ways in which they typically transform inputs into outputs of various kinds. Although the user's intentions and the context in which the artifact is being used also play a role in determining the outcome of a technologically assisted action, the intentionality embedded in the artifacts themselves is not an eliminatable component of

Source: From *Ethics and Technology, Encyclopedia of Science*, Vol. a–c, Macmillan Reference, Gale, a part of Cengage Learning.

the overall explanation of what takes place. This kind of extended notion of intentionality has been used to describe artificially intelligent computer programs and robots, but these authors think that the notion of surrogate agency, or derived intentionality, can be extended to designed artifacts of all kinds. If they are right, it opens up a rich new philosophical perspective on the designed world that we live in.

FOCUS QUESTIONS

1. What do Johnson and Powers mean when they claim that we are living in the anthropocene era?
2. What is a "reason explanation," and why is it necessary for the moral appraisal of action?
3. In what sense can artifacts be said to possess intentionality? How does the intentionality of artifacts differ from that of human agents?
4. What are some examples of how the explanation of a complex action requires reference to the threefold intentionality of designers, artifacts, and users?
5. Does the attribution of intentionality to artifacts entail that designers and users are relieved of moral responsibility? Explain why or why not.

KEYWORDS

anthropogenic, artifactual platform, intentionality, moral agency, surrogate agents, technological function

In this paper we present a program for future study of ethics and technology. Most generally, the analysis involves understanding the role of technology in moral action. On the one hand, technology shapes and is shaped by moral thought and action; on the other, this shaping is rarely acknowledged, let alone understood, by moral philosophers. Thus the program sketched here is aimed at making technology visible as an element of moral philosophy. We lay out a line of reasoning that uncovers the intentionality of the design of technological artifacts, and then we compare human moral action to features of the design and use of technological artifacts. This line of reasoning provides the groundwork for extensive future research. The program description is both a plan of study for our own research as well as a call for other scholars to turn their attention to the issues outlined.

In thinking about the nature of a technology, we argue that traditional philosophical theories of human action and ethics can be usefully extended to technology. Contemporary action theory has suggested a causal model of intentional behavior in humans, and we believe that (with modification) this model is applicable to technology. Indeed, when technology is viewed in relation to a causal model of intentional behavior, the moral nature of technological agency becomes apparent. Similarly, traditional notions from ethics, such as goodness, responsibility, and accountability, can be extended in order to understand technology in a new light.

THE ARTIFACTUAL PLATFORM

The world in which humans act and live is a world filled with human-made objects. In addition to the objects of the natural world, these human-made objects provide an enabling and inhibiting background for human thought and action, and for all of the arrangements of human life. This background influences and informs what we think, how we act, and how we arrange ourselves into units, organizations, and institutions.

By noting the presence of human-made objects, we introduce a distinction between the human-made and the natural world, though we readily admit the two are intertwined. Indeed, they are often so intertwined that it is difficult to separate them. The natural world has been dramatically affected by human activity, and technology is, at least in part, the manipulation of natural potential. Scientific research from the late twentieth and early twenty-first centuries suggests there is very little left of a natural world that is untouched by human agency; the balance, over human history, has clearly shifted toward a relatively larger class of human-made objects. In other words, we are living in the anthropocene, on an increasingly anthropogenic planet (Allenby 2004).

Even though, as a matter of ontology, it will be increasingly difficult to maintain a distinction between the classes of human-made and natural objects, the difference remains significant. The human-made world could be otherwise, and the future human-made world is, to some extent, a matter of human choice and human action. Indeed, work in "normative" design and engineering, seen in the universal design, green engineering, and appropriate technology movements, presupposes that there are morally better (and worse) ways to create the future human-made world. The analysis herein provides these normative enterprises with a philosophical footing.

Moral philosophy has always presumed the natural world as the background for human action and morality, but has failed to recognize the powerful role of the human-made world in moral thought and behavior. Rather than focusing on the background, moral philosophy has concentrated attention on human agency, and the presumption has been that moral action (through human beings) is part of the embodied world. The embodied world has been understood to consist both of natural things and human bodies, though, to be sure, some ethicists have acknowledged that morality might be different if humans had different sorts of bodies or acted in a natural world ordered in a different way. Moral philosophers have considered a typical action to consist of an agent (an embodied being) moving his or her body in some way, even if only in a very small way—a wink, a bit of pressure on a trigger, and so on. If the agent does not move his or her body in some way, then there is no action. Even speech acts require movement of the speech organs, and most philosophers have recognized that humans can commit moral wrongs with mere words.

So our starting place is the idea that human agency operates in an embodied world, noting how the embodied world includes both human-made and natural objects. But we want to call attention to the *normative* features of the human-made part and come to grips with the moral importance of technology in constituting the background for human action. We will call the human-made part of the embodied world, as far as it concerns human action, the *artifactual platform*. This platform is the class of constructed objects and systems of objects that are created by and come to influence human action.

Often, descriptions of action incorporate human-made objects into the action. For instance, when we say "John shot Bill," use of a gun is implicit; when we say "Mary flew to London," use of an airplane is presumed; and so on. This feature of descriptive language is what Joel Feinberg (1970) has called the "accordion effect." We can choose an expanded description that includes the artifact, or a collapsed version that conceals it.

When those who study action from the normative point of view use narrow or collapsed descriptions, the technological component is glossed over. What is missed is that particular movements of an agent's body could not have had their associated effects were it not for an artifact. Noting the artifacts involved in moral behavior is the first step in gaining a better understanding of the role of the artifactual platform in morality. Becoming aware of this platform allows us to see that a good deal of moral behavior is action *with* technology. In this respect, moral actions, agents, and patients are not sufficient for an ontology of morality; artifacts are also part of the moral world. The task of understanding the role of artifacts in morality is, then, a matter of recognizing the difference it makes for humans to live in a world with the particular artifacts that currently exist or might exist in the future.

Nevertheless, realizing that moral action takes place *with technology*, and on or from an artifactual platform, does not go far enough. As indicated, technological artifacts with their particular features are matters of human choice. Just as humans deliberate about and choose their actions, some humans (artisans and engineers) deliberate about and create artifacts; other humans (consumers and users) choose and employ artifacts that enable and constrain moral action. Human agency is significantly affected by technological artifacts. It may be augmented, constrained, or merely altered. The design, availability, and employment of technology shapes what humans can do, and what they end up doing.

What, then, is the significance of technology? Technology expands and constrains the range of human moral behavior, and changes the character of that behavior. Technology is far from neutral in its combination with human behavior. Can one say that it has moral agency? This question can be pursued by considering relations between human moral agency and technology.

THE MORAL AGENCY OF TECHNOLOGY

The question of the moral agency of technology can be used as an entry point for exploring the role of technology in morality. Grounding it in philosophical concepts, the analysis starts with the traditions of ethical theory and action theory and the accounts of human moral agency they provide. In ethical theory, the standard account of the responsibility of moral persons (acting without technology) says that individuals are primarily responsible for their voluntary, intended behaviors. In action theory, there is a broader account of intentionality, in which intentional states ("intendings" as well as desires, beliefs, plans, etc.) are the causes of action. The intentionality of these states is a property that relates them to states of affairs and objects in the actual world and in possible worlds. Intentionality, then, is "aboutness" or directedness. On this view, voluntary action or intended behavior is understood to be outward behavior caused by a complex of internal mental states. By stipulating the specific kind of intending, desiring, and believing that causes a particular action, philosophers have distinguished moral action from nonmoral behavior. Because the outward behavior in moral action is the result of these internal mental states, it is amenable both to a causal explanation and to a "reason explanation" (see Davidson 2001). That is, when we ask why someone acted in a particular way, he or she can offer antecedent intendings, beliefs, desires, and other intentional states as reasons for the action.

The standard philosophical account is spelled out in contemporary work in ethical theory and action theory, but the roots of the account are much older. The subject matter of moral appraisal even as far back as Aristotle (384–322 B.C.E.) has been understood to be intended, voluntary behavior. This is action, conduct, or the commission of a deed, as opposed to "mere" reaction or nonvoluntary behavior. In contemporary action theory, Aristotle's basic view is elaborated upon, and this produces the following conditions for moral action. First, there is a potential agent with an internal state. The internal state consists of intentional mental states, one of which is, necessarily, an intending to act. Together, the intentional states (e.g., belief that X is possible, desire to X, plus an intending to X) constitute a reason for X-ing. Second, there is an outward, embodied event—the agent does something, moves his or her body in some way. Third, the internal state is the cause of the outward event; that is, the movement of the body is rationally directed and is an action insofar as it is caused by an internal state. Fourth, the outward action has an outward effect. Finally, the effect has to be on a patient—the recipient of an action that can be harmed or helped. Moral patients are typically human beings, but the class may include other beings or things as well. Some ethicists now include higher functioning animals, entire species, and even ecosystems in the class of moral patients, and clearly technology does seriously affect ecosystems and nonhuman animals.

The convergence of these parts of ethical theory and action theory has produced a plausible account of the connection between thought and action, and has helped locate the focal point of moral agency. We adopt this account as the framework in which to consider the moral agency of technology. In other words, whether or not or in what ways technology has moral agency can best be revealed by comparing features of technology with the standard account of moral action as derived from ethical theory and action theory.

Interesting work has been done in the late twentieth and early twenty-first centuries along these lines, as philosophers have turned to consider the possibility of nonhuman moral agents (Allen, Varner, and Zinser 2000, Floridi and Sanders 2001, Brooks 2002, Kurzweil 1999, Danielson 1992). Most attention has been given to artificially intelligent computers as the best candidates for agency. Computers have drawn attention in part because of the interest in the precise nature of intelligence. Some philosophers of artificial intelligence (AI) seem to think that intelligence can emerge out of the complex states of computers. This view implies that the ability of a computer to generate intentional states on its own would go a long way toward making it like a human moral agent. (Researchers in AI are primarily interested in engineering robotic computers to do things such as sense, recognize, navigate, and modify, and not, in the main, concerned with the deeper implications of AI for a philosophical account of intelligence.) A thrust of the account here is to draw attention away from the project of considering intelligence and computers, and instead to explore technological artifacts more broadly, as entities that have intentional states that are not mental states.

At the heart of our argument for the moral significance of technology is the claim that artifacts have intentionality, the property of "aboutness" or directedness toward the actual world and a future designed world. One of the reasons so little attention has been given to ethics and technology seems to be a failure to recognize the intentionality designed into technological artifacts. On the one hand, the only type of intentionality of interest to ethicists has been the type found in the mental states of *human* agents. With its focus on human agents, ethical theory has not recognized the importance and relevance of the design and use of technological artifacts by human agents. On the other hand, scholars in science and technology studies have introduced the idea of technology having a kind of agency (Law 1987, Callon 1986). However, they have not recognized the ethical implications of this move. Nor have they related technological agency to the broader philosophical literature on action. The argument in this essay brings ethical theory and action theory to bear on the moral agency of technology.

Because the program outlined here builds on our claim that artifacts have intentionality, it will be helpful to discuss the theoretical apparatus traditionally used to describe intentionality in moral action. In order for a human action to be both open to "reason explanation" and subject to moral appraisal, there must be in the agent some collection of intentional mental states connected to the action in some fairly specific ways. Agents are subject to moral appraisal in virtue of those intentional acts that have morally relevant effects on moral patients. Intentional acts are caused by a variety of intentional states and/or entities: beliefs, desires, intendings, maxims, plans, and the like. An agent is a being who acts, with the cause of the action originating in the agent's mind as the complex of intentional states. The cause of the action is the primary reason for the action, and the cause as a whole can be seen as a collection of intentional states that serve as a "reason explanation" of the action. Intentional entities are entities that are capable of having intentional states; intentional actions are those actions that are caused by intentional states.

Our extension of this view of agency does not entail that artifacts have mental states or the ability to intend. We claim only that artifacts have intentionality or directedness at users and environments, and that this intentionality is causally efficacious. In proposing that intentionality is designed into technological artifacts, we avail ourselves of a quite general definition of intentionality, according to which it is the property of something, such that it is directed at or represents an object or state of affairs. The term *intentionality* is broadly construed so that intentional entities can be states of mind, sentences, speech acts, maps, or any designed object. Though this view of intentionality is quite broad, we nonetheless agree with the traditional view that humans are intentionality-generating beings. Their states of mind are directed at or about objects and states of affairs, and it is this original power of mind as intentionality generating that accounts for the intentionality in nonmental entities.

Humans have the ability to externalize their intentional states in speaking and writing. Spoken and written declarative sentences are intentional, just as are the beliefs that they express. While sentences and signs originate in the processes of the mental realm, these entities come into being only when they are expressed outwardly. Clearly, some intentional entities remain *internal* to humans, such as mental states of belief, desire, and visual perception. Internal intentional states explain the actions of human moral agents in that the intentional entities cause the actions and count as reasons why the agent committed the act. As for the external intentional entities, once they come into being and are (by definition) physically separated from the human who generated them, they still rely on a community of intentionality-generating beings (interpreters) in order to be intentional—in order for their intentionality to be grasped. Examples are maps, chairs, sentences in a natural language, and works of art. External intentional entities, like their internal counterparts, can cause and explain action. For example, the stop sign causes drivers to step on the brakes and bring their vehicles to a stop; the speech act of commanding individuals to behave in a certain way may cause individuals to do what is commanded; and so on.

The internal/external distinction in intentional entities takes into consideration the kinds of intentionality in human minds, in tangible expressions such as sentences and speech acts, and in representational states that are found in designed artifacts. Internal intentional states are those that necessarily remain mental; external intentional states, by contrast, are expressed in the form of entities that exist outside of the mind. An internal intentional state such as a belief often leads to an external intentional entity by means of a process not yet fully understood, but still assumed to be causal in nature. We argue that designed artifacts such as maps, computer programs, cars, and the like are externalized expressions of internal intentional states. They are intentional entities that cause action with morally relevant effects.

The most difficult part of the account here is the claim that things other than mental states can be about, be directed at, or represent objects and states of affairs. This claim seems noncontroversial when applied to sentences, speech acts, and maps. For instance, John R. Searle (2001) describes maps and house blueprints as intentional entities. Thus it should not be controversial when it comes to technological artifacts. While we claim that technological artifacts are intentional entities, we acknowledge that in the standard account of agency and action, agents have a specific intentional state of intending to perform a particular action, plus some more basic intentional states such as beliefs and desires. Because we claim that artifacts are intentional entities, the obvious question is what kind of intentionality do they have? That is, do they have something akin to the basic intentional states of humans, such as beliefs and desires, or something like the specific states of intending?

THE FUNCTIONALITY AND INTENTIONALITY OF ARTIFACTS

Our argument for the intentionality of technological artifacts is based on a particular understanding of the intentional states that artifacts can have. These intentional states cannot be fully understood without reference to the functions of the artifact. Accordingly, our account of the functionality of artifacts will be developed by answering three questions. What are functions in an artifact? How do they get into the artifact? What do users do with functions?

What Are the Functions in an Artifact?

Typically artifacts are thought to have functions, and their functionality is framed in terms of purposive or teleological explanation. While we do not reject this approach, we want to suggest a different view—one that allows for the flexibility we find in the design and use of artifacts. We base our understanding of the functionality of artifacts on the model of mathematical functions. An artifact has a function when it takes some input from a domain of human behaviors and produces a result within a range—what we generically call the output. The behavior of the user with the artifact fits the mathematical model of functions in that it consists of a relational triple: input, rule of transformation, and output. In the case of both mathematical functions and artifacts, one of two things can happen in the functional transformation. Either an input maps onto exactly one output (in which case the relation is one-to-one), or many different inputs map onto one output (a many-to-one relation). The definition of a function precludes the possibility that a particular input will deliver varying outputs (except in the case of artifacts such as slot machines whose one output is to produce varying outputs). This is an important condition for mathematical functions as well as artifactual ones. An artifact ceases to be useful (or even sometimes safe) when its output is unpredictable (except, again, when unpredictability is the designed output), and this is exactly what happens when a user gets different outputs for the exact same input on different occasions.

Here is an example of a technological function. A designer of a braking system for cars would model input by considering reaction times, leg position, pedal pressure, and stopping force for drivers who wish to control a typical car by pressing on the brake pedal. This process of design begins to reveal how the artifact becomes intentional; the input model is "about" driver capabilities and driving conditions—what we can gloss as "input" and "environment" aspects of the model. The transformation rule for the function, which is embodied in the mechanical parts of the braking system, turns those anticipated inputs into a result: The car slows at an appropriate speed. This is how the intentional states are actually manifested in the artifact; they are "materialized" in the way the artifact transforms the input. A successful braking system will incorporate realistic reaction times and pressures for the vast majority of drivers, and will reliably transform those inputs into the safe braking of a car under most conditions. A proper braking system will not map the different outcomes "stop the car" and "accelerate the car" to the exact same driver behavior. Design functions, like mathematical functions, are not one-to-many relations.

When an artifact *appears* to function differently with the same inputs, either the artifact is broken or there is a mistake about the sameness of inputs. The input mode for many complex artifacts such as computers is context dependent. For example, when the input of "striking the return key" on the keyboard yields different results at different times, this is because the computer is in different states during the respective inputs. In some programs, a query can be answered affirmatively by striking the return key. In others—word processors, for example—striking the return key places a hard return in a document. The lesson is that inputs are always tied to context. The condition that the artifactual functions borrow from mathematical ones reveals that there will never be more than one output for an *input in a context.* We may get spaces in some word-processing documents when we push the return key, and affirmations to queries when running other programs, but we will never get spaces sometimes and affirmations other times, in the exact same input context.

How Do Functions Get into an Artifact?

Crucial to this account is the fact that transformation rules of functions cannot be built into artifacts without applying intentional models of users and the world in which they operate.

There are two immediate senses in which the intentionality that begins with design is connected to technological artifacts in use. The act of design always requires intentionality—the ability of a designer to represent, model, perceive, and the like. Similarly, the use of an artifact—grasping a tool, following the user's guide—requires typical forms of cognition that feature intentionality. But there are deeper ways intentionality connects to designed functions and uses, ways that go beyond the intentionality of designers and users. When designers design artifacts, they poise them to behave in certain ways. Those artifacts *remain* poised to behave in those ways. They are designed to produce unique outputs when they receive inputs. They are directed at states of affairs in the world and will produce other states of affairs in the world when used. The telephone is "about" typical human fingers and ears, auditory capacities, and the physics of sound—it is intentional with respect to certain organisms and their environments. In a complicated way, the intentionality of the telephone is required to make it work as a communication device. But the telephone is also directed at certain social facts; it is about a world in which individuals want to talk with others who are beyond the reach of (unassisted) human voices. The telephone also requires that users memorize or keep a record of numbers attached to persons. Otherwise, a potential caller will not be able to use the telephone. Long after the designer has poised the artifact, the functions still reside in it and make complex actions possible. The argument here receives support from an analysis by Fred Dretske (1989) of what he terms the "design problem," as exemplified by how to get a mechanical system to do something that its designers find important, such as how to get a temperature indicator to be a switch for turning on a furnace.

What Do Users Do with Functions?

Users do not merely comply with the behavioral requirements designed into artifacts; they do not merely "satisfy" the model of use. They can add to the functions of an artifact by envisioning an unanticipated input that yields a novel output. This envisioning itself begins as an intentional state in the user, but it is then manifest in outward ways. An example of this is when someone picks up a television and throws it at an attacker to stop the attack. Here the user sees that by providing a particular kind of input (lifting and throwing), the television can be used to produce an output that it was not originally designed to produce.

The intentional states of artifacts are the result of the work of the artifact designer; designers *mold* intentionality into artifacts by concretizing the intentional models so that they enable the transformations promised by the functions. Users then deploy these functions by supplying inputs to the artifacts, under the prescribed conditions. Our argument is thus more than that the intentionality of designers and users becomes operative when artifacts get put to use. Our claim is that artifacts are in some sense chunks of intentionality, externalized by artifact designers and deployed by users in particular contexts.

When the intentionality and functionality of artifacts are seen in this light, it becomes difficult to locate precisely the agency in human actions with technological artifacts. There is intentionality in the mind of the artifact user, in the intentional states and functions of the artifact, and in the designer who created the intentionality and functionality embodied in the artifact. What may begin as the intentional model of a designer gets molded into an artifact and then deployed by the user. Hence, there is a complex of agency with human and nonhuman components.

We thus acquire a picture of moral action with technology as a complex combination of the intentionality of artifact designer, the intentionality of the artifact, and the intentionality of the user. Does this mean that artifacts are moral agents? If we return to the standard account of moral agency, it is now clear that artifacts meet most but not all of the conditions. Remember that on the standard account, human moral agency includes the stipulation of a potential agent with internal mental states, and one of these states is an intending to act. The agent does something, moves his or her body in some way, such that the internal states are the cause of the movement. The internal, mental states are thus also the reason for the action. The movement or behavior has an effect on a moral patient, someone or something that can be harmed (or helped).

Our analysis of human-action-with-artifact overlaps significantly with standard (nontechnological) human action, even though it locates agency in the triad of designer, artifact, and user. We have found that intentional states are spread out over designers, artifacts, and users, so that the action of the human-agent-with-artifact is caused by intentional states in each member of the triad. A complete reason explanation must include an account of the intentional states and functions of the artifact, because these states and functions play a causal role in the eventual action. The causal role of the artifact is necessary, but not sufficient, for the effect on the moral patient. True, artifacts alone are not agents, nor are their intentional states in any way internal mental states. Likewise, artifacts alone do not intend. But the intentional states of artifacts shape and cause external or embodied movement, both in terms of functional inputs of users and in terms of artifactual output. And intentional, caused, embodied movement can have morally relevant effects on patients. Thus, the intentionality and functionality of artifacts are important components of a full picture of moral action.

This account has implications for the notion of moral responsibility. Because philosophers and others may resist the idea of any kind of agency or even intentionality being attributed to technology because it may appear to deflect responsibility from human actors, it is appropriate to consider the issue of responsibility in a case study. Can technological artifacts be said to bear moral responsibility, or even to be morally good or bad entities?

AN ILLUSTRATION: THE MORAL EVALUATION OF COMPUTERS

At first glance, the idea of artifacts bearing moral responsibility appears implausible. There is, however, a form of human moral responsibility that is applicable to certain kinds of computer systems that may have broader application to other technologies. We refer here to the responsibility of human surrogate agents to their clients. Human surrogate agents are those who act on behalf of others. For example, lawyers, tax accountants, estate executors, and managers of performers and entertainers pursue the interests of their clients. The behavior of these agents is evaluated in terms of how well they pursue their client's interest while staying within the constraints and expectations associated with their roles. Like surrogate agents, computer systems pursue interests of their users; hence, their behavior can be evaluated in terms of how well they pursue the interests of their users.

If computer systems can be understood as surrogate agents for their human users, it would seem that role morality can be extended to computer systems, and this is a reason for attributing moral responsibility to computer systems and for morally evaluating such systems. In essence, the suggestion here is that the concept of role morality can be understood as a set of constraints on behavior, based on the interests of others, and can be applied to the functionality of particular computer systems. Just as human surrogate agents are evaluated in terms of whether they adequately understand and represent the point of view of their clients, one can evaluate computer systems in terms of how they represent and pursue the user's interests. Such an evaluation would involve many aspects of the system, including what it allows as user input and how it goes about implementing the interests of the user.

Consider the search engine surrogate that pursues a user's interest in finding web sites on a particular topic. Whether the search engine lists web sites in an order that reflects highest use, or fails to list some sites, or gives priority to sites for which the owner has paid to be listed—all of this can have moral implications (Introna and Nissenbaum 2000). We might say, then, that the computer system takes on a third-person, interested perspective, either of the user or of someone else. Several important questions arise. Does the system act on the actual user's interests, or on a restricted conception of the user's interests? Does the system competently pursue the user's interests, without pursuing other, possibly illegitimate interests such as those of advertisers, computer hardware or software manufacturers, government spying agencies, and the like? Are faulty or buggy computer systems analogous to misbehaving human surrogate agents? Do they fail to do the tasks (or to adequately do the tasks) that users employ them to do?

The foregoing suggests the kind of moral evaluation that can be made when computer systems are seen as surrogate agents. Tax preparation programs perform like tax advisers; contract-writing programs perform some of the tasks of attorneys; Internet search engines seek and deliver information like information researchers or librarians. Other types of programs and computer systems serve the interests of users, but there are no corresponding human surrogate agents with whom to compare them. Spyware programs uncover breeches in computer security, but when they do so for the user, they do not replace the tasks of a private detective or security analyst. Increasingly, computer systems do more for us than human surrogates could do. This is why it is all the more important to have a framework for morally evaluating computer systems, especially a framework that acknowledges that computer systems can do an incompetent job of pursuing the interests of their users and can misbehave in their work on behalf of users.

To claim that computer systems (and possibly other technologies) have moral responsibility and can be morally evaluated is *not* to claim that the responsibility or blameworthiness of users or system designers is thereby diminished. We anticipate that the standard response to our argument will be that the attribution of responsibility to various agents is a zero-sum situation—that designers are "let off the hook" when we turn to the moral evaluation of computer systems. In response, we deny that moral evaluation is zero sum. Computer systems behave. Their behavior is intentional, and it can have effects on humans and can be morally appraised independently of an appraisal of their designers' behavior. What the designer does and what the computer does (in a particular context) are different, albeit closely related. To think that only human designers are subject to morality is to fail to recognize that technology has intentionality, and its intentionality plays a causal role in the effects that computer systems can have on moral patients.

So the point of emphasizing the moral responsibility and moral evaluation of computer systems is not to deflect responsibility away from system designers or users. Because a computer system is conceptually distinct from the computer system designer and user, all three should come in for moral scrutiny. Computer systems are an interesting case here because they are becoming increasingly sophisticated, in both technical and social dimensions. Though the first computer systems may have been simple utilities or "dumb" technologies designed to help humans connect phone calls, calculate bomb trajectories, and do arithmetic, computer systems are increasingly taking over roles once occupied by human surrogate agents. This continuous change would suggest that, somewhere along the way, computer systems changed from mere tool to component of a complex agent. Now, it can no longer be denied that computer systems have displaced humans—both in the manufacturing workforce, as has long been acknowledged, and more recently in the service industry. It would be peculiar, then, for users to recognize that computers have replaced human service workers who have always been supposed to have moral constraints on their behavior, but to avoid the ascription of similar moral constraints to computer systems.

We introduced this discussion of computer systems as a way of opening up the possibility of technology bearing moral responsibility and being subject to moral evaluation. The challenge of the program we propose is to explore this territory in relation to both smart as well as more mundane (less complicated) technologies. The larger program will have to come to grips with the triad involved in moral action and agency: designers, artifacts, and users.

CONCLUSION

The line of reasoning developed here sketches an account of the role of technology in moral action. We began with the distinction between natural and human-made objects and noted that moral philosophy has neglected the importance of the artifactual platform in which human action occurs. We argued that artifacts have intentionality and gave an account of this intentionality using the functionality of artifacts and their directedness at states of affairs in the world; in this way, artifacts are comparable to speech acts. Building on our account of the intentionality of artifacts, we considered whether artifacts have moral agency. Here we argued that there are three forms of intentionality at work in moral action with technology: the intentionality of the artifact designer, the intentionality of the artifact, and the intentionality of the artifact user. Allowing for the agency of artifacts does not diminish the responsibility of human actors. To address the issue of the responsibility and moral evaluation of artifacts, we examined computer systems as surrogate agents. We argued that the responsibility of human surrogate agents provides a good model for making sense of the responsibility of computer systems. Computer systems can be morally evaluated in terms of their roles in relation to users. We have long known that computer systems can err; our account suggests that they can also misbehave.

The set of issues discussed here constitute a program for future research. Technology has not been a significant focus in moral philosophy, and yet it shapes the human moral universe in significant ways. Attention to technology promises to open up a range of interesting, complex, and important philosophical issues.

BIBLIOGRAPHY

Allen, Colin; Gary Varner; and Jason Zinser. (2000). "Prolegomena to Any Future Artificial Moral Agent." *Journal of Experimental and Theoretical Artificial Intelligence* 12(3): 251–261.

Allenby, Braden R. (2004). "Engineering and Ethics for an Anthropogenic Planet." In *Emerging Technologies and Ethical Issues in Engineering.* Washington DC: National Academies Press.

Brooks, Rodney A. (2002). *Flesh and Machines: How Robots Will Change Us.* New York: Pantheon.

Callon, Michel. (1986). "Some Elements of a Sociology of Translation: Domestication of the Scallops and the Fishermen of St. Brieuc Bay." In *Power, Action, and Belief: A New Sociology of Knowledge?* ed. John Law. London: Routledge and Kegan Paul.

Danielson, Peter. (1992). *Artificial Morality: Virtuous Robots for Virtual Games* London Routledge.

Davidson, Donald. (2001). *Essays on Actions and Events*, 2nd edition. Oxford: Clarendon Press.

Dretske, Fred. (1989). "Reasons and Causes" *Philosophical Perspectives* 3: 1–15.

Feinberg, Joel. (1970). "Action and Responsibility" Chap 6 in *Doing and Deserving Essays in the Theory of Responsibility.* Princeton, NJ: Princeton University Press.

Flondi, Luciano, and J. W. Sanders. (2001). "Artificial Evil and the Foundation of Computer Ethics." *Ethics and Information Technology* 3(1) 55–66.

Introna, Lucas D., and Helen Nissenbaum. (2000). "Shaping the Web: Why the Politics of Search Engines Matters." *Information Society* 16(3): 169–185.

Johnson, Deborah G., and Thomas M. Powers. (2005). "Computers as Surrogate Agents." In *Information Technology and Moral Philosophy*, eds. Jeroen Van Den Hoven and John Wechert. Cambridge: Cambridge University Press.

Kurzweil, Ray. (1999). *The Age of Spiritual Machines: When Computers Exceed Human Intelligence.* New York: Viking.

Law, John. (1987). "Technology and Heterogeneous Engineering: The Case of Portuguese Expansion." In *The Social Construction of Technological Systems*, eds. Wiebe E. Bijker, Thomas P. Hughes, and Trevor J. Pinch. Cambridge, MA: MIT Press.

Searle, John R. (2001). *Rationality in Action.* Cambridge, MA: MIT Press.

PART TWO

Contemporary Technology and the Future

2.1 GLOBALIZATION AND ECONOMIC DEVELOPMENT

2.1.1 The World Is Flat

THOMAS L. FRIEDMAN

Thomas Friedman, the Pulitzer Prize–winning foreign affairs columnist for the *New York Times,* is one of the most astute and prolific observers of the relationship between technology and globalization. In his previous book on this topic, *The Lexus and the Olive Tree: Understanding Globalization* (1999), a portion of which was reprinted in the last edition of this reader, Friedman argued that "globalization has its own defining technologies: computerization, miniaturization, digitization, satellite communications, fiber optics, and the Internet, which reinforce its defining perspective of integration." His view at that time was that these technologies have changed the rules of the game for multinational corporations by making innovation and the ability to adapt to rapid change the keys to success in the global marketplace.

But six years later in his *The World Is Flat: A Brief History of the Twenty-First Century* (2005), Friedman has deepened and sharpened his analysis of the synergies created by these technological innovations and advances the claim that at the beginning of the twenty-first century we are embarking on a new age of globalization, what he calls Globalization 3.0, that is flattening out the global playing field even more dramatically. The key "flatteners" are information technologies that allow for new forms of collaboration and cooperation from widely dispersed groups of individuals. These technologies, he thinks, are producing a "triple convergence" that is already transforming the way in which millions of people around the world are living and working. It is particularly important in Friedman's view that young people become aware of these changes because they are (1) empowering millions of tech-savvy young people from China and India, as well as young people from such developed countries as the United States, Canada, Western Europe, and Japan and (2) challenging them all to learn the new rules of the global economic system.

FOCUS QUESTIONS

1. What are Friedman's three eras of globalization, and what are their distinctive characteristics?
2. What were the key technological innovations that "flattened" the world, and how do they function to enable new forms of collaboration?
3. What are the three convergences made possible by these flattening technologies and their applications?

Source: From talk given to Carnegie Council For Ethics and International Affairs, April 6, 2005. Copyright © 2005. Reprinted by permission of the Carnegie Council on Ethics and International Affairs, www.carnegiecouncil.org.

4. Compare Friedman's analysis of the economic importance of these new information technologies to the analysis of the potential for new forms of deliberative democracy discussed by Cass Sunstein in Selection 2.2.1.

KEYWORDS

convergence, globalization, Netscape, open sourcing, outsourcing, supply chains, workflow

Let me give you the brief thesis. The first chapter of the book is called, appropriately, "While You Were Sleeping." As I pointed out in the *Times Magazine* the other day, the main argument here is that Christopher Columbus set sail in 1492 looking for, as we all know, a shorter route to India. That is where he was going. He had the *Nina,* the *Pinta,* and the *Santa Maria.* He never did find India, but he called the people he met Indians, nevertheless. He came home and told his wife, "Honey, I've accidentally discovered that the world is round."

I set off for India 512 years later. I knew just which direction I was going. I went east. I had Lufthansa business class and a GPS satellite that popped up in my seat. I came home and reported to my wife—and only my wife, and only in a whisper—"Honey, I've discovered accidentally that the world is flat."

The first chapter is really about all the encounters I had, first in India and then beyond. I kept going east, to Dalian, China, which is now the outsourcing capital of Japan. Japanese-speaking Chinese, by the tens of thousands, are now doing the backroom operations for many global companies, including G.E. and Microsoft, from Dalian, China, for the Japanese market.

Then I kept going east, to the McDonald's franchises that are in a pilot operation, where if you drive up to the McDonald's now and you say, "I want three milkshakes and four Big Macs and eighteen fries," you are actually talking to someone in Colorado—you are not talking to someone at that McDonald's—who is taking down your order electronically, and taking your picture, incidentally, and zapping your picture and your order to a processor inside that McDonald's, who actually prepares the food and hands it to you, corresponding to your picture. McDonald's discovered they saved thirty seconds on every order when they did that and drove their error rate down to massively low levels.

I kept going east. I called JetBlue to make a reservation. I knew what was going on. After I tried to make my reservation, I said to the woman on the phone, "Ma'am, could I ask you your name?" She said, "Sure. My name is Betty." I said, "Betty, where are you right now?" She said, "Honey, I'm up in my bedroom in Salt Lake City. I'm in my slippers and my bathrobe, and I'm looking out at this beautiful winter scene." David Neeleman, the founder of JetBlue, has set up a reservation system that basically is people—housewives and retirees—in Salt Lake City. If you call JetBlue, that is who you are talking to. It is a completely home-based reservation system.

As I kept moving east and seeing these flattening forces, I finally ended up back home in Washington, D.C.

Now, the basic meta-argument I make in this first chapter is that there have been three great eras of globalization. One I call Globalization 1.0. It was from 1492 to about 1800. It shrunk the world from a size large to a size medium. That era of globalization was built primarily around countries globalizing. The agent of globalization was Spain discovering America, Great Britain colonizing India, and Portugal in the East Indies and East Asia.

The second great era of globalization, I would argue, is around 1820, 1825—that was really the beginning of global arbitrage—until the year 2000. That era shrunk the world from a size medium to a size small. That era of globalization was built around companies globalizing. That was the dynamic agent, companies globalizing for markets and for labor.

What I am arguing in this book is that while you were sleeping—certainly while I was sleeping—we actually entered Globalization 3.0, which began in the year 2000—by accident, right at the turn of the millennium. This era is shrinking the world from a size small to size tiny, and leveling and flattening the playing field at the same time.

What is unique about this era is that it is not built around countries, and it is not built around companies. It is built around individuals. The new "new" thing about this era of globalization is that the dynamic agent is the individual and the small group's ability to globalize. Be advised, it is not going to be a bunch of white Western individuals. It is going to be individuals of all colors of the rainbow.

The second chapter of the book is the longest chapter. It is a third of the book. It is the one that took me the most time and really forced me to retool myself. It is a whole chapter devoted to answering that question that burned in me when I was doing those interviews in India. That question was, how did this happen?

That chapter is called "The Ten Days That Flattened the World"—it is really "The Ten Forces That Flattened the World." This is my attempt to explain what the forces were that created this level playing field. I have come up with ten. Let me go through them very quickly.

Day 1: The first flattener is 11/9—not 9/11, 11/9. In a wonderful cabalistic accident of dates, the Berlin Wall came down on 11/9, November 9, 1989. The fall of the Wall was a huge flattener. When the Wall was there, it was very hard—in fact, it was impossible—to actually see the world as a single flat space. But when the Wall was removed, suddenly you could see from one end of the world, metaphorically, to the other.

I daresay if you did a LexisNexis search of the term "globalization," before the Berlin Wall, you would find it rarely used, because, after all, who could have a global policy? You could have an Eastern policy, you could have a Western policy, but it was very hard to have a global policy when there was a wall in the way. So the fall of the Wall was hugely important for us to perceptually see and think of the world as a single space.

What I call this first flattener is, "When the Wall came down and the Windows came up." Windows operating system 3.0 shipped six months after the fall of the Berlin Wall. Those two things happened at the same time, giving us a universal graphical user interface from one end of the world to the other, to look at the world through. That was the first flattener.

Day 2: The second flattener occurred on 8/9/95, which I consider to be as important a day in our lifetime as the fall of the Berlin Wall. 8/9/95, August 9, 1995, is the day a small company in Mountain View, California, called Netscape, went public. Netscape's IPO was a transformative day in our lifetime, for three reasons:

1. Netscape going public gave us the Internet browser. The browser is that thing that allows us to illuminate and illustrate all the data, information, words, and music that are in those Web sites. It is what allowed us to browse the Internet and visually see what was there. It was a huge breakthrough, an invention by Mark Andreessen from the University of Illinois. That going public basically made the Internet open and accessible to everyone from grandma and grandpa to a five-year-old grandchild. It essentially gave us the Internet.

2. It gave us—this is a little more technical—a set of transmission protocols, kind of digital pipes, that made the Internet interoperable. You may recall, when you first started using the Internet, that you were on CompuServe and your wife was on AOL, and you had a hard time communicating. What Netscape did was, basically, commercialize a set of open standards that really made the Internet interoperable.

3. Third and most importantly, Netscape triggered the dot-com boom, which triggered the dot-com bubble, which triggered the crazy, wild, ridiculous, massive overinvestment in fiberoptic cable—$1 trillion in five years. Netscape came out at $28.00. It opened at $71.00. It closed the first day at $56.00. People all over America looked at that and said, "There is gold over them there hills." That started the dot-com

boom. That prompted every yahoo from Global Crossing to Lucent, to your local telephone company, to think that the demand for bandwidth is going to be infinite, and if the demand is going to be infinite, you can't lay down enough fiberoptic cable under the ocean and around the world. So every one of these companies tried to do just that. You and I, with our investment dollars, paid for it. The accidental result was that within five years of Netscape going public, Bangalore and Beijing and the Bronx had become next-door neighbors. We drove down the cost of transmitting words and music and data between all these points to zero. What the Netscape moment did, in sum, was bring people-to-people connectivity. People were able to connect with people elsewhere like never before.

Day 3: The next flattener I simply call **work-flow.** It is really my summary of all the software and standards—standards are very important—that connected all that bandwidth from those fiber-optic cables with all those PCs. Workflow is very important. Again, if you go back to the early 1990s, you may recall that the Carnegie Council here—their inventory department was running Microsoft Windows, but their membership department was running Novell. Each department was more efficient, because they were working on computers. There was just one problem: Their Novell computers couldn't talk to their Windows computers. So they were never as productive as they could be.

There was a revolution going on in the late 1990s, thanks to all kinds of digital pipes and things like middleware, that enabled applications to talk to applications. Suddenly, everyone's inventory department could talk to everyone's sales department without ever thinking about it. More importantly, Carnegie's sales department and inventory department could talk to the UN's inventory and sales departments, no matter what machine they were operating on and no matter what software they were running. That was a huge, huge revolution, because when applications could talk to applications, suddenly we could work together in whole new ways.

After these first three flatteners, we get what I call the "genesis" of the flat world. It happened right at the end of the 1990s when, suddenly, people could talk to people like never before and, at the same time, applications could talk to applications like never before. Put those two together and, willy-nilly, you have a global platform for multiple forms of collaboration. Suddenly, people can collaborate on more kinds of work, in more different ways, on more different days, and from more different places than ever before. The next six flatteners are the new forms of collaboration that immediately sprung from this platform.

Day 4: The first new form of collaboration was **outsourcing.** Suddenly, I can take the Carnegie Council's accounting department and move it to North Dakota, to Arizona, or to Bangalore, because when people-to-people and application-to-application can connect, I can move it anywhere—where the most efficient, effective, or cheapest producer can operate it.

Day 5: The second new form of collaboration was what I simply call **offshoring.** This existed before, but it has gone to a whole new level, basically, thanks to the flattening of the world. Offshoring is when I take my factory from Canton, Ohio, and move it lock, stock, and barrel to Canton, China, where it then gets integrated into my whole production operation. Offshoring dates from when China joined the World Trade Organization and from when India began to remediate all our computers for Y2K.

Day 6: The third great new form of collaboration is **open sourcing.** Now, I have a bunch of geeks sitting at home working for free, writing the next operating system, called Linux. How would you like to be Bill Gates? Your whole business model all these years—you are a tough businessman—is that anybody who comes up and tries to compete with you, you undercut them, because you are big and tough and you are Microsoft. Then one day you discover that your main competitor—Linux now has 15 percent of the operating-system market—is selling your product for free. It is kind of hard to undercut that, especially when all your other competitors are funding people to work on it for free, so they can get into your cash hoard. This is a whole new model of production. Some of you, I am sure, have kids in college. Ask them how many of them have downloaded Firefox. Firefox is a new browser. As we all know, the browser on all our computers is Internet Explorer, made by Microsoft. Through a very interesting collaboration last year, a nineteen-year-old at Stanford, working with a twenty-four-year-old in New Zealand, never having met face to face, collaborated in an open-source forum. The new browser they created was downloaded 10 million times in the first month. Firefox now has 5 percent of the browser market. In the book, I profile a remarkable young man, Brian Behlendorf, who was the leader of the Apache movement. All your computers basically operate on a Web server. The Web server is what goes to that Web site when you tell it to, to get the information there. Every Web site has to have a Web server to serve it up to your computer. The Web server that really runs 75 percent of the computers in America is called Apache. The chief of the Apache tribe is a young man named Brian Behlendorf. These people, in an open-source forum, produced a Web server that was so good, it basically prompted IBM to throw out its Web server and pay its own engineers to join the open-source chat room of Apache that produced today's standard Web server.

Open sourcing, a whole new form of collaboration. It is not just about Web servers. I use Wikipedia constantly. I don't know how many of you have used Wikipedia. It is an open-source dictionary and encyclopedia, where people simply contribute the entries on their own. It is self-corrective. If you have never dipped into the open-source world, I urge you to do so. It is going to be, I think, the main post-industrial forum of creative innovation.

Day 7: The fourth new form of collaboration I call **supply-chaining.** "Supply-chaining" is simply my word for Wal-Mart. Wal-Mart has designed a global supply chain down to the last atom of efficiency, so if you take an item off the shelf in Brooklyn, another is immediately made in Shenzhen, China. As you may have heard, if Wal-Mart were a country, it would be China's eighth-largest trading partner today.

Day 8: The fifth new form of collaboration that sprung off this platform I call **insourcing.** I had the most fun learning about this, actually. Insourcing is what UPS does. If you think the folks in the funny brown shorts in the funny brown trucks are just delivering packages, then you have not been paying attention to the little new logo on the side of that funny brown truck. You know what it says now? It doesn't say, "Packages delivered." It says, "Your world synchronized." What UPS does now is go inside your company—it is why I call it insourcing—and take over your whole internal logistics operation right up to your neck.

My favorite example: If you have a Toshiba laptop and your Toshiba laptop breaks, what do you do? You look at the warranty. It says, "Call 1-800-HELP." So you call 1-800-HELP, and when you call there, they tell you to take your Toshiba laptop down to the UPS store and send it to Toshiba, and they will repair it and send it back. What you don't know is that your Toshiba laptop goes from the UPS store to the UPS hub at Louisville Airport in Kentucky, their global headquarters, where in a clean room, in a hangar, at Louisville Airport, your Toshiba laptop is repaired by a UPS employee. Your Toshiba laptop never goes back to Toshiba. They don't want to see it. They insource all of it to UPS.

You call nike.com, go online to order a pair of sneakers for your kids. UPS answers that email. UPS picks and packs the shoes. UPS ships them. UPS bills them, and UPS collects the money. You see the Papa John's Pizza truck go by. Guess who is driving? It ain't Papa John's. It is someone in funny brown shorts working for UPS.

There are whole companies today—and you would be shocked to know how many—who never touch their products anymore. They have been completely insourced to UPS or FedEx or DHL. This is a huge flattener going on. To do this requires an enormous number of standards, in order to make this operate at a seamless level.

Day 9: The last new form of collaboration I call **informing.** Informing is what Google, Yahoo, and Microsoft Search do. They allow you to collaborate now with data all by yourself. I had a research assistant, my assistant in Washington, who worked with me on this book. But my real research assistant for this book was a person named Google. I was able to mine all my data all by myself. I was able to inform myself. Inform me: that is what Google does; it is what TiVo does. It allows you to inform and entertain yourself—a whole new form of collaboration.

Day 10: The tenth I simply call the **"steroids."** The steroids are voice-over-the-Internet and wireless. What the steroids are doing is turbo-charging all six of these new forms of collaboration and now allowing you to do any one from anywhere with any device.

So those are the ten days that flattened the world. You will understand why it took me a long time (a) to figure that out, and (b) to go down to UPS and Wal-Mart and do all the research around this, so that I was able to understand them enough to explain it to myself and, hopefully, to you.

The third chapter of the book is really the core thesis. It is called "The Triple Convergence." The triple convergence is basically what, I argue, is the pivot point for the flattening of the world. The first convergence was that sometime around 2000, all ten of these flatteners started to converge. The complementarities between them all suddenly started to work together. The informing drove the outsourcing; the outsourcing drove the insourcing; the insourcing drove the supply-chaining; the supply-chaining drove the offshoring. All started to work together at a tipping point, and the result was a Web-enabled global platform for multiple forms of collaboration and sharing of knowledge—irrespective of distance, of geography, and increasingly, even of language. We are just at the beginning of this.

The second convergence—as I said, it was a triple convergence—was the fact that we are now at the beginning of learning to what I call "horizontalize" ourselves. We are going from a world where value was created almost exclusively in command-and-control silos, from the top down, to a world where value is going to increasingly be created by connect-and-collaborate, horizontally. We are going from a vertical value-creation model to a horizontal value-creation model. To get the most out of this, you have to change all your habits.

The Stanford economist Paul David wrote a famous essay on electrification. He asked, when electricity came out, why didn't we get a burst of productivity? His answer was, because people had to change all their habits. They had to change the very architecture of buildings in order to accommodate small electric motors. It was only after twenty years, when everyone changed their habits from steam engines and their architecture and their business-management processes, did we get the explosion of productivity from electrification.

I would argue the same is going to have to happen with "horizontalization," as we move from vertical to horizontal. An example I like to give from this—and it is a very vivid one—happened to me when I was starting to write this book. My daughter goes to school in New Haven. I live in Bethesda, Maryland. Last spring, I was going to visit her, taking her some spring clothes. To get from Bethesda, Maryland, to New Haven is a total pain in the behind. You have to drive to BWI Airport in Baltimore, take Southwest Airlines to Hartford, and then drive an hour from Hartford to New Haven.

You don't look like a Southwest crowd to me, but never mind. If you have flown Southwest, you may know that on Southwest Airlines you don't get an assigned seat; you just get a ticket that says A, B, or C. You do not want to be a C on Southwest Airlines. You don't even want to be a B if you are carrying two bags of carry-on for your daughter and want to find room in the bin overhead or not get stuck in the middle seat.

No problem. I am a hip guy. I did the e-ticket thing. I got to Southwest Airlines ninety-five minutes before my flight. I put my credit card in the Southwest e-ticket machine. Out came my ticket, and it said B. I said, "This thing is rigged! This is fixed! This is worse than Las Vegas! There is no way I'm a B! I'm here ninety-five minutes before this flight. There is no way I'm a B!" I kicked the thing, went and got my Cinnabon and stewed in the back of the B line. So I was sitting at the gate for forty-five minutes in the back of the B line. Then they called the flight. Then I saw it. All the A's were getting on with what looked to me like crumpled pieces of white printer paper, as if they had downloaded their boarding passes at home and printed them out on their home computers.

What, of course, I didn't know was that Southwest Airlines had just instituted a program where at 12:01 A.M. the night before, because of the convergence, that first convergence, they could make their customers their employees. They could get you to stay up until 12:01 A.M. the night before, and if you valued your time, in effect, pay Southwest Airlines to be their employee and download your boarding pass and your barcode on your own home printer paper the night before. I looked at that, friends, and I said, "Friedman, you are so twentieth-century. You are so Globalization 2.0."

Think about it. In our lifetime, we went from a ticket agent, in Globalization 1.0, a physical person who stood before you, to the e-ticket machine, to you becoming the ticket agent. You just saw us go from Globalization 1.0, to 2.0, to 3.0, in a decade. That transition is happening in every business. I can't tell you how many CEOs I spoke to who all told me the same thing, like they were preprogrammed: "I've had to do the most amazing thing in order to stay alive in this business."

That is the second convergence. I had to learn to "horizontalize" myself. I had to learn to collaborate totally differently with Southwest Airlines to get the productivity boost for myself and for Southwest Airlines. We are just at the beginning of that.

The third convergence—I said there were three—is that right when the world was flattened, what accidentally happened was that 3 billion people who were out of the game walked onto the playing field—from India, China, and the former Soviet empire. When do they walk onto the playing field, friends? Just when it has been flattened. Just when they can plug and play, connect and collaborate, more directly with your kids and mine than ever before in the history of the planet.

Oh, there are 3 billion of them, but only 5 percent can plug and play. Excuse me, that is 150 million by my math. That is the exact size of the American workforce. Also, they can plug and play much more quickly, because they have no embedded legacy systems. That is why there are more cell phones in China today than there are people in America. They can go straight to the latest technology.

The simple thesis of this book is that the triple convergence of this flattened world with these new businesses processes, with these 3 billion new players, is defining the course of the twenty-first century. Let me simply close by saying that this triple convergence happened to coincide with a political "perfect storm." The political perfect storm was called Enron. Enron, 9/11, and the dot-com bust made a lot of morons think and write that globalization was over. Actually, just the opposite was happening. 9/11 completely distracted us—most of all, myself—from everything that was going on. Enron made it so that every business executive was guilty until proven innocent; therefore, none of them wanted to talk about any of this.

When I went around and interviewed people for this book, it was a bit like being in a science fiction movie. They are like pod people, all these CEOs. I learned everything that I know for this book from them. They know just what is going on. But nobody has told the kids. Nobody is talking about this. So we are at one of the great inflection points, I would argue, in our history. I think this is going to be as big as Gutenberg when it plays out. And nobody is talking about it.

2.1.2 In Defense of Globalization

JAGDISH BHAGWATI

Even though the process of globalization through the integration of the world economy began with technological developments in transportation and communications, Jagdish Bhagwati, an economist at Columbia University, claims that today's version of this phenomenon is markedly different from what had existed for a number of reasons. Instead of having technology as the change agent today, Bhagwati builds the case that recent governmental policy shifts have made the changes we see today possible. The author considers various factors that contributed to the negative view of capitalism and its ability to contribute to solving issues of social injustice held by some, including not only young skeptics but also some intellectuals as well as a few very successful capitalists. The increasing power and influence of multinational organizations are examined, and the views of various groups are considered in an attempt to determine the extent to which social groups feel they are benefiting from or being disadvantaged in this changing world. Bhagwati's generally positive view of globalization is tempered somewhat when he acknowledges that unbridled capitalism and globalization might negatively impact communitarian values. Viewing the world through economic lenses, Bhagwati extols the virtues of efficiency in the marketplace even though he appears to be somewhat uneasy with the type of world that might be created if the forces of global capitalism remain unchecked.

FOCUS QUESTIONS

1. What are Bhagwati's key arguments against those who attempt to portray the current stage of globalization as antidemocratic and antiegalitarian? Why are you either inclined to accept or reject his view of the overall benefits of unbridled capitalism and free trade? Discuss.
2. Contrast the generally positive opinions expressed in this article with the concerns over the privatization of the commons raised by the International Forum on Globalization article (Selection 2.1.4). With which point of view are you more inclined to agree and why?
3. How does Bhagwati justify his overwhelmingly positive view of globalization and capitalism? Are you as convinced as he is that the society is not sacrificing "communitarian values" for the apparent self-interest of capitalism? What do you feel might eventually happen to our society if his optimistic view is proven wrong?
4. Discuss both the positive and negative views of globalization presented in this article with the points made in the Friedman article (selection 2.1.1) and the Stiglitz article (selection 2.1.3).

Source: *In Defense of Globalization* by Jagdish Bhagwati, pp. 10–27, a Council on Foreign Relations Book. Copyright © 2004 by Jagdish Bhagwati. Reprinted by permission of Oxford University Press, Inc.

KEYWORDS

commodification, communitarianism, deconstructionism, fair trade, free trade, global integration, imperialism, invisible hand, mercantilism, monopolies, multinationals, usury, xenophobia

GLOBALIZATION TODAY: DIFFERENT FROM YESTERDAY

If globalization's perils tend to be exaggerated [by some]..., they are also understated by many who say, "Well, we have always had globalization, and it is no big deal." True, rapid integration of the world economy occurred in the late nineteenth and early twentieth centuries. We can go back to the end of the nineteenth century, for instance, and find that trade, capital flows, and migrations were no less then than they are today. If multinationals bother you, then just think of the great East India Company, which virtually paved the way for the British conquest of India, and the Dutch East Indies Company, which dominated Indonesia. Trade grew rapidly along with European outward expansion, as did settlements in the new areas opened up by exploration and conquest. Capital flowed profusely, financing the building of railways in Africa and the extraction of minerals worldwide. Many historians have noticed that the years spanning the two world wars were an interruption of the upward trends in the expansion of world trade and investment, and that it is possible to interpret the postwar liberalization of trade and investment flows as leading to a resumption of the trends set into motion prior to World War I. But all this misses the fact that there are fundamental differences that give globalization today a special, and at times sharp, edge.

First, the earlier integration of the world economy was driven more by technological developments in transportation and communications than by policy changes. It's true that British prime minister Robert Peel repealed the Corn Laws in 1846, bringing free trade unilaterally to England in the first dramatic move away from mercantilism. We also know that in various ways many European nations, notably France, followed suit with some trade liberalizations of their own, though historians have not yet decided whether their actions were induced by the example of Britain's success with free trade, as expressly predicted by Peel.

But none of these policy changes did as much to integrate the world economy in the latter half of the century as did emerging technological revolutions in transportation by railways and in the oceans. Technological advances in these sectors rapidly reduced costs of transport and communication continually through the nineteenth century. Martin Wolf, the *Financial Times* columnist, has observed: "The first transatlantic telegraph was laid in 1866. By the turn of the century, the entire world was connected by telegraph, and communication times fell from months to minutes."[1]

Of course, the rate of technological change in moving goods and services and knowledge cheaply and rapidly across nations has continued unabated, even accelerating according to some observers. Thus, Wolf writes: "The cost of a three-minute telephone call from New York to London in current prices dropped from about $250 in 1930 to a few cents today. In more recent years, the number of voice paths across the Atlantic has skyrocketed from 100,000 in 1986 to more than 2 million today. The number of Internet hosts has risen from 5,000 in 1986 to more than 30 million now."[2]

But today's most dramatic change is in the degree to which governments have intervened to reduce obstacles to the flow of trade and investments worldwide. The story of globalization today must be written in two inks: one colored by technical change and the other by state action. In fact, even the early postwar hostility toward global integration in many of the poor countries has, as already remarked upon, yielded steadily to the progressive embrace of globalization. But this fact forces upon our attention a disturbing observation: governments that can accelerate globalization can also reverse it. Herein lies a vulnerability that cannot be dismissed complacently. The earlier globalization, in the end, was interrupted for almost a half century with rising trade barriers epitomized by the infamous 1934 Smoot-Hawley Tariff of the United States and declining trade flows and investments after World War I through to the Great Crash of 1929 and World War II.

Second, the new information technologies have created a landscape where movements of services and capital are faster by several orders of magnitude. The rapidity with which huge amounts of funds moved out of East Asia within less than a week in 1998, the precipitous outflows from Mexico in November 1994, and many other instances of substantial and rapid-fire outflows of capital have created immense management problems that elude the grasp of countries that face difficult developmental weaknesses and challenges but want to embrace financial globalization or are forced to do so. Financial panics, crashes, and manias are nothing new, as the renowned economist Charles Kindleberger has reminded us; but their magnitudes and the speed at which they arrive are indeed qualitatively a different, and potentially more dangerous, phenomenon.

Third, the sense of vulnerability, or economic insecurity, is arguably greater today than in earlier periods because the growing integration of nations worldwide into the international economy has intensified competitive pressures from actual and potential rivals elsewhere. In Adam Smith's time, over two centuries ago, orange producers in the tropics had little worry about competition from Glasgow even though oranges could be grown in glass houses: the cost difference would be so high that the tropical farmers felt secure behind a solid buffer of competitive advantage. England's producers of manufactures also enjoyed easy dominance in many cases because England was ahead of all on industrialization. But today, in most commodities and activities, technology matters and has diffused greatly, both because many have access to similar pools of knowledge and because multinationals can take scarce knowledge almost everywhere if they choose, as they often do, and they do produce globally. The buffer has therefore shrunk dramatically in most activities, and international competition is fierce and feared.

The inevitable effect has been to prompt firms everywhere to worry about "fair trade." Each looks over his foreign rival's shoulder to see if any difference in domestic policy or institutions gives this competitor an "unfair" advantage. The result has been a growing demand for ironing out any such differences, including in labor and environmental standards, as firms seek "level playing fields," ignoring the fact that it is differences, whether of climate and skills or of domestic institutions and policies reflecting local conditions, that lead to beneficial trade among nations.

While these demands, familiar in the rich countries for the most part, have transformed the debate on globalization, and their many ramifications will be subjected to critical examination at different places in this book ... the other important implication of intensified world competition is that it has exposed producers in the poor countries to increased risks as a result of shifting to world markets in search of greater prosperity. Thus farmers who shift from traditional staples to cash crops because of higher returns at current prices face the prospect that this shift will lead them into ruination if rivals elsewhere with lower prices suddenly move into the market: a phenomenon that is more likely in a world with many potential suppliers with small margins of difference in competitiveness. Since few farmers in the poor countries are likely to take these downside possibilities into account, sudden misery is a possibility that has at times resulted from the shift to global markets. The absence of institutional support to handle these downsides ... has become a major source of worry.

Finally, fears that globalization intensifies interdependence among nation-states and increasingly constrains their ability to provide for the welfare of their citizens have a salience that did not quite obtain in the earlier period. The growth of the welfare state in the twentieth century—even though we had elements of it starting earlier, as with social security, whose origins go back to Bismarck in Germany—has created a mind-set, an ethos, where the state is expected to be responsible for the welfare of its citizens. The novel fear today is that globalization places limits on the freedom to discharge this critical responsibility.

And so the complacent view that there is nothing new about globalization is simply wrong. We do need to look at the phenomenon closely, seeking to analyze and address the fears that are novel and indeed appear to be plausible at first blush.

A TRILOGY OF DISCONTENTS

Anti-Capitalism

As the twentieth century ended, capitalism seemed to have vanquished its rivals. Francis Fukuyama's triumphalism in his celebrated work *The End of History and The Last Man* (1990) was like a primeval scream of joy by a warrior with a foot astride his fallen prey.[3] It was not just the collapse of communism in Europe and China's decisive turn away from it. As the energetic anti-globalization NGO Fifty Years Is Enough laments, even the Swedish model (with its enhanced Social Democratic commitment to the welfare state, backed by a markedly progressive and redistributive tax system) had lost its appeal. The much-advertised model of "alternative development" in the Indian state of Kerala, with its major emphasis on education and health and only minor attention to growth, had also run into difficulties, much as President Julius Nyerere's celebrated socialist experiment in Tanzania had run the country's economy into the ground. This vanishing of different possibilities has led to what I have called the tyranny of the missing alternative, provoking a sense of anguished anti-capitalist reactions from both the old and the young.

The old among the disenchanted are few, and so they perhaps matter less than the young, who are many. They are among the anti-capitalists of the postwar years, ranging from socialists to revolutionaries. The communists and Marxists are captive to a nostalgia for their vanished dreams.

When the World Economic Forum met in Davos, Switzerland, in February 2001, there was an anti-Davos meeting in Brazil at the same time.[4] The rhetoric in Brazil was one of revolution. I recall George Soros, who properly considers himself to be a progressive financier, going into a debate from Davos on the video monitor with some of the anti-Davos participants. I recall his frustration, indeed astonishment, when he realized that he was seen as the enemy, not a friend, much as U.S. Democrats were chagrined that Ralph Nader thought during the last presidential election that they were no different from the Republicans.

Soros, who had not previously interacted with these groups, just did not get it: as far as these anti-capitalist revolutionaries are concerned, anyone who is into stocks and bonds should be put *in* stocks and bonds. Indeed, these groups, who were memorializing Che Guevara and listening to Ben Bella, were the exact antitheses of the Arthur Koestlers of the world, who wrote of the god that failed. They were working from a script about the god that died but will come again, much like born-again Christians. They only had to keep the faith.

But we who favor globalization must also confront the young. And if you have watched the streets of Seattle, Washington, Prague, Montreal, and Genoa, where the anti-globalizers have congregated with increasing militancy, or if you see their impassioned protests on the campuses, as I have watched the Anti-Sweatshop Coalition's activities at my own university (Columbia), there can be no doubt that we have here a phenomenon that is truly important in the public space and also more potent: the nostalgia of the fading generation cannot compete with the passions of the rising generation.

So how is the discontent of the young to be explained? Of course, a rare few among them share their predecessor's revolutionary bent. Consider Global Exchange, an NGO that describes itself as a "human rights group"—this is the in term, much as "socialism" was three decades ago, and its moral resonance immediately gets you onto higher ground and gives you a free pass with the media and the public. It professes radical politics and gets endorsement from the great linguist and activist Noam Chomsky, among other left intellectuals. Its pronouncements on the World Trade Organization are dramatic and drastic: "the WTO only serves the interests of multinational corporations" and "the WTO is killing people."[5]

But Global Exchange and its radical chic are really a fringe phenomenon. There are several explanations, other than strong socialist convictions, of what animates the young in particular. Each may explain part of the reality, while collectively they provide a more complete explanation.

1. Far too many among the young see capitalism as a system that cannot address meaningfully questions of social justice. To my generation, and that of the British left-learning intellectuals such as George Bernard Shaw that preceded it, the Soviet model was a beguiling alternative. Indeed, my much-translated 1966 book *The Economics of Underdeveloped Countries* contains a distinct nod toward the Soviet Union: "The imagination of many ... nations has been fired, perhaps most of all, by the remarkable way in which the Soviet Union has raised itself to the status of a Great Power by its own bootstraps and in a short span of time."[6] How appalling a misjudgment this view of the Soviet alternative seems today, and how commonplace it was then!

That capitalism may be viewed instead as a system that can paradoxically destroy privilege and open up economic opportunity to the many is a thought that is still uncommon. I often wonder, for example, how many of the young skeptics of capitalism are aware that socialist planning in countries such as India, by replacing markets systemwide with bureaucratically determined rations of goods and services, worsened rather than improved unequal access because socialism meant queues that the well-connected and the well-endowed could jump, whereas markets allowed a larger number to make it to the check-out counter. I have always been astonished at the number of well-meaning socialists, whose aspirations I admire, who continue to fall for the erroneous view that controls and direct allocations are an appropriate answer to inequality.

2. But the anti-capitalist sentiments are particularly virulent among the young who arrive at their social awakening on campuses in fields other than economics. English, comparative literature, and sociology are fertile breeding grounds.

Thus, deconstructionism, espoused by the French philosopher Jacques Derrida, has left the typical student of literature without anchor because of its advocacy of what amounts to an endless horizon of meanings. Terry Eagleton, the sympathetic chronicler of modern literary theory, has written: "Derrida is clearly out to do more than develop new techniques of reading: deconstruction is for him an ultimately political practice, an attempt to dismantle the logic by which a particular system of thought, and behind that a whole system of political structures and social institutions, maintains its force."[7]

True, Derrida's technique will deconstruct any political ideology, including Marxism. Typically, however, it is focused on deconstructing and devaluing capitalism rather than Marxism, often with nihilistic overtones, which creates the paradox that many now turn to anarchy not from Bakunin but from Derrida.

The near-nihilist influence of the deconstructionism of Derrida in feeding anti-capitalism has been matched by the equally profound influence of Michel Foucault: these have amounted to a double whammy, courtesy of Paris, Foucault's emphasis on discourses as instruments of power and dominance has also led to what is often described as an "anti-rational" approach that challenges the legitimacy of academic disciplines, including economics, and their ability to get at the "truth." There is little doubt that the language of power, and the focus on it, feeds in turn the notion, discussed later, that corporations will dominate and exploit the workers under the liberal rules that define capitalism, and by extension, globalization.[8]

The heavy influence of Marxist texts on students of literature, on the other hand, has been beautifully captured by V. S. Naipaul in his compelling portrait in *Beyond Belief* of the Pakistani guerrilla Shabaz, who went from studying literature in England to starting a revolution in Baluchistan that failed:

> There were close Pakistani friends at the university. Many of them were doing English literature, like Shabaz; it was one of the lighter courses, possibly the lightest, and at this time it was very political and restricted. It was encouraging Marxism and revolution rather than wide reading. So Shabaz and his Pakistani friends in their Marxist study group read the standard (and short) revolutionary texts, Frantz Fanon, Che Guevara. And while they read certain approved Russian writers, they didn't read or get to know about the Turgenev novels, *Fathers and Sons* (1862) and *Virgin Soil* (1877), which dealt with conditions not unlike those in feudal Pakistan, but questioned the simplicities of revolution.[9]

Feeding the anti-globalization movement are also the post-colonial (poco) theorists, who, following Edward Said's pathbreaking writings, have a profound suspicion of Western scholarship as an objective source of interpretation and conceptualization of the colonial societies that were part of the global polity that European expansion created. That suspicion breeds hostility both to Western disciplines such as economics and to the threat that they see from them to the cultures of the communities and nations that have succeeded the colonial rule.

Thus the post-colonial theorists become natural allies of the deconstructionists, the diverse post-modernists (pomos), the Foucault cultists, and the Marxists, in their anti-globalization sentiments in the literature departments. The cauldron draws its boiling waters from many spigots.

As for sociology, many of its students are influenced equally by the new literary theory and the old Marxism. They stand in contempt of economic argumentation that would refute their rejectionist beliefs about capitalism by asserting that economics is about value whereas sociology is about values. But they are wrong today on both counts.

Economists will retort that as citizens they choose ends, but as economists they choose the (best) means. Moreover, accused of indulging the profit motive, they respond with the Cambridge economist Sir Dennis Robertson that economics is addressed heroically to showing how "man's basest instincts," not his noblest, can be harnessed through appropriate institutional design to produce public good. Adam Smith would surely have died an unsung hero if he had peddled the pedestrian argument that altruism led to public good.

The presumption that sociology is a better guide to virtue than economics is also misplaced. Certainly its related discipline, social anthropology, has traditionally leaned toward preserving cultures, whereas economics in our hands is a tool for change.[10] When I studied in England I was fascinated by social anthropology and deeply buried in the writings of the legendary A. R. Radcliffe-Brown and many others, but I still wound up preferring economics for my vocation. What other choice could really have been made by a young student from a country afflicted by economic misery? Indeed, if reducing poverty by using economic analysis to accelerate growth and therewith pull people up into gainful employment and dignified sustenance is not a compelling moral imperative, what *is*?

But I should add that many of these students are also susceptible to the bitingly critical view of economics as an apologia for capitalism that was brilliantly propounded by Rosa Luxemburg in her classic essay "What Is Economics?"—the first chapter of a proposed ten-chapter work, only six chapters of which were found in her apartment after her murder. She had argued that "the new science of economics," which had reached the status of an academic discipline in Germany, was tantamount to an attempted legitimation of the "anarchy of capitalist production" and was essentially "one of the most important ideological weapons of the bourgeoisie as it struggles with the medieval state and for a modern capitalist state." The "invisible hand," with its rationalization of markets, had a hidden agenda, hence it lacked plausibility. This analysis attracts many.

3. But I also think that an altogether new factor on the scene that propels the young into anti-capitalist attitudes comes from a different, technological source in a rather curious fashion. This is the dissonance that now exists between empathy for others elsewhere for their misery and the inadequate intellectual grasp of what can

be done to ameliorate that distress. The resulting tension spills over into unhappiness with the capitalist system (in varying forms) within which they live and hence anger at it for its apparent callousness.

Today, thanks to television, we have what I call the paradox of inversion of the philosopher David Hume's concentric circles of reducing loyalty and empathy. Each of us feels diminishing empathy as we go from our nuclear family to the extended family, to our local community, to our state or county (say, Lancashire or Louisiana), to our nation, to our geographical region (say, Europe or the Americas), and then to the world. This idea of concentric circles of empathy can be traced back to the Stoics' doctrine of *oikeiosis*—that human affection radiates outward from oneself, diminishing as distance grows from oneself and increasing as proximity increases to oneself. In the same vein, Hume famously argued that "it is not contrary to reason to prefer the destruction of the whole world to the scratching of my finger" and that "sympathy with persons remote from us is much fainter than with persons near and continguous."[11]

Similarly, his contemporary Adam Smith wrote in 1760 in *The Theory of Moral Sentiments,* which is as celebrated among moral philosophers as *The Wealth of Nations* is among economists:

> Let us suppose that the great empire of China, with all its myriads of inhabitants, was suddenly swallowed up by an earthquake and let us consider how a man of humanity in Europe, who had no sort of connexion with that part of the world, would be affected upon receiving intelligence of this dreadful calamity. He would, I imagine, first of all express very strongly his sorrow for the misfortune of that unhappy people, he would make many melancholy reflections upon the precariousness of human life and the vanity of all the labors of man which could thus be annihilated in a moment. He would too, perhaps, if he was a man of speculation, enter into many reasonings concerning the effects which this disaster might produce upon the commerce of Europe and the trade and business of the world in general. And when all this fine philosophy was over, when all these humane sentiments had been once fairly expressed, he would pursue his business or pleasure, take his repose or his diversion, with the same ease and tranquility as if no such accident had occurred.
>
> The most frivolous disaster which could befall himself would occasion a more real disturbance. If he was to lose his little finger tomorrow, he would not sleep to-night; but, provided he never saw them, he would snore with the most profound security over the ruin of a hundred million of his brethren. The destruction of that immense multitude seems plainly an object less interesting to him than this paltry misfortune of his own. To prevent, therefore, this paltry misfortune to himself would a man of humanity be willing to sacrifice the lives of a hundred million of his brethren, provided he had never seen them?[12]

What the Internet and CNN have done is to take Hume's outermost circle and turn it into the innermost. No longer can we snore while the other half of humanity suffers plague and pestilence and the continuing misery of extreme poverty. Television has disturbed our sleep, perhaps short of a fitful fever but certainly arousing our finest instincts.[13] Indeed, this is what the Stoics, chiefly Hierocles, having observed the concentric circles of vanishing empathy, had urged by way of morality: that "it is the task of a well tempered man, in his proper treatment of each group, to draw circles together somehow towards the centre, and to keep zealously transferring those from the enclosing circles into the enclosed ones."[14]

At the same time, the technology of the Internet and CNN, as Robert Putnam has told us, has accelerated our move to "bowling alone," gluing us to our TV sets and shifting us steadily out of civic participation, so that the innermost circle has become the outermost one.

So the young see and are anguished by the poverty and the civil wars and the famines in remote areas of the world but often have no intellectual training to cope with their anguish and follow it through rationally in terms of appropriate action. Thus, as I watched the kids dressed as turtles at Seattle, during the riotous 1999 WTO ministerial meeting, protesting against the WTO and the Appellate Body's decision in the shrimpturtle case, I wondered how many knew that the environmentalists had really won that decision, not lost it. The ability to unilaterally impose requirements on foreign shrimpers on the high oceans to use turtle-excluding devices (nets with narrow necks), failing which imports of shrimp would be disallowed, was upheld, not denied. When I asked, of course, no one knew the facts, and so they did not really understand what they were protesting. When I mischievously asked some if they had read Roald Dahl's famous story "The Boy Who Talked with Animals," about a boy who freed a giant turtle and sailed away on it into the far ocean, they shook their turtle heads.[15] It has become fashionable to assert that the demonstrating youth know much about the policies they protest; but that is only a sentiment of solidarity with little basis in fact. True, there are several serious NGOs with real knowledge and serious policy critiques, such as the World Wildlife Fund, and I shall presently consider their phenomenal growth and the opportunity they present for making economic and social well-being a shared success between the agents of economic globalization and the civil society—the two great phenomena as we enter the twenty-first century. But they are not the tumultuous many who are agitating in the streets.

4. Overlaying the entire scene, of course, is the general presumption that defines many recent assertions by intellectuals that somehow the proponents of capitalism, and of its recent manifestations in regard to economic reforms such as the moves to privatization and to market liberalization (including trade liberalization), are engaged, as Edward Said claims, in a "dominant discourse [whose goal] is to fashion the merciless logic of corporate profit-making and political power into a normal state of affairs." Following Pierre Bourdieu, Said endorses the view that "Clinton-Blair neoliberalism, which built on the conservative dismantling of the great social achievements in health, education, labor and security of the welfare state during the Thatcher-Reagan period, has constructed a paradoxical *doxa*, a symbolic counterrevolution."[16] In Bourdieu's own words, this is "conservative but presents itself as progressive; it seeks the restoration of the past order in some of its most archaic aspects (especially as regards economic relations), yet it passes off regressions, reversals, surrenders, as forward-looking reforms or revolutions leading to a whole new age of abundance and liberty."[17]

But, frankly, this view stands reality on its head. Of course, we have known since Orwell that words do matter, and the smart duelists in the controversies over public policy will often seize the high ground by appropriating to themselves and their own causes, before their adversaries do, beguiling words such as *progressive*. Thus, believe it or not, protectionists in trade have been known to ask for "tariff reform"; today, they ask for "fair trade," which no one can deny except for the informed few who see that it is used to justify unfair trade practices. Phrases such as "corporate profit making" and "trickle-down" do the same for the friends of Bourdieu, creating and fostering a pejorative perception of the market-using policy changes that they reject.

It is therefore not surprising that today's critics turn to the same linguistic weapons as the anti-capitalist forces of yesterday. But let us ask: is it "conservative" or "radical" to seek to correct, in light of decades of experience and in the teeth of entrenched forces, the mistakes and the excesses of past policies, no matter how well motivated? In fact, as reformers know only too well, it takes courage and élan to challenge orthodoxies, especially those that are conventionally associated with "progressive" forces.

As for the policies themselves, the fierce binary contrast drawn by Bourdieu is an abstraction that misses the central issues today. The debate is really not about conservative counterrevolution and the enlightened past order. It is rather about shifting the center of gravity in public action more toward the use of markets and less toward dirigisme. It is not about "whether markets"; it is about where the "limits to markets" must be drawn. This is a question that, as will be discussed, provokes spirited complaints from the recent communitarians who wish the limits to markets to be drawn more tightly.

The present-day turn toward reforms in the developing countries is also prompted by excessive and knee-jerk dirigisme. As I often say, the problem with many of these countries was that

Adam Smith's invisible hand was nowhere to be seen. Their turn to economic reforms is to be attributed not to the rise of "conservatism" but to a pragmatic reaction of many to the failure of what a number of us once considered to be "progressive" policies that would lift us out of poverty, illiteracy, and many other ills. As John Kenneth Galbraith once said about Milton Friedman—and here I take only the witticism and not sides—"Milton's misfortune is that his policies have been tried."

ANTI-GLOBALIZATION

Anti-capitalism has turned into anti-globalization among left-wing students for reasons that are easy to see. After all, Lenin wrote extensively about imperialism and its essential links to capitalism, and present-day writers such as Immanuel Wallerstein have seen the growing integration of the world economy in related ways as the organic extension of national capitalism.[18]

Lenin's views on imperialism provide an insight into a principal reason why anti-globalization is seen by those on the left so readily as following from anti-capitalism. In his famous work *Imperialism: The Highest Stage of Capitalism,* Lenin stated that the distinctive characteristics of capitalism in the form of monopolies, oligarchy, and the exploitation of the weak by the strong nations compel us to define it as "parasitic, decaying capitalism."[19] Nikolai Bukharin, for whose work *Imperialism and the World Economy* Lenin wrote a preface, considered that imperialism with its attendant globalization of the world economy is little more than capitalism's "[attempt] to tame the working class and to subdue social contradictions by decreasing the steam pressure through the aid of a colonial valve"; that "having eliminated [through monopolies] competition within the state, [capitalism has] let loose all the devils of a world scuffle."[20]

The notion that globalization is merely an external attenuation of the internal struggles that doom capitalism, and that globalization is also in essence capitalist exploitation of the weak nations, provides not only an inherent link between capitalism and globalization but also makes globalization an instrument for the exploitation of the weak nations. And this certainly has resonance again among the idealist young on the left. Capitalism seeks globalization to benefit itself but harms others abroad. The Lenin-Bukharin argument then leads, as certainly as a heat-seeking missile reaching its target, to anti-capitalist sentiments.

Anti-Corporation Attitudes

But central to that perspective is the notion, of course, that it is the "monopolies" (for that is indeed how the multinationals are often described even today in much of the anti-globalization literature) that are at the heart of the problem: they do not benefit the people abroad; they exploit them instead. Indeed, this notion of globalization as an exploitative force that delays the doomsday for capitalism at home and harms those abroad has captured some of the more militant among the naive youth today.

The anti-corporation attitudes come to many others who are not aficionados of left-wing literature, also from the obvious sense that multinationals are the principal agents and beneficiaries of capitalism and of globalization.[21] Yet others find it plausible that multinationals must necessarily be bad in a global economy because global integration without globally shared regulations must surely amount to an advantageous playing field for multinationals. These corporations would then be able to seek profits by searching for the most likely locations to exploit workers and nations, thereby putting intolerable pressure on their home states to abandon their gains in social legislation. This is what is known as a race to the bottom. Indeed, this view is so credible that even a shrewd and perceptive intellectual such as Alan Wolfe, who sees through cant better than most, has recently written disapprovingly and casually of the "policies of increasingly rapacious global corporations."[22]

These anti-corporation arguments are not supported by the facts. But many believe them. And they zero in with a "gotcha" mentality, seizing on every venal misdeed of a multinational they can find, seeking to validate through these specific examples their general anti-corporation biases. This surely accounts for the return of Ralph Nader, the great scourge of manifest misdeeds by corporations. It has also magically transformed Julia Roberts, whose triumph in *Pretty Woman* reflected chiefly her marvelous good looks, into an acclaimed actress in *Erin Brockovich* and introduced the gifted actor Russell Crowe to celebrity on the screen in *The Insider,* both movies where a David takes on the Goliath in shape of a truly venal corporation.

The anti-corporation militancy that is on the rise among the young anti-globalizers is also strategic. We have witnessed the brilliant way in which the anti-globalizers managed to use the meetings of the international agencies such as the World Bank, the IMF, and particularly the WTO (originally the GATT), the pride of progressive architectural design regarding the management of the world economy and the permanent legacy of legendary men of vision, to protest and to profess their anti-globalization sentiments. After all, these meetings were where the world's media gathered. What better place to create mayhem and get attention from the vast multitude of reporters looking for a story? So while the old guerrillas struck where you least expected them, these new guerrillas have struck where you most expected them: at these meetings.

The same strategic sense has been displayed in going after the corporations as well. Nike and Gap, two fine multinationals, now have a permanent set of critics, with newsletters and websites worldwide. With Nike and Gap having overseas operations in numerous locations, it is not possible to avoid lapses altogether from whatever is defined as good behavior: the host governments often force the hiring of domestic managers who are regrettably part of cultures that are not as egalitarian and mindful of the dignity of others working below them as the West would like them to be. When lapses occur, these firms become obvious targets in a propaganda war that is stacked against them. Naomi Klein, the Canadian writer, admits frankly that, faced with the amorphous but overwhelming phenomenon of globalization, the only way to get at it is to latch on to something concrete and targetable.[23]

The same strategic thought recurs in the writings of other anti-capitalist activists. Thus the Nicaragua Solidarity Network of Greater New York reported that in Brazil "[o]n Mar. 8 [2001], International Women's Day, women linked to landless rural worker movements in Rio Grande do Sul state gathered in front of a McDonald's restaurant in Porto Alegre, the state capital, to protest Nina ... Tonin, a member of the National Board of Directors of the Movement of Landless Rural Workers (MST), said the group chose McDonald's because it is '*a symbol of the intervention politics of the big monopolies operating in Brazil*'"[24]

So they go after the corporations that spread and constitute the globalization that is reprehensible We then also see teenagers carrying placards outside Staples, the office products chain that has succeeded immensely throughout the United States, and demonstrating in front of Starbucks while their more militant adult friends threw stones through the coffee chain's windows in Seattle. I talk with them at every opportunity, I find enthusiasm, even idealism, but never any ability to engage concretely on the issues they take a stand on. But then the Kleins of the anti-globalization movement are not fazed, it is all strategic, it is in a good cause.

Indeed, it is hard to understand the deep and unyielding hostility to multinational corporations, manifest on the streets and on campuses, except by analogy to earlier times. Perhaps the classic parallel is with the stigma attached to usury in medieval times interest and moneylenders then, as profits and corporations now, invited implacable hostility. The exaction of interest was forbidden by ecclesiastical and civil laws, its practice turned into a crime. Even as trade and globalization increased with mercantile expansion and laws began to change (with occasional relapses), usury remained beyond the pale, contrary to conventional and persistent norms.

> By 37 *Henry VIII, cap. ix,* the old laws against usury are, indeed, abolished, and a rate of ten percent is indirectly legalized by the fixing of severe

penalties for any rate higher; but the practice is condemned, and classed with corrupt bargains.... In 1552, however, by *6 Edward VI, cap. xx,* the act of Henry VIII is annulled ... and severe penalties are enacted against any usury what ever, "forasmuch as Usurie is by the word of God utterly prohibited, as a vyce most odious and detestable..." In 1570, by *13 Elizabeth, cap. viii, 6 Edward VI* is annulled and *37 Henry VIII re-enacted, but* "forasmuch as all Usurie, being forbidden by the Law of God is synne and detestable ..." It is expressly provided that all offenders shall "also be punished and corrected according to the ecclesiastical laws heretofore made against usury."[25]

OTHER IDEOLOGICAL AND INTELLECTUAL SOURCES OF ANTI-GLOBALIZATION

While the sources of anti-globalization rooted in anti-capitalism in the diverse ways set out so far are dominant in the current discourse, there are others, not quite so influential, that cannot be ignored.

The Right

In this variegated landscape, complementing those who lean on the left are forces on the right. Thus for every Ralph Nader there is a Pat Buchanan. But the Buchanans are instead knee-deep in xenophobia and crude assertions of national identity and sovereignty. These beliefs lead directly to proposals to isolate America from commerce by building tariff walls. Thus in the 1990s Buchanan called for tariffs against the Japanese, asking for a 10 percent tariff on every Japanese import, and has argued recently against letting Chinese imports freely into the United States.[26] Interestingly, the right-wing extremists in India's ruling Bharatiya Janata Party are also fanatically for self-reliance in trade and incoming foreign investment.

The anti-globalization sentiments on the right extend easily to anti-immigration attitudes, whereas the left's fascination with anti-globalization rarely extends to a fortress mentality on immigration. While some liberal environmental groups slide into anti-immigration rhetoric when they argue that immigration adds to environmental problems, the general posture of the liberal anti-globalization groups is one of benign neglect. Surprisingly, however, there are a rare few progressive segments of the anti-globalization movement that are for free immigration. The anthropologist David Graeber has drawn attention to the Italian group Ya Basta!, whose platform includes guaranteed free movement of people across borders: an objective that has simply no political salience or social resonance, to be brutally frank.

Communitarianism and Limits to Markets

The "liberal international economic order," as the spread of capitalism and markets worldwide is sometimes described, has also been challenged by political philosophers of influence, these coming from the Anglo-Saxon campuses rather than from the banks of the Seine. Thus, communitarians in the United States such as Michael Sandel of Harvard and Michael Walzer of Princeton's Institute for Advanced Study have tried to define limits on the use of markets.

To illustrate, Sandel has objected to the use of global-efficiency-enhancing international trade in permits for carbon dioxide emissions among members of the Kyoto treaty on global warming. With such trade, Brazil would be able to reduce its emissions but effectively sell the reduction achieved as a tradable permit to the United States, which would then credit it as a contribution toward the fulfillment of its own target of emission reductions, thus reducing by the traded amount the emission reduction it had to achieve. This trade would mean that a country where the real cost of reducing carbon dioxide emissions is higher would be able to buy the tradable permits from one where the real cost was lower: the world cost of reducing emissions would obviously fall with such trade. But Sandel once argued in a *New York Times* op-ed article why it was "immoral" to buy the rights to pollute: we expect everyone in a community to make a shared effort toward such goals.[27] A good example would be that our community would be offended if the rich boys could buy their way out of fighting a war (though one must admit that the substitution of a professional army for conscription is precisely a case where that communitarian sense has given way to the notion of efficiency). Sandel himself produces the example of parking spaces for handicapped people. The community would be offended if the rich could buy permits to use such spaces. But here again, the rich can always park their BMWs in these spaces and pay the fines if caught. To my knowledge, no one threatens that the luxury cars illegally parked in these spaces will be destroyed and the violators will be incarcerated, thus raising the effective price paid for such spaces by the rich to levels that really do amount to prohibition. In short, while communitarian principles do intrude frequently to place limits on markets, and hence on the principle of efficiency that markets help to implement, the communitarian spirit itself is subject to limits in practice.

It is likely that the extent of communitarian limits on markets will erode with capitalism taking hold. This is what Marx had in mind as he observed what he called the "commodification" process—what economists call increased commercialization. Thus, the balance between altruism, love, duty, and the other virtues, on one hand, and pursuit of self-interest, on the other hand, may shift away from those virtues as capitalism progresses. For instance, love may become sex, with reverence and mystique yielding to gratification. It is hard to see this in one's own culture, but during O. J. Simpson's trial I was struck by the fact that when newspapers described how he had been looking through the window as Nicole made love to her boyfriend, they all said that she and her friend had had dinner, come home, had coffee, and then "had sex." Mind you, none said they had "made love." So making love was reduced to having sex, the way they had dinner and then coffee. And, just as you might remark that the coffee was an espresso, the reports added that the sex was oral!

But the communitarians surely exaggerate the commodification that markets wreak. There is movement the other way too, and often it comes about because of the rapid pace of technical change, which has accelerated both the pace of economic globalization and that of globalized civil society. The cloning debate shows how societies will seek to place limits on what will be left to markets.

In the world as we know it, therefore, both communitarian and liberal principles coexist in varying forms. The important question is not whether we should have one or the other but whether capitalism and globalization are such an inexorable force that they propel society into a headlong rush away from traditional communitarian values and ways. The evidence for such an alarmist conclusion is not compelling.

Anti-Americanism

Yet another source of anti-globalization sentiments is the resentment that comes from the rise of the United States to a military and economic hegemony so unprecedented that the French call America, with which they have a notorious love-hate relationship, a hyperpower, as if being called a superpower is no longer the highest accolade.

Since this hegemony is exercised in the global context, the resentment of the United States follows worldwide. The loss of the Soviet Union as a countervailing superpower is mourned, even as the collapse of the scourge of communism is celebrated. The anti-Americanism that American power and its exercise—no matter how benign and invited—creates is then an important source of anti-globalization sentiment. Throwing sand into the gears of globalization is seen as a way to spit on American hegemony, if not to limit the exercise of it in the political, cultural, and economic domains.

NOTES

1. Martin Wolf, "Will the Nation-State Survive Globalization?" *Foreign Affairs* **80**, 1(2001), 181–82.
2. Ibid., 182.
3. Francis Fukuyama, *The End of History and the Last Man* (New York: Free Press, 1992).
4. This meeting in Porto Alegre has now become an annual, parallel affair and describes itself as the World Social Forum, in contrast to the World Economic Forum of Davos. The contrasting

choice of terminology is clearly intended to suggest that they are for social outcomes and for humanity, whereas their opponents are for profits and against humanity.

5. See http://www.globalexchange.org/campaigns/rulemakers/topTenReasons.html.
6. Jagdish Bhagwati, *The Economics of Underdeveloped Countries* (London: Weidenfeld and Nicolson, 1966), Chapter 1. I must add two vignettes about this first book of mine. First, its Chapter 1 is titled "Poverty and Income Distribution." Second, I had the curious satisfaction of getting back at a social-democratic critic, Dr. Louis Emmerij, when I gave a keynote speech at Antwerp many years ago. When I had talked about poverty and how to address it, he got up and said that it was good to see that Professor Bhagwati was "finally" turning to poverty. So I retorted, "As it happens, I was rereading my 1966 book on underdeveloped countries last week to write my speech today, and I am sorry to have to tell you that the first chapter was concerned precisely with poverty."

   Besides, I must say that the book contained a moving photograph of a malnourished, starving child in Africa. At a time when it was fashionable to equate developmental analysis with esoteric questions such as the optimal choice of techniques, where the modeling was used to arrive at the disastrous conclusion that capital-intensive techniques were appropriate in poor countries, as they would raise savings and lead to faster growth, it seemed like heresy and a betrayal of economics to focus directly on poverty and pestilence and to concretize them with telling pictorial evidence. In fact, John Chipman, a world-class economist at the University of Minnesota and a fine friend, wrote to me at the time that he had heard a colleague exclaim: "Bhagwati has gone bananas; he has published a book with a picture of a starving chiid in it!"
7. Terry Eagleton, *Literary Theory: An Introduction*, 2nd. ed. (Minneapolis: University of Minnesota Press, 2001), 128.
8. See also the quote from Edward Said further below. Blair Hoxby has reminded me that, earlier than Foucault, these antirational views may be traced to Theodor Adorno and Max Horkheimer's *Dialectic of Enlightenment*, first published in German in 1944.
9. V. S. Naipaul, Beyond Belief: Islamic Excursions Among Converted Peoples (New York: Vintage, 1999), 276.
10. Today social anthropology has moved into a more liberal stance, under the influence of post-colonial and post-modern theorists. Nonetheless, it is not free from its status quo bias on culture, which seeks to value rather than vanquish the old, and to be skeptical and suspicious of change. The influence on policy of this discipline has revived as social anthropologists have found their way into foundations, the World Bank, and several NGOs.
11. David Hume, *A Treatise of Human Nature* (London: J. M. Dent, 1911), **2**: 128. See also David Hume, *An Enquiry Concerning the Principles of Morals*, ed. J. B. Schneewind (Indianapolis Hackett, 1983): "Sympathy, we shall allow, is much fainter than our concern for ourselves, and sympathy with persons remote from us, much fainter than with persons near and contiguous" (49); and "It is wisely ordained by nature, that private connexions should commonly prevail over universal views and considerations, otherwise our affections and actions would be dissipated and lost, for want of a proper limited object Thus a small benefit done to ourselves, and our near friends, excites more lively sentiments of love and approbation than a great benefit done to a distant commonwealth" (49).
12. Adam Smith, *The Theory of Moral Sentiments* ed. D. Raphael and A. L. Macfie (Oxford Clarendon, 1976), 136–37.
13. This new consciousness of ills elsewhere, and the aroused conscience that often goes with it, does not imply that remedial action will necessarily follow Famines, pestilence, war crimes, and much else that plagues humanity has continued to our great embarrassment and sorrow.
14. Hierocles, in A. A. Long and D. N. Sedley, eds., *The Hellenistic Philosophers* (Cambridge: Cambridge University Press, 1987). The quote from Hierocles is from Fonna Forman-Barzilai, "Adam Smith as Globalization Theorist," available at http://www.ciaonet.org/olj/cr/cr_vl4_4_fof01.pdf, 4.
15. This delightful story has been reprinted as the lead story in Roald Dahl's collection *The Wonderful Story of Henry Sugar* (New York: Puffin, 1988).
16. Edward W. Said, "The Public Role of Writers and Intellectuals," *The Nation*, September 17, 2001, no 8, vol **273**, 27.
17. Ibid.
18. Immanuel Wallerstein, "Development: Lodestar or Illusion?" in Leslie Sklair, ed., *Capitalism and Development* (London: Routledge, 1994).

19. V. I. Lenin, *Imperialism: The Highest Stage of Capitalism* (Moscow, USSR: Progress Publishers, 1982; 18th printing) chapter 8, titled "Parasitism and Decay of Capitalism," 96.
20. Nikolai Bukharin, *Imperialism and World Economy* (New York: Howard Fertig, 1966), 169.
21. Chapter 12 offers a comprehensive analysis of corporations and their role in today's globalized economy. Arguments such as effects on local culture are addressed in Chapter 9.
22. Alan Wolfe, "The Snake: Globalization, America, and the Wretched Earth," *The New Republic*, October 1, 2001, 31.
23. Naomi Klein, *No Logo: No Space, No Choice, No Jobs* (New York: Picador, 2002).
24. Nicaragua Solidarity Network.
25. Elmer EdgarStoll, "Shylock," *Shakespeare Studies* (New York: Stechert, 1927). Quoted in *The Merchant of Venice*, ed. Kenneth Myrick (New York: Signet Classic, 1987), 165.
26. See my op-ed article "What Buchanan Owes Clinton," *New York Times*, February 22, 1996. The melodramatic tide, chosen (as always) by the newspaper, reflected the fact that I was pointing to some parallels between Buchanan's demands and the Clinton administration's Japan-bashing attitudes and the proposals of some of the administration's supporters who had in fact asked for even higher tariffs against the Japanese. The situation was ironic, in my view; a liberal administration sharing the views of a xenophobe!
27. Michael Sandel, "It's Immoral to Buy the Right to Pollute," *New York Times*, December 15, 1997.

2.1.3 Making Globalization Work

JOSEPH E. STIGLITZ

Winner of the 2001 Nobel Prize in economics, Columbia University Professor Joseph Stiglitz provides a less rosy picture of the fairness of the current pattern of globalization. During the 1990s, he chaired President Bill Clinton's Council of Economic Advisers and served as the chief economist at the World Bank. In both these jobs, he had an excellent vantage point for understanding how globalization really works. It predictably produces both "winners" and "losers," but under the current rules of international trade, there are more losers than winners, and the winners are doing nothing to compensate the losers.

In his earlier book, *Globalization and Its Discontents,* he analyzed how multilateral institutions such as the World Bank and the International Monetary Fund (IMF) affected policy and the lives of ordinary people. In his new book, *Making Globalization Work,* Stiglitz seeks to diagnose the reasons why globalization has not made everyone better off, and he offers a detailed analysis of what needs to be fixed in the current international economic system in order to create a fairer world. His focus is on what needs to be done to make this process work for the poor and for developing countries. He tells us why changes are needed in governmental policies, the world economic institutions, the rules of the game, and the general mind-sets of the public at large. He argues that a "one size fits all" solution does not work for everyone, yet he also understands that there are systematic reasons why the current rules of globalization are not working to help those in greatest need.

Source: From "Making Globalization Work," a Carnegie Council on Ethics and International Affairs lecture, delivered October 5, 2006 by Joseph Stiglitz. Copyright © 2006. Reprinted by permission of the Carnegie Council on Ethics and International Affairs, www.carnegiecouncil.org.

FOCUS QUESTIONS

1. What in Stiglitz's view are the main reasons why the current system of globalization is not working better than it is to help lift the world's poor?
2. What does he mean when he says, "Too often, notions of fairness stop at the border"? What are the examples that he uses to illustrate this point?
3. What is intellectual property, and how is it different from other kinds of property? Why are there special rules in international trade agreements about it?
4. Why was Stiglitz pleased to find that one of his books had been pirated? How does his view relate to the idea of copyleft licenses discussed by Sunstein?
5. In the end, Stiglitz says he is optimistic about changing the current economic system to make it fairer. Do you agree that there are reasons for such optimism?

KEYWORDS

Cold War, debt crisis, debt relief, economic globalization, GDP, IMF, intellectual property, NAFTA, political globalization, power politics, tariffs, TRIPs, World Bank

A lot of economists have talked about the advantages of globalization—Adam Smith talked about it—creating larger markets, larger markets expand opportunities. But they don't talk about some of the other adverse consequences, which I will focus on more narrowly, and the fact, for instance, that inequality is growing in most countries around the world.

It is not an accident. It has to do very clearly with globalization and, in particular, with the asymmetric ways in which globalization has been pursued in the last twenty-five or thirty years, both the asymmetries between developed and less-developed countries; the asymmetries between capital and labor; between natural persons, people as we know them, and artificial persons like corporations.

In a way, the title of the book summarizes the book. *Making Globalization Work* suggests that something is not working, and a great deal of the book is devoted to trying to describe and diagnose what is not working. It also says there is a note of optimism, that I actually think that the arguments that were made about what globalization could do had a certain validity to them, that there are things that could be done to make globalization work—some small, some large; some that could be undertaken rather quickly, some that are actually going on as I'm talking, and others that will take years to accomplish. But there is a rich agenda which would enable globalization to work, or at least work better, for more of the people around the world.

The book differs from my earlier, book, as in that one I focused on the IMF and the World Bank. I had just come out of the World Bank and I had a certain passion for describing what I had seen. What this book points out is that globalization is much broader than that. It involves a whole range of issues, from intellectual property, trade, multinational corporations, how we manage the environment, natural resources, oil, as well as the global financial system. In a sense, globalization is the sum total of all of those. While there are some underlying forces that affect the shaping of all of these—and I have tried to analyze that—that one actually has to go in and try to talk about each of these, to think about them each separately and think about what can be done to make globalization work in each of those areas.

What I'm going to try to do is, first, in this talk to describe some of the ways in which globalization has not been working, to describe some of the broad macro explanations for why it hasn't been working, and then look at one or two of these, depending on the time, and hope you read the rest of the book to find the other ones, and just give a hint of the kinds of issues. I will talk about probably some that have gotten some attention, some that have not.

At the beginning of the modern debate on globalization twenty years ago, the view was that globalization would make everybody better off. So when in Seattle at the beginning of what was supposed to be a new round of trade talks, riots broke out, rather than the beginning of what I think President Clinton wanted to be called the Clinton Round, a lot of people were surprised, because everybody was supposed to be made better off.

Some economists responded by saying, "This is not a problem of economics; it's a problem for psychiatry. Why was it that people were better off and unhappy?" But actually, as we looked at the data, it was clear that they were unhappy because they should be unhappy. They were being made worse off.

At the last round of trade negotiations, the Uruguay Round, for the poorest countries of the world, it wasn't that they got a small share of the gains—everybody expected that; that's power politics—but they actually wound up worse off than they had been before, it was so unbalanced, so asymmetric.

The hope of globalization was that it was like a rising tide lifts all boats, and so the poorest would see themselves go up. But in the way it was managed, it might be more likened to a riptide knocks over the weakest boat, and without life vests, without safety nets, a lot of the people in those weaker boats drowned.

That is, in a sense, what has happened. The divergence between the richest countries and the poorest has increased, in spite of a well-defined economic theory that said they ought to narrow.

Even closer to home, the divergence between Mexico and the United States has increased in recent years, since NAFTA. One of the arguments for NAFTA, for a North American Free Trade Agreement, was that it was supposed to reduce that gap and reduce, therefore, migration pressure. It didn't do that. And actually, as we looked and studied what happened to NAFTA, some of the provisions of NAFTA actually contributed to the problem.

Now, let me make clear, NAFTA is called the North American Free Trade Agreement, but it was not a free trade agreement. A free trade agreement would be very easy to write; you could write it in about three pages: we have no tariffs, they have no tariffs; we have no non-tariff barriers, they have no non-tariff barriers; we have no subsidies, they have no subsidies. It would be a couple of pages. Lawyers would be out of business; they couldn't write. But, in fact, if any of you know some of these free trade agreements, such as the Uruguay Round, they go on for thousands of pages. In fact, almost no one knows what's in them—you might know your own little provision. That gives an opportunity for all kinds of special interests to stuff in things that shouldn't be there.

That happened in NAFTA. There were things there that actually we didn't discover until later, that no one in the White House talked about, and that everybody in the White House, had they talked about them, would have opposed. It was so complex. A particular provision was on Chapter 11, on investor protection, which was really an anti-environmental provision. Never discussed.

There is a recent book by Tom Friedman that has gotten a lot of attention and sold very well, called *The World Is Flat*. One of the themes of my book is not only is the world not flat, but it is in many ways getting less flat. Two of the reasons it is getting less flat are: some of the rules of the game, like the Uruguay Round, made it tilted against the developing countries; but also, one of the things that Tom rightly emphasizes is that new technologies have changed the global landscape, and there are some enormous successes, and we shouldn't underestimate the importance of those. They impose challenges, but they are successes.

China and India have been doing very well, and there is a convergence at that part of the income distribution. China has been growing at 9.7 percent for thirty years—enormous. If you compare it with what happened in the Industrial Revolution or any period in history, it's an order of magnitude higher, and they managed it in ways to ensure that hundreds of millions of people moved out of poverty, even though there was growing inequality. India has been growing at 5-to-6 percent for a quarter-century.

One of the things that led to the success of these countries was heavy investments in technology and education. But those at the bottom in Africa typically don't have the resources, don't have the knowledge, to take advantage of these new technologies. As a result, the gap between them and the rest of the world is actually increasing.

As another example or manifestation of the way that globalization isn't working out in the way that we would have thought, if you saw a world in which water was moving uphill, you would say something's peculiar about that world; antigravity—you could make a science fiction movie. But in economics the corresponding notion is money ought to be going from rich countries to poor countries—poor countries where it is scarce, rich countries where it is relatively abundant, sort of a standard economic model. In fact, in recent years money has been flowing from the poor countries to rich countries. Again, standard economic theory says rich countries can bear risk better than poor countries and financial markets pride themselves in their ability to slice and dice risk and move from those less able to those more able to bear it, and that means move it from the poor to the rich.

But the debt contracts that are signed around the world, typically by poor countries, involve short-term contracts denominated in hard currencies. The result of it is that the poor countries bear an enormous amount of risk associated with interest rate and exchange rate volatility, and that has meant there have been large numbers of crises.

If there were only one or two countries that had a debt crisis, you could blame the government. Every country, even a democratic government, knows that it can have bad political leaders. A country can go from a 2 percent surplus to a 4 percent deficit of GDP in the space of three or four years. So we know that can happen anywhere in the world, and it can happen in the developing world.

But the thing about developing country debt is it's not just one or two countries; it's country after country. When you see something happening to country after country, you have to say there's something systemic about it, there's something systemic that leads countries to have more debt than they can bear. And while it is good news what happened at Gleneagles a year and a half ago, debt relief, the third time in a decade, the fact that it was the third time in a decade suggests that unless we get at the underlying problems, we will have to have more and more debt relief. The discussion at Gleneagles highlighted the problem. People talked about debt relief, but no one talked about the systemic sources of the problem and doing anything about those systemic sources.

Economists like to think that we know more about growth and what makes successful growth than we did thirty years ago—I mean what have we been doing if we haven't learned something about that?—and we think that there are better institutions. We worked hard to create successful market institutions around the world. If that's true, you would have thought that you would have had faster and more stable economic growth.

But actually, it is exactly the contrary. The countries that followed the advice of the IMF, the World Bank, have actually done more poorly recently than they did in the past before they found out how to manage their economies. So in the 1990s, growth in Latin America was just half of what it was in the 1950s, 1960s, and 1970s, before we taught them what to do.

In the case of Brazil, it had grown at 5.7 percent for seventy-five years before 1980. Now what's so striking is you go down to Brazil and they are happy if they can get growth up to 3 percent, 2.5 percent—that's a big success—and the government says, "We turned the economy around." In Brazil, actually the last government succeeded in inventing a new concept. In East Asia, they had export-led growth; exports grew and the economy grew. Brazil in the last four years had a new concept, which I call export-led non-growth. Their exports doubled and the economy managed to stagnate—grow a little bit, but not what we had hoped.

Stability, the same issue. A hundred countries have had crises in the last thirty years. It's more unusual not to have had a crisis than to have had one. I could go on, but I think the picture is clear, that in many ways globalization has not fulfilled what people had hoped, and done it so systematically that you have to say it's not just a problem of one country, it's something about the system.

The next question I turn to is: Why has globalization not worked out as well? As I say, much of my analysis is looking at the specific issues, but I wanted to spend a few minutes talking about what I see as the broad problem.

That is very simple. To put it in a sentence, economic globalization has outpaced political globalization. Economic globalization has meant we are more interdependent, more integrated, as a global economy; and more integration, more interdependence, means there is more need for cooperative action. We have to do things together—set standards, set rules of the game. But we don't have the political institutions by which to do that democratically, nor the mindset to do it in ways that are fair. Too often, notions of fairness stop at the border.

I could see that very clearly when I was in Washington, where when we were talking about domestic policies we would always talk about what was efficient and what was fair. Internationally, when we sent our trade ministers to Geneva, we never said, "Come back with a fair trade agreement." If they had done that, they would have been fired. We said, "Do the best deal for America," and what we really meant was "Do the best deal for those special interests who are breathing down our back and giving us big campaign contributions." That's why you see such inconsistencies.

The big issue in the Clinton Administration in the beginning years was access to health. One of the bad guys in that debate was the drug companies, the high drug prices that meant that many Americans could not get access to the medicines they needed, and we were really scrapping with the drug companies—you could see it. Internationally, we were in bed with the drug companies.

The Uruguay Round TRIPs Agreement, which is Trade-Related Intellectual Property, has nothing to do with trade. They just put "trade-related" because they had to put that in there to have it in a trade agreement. That was the real ingenuity. There was already an intellectual property organization, called WIPO, the World Intellectual Property Organization. But they wanted the trade ministers to do it because the trade ministers didn't know anything about intellectual property, and that meant they were much more vulnerable to the influences of the special interests.

They put in provisions that were explicitly designed to reduce access to generic medicines. Just to highlight why that's important, a generic AIDS medicine, for instance, costs under $300 for a year's treatment. The brand name is $10,000. If your income is $500 a year or $300 a year, or even $5,000 a year, you can't afford $10,000 a year for the brand name. So when they were signing that agreement in Marrakesh, they were signing the death warrants for thousands of people in sub-Saharan Africa. That was the consequence.

I think what made things worse in many ways was the end of the Cold War, which in other respects was a great thing. During the Cold War, we had to compete for the hearts and minds of those in the Third World, or at least we wanted to make sure they didn't go to the other side. So we gave money to Mobutu in the Congo, knowing that the money that we lent to him, gave to him, was going to Swiss bank accounts. It wasn't designed to help the country develop. It was to make sure that he wasn't on the other side. We would support Pinochet in Chile, knowing what he was doing, but again the principle was that the enemy of our enemy was our friend.

At the end of the Cold War, we had an opportunity to try to reframe the international economic order more in accord with our principles, our values, or we had the opportunity to say that, unfettered with competition from Russia, we could try to shape it in our economic interest. Unfortunately, we chose the latter course. That was why we went ahead, not long after the end of the Cold War. It's not an accident that the agreement that comes out right after the end of the Cold War was so unfair to the poorest countries of the world. We were no longer competing for their affections.

The other reason I think that globalization has come out so poorly is that we were to a large extent Pollyannaish about what it would bring, that everybody would be better off. Actually, economic theory had always made clear that not everybody would win. What economic theory had said is that the gainers could compensate the losers—in other words, the country as a whole would be better off. If it were managed fairly, the country as a whole would be better off, so much better off that those who won could compensate the losers. But no one ever said that they would compensate the losers.

The theory predicted that there would be potentially very big losers. The way to see that most simply is to think through what it would mean if we had full integration, full globalization, in a model of the kind that the advocates of globalization always talk about, free markets working perfectly.

We know what that would mean. That would mean unskilled wages everywhere in the world would be exactly the same. That's what we mean by a fully integrated market. That means the unskilled wages in the United States and the unskilled wages in India would be exactly the same, roughly equal to the average of the two. That means that there would be huge downward pressures on unskilled wages in the United States.

Now, this is an obvious implication of full integration that none of the advocates of globalization have tried to advertise, for an obvious reason—because there are a lot of people who would be very unhappy knowing that this was happening. The fact is that there are actually a number of forces that are simultaneously depressing wages at the bottom, or even the middle. I don't want to pretend that globalization is the only one—technology is another. But these forces are real, and they're not short term. In the United States, real wages at the bottom today are about 30 percent below what they were thirty years ago. So this is not a one-year trend. And it is not going to be reversed.

More disturbing is even in the middle in the last six years real incomes have fallen. So, while GDP in the United States is higher than it was six years ago, the median American is actually worse off than he was six years ago. You see a number of articles now talking about that.

And as I say, while there are a number of forces that have contributed to this, globalization is one of the forces, but it's one that people feel like they can do something about. Now, some people talk about globalization as being inevitable; it's like cod liver oil, that you just have to take it and swallow it; it may be bitter, but you have to get used to it. But that's not true.

Globalization is measured by the ratio of trade to GDP or capital flows to GDP. It was stronger before World War I than it was in the inter-war period. We all know about the Smoot-Hawley tariffs, where we withdrew from globalization. If a majority of Americans feel—a majority of people around the world feel—that they are losing from globalization, there really is a risk of a backlash. So it behooves, I think, those who are advocating globalization to actually try to make sure that it is reshaped so that there are more winners and fewer losers.

When the young students in France went on protest last spring, they were protesting about the fact that wages and benefits were being lowered. The response was, "you have to do this because of globalization." Then they scratched their heads and they said, "Well, you told us that globalization was going to make us better off." They said, "How can lower wages and less job protections make us better off?"

Sometimes the answer will come back, "Well, you have to be patient." But then, of course, Keynes' famous quip comes to mind: "In the long run we're all dead." If we are talking about forces, that over thirty, forty years real wages have fallen by a third, that's a working lifetime.

So what I've tried to do is to sketch very briefly some of the underlying forces that are leading to globalization not working out in the way that it had been hoped. Let me try to talk now about how this plays out in a couple of specific contexts.

One of them is intellectual property. Why is intellectual property even on the table? Why is it a globalization issue? Well, it's a globalization issue because it was made a globalization issue. It was an issue where the United States said, "There have to be high uniform, or close to uniform, standards of intellectual property around the world." In the Uruguay Round, we forced all the countries to adopt our intellectual property standards. Therefore, it became a globalization issue because we were forcing that as a standard.

That is true of a lot of the areas of globalization. One of the complaints is that country sovereignty is being reduced; they can't have the intellectual property regime that they want, or other areas, because under globalization we have to have certain standards.

As an academic, obviously I have some sympathy with intellectual property. It's the way we get some of our rewards. I will tell you a little story that illustrates perhaps, though, my ambivalence.

About twenty years ago, I got a letter from a Chinese publisher wanting me to write an introduction to a pirated edition of my textbook. I was very enthusiastic about it. You know, I had written the book not only to make money, but also for influence, of having ideas. I figured if one-tenth of 1 percent of the Chinese read this book, that's a big audience. You are talking about a billion people, and with one-tenth of 1 percent you really can have some effect. So I went ahead, thought I would do it, and was very enthusiastic. But I thought before doing it I should check with my publisher, which was Norton, and they went ballistic.

As another example, around the same time I was in Taiwan for a conference and I had a little time to go to a bookstore. Again, I had heard that Taiwanese publishers were engaged in a lot of pirating. As I walked through the bookstore, I had a little debate in my mind: Would I be unhappier if when I got to the bookstore they had pirated my book and had stolen my property, my intellectual property; or if they hadn't stolen my book, because if they hadn't stolen my book, that meant that my ideas were not being disseminated, they had ignored me. By the time I got to the bookstore, I had finished the debate and I decided that I really wanted them to have stolen my book. And they had. So I actually felt very pleased.

Academics believe in the importance of spreading ideas. Thomas Jefferson talked about it much more poetically than I can. It's in the Jefferson Memorial. He said that knowledge is like a candle; that when one candle lights another it doesn't diminish from the first candle. So the way economists say this is that knowledge is a public good—zero marginal cost, to put it in very unpoetic terms.

What does that mean? That means that efficiency requires that you not restrict the use, you disseminate it, you let everybody use it. Yet, the intellectual property system—the patent system, copyright—is based on restricting use.

This is very different from ordinary property. Property rights—many of you know, the big discussion of property rights—are associated with increasing economic efficiency. Intellectual property rights are concerned with decreasing economic efficiency, restricting use of something that is a public good. But it's even worse than that; they give a monopoly power. And we all know the enormous distortions associated with monopoly.

So here we have in the Constitution of the United States a provision saying you're going to create intellectual property that is going to restrict something that is a public good, and create an enormous monopoly distortion. Why do you do it? Well, you do it because you hope that it will somehow stimulate innovation. Intellectual property is extremely complex—what can be patented, how long it can go, the scope, the conditions. The most important ideas can't be patented. Einstein's idea on $E = mc^2$ could not be patented. In economics, one of the most important ideas in recent years has been the theory of asymmetric information, and that can't be patented. So a lot of the most important ideas can't be patented.

If you don't get it right, you get the disadvantages of monopoly but not the advantages of innovation. The Council of Economic Advisers and the Office of Science and Technology in the White House both came to the conclusion that TRIPs had got it wrong, that we were getting monopoly but not innovation—in fact, it can actually stifle innovation.

I explain it in the book by giving two stories. The two most important innovations in the

19th century, the automobile and the airplane, and both were almost stifled by the patent system. It was just luck, and in one case the government taking over, saying, "We won't let the patent lawyers destroy us," because of World War I, where they seized the patents back and formed a patent pool, that we have the airplane today.

So patents can have a very negative effect. Right now they are having a very negative effect in the software industry. Why is this important? Well, as I said before, in the area of drugs the intellectual property regime was designed to make generic medicines less successful—in other words, less affordable to those in the developing countries. And it worked. But it worked in the sense of denying access to medicine.

Did it work on the other side? We got the disadvantages of monopoly. What about innovation? The answer is almost none. The drug companies spend far more money on advertising and marketing than they do on research, far more money on research on lifestyle drugs, like hair or other things, than they do on lifesaving drugs, and almost no money on the lifesaving drugs that are of concern to the developing countries, with hundreds of millions of people affected by malaria and other tropical diseases.

In the book I describe an alternative system for financing innovation. Innovation doesn't come costlessly, so you can't just say, "Let's just have people innovate." It requires incentives; it requires finance. But a far better system is a prize system, where you ascertain what are the diseases that we care about, malaria and diseases that affect hundreds of millions of people, and you say, "If you discover that, you'll get a big prize. If you discover something less important, you get a small prize. But then we'll use the force of the market economy to distribute it at as low a price as possible." As opposed to the current system, where you use monopoly to reduce the production and raise the price, this is based on increasing the production and lowering the price. I am going to argue this is a far better way of organizing our health care innovation system than the current one.

What I've tried to do is I go through each of the other areas. One of the ones I talk about, for instance, is global warming. Kyoto was a major success. But 75 percent of the emissions are left out, so clearly it is not going to work. I give some proposals of how we can make a global system for global warming actually work.

I talk about natural resources. Why is there a natural resource curse, where, on average, countries with more resources grow more slowly rather than faster? A real paradox. I suggest what we can do to convert resources into the blessing that they ought to be.

Global financial instability, an enormous amount of it everywhere. It has not gone down; it has gone up. Some of you may have seen I had an Op-Ed, a very brief one, in *The New York Times* two days ago, where I tried to talk about why the kinds of things on the table are only focusing on systematic relief, likely to make things even worse, and why you need a systemic reform.

Let me just conclude. One of the criticisms I've sometimes gotten is aren't I too Utopian, too optimistic, about reforms. I describe all of the problems and the forces that lead to them. Why do I think change is going to happen?

I think the answer is actually fairly simple. Change is going on. Globalization is a dynamic force, it's a fluid force. The question isn't whether there will be change; the question is whether when there will be a crisis, we respond to the crisis by some patchwork; it will work for a little while, then we'll have another crisis. Or whether we try to identify the problems, think rationally about them, realizing that we have at various times opportunities to make some of these reforms, and then try to do it in a more systematic way.

This book is offered on the written idea that there are at least a number of these changes that are feasible, would make a difference, and, given the enormous forces of dissatisfaction with globalization, actually I think there could be a political consensus behind it. So I am optimistic that we actually can make at least some of these changes that would make globalization work, or at least work a lot better than it has been.

2.1.4 What Should Be Off-Limits to Globalization?

INTERNATIONAL FORUM ON GLOBALIZATION

Since Garrett Hardin published his seminal essay "The Tragedy of the Commons" in 1968 (Selection 2.5.1), much has changed in the world. Even though Hardin's article emphasized the potentially negative impact of population growth on our planet, his basic concern was the urgent need to address the ethics of unrestrained self-interest in a shrinking and increasingly interdependent world. Changes in the international system, such as those described by Thomas Friedman (Selection 2.1.1), suggest that since the end of the cold war, multinational corporations have become increasingly powerful and influential actors in international affairs. In the continual search for increased profits, companies, both large and small, have attempted to commodify natural resources, such as water and seeds for food crops, which until recently had been either free or available at very low cost. This article, published by the International Forum on Globalization, a group of economists, scholars, activists, and others concerned with the long-range impact of economic globalization, argues that the value of preserving the commons is being ignored in the rapidly accelerating search for financial gain. If this trend is allowed to continue unchecked, it could have irreversible negative consequences for our planet. The future of humanity could be at stake if human rights and democratic local control are not respected in decisions over what is and is not for sale in the global marketplace.

FOCUS QUESTIONS

1. How do the authors of this article define the notion of the "commons"? What are some examples of the kinds of things that traditionally have been thought to belong to the commons? What are some examples of the kinds of things the authors believe should belong to the "modern commons"?
2. Which of the current threats to the commons discussed in this article do you think is the most serious? Explain why. To what extent do you think citizens of the developed world are aware of these threats? Would you be willing to take action, and what price might you be willing to pay to protect people in the less-developed nations and indigenous peoples from these threats?
3. Critically evaluate the specific proposals to protect the commons, found at the end of this article. What could motivate different interest groups either to welcome or oppose such changes, and on what might they base their rationale for their positions? Explain.
4. Compare the position on globalization taken in this reading to that found in Jagdish Bhagwati (Selection 2.1.2). Where do you stand on the debate over the limits of globalization? Discuss.

Source: From "The Commons: What Should be Off-Limits to Globalization?" in *Alternatives to Economic Globalization: A Better World is Possible*, by The International Forum on Globalization, pp. 79–104. Copyright © 2002 by International Forum on Globalization. Reprinted by permission of Berrett-Koehler Publishers, Inc.

KEYWORDS

biodiversity, biopiracy, commodification, the commons, enclosure, human rights, indigenous people, NAFTA, subsidiarity, sustainability, TRIPs

As recently as two decades ago, large parts of the world were not part of economic globalization. The majority of people in the world still lived off the land, many with little dependence on outside markets. In many rural areas, seeds were exchanged as the collective property of the community, not the private property of Monsanto or Cargill. Many of the three hundred million indigenous people in the world lived in complete isolation from global trade activity. Most municipal water systems were under local government or community control. Much of the economic activity in the Soviet Union, Eastern Europe, and China was not linked to global markets. Most developing countries restricted foreign investment in their banking, insurance, and other critical economic sectors. Most stock markets were national, closed to global investors. Even though global corporations clamored to enter each of these domains, national and local governments and communities maintained strong barriers.

All of that has changed. Under two decades of market fundamentalism, introduced by Ronald Reagan, Margaret Thatcher, Helmut Kohl, and their counterparts elsewhere, the boundaries came crashing down. Some of this was seen in dramatic fashion on CNN in living rooms around the world, such as the destruction of the Berlin Wall. Some happened in the face of remarkable citizen opposition, such as the passage of NAFTA in 1993 and the WTO in 1994. Other battles over the global spread of corporate control occurred on the local stage, such as the determined fight by Bolivian workers and peasants to keep the municipal water system in Cochabamba out of the hands of Bechtel and the struggles of Indian peasants against the Cargill and Monsanto assertions of property rights over their seeds. During these two decades, global corporations—with the strong support of many national governments—forcefully asserted their right to any market anywhere. And today their reach has extended into virtually every domain of even remote rural communities around the world.

One of the most critical points of unity among the authors of this document is that this encroachment of corporate globalization into every aspect of life and the environment must stop. We seek to shift the framework of the overall debate on globalization in this sense: we believe that many aspects of social and economic life around the world should be off-limits to the processes of economic globalization. In this chapter, we offer the beginnings of a framework for choosing which arenas should be off-limits to which aspects of economic globalization.

On one level, there is already agreement across the spectrum of the globalization debate that certain goods and services should be kept out of trade. For example, governments around the world have created a global convention to ban trade in hazardous wastes. Likewise, there is a global convention against the trafficking of endangered species. And there is growing global action against the trafficking across borders of women sold into sexual bondage.

Now, the International Forum on Globalization would like to expand the debate beyond the "pernicious" goods mentioned above to include the rights of peoples and obligations of nations concerning what has traditionally been called *the commons.*

In this chapter, we offer an overview of the many notions of the commons around the world and spell out the current threats of economic globalization to commons such as freshwater, the genetic commons, communal lands, and others. We then introduce the concept of the modern commons—that is, the role of governments in carrying out a sacred public trust to perform certain key services that were once the province of communities and families but have been captured by and subsumed into the nation-state. We argue that selling off these services to global corporations—which operate on an entirely different set of priorities than the public interest—is a grave violation of these modern commons, many of which should never be commodified. We argue that they are also obligations of governments as trustees of the common rights and services of people. Finally, we offer a few ideas on how the commons might be protected from the worst aspects of economic globalization.

We offer these suggestions in the spirit of opening up a complex discussion. We do not pretend to present the final answers.

UNDERSTANDING THE COMMONS

Much of the thrust of economic globalization over these decades has been driven by global corporations pushing to develop and market every type of natural resource. In a world where natural resources were already seriously overexploited, corporations have attempted to convert every remaining nook and cranny of the natural world and human experience into commodified form.

Now, areas of life traditionally considered out of bounds are being considered for monetized activity, private ownership, or global trade. These are aspects of life that had been accepted since time immemorial as collective property, or the common heritage of all peoples and communities, existing for everyone to share as they have for millennia. These are what have been known as the commons.

Obvious among them are the air we breath, the freshwater we drink, the oceans and the diverse wildlife and plant biodiversity of the world, the genes all creatures pass to following generations, the stores of human knowledge and wisdom, the informal support systems of the community, the seeds that communities use for replanting, the public square, shared languages and culture, and among indigenous peoples, communal lands that have been worked cooperatively for thousands of years.

Some commons are gifts from the bounty of nature and are crucial to the survival of people and the earth. Most cultures have innumerable rituals to celebrate these gifts and rules or taboos against harming them. Other commons are new, including, for example, the broadcast spectrum or the Internet. Still others are ancient, such as the common grazing meadows of Africa, Europe, and Asia, folklore, and cultural artifacts.

Some commons may be thought of as global, such as the atmosphere, the oceans, outer space, and because they have no territorial claimants, Antarctica and the moon. Others may be thought of as community commons: public spaces, common lands, forests, the gene pool, local innovative knowledge with respect to medicinal plants, and seeds that communities have developed over centuries.

Author Jonathan Rowe of California's Tomales Bay Institute points out that the key characteristic of all aspects of the commons is that they belong to everyone. No one has traditionally had exclusive rights to them. We have inherited them jointly; they are our common heritage. They "are more basic to our lives than the state or the market," says Rowe. He goes on to say, "One cannot imagine a life without air fit to breathe, oceans rich with life, free clean water, a vibrant biodiversity. These are things we have always taken for granted. The commons have the quality of always having been there, one generation after another, available forever to all."

Later in this chapter, we will advocate for yet another category—the "modern commons" of public services like health, water purification and distribution, education, information, each of which was once achieved informally within small local and indigenous communities that have since been absorbed by the state and are also now on tap for privatization.

The modern nation-state has also taken onto itself the collective security of its citizens, which in a less technologically oriented and mobile world was once the province of communities. In that context, we need to discuss the varieties of security protection that a modern state is obliged to offer in addition to its obvious military roles. Since adopting the Universal Declaration of Human Rights in 1948, the United Nations has helped governments define basic human rights. Governments are obligated to protect human rights, as well as food security, as fundamental to life.

Protection of cultural diversity is also a basic duty and right. Nothing in the global trading system should ever be permitted to reduce these fundamental priorities. (At present, many elements of the WTO and other trade agreements work directly against countries that try to protect these fundamental rights, which we now propose as part of the modern commons.)

Precise categorization of each type of commons is difficult to achieve because many cross several categories—for example, river water (which may pass through several regions and countries), biodiversity (which may be local or national), the broadcast spectrum (which may be local, national, or international), and the genetic structures of life. Similarly, protections against trade that destroys the commons—toxins, armaments, and so on—must be national and international.

Nonetheless, the purpose of this discussion is to lay on the table one central principle:

> Any global trading system needs to recognize and yield to the primary notion that not every aspect of experience should be subject to its centralized rules, and many aspects should never be included in global trade or investment of any kind or in the rules that govern trade and investment.

Such complex questions are usually omitted from discussions about global trading systems, which usually keep their focus on new resources, expansion, and profit. But these questions must be addressed if any kind of social or environmental sustainability is to be obtained. How can communal spaces be effectively protected? Do any effective instruments now exist? What new ones can be proposed? How do we define the areas of the commons, common heritage, or government services that should *never* be subject to trade—or at least never be subject to the authority of global agreements that impinge on local or national sovereignty? What are the obligations of nation-states in the modern world? What goods are too dangerous—toxins, weapons, and drugs, for example—to be allowed into the global trade system at all? Should we establish taboos for certain kinds of trade?

CURRENT THREATS TO THE COMMONS

The conversion of the commons into commodified, privatized, "enclosed" form has been under way for centuries ... In the current context, the main engines of this conversion are the global corporations and the global bureaucracies that increasingly have served these corporations. With the help of the new global trade and finance bureaucracies, corporations are finding opportunities in some virgin territory that most humans never thought could possibly be fodder for corporate enterprise. Here are a few examples.

Threats to the Freshwater Commons

Unthinkable as it may seem, freshwater—a common heritage basic to the survival of all human beings—is being opened up to private ownership, commodification, export, and trade. It's as if water were an ordinary commodity, like new computer parts or car tires, rather than a shared, irreplaceable, and limited resource needed by all creatures of the earth.

In many parts of the world, the rights to fresh-water in rivers, streams, and lakes are being sold to giant transnational corporations like Bechtel, Vivendi, and others. (Before its collapse, Enron was also a main player in water deals.) These firms have started charging users for every drink of water or liter of irrigation. For people who cannot pay the fees—and many cannot—they, their families, and their fields go thirsty.

Private corporations around the world have identified freshwater as the last great untapped natural resource to be exploited for profit. They are quickly taking control of water and water services to kick-start trade in what authors Maude Barlow and Tony Clarke have labeled *blue gold*. Indeed, water is becoming just as important as a prior era's black gold—oil.

Companies have been able to proceed aggressively because water has been defined as a tradable commodity by both NAFTA and the WTO. Once the tap is turned on—that is, once any deals are made by *any* state or municipality in a country to privatize water or water services—the tap cannot be turned back off without violating corporate rights. The WTO contains specific provisions prohibiting the use of export controls to prevent the export of water, and NAFTA contains a clause (chapter 11 of NAFTA) that gives companies the right to sue governments for lost *future* profits. This applies, for example, in cases where governments try to stop water export. Water services are also among those slated to be labeled as a commodity in the new General Agreement on Trade in Services (GATS), under a new category called "Environmental Services."

Once water is privatized, commodified, and put on the open market, it is not available to everyone who needs it but only to those who pay. Right now, contrary to popular understanding, most of the world's freshwater is used by corporate industrial agriculture and in manufacturing, such as in the computer industry for manufacture of computer chips. Relatively little is left for drinking or small-scale farming.

Already, the privatization of water has been the subject of enormous angry protests in many countries, notably Bolivia, South Africa, Canada, and elsewhere. In Cochabamba, Bolivia, for example, hundreds of thousands of people rose up against the fees being charged by Bechtel Corporation after it gained control of the municipality's water distribution system and immediately raised prices. On the brink of a revolution, the Bolivian government finally cancelled its agreement with Bechtel, which responded by suing the government under investment rules of a Bolivia-Netherlands trade agreement that mirror the NAFTA rules. As we go to press, the case is still pending.

Threats to the Genetic Commons

Another commons that few people ever thought could be subject to privatization and development is the genetic commons—the vast building blocks of all life on earth. Yet this too is now subject to reinvention through genetic engineering and transformed into patentable commodities.

The late David Brower of Earth Island Institute once called the genetic commons "the last untapped wilderness on earth," but that is no longer true. Like our great forests, the genetic commons are on the verge of rampant commercial intervention. In some areas, like agriculture, the process is well under way. Third World agriculture activists call it *biopiracy.*

According to Andrew Kimbrell of the International Center for Technology Assessment, "Corporations are now scouring the globe seeking valuable plant, animal, and human genes that they can claim as their own private property, as if they invented them. Thousands of gene patents have already been given to corporations, which are now able to patent whole life forms and own them."

Most of this activity falls within the life science industries. Corporations like Monsanto, Novartis, DuPont, Pioneer, and others have benefited enormously from the WTO's TRIPs [trade-related aspects of intellectual property rights] agreement, which confirms their ability to patent plant and seed varieties according to their genetic makeup. Even though these varieties were developed over centuries by indigenous farming communities that shared them with one another freely in a process that is at the core of these cultures, now fees must be paid to use them.

Global corporations insist that this valuable genetic material should not be locked up by small communities but that the whole world should have access to it. Indeed, corporations use the language of the global commons until such time as they confirm their monopoly patents on the material. At that point, all arguments in defense of the commons are abandoned. Instead, the corporations then argue that *they* should be permitted to lock up these genetic materials through patents in order to have a chance of recouping their research investment—for the benefit of all humanity.

Pharmaceutical corporations are especially eager for access and the rights to patent genetic materials. Their representatives travel the globe, exploring traditional native remedies in jungles and fields. They also extract blood and scrape "buccal mucosa" from the skin of native peoples wherever they can, hoping to find genes that contain natural resistance to certain maladies. Usually they accomplish this without disclosing why they are doing it or how much profit they stand to make from their findings and their patents. Among indigenous peoples, the right of "free and prior informed consent" has now become a major international demand before governments can bring in development projects and before companies are permitted to enter.

The cynicism of such practices became especially clear when global pharmaceutical corporations refused to set aside the rules of the WTO's TRIPs agreement in South Africa to permit low-cost, locally developed AIDS drugs to be substituted for the expensive patented varieties they controlled. Only after intense global protest did the patent holders agree to lower prices for AIDS victims there. But the TRIPs rules remain in force for all other instances.

The authors of this document believe that seeds, medicines, and other genetic materials that have been developed in communities for centuries or millennia should always be subject to community control. Any agreement with outsiders to use these materials must be on the basis of fair and equal negotiations on a case-by-case basis, after full discussion of all the relevant facts.

Threats to Communal Lands

In hundreds of cultures around the world, the notion of private, individual land ownership is anathema. Communal land ownership—or no land ownership—is traditional practice and belief among indigenous and farming communities on every continent. This worldview is fundamental to these millions of people, their cultures, their agriculture, and their economic, political, and spiritual practices. In peasant farming communities of South America and Asia and in indigenous communities everywhere, the notion that an individual or corporation could legally gather under its own authority large fruitful tracts of land—thus depriving the people who shared it for millennia—is outrageous beyond all understanding.

Native American activist Winona La Duke has described the land ownership issue among indigenous peoples by pointing out that in her own Ojibway culture, the term *nishnabe akin* means "the land to which the people belong." It is a notion that is the exact opposite of Western ideas about land ownership. It is also at the heart of many teachings about humans and land being in *relationship* with each other, with reciprocal obligations.

In contrast, the new trade agreements and policies of international banks and corporations are designed to delegitimize the authority of any such reciprocal arrangements and to solidify private ownership so that land can be more easily bought and exploited. For example, one of the United States' specific demands in NAFTA negotiations with Mexico was that Mexico break up the traditional *ejidos* of the Mayan corn farmers, the system of communal land ownership that began with the successful Zapatista revolution of the early 1900s.

The history of the "enclosure" of the commons is largely devoted to the privatization of communal lands throughout the planet. In most places, the process is so far along that it is rarely publicly argued. However, this has begun to change as mass movements like Brazil's landless peasant movement (Movement of Landless Rural Workers) and other such movements around the world have demanded dramatic land reforms and redistribution under the principle that land, like water, is basic for sustenance.

Appropriation of the Global Commons for Waste Sinks

Ownership and privatization are not the only threats to the commons. There is also the effective appropriation of particular global commons as free dumping grounds and waste sinks for the activity of global corporations.

The atmosphere, oceans, and even outer space have become dangerously polluted, freely appropriated by oil, energy, shipping, and toxic industries as convenient sites to dump effluents and wastes. In the case of automobiles, ships, and the fossil fuel industry, it is an intrinsic result of the technologies that effluents rise to the atmosphere.

When similar pollution takes place in a local commons or inside national borders—say, local smokestack emissions or runoff into rivers—government agencies exist specifically to try to do something about it. This is not to say these agencies do a good job of regulating such activity—they do not—but at least they offer an authority to address the matter and a place where citizens may focus their complaints.

When it comes to the global commons, however, few such agencies exist. There have been some efforts over the last half-century to apply some pollution regulations. The Kyoto Protocol on Global Warming, the Montreal Protocol on Substances That Deplete the Ozone Layer, the United Nations Convention on the Law of the Sea, the Stockholm Convention on Persistent Organic Pollutants agreement, among other multilateral environment agreements (MEAs), are efforts to control impacts on global commons. But all have suffered from tremendous political resistance, weak regulatory regimes, and poor enforcement ability. Still, MEAs remain one hope for rational international recognition, on a case-by-case basis, of the collective rights to maintain the commons in a condition that serves all people and the planet's other species.

An important problem, however, is that when such agreements do begin to make progress in limiting corporate activity, the World Trade Organization can threaten to negate them by asserting its own superior authority on behalf of the primacy of global trade activity. For example, at the November 2001 WTO ministerial meeting in Doha, Qatar, the WTO made explicit its intentions to codify its superiority to MEAs, potentially wiping out generations of effort.

Other solutions to the problem have also been proposed. They include a variety of trust agreements where certain commons would be held as the explicit property of all people in trust for the future. Any encroachments would have to go through very complex permission procedures, thus at least slowing and making visible the problems before they occur.

Sadly, there are hundreds of examples of threats to the commons of the kind we have given here. All reflect increased global pressure on remaining pristine areas. Fortunately, however, there is also increased popular resistance to these encroachments. New methods and instruments must be found or created to prevent continued destruction.

THE TRADITION OF THE COMMONS

In most parts of the world, the tradition of the commons is ages old, though it varies from place to place and culture to culture. These are a few examples.

Europe

In Europe, the concept of the commons dates back at least fifteen hundred years. It referred to commonly shared areas of land and resources enjoyed by all members of village communities, including pasture for the grazing of animals, water from streams and lakes, and all the products of field and forest that people used to sustain their lives. The notion that any of these could be enclosed or turned into the private property of individuals or institutions like corporations was, at first, unthinkable.

The commons deteriorated over time in feudal Europe. There were struggles over definitions of the commons, and large parts of them were appropriated through military force by feudal lords and kings. Still, vast areas remained available for village use as traditional common areas.

As trade developed between regions, and especially with the rise of a large European-wide market for wool, lords and merchants increasingly sought to ensure and expand their own supply by privatizing more and more of the common areas, most importantly land. As they succeeded in enclosing ever larger areas, peasant communities began to lose access to resources they had previously taken for granted. Self-sustainability became more difficult. Rather than remaining as subsistence farmers who also traded in local markets, peasants increasingly became "cottagers"—small artisanal producers—or sought day-labor jobs with the large landowners on lands they had formerly shared. With the coming of the Industrial Revolution, cottage industries declined, and people were entirely removed from their land and sources of sustenance. They became factory workers with no connection to the land. The peasants thus evolved into the proletariat.

Some mainstream economists have justified and praised this conversion of the commons to private property as a way of establishing clear ownership and therefore the ability to protect resources from exploitation. But this justification for what was essentially robbery of shared common resources ignores two important facts. First, the people whose lives depended on the commons were almost always excellent caretakers of it and remained so over many centuries. In fact, it was basic to the survival and success of the commons that the entire community shared its values as well as its sustaining virtues and helped protect and preserve it. Second, the people who enclosed the commons, appropriating it for private use, were nearly always outsiders, absentee owners with little personal dedication to nurturing, conserving, or taking care of these resources for the future. The reason they sought private ownership was to exploit the resources as fast as possible. They did not try to own it in order to save it, the assertion of mainstream economists notwithstanding. Rather, they usually pillaged and polluted it.

With the advent of corporate ownership and rights of private property, ownership was made still more abstract or removed from resources, which were increasingly understood only in quantifiable, objective terms. Forests, for example, were no longer appreciated for their community sustainability, the biodiversity they fostered, or their spiritual contexts. Instead, they became "board-feet," ripe for exploitation. That is certainly the situation we face today, in its most amplified form.

Indigenous Communities

In other parts of the world, terms like *commons* were not well-known, but the concepts of shared community use and protection of common resources were basic, endemic, understood and respected by entire societies.

Among indigenous peoples around the world, virtually all political, social, and spiritual values have traditionally been so deeply intertwined with the values and teachings of the natural world that these societies say they are inseparable. It is not really a question of a community commons, as understood by the Europeans. It is more that all creatures—human as well as plant and animal—are directly related, equal, and with equal rights to exist in a fulfilling manner. All economic, political, and spiritual teachings are rooted in that primary relationship.

It is little wonder, therefore, that invading societies—at least those that did not actually slaughter the native populations—made enormous efforts to undermine and destroy their commitment to their traditional relationships to land and nature. That was the only way they could succeed in getting their hands on the resources they desired.

Native peoples were pushed to separate from their lands in hundreds of different ways. Primary among these efforts was the aggressive attempt to undermine traditional religious values and cosmologies as well as traditional native stories and teachings about the need to live in harmony with, and as part of, nature. The actions of missionaries throughout the Americas, the Pacific Islands, and Africa are well-known in this context. They actively helped shift the traditional value system toward a new and more hierarchical view of humans and nature and toward the individualistic notion of private property. In the United States, Australia, and elsewhere, "reeducation" also played an important role—that is, young people were forcibly removed from their traditional communities and placed into boarding schools that did not allow native languages or teachings. The result was a kind of self-loathing that undermined native cultures and their traditional collective economic values.

Equally important were legal maneuvers, such as requiring adjudicatory land title. Since native societies did not traditionally conceive of themselves as "owners" of land but as part of it as a community, "title" and "ownership" of land were an absurdity, but one which they were required to address. The histories of the relationships between invading and native societies are replete with stories of how legalistic maneuvering succeeded in separating Indians from millions of acres of land they formerly enjoyed in a collective manner. These acts of removal and separation continue to this day, notably in the United States.

One particularly appalling recent example is the U.S. Congress's creation of the Alaska Native Claims Settlement Act (ANCSA), purported to be a guarantor of native land rights in Alaska, where these rights had never been abrogated. In fact, ANCSA was the final step in extinguishing the native relationship and rights to enjoy the lands in the traditional manner. Rather than native Alaskans being granted title, or simply granted recognition of "aboriginal rights of ownership" as requested, the Alaskan lands were divided and made into native corporations, managed by native boards of directors, who were given ownership of the lands. But in order to survive, these corporations needed to cut down their forests or exploit their minerals just as any corporation would. These corporate acts, albeit carried out by natives, were contrary to their prior indigenous values. So for the larger society, the desired outcome was achieved; the communal relationship to nature was removed and replaced by an exploitative one, thus providing new fodder for global corporations.

The global invasion of communally held native lands—which has happened on every continent and continues today—has had terrible outcomes, from destruction of the traditional reciprocal relationship between humans and nature to major social breakdowns.

The conflict of values endemic to these pressures over ownership of common lands and resources was very well described in the book *A Basic Call to Consciousness,* published in 1977 by the Iroquois Nation, in a submission to the United Nations Conference on Indigenous Peoples. Here are some short excerpts:

> The majority of the world does not find its roots in Western culture or tradition. The majority of the world finds its roots in the natural world, and it is the natural world, and the tradition of the natural world, which must prevail.
>
> ...
>
> The original instructions direct that we are to express a great respect, an affection, and gratitude toward all the spirits which create and support life. When people cease to respect and express gratitude for these many things, then all life will be destroyed.
>
> ...
>
> To this day the territories we still hold are filled with trees, animals, and the other gifts from the Creation. In these places we still receive our nourishment from our Mother Earth. Many thousands of years ago, all the people of the world believed in the same way of life, that of harmony with the universe. [But] the way of life known as Western Civilization is on a death path on which their own culture has no viable answers.
>
> ...
>
> The Indo-European people who have colonized our lands have shown very little respect for the things that create and support life. We believe that these people ceased their respect for the world a long time ago. The air is foul, the waters poisoned, the trees dying, the animals disappearing. Even the systems of weather are changing. Our ancient teachings warned us that if Man interfered with the natural laws, these things would come to be.
>
> ...
>
> The traditional native people hold the key to the reversal of the processes in Western Civilization Our culture is among the most ancient continuously existing cultures in the world. We are the spiritual guardians of this place. We are here to impart this message.

Asia

Traditional societies everywhere on the planet share values similar to the ones expressed by the North American Iroquois leadership. Concepts like Mother Earth combined with belief in non-hierarchical, nonownership-based communal relationships to field and forest can be found among all peoples who still live in a direct relationship with the earth.

Most people in India today still derive their livelihoods and meet their survival needs from the biological resources of the country, as forest dwellers, farmers, fisherfolk, healers, and livestock owners. Indigenous knowledge systems in medicine, agriculture, and fisheries are the primary basis for meeting their food, health, and cultural needs. In these traditional communities, the biodiversity of the forests and fields and the historic innovations of plant life for food and medicinal purposes have never been seen as the individual property of any person or family but as community resources available to all people. None can be excluded, and neither the state nor any other economically powerful entity can monopolize use of any aspect of the commons, biologically or intellectually.

There is a vibrant struggle in India today over the commons—not only the biological commons (land, forests, water) that have been the basis of sustainability for a great majority of India's population to the present time but also the *intellectual commons.* This refers to the cumulative knowledge that agricultural communities have collected and freely shared for centuries, as well as the innovations they have achieved in developing plant varieties for food and medicine. Global biotech and pharmaceutical companies have been aggressively patenting these examples of the intellectual commons, preventing their common use, and privatizing them for their own purposes. This invasion has led to a level of outrage on the part of India's farmers, indigenous people, and peasant communities that has brought literally millions of people onto the streets in protest against the World Trade Organization's TRIPs agreement, which protects the rights of corporations to engage in these practices.

Community rights to control the biological and intellectual commons are recognized in law as sui generis rights—equivalent to a patent, but recognizing roots in a community rather than an individual. This system is based in part on usufruct rights, which entitle farmers and laborers access to resources needed for their own sustenance, such as common pastures, water, and biodiversity. Sustainability and justice are inherent in such a system of usufruct rights because there are physical limits on how much any one person can labor; hence there are limited returns for labor, unlike capital and private property.

The battle over the biological and intellectual rights of farmers in India, and against the WTO's TRIPs agreement, comes at the end of a long and painful history of prior enclosures of the commons in India. The policy of deforestation and enclosure of the commons in India began in 1865, when the Indian Forest Act authorized the government to declare forests as "unmeasured" lands or "reserves" for state use. This began what was called the scientific management of forests, but it was really the first step in a long series of moves to remove forests from people and convert them to commodities available for private ownership. Peasant communities that had formerly sustained themselves based on the forests' resources were forced to produce indigo instead of food and pay taxes for salt. They experienced the rapid erosion of their usufruct rights to food, fuel, and livestock pastures, as well as forests and sacred sites. This was a primary cause of their later impoverishment, which led directly to their resistance to further erosion of their common rights by global biotech corporations.

THREATS TO THE "MODERN COMMONS"

In most developed countries, it is hard to remember the time when the central political and economic unit was the local community or when resources were commonly shared. Over the past several centuries, political, economic, and technological evolution in much of the world has conspired to bring far more specialization and industrialization of economic activity, far less economic and social self-reliance, and far greater dependence on dominant centralized political units—cities, states, provinces, and national governments—to provide for the common fundamental needs and services that people require, such as education, transportation, health care, environmental protection, security, and the certainty that there will be sufficient food, housing, and work.

All governments now acknowledge their responsibility in these matters, though they perform them with varying levels of success. Canadians and Danes tend to believe their governments have performed well, at least until recently, whereas Russians and Burmese may not feel this way. Most governments get mixed grades on these matters—good in some ways, bad in others. The United States, for example, has kept its economic and sanitation performance generally high but has been very poor in matters of health care and transportation, and its delivery of these services is marked by extreme inequality. Maude Barlow's forthcoming book, *Profit Is Not the Cure,* details the impact of the World Bank, the IMF, the WTO, and their market-opening policies on the erosion of health care services all over the world, and she chronicles the private sector firms that have benefited. Two decades of these policies have left a legacy of unequal access and health crises for the poor worldwide.

The United Nations Universal Declaration of Human Rights asserts that in addition to the services that nations are expected to perform, governments are also expected to ensure certain basic human rights, religious and political freedoms, and the right to *meaningful* work at fair wages with human dignity. In fact, the U.N. declaration asserts that every person on the planet has an "inherited right to citizenship," which includes health care, education, and work. Moreover, every government has the duty to *defend* the fundamental human rights of every one of its citizens, even beyond its borders. Such assertions also imply that governments have the duty to protect their own ability to perform these services and ensure these fundamental rights against attempts to weaken them.

The authors of this report believe that these services and protections qualify as a kind of "modern commons," in which the state has assumed the responsibility for the common good that once resided in local communities. Even as more power devolves back toward the local—an outcome most of us support—we believe that states have a vital role to play in protecting the community stewardship of both traditional and modern commons. The performance of these responsibilities, however, is now under tremendous threat from global economic institutions.

Great pressure is being applied to national governments by corporations and global bureaucracies to privatize and commodify most public services. Global corporations seek to put them in the same category of commercial activity as toothpaste, cars, real estate services, or movies, provided by private industry at market rates.

Yet there are profound differences between the sacred trust arrangement of governments to provide for basic needs and rights and the private, contracted provision of products, entertainment, and commercial services. Corporations operate from a hierarchy of values that requires profit and growth. Yet as corporations make inroads as providers of health, education, water, or food security, the delivery of these services will go only to people who can pay the market rate. The many who cannot will essentially fall out of the system. *Hence, we would argue that any acts that separate governments from their obligation to provide for all people regardless of economic status are to be prevented.*

Similarly, any efforts by global bureaucracies to *require* that governments privatize such services should be resisted by governments and activists alike—and ultimately banned. At this moment, the current WTO negotiations in Geneva over the expansion of the General Agreement on Trade in Services (GATS) are a case in point.

If the GATS agreement is finalized, then most of the services we have listed here as fundamental rights of citizens and obligations of governments will be subsumed under the new rules of GATS. In other words, corporations will have the right to establish a commercial presence and operate what have until now been domestic services inside countries. These include health care, elder care, child care, water purification and delivery, education, prisons, domestic rail and air transportation, public broadcasting, parks, museums and cultural institutions, social security and welfare programs, and public works of all kinds. As mentioned [earlier], the United States or Canada might find ExxonMobil running public broadcasting while Mitsubishi runs social security; France might have Disney operating the Louvre; Enron or WorldCom could be running the German health care system; and Shell Oil could be in charge of the Japanese railroads and perhaps child rearing as well. Such outcomes are not unrealistic: as we already mentioned, U.S. giant Bechtel was on the verge of running a significant piece of Bolivia's water delivery system until recently, nearly causing a revolution because of its prices to the poor.

The U.N. Covenant on Economic, Social, and Cultural Rights includes the right to education and health. Of all services, these are shaping up as the most potentially lucrative for the global corporations pushing the GATS agreement. Global expenditures on education now exceed \$2 trillion, and global expenditures on health care exceed \$3.5 trillion. Global corporations are aiming at nothing less than the dismantling of public education and health care systems. Already they have succeeded in lobbying over forty countries, including all of Europe, to be listed in the GATS.

The obligation of governments to provide services for their citizens may soon be reduced to whether some distant corporation will or will not charge an affordable rate for people to send their children to school or to a doctor.

In our view, no global agreement should have the power to forcibly intervene in the trust agreement between governments and citizens.

Of course, there are many other threats to basic social programs and services and basic rights to food and health, aside from the upcoming GATS agreement. [Earlier], we discussed the structural adjustment programs of the World Bank and the International Monetary Fund. To be eligible for development loans or debt relief, dozens of developing countries were forced to abandon a multitude of social programs and allow for-profit foreign corporations to enter, commercialize, and privatize these operations to the detriment of local people.

We have also discussed the WTO's TRIPs agreement, which enables global corporations to claim intellectual property rights over the genetic heritage of people and communities and to redefine the role and form of agriculture. Farming and the community way of life it has sustained are becoming dominated by global corporations who have rendered farmers dependent on them for seeds, fertilizers, pesticides, and herbicides. Structural adjustment programs have also played a big role in this shift in agriculture, requiring nations to convert their farms to export-oriented, specialized production and permit entry of global corporations that accelerate the process. This has driven farmers off lands where they formerly grew food for their communities and has increased hunger and migration.

Because food security is one of the most fundamental human rights, every government has an interest in ensuring it as an essential foundation for social stability and public health. We believe this means that no development banks or trade agreements should be given the right to *require* that any country revamp its agricultural production systems, allow foreign entry and investment, or open itself to cheaper food from abroad to its own detriment. Of course, any country may choose to allow such entry if conditions warrant, but it should not be *forced* to do so.

Cultural diversity and integrity is another area that can be seen as part of the commons and is arguably a fundamental right that should be protected by nations. It too is now threatened in many ways by global trade agreements. The right of social, religious, cultural, and indigenous groups to preserve their practices, beliefs, artifacts, and artistic expressions is crucial to maintaining diversity within and among nations and in the world. This also applies to the efforts of nation-states to prevent foreign domination of their own national cultural expressions, through media and artistic creations. Many countries, notably Canada and France—both deeply concerned about retaining film and television industries in domestic hands—have been fighting strenuously to retain their rights to protect their own cultures.

Current WTO trade law subjects culture to the disciplines of the agreement, including "national treatment," "most favored nation," and the prohibition against quantitative restrictions. (All of these WTO rules open up countries to foreign media and other cultural products, often to the detriment of local cultural expressions, which can be overpowered.) There have been several complaints over culture at the WTO since its inception. All have had the effect of limiting the right of a state to protect its cultural industries. The most significant was a 1997 ruling in which the United States successfully forced Canada to abandon protections of its magazine industry, even though American magazines already made up 85 percent of all of those available at Canadian newsstands. Then—U.S. trade representative Charlene Barshefsky said the decision would serve as a useful weapon against Canada's and other countries' protection of their film, books, and broadcasting industries.

The United States is taking such a hard line because any exemption for Canada would set a negative precedent for other countries, especially in the developing world, where cultural protection is an emerging issue. The fact that the effort to undermine these protections failed at the Seattle WTO ministerial meetings does not mean the problems are over. Both the GATS and the TRIPs agreement will have a direct impact on the telecommunications sector, including the Internet, digital and e-commerce spheres, public broadcasting, patents, trademarks, and copyright law. All are now on the table. They should be taken off.

In sum, we argue that in all of the preceding issues, nation-states and communities should not be subjected to the rules of global trade agreements or multilateral institutions like the WTO or the IMF. Trade in these areas should be subject to national and local decision-making processes alone. Only in this way will it be possible for nations to act on behalf of the common interests of their citizens and to fulfill their own obligations to them.

PROPOSALS

At the start of this chapter, we said that the issues raised here—the preservation outside of the global trading system of the remaining nonmonetized, nonprivatized commons and the governmental trust in preserving fundamental services and rights (the modern commons)—would be nuanced and complex. We proceeded from the principle that not every aspect of human experience or nature should be commodified or subjected to the rules of global trade regimes that require adherence to the global free trade model. However, defining exactly which aspects to exclude, and precisely when, is not simple and needs to be the subject of continuing discussion and debate. Stimulating that discussion has been our main purpose in this chapter.

To further the process, we end the chapter with a short list of broad policies consistent with the ten principles for sustainable societies.

The Authority of Trade Agreements Must Be Narrowly Defined Global trade bureaucracies and international financial agencies should not have authority over state or national decision making when it comes to the commons, natural heritage resources, the preservation of national choice in domestic services, or fundamental human rights. Trade and investment agreements should not be allowed to require a national or state government to privatize or commercialize remaining areas of the commons or public services, or to force countries to open up these areas to foreign investment and competition, either by imposing rules requiring governments to conform or penalizing them for not doing so.

Decisions on Common Property Resources and Public Services Should Be Local or National Decisions about common property resources and public services should be reserved to the localities and nations involved, consistent with the principle of subsidiarity. Local commons are the province of local communities. National commons should be subject to national democratic decision-making processes. Global commons should be addressed by multilateral agreements on issues of sustainability and equitable access. No commons—whether local, national, or global—are the proper subject of a multilateral trade agreement. Decisions about the ownership, control, and operation of fundamental public services—including health care and hospitals, water management and delivery, natural resource use, education, transportation, public broadcasting, agriculture and food security, culture, social security, welfare, military, police, and jails—should be specifically excluded from multilateral trade and investment agreements.

Some nations and communities may determine that it is in their public interest to contract for private operation of some of these resources and public services. Indeed, there is sometimes a role for private ownership and markets to play in the management, allocation, and delivery of certain common heritage resources—including land, seeds, and water—but only in a framework of effective, democratically accountable public regulation that guarantees fair pricing, equitable access, quality, and public stewardship. However, decisions in these matters are properly local or national and have no place being prescribed by global trade and investment regimes concerned only with advancing private commercial interests. Nor is it acceptable for any international agreement to dictate actions by local or national jurisdictions that would result in excluding individuals or communities from equitable access to services and resources, such as clean water, that are essential to life and health.

Things Fundamental to Life and, Human Survival Should Not Be Privatized or Monopolized Certain aspects of the commons that are basic to survival should not be privatized or subject to trade agreements. These include the atmosphere, bulk freshwater, and the genetic and molecular building blocks of life (including the human genome). It may be permissible to patent truly distinctive seed varieties created by privately funded research, for a limited period of time, but the patenting of naturally occurring seeds or seed varieties developed by farming communities or by publicly funded research should not be allowed.

Some Aspects of Life Should Not Be Patented or Otherwise Monopolized Here we include some areas of life that *are* now partly privatized and traded but should never be subject to corporate *patent* rights or monopoly ownership as offered by TRIPs. At present, these include genes, seeds, plant varieties, and animal breeds—with the possible exception of temporary rights to the exclusive production and sale of distinctive plant and animal varieties created through privately funded breeding programs. The general principle is this: No patents on life. There is also a need to rethink patent rules on life-sustaining pharmaceuticals—for example, AIDS drugs—to ensure fair pricing and access by all who need them, without regard to financial means.

The Right of Countries to Choose Not to Import or Export Goods They Deem Harmful and Pernicious Should Be Protected; Trade in Certain Pernicious Goods May Properly Be Prohibited by International Agreement A country properly has the right to ban the import or export of certain goods that it considers to present a threat to health and safety, including GMOs, toxins, weapons, and addictive drugs, as well as tobacco and alcohol, for which existing trade agreements now prohibit exclusions. Some currently traded goods are so harmful to the environment, public health, safety, peace, and the global commons that it may be appropriate to create an international agreement to ban them entirely. Candidates would include toxic and nuclear wastes, endangered species, land mines, and sex workers. Such issues, however, are appropriately addressed by international forums and agreements devoted specifically to these topics, not by specialized trade bodies or trade and investment agreements.

International Agreements Are Needed to Protect Global and Transnational Commons Because certain activities in one country can have serious consequences for common resources in other countries, a system is needed to regulate them. For conditions like acid rain, air pollution, ozone depletion, ocean pollution or overexploitation, climate change, and so on, or where common resources such as rivers serve multiple jurisdictions, negotiations are needed on a bilateral or multilateral basis to protect the threatened commons and secure a just and equitable allocation of benefits. These negotiations should take place in forums dedicated to dealing with such issues and should be placed outside the jurisdiction and authority of trade bodies.

2.2 COMPUTERS, INFORMATION, AND SURVEILLANCE TECHNOLOGIES

2.2.1 Many Working Minds: Wikis, Open Source Software, and Blogs

CASS R. SUNSTEIN

In this selection, University of Chicago law professor Cass R. Sunstein examines a variety of different methods currently in use by which many creative minds can collaborate freely to produce valuable products and services. His interest in this subject is motivated by a recognition that such distributed collaboration made possible by computers and the Internet allows for a new kind of deliberative democracy that is coming to have increasing social importance. Wikis and open source software, for instance, have come to be called the "blogosphere" and are somewhat "miraculous" in that they depend on the spontaneous formation of cooperative virtual communities of information workers. What is astonishing about these phenomena is that a great many people are willing to contribute their time and talent to such collaborative projects without the promise of economic rewards for their labors. What motivates people to do this? How can we harness this creative energy and talent in order to solve other social problems that we face? The possibilities suggested by what has been done so far are endless.

FOCUS QUESTIONS

1. Sunstein employs an analogy between the way in which free markets set prices and the ways in which wikis and blogs consolidate dispersed knowledge. What are the points of similarity he identifies? What are the important differences?
2. How do wikis work to prevent vandals from corrupting the information that is contained in them?
3. What are some advantages of copyleft licenses, like the General Public License, or the Creative Commons License over traditional copyright for intellectual property like software? What are some disadvantages?
4. What are some advantages of blogs over traditional media sources? What are some of the disadvantages?

KEYWORDS

blogs, BIOS, collaborative filtering, copyright, copyleft, Creative Commons Licence, FOSS, information cocoons, Linux, Wikipedia

---

Editor's note: The section on open source software has been removed from this reading. Interested readers should consult the original.

Source: From *Infotopia: How Many Minds Produce Knowledge*, by Cass R. Sunstein, pp. 147–196. Copyright © 2006 Oxford University Press. Reprinted by permission.

WIKIS, WIKIPEDIA, FLU WIKI, AND BEYOND

Wiki World

A wiki is a Web site that allows any user to add material and to edit and delete what previous users have done. The term comes from the Hawaiian word *wikiwiki,* which means "fast" or "speedy." (That term may well come from the English word "quick"; if "quick" were translated into Hawaiian phonology, *wiki* or *kiwiki* would be the result.) The concept of the wiki originated with Ward Cunningham, who sought to produce "the simplest online database that could possibly work." In 1994, Cunningham developed the initial wiki server, which provided an exceptionally easy means of editing and which invited contributions from anyone who wanted to edit or add material.

In the enthusiastic words of Cunningham and his coauthor Bol Leuf, "Wiki is *inherently democratic*—every user has exactly the same capabilities as any other user." Cunningham's own wiki is thoroughly democratic in that sense. Other wiki software, such as the widely used Media Wiki, includes special support for "administrators" with greater powers than other users. Nonetheless, wikis are democratic in the sense that they permit anyone to edit pages.

At first glance, the democratic quality of wikis seems to be a big problem. If anyone in the world can make changes, isn't the text vulnerable to pranks and even destruction? Isn't some kind of security needed to protect against malevolent people? Cunningham and Leuf say that "experience shows that in fact little damage is done to wiki content even in the absence of security mechanisms." If this is so, it is not because of economic incentives, as in prediction markets. It is because most people really want the process to work. An important current use of wikis is to create documentation for technical projects, and many free and open source software projects now use wiki as the preferred format for creating such documentation.

Wikipedia

Of course, software projects are not everyone's cup of tea. To date, the most notable wiki, by far, is Wikipedia, a free, Web-based encyclopedia that attempts to take advantage of the information held by its tens of thousands of contributors ("Wikipedians"), who add to and edit the encyclopedia. (Try it, if you like; it's easy.) Wikipedia is written and edited by these numerous volunteers, who can change and add articles however they wish. Its remarkable goal is nothing less than "to distribute a free encyclopedia to every single person on the planet in their own language."

Wikipedia is growing at an explosive rate, and any numbers will rapidly become obsolete. At the present time, there are more than 2 million articles, approaching 1 million in English (amounting to more than 200 million words) and the rest in about two hundred other languages, of which only about half are active. (There is a Wikipedia in Klingon, the fictional language of a race of violence-prone but basically honorable humanoids created on the television show *Star Trek.*) There are nine "major" Wikipedias, with more than fifty thousand articles; twenty-one minor Wikipedias, with more than ten thousand articles; the rest are less active. Interestingly, the growth of the Arabic Wikipedia has been slowed by virtue of the fact that most Arabic Internet users speak English well, and they have been writing Wikipedia entries for the English Wikipedia.

Tens of millions of people visit Wikipedia every day, making it one of the world's most popular sites, more popular than the *New York Times* and even PayPal. The number of visitors, like the number of articles, is rapidly growing. The range is astonishing. If a person suddenly achieves public importance—through election, appointment, or sheer celebrity—it is almost certain that Wikipedia will have a relevant article almost immediately. The article is often detailed; it is nearly always highly informative.

Wikipedia grows out of an old-fashioned, less imaginative, and now-abandoned project, Nupedia, an early effort to create a free encyclopedia on the Internet. Nupedia was structured like an ordinary encyclopedia, with expert writers and a system of peer review. Unfortunately, if also unsurprisingly, the process of writing Nupedia proved exceptionally slow. As a result, Jimmy "Jimbo" Wales, the founder of Nupedia, was persuaded to supplement it with a more informal project, in which ordinary people could write and edit entries. Started on January 10, 2001, Wikipedia had one thousand articles by February, ten thousand by September 7, and forty thousand by August 30, 2002. As early as May 2001, Wikipedias were created in many other languages, including Catalan, Chinese, Dutch, German, Esperanto, French, Hebrew, Italian, Portuguese, Spanish, and Swedish.

It is an understatement to say that Wikipedia generally works. In terms of sheer volume, it dwarfs the *Encyclopedia Britannica*. The number of articles is extraordinary. True, the quality does not always match the quantity; you can easily find articles that are thin or amateurish or that contain significant omissions and errors. But for the most part, the quality tends to be high as well. Specialists are regularly surprised to see a great deal of accuracy, as well as astounding currency, in Wikipedia entries; the millions of visitors are responding to the fact that they have a lot to learn. In a way, this is a real mystery. Why is Wikipedia so successful?

An essential part of the answer is that large numbers of knowledgeable people are willing to participate in creating Wikipedia, and whatever errors they make usually receive rapid correction, simply because so many minds are involved. The involvement of many people ensures that Wikipedians are able to produce a much more comprehensive resource than a small group could, even a small group of experts. Amazing but true: Wikipedia is revised hundreds of times every hour. At last count, more than seven hundred articles were being added every *day*. Wikipedia is thus able to elicit widely dispersed information. But the large set of contributors disguises some distinctive features of this particular wiki. For the English edition, over half of the edits are done by 0.7 percent of all users—a mere 524 people. The most active 2 percent of users, that is, fewer than fifteen hundred people, have done almost three-quarters of all edits. For the Spanish Wikipedia, 8.1 percent of all users produce more than 90 percent of edits. Wikipedia thus combines huge numbers of occasional volunteers with a not-so-huge core of frequent editors.

Wikipedia is in part a deliberative forum, with reason-giving by those who disagree and with deliberative "places" to accompany disagreement. In fact, every page on Media Wiki, used by Wikipedia, includes an accompanying "talk" page. This means that every entry in the encyclopedia can be used as a deliberative space—and many entries are so used.

Wikipedia also has the huge advantage of cumulative knowledge. An initial entry might be thin. In fact, thin entries are described as "stubs," inviting more sustained treatment. In Wikipedia's own words, "Stubs are articles which have not yet received substantial attention from the Wikipedia editors. They have been created, but don't yet contain enough information to be truthfully considered articles. The community believes that stubs are far from worthless. They are, rather, the first step articles take on their course to becoming complete." Over a short period of time, stubs and thin entries do become much thicker.

It is even possible to think of Wikipedia as an exceptionally fast-moving tradition: Everyone who edits is standing on the shoulders of those who were there earlier. It isn't easy to write an entry from scratch, especially on a technical topic. But if thousands of people are in a position to make small additions and improvements, an initial skeleton can rapidly become a full body. In the anyone-can-edit words of the site itself, "We are working together on statements of what is known (what constitutes free human knowledge) about various subjects. Each of us individually benefits from this arrangement. It is difficult to single-handedly write *the perfect article*, but it becomes easier when working together.... We *assume that the world is full of reasonable people* and that collectively they can arrive eventually at a reasonable conclusion, despite the worst efforts of a very few wreckers." Quality control occurs through a kind of peer review, in which new edits appear on a "recent changes" page that is often examined by many people each day.

This attitude leads to a distinctive and, in a way, remarkable attitude toward authorship.

On Wikipedia, no person considers himself "the" author of an entry. With wikis in general, the concept of authorship is discouraged and, in a way, senseless; it is disconnected from the very notion of a wiki. Many people consider it "unwiki" to proclaim authorship, or principal authorship, of an entry. Blogs, which I take up shortly, are very different on this count. To be sure, many bloggers release their content under a special kind of license, known as a Creative Commons License, which generally allows free distribution of copyrighted works so long as credit is given. (The development of the Creative Commons License, launched by Lawrence Lessig, is worth emphasizing; because copying is permitted without causing copyright problems, this license promotes access to material by many minds. Wikipedia uses the GNU Free Documentation License, which also rejects standard copyright restrictions in favor of much freer use.) But bloggers usually protect their authorship by asking that they be credited for ideas and texts. Wikipedia works even though authorship is not rewarded or even claimed.

Of course, there are risks of error, partiality, and vandalism on wikis. People may believe that something is true about evolution, or George W. Bush, or Fidel Castro, or life on other planets, or the Catholic Church, but the belief may be mistaken. Wikipedia works because those who know the truth, or something close to it, are usually more numerous and more committed than those who believe in a falsehood. The site explains, again in prose that anyone can edit, "In all honesty, Wikipedia has a fair bit of well-meaning, but ill-informed and amateurish work. In fact, we welcome it—an amateurish article to be improved later is better than nothing. In any case, when new hands (particularly, experts on the subjects in question) arrive and go to work, the amateurish work is usually straightened out. Really egregious errors are fixed quickly by the thousands of people who read Wikipedia every day. In general, the worse the error, the faster it will be noticed and fixed."

This may be an excessively sunny view of the situation. Some of the entries aren't very good. In areas that involve technology, Wikipedia tends to shine, often outperforming ordinary encyclopedias—a tribute to the technology-savvy participants that it attracts. But in my own field of law, the quality is more mixed, especially in complex areas. Even in law, however, most of the entries are at least serviceable, and it is true that those that are really bad tend to be corrected, often promptly, especially when and because certain pages are watched by editors and authors.

There is a deeper issue. In some areas, what is true is greatly disputed, and it is hard to find an impartial arbiter. If anyone in the world can serve as an editor, partisans should be able to move content in their preferred directions, making entries quite unreliable. We could easily imagine a situation in which liberals or conservatives skew relevant articles, hoping to influence opinions and perhaps even the outcome of elections. In response to this risk, Wikipedia maintains a general policy of neutrality, and in the event that the policy seems to be violated, Wikipedia offers an ingenious solution: a red "Stop Hand," supplemented by the simple statement, "The neutrality of this article is disputed." In fact, there is a (very) long list of articles whose neutrality is disputed. A recent list, with more than twelve hundred entries, included articles on Jimmy Carter, monogamy, libertarianism, lawyer, Noam Chomsky, Nation of Islam, Palestinian National Authority, Richard Nixon, persecution of Christians, rape, sexism, terrorism, Vietnam War, Fidel Castro, sport utility vehicle, AIDS conspiracy theories, and New Jersey(!). The large number of disputed articles is causing some consternation in the Wikipedia community.

When active debates are occurring about the content of articles, it is necessary to have good norms to provide some discipline. The term "Wikiquette" refers to the etiquette that Wikipedians follow. Wikiquette helps to ensure that the active debates are transferred to separate "talk pages." These are the deliberative forums on Wikipedia, in which those who disagree explain the basis for their disagreement. What is noteworthy is that the articles themselves are (mostly) solid, and that partisan debates have a specifically designed location. Sometimes those debates end up producing shared judgments that can, in turn, be found in articles.

To be sure, vandalism is a potentially serious problem. As Wikipedia is constructed, only an administrator can permanently delete pages. But anyone in the world can make a temporary change or deletion, which will show up on any computer in the world with Internet access. Spamming is also possible. People might alter an entry to make it a string of obscenities, or to turn it into nonsense, or to insert deliberate errors, or simply to cause chaos. In 2005, one vandal wrote that John Seigenthaler Sr., a prominent journalist, may have been involved in the assassination of both President John F. Kennedy and his brother Robert Kennedy; this erroneous statement stayed on Wikipedia for four months before it was taken down. Another vandal has repeatedly added images of Darth Vader to various pages; yet another added fake death notices to the pages of prominent Democratic politicians; other vandals have created nonsense pages. But in general, Wikipedia has done exceedingly well in combating these problems. It describes its own practice as "something along the lines of vigilante justice." This means that individual readers can "revert" the page to the most recent good version or mark the page as one that ought to be deleted.

Readers are also permitted to identify persistent vandals and to suggest that they be added to the "vandalism in progress" page. Such vandals can eventually be blocked by Wikipedia's technology (allowing IP blocking or username blocking). Wikipedia works because the vandals are hopelessly outnumbered by those who want to make the project work.

Why Wikis Work (or Not)

It is tempting and helpful to explain the success of Wikipedia through Hayek's distinctive lens. Jimmy Wales himself has drawn the connection, saying, "Hayek's work on price theory is central to my own thinking about how to manage the Wikipedia project. Possibly one can understand Wikipedia without understanding Hayek.... But one can't understand my ideas about Wikipedia without understanding Hayek." Certainly, Wikipedia entries often aggregate the information held by numerous people in a way that connects closely to Hayek's claims about the price system. If information is widely dispersed, and if no single "planner" has access to what is known, then Wikipedia's method of operations has the same general justification as the price system. As central planners relate to markets, so, in a way, do standard encyclopedias relate to Wikipedia.

Indeed, we can go much further. Perhaps any particular article, at any particular time, should be seen as a kind of "price" that is a product of many minds and that might be altered, at least to some extent, by any interested person. As we have seen, a price is a result of the judgments and tastes of a large number of consumers. An article on Wikipedia or any other wiki has the same characteristic.

But this is only a metaphor. Wikipedia does not involve or set prices, and here there is an initial and major difference between wikis on the one hand and the price system on the other. In addition, most Wikipedians do not stand to gain or lose by adding information. There are no trades and no mutually advantageous deals. The economic incentive that underlies market behavior usually plays no role in Wikipedia. For many users, participation is attributable not to self-interest, but to other motivations, including people's desire to see their words in print, the value of self-expression, and the apparently widespread desire to be helpful and constructive. To the extent that the economic incentive is generally more reliable than these motivations, Wikipedia's success may not be so easy to replicate. But for many wikis, money and self-interest are apparently less important than economists, at least, tend to think.

A qualification: It is possible to become an enfranchised voter in major decisions about Wikipedia's future (consider the question whether Wikimedia should create a new service of one or another kind). Those who make enough edits to be considered active users obtain the franchise. Some Wikipedians make large numbers of small edits (involving grammar and spelling) to obtain this more powerful status. In this sense, status and reputation can play a significant role in wiki communities, a point to which I return in the context of open source software.

There is another difference between the price system and wikis. In wikis, the last editor can be a self-appointed dictator; in the price system, individual consumers almost never have any such role. If you really like chocolate ice cream, you will probably buy a lot of chocolate ice cream, but your purchases will not much affect the price. But on Wikipedia, you can delete an entry or enter false information, at least until you are caught. If you are confused and add errors, those errors can dominate the story, whatever your predecessors said. I have emphasized that Wikipedia has safeguards against vandalism and that Wikipedians are good at correcting errors. But the last editor has an authority far greater than that of the last purchaser or seller of a product.

For this reason, it should be easy to see that Wikipedia need not always incorporate the multiple diverse views of its editors. Because the last editor can appoint himself as sovereign, no aggregation may occur at all (even though editors who behave inappropriately end up with a brief reign). In the price system, an individual consumer cannot easily become a self-appointed sovereign. President John F. Kennedy's father is said to have purchased forty thousand copies of his son's book, *Profiles in Courage,* to put that book on the best-seller list; but such behavior is rare in markets. Because Wikipedia uses a "last in time" rule, because no literal price is created, and because economic incentives are not directly involved, Hayek's central arguments about that "marvel," the price system, do not apply, at least not directly.

In this light, we can easily imagine a society in which Wikipedia would not work. Imagine what science fiction writers call a parallel world, one very much like our own but in which many or most contributors to Wikipedia are confused, error-prone, partisan, or eager to engage in vandalism. Here the wrongdoers would triumph, creating error and confusion or worse. The good-faith contributors would be overwhelmed. Nor is this world entirely hypothetical. Some wikis have run into problems as a result of these very problems. In 2005, the *Los Angeles Times* announced that it would begin to run on its Web page "wikitorials," editorials that would operate as wikis, in the sense that all readers could edit them. With evident (charming? naïve?) optimism, the editors said that they were seeking "a constantly evolving collaboration among readers in a communal search for truth."

The opening editorial, involving the Iraq war, was called "War and Consequences," and it was accompanied by a wikitorial titled "Dreams about War and Retribution." Readers were invited to "rewrite the editorial yourself if they thought that something could be improved. In just two days, the wikitorial was edited more than 150 times, in a way that significantly increased its length and scope. But on the third day, the site was flooded with pornography, and the newspaper eventually lost its technological battle with the vandals. The *LATWiki Main Page* was replaced with this somewhat mournful text: "Where is the wikitorial? Unfortunately, we have had to remove this feature, at least temporarily, because a few readers were flooding the site with inappropriate material. Thanks and apologies to the thousands of people who logged on in the right spirit."

Wikis and More Wikis

This is a story of how the wiki form might go wrong. But we should not bow to pessimism, even for wikitorials. Other newspapers are running experiments in just this vein; with better protection against vandals, perhaps the experiments will work, or at least generate some interesting results. For its article on Wikipedia, *Esquire* magazine tried a creative approach: Its author, A. J. Jacobs, posted a badly written, typo-pervaded, error-filled first draft of the article on Wikipedia itself and asked Wikipedians to improve it. The draft was edited 224 times in the first twenty-four hours after it was posted, and another 149 times in the following twenty-four hours. After the article was "locked," it was published in the magazine—and it is quite excellent.

[Earlier], I mentioned dKosopedia, "the free political encyclopedia," which offers a good deal of information about political issues. At the time of the present writing, the Politics.ie wiki is both more specialized and far more advanced; it attempts to create a comprehensive resource of information relating to Irish politics, and anyone can edit it. Detailed materials can be found about the Labour Party, Sinn Fein, the Green Party, Michael Collins, and much more. Recent events are catalogued as they occur. Wikis devoted to science, in general and in particular areas, are easy to find; a general science wiki was created in 2005. An entire wiki focuses on the politics of open source software adoption. All are warmly invited to participate: "In keeping with the open structure and spirit of wiki collaboration, we invite you to build on this account of free and open source software politics—adding to or revising the existing accounts, branching out into new accounts of other contexts and processes, or linking to relevant external sources." On Wikicities.com, it is possible to find well over three hundred wikis. Some of these involve entertainment. Wikis are devoted to *Star Trek* (as of this writing, with a disappointing lack of detail), *Star Wars* (same parenthetical), and *Lord of the Rings* (no comment!). Others involve general topics in which many people are interested, such as insurance, cancer, globalization, and genealogy (not to mention shopping).

An especially interesting wiki is the World Wind Wiki. On this site, it is possible to "zoom from outer space to any place on earth. World Wind leverages satellite imagery and elevation data to allow users to experience Earth terrain in visually rich 3D, just as if they were really there. Virtually visit any place in the world. Look across the Andes, into the Grand Canyon, over the Alps or along the African Sahara." Numerous users add relevant information, allowing the site to accumulate new facts and data. Lawrence Lessig has posted his influential 2000 book, *Code, and Other Laws of Cyberspace,* as a wiki, and a number of changes have been made.

Some of the most promising efforts are building directly on the Wikipedia model. Wikipedia itself has a range of sister projects, including Wikispecies (a directory of species), Wiktionary (a dictionary and thesaurus), Wikisource (a collection of primary source documents that anyone can edit), and Meta-Wiki (a Web site about the various projects of the Wikimedia Foundation). There are countless other possibilities in this vein. For example, many people have been concerned about the risk of a flu epidemic. State-of-the-art information can be found at Flu Wiki, a Web site that anyone can edit. Flu Wiki offers articles about prevention, diagnosis, treatment, and much more. As of this writing, a Flu Wiki can be found not only in English, but also in French, Spanish, and Turkish.

As an especially colorful example of the same basic form, consider the Urban Dictionary. The Urban Dictionary defines itself as "a slang dictionary with your definitions." There is no deliberation here, but it operates as a wiki; anyone can add or edit the existing definitions. The word "cool," for example, has fifty-eight definitions (as of September 2005), from the not terribly exciting "cold or having an overall cold temperature" to the somewhat better "laid back, relaxed, not freaked out, knows what's goin on." For its part, the word "cold" has, as one of its definitions, "more than cute and more than sexy its kind of like calling someone a dime." The word "dime" (for those who are puzzled and really want to know) has forty-seven definitions of its own. I won't test the reader's patience, or moral commitments, with further details. But for those who are interested in contemporary American slang, the Urban Dictionary actually provides an excellent place to start (and usually to end). It does so precisely because it aggregates highly dispersed information, as a slang dictionary should.

As a promising variation on the idea that anyone can edit, consider ohmynews.com, an online newspaper that wants to make "every citizen a reporter." The paper was founded by Oh Yeon Ho, a Korean who sought to transform what he called the "closed and elite journalistic culture." Frustrated by that culture, he created a new forum, in which anyone could submit articles. As of late 2005, ohmynews.com had a professional staff of seventy-five people, including forty-five reporters, and an official "staff" of thirty-nine thousand citizen reporters! Every day, more than two hundred articles are submitted to ohmynews.com, and about 70 percent of the submissions are published. Writers receive a small, nominal payment. As in the case of Wikipedia, people contribute for nonmaterial reasons. Unlike in the case of Wikipedia, the professional staff imposes filters, designed to ensure decent writing and accuracy. But the advantage of ohmynews.com is that it invites everyone to contribute, and in that sense promises to provide a wide range of information.

In Korea, ohmynews.com has had a substantial effect on some political disputes, and its English edition is now flourishing. It counts as a genuine success. We might expect many more ventures in this vein.

Many businesses are now using wikis. E-mail can be time-consuming and cumbersome. It is often much better to create a wiki, producing a document that anyone can edit. Walt Disney, Eastman Kodak, Yahoo, Oxford University Press, and parts of the U.S. military have used private workspace wikis, in which employees can discuss one another's work and also make immediate editorial changes in documents. An artificial intelligence company, Soar Technology Inc., which works for the Office of Naval Research, reports that wikis cut the time required to finish projects by 50 percent. Some people project that in the next five years, wikis will be used by most businesses in the United States.

The quality of the wiki form is immensely variable. It will be exceptionally interesting to see how the form evolves over time. We could easily imagine amplification of errors, hidden profiles, cascade effects, and group polarization on wikis and their cousins (not excluding ohmynews.com and wikitorials). But my hunch is that the diversity of views, along with a widespread desire to cooperate, will ensure many successes, especially but not only within working groups. Of course, many experiments fail. But the explosive growth of Wikipedia, and of wikis in general, suggests that more and even better developments are on the way.

BLOGS

One of the most unanticipated developments of the first years of the twenty-first century was the remarkable rise of Weblogs, which can serve to elicit and aggregate the information held by countless contributors. Weblogs, or blogs, have been growing at a truly astounding rate, so much so that any current account will rapidly grow out of date. At the present time, more than 50 million blogs are up and running. Tens of thousands blogs are created each day, with a new one every 2.2 seconds. (Question: How many blogs are created in the time it takes to read a short book?) In recent years, the most highly rated political blogs—including Atrios, Instapundit, and Daily Kos—have received at least several tens of thousands of visitors *each day*. The worlds of law and politics are full of blogs, and my own institution, the University of Chicago Law School, has its own Faculty Blog, dealing (most of the time) with questions of law.

Stories

Every well-known blog has its own story, often full of some combination of talent, luck, and coincidence. Consider Instapundit, run by Glenn Reynolds, a professor of law at the University of Tennessee. Before becoming a blogger, Reynolds was a moderately well-known law professor with several strong publications. On August 8, 2001, he began Instapundit, in part inspired by his Internet law class. Since that point, his blog has grown into one of the largest on the Internet, attracting more than one hundred thousand visits per day. As a result of his remarkable success, Reynolds is sometimes referred to as "the Blogfather."

Reynolds provides commentary of varied length, sometimes merely linking to an interesting story or post found elsewhere, and sometimes explaining his own point of view at length. His own views are eclectic. He has also expanded into the mainstream, blogging at GlennReynolds.com for MSNBC, and his writings have appeared in many traditional outlets, including the *Washington Post* and the *Wall Street Journal*; he also writes regularly for the Fox News Web site. (Full disclosure: Reynolds invited me to post on his site on msnbc.com for a week in 2004, and it was astounding to receive the range of e-mail responses, by turns smart, funny, enraged, helpful, nutty, and incoherent.)

Blog Triumphalism?

Bloggers have occasionally had an impact on real-world events, and their impact may be growing. Drawing from the account of blogging enthusiast Hugh Hewitt, let us consider a few examples:

- Bloggers deserve significant credit for the 2004 "Rather-gate" scandal, in which Dan Rather used what seemed to be authentic memoranda to offer embarrassing disclosures about the military service of President George W. Bush. The memoranda indicated that Bush had failed to do his duty, and indeed had refused to obey direct orders. Careful bloggers showed that the memoranda could not possibly be authentic. Only one day after the broadcast, a blogger known as Buckhead wrote, "Every single one of these memos to file is in a proportionally spaced font, probably Palatino or Times New Roman. In 1972 people used typewriters for this sort of thing, and typewriters used monospaced fonts.... I am saying these documents are forgeries, run through a copier for 15 generations to make them look old." Additional bloggers worked hard to confirm the accusation. As Hewitt notes, bloggers "exposed the fraud with breathtaking speed and finality."

• In 2002, Trent Lott, Senate majority leader, spoke at a birthday party for Senator Strom Thurmond. Lott said of Mississippi, his own state, "When Strom Thurmond ran for president, we voted for him. We're proud of it. And if the rest of the country had followed our lead, we wouldn't have had all these problems over all these years, either." This was a genuinely scandalous statement; Thurmond had run on a racist, pro-segregation platform, and the Senate majority leader seemed to be saying that if Thurmond had won, the nation would have been problem-free. But somehow the remarks were ignored—except on the blogosphere. A blogger named Atrios gave serious coverage to the comments, which were then picked up on talkingpointsmemo.com, and the building momentum proved unstoppable. Lott was forced to resign as majority leader.

• In 1979, John Kerry said, "I remember spending Christmas Eve of 1968 five miles across the Cambodian border being shot at by our South Vietnamese allies who were drunk and celebrating Christmas." In the 2004 election, the blogosphere was full of stories about whether Kerry had really spent Christmas Eve in Cambodia, and indeed whether he had been in Cambodia at all. The doubts raised questions about the credibility of Kerry's statements about his record in the Vietnam War. Focusing on the claim of Christmas Eve in Cambodia, one blogger, RogerLSimon.com, objected to the prospect of having someone "who sounds like a pathetic barroom blowhard" as president of the United States, especially "in a time of war. People like this start to believe their own lies." A liberal blogger, Matthew Yglesias, said, "It certainly looks bad from here, and I haven't seen a good explanation yet, perhaps because there isn't one." Eventually, the Kerry campaign acknowledged that Kerry had not been in Cambodia on Christmas in 1968. Hewitt writes: "The Christmas-Eve-not-in-Cambodia became shorthand for Kerry's fantasy life, and suddenly the Swift Vets," who savagely attacked Kerry's honesty and patriotism, "had credibility, as Internet donations flowed into their coffers."

Whatever one thinks of these events, bloggers appear to have influenced the public stage, driving media coverage and affecting national perceptions of national questions. And of course, there is much more. In my own area of law, bloggers offer quick and insightful analyses of legal events. Those analyses are widely read, and they can influence media coverage as well. When bloggers err on legal questions, their errors are often corrected. To take just one example: The Volokh Conspiracy, an extremely popular law-related Web site, often provides discussions of important Supreme Court decisions, sometimes on the day those decisions are announced. These discussions put the Court's decisions in context and typically provide illuminating criticisms. If the analysis seems to go wrong, the author is immediately notified, and a correction or debate usually ensues. Other events in law and politics often receive instructive and immediate attention.

In law and policy more broadly, Nobel Prize winner Gary Becker and court of appeals judge Richard A. Posner have run a blog (named, not so imaginatively, the Becker-Posner blog) that offers substantive discussions of such issues as global warming, property rights, health insurance, terrorism, and bankruptcy reform. Becker and Posner receive thousands of visitors each week, and those visitors offer insightful comments and corrections.

Of course, there is a great deal more. Bloggers frequently deliberate with one another, exchanging information and perspectives. Becker and Posner regularly feature debates between the two. The Volokh Conspiracy is run by law professor Eugene Volokh, but it has a number of contributors with different perspectives. Disagreement among the contributors is common; a debate on same-sex marriage or the future of the Supreme Court is far from unusual. Discussion and argument occur every day across blogs, not just within them. Because of their openness, speed, and flexibility, some people believe that blogs will come to replace, at least in part, the discussions of law and politics that can now be found in traditional academic journals. The very fact that an analysis can be done in an hour or a day might seem to make such journals obsolete.

In addition, many blogs offer public space for comments by anyone who cares to participate. If a blogger makes an error, or merely appears to make an error, there is a good chance that someone will complain. Often the comment sections take on lives of their own, offering vigorous debates on topics only lightly explored by the post that inspired them. In the University of Chicago Law School, one of the most interesting developments is the extensive use of the comment section, in which people often engage with one another, and not so much with the post that originally triggered their exchange.

Indeed, the blogosphere might be seen as a kind of gigantic town meeting, or series of such meetings. The presence of many minds is especially important here. If countless people are maintaining their own blogs, they should be able to act as fact-checkers and as supplemental information sources, not only for one another but also for prominent members of the mass media. If hundreds of thousands of people are reading the most prominent blogs, then errors should be corrected quickly. In addition, the blogosphere enables interested readers to find an astounding range of opinions and facts. Judge Posner has gone so far as to invoke Hayek's argument about the price system on behalf of blogs, emphasizing their potential to reveal dispersed bits of information. In Judge Posner's words:

> Blogging is ... a fresh and striking exemplification of Friedrich Hayek's thesis that knowledge is widely distributed among people and that the challenge to society is to create mechanisms for pooling that knowledge. The powerful mechanism that was the focus of Hayek's work, as of economists generally, is the price system (the market). The newest mechanism is the "blogosphere." There are 4 million blogs. The Internet enables the instantaneous pooling (and hence correction, refinement, and amplification) of the ideas and opinions, facts and images, reportage and scholarship, generated by bloggers.

Not Hayek: Problems in the Blogosphere

But Judge Posner's use of Hayek misses the mark, and we should therefore resist blog triumphalism. Indeed, the very problems that infect deliberation can be found on the blogosphere, too. The world of blogs is pervaded by the propagation of errors, hidden profiles, cascades, and group polarization.

Even the best blogs lack anything like prepublication peer review, and their speed and informality often ensure glibness, superficiality, confusion, and blatant errors. Many blogs in law and politics are close to talk radio, or to brisk and irresponsible conversations over the lunch table. (Granted, that is part of what makes them fun.) Sometimes falsehoods spread like wildfire, as informational and reputational cascades lead to widespread mistakes. Confidently stated errors have proliferated on countless topics, including the plans of Israel and Iran, the likely Supreme Court nominees of President George W. Bush, and the political views (and corruption, or worse) of both Republicans and Democrats. Group polarization is easy to find on blogs; the conservative-leaning Volokh Conspiracy, despite its civility, intelligence, and overall high quality, is an occasional example, with commentators sometimes leading one another to more extreme versions of what they thought before discussions began.

The blogosphere does not produce prices, which aggregate, in one place, a wide range of opinions and tastes. It certainly does not work as open source software does. It does not produce a giant wiki, aggregating dispersed information. Instead, it offers a stunningly diverse range of claims, perspectives, rants, insights, lies, facts, falsehood, sense, and nonsense.

Participants in the blogosphere usually lack an economic incentive. They are not involved in any kind of trade, and most of the time they have little to gain or to lose. If they spread falsehoods, or simply offer their opinion, they do not sacrifice a thing. Perhaps their reputation will suffer, but perhaps not; perhaps the most dramatic falsehoods will draw attention and hence readers. Most bloggers do not have the economic stake of those who trade on prediction markets. True, some bloggers attract advertising, and many blogs aggregate a lot of information; instapundit.com, for example, assembles material from many sources. But it is not possible to find a Superblog, in general or in particular areas, that corresponds to Wikipedia or open source software. In other words, we lack a blog that succeeds in correcting errors and assembling truths. Those who consult blogs will learn a great deal, but they will have an exceedingly hard time separating falsehoods from facts.

By their very nature, blogs offer rival and contentious positions on facts as well as values. In many ways, this is a virtue, for people who are curious can find a wide range of views, including those that oppose their own. But if truth is to emerge, it is because of the competition of the marketplace of ideas, and the discussion thus far suggests that this particular marketplace is far from reliable. One of the undeniable effects of blogs is to spread misunderstandings and mistakes. If deliberating groups propagate error and leave hidden profiles, we can be sure that those who write or read blogs will do the same thing.

To return to one of my primary themes: A particular problem arises if people are reading blogs that conform to their own preexisting beliefs. If this is so, polarization is inevitable. Liberals reading liberal blogs will end up more liberal; conservatives will become more conservative if they restrict themselves to conservative blogs. The Colorado experiment, involving group polarization, finds itself replicated in the blogosphere every day, with potentially harmful results. People sometimes go to extremes simply because they are consulting others who think as they do. The rise of blogs makes it all the easier for people to live in echo chambers of their own design. Indeed, some bloggers, and many readers of blogs, live in information cocoons.

Can anything be done about this? Here's one idea: Public-spirited bloggers would do well to offer links to those whose views are quite different from their own. Liberal blogs could more regularly link to conservative ones, and vice versa. We could easily imagine explicit or implicit "deals" among bloggers with competing opinions, producing mutual linking. Such deals would increase the likelihood that people will be exposed to different perspectives; they would also reflect a healthy degree of mutual respect.

Of course, blogs do add to the range of available views, and they certainly hold out the promise of aggregating information held by large numbers of people. As Posner suggests, blogging could operate as an extraordinary method for collecting dispersed knowledge. Sheer numbers could and do play a large and beneficial role here, because information aggregation is likely to work best when many minds are involved; but it is also important that reasons and information are being exchanged in a way that can lead to corrections and real creativity. To some extent, this is happening already. But whereas the price system automatically collects dispersed information, and open source software contains a remarkable system for aggregating with filters, and Wikipedia provides an aggregating mechanism with both formal and informal safeguards, blogs offer no filters, and the only safeguards come from the discipline of the market for ideas.

Evidence

What do we actually know about the blogosphere? All too little. The empirical analysis remains in its earliest stages. But there is good evidence that many bloggers are mostly linking to like-minded others, and that when they link to opinions that diverge from their own, it is often to cast ridicule and scorn on them.

One study explores the degree to which conservative and liberal bloggers interact with each other. Focusing on fourteen hundred blogs, the study finds that 91 percent of the links are to like-minded sites. Hence, the two sides sort themselves into identifiable communities. For example, powerlineblog.com, a conservative blog, is linked to by only twenty-five liberal blogs, but by 195 conservative blogs. Dailykos.com, a liberal blog, is linked to by forty-six conservative blogs, but by 292 liberal blogs. In the aggregate, the behavior of conservative bloggers is more noteworthy in this regard; they link to one another far more often and in a denser pattern.

The study's authors also examined about forty "A-List" blogs, and here, too, they found a great deal of segregation. Sources were cited almost exclusively by one side or the other. Those sites with identifiable political commitments, such as Salon.com and NationalReview.com, were almost always cited by blogs on the same side of the political spectrum.

Another study, by Eszter Hargittai, Jason Gallo, and Matt Kane, offers more detailed support for the same general conclusions. Examining the behavior of forty popular blogs, half liberal and half conservative, Hargittai and her coauthors find that like-minded views receive a great deal of reinforcement. On the "blogrolls," referring readers to other blogs, conservatives are far more likely to list other conservatives, and liberals are far more likely to list other liberals. When blogs refer to discussions by other bloggers, they usually cite like-minded others. To be sure, there is a significant amount of cross-citation as well. But—and here is perhaps the most striking finding—a significant percentage of the cross-citations simply cast contempt on the views that are being cited. In this way, real deliberation is often occurring within established points of view, not across them.

The general conclusion is that in the blogosphere, there is a significant divide among politically identifiable communities. Liberals and conservatives do not usually link to one another. Much of the time, they do not even discuss the same topics. To be sure, many people are using the blogosphere to learn about different views and new topics. Just like the Internet of which it is a part, the blogosphere increases the range of options, and this is a great virtue, above all for curious and open-minded people. On balance, the blogosphere, like the Internet more generally, is certainly good for democracy because it increases information. But if linking behavior on blogs can be taken as a proxy for information filtering, it is reasonable to think that many readers are obtaining one-sided views of political issues.

The construction of information cocoons and echo chambers is a real problem for a democracy, not least because amplification of errors, hidden profiles, cascade effects, and polarization are inevitable. For many people, blunders and extremism are highly likely, not in spite of the blogosphere but because of it.

CREATIVE FUTURES FOR MANY MINDS

It is possible to imagine many different efforts to aggregate dispersed information. Experiments in this vein are cropping up all the time. Consider a few of many examples.

Slashdot, the largest community-driven technology site on the Internet, has long identified itself as "news for nerds, stuff that matters." Slashdot is, among other things, an edited compilation of news abstracts, focusing on a wide range of topics related to technology. A first-time visitor to Slashdot will notice that the site resembles an ordinary news site, with story headlines, synopses, and links to follow. But its real value lies in the fact that it permits its users to discuss both news articles and one another's posts. Specifically, Slashdot users can spark discussions by posting ideas and responses to particular articles, thus facilitating discussion.

Of course, the system is vulnerable to irrelevant, silly, and abusive comments. Slashdot's ingenious response is a "moderation system," by which users judge comments and rank them by score. At first, the founders of Slashdot moderated posts themselves. But as the user base expanded, the job of moderating became unmanageable and was therefore delegated to users. As a result, a group of moderators has been selected from a pool of active users. Many minds thus evaluate the contributions of many minds.

As the system operates, all comments are scored on an absolute scale from –1 to 5. Logged-in users start at 1 (although this can vary from 0 to 2 based on their prior actions), and anonymous users start at 0. Moderators can add or deduct points from a comment's score, thus influencing whether a comment will be immediately visible to a reader. (Confession: Slashdot had a discussion of my 2001 book, *Republic.com;* as the author, I ventured a nonanonymous comment, which was ranked very low: 0, as I recall. True, I probably deserved the low ranking.)

Of course, there is a risk that the moderators will promote an agenda of their own. To combat that risk, Slashdot has produced the ingenious mechanism of "metamoderation," which operates as a review process of the moderation system. Instead of rating the usefulness of a comment, metamoderation rates the fairness and accuracy of the moderator's judgment. According to the metamoderation statistics, 92 percent to 93 percent of moderations are judged fair. (Hence, it is not necessary, to date, to create meta-metamoderation, reviewing the metamoderators!)

Slashdot explores a wide range of questions relating to technology, but more specialized aggregations, involving goods and activities of relevance to everyday life, are easy to imagine. An obvious question, of potential interest to many people, is this: How might many minds be enlisted in the evaluation of products and services? Angie's List, founded by Angie Hicks, is one attempt at an answer; it collects and distributes detailed customer satisfaction reports on local businesses in over twenty-six major cities. For a $10 sign-up fee and a $5.95 monthly charge, subscribers can find reviews of neighborhood service providers and contractors. Members are able to read what other customers are saying about a business before hiring them.

Angie's List is hardly a new concept. The Better Business Bureau has a similar service, giving companies either a satisfactory rating or listing their number of complaints. But Angie's List provides a great deal of inside information through its rating system, which gives the subscriber the most recent reports on numerous companies. There are countless analogues on the Internet, as customers evaluate a wide range of products—cars, books, and more—and allow the evaluations to be aggregated to produce useful information. (Recall the Condorcet Jury Theorem.)

There are many other methods for obtaining the evaluations of large numbers of people. Visited by millions of people every month, Rotten Tomatoes aggregates the reviews of approved critics about movies, DVDs, and video games. The site is *not* open to all reviewers: Movie reviews are posted by critics from "accredited media outlets and online film societies." Before a critic is allowed to post on the site, she must complete an application and be certified by the owners of the site that she is a bona fide movie critic.

Views are aggregated on Rotten Tomatoes through two methods: the "Tomatometer" and the "Average Rating." The Tomatometer is a measure of how highly recommended a given film is, while the Average Rating is a more precise measure of the quality of the movie. The Average Rating score is simply the average of each critic's 1–10 rating of a given film. The Tomatometer score indicates the percentage of "Approved Tomatometer Critics" who have recommended a movie. A movie is deemed to be "Fresh" if its Tomatometer score is 60 percent or greater, and it is branded as "Rotten" if its score is below 60 percent. Additionally, a movie is deemed "Certified Fresh" if it has a Tomatometer score of 75 percent or higher after having been reviewed by twenty or more critics. Numerous people consult Rotten Tomatoes, apparently on the Condorcetian theory that the average view is likely to be highly reliable.

An alternative method can be found on eBay, which contains an especially admired system for providing feedback on transactions. After a transaction is completed, both the buyer and the seller are given the opportunity to leave comments about the transaction, and to rate the transaction as "positive," "negative," or "neutral." EBay tallies the scores (with a positive being worth +1, a neutral being worth zero, and a negative being worth –1) and prominently places the user's "feedback rating" next to her user ID. For each user, eBay also reveals the percentage of total feedback that is positive.

In addition, eBay allows users to post brief messages explaining their feedback ratings, and if the feedback is neutral or negative, the recipient is allowed to reply to the message. The eBay site allows users to see the feedback that a user has left for others—if, for example, one user appears overeager to leave negative feedback, other users might choose not to do business with that person. One of the valuable features of the eBay feedback mechanism is that both buyers and sellers—even those who use eBay infrequently—almost universally participate in the feedback process. Indeed, eBay goes so far as to send reminder emails to users who have not yet left feedback for a completed transaction.

It would be easy to imagine many uses for mechanisms of this kind. Lior Strahilevitz, for example, has suggested that communities might build on the use of "How am I driving?" bumper stickers by commercial truckers, creating general use of such stickers with the goal of decreasing highway accidents by enlisting many minds. The possibilities seem endless.

I have covered many areas in this chapter, and it will help to offer a summary by way of conclusion.

Even though the price system is not involved, Wikipedia works extraordinarily well, because so many people are both willing and able to cooperate. The wiki form allows anyone to edit and thus provides an exceptional opportunity to aggregate the information held by many minds. Wikipedia itself offers a series of deliberative forums in which disagreements can be explored. But we can also identify conditions under which wikis will do poorly. If vandals are numerous, if contributors are confused or prone to error, or if people are simply unwilling to devote their labor for free, the success of Wikipedia will not be replicated. Fortunately, the conditions for wikis are often good; hence there are numerous opportunities for using the wiki form to aggregate knowledge.

Of the new methods I have explored here, including prediction markets, open source software may well be the most unambiguous success. A number of factors have made this possible. Many people are willing and able to contribute, sometimes with the prospect of economic reward, sometimes without any such prospect. It is often easy to see whether proposed changes are good ones. For open source projects, filters are put in place to protect against errors. The problems associated with deliberation can be reduced because we are often dealing with eureka-type problems, where deliberation works well. Open source projects typically combine deliberation with access to widely dispersed information and creativity. For this reason, they provide an exciting model, one that might well be adapted to many domains.

It is true that one cannot say, in the abstract, whether open source methods will work better than proprietary ones. For many commodities, internal labor and deliberation, with a direct profit motive, will be best. The success of open source software does, however, give reason to explore the use of the same approach in many other arenas, through a system that includes significant deliberation and numerous contributors.

With respect to the blogosphere, the picture is mixed, notwithstanding Posner's enthusiastic invocation of Hayek. The immense range of voices unquestionably adds to the stock of perspectives and information in a way that can and does correct social errors. A larger marketplace of ideas is a better marketplace of ideas. On the other hand, the world of blogs is full of many things, including mistakes, confusion, and sheer rage. In many domains, people understand much more because of the existence of blogs. But in some domains, they understand less.

2.2.2 The Consequences of the Information Revolution

MAX BOOT

Most of us are familiar with the consequences of the information revolution on civilian life—personal computers, the Internet, blogs, online shopping, and so forth—but unless one is a member of the military, one probably has only a hazy idea of the effect of information and communications technologies (ICT) on the battlefield. Many authors have talked about a "revolution in military affairs" brought about by the integration of advanced ICT capabilities into the arsenals of modern armies, but few have studied its effects and understood its consequences and limitations as thoroughly as Max Boot, a defense analyst and military historian. In this reading taken from his book *War Made New: Technology, Warfare, and the Course of History—1500 to Today,* Boot provides a glimpse into the awesome powers of the U.S. military machine and, in particular, the additional capabilities for land, sea, and air warfare made possible by the use of advanced ICT. The current military might of the United States is unparalleled in history; however, the armed forces remain stymied in Iraq and Afghanistan by irregular forces using tactics of asymmetrical warfare against our high-tech forces. Moreover, the same information technologies that we use can also be used by terrorists to wreak havoc on our twenty-first-century information economy. Boot suggests that to counter these new threats we need to think beyond "technological fixes" toward a paradigm shift in the way in which we prepare for and wage war.

FOCUS QUESTIONS

1. How have the advanced communication technologies employed by U.S. land forces allowed them to overpower more numerous adversaries? What is the "Achilles heel" of these technologies in counterinsurgency operations?
2. Why is the advantage that the U.S. military has in space slowly eroding? What can potential adversaries do to shield themselves from satellite surveillance?
3. In what ways does America's reliance on high-tech systems create vulnerabilities of its own? What kind of countermeasures does Boot think are needed to meet these new kinds of threats?
4. What is meant by the "tooth to tail" ratio, and what needs to be changed in the way in which military bureaucracies operate in order to reduce these ratios?

KEYWORDS

FORCEnet, Future Combat System, legacy systems, smart bombs, space warfare, the fog of war, visual stealth technology

Source: From *War Made New: Technology, Warfare, and the Course of History—1500 to Today*, Part IV: *The Information Revolution*, by Max Boot, pp. 419–436. Copyright © 2006 Gotham Books. Reprinted by permission of Penguin Group (USA) Inc.

It is tempting to argue, based on the difficulties that U.S. forces have encountered in Iraq (and the similar problems of the Israeli Defense Forces in Lebanon, the West Bank, and Gaza Strip), that the effect of the Information Revolution on warfare has been overstated by some enthusiasts. There is some truth to this—there *has* been an awful lot of hype—but it would be a mistake to go too far in dismissing the results of recent advances. That would be akin to denying the effect of the Industrial Revolution in the early 1900s simply because the British had a lot of trouble subduing the Boers. Improvements in technology have always had a more immediate impact on conventional than on irregular warfare. But that doesn't mean that the art of war has remained static. Indeed the tactics of Islamist guerrillas, who rely so heavily on the Internet, cell phones, and satellite television—all of which barely existed in 1980—show just how much things have changed.

Not all of the changes wrought by the Information Age are obvious at first glance, because the basic military systems of the early twenty-first century look roughly similar to their predecessors of the Second Industrial Age. Military analyst Michael O'Hanlon notes that "basic propulsion systems and designs for aircraft, ships, and internal-combustion vehicles are changing much more gradually than in the early twentieth-century, when two of those three technologies had only recently been invented." The average speed of a U.S. Navy destroyer, for instance, has not increased in the past one hundred years. The U.S. Air Force continues to rely on B-52H bombers last built in 1962. And the Marine Corps still uses helicopters that flew in the Vietnam War. What has been changing with great rapidity since the mid-1970s is the communications, targeting, surveillance, and ordnance technology that can make such "legacy" systems considerably more potent.

Land Warfare Advanced armies are still structured, as they have been since the 1940s, around armored forces complemented by infantry troops who move by armored vehicle, truck, and aircraft. The best tank in the world is probably the American Abrams (of which the U.S. has nine thousand), but the British Challenger II, the German Leopard II, the Israeli Merkava Mk. 4, and the Russian T-80 and T-90 come within striking distance. All modern tanks have stabilized turrets, night-vision capabilities, laser range-finders, and targeting computers that allow them to fight in conditions—on the move or in the dark—that would have stymied earlier models. In addition, composite or reactive armor offers far more protection than in years past, and main guns firing depleted uranium rounds have far more penetrating power. Armored personnel carriers and infantry fighting vehicles, such as the American Bradley Fighting Vehicle and Stryker and the Russian BMP and BTR, are essentially light tanks, some running on wheels, others on tracks, that sacrifice armor and armaments for extra room to carry infantry, command-and-control suites, or other cargo. Self-propelled artillery and rocket systems are also mounted on armored chassis.

Armored vehicles have improved over the years. But so have antiarmor weapons. These range from heavy missiles such as the U.S. Hellfire and Russian Ataka-V fired from vehicles or aircraft to handheld versions such as the U.S. Javelin, the Franco-German Milan, and the Russian Kornet. In addition, even the most advanced tanks can be disabled by other tanks, massive mines, aerial bombs, or artillery shells. The full impact of advances in antiarmor technology has not yet become apparent, because the forces that have fought modern tanks in recent years—Iraqis, Palestinians, Chechens—have not possessed the latest defensive weapons. But the U.S. success in wiping out Iraqi tanks from standoff ranges suggests that, in the constant struggle between offense and defense, the advantage may have shifted against heavy armor.

The U.S. Army is responding to these changes by budgeting at least $124 billion to develop a Future Combat System that is supposed to replace much of its current armored force with a family of lighter vehicles, manned and unmanned, that will have stealth designs that will make them harder to detect and hybrid-electric engines that will lessen their fuel requirements—one of the chief disadvantages of the gas-guzzling Abrams, because it increases demands on vulnerable supply lines. Future vehicles will feature advanced composite armor designed to deliver more protection than current models for the same amount of weight, but they will rely for protection less on armor and more on locating and destroying the enemy before they are attacked. Critics believe this is placing too much faith in "perfect situational awareness," and that these vehicles will not be of much use against guerrillas who can strike with no warning.

As usual, the infantryman's tools have changed least of all. A modern soldier has better protection than his forefathers if he wears Kevlar body armor, but his firepower—which comes primarily from a handheld assault rifle like the M-16 or AK-47 and from a variety of crew-served mortars and machine guns—does not vary significantly from that of a G.I. in World War II. A replacement for the M-16 known as the XM29 is under development but it is hardly revolutionary. In addition to shooting the same 5.56 mm rounds as the M-16 out of one barrel, it will have another barrel that can fire 20 mm high-explosive airburst projectiles to a range of half a mile. These mini grenades will come with embedded microchips that will control when they explode, allowing them to kill enemy fighters who might be lying flat on the ground or hiding behind a berm. Alternatively, nonlethal projectiles like rubber balls could be substituted for crowd-control situations. This is not terribly different from the capability afforded by grenade launchers attached to today's M-16s. Electronic guns that are capable of spitting out a million rounds a minute have also been developed. They might permit a soldier to stop an incoming rocket-propelled grenade with a solid wall of lead. But such weapons are years away from being fielded.

Unfortunately for Western infantrymen, the proliferation of small arms can put low-tech foes on an almost equal footing with the representatives of the most advanced militaries. There are 250 million military and police small arms knocking around the world, and more are being manufactured all the time by at least 1,249 suppliers in ninety countries.

The salvation of Information Age infantry, at least when they are conducting conventional operations, is their ability to use a wireless communications device to call in supporting fire on exact coordinates. It is doubtful that any military force will again enjoy the preponderance of power of a Kitchener at Khartoum, but Americans dropping JDAMs on Afghan tribesmen armed with Kalashnikovs—or even on Iraqi soldiers with outdated T-72 tanks—came close. The American edge decreases considerably, however, when its troops have to deploy for peacekeeping or counterinsurgency operations that leave them exposed to low-tech ambushes.

Naval Warfare Navies remain divided, as they have been since the dawn of the Second Industrial Age, into aircraft carriers, submarines, and surface ships. The major difference is that blue-water naval competition has disappeared after more than five hundred years. No one even tries to challenge the U.S. Navy anymore on the high seas. Virtually every other navy in the world is little more than a coastal patrol force.

The U.S. has twelve aircraft carriers, nine of them *Nimitz-class*, nuclear-powered supercarriers that can carry more than seventy high-performance aircraft such as the F/A-18E/F Super Hornet. A tenth supercarrier is in the works. No one else has a single one. France has the world's only other nuclear-powered aircraft carrier, the *Charles de Gaulle*, but it's half the size of the *Nimitz*. Russia has one aircraft carrier, the *Admiral Kuznetsov*, that rarely leaves port, and it has sold another one, the *Admiral Gorshkov*, to India. Britain has three small *Invincible-class* aircraft carriers that are used only for helicopters and vertical-takeoff Harrier jets. France, Italy, Spain, Japan, and South Korea have similar helicopter carriers in the works. These ships are comparable to the U.S. Navy's twelve amphibious assault ships, which transport helicopters, jump jets, and marines.

Whenever they leave port, U.S. capital ships are surrounded by surface and submarine escorts. Twenty-four *Ticonderoga-class* cruisers and forty-five (and counting) *Arleigh Burke-class* destroyers come equipped with Aegis phased-array radar that can track up to nine hundred targets in a three-hundred-mile radius. These surface combatants can also operate on their own or in conjunction with smaller vessels such as frigates and minesweepers.

In World War II, ships that didn't carry aircraft were limited to firing torpedoes or heavy guns with a range of less than thirty miles. Starting in the 1960s some submarines were equipped with intercontinental range ballistic missiles, but their targeting was so imprecise that it made no sense to equip them with conventional warheads. Ballistic-missile subs became a mainstay of nuclear deterrence. The development of accurate cruise missiles starting in the 1970s allowed submarines and surface combatants to hit land targets hundreds of miles away with conventional ordnance. Improvements in torpedo design, including the development of rocket-propelled supercavitating torpedoes, also allow submarines to do more damage in their traditional ship-fighting role.

The U.S. has the world's largest fleet of nuclear-powered attack submarines (54) and nuclear-powered ballistic-missile subs (16). Russia is next, with 37 attack submarines and 14 ballistic missile subs. Britain has 15 nuclear-powered submarines, followed by France with 10, and China with six. Not only are U.S. submarines more numerous but they are also more advanced, the most sophisticated being three 1990s-vintage Seawolfs described by one defense analyst as "the fastest, quietest, and most heavily armed undersea vessels ever built."

Because of the growing power of each of its vessels and the lack of competitors, the U.S. Navy has consolidated its high seas hegemony even while its fleet has shrunk from almost five hundred ships in the 1980s to fewer than three hundred in the early years of the twenty-first century. The potency of U.S. naval vessels is increased by linking together sensors and weapons systems with a tactical Internet known as FORCEnet.

While the U.S. Navy probably will remain unchallenged in blue waters, it faces greater threats as it gets closer to shore. Here water currents, thermal layers, and various obstacles can interfere with even the most advanced sensors, and a variety of defensive weapons systems lurk in wait.

More than seventy-five thousand antiship missiles are owned by seventy countries. A few are ballistic, but most are of the cruise-missile variety. Their potency was proved in 1987 when French-made Exocets fired by an Iraqi aircraft crippled the USS *Stark*, a Perry-class frigate, killing thirty-seven sailors. Earlier, Argentinian-owned Exocets sank two British ships during the Falkland Islands War (1982). Newer antiship cruise missiles such as the Russian-made Yakhont, Sunburn, and Uran are even deadlier because they have faster speeds, greater stealth capabilities, and more accurate, GPS-enhanced targeting. Russia is selling these missiles to customers abroad and some nations, such as China, are developing their own versions.

U.S. warships have sophisticated defensive systems to guard against air attack: Incoming missiles can be deflected by electronic countermeasures, flares, or chaff, or destroyed by naval aircraft, sea-to-air Standard missiles, or, as a last resort, by rapid-fire, radar-guided Phalanx guns. But, like the *Stark*, a warship could be caught by surprise or overwhelmed by a flurry of missiles coming from different directions.

Even more worrisome from an American viewpoint is the fact that transport ships and fuel tankers which have to replenish a fleet at sea have no protection when they are outside the defensive range of a battle group. They are as vulnerable as supply convoys on the roads of Iraq. Because a supercarrier has only about a three-day stockpile of JP-5 jet fuel (6,500 barrels a day are needed during combat operations), the most powerful warship in history could be rendered useless if its fuel tankers were sunk. The cargo container ships upon which global commerce depends also have no antimissile protection. A country or even a subnational group armed with cruise missiles could wreak havoc on the world's shipping lanes at chokepoints like the Straits of Hormuz or Malacca.

The threat to shipping, civil and military, is increased by diesel submarines. The latest diesel submarines have ultraquiet electric engines that make them hard to detect with sonar, and they are much cheaper to buy or produce than a nuclear-powered submarine. Russia has exported Kilo-class diesel-electric subs to China, India, Iran, and Algeria, among others. China is producing its own *Song-class* diesel submarines in a bid to challenge U.S. naval hegemony by using the same strategy that Germany, with its U-boats, once used to challenge British dominion of the waves. U.S. antisubmarine defenses are quite sophisticated, especially in open waters, but even American sensors can have trouble tracking quiet diesel subs in noisy coastal waters.

Mines, which can be scattered by submarines or other vessels, represent another major threat to shipping. More than three hundred different varieties are available on the world market. They can be triggered by changes in magnetic fields, acoustic levels, seismic pressure, or other factors. Some come equipped with microelectronics that allow them to distinguish between different types of ships, while others have small motors that allow them to move around. This makes it difficult to certify that a shipping channel is free of mines—it may have been safe an hour ago, but not anymore. Demining technology has lagged behind; the U.S. Navy, for one, has never placed much emphasis on lowly minesweepers. It has paid a price for this neglect. In 1987, during operations to prevent Iran from closing the Persian Gulf, an Iranian mine of World War I design nearly sank the frigate *Samuel Roberts.* Four years later, in the Gulf War, the cruiser USS *Princeton* and the amphibious landing ship *Tripoli* were nearly blasted apart by Iraqi mines. And even a cheap motorboat packed with explosives can pose a significant threat to a modern warship. The USS *Cole,* an *Arleigh Burke-class* destroyer, was badly damaged in such a terrorist attack in the port of Aden, Yemen, in 2000.

All of these threats could be largely negated if U.S. fleets were to stay far out at sea, but they have to approach fairly close to land to launch aircraft or missiles with operational ranges of only a few hundred miles. Moreover, the places where the U.S. Navy is likely to fight in the future are dangerously narrow. The Persian Gulf is only thirty miles wide at its narrowest point, the Taiwan Strait only one hundred miles wide.

To maintain its dominance, the U.S. Navy regularly updates the electronics and weapons aboard its warships even as the hulls and propulsion systems remain unchanged. It also plans to build a variety of unmanned vessels along with a CVN-21 aircraft carrier to replace the *Nimitz-*class, a *Zumwalt-class* DD(X) destroyer to replace *Oliver Hazard Perry-class* frigates and *Spruance-*class destroyers, a CG(X) cruiser to replace the *Ticonderoga-class* cruisers, and a smaller and speedier Littoral Combat Ship with no direct parallel in today's fleet that would focus on clearing mines, hunting submarines, and fighting terrorists in coastal waters. All of these new vessels will have improved defenses and information-processing tools as well as "plug and play" capacity that will allow them to be quickly reconfigured for different missions. They will also incorporate composite materials, stealthier designs, and electric propulsion to make them harder to detect, though an aircraft carrier with a 4.5-acre flight deck can never exactly hide.

Whether all of these warships are truly needed, given the U.S. Navy's already substantial lead over all competitors, remains an open question. A program to develop giant sea bases—perhaps akin to offshore oil-platforms—that would allow American ground and air forces to operate overseas might be of greater use, given the growing difficulty the U.S. has had in gaining basing and overflight rights from other countries.

Aerial Warfare Fighters such as the American F-15 and the Russian MiG-29 were designed in the 1970s for air-to-air combat, but this has become almost as rare as ship-to-ship actions. Since the Israelis destroyed much of the Syrian air force in 1982, and the U.S. and its allies made similarly quick work of the Iraqi air force in 1991, few if any aircraft have been willing to challenge top-of-the-line Western militaries. (The U.S. Air Force has not produced an ace—an airman with at least five aerial kills—since 1972.) That may change with the sale to China of the Russian-built Sukhoi Su-30, whose performance characteristics are said to exceed those of the F-15C, but the F/A-22 Raptor, the F-35 Joint Strike Fighter, and the Eurofighter should restore the Western edge. The odds of future aerial dogfights are, however, slim.

Modern surface-to-air missiles pose a more immediate danger, because they are cheaper and easier to operate. The U.S. and its allies have developed effective methods of neutralizing most existing air defenses. In addition to jammers, radar-seeking missiles, and decoys, the U.S. employs stealth technology, first used on the F-117 Nighthawk, then on the B-2 Spirit, and now on the F/A-22 and F-35. Future aircraft may be designed with "visual stealth" technology to render them almost invisible even in daylight.

No other nation has deployed any stealth aircraft. But advanced sensor networks may be able to detect first-generation stealth planes. The Serbs actually managed to shoot down an F-117 in 1999.

None of the most sophisticated surface-to-air missiles, such as Russia's double-digit SAMs (SA-10, SA-15, SA-20), was available to Iraq, Serbia, Afghanistan, or other states that the U.S. has fought in recent years, but they are being sold to other customers. So are shoulder-fired antiaircraft missiles such as the American FIM-92 Stinger, British Starstreak, French Mistral, Chinese Qianwei-2, and Russian SA-7 Grail, SA-14 Gremlin, SA-16 Gimlet, and SA-18 Grouse. There are at least one hundred thousand such systems in the arsenals of over one hundred states and at least thirteen nonstate groups such as Hezbollah, the Revolutionary Armed Forces of Colombia (FARC), and the Tamil Tigers. The best models have a range of 23,000 feet.

The potential of hand-carried missiles was demonstrated in the 1980s when Stingers took a significant toll on Soviet aircraft in Afghanistan. The threat is serious enough for the U.S. to rely increasingly on unmanned drones for high-risk missions and to mandate that manned aircraft in war zones stay above 15,000 or 20,000 feet. SAMs pose an especially great threat to helicopters, which don't have the option of flying that high, and for airplanes taking off or landing. Three cargo aircraft leaving Baghdad International Airport have been seriously damaged by missiles, and, while all of them survived, several U.S. helicopters hit with SAMs in Iraq and Afghanistan did not. An Israeli jetliner was almost shot down in Mombasa, Kenya, in 2002 by al Qaeda operatives firing an SA-7. Only the terrorists' targeting error prevented the deaths of 271 passengers and crew. Other civilian airliners are sure to be less lucky.

Assuming that warplanes can reach their destination, the growing precision of bombs and missiles has made it possible to take out targets with fewer and smaller munitions than ever before. (The U.S. Air Force's latest bomb carries only fifty pounds of explosives.) Weapons are getting smarter all the time. The U.S. Sensor-Fuzed Weapon, first employed in the Iraq War, disperses forty "skeet" antiarmor warheads that use infrared and laser sensors to find and destroy armored vehicles within a thirty-acre area. The Tactical Tomahawk, which entered production in 2004, can loiter up to three hours while searching for targets and receive in-flight retargeting instructions.

The U.S. preponderance in smart bombs and missiles helps to compensate for the relatively small size of its manned bomber force. As of 2005, the U.S. Air Force had only 157 long-range bombers (B-52s, B-ls, B-2s), a considerable reduction not only from World War II (when the U.S. had 34,780) but also from the end of the Cold War (360). While few in number, each B-2 can perform the work of thousands of B-29s by "servicing" eighty "aim points" per sortie.

Tankers such as the KC-10 and KC-135 vastly extend the range and effectiveness of combat aircraft. Cargo-lifters like the U.S. C-5, C-17, and C-130 and the Russian An-70 and An-225 also perform a valuable, if unglamorous, role in projecting military power around the world. The U.S. owns 740 tanker aircraft and 1,200 cargo aircraft, far more than any other country. A lack of such support aircraft makes it difficult for even the relatively sophisticated European militaries to move their forces very far.

A host of other aircraft, ranging from JSTARS and AWACs to Rivet Joint and Global Hawk, perform surveillance and electronic-warfare missions in support of combat forces. Their numbers have been growing: While there were only two JSTARS in the Gulf War, in the Iraq War there were fifteen. But commanders have become so dependent on these systems that there never seem to be enough to go around. These, too, are vital U.S. assets that few other nations possess.

Space Warfare A growing amount of surveillance, communications, and intelligence work is being performed by unmanned aircraft and satellites. In 2001 the U.S. had an estimated 100 military satellites and 150 commercial satellites in orbit, as much as the rest of the world combined. The U.S. spends more than $15 billion a year on space, some 90 percent of the global total. The most advanced U.S. surveillance satellites are said to be able to pick out a six-inch object from 150 miles above. A new generation of satellites utilizes stealth technology to make it more difficult for other countries to track their progress and thus to hide equipment from American eyes.

The advantage the U.S. military derives from mastery of space is slowly eroding, however. The Global Positioning System developed by the Defense Department is now widely available for countless commercial applications that have spawned a $30-billion-per-year industry. A potential enemy could use GPS signals to locate targets in the U.S. the same way the U.S. military uses it to locate targets in Iraq or Afghanistan. The U.S. could jam or degrade GPS signals in wartime, but it would have to do so very selectively for fear of imposing a severe toll on the economy, because GPS devices are now essential for civil aviation, shipping, and other functions. In any case, the European Union in cooperation with China is launching its own GPS constellation, known as Galileo, that would be outside of U.S. control.

This is part of a trend of more and more countries—at least forty to date—lofting their own satellites. But getting access to space no longer requires having your own satellite. A growing number of private firms with such names as Google Earth, Keyhole, DigitalGlobe, and Space Imaging sell or give away high-resolution satellite photos via the Internet. The best of these offer imagery of sufficient quality to identify objects eighteen inches wide. The Israeli-owned ImageSat International offers customers the opportunity to redirect its EROS-A imaging satellite (launched in 2000 aboard a Russian rocket) and download its data in total secrecy with few if any restrictions. Its CEO boasts, "Our customers, in effect, acquire their own reconnaissance satellite ... at a fraction of the cost that it would take to build their own." The private satellite industry is becoming so pervasive that the U.S. military has turned to it to provide some of its own imaging (typically low-resolution pictures used for mapping) and much of its communications needs.

Targets identified from space could be attacked either with terrorist (or commando) strikes or with the growing number of missiles proliferating around the world. More than two dozen nations have ballistic missiles and by 2015 at least a dozen will have land-attack cruise missiles. Either type of projectile could be topped with chemical, biological, or nuclear warheads. At least eight countries already have nuclear weapons and more are trying to get them, in part to offset the tremendous U.S. advantage in conventional weaponry.

In response, the U.S. is working on a variety of missile defenses. The most advanced are the ground-based Patriot Advanced Capability 3 and the sea-based Standard Missile 3, which already have been deployed to protect U.S. troops overseas. The deployment of a long-heralded system designed to protect the U.S. homeland against long-range missiles began in 2004 with the installation of interceptors in Alaska. Eventually, the U.S. plans to field a multilayered defense using a variety of sensors and weapons on land, sea, air, and space. Also in the works are systems designed to defeat low-flying cruise missiles, which are hard to distinguish from ground clutter.

FOG FORECAST

The changes wrought by the Information Revolution are still in their early stages and have serious limitations. Even the best surveillance systems can be thwarted by simple countermeasures like camouflage, smoke, and decoys, by bad weather, or by difficult terrain like the deep sea, mountains, or jungles. Sensors have limited ability to penetrate solid objects, so they cannot tell what is happening in underground bunkers such as those that North Korea and Iran use to hide their nuclear weapons programs. Urban areas present a particularly difficult challenge: There are far more things to track (individuals) and far more obstructions (buildings, vehicles, trees, signs) than at sea or in the sky—and figuring out whether a person is a civilian or an insurgent is a lot harder than figuring out whether an unidentified aircraft is a civilian airliner or an enemy fighter. It is harder still to figure out how hard enemy soldiers will resist or what stratagems they will employ. No machine has yet been invented that can penetrate human thought processes. Even with the best equipment in the world, U.S. forces frequently have been surprised by their adversaries.

Some strategists expect that advances in information technology will greatly diminish if not altogether obliterate some of these difficulties. The Pentagon is creating a Global Information Grid that will pool data from all U.S. assets, whether an infantryman on the ground or a satellite in space. The ultimate goal: to provide a perfect operational picture—a "God's-eye view" of the "battlespace."

This ambitious objective could be furthered by the development of better microwave radars that could see through walls, foliage, or soil; cheaper, more pervasive sensors that could provide 24/7 coverage of the battlefield; better data compression and transmission techniques that could allow more bytes to be sent much faster; and more powerful computers that might make it possible to create, for example, a real-time, three-dimensional model of a city showing all the people who reside in it. Not only are electronic computers getting more powerful in accordance with Moore's Law, but even greater leaps in computing power may be achieved using biological computers that rely not on electronic components but on DNA, individual molecules, or proteins; optical computers that use light rather than electricity; and quantum computers that exploit the atomic properties of matter. Some scientists speculate that by using such methods a billionfold increase in computing power is possible. "That means you could hold the power of all earth's present computers in the palm of your hand," says Stan Williams of Hewlett-Packard.

Yet no matter how far information technology advances, it is doubtful that the Pentagon will ever succeed, as some Utopians dream, in "lifting the fog of war." The fallibility of American soldiers and the cunning of their enemies will surely continue to frustrate their best-laid plans. Indeed, America's growing reliance on high-tech systems creates vulnerabilities of its own: Future enemies have strong incentives to attack U.S. computer and communication nodes. Strikes on military information networks could blind or paralyze the armed forces, while strikes on civilian infrastructure, such as banking or air-control systems, could cause chaos on the home front.

Safe to say, adversaries will figure out ways to blunt the U.S. informational advantage. From Operation Anaconda in Afghanistan to numerous misadventures in Iraq, they already have.

AMERICA'S UNPARALLELED POWER

While various setbacks in the war on terror underscore the limits of American power, it is important not to lose sight of the bigger picture: The dawn of the Information Age has coincided with a period of American global hegemony. Part of the explanation lies in U.S. economic strength and its "soft power." But Europe and Japan are rich, too, yet their global sway lags far behind. What they lack is America's military strength.

In the early years of the twenty-first century the United States enjoys a preponderance of military power greater than that of any other nation in history. Rome was rivaled in land power by Carthage, Persia, and other states, and its sphere of control never extended far beyond western Europe and the Mediterranean region. Britain was rivaled in naval power by the Netherlands, France, and later Germany, and it was never dominant on land. Today America is rivaled in land, sea, and air power by ... no one. Although the dominance of U.S. forces can still be challenged when they come into close contact with the enemy on his home turf, they are undisputed masters of the "commons" (sea, air, space), which allows them to project power anywhere in the world at short notice. In the words of journalist Gregg Easterbrook, "The American military is now the strongest the world has ever known, both in absolute terms and relative to other nations; stronger than the Wehrmacht in 1940, stronger than the legions at the height of Roman power."

What accounts for this huge military edge? Not manpower. The U.S. armed forces in 2006, with about 1.4 million active-duty personnel and 1.2 million reservists, were hardly the biggest in the world. NATO's European members and China each had roughly 2.2 million men and women under arms. Other nations—North Korea with 1 million active-duty soldiers and 4.7 million reservists, Russia with 960,000 on active duty and 2.4 million in the reserves—were not far behind. In any case, because the U.S. armed forces typically do their fighting overseas, they seldom enjoy a numerical advantage in their theater of operations. Whether in Iraq or Afghanistan, they have usually been outnumbered.

In the Information Age the U.S. edge lies in quality, not (as it did during the Second Industrial Age) in quantity. Both its soldiers and their equipment are among the best on earth. The U.S. armed forces are not the only Information Age military—Britain, France, Japan, Singapore, Australia, Sweden, and other nations have followed in its wake—but they have gone the furthest fastest.

Among other nations, Israel's success in harnessing the Information Revolution has been particularly consequential. The balance of power in the Middle East shifted sharply in Israel's favor following the Yom Kippur War, because it modernized its military to a far greater extent than its neighbors did. This helps to explain why no Arab nation has mounted a conventional attack on Israel since 1973.

The United States' success in harnessing the Information Revolution produced its profoundest effects without a shot being fired. Aware that the Soviet Union could not keep up with U.S. military advances in the 1980s, Mikhail Gorbachev responded with perestroika and glasnost, reform efforts that spun out of control and ultimately consigned the Soviet Union to the ash heap of history. The demise of the USSR set the stage for the U.S. military dominance that has underpinned the current era of globalization, which has been remarkably devoid of conflict between states.

Wars between states have declined in size and frequency for a variety of reasons, not the least being the integration of old adversaries like France and Germany into the European Union, the international norms propagated by the United Nations Charter, the spread of capitalism and democracy across the world, and the deterrence provided by nuclear weapons. But surely another part of the explanation is that few states feel free to challenge the Pax Americana. Several of those that have tried, including Panama, Serbia, Afghanistan, and Iraq, have seen the downfall of their regimes. "War, let alone 'decisive war' between major states, currently is enjoying an off season for one main reason," writes British strategist Colin Gray. "So extreme is the imbalance of military power in favor of the United States that potential rivals rule out policies that might lead to hostilities with the superpower."

ACCESS DENIED?

It is doubtful that any country will mount a full-spectrum challenge to U.S. military capabilities in the foreseeable future. The entry barriers are simply too high, especially for air, sea, and space systems. *Virginia-class* nuclear submarines cost $2.4 billion, *Nimitz-class* aircraft carriers go for $6 billion, and the F-35 Joint Strike Fighter program will cost at least $245 billion. The U.S. spends around $500 billion a year on its military, almost as much as the rest of the world combined. In fact, the U.S. spends more simply on the research, development, testing, and evaluation of new weapons—$71 billion in 2006—than any other country spends on its entire armed forces. (By way of comparison, the top three spenders after the U.S. are Russia, whose defense budget in 2003 was estimated at $65 billion; China, at $56 billion; France, at $45 billion; and Japan and the United Kingdom, at $42 billion each.)

It is not only U.S. hardware that's hard to replicate; so is the all-volunteer force that makes it work. Operating high-tech military equipment requires long-service professionals, not short-term conscripts. Countries as diverse as Vietnam, China, Germany, and Russia are emulating the Anglo-American model by downsizing their forces and relying less on draftees. Many other nations have abolished the draft altogether. The U.S. military's edge lies not simply in recruiting high-quality personnel but in its methods for training and organizing them. Initiatives undertaken in earlier decades, such as setting up realistic training centers to simulate combat conditions and forcing the services to work more closely together (the Goldwater-Nichols Act), continue to bear fruit. Few other armed forces have made comparable reforms. Writes one scholar: "The superb U.S. all-volunteer military force … is a unique human and institutional asset that less capable foreign rivals can neither copy nor steal."

But a potential adversary does not need to duplicate U.S. force structure in order to challenge it. The United States faces a growing "asymmetric" threat both from other states and from substate groups.

As we have seen, a variety of off-the-shelf missiles can threaten U.S. tanks, surface ships, and aircraft, especially when they get close to hostile territory. The power of smart munitions is outstripping the protection afforded by speed or armor. After 2010, write defense analysts Michael Vickers and Robert Martinage, "the survivability of aircraft carriers, high-structure surface combatants [e.g., tanks], and non-stealthy aircraft of all types could increasingly be called into question as maritime, over-the-horizon 'area denial' capabilities and extended-range air defense systems continue to mature."

Also vulnerable are the ports, airfields, and bases that the U.S. uses to project its power overseas. Imagine how much damage Saddam Hussein could have done in 2003 if he had been able to annihilate the one port in Kuwait that was being used to disembark coalition troops or the large desert bases in Kuwait where over one hundred thousand British and American troops gathered prior to the invasion of Iraq. The Pentagon's 2001 Quadrennial Defense Review warned that "[f]uture adversaries could have the means to render ineffective much of our current ability to project military power overseas."

If the U.S. armed forces could not count on safe, assured access to overseas bases they would have to radically change the way they do business. It would no longer be practical to rely on large land armies or lots of short-range combat aircraft operating out of vulnerable forward bases supplied by equally vulnerable cargo ships, trucks, and aircraft. The U.S. Army might be forced to rely on a small number of commandos supported by long-range aircraft and missiles—the Afghanistan model. The navy might have to depend more on submarines and the air force on stealth aircraft. All the services might have to make greater use of unmanned vehicles. The battlefield, which has been growing less crowded for centuries, might empty out even further as small units try to conceal themselves from ubiquitous sensor networks, emerging only briefly to launch lightning strikes before they go back into hiding.

This has become known as the "swarming" scenario, and it has attracted support from the likes of military historian Alexander Bevin, who writes, "Large concentrations of troops and weapons are targets for destruction, not marks of power, and [in the future] they no longer will exist…. Military units, to survive, must not only be small, but highly mobile, self-contained, and autonomous."

Even if these predictions are accurate, however, no timeline is attached. Timing matters. After all, everyone knows that a bull market will be followed by a bear market, but the key to making money in stocks is knowing when that transition will occur. Likewise, the key to winning future wars is knowing when to move from one form of military to another. A premature decision to change (such as the U.S. Army's Pentomic design in the 1950s) can leave one unprepared to fight and win wars that actually occur, Vietnam being the classic example.

In any case, it is doubtful that a complete shift to "swarming" will ever take place. Winning wars, as distinct from winning battles, will continue to require controlling territory, which in turn will require a substantial presence of ground troops, as the U.S. has learned in Afghanistan and Iraq. No wonder weapon will alter this fundamental reality.

"AMERICAN HIROSHIMA"

Even as strategists look to the future, armed forces must not lose sight of the threats of the moment, and they do not come for the most part from traditional militaries. They come largely from terrorist groups—some with state sponsorship, others without—that utilize the fruits of modern technology to their advantage.

"Irregular" attacks carried out by tribes, clans, or other nonstate actors are as old as warfare itself; they long predate the development of modern armed forces and the nation-state. The religious fanaticism that animates so many of today's terrorists and guerrillas is equally ancient. But technological advances have made such attacks far more potent than in the past. The progeny of the Second Industrial Revolution—assault rifles, machine guns, mortars, rocket launchers, land mines, explosives—long ago spread to the remotest corners of the globe. Fighters who a century ago might have made do with swords and muskets now have access to cheap and reliable weapons, such as the AK-47, capable of spewing out 100 bullets a minute. More advanced technologies, from handheld missiles to chemical, biological, and nuclear weapons, give even a small group of insurgents the ability to mete out far more destruction than entire armies could a century ago. And thanks to modern transportation and communications infrastructure—such as jumbo jets, the Internet, and cell phones—insurgents have the capability to carry out their attacks virtually anywhere in the world.

September 11, 2001, showed the terrifying possibilities of such unconventional warfare. It is easy to imagine that in the future super-terrorists will be able to kill hundreds of thousands, even millions, with effective weapons of mass destruction. All of the materials, as well as the know-how, needed to craft such devices are all too readily available.

Chemical and biological threats will be discussed in Chapter Thirteen, but nuclear weapons, more than any other kind, have the ability to trump U.S. military hegemony. The atomic bomb is more than sixty years old. It belongs to an age of rotary-dial telephones and fin-winged cars. It is a miracle that it has not been used in anger since 1945, but that streak won't last forever. And while Information Age technology offers a reasonable chance of stopping a nuclear-tripped missile, there is much less probability of stopping a terrorist with a nuclear suitcase. (Yes, nuclear bombs have gotten smaller, just like computers.) There is little in theory to prevent al Qaeda from carrying out its oft-expressed desire to create an "American Hiroshima." In the words of a retired four-star general who once ran antinuclear terror programs for the Department of Energy: "It is not a matter of if, it's a matter of *When.*"

The most important challenge for the armed forces of the U.S. and its allies in the post-9/11 world is to "leverage" their advantage in conventional weaponry to deal with an unconventional threat. Information technology can be an important part of this task. Embedded microchips can track the 18 million cargo containers moving around the world and prevent terrorists from using them to smuggle weapons. Computerized cameras scanning a crowd may be able to pick out a terrorist based on facial recognition patterns. Doglike sniffing machines may be able to recognize suspects by their body odor. Powerful computers utilizing artificial intelligence programs can sift vast reams of digital data to pick out information about terrorist plots—if concerns about violating the privacy of innocent people do not get in the way. A variety of unobtrusive sensors can warn of the presence of explosives or chemical, biological, or nuclear weapons. Handheld computer translating devices such as the Phraselator already in use by U.S. troops can bridge some of the language gap between Western operatives and the regions where they operate.

But in the final analysis, having the best technology is not enough to defeat the most ruthless terrorists. In fact, most of the expensive weapons systems being purchased by the U.S. and its allies are almost completely irrelevant to the war against terrorism. Smart bombs can be useful for killing the enemy once he's been located. But figuring out who the enemy is, where he is, and what he is up to—that requires smart *people.*

Various remedies have been proposed to fix the obvious American weakness in this area: Requiring more foreign-language training for the armed services. Recruiting more spies. Setting up a military school devoted to civil governance. Creating an agency tasked with "nation-building." Appointing "cultural scouts"—an enhancement of the existing Foreign Area Officer program, which is widely seen as a career dead end—who would spend long periods of time in foreign lands. These are all good ideas and some are beginning to be implemented, but they are harder to enact than a decision to buy a new weapons system. They require changing the culture of the Defense Department and other government agencies, which have not stressed skills in counter-insurgency, human intelligence, or nation-building.

TOOTH AND TAIL

While the U.S. armed forces have made some major strides in recent decades, especially in getting branches to work more closely together, they still have a long way to go before they have an organizational structure that makes the most effective use of their high-tech equipment. The army, although putting greater emphasis on more nimble, four-thousand-person brigades, still maintains a divisional structure that dates back to the First Industrial Age, while the basic units of the navy (carrier groups) and the air force (squadrons and wings) date back to the Second Industrial Age. All of the services employ a personnel system developed more than one hundred years ago that treats individuals as interchangeable cogs in a giant machine. Army officers have traditionally spent an average of only eighteen months at each duty station during the course of a twenty-five-year career, making it difficult to build true expertise in such complex areas as foreign cultures.

Another problem is a cumbersome procurement process that costs too much and takes too long to deliver new equipment. The U.S. paid a heavy human cost for those shortcomings in Iraq, where body armor, armored Humvees, and IED-jamming devices were slow to arrive. The time and expense involved in producing new weapons systems have increased severalfold since the 1970s, even as the private sector has been able to produce products like cell phones and microchips faster and more cheaply. "In order to stay ahead of adversaries with access to technologies available in the global marketplace, the DOD [Department of Defense] needs to shorten the timeframe from concept to testing," writes Lieutenant Colonel Augustus Way Fountain III, a chemistry professor at West Point. That's exactly what the best-run companies—the Microsofts and the Wal-Marts—have done, but the U.S. armed forces (and most others, for that matter) have lagged behind.

In general, the U.S. military is hindered by a sluggish, bloated bureaucracy that has resisted countless reform efforts. "We're No. 1 in the world in military capabilities," says David, M. Walker, head of Congress's Government Accountability Office. "But on the business side, the Defense Department gets a D—giving them the benefit of the doubt. If they were a business, they wouldn't be in business."

Some statistics buttress the point. The "tooth to tail" ratio in the U.S. military—the number of support personnel as opposed to actual trigger-pullers—varies from 12:1 for the Army and Marine Corps, to 15:1 for the Navy, and 32:1 for the Air Force. "An astounding 70 percent of the defense budget is spent on overhead and infrastructure (the bureaucratic 'tail'). Only 30 percent directly reaches our combat forces in the field (the 'tooth')," writes retired Admiral Bill Owens. "No community would tolerate 7 out of every 10 police officers sitting at their desks pushing paper. The nation should not tolerate such a ratio in the military."

What makes this unwieldy setup so intolerable is that it can stymie the potential of even the most advanced information technologies. Retired Marine Colonel T. X. Hammes notes that

> most commanders must submit their intelligence requirements up the chain of command. Each level validates, consolidates, and prioritizes the requests, which are then fed through the centralized staff system to task the assets that will actually collect against the requests. The information is collected, passed to another section for analysis, then put in the form of a usable product, and finally disseminated through the same cumbersome system. Thus, the premier benefit of the Information Age—immediate access to current intelligence—is nullified by the way we route it through our vertical bureaucracy.

The good news, from the American perspective, is that many potential enemies (e.g., China or North Korea) are encumbered by even more sclerotic bureaucracies. The bad news is that this is not true of nimble, networked groups like al Qaeda. To fight them effectively, the U.S. military will have to display more of the decentralized decision-making that it showed in Afghanistan in the fall of 2001. This will not be easy to do because modern command and control technology is a two-edged sword: It can be used to centralize or decentralize. It will always be difficult for a senior military or political leader to resist the temptation to micromanage operations from afar—a style of leadership that modern communications technology has made easier, but no more effective, than in the past.

Veteran journalist Robert Kaplan rightly calls "the dinosauric, vertical bureaucracy of the Industrial Age...the greatest single impediment to America's ability to wage a successful worldwide counter-insurgency." Unless the U.S. government can streamline its Industrial Age bureaucracy and become a networked organization, it may find that even purchasing the latest and best technology will not offer sufficient protection against the country's foes.

2.2.3 Bigger Monster, Weaker Chains

JAY STANLEY AND BARRY STEINHARDT

George Orwell's chilling novel *1984* depicts a society ruled by a totalitarian government bent on total manipulation and control of what people think and where every person is being constantly watched by Big Brother. When Orwell published his novel in 1949, the technologies that made such a dystopia possible were still in the realm of science fiction. But since that time, technological advances in digital cameras, computers, global positioning satellites, "data-mining," and other surveillance technologies have made "total information awareness" a real possibility. In addition, in response to the terrorist attacks of September 11, 2001, the U.S. government has increased its surveillance activities in the name of national security while keeping the details of what they have been doing secret from the general public. Civil libertarians, such as the authors of this report prepared for the American Civil Liberties Union in 2003, are alarmed at the erosion of personal privacy that these technological and political developments portend. Americans, they argue, are being increasingly watched, tracked, and recorded, both by private corporations and by a security-obsessed government. They fear that "privacy, while not dead, is on life support" and argue that the best way to prevent the emergence of a "surveillance society" is to enact strong new privacy laws based on the constitutional principle of the Fourth Amendment, laws that do not leave the right to privacy at the mercy of advancing technology.

FOCUS QUESTIONS

1. What are some ways in which private corporations are increasingly using data surveillance to track and record our daily activities? Are you at all troubled by this trend toward the consolidation and commodification of personal information? Why or why not?

Source: *Bigger Monster: Weaker Chains: The Growth of an American Surveillance Society*, by Jay Stanley and Barry Steinhardt, January 2005. American Civil Liberties Union Technology and Liberty Program. Reprinted by permission of the American Civil Liberties Union.

2. The authors claim that the post-9/11 legislation such as the USA Patriot Act expanded the government's authority to spy on its own citizens while weakening the system of judicial checks and balances on those powers. Explain why the authors think this is the case.
3. Why are the authors concerned about the possibility of a national ID card linked to a national database containing personal information about every citizen? Do you share their concerns, or do you believe that such a step would help the government protect us from criminals and terrorists? Where does the proper balance lie between personal privacy and national security?
4. Discuss this reading in light of the readings by Langdon Winner (Selection 1.2.2) and Claire Hope Cummings (Selection 2.4.4). Whose political values are embedded in the new surveillance technologies?

KEYWORDS

biometrics, Carnivore, data profiling, data surveillance, digitization, Echelon, genetic information, GPS, PATRIOT Act, privacy, RFID chips, TIPS, video surveillance

THE GROWING SURVEILLANCE MONSTER

In the film *Minority Report,* which takes place in the United States in the year 2050, people called "Pre-cogs" can supposedly predict future crimes, and the nation has become a perfect surveillance society. The frightening thing is that except for the psychic Pre-cogs, the technologies of surveillance portrayed in the film already exist or are in the pipeline. Replace the Pre-cogs with "brain fingerprinting"—the supposed ability to ferret out dangerous tendencies by reading brain waves—and the film's entire vision no longer lies far in the future. Other new privacy invasions are coming at us from all directions, from video and data surveillance to DNA scanning to new data-gathering gadgets.

Video Surveillance

Surveillance video cameras are rapidly spreading throughout the public arena. A survey of surveillance cameras in Manhattan, for example, found that it is impossible to walk around the city without being recorded nearly every step of the way. And since September 11 the pace has quickened, with new cameras being placed not only in some of our most sacred public spaces, such as the National Mall in Washington and the Statue of Liberty in New York harbor, but on ordinary public streets all over America.

As common as video cameras have become, there are strong signs that, without public action, video surveillance may be on the verge of a revolutionary expansion in American life. There are three factors propelling this revolution:

1. **Improved technology.** Advances such as the digitization of video mean cheaper cameras, cheaper transmission of far-flung video feeds, and cheaper storage and retrieval of images.

2. **Centralized surveillance.** A new centralized surveillance center in Washington, DC, is an early indicator of what technology may bring. It allows officers to view images from video cameras across the city—public buildings and streets, neighborhoods, Metro stations, and even schools. With the flip of a switch, officers can zoom in on people from cameras a half-mile away.[1]

3. **Unexamined assumptions that cameras provide security.** In the wake of the September 11 attacks, many embraced surveillance as the way to prevent future attacks and prevent crime. But it is far from clear how cameras will increase security. U.S. government experts on security technology, noting that "monitoring video screens is both boring and mesmerizing," have found in experiments that after only 20 minutes of watching video monitors, "the attention of most individuals has degenerated to well below acceptable levels."[2] In addition, studies of cameras' effect on crime in Britain, where they have

been extensively deployed, have found no conclusive evidence that they have reduced crime.[3]

These developments are creating powerful momentum toward pervasive video surveillance of our public spaces. If centralized video facilities are permitted in Washington and around the nation, it is inevitable that they will be expanded—not only in the number of cameras but also in their power and ability. It is easy to foresee inexpensive, one-dollar cameras being distributed throughout our cities and tied via wireless technology into a centralized police facility where the life of the city can be monitored. Those video signals could be stored indefinitely in digital form in giant but inexpensive databases, and called up with the click of a mouse at any time. With face recognition, the video records could even be indexed and searched based on who the systems identify—correctly, or, all too often, incorrectly.

Several airports around the nation, a handful of cities, and even the National Park Service at the Statue of Liberty have installed face recognition. While not nearly reliable enough to be effective as a security application,[4] such a system could still violate the privacy of a significant percentage of the citizens who appeared before it (as well as the privacy of those who do not appear before it but are falsely identified as having done so). Unlike, say, an iris scan, face recognition doesn't require the knowledge, consent, or participation of the subject; modern cameras can easily view faces from over 100 yards away.

Further possibilities for the expansion of video surveillance lie with unmanned aircraft, or drones, which have been used by the military and the CIA overseas for reconnaissance, surveillance, and targeting. Controlled from the ground, they can stay airborne for days at a time. Now there is talk of deploying them domestically. Senate Armed Services Committee Chairman John Warner (R, VA) said in December 2002 that he wants to explore their use in Homeland Security, and a number of domestic government agencies have expressed interest in deploying them. Drones are likely to be just one of many ways in which improving robotics technology will be applied to surveillance.[5]

The bottom line is that surveillance systems, once installed, rarely remain confined to their original purpose. Once the nation decides to go down the path of seeking security through video surveillance, the imperative to make it work will become overwhelming, and the monitoring of citizens in public places will quickly become pervasive.

Data Surveillance

An insidious new type of surveillance is becoming possible that is just as intrusive as video surveillance—what we might call "data surveillance." Data surveillance is *the collection of information about an identifiable individual, often from multiple sources, that can be assembled into a portrait of that person's activities.*[6] Most computers are programmed to automatically store and track usage data, and the spread of computer chips in our daily lives means that more and more of our activities leave behind "data trails." It will soon be possible to combine information from different sources to recreate an individual's activities with such detail that it becomes no different from being followed around all day by a detective with a video camera.

Some think comprehensive public tracking will make no difference, since life in public places is not "private" in the same way as life inside the home. This is wrong; such tracking would represent a radical change in American life. A woman who leaves her house, drives to a store, meets a friend for coffee, visits a museum, and then returns home may be in public all day, but her life is still private in that she is the only one who has an overall view of how she spent her day. In America, she does not expect that her activities are being watched or tracked in any systematic way—she expects to be left alone. But if current trends continue, it will be impossible to have any contact with the outside world that is not watched and recorded.

The Commodification of Information

A major factor driving the trend toward data surveillance forward is the commodification of personal information by corporations. As computer technology exploded in recent decades, making it much easier to collect information about what Americans buy and do, companies came to realize that such data is often very valuable. The expense of marketing efforts gives businesses a strong incentive to know as much about consumers as possible so they can focus on the most likely new customers. Surveys, sweepstakes questionnaires, loyalty programs and detailed product registration forms have proliferated in American life—all aimed at gathering information about consumers. Today, any consumer activity that is *not* being tracked and recorded is increasingly being viewed by businesses as money left on the table.

On the Internet, where every mouse click can be recorded, the tracking and profiling of consumers is even more prevalent. Web sites can not only track what consumers buy, but what they *look at*—and for how long, and in what order. With the end of the Dot Com era, personal information has become an even more precious source of hard cash for those Internet ventures that survive. And of course Americans use the Internet not just as a shopping mall, but to research topics of interest, debate political issues, seek support for personal problems, and many other purposes that can generate deeply private information about their thoughts, interests, lifestyles, habits, and activities.

Genetic Privacy

The relentless commercialization of information has also led to the breakdown of some longstanding traditions, such as doctor–patient confidentiality. Citizens share some of their most intimate and embarrassing secrets with their doctors on the old-fashioned assumption that their conversations are confidential. Yet those details are routinely shared with insurance companies, researchers, marketers, and employers. An insurance trade organization called the Medical Information Bureau even keeps a centralized medical database with records on millions of patients. Weak new medical privacy rules will do little to stop this behavior.

An even greater threat to medical privacy is looming: genetic information. The increase in DNA analysis for medical testing, research, and other purposes will accelerate sharply in coming years and will increasingly be incorporated into routine health care.

Unlike other medical information, genetic data is a unique combination: both difficult to keep confidential and extremely revealing about us. DNA is very easy to acquire because we constantly slough off hair, saliva, skin cells and other samples of our DNA (household dust, for example, is made up primarily of dead human skin cells). That means that no matter how hard we strive to keep our genetic code private, we are always vulnerable to other parties' secretly testing samples of our DNA. The issue will be intensified by the development of cheap and efficient DNA chips capable of reading parts of our genetic sequences.

Already, it is possible to send away a DNA sample for analysis. A testing company called Genelex reports that it has amassed 50,000 DNA samples, many gathered surreptitiously for paternity testing. "You'd be amazed," the company's CEO told *U.S. News & World Report.* "Siblings have sent in mom's discarded Kleenex and wax from her hearing aid to resolve the family rumors."[7]

Not only is DNA easier to acquire than other medical information, revealing it can also have more profound consequences. Genetic markers are rapidly being identified for all sorts of genetic diseases, risk factors, and other characteristics. None of us knows what time bombs are lurking in our genomes.

The consequences of increased genetic transparency will likely include:

- **Discrimination by insurers.** Health and life insurance companies could collect DNA for use in deciding who to insure and what to charge them, with the result that a certain proportion of the population could become uninsurable. The insurance industry has already vigorously opposed efforts in Congress to pass meaningful genetic privacy and discrimination bills.

- **Employment discrimination.** Genetic workplace testing is already on the rise, and the courts have heard many cases. Employers desiring healthy, capable workers will always have an incentive to discriminate based on DNA—an incentive that will be even stronger as long as health insurance is provided through the workplace.

• **Genetic spying.** Cheap technology could allow everyone from schoolchildren to dating couples to nosy neighbors to routinely check out each other's genetic codes. A likely high-profile example: online posting of the genetic profiles of celebrities or politicians.

Financial Privacy

Like doctor–patient confidentiality, the tradition of privacy and discretion by financial institutions has also collapsed; financial companies today routinely put the details of their customers' financial lives up for sale.

A big part of the problem is the Gramm-Leach-Bliley Act passed by Congress in 1999. Although Gramm-Leach is sometimes described as a "financial privacy law," it created a very weak privacy standard—so weak, in fact, that far from protecting Americans' financial privacy, the law has had the effect of ratifying the increasing abandonment of customer privacy by financial companies.

Gramm-Leach effectively gives financial institutions permission to sell their customers' financial data to anyone they choose. That includes the date, amount, and recipient of credit card charges or checks a customer has written; account balances; and information about the flow of deposits and withdrawals through an account. Consumers provide a tremendous amount of information about themselves when they fill out applications to get a loan, buy insurance, or purchase securities, and companies can also share that information. In fact, the only information a financial company may NOT give out about you is your account number.

Under Gramm-Leach, you get no privacy unless you file complex paperwork, following a financial institution's precise instructions before a deadline they set, and repeating the process for each and every financial service provider who may have data about you. And it is a process that many companies intentionally make difficult and cumbersome; few let consumers "opt out" of data sharing through a Web site or phone number, or even provide a self-addressed envelope.

Gramm-Leach is an excellent example of the ways that privacy protections are being weakened even as the potential for privacy invasion grows.

New Data-Gathering Technologies

The discovery by businesses of the monetary value of personal information and the vast new project of tracking the habits of consumers has been made possible by advances in computers, databases and the Internet. In the near future, other new technologies will continue to fill out the mosaic of information it is possible to collect on every individual. Examples include the following:

• **Cell phone location data.** The government has mandated that manufacturers make cell phones capable of automatically reporting their location when an owner dials 911. Of course, those phones are capable of tracking their location at other times as well. And in applying the rules that protect the privacy of telephone records to this location data, the government is weakening those rules in a way that allows phone companies to collect and share data about the location and movements of their customers.

• **Biometrics.** Technologies that identify us by unique bodily attributes such as our fingerprints, faces, iris patterns, or DNA are already being proposed for inclusion on national ID cards and to identify airline passengers. Face recognition is spreading. Fingerprint scanners have been introduced as security or payment mechanisms in office buildings, college campuses, grocery stores and even fast-food restaurants. And several companies are working on DNA chips that will be able to instantly identify individuals by the DNA we leave behind everywhere we go.

• **Black boxes.** All cars built today contain computers, and some of those computers are being programmed in ways that are not necessarily in the interest of owners. An increasing number of cars contain devices akin to the "black boxes" on aircraft that record details about a vehicle's operation and movement. Those devices can "tattle" on car owners to the police or insurance investigators. Already, one car rental agency tried to charge a customer for speeding after a GPS device in the car reported the transgression back to the company. And cars are just one example of how products and possessions can be programmed to spy and inform on their owners.

- **RFID chips.** RFID chips, which are already used in such applications as toll-booth speed passes, emit a short-range radio signal containing a unique code that identifies each chip. Once the cost of these chips falls to a few pennies each, plans are underway to affix them to products in stores, down to every can of soup and tube of toothpaste. They will allow everyday objects to "talk" to each other—or to anyone else who is listening. For example, they could let market researchers scan the contents of your purse or car from five feet away, or let police officers scan your identification when they pass you on the street.

- **Implantable GPS chips.** Computer chips that can record and broadcast their location have also been developed. In addition to practical uses such as building them into shipping containers, they can also serve as location "bugs" when, for example, hidden by a suspicious husband in a wife's purse. And they can be implanted under the skin (as can RFID chips).

If we do not act to reverse the current trend, data surveillance—like video surveillance—will allow corporations or the government to constantly monitor what individual Americans do every day. Data surveillance would cover *everyone,* with records of every transaction and activity squirreled away until they are sucked up by powerful search engines, whether as part of routine security checks, a general sweep for suspects in an unsolved crime, or a program of harassment against some future Martin Luther King.

Government Surveillance

Data surveillance is made possible by the growing ocean of privately collected personal data. But who would conduct that surveillance? There are certainly business incentives for doing so; companies called data aggregators (such as Acxiom and ChoicePoint) are in the business of compiling detailed databases on individuals and then selling that information to others. Although these companies are invisible to the average person, data aggregation is an enormous, multi-billion-dollar industry. Some databases are even "co-ops" where participants agree to contribute data about their customers in return for the ability to pull out cross-merchant profiles of customers' activities.

The biggest threat to privacy, however, comes from the government. Many Americans are naturally concerned about corporate surveillance, but only the government has the power to take away liberty—as has been demonstrated starkly by the post-September 11 detention of suspects without trial as "enemy combatants."

In addition, the government has unmatched power to centralize all the private sector data that is being generated. In fact, the distinction between government and private-sector privacy invasions is fading quickly. The Justice Department, for example, reportedly has an $8 million contract with data aggregator ChoicePoint that allows government agents to tap into the company's vast database of personal information on individuals.[8] Although the Privacy Act of 1974 banned the government from maintaining information on citizens who are not the targets of investigations, the FBI can now evade that requirement by simply purchasing information that has been collected by the private sector. Other proposals—such as the Pentagon's "Total Information Awareness" project and airline passenger profiling programs—would institutionalize government access to consumer data in even more far-reaching ways.

Government Databases

The government's access to personal information begins with the thousands of databases it maintains on the lives of Americans and others. For instance:

- The FBI maintains a giant database that contains millions of records covering everything from criminal records to stolen boats and databases with millions of computerized fingerprints and DNA records.

• The Treasury Department runs a database that collects financial information reported to the government by thousands of banks and other financial institutions.

• A "new hires" database maintained by the Department of Health and Human Services, which contains the name, address, social security number, and quarterly wages of every working person in the U.S.

• The federal Department of Education maintains an enormous information bank holding years worth of educational records on individuals stretching from their primary school years through higher education. After September 11, Congress gave the FBI permission to access the database without probable cause.

• State departments of motor vehicles of course possess millions of up-to-date files containing a variety of personal data, including photographs of most adults living in the United States.

Communications Surveillance

The government also performs an increasing amount of eavesdropping on electronic communications. While technologies like telephone wiretapping have been around for decades, today's technologies cast a far broader net. The FBI's controversial "Carnivore" program, for example, is supposed to be used to tap into the e-mail traffic of a particular individual. Unlike a telephone wiretap, however, it doesn't cover just one device but (because of how the Internet is built) filters through *all* the traffic on the Internet Service Provider to which it has been attached. The only thing keeping the government from trolling through all this traffic is software instructions that are written by the government itself. (Despite that clear conflict of interest, the FBI has refused to allow independent inspection and oversight of the device's operation.)

Another example is the international eavesdropping program codenamed Echelon. Operated by a partnership consisting of the United States, Britain, Canada, Australia, and New Zealand, Echelon reportedly grabs e-mail, phone calls, and other electronic communications from its far-flung listening posts across most of the earth. (U.S. eavesdroppers are not supposed to listen in on the conversations of Americans, but the question about Echelon has always been whether the intelligence agencies of participating nations can set up reciprocal, back-scratching arrangements to spy on each others' citizens.) Like Carnivore, Echelon may be used against particular targets, but to do so its operators must sort through massive amounts of information about potentially millions of people. That is worlds away from the popular conception of the old wiretap where an FBI agent listens to one line. Not only the volume of intercepts but the potential for abuse is now exponentially higher.

The "Patriot" Act

The potential for the abuse of surveillance powers has also risen sharply due to a dramatic post-9/11 erosion of legal protections against government surveillance of citizens. Just six weeks after the September 11 attacks, a panicked Congress passed the "USA PATRIOT Act," an overnight revision of the nation's surveillance laws that vastly expanded the government's authority to spy on its own citizens and reduced checks and balances on those powers, such as judicial oversight. The government never demonstrated that restraints on surveillance had contributed to the attack, and indeed much of the new legislation had nothing to do with fighting terrorism. Rather, the bill represented a successful use of the terrorist attacks by the FBI to roll back unwanted checks on its power. The most powerful provisions of the law allow for:

• **Easy access to records.** Under the PATRIOT Act, the FBI can force anyone to turn over records on their customers or clients, giving the government unchecked power to rifle through individuals' financial records, medical histories, Internet usage, travel patterns, or any other records. Some of the most invasive and disturbing uses permitted by the Act involve government access to citizens' reading habits from libraries and bookstores. The FBI does not have to show suspicion of a crime, can gag the recipient of a search order from disclosing the search to anyone, and is subject to no meaningful judicial oversight.

- **Expansion of the "pen register" exception in wiretap law.** The PATRIOT Act expands exceptions to the normal requirement for probable cause in wiretap law.[9] As with its new power to search records, the FBI need not show probable cause or even reasonable suspicion of criminal activity, and judicial oversight is essentially nil.

- **Expansion of the intelligence exception in wiretap law.** The PATRIOT Act also loosens the evidence needed by the government to justify an intelligence wiretap or physical search. Previously the law allowed exceptions to the Fourth Amendment for these kinds of searches only if "the purpose" of the search was to gather foreign intelligence. But the Act changes "the purpose" to "a significant purpose," which lets the government circumvent the Constitution's probable cause requirement even when its main goal is ordinary law enforcement.[10]

- **More secret searches.** Except in rare cases, the law has always required that the subject of a search be notified that a search is taking place. Such notice is a crucial check on the government's power because it forces the authorities to operate in the open and allows the subject of searches to challenge their validity in court. But the PATRIOT Act allows the government to conduct searches without notifying the subjects until long after the search has been executed.

Under these changes and other authorities asserted by the Bush Administration, U.S. intelligence agents could conduct a secret search of an American citizen's home, use evidence found there to declare him an "enemy combatant," and imprison him without trial. The courts would have no chance to review these decisions—indeed, they might never even find out about them.[11]

The "TIPS" Program

In the name of fighting terrorism, the Bush Administration has also proposed a program that would encourage citizens to spy on each other. The Administration initially planned to recruit people such as letter carriers and utility technicians, who, the White House said, are "well-positioned to recognize unusual events." In the face of fierce public criticism, the Administration scaled back the program, but continued to enlist workers involved in certain key industries. In November 2002 Congress included a provision in the Homeland Security Act prohibiting the Bush Administration from moving forward with TIPS.

Although Congress killed TIPS, the fact that the Administration would pursue such a program reveals a disturbing disconnect with American values and a disturbing lack of awareness of the history of governmental abuses of power. Dividing citizen from citizen by encouraging mutual suspicion and reporting to the government would dramatically increase the government's power by extending surveillance into every nook and cranny of American society. Such a strategy was central to the Soviet Union and other totalitarian regimes.

Loosened Domestic Spying Regulations

In May 2002, Attorney General John Ashcroft issued new guidelines on domestic spying that significantly increased the freedom of federal agents to conduct surveillance on American individuals and organizations. Under the new guidelines, FBI agents can infiltrate "any event that is open to the public," from public meetings and demonstrations to political conventions to church services to 12-step programs. This was the same basis upon which abuses were carried out by the FBI in the 1950s and 1960s, including surveillance of political groups that disagreed with the government, anonymous letters sent to the spouses of targets to try to ruin their marriages, and the infamous campaign against Martin Luther King, who was investigated and harassed for decades. The new guidelines are purely for spying on Americans; there is a separate set of Foreign Guidelines that cover investigations inside the U.S. of foreign powers and terrorist organizations such as al Qaeda.

Like the TIPS program, Ashcroft's guidelines sow suspicion among citizens and extend the government's surveillance power into the capillaries of American life. It is not just the reality of government surveillance that chills free expression and the freedom that Americans enjoy. The same negative effects come when we are constantly forced to wonder whether we *might* be under observation—whether the person sitting next to us is secretly informing the government that we are "suspicious."

THE SYNERGIES OF SURVEILLANCE

Multiple surveillance techniques added together are greater than the sum of their parts. One example is face recognition, which combines the power of computerized software analysis, cameras, and databases to seek matches between facial images. But the real synergies of surveillance come into play with data collection.

The growing piles of data being collected on Americans represent an enormous invasion of privacy, but our privacy has actually been protected by the fact that all this information still remains scattered across many different databases. As a result, there exists a pent-up capacity for surveillance in American life today—a capacity that will be fully realized if the government, landlords, employers, or other powerful forces gain the ability to *draw together* all this information. A particular piece of data about you—such as the fact that you entered your office at 10:29 AM on July 5, 2001—is normally innocuous. But when enough pieces of that kind of data are assembled together, they add up to an extremely detailed and intrusive picture of an individual's life and habits.

Data Profiling and "Total Information Awareness"

Just how real this scenario is has been demonstrated by another ominous surveillance plan to emerge from the effort against terrorism: the Pentagon's "Total Information Awareness" program. The aim of this program is to give officials easy, unified access to every possible government and commercial database in the world.[12] According to program director John Poindexter, the program's goal is to develop "ultra-large-scale" database technologies with the goal of "treating the world-wide, distributed, legacy databases as if they were one centralized database." The program envisions a "full-coverage database containing all information relevant to identifying" potential terrorists and their supporters. As we have seen, the amount of available information is mushrooming by the day, and will soon be rich enough to reveal much of our lives.

The TIA program, which is run by the Defense Advanced Research Projects Agency (DARPA), not only seeks to bring together the oceans of data that are already being collected on people, but would be designed to afford what DARPA calls "easy future scaling" to embrace new sources of data as they become available. It would also incorporate other work being done by the military, such as their "Human Identification at a Distance" program, which seeks to allow identification and tracking of people from a distance, and therefore without their permission or knowledge.[13]

Although it has not received nearly as much media attention, a close cousin of TIA is also being created in the context of airline security. This plan involves the creation of a system for conducting background checks on individuals who wish to fly and then separating out either those who appear to be the most trustworthy passengers (proposals known as "trusted traveler") or flagging the least trustworthy (a proposal known as CAPS II, for Computer Assisted Passenger Screening) for special attention.

The *Washington Post* has reported that work is being done on CAPS II with the goal of creating a "vast air security screening system designed to instantly pull together every passenger's travel history and living arrangements, plus a wealth of other personal and demographic information" in the hopes that the authorities will be able to "profile passenger activity and intuit obscure clues about potential threats." The government program would reportedly draw on enormous stores of personal information from data aggregators and other sources, including travel records, real estate histories, personal associations, credit card records, and telephone records. Plans call for using complex computer algorithms, including highly experimental technologies such as "neural networks," to sort through the reams of new personal information and identify "suspicious" people.[14]

The dubious premise of programs like TIA and CAPS II—that "terrorist patterns" can be ferreted out from the enormous mass of American lives, many of which will inevitably be quirky, eccentric, or riddled with suspicious coincidences—probably dooms them to failure. But failure is not likely to lead these programs to be shut down—instead, the government will begin feeding its computers more and more personal information in a vain effort to make the concept work. We will then have the worst of both worlds: poor security and a super-charged surveillance tool that would destroy Americans' privacy and threaten our freedom.

It is easy to imagine these systems being expanded in the future to share their risk assessments with other security systems. For example, CAPS could be linked to a photographic database and surveillance cameras equipped with face recognition software. Such a system might sound an alarm when a subject who has been designated as "suspicious" appears in public. The Suspicious Citizen could then be watched from a centralized video monitoring facility as he moves around the city.

In short, the government is working furiously to bring disparate sources of information about us together into one view, just as privacy advocates have been warning about for years. That would represent a radical branching off from the centuries-old Anglo-American tradition that the police conduct surveillance only where there is evidence of involvement in wrongdoing. It would seek to protect us by monitoring *everyone* for signs of wrongdoing—in short, by instituting a giant dragnet capable of sifting through the personal lives of Americans in search of "suspicious" patterns. The potential for abuse of such a system is staggering.

The massive defense research capabilities of the United States have always involved the search for ways of outwardly defending our nation. Programs like TIA[15] involve turning those capabilities inward and applying them to the American people—something that should be done, if at all, only with extreme caution and plenty of public input, political debate, checks and balances, and Congressional oversight. So far, none of those things have been present with TIA or CAPS II.

National ID Cards

If Americans allow it, another convergence of surveillance technologies will probably center around a national ID card. A national ID would immediately combine new technologies such as biometrics and RFID chips along with an enormously powerful database (possibly distributed among the 50 states). Before long, it would become an overarching means of facilitating surveillance by allowing far-flung pools of information to be pulled together into a single, incredibly rich dossier or profile of our lives. Before long, office buildings, doctors' offices, gas stations, highway tolls, subways and buses would incorporate the ID card into their security or payment systems for greater efficiency, and data that is currently scattered and disconnected will get organized around the ID and lead to the creation of what amounts to a national database of sensitive information about American citizens.

History has shown that databases created for one purpose are almost inevitably expanded to other uses; Social Security, which was prohibited by federal law from being used as an identifier when it was first created, is a prime example. Over time, a national ID database would inevitably contain a wider and wider range of information and become accessible to more and more people for more and more purposes that are further and further removed from its original justification.

The most likely route to a national ID is through our driver's licenses. Since September 11, the American Association of Motor Vehicle Administrators has been forcefully lobbying Congress for funds to establish nationwide uniformity in the design and content of driver's licenses—and more importantly, for tightly interconnecting the databases that lie behind the physical licenses themselves.

An attempt to retrofit driver's licenses into national ID cards will launch a predictable series of events bringing us toward a surveillance society:

- Proponents will promise that the IDs will be implemented in limited ways that won't devastate privacy and other liberties.

• Once a limited version of the proposals is put in place, its limits as an anti-terrorism measure will quickly become apparent. Like a dam built halfway across a river, the IDs cannot possibly be effective unless their coverage is total.

• The scheme's ineffectiveness—starkly demonstrated, perhaps, by a new terrorist attack—will create an overwhelming imperative to "fix" and "complete" it, which will turn it into the totalitarian tool that proponents promised it would never become.

A perfect example of that dynamic is the requirement that travelers present driver's licenses when boarding airplanes, instituted after the explosion (now believed to have been mechanical in cause) that brought down TWA Flight 800 in 1996. On its own, the requirement was meaningless as a security measure, but after September 11 its existence quickly led to calls to begin tracking and identifying citizens on the theory that "we already have to show ID, we might as well make it mean something."

Once in place, it is easy to imagine how national IDs could be combined with an RFID chip to allow for convenient, at-a-distance verification of ID. The IDs could then be tied to access control points around our public places, so that the unauthorized could be kept out of office buildings, apartments, public transit, and secure public buildings. Citizens with criminal records, poor CAPS ratings or low incomes could be barred from accessing airports, sports arenas, stores, or other facilities. Retailers might add RFID readers to find out exactly who is browsing their aisles, gawking at their window displays from the sidewalk or passing by without looking. A network of automated RFID listening posts on the sidewalks and roads could even reveal the location of all citizens at all times. Pocket ID readers could be used by FBI agents to sweep up the identities of everyone at a political meeting, protest march, or Islamic prayer service.

CONCLUSION

If we do not take steps to control and regulate surveillance to bring it into conformity with our values, we will find ourselves being tracked, analyzed, profiled, and flagged in our daily lives to a degree we can scarcely imagine today. We will be forced into an impossible struggle to conform to the letter of every rule, law, and guideline, lest we create ammunition for enemies in the government or elsewhere. Our transgressions will become permanent Scarlet Letters that follow us throughout our lives, visible to all and used by the government, landlords, employers, insurance companies and other powerful parties to increase their leverage over average people. Americans will not be able to engage in political protest or go about their daily lives without the constant awareness that we are—or could be—under surveillance. We will be forced to constantly ask of even the smallest action taken in public, "Will this make me look suspicious? Will this hurt my chances for future employment? Will this reduce my ability to get insurance?" The exercise of free speech will be chilled as Americans become conscious that their every word may be reported to the government by FBI infiltrators, suspicious fellow citizens or an Internet Service Provider.

Many well-known commentators like Sun Microsystems CEO Scott McNealy have already pronounced privacy dead. The truth is that a surveillance society does loom over us, and privacy, while not yet dead, is on life support.

Heroic measures are required to save it.

Four main goals need to be attained to prevent this dark potential from being realized: a change in the terms of the debate, passage of comprehensive privacy laws, passage of new laws to regulate the powerful and invasive new technologies that have and will continue to appear, and a revival of the Fourth Amendment to the U.S. Constitution.

1. Changing the Terms of the Debate

In the public debates over every new surveillance technology, the forest too often gets lost for the trees, and we lose sight of the larger trend: the seemingly inexorable movement toward a surveillance society. It will always be important to understand and publicly debate every new technology and every new technique for spying on people. But unless each new development is also understood as just one piece of the larger surveillance mosaic that is rapidly being constructed around us, Americans are not likely to get excited about a given incremental loss of privacy like the tracking of cars through toll booths or the growing practice of tracking consumers' supermarket purchases.

We are being confronted with fundamental choices about what sort of society we want to live in. But unless the terms of the debate are changed to focus on the forest instead of individual trees, too many Americans will never even recognize the choice we face, and a decision against preserving privacy will be made by default.

2. Comprehensive Privacy Laws

Although broad-based protections against government surveillance, such as the wiretap laws, are being weakened, at least they exist. But surveillance is increasingly being carried out by the private sector—frequently at the behest of government—and the laws protecting Americans against non-governmental privacy invasions are pitifully weak.

In contrast to the rest of the developed world, the U.S. has no strong, comprehensive law protecting privacy—only a patchwork of largely inadequate protections. For example, as a result of many legislators' discomfort over the disclosure of Judge Robert Bork's video rental choices during his Supreme Court confirmation battle, video records are now protected by a strong privacy law. Medical records are governed by a separate, far weaker law that allows for widespread access to extremely personal information. Financial data is governed by yet another "privacy" law—Gramm-Leach—which as we have seen really amounts to a license to share financial information. Another law protects only the privacy of children under age 13 on the Internet. And layered on top of this sectoral approach to privacy by the federal government is a geographical patchwork of constitutional and statutory privacy protections in the states.

The patchwork approach to privacy is grossly inadequate. As invasive practices grow, Americans will face constant uncertainty about when and how these complex laws protect them, contributing to a pervasive sense of insecurity. With the glaring exception of the United States, every advanced industrialized nation in the world has enacted overarching privacy laws that protect citizens against private-sector abuses. When it comes to this fundamental human value, the U.S. is an outlaw nation. For example, the European Union bars companies from evading privacy rules by transferring personal information to other nations whose data-protection policies are "inadequate." That is the kind of law that is usually applied to Third World countries, but the EU counts the United States in this category.

We need to develop a baseline of simple and clear privacy protections that crosses all sectors of our lives and give it the force of law. Only then can Americans act with a confident knowledge of when they can and cannot be monitored.

3. New Technologies and New Laws

The technologies of surveillance are developing at the speed of light, but the body of law that protects us is stuck back in the Stone Age. In the past, new technologies that threatened our privacy, such as telephone wiretapping, were assimilated over time into our society. The legal system had time to adapt and reinterpret existing laws, the political system had time to consider and enact new laws or regulations, and the culture had time to absorb the implications of the new technology for daily life. Today, however, change is happening so fast that none of this adaptation has time to take place—a problem that is being intensified by the scramble to enact unexamined anti-terrorism measures. The result is a significant danger that surveillance practices will become entrenched in American life that would never be accepted if we had more time to digest them.

Since a comprehensive privacy law may never be passed in the U.S.—and certainly not in the near future—law and legal principles must be developed or adapted to rein in particular new technologies such as surveillance cameras, location-tracking devices, and biometrics. Surveillance cameras, for example, must be subject to force-of-law rules covering important details like when they will be used, how long images will be stored, and when and with whom they will be shared.

4. Reviving the Fourth Amendment

> *The right of the people to be secure in their persons, houses, papers, and effects, against unreasonable searches and seizures, shall not be violated, and no warrants shall issue, but upon probable cause, supported by oath or affirmation, and particularly describing the place to be searched, and the persons or things to be seized.*
>
> Fourth Amendment to the U.S. Constitution

The Fourth Amendment, the primary Constitutional bulwark against Government invasion of our privacy, was a direct response to the British authorities' use of "general warrants" to conduct broad searches of the rebellious colonists.

Historically, the courts have been slow to adapt the Fourth Amendment to the realities of developing technologies. It took almost 40 years for the U.S. Supreme Court to recognize that the Constitution applies to the wiretapping of telephone conversations.[16]

In recent years—in no small part as the result of the failed "war on drugs"—Fourth Amendment principles have been steadily eroding. The circumstances under which police and other government officials may conduct warrantless searches have been rapidly expanding. The courts have allowed for increased surveillance and searches on the nation's highways and at our "borders" (the legal definition of which actually extends hundreds of miles inland from the actual border). And despite the Constitution's plain language covering "persons" and "effects," the courts have increasingly allowed for warrantless searches when we are outside of our homes and "in public." Here the courts have increasingly found we have no "reasonable expectation" of privacy and that therefore the Fourth Amendment does not apply.

But like other Constitutional provisions, the Fourth Amendment needs to be understood in contemporary terms. New technologies are endowing the government with the 21st century equivalent of Superman's X-ray vision. Using everything from powerful video technologies that can literally see in the dark, to biometric identification techniques like face recognition, to "brain fingerprinting" that can purportedly read our thoughts, the government is now capable of conducting broad searches of our "persons and effects" while we are going about our daily lives—even while we are in "public."

The Fourth Amendment is in desperate need of a revival. The reasonable expectation of privacy cannot be defined by the power that technology affords the government to spy on us. Since that power is increasingly limitless, the "reasonable expectation" standard will leave our privacy dead indeed.

But all is not yet lost. There is some reason for hope. In an important pre-9/11 case, *Kyllo vs. U.S.*,[17] the Supreme Court held that the reasonable expectation of privacy could not be determined by the power of new technologies. In a remarkable opinion written by conservative Justice Antonin Scalia, the Court held that without a warrant the police could not use a new thermal imaging device that searches for heat sources to conduct what was the functional equivalent of a warrantless search for marijuana cultivation in Danny Kyllo's home.

The Court specifically declined to leave Kyllo "at the mercy of advancing technology." While *Kyllo* involved a search of a home, it enunciates an important principle: the Fourth Amendment must adapt to new technologies. That principle can and should be expanded to general use. The Framers never expected the Constitution to be read exclusively in terms of the circumstances of 1791.

NOTES

1. Jess Bravin, "Washington Police to Play 'I Spy' with Cameras, Raising Concerns," *Wall Street Journal*, Feb. 13, 2002.
2. See http://www.ncjrs.org/school/ch2a5.html.
3. See http://www.scotcrim.u-net.com/researchc2.htm.
4. The success rate of face recognition technology has been dismal. The many independent findings to that effect include a trial conducted by the U.S.

military in 2002, which found that with a reasonably low false-positive rate, the technology had less than a 20% chance of successfully identifying a person in its database who appeared before the camera. See http://www.aclu.org/issues/privacy/FINALl Final Steve King.pdf, 17th slide.

5. Richard H. P. Sia, "Pilotless Aircraft Makers Seek Role for Domestic Uses," *CongressDaily*, Dec. 17, 2002.
6. Data surveillance is often loosely referred to as "data mining." Strictly speaking, however, data mining refers to the search for hidden patterns in large, pre-existing collections of data (such as the finding that sales of both beer and diapers rise on Friday nights). Data mining need not involve personally identifiable information. Data surveillance, on the other hand, involves the collection of information about an identifiable individual. Note, however, that when data surveillance is carried out on a mass scale, a search for patterns in people's activities—data mining—can then be conducted as well. This is what appears to be contemplated in the Total Information Awareness and CAPS II programs (see below).
7. Dana Hawkins, "As DNA Banks Quietly Multiply, Who Is Guarding the Safe?" *U.S. News & World Report*, Dec. 2, 2002.
8. Glenn R. Simpson, "Big Brother-in-Law: If the FBI Hopes to Get the Goods on You, It May Ask ChoicePoint," *Wall St. Journal*, Apr. 13, 2001.
9. The expanded exception involves what are called "pen register/trap & trace" warrants that collect "addressing information" but not the content of a communication. Those searches are named after devices that were used on telephones to show a list of telephone numbers dialed and received (as opposed to tapping into actual conversations). The PATRIOT Act expands the pen register exception onto the Internet in ways that will probably be used by the government to collect the actual content of communications and that allow nonspecific "nationwide" warrants in violation of the Fourth Amendment's explicit requirement that warrants "must specify the place to be searched."
10. In August, the secret "FISA" court that oversees domestic intelligence spying released an opinion rejecting a Bush Administration attempt to allow criminal prosecutors to use intelligence warrants to evade the Fourth Amendment entirely. The court noted that agents applying for warrants had regularly filed false and misleading information. In November 2002, however, the FISA appeals court (three judges chosen by Supreme Court Chief Justice William Rehnquist), meeting for the first time ever, ruled in favor of the government.
11. See Charles Lane, "In Terror War, 2nd Track for Suspects," *Washington Post*, Dec. 1, 2002. Online at http://www.washingtonpost.com/wp-dyn/articles/A58308-2002Nov30.html.
12. See "Pentagon Plans a Computer System That Would Peek at Personal Data of Americans," *New York Times*, Nov. 9, 2002, "US Hopes to Check Computers Globally," *Washington Post*, Nov. 12, 2002, "The Poindexter Plan," *National Journal*, Sept. 7, 2002.
13. Quotes are from the TIA homepage at http://www.darpa.mil/iao/index.htm and from public 8/2/02 remarks by Poindexter, online at http://www.fas.org/irp/agency/dod/poindexter.html.
14. Robert O'Harrow Jr., "Intricate Screening of Fliers in Works," *Washington Post*, Feb. 1, 2002, p. A1.
15. The TIA is just one part of a larger post-9/11 expansion of federal research and development efforts. The budget for military R&D spending alone has been increased by 18% in the current fiscal year to a record $58.8 billion. Bob Davis, "Massive Federal R&D Initiative to Fight Terror Is Under Way," *Wall Street Journal*, Nov. 25, 2002.
16. In 1967 the Supreme Court finally recognized the right to privacy in telephone conversations in the case *Katz v. U.S.* (389 US 347), reversing the 1928 opinion *Olmstead v. U.S.* (277 US 438).
17. 190 F.3d 1041, 2001.

2.2.4 In Praise of Big Brother: Why We Should Learn to Stop Worrying and Love (Some) Government Surveillance

JAMES STACEY TAYLOR

In the previous selection, "Bigger Monster, Weaker Chains" (2.2.3), Jay Stanley and Barry Steinhardt decry the growing use of surveillance technologies that they see as a threat to privacy. Not everyone agrees, however, that increased surveillance by governments and corporations is such a bad thing. James Stacey Taylor presents a contrarian view in which he argues that what matters is *not* whether someone is watching over you but *what* they do with the information obtained by contemporary surveillance technologies. Rather than opposing the use of these technologies for gathering personal information, we should encourage their use as long as we observe the distinction between the surveillance itself and the question of who is permitted to access the gathered information and the ways in which that information is used. This argument is based on the principle of polypotency of technologies under which the same technology can be used for good or bad purposes. Stacey's argument turns on our accepting the idea that, with proper legal safeguards against governmental abuse, omnipresent surveillance can actually promote important social benefits such as deterring crime and lessening the need to subpoena reluctant witnesses to testify in trials. He argues that, rather than violating rights, the morally legitimate use of surveillance technologies can actually make us safer and enhance our autonomy and privacy.

FOCUS QUESTIONS

1. What is Taylor's argument for thinking that use of surveillance technologies by the state should be morally acceptable to both rights theorists and consequentialists?
2. Under what circumstances should the state be permitted to access the personal information that it gathers through the use of constant surveillance? What limitations and safeguards does Taylor propose to minimize abuse of these powers?
3. Does it matter what kind of government employs surveillance technology to monitor personal behavior? Should U.S. citizens be wary of increased reliance on these technologies by their own government?
4. Can a person be harmed by being spied upon if he or she does not know that this is happening? Do you agree with Taylor's view? Explain.
5. Comparing the argument in this reading with the previous one, which do you think has the better argument? Explain.

KEYWORDS

autonomy, consequentialism, dystopic, harm principle, libertarianism, privacy, surveillance

Source: From "In Praise of Big Brother: Why We Should Learn to Stop Worrying and Love (Some) Government Surveillance," by James Stacy Taylor. Revised version. Original version published in *Public Affairs Quarterly* 19, no. 3 (2005): 227–246. Reprinted by permission.

In recent years surveillance technology has undergone a revolution. Spy satellites are now so accurate that they can be used to track the movements of individual people, and even read license plates on cars. It is now simple to intercept faxes, pager messages, and telephone messages, for rooms to be bugged, and for tracking devices to be installed on vehicles, goods, and even individual persons. Spyware software can now be covertly and remotely implanted onto Internet-linked computers to monitor the keystrokes that their users make and the websites that they visit. And in many areas of the developed world persons now live much of their public lives under the panoptic gaze of closed-circuit television monitors that record their every move.

This revolution in surveillance technology is often regarded with horror. Discussions of its ethical implications frequently draw analogies between it and Big Brother's sinister surveillance of the citizens of Oceania in George Orwell's *1984*. Worse yet, as many of the participants in such discussions note, the surveillance capabilities that are now available to governments and corporations dwarf that which Big Brother had access to. In *1984*, people could be sure that they could not be watched by Big Brother's telescreens if they were in a crowd.[1] Face-recognition software now renders such a hope futile. In *1984* people could escape the omnipresence of Big Brother's telescreens by going out of the cities and into the country, where they only had to take care that their conversations were not monitored by hidden microphones.[2] Such escape is now impossible, for spy satellites can be used to monitor people wherever they go.

With the dystopic vision of *1984* lurking in the background, it is clear that one need not possess any pronounced Luddite tendencies to oppose the expanding use of surveillance technology. It will be argued in this paper, however, that rather than opposing such an expansion of surveillance technology, its use should be *encouraged*—and not only in the public realm. Indeed, the State should place all of its citizens under surveillance at all times and in all places, including their offices, classrooms, shops—and even their bedrooms.

AN OVERVIEW OF THE ARGUMENT

At first sight, the conclusion that the State should place all of its citizens under constant surveillance is alarming. Yet this alarm can be dispelled once it is realized that this conclusion flows naturally from the plausible and widely held view that, in certain circumstances, it is morally permissible for the State to secure information about past events. It is, for example, widely held that in certain circumstances it is morally permissible for the State to compel witnesses to testify about past events in criminal trials. The State, however, can only use hindsight to determine what information it is morally permitted to have access to, for it will only become clear in retrospect what information is relevant to (for example) solving a crime or judging mitigating circumstances. To ensure that it gleans all of the information that it is morally permitted to access, then, the State can gather information about all events that occur, provided it only accesses that which it is morally permitted. Given this, then, the State is in principle morally permitted to place its citizens under constant surveillance. The purpose of this paper is not, however, only to show that the State is morally permitted to place its citizens under constant surveillance. It is also to show that a situation in which the State used such surveillance would be morally *preferable* to one where it did not. To establish this it will be shown that under such a system of surveillance it is likely that crime will decrease, that justice will be better served, and that fewer costs will be imposed on witnesses. Finally, four objections to the use of such a system of State surveillance will be examined and rejected: that it would be open to abuse, that it is not morally permissible for the State to secure information about past events, and that such surveillance would violate citizens' privacy, or autonomy, or both.

Before moving to develop the above argument in favor of constant State surveillance an important initial clarification is in order. This argument is based on two claims: (i) that if it is ever morally permissible for the State to secure information about past events, then it is morally permissible for it to do so through the use of surveillance devices, and (ii) that in some cases it is permissible for the State to secure information about past events. As it stands, however, it is not clear whether (ii) is the claim that the State's acquisition of information respects a person's moral rights (e.g., to privacy or autonomy), or the claim that in some cases the consequences of securing such information justify the State's acquisition of it. That is, it is not clear whether this argument is one that would be acceptable to a rights theorist, or only to a consequentialist.[3] This unclarity can be dispelled once it is recognized that the argument presented here is compatible with *both* a rights-based and a consequentialist approach to ethics.[4] This argument is acceptable to a rights theorist because, as will be argued below, when the State is morally permitted to access information it will not violate anyone's rights in so doing. If the arguments below are sound, then claim (ii) will be true if one accepts a rights-based approach to ethics. This argument is also acceptable to consequentialists, who could also accept claim (ii).[5] For a consequentialist to accept (ii) it must be the case that there is at least *one* time at which it is clear that the consequences justify the State's acquisition of information about a certain past event. And, as will be argued below, such a situation is simple to envisage. As such, the argument of this paper is amenable to both rights theorists and consequentialists alike.[6]

SURVEILLANCE AND TESTIMONY

Despite appearances, then, the conclusion that there is no principled reason why a State should not place all of its citizens under constant surveillance is by no means a radical one. It is merely an extrapolation of the widely accepted view that, under certain circumstances, it is morally permissible for agents of the State to secure information about past events. It is, for example, widely accepted that it is morally permissible for judges to subpoena witnesses to require them to disclose information. It is also widely accepted that it is morally permissible for judges to permit law enforcement agencies to install surveillance devices to monitor the activities of persons they suspect of criminal activity, provided that such agencies demonstrate that they have probable cause for their suspicions.[7] The claim that it is morally permissible for agents of the State to secure information about past events is thus innocuous.[8] Moreover, if it is morally permissible for agents of the State to secure information about past events through the subpoenaing of witnesses or the use of surveillance devices, then there should be no moral bar to their gaining such information through securing access to records of past events that might have been generated by preexisting surveillance devices. (Provided, of course, that in securing such information the agents of the State are subject to the same restrictions on their powers that are in place with respect to their subpoenaing of witnesses or the placing of suspects under surveillance.)

However, that it is morally permissible for agents of the State to secure access to information about past events that has been gathered through the use of surveillance devices does not show that it is morally permissible for the State to place its citizens under constant surveillance. To reach this further conclusion it must first be noted that it cannot (typically) be known in advance what information it would be morally permissible for the agents of the State to have access to. Instead, one can only use hindsight to determine what events it would be morally permissible for them to access information about. For example, it could not have been predicted that knowledge of the actions performed by Billy Nolan Lovelady, a worker at the Texas Square Book Depository in Dallas on 22nd November, 1963, would be relevant to assessing who assassinated the president of the United States. However, the defenders of Lee Harvey Oswald (who was accused of this assassination) claimed that at the time of the shooting Oswald was standing unarmed in the doorway of the Texas Square Book Depository and produced a photograph purporting to prove this. Once this had occurred, knowledge of Lovelady's actions became relevant in showing that the man in the photograph who was claimed to be Oswald was actually Lovelady. In this situation, then, it was morally permissible for agents of the State to take steps to secure information about Lovelady's whereabouts at the time in question to disprove Oswald's alibi—and this could not have been predicted beforehand.

As well as it being clear that one usually cannot know in advance what information the agents of the State are morally permitted to secure, it is also clear that once it becomes evident what information they are permitted to secure, gathering this is frequently difficult—as the continuing controversy over "who shot JFK?" indicates. Putting these two facts together, then, it is evident that there should be no moral bar against the agents of the State installing surveillance devices to secure all the information that they might potentially be permitted to secure access to, provided that *they only access the information thus gathered in circumstances where this access is morally permissible.* Thus, since it is *potentially* morally permissible for agents of the State to secure information about events no matter when or where they take place, it is morally permissible for the State to subject its citizens to surveillance at all times and in all places, provided that the information thus gathered is only accessed in the morally appropriate circumstances.

FURTHER CLARIFYING THE ARGUMENT

Yet despite the above disclaimer that this argument is by no means as radical as it appears the conclusion that it is morally permissible for the State to subject its citizens to constant surveillance might still seem chilling. To alleviate this concern the above pro-surveillance argument should be clarified in two ways. First, it must be emphasized that although this argument leads to the conclusion that it is morally permissible for the State to place its citizens under constant surveillance, it does *not* lead to the conclusion that it is morally permissible for the State to have access to *all* of the information that its surveillance devices secure. Instead, this argument leads only to the conclusion that the State should have access to the information recorded by these devices that it is *morally permissible* for it to have access to. Of course, the question of the extent to which the State is morally permitted to secure information about the actions of its citizens, or the events that they are involved in, is a vexed one. It is, for example, debatable as to how far the privilege that is accorded to information divulged within certain professional relationships (such as those between clergy and penitents,[9] doctors and patients,[10] lawyers and clients,[11] counselors and clients,[12] or journalists and sources[13]) should extend, and for what reasons (if any) such privilege should be trumped by other considerations.[14] It is also debatable as to whether the increased powers accorded to law enforcement agencies by the Patriot Act to secure information about suspects or "persons of interest" are morally legitimate.[15] However, it must be stressed that the question of *what* information the State that subjects its citizens to constant and universal surveillance should have access to is separate from the question of *whether it is morally permissible* to *place them under surveillance at all*—and it is the *latter* question that is at issue here.

The second way in which this pro-surveillance argument must be clarified is related to the first. In cases where agents of the State *are* morally permitted to access information about the actions of others the information that they are morally permitted to secure is limited to the *minimum* that is needed for them to achieve the legitimate purposes for which they need it. Accordingly they are not morally permitted to have access to, for example, videotaped records of the actions of others if the information that they are morally permitted to secure could be gleaned from an automatic transcription of such videotape. Thus, although it might be morally permissible for an agent of the State to secure detailed information about a criminal defendant's past adultery if this is relevant to the State's case against him in a criminal trial, it does not follow that it is also morally permissible for this agent to watch a videotape of the defendant in the act. Similarly, the agents of the State would only be morally permitted to place citizens under surveillance in private areas such as their homes or offices if they could achieve this without accessing more information than they were morally permitted to access. It would thus not be morally permissible, for example, for the agents of the State to enter a person's house to install surveillance devices in it. This is because in doing so they would access more information than they were morally permitted to access (e.g., they would find out information about his domestic habits and the interior of his home during the installation process) for the installation of such devices would have to occur *before* there were reasons to believe that the State was morally permitted to secure such information to detect and prosecute criminal activity. Indeed, it is likely that, with respect to the interiors of the homes of most of the State's citizens, such reasons will never be forthcoming.

This second clarification of the above pro-surveillance argument is important in three respects. First, it underscores the fact that this argument does not cede to the State any information-gathering powers that it does not already enjoy. Second, it emphasizes that the conclusion of this argument is a parsimonious one, insofar as it only supports the State's securing the *minimum* amount of information that it needs for its morally legitimate purposes. This argument will thus *not* support the use of any surveillance devices that enable the State to secure more information than is necessary for its morally legitimate purposes. As such, although this argument does show that the State is morally permitted to use surveillance devices to gather information about events that occur in private areas (such as private offices and houses) it restricts its use of such devices to those whose use does not necessitate the State's securing any more information than it is morally permitted to secure. Thus, as noted above, this argument will not support the installation of surveillance devices in, for example, persons' homes without their consent. Although it does support the use of any technology, such as, for example, infrared thermal imaging systems that record the movements of persons in their homes, which could secure information about the events that occurred to them, that would not entail the State's securing of information that it was not entitled to.[16] Similarly, this argument will also support the use of future surveillance technology that can similarly be used to record events that occur in persons' homes without having to enter them. Finally, and in a related vein, once it becomes possible for surveillance technology automatically to provide a written narrative of events, the use of any type of surveillance technology that provides *more* than this information, such as, for example, manned closed-circuit television monitors and videotapes, will *cease* to be morally justified by the above pro-surveillance argument. Rather than justifying the *expansion* of the State's powers of surveillance, then, the above pro-surveillance argument will instead eventually justify their *curtailment.*

THE ADVANTAGES OF UNIVERSAL STATE SURVEILLANCE

If the above pro-surveillance argument is sound, then it is morally permissible for a State to subject its citizens to constant surveillance. Given the horror with which the current proliferation of surveillance devices is usually greeted, this conclusion is not likely to be a popular one. However, before turning to rebut the objections that it will be faced with, some of its advantages should be outlined.

The most obvious advantages to the State's installing such a surveillance system would result from the fact that witnesses would no longer be needed in either criminal or civil cases, for their testimony would be supplanted by information supplied by surveillance devices. Unlike witness testimony, this information would be accurate. It would, for example, be unaffected by any biases (whether conscious or unconscious) that human witnesses might be subject to and which could taint their testimony. It would also be free from distortions, whether deliberate (e.g., the witness is lying, or omitting parts of the truth) or accidental (e.g., the witness has a faulty memory). Moreover, the juries and judges to whom the information taken from surveillance devices would be presented in a court could take it at its face value, rather than having subjectively to assess its accuracy in the light of the perceived reliability of the witness from whom it was taken. Furthermore, the fact that witnesses would no longer be needed under a system of constant and universal State surveillance would also benefit those who would otherwise have served in this capacity. Most obviously, they would no longer be burdened with the task of testifying, which might have required them to travel, or to take time off work. They would also be relieved from any threats that they might have faced from persons who would be adversely affected either by their testimony (e.g., the defendants, or their associates) or by its lack (e.g., the prosecutors).

A system of constant State surveillance would have other advantages, too. Under the current criminal justice system, a wealthy defendant who is innocent of the charges that she is faced with can use her wealth to hire private investigators to demonstrate her innocence, either by finding persons who witnessed the crime of which she is accused or by finding persons who can provide her with a legitimate alibi. This option is not open to poorer defendants who are similarly innocent, but who cannot afford to hire private investigators. Since this is so, innocent, poor defendants are more likely than innocent, wealthy defendants to accept plea-bargains, or to be convicted of crimes that they did not commit. If, however, a poor person were to be accused of a crime in a State that subjected its citizens to constant surveillance, the judge in her case would be morally justified (indeed, would be morally *required*) in enabling the defense to secure information that would prove her innocence, and that would have been gathered by the State's surveillance devices. A State's use of constant surveillance could thus reduce the number of persons who are wrongfully convicted. This would not only be good in itself, but it would also lead to a more equitable justice system, for the disparity in wrongful conviction rates between the wealthy, who could use their wealth to prove their innocence, and the poor could be eliminated.

In addition to these advantages constant State surveillance would also benefit the State's citizenry at large, by serving as a deterrent to crime. This would not be because the citizens who lived under State surveillance would never know when they were being watched, and so would refrain from committing crimes for fear of being caught in the act, as would persons in both *1984* and Jeremy Bentham's Panopticon.[17] As is clear from the second clarification of this pro-surveillance argument, above, this argument does not justify the State watching its citizens, for in doing so it would acquire more information about them than it is morally permitted to acquire. However, were the State to subject its citizens to the degree of surveillance that would be justified on the above argument, its citizens would know that whenever a crime was committed its performance would be recorded, and so its perpetrator would be likely to be apprehended. This knowledge would deter many potential criminals from committing crimes.[18] It would also deter law enforcement officers from extending the limits of their authority.[19] To be sure, the knowledge that one's criminal act would be recorded would not deter all potential criminals from committing crimes. Some persons would still commit crimes of passion, and of anger; others would succumb to the temptation to commit an opportunistic theft, act under the influence of drugs or alcohol, or act on the belief that they would not be caught. But most persons would simply judge the commission of crime not worthwhile once they realized that they were subject to constant State surveillance, and so such surveillance would serve as an effective deterrent to most criminal activity.

TWO INITIAL OBJECTIONS

Despite the advantages that would accrue to a system of constant State surveillance of the type that is defended above, there are two immediate objections that its proponents must face. The first is that such a surveillance system would be open to abuse. The second denies the claim that it is morally permissible for agents of the State (e.g., judges) to compel witness testimony or authorize information-gathering surveillance.

The Objection from Potential Abuse

The most obvious objection to a system of constant State surveillance is that it would be open to abuse. Jay Stanley and Barry Steinhardt, for example, note that the FBI's "Carnivore" program, which is "supposed to be used to tap into the email traffic of a particular individual," will filter through "all the traffic on the Internet Service Provider to which it has been attached"—and they note, "the only thing that is keeping the government from trolling through all this traffic are software instructions written by the government itself."[20] Similarly, they note that under the PATRIOT Act the FBI need not show any probable cause (or even reasonable suspicion of criminal activity) to gain access to "individuals' financial records, medical histories, Internet usage, travel patterns, or… other records"—a situation that is ripe for abuse.[21] It must be admitted that, in practice, a system of constant State surveillance *is* likely to be abused to some extent.[22] However, if one adopts a rights-based understanding of claim (ii) above (i.e., if one holds that such a system of State surveillance is permissible as it does not in itself violate persons' moral rights), the theoretical force of this objection can be rebutted. On such an understanding of claim (ii) one could first note that this abuse-based objection gets its force from the view that such abuse would violate persons' moral rights. The proponent of a rights-based understanding of claim (ii) would certainly agree with this underlying view and would join with its advocates in condemning such abuse. However, the rights theorist who was in favor of such a system of State surveillance would also note that the condemnation of the *abuse* of State surveillance is not to condemn State surveillance *itself*. To condemn the use of *x* for the purposes of *y*, where *y* violates persons' rights (e.g., to privacy or autonomy), is *not* also to condemn the use of *x* for the purposes of *z*, where *z* does *not* violate persons' rights. Thus, a rights theorist who was a proponent of State surveillance could argue that to offer the possibility of abuse as an objection to constant State surveillance is to confuse the moral status of different possible uses of such surveillance. This is not, of course, either to downplay the badness of any abuse that might take place or to avoid the question of what practical measures should be imposed to attempt to minimize it. However, it is important to note that to object to a system of surveillance on the grounds that it could be abused is not to object to the surveillance itself, unless one believes (and can show) that the abuse in question would necessarily occur.

If one adopts a consequentialist understanding of claim (ii), however, defending the use of constant State surveillance against this objection is more difficult. This is because the likelihood of such abuse together with the likelihood of such abuse causing harm must be weighed against the benefits (as outlined above) that such a system is likely to provide. And, given that such a system has not yet been implemented, such a weighing and balancing of its relative costs and benefits will be difficult to assess with certainty. As such, then, the moral legitimacy of such a system would depend upon the political context in which it was proposed. If there is good reason to believe that little harm will accrue from the abuse of such a system of surveillance and there is reason to believe that it would bring important benefits to the citizens of the State in which it is installed, the possibility of its abuse should not deter consequentialists from endorsing the above pro-surveillance argument. Thus, it seems that installing a system of State surveillance in a State that possessed little power, a State that was too weak to exercise its power, or a State that had strict limits placed upon its power *and* that adhered to them would be justified on a consequentialist understanding of claim (ii). However, installing a system of State surveillance in a State that possessed considerable power over its citizens, that was strong enough to exercise such power, or that either had little restraints imposed upon it in its dealing with its citizens, or that had such restraints but frequently failed to adhere to them would be unlikely to be justified on a consequentialist understanding of claim (ii).[23]

Compelling Testimony Is Morally Impermissible

Both the rights theorists and the consequentialists who support the introduction of a system of constant State surveillance can thus meet the objection that such a system might be abused—although it should be noted that the consequentialist's response is such that the imposition of such a system would not be justified in some States. What, then, of the second objection that those who support the introduction of such a system of State surveillance are faced with: that it is not morally permissible for the agents of the State (e.g., judges) to compel witness testimony or authorize information-gathering surveillance with probable cause? This second objection is less plausible than the first. As was noted in the initial clarificatory section of this essay, the above pro-surveillance argument is a *conditional* argument, such that *if* it is ever morally permissible for an agent of the State (e.g., a judge, or a prosecutor) to secure information from a witness about past events, *then* it is morally permissible for her to use State surveillance devices to secure the same information. For the antecedent clause of this argument to be true all that needs to be true is that *in at least one case* it would be morally permissible for a judge to secure information from a witness. And this latter claim is very plausible indeed, for both rights theorists and consequentialists alike. To see this, assume that Lee Harvey Oswald really was innocent of the assassination of John F. Kennedy, and, to prove his innocence, needed to secure the photograph that was taken of him standing in the doorway to the Texas School Book Depository at the time of the shooting. Assume also that the owner of this photograph disliked Oswald, and wanted to see him wrongly convicted. Here, it would clearly be morally permissible for the judge in Oswald's case to require that the owner of the photograph produce it in evidence. This claim becomes even stronger if the production of this photograph would cost its owner nothing but the frustration of his desire to see Oswald wrongly convicted; if, for example, the judge sent a messenger over to the house of the owner of the photograph to collect a copy of it, that he paid for this, and so on. Of course, extreme libertarians who oppose *any* form of interference by the State in the lives of its citizens would still hold that even this minimal interference in the life of the owner of the photograph is morally impermissible, and that under no circumstances should private individuals be required to give up any information, or any evidentiary items, that they might happen to possess.[24] It is not easy to provide a definitive rebuttal to this extreme libertarian position.[25] However, the advantages that this strict libertarian position possesses in terms of its ease of defense are, for most persons (rights theorists and consequentialists alike), greatly outweighed by its highly counterintuitive results. (Or, at least, results that are counterintuitive to everyone *but* an extreme libertarian!) It is simple to construct examples in which the ill effects that result from a person's refusal to produce an item of information in evidence are vast, and where the costs to him of supplying this information are tiny. Imagine, for example, a case in which ten men will be executed for a crime that they did not commit unless a man who for idiosyncratic reasons of his own dislikes discussing what clothes he wore in the past discloses to their judge which clothes he wore on the day of the crime. In this case the clothes that the uncooperative witness wore are, for some reason, crucial to establishing whether it is the accused, or another group of ten men, who committed the crime in question. Clearly, in this case it would be counterintuitive to claim that the judge was not justified in requiring this man to reveal what clothes he wore on the day in question. As examples such as this multiply against the extreme libertarian's position, with the ill effects of the failure to produce the information increasing, and the costs involved in its provision decreasing, the claim that it is not morally permissible for a judge to impose the costs in question on the person withholding the information becomes increasingly implausible. And, once one accepts that for *any* case outlined in an example such as this, it would be morally permissible for a judge to secure the information in question, then one will have granted the truth of the antecedent claim on which this conditional argument in favor of surveillance rests. That is, once one grants that for any given case that it would be permissible for a judge to secure the withheld information, then one must also grant that it would be permissible to use State surveillance to secure the same information. And, since the State cannot tell where or when the actions or events that this information pertains to would occur, one would then also have to grant that the State would be justified in gathering information about *all* actions and events that occur, with, of course, the proviso that it can only *access* that which it is morally permissible for it to access. Unless one wishes to endorse the extreme libertarian's highly counterintuitive claim that under no circumstances at all can a judge secure information from a witness that is relevant to a case in his court, then, one should reject this second objection to the above pro-surveillance argument.

SURVEILLANCE, PRIVACY, AND AUTONOMY

The two most obvious and immediate objections to the above pro-surveillance argument can thus be met. However, it still faces two more. The first of these is based on the claim that such a surveillance system would violate the privacy of those subjected to it. The second is based on the claim that it would illegitimately compromise their autonomy.[26]

Both of these objections have been leveled by Stanley and Steinhardt against the increase in surveillance in the United State under the administration of George W. Bush. According to Stanley and Steinhardt, both "Privacy and liberty in the United States are at risk," as it is "at risk of turning into a Surveillance Society."[27] As was noted above in discussing the consequentialist understanding of claim (ii) in response to the objection that a system of State surveillance of the type outlined above could be abused, the worries that Stanley and Steinhardt express would be legitimate ones in certain political contexts—including that which they are explicitly addressing. However, were the system of surveillance that is outlined above to be installed in a State that would be unlikely to abuse it, neither of their objections would be sound.

The objection that constant State surveillance would violate the privacy of those subject to it rests on a failure to acknowledge the legitimate limits of the proposed surveillance. On the system of surveillance argued for above the State would only be permitted to access the information that its surveillance devices gather *when it is morally permissible for it to do so*. As such, the State's use of such a surveillance system would not enable it justly to access any more information than it is morally permitted to access already. This point is not reiterated to defend the system of State surveillance advocated above on the grounds that it would not violate the privacy of its citizens any more than this is violated already. Rather, it has been reiterated to provide the basis for a *stronger* defense of this system of State surveillance: *that it would not violate the citizens' privacy at all.*

To develop this strong defense of the system of State surveillance advocated above it must be recognized that privacy is both a relative notion and a normative notion. A certain item of information is private *relative to* a certain person, if that person cannot *legitimately* (a normative concept) require that that item of information be disclosed to her.[28] For example, my use of the checking account that I share with my wife is not private with respect to her, for she can legitimately require that I disclose my use of it to her. However, it is private with respect to my colleagues, who cannot legitimately require that I disclose my use of it to them. Similarly, the examination score of a student in my class is not private with respect to the student, since she can legitimately require its disclosure, but it is private with respect to my wife, who cannot. Given, then, that privacy is both a *relative* notion and a *normative* notion, and since, according to the pro-surveillance argument above, the agents of the State can only access those items of information that they are morally permitted to access, it is clear that the above pro-surveillance argument does not justify the violation of the privacy of the State's citizens. According to that argument, the only time at which the State could permissibly access information about actions or events would be when it was morally permitted to do so; that is, when it could *legitimately* require that this information be disclosed to it. This being so, under the system of State surveillance argued for above, the State could only access information that is *not* private relative to it. Thus, in accessing such information the State would not violate the privacy of its citizens.[29]

Just as constant and universal State surveillance of the sort argued for above would not violate the privacy of the persons subject to it, nor would it compromise their autonomy—although it is easy to see why one might think that it would. In *1984* Oceania's citizens adjusted their behavior when they were in the presence of telescreens to conform to the way that they believed that Big Brother's Party wanted them to behave.[30] Were they not to do this, and were they to be observed by agents of Big Brother during their refusal to conform, they risked severe punishment. To avoid the penalties that the Party would impose on them if they failed to conform to its expectations, then, Oceania's citizens ceded a degree of control over their actions to the Party. That is, when they acted out of fear that Party members were observing them, and so acted to conform to the Party's view of how they should behave, the citizens of Oceania satisfied their individual first-order desires to "Perform the actions that the Party wants me to perform." To the extent that they thus ceded control to the Party, then, Oceania's citizens were other-directed, and so heteronomous, rather than being self-directed, and so autonomous.[31] Thus, in *1984*, Big Bother's citizens suffered from compromised autonomy as a result of being subjected to (or potentially subjected to) State surveillance.[32]

Fortunately, however, the citizens of a State that utilized the type of constant surveillance that would be justified on the above pro-surveillance argument would not similarly suffer from compromised autonomy. As noted earlier such a surveillance system would not utilize the type of in-person surveillance that was used by Big Brother's Party in *1984*. Instead, it would merely record the actions of the citizens and the events that they participated in. Since this is so, most of the citizens subject to this form of State surveillance would not believe that they needed to alter their behavior to conform to the State's view of how they should act (were the State even to hold such a view) for they would recognize that the State would not actually be watching them. Moreover, if they were law-abiding then they would also recognize that the chances of the State having just cause to access information about their actions would be very slim indeed. Free from the pressure to conform of the sort that was imposed upon the citizens of Oceania, then, most citizens whose State subjected them to constant and universal surveillance of the type outlined above would *not* cede control over their acts to the State. The citizens of such a State would thus not become heteronomous with respect to their behavior, as did the citizens of Oceania. Instead, they would retain their autonomy with respect to it. Moreover, the claim that most citizens placed under constant State surveillance would not suffer from any diminution in their autonomy is not merely a speculative one. Persons subjected to surveillance are unlikely to alter their behavior once they become used to being "on tape" (unless they previously performed acts that they believed that they should not have been performing) when they realize that there is little chance that the information that the surveillance devices record would ever be required, and so there is little chance of their actions ever being observed.[33]

Of course, not all the citizens of a State that utilized the type of surveillance advocated above would retain full autonomy with respect to all of their actions. The exceptions would be those who are criminally inclined, and who, as a result of being placed under State surveillance, would alter their behavior by refraining from committing crimes. Such persons would suffer from compromised autonomy with respect to their deliberate omission of criminal activity, insofar as they alter their behavior solely to avoid incurring criminal penalties. Yet, given that the actions that these persons refrain from performing are criminal ones, the diminution in autonomy that these persons would experience as a result of being placed under State surveillance is one that it is morally legitimate to inflict upon them.[34]

CONCLUSION

It is now time to take stock. Although it is often claimed that the recent proliferation of surveillance technology is turning the West into an "Orwellian nightmare" it was argued in this paper that, rather than condemning the prospect of constant State surveillance, we should instead welcome it—provided that we lived in a State where its abuse would be unlikely.[35] Such surveillance would not, however, involve any expansion of State power into the lives of its citizens. If, under certain circumstances, it is morally permissible for judges to secure information relevant to their cases from witnesses, then, under the same circumstances, it should also be morally permissible for them to secure this information through the use of surveillance devices. Constant State surveillance is thus no different in principle than the current system of subpoenaing witnesses. Moreover, the State's use of such surveillance would be morally *preferable* to the subpoenaing of witnesses. It would, for example, avoid the need to impose costs on those who would otherwise be called as witnesses, and it would result in the provision of more accurate information. There are, of course, practical concerns that must be addressed before any such State surveillance system is put in place. But since, as has been argued in this paper, there is no *principled* reason to oppose such a system, but there is reason to endorse it, once worries about the possibility of such a system surveillance being abused are laid to rest the road would be clear for its introduction. Big Brother would then indeed be watching over us. But, unless one has criminal tendencies, this should be a cause for relief, rather than concern.[36]

NOTES

1. George Orwell, 1984 (London: Seeker and Warburg, 1987), 119.
2. Ibid., 123.
3. I thank an anonymous referee for pressing me on this point.
4. Note, however, that owing to the possibility that a constant and universal system of State surveillance will be subject to abuse it will be easier to justify such a system if one adopts a rights-based approach to ethics than if one adopts a consequentialist approach. This is discussed more fully below.
5. At least, if one accept a plausible version of consequentialism, such that human well-being is the good to be maximized.
6. A further clarification is also in order. Since claim (ii) can be accepted by both rights theorists and consequentialists, the fact that the arguments for the view that a system of State surveillance is morally preferable to the absence of such a system are based on the good consequences that such a system would have does not preclude rights theorists from accepting these arguments. A rights theorist could endorse such consequentialist reasoning, provided that such a system of State surveillance would respect those moral rights that she believes that persons possess.
7. That Anglo-American common law recognizes these exemptions to personal privacy was noted by Warren and Brandeis in their seminal article "The right to privacy [The implicit made explicit]," in Ferdinand D. Schoeman, ed., *Philosophical Dimensions of Privacy: An Anthology* (Cambridge, Cambridge University Press, 1984), 78, 88–89. Warren's and Brandeis's approval of, and lack of defense of, such exemptions indicates both that they found them to be morally permissible, and also that they assumed (as it is also assumed in the arguments in this paper) that this view would be so widely accepted as to need no defense.
8. Although the claim that, under certain circumstances, judges are morally permitted to compel witnesses to testify and to permit law enforcement agencies to monitor suspects is innocuous, the question of under what circumstances such compulsion and surveillance is morally permissible is a contentious one. As will be noted below, however, the arguments in this paper rest only on the innocuous view *that in some circumstances* such compulsion and surveillance is morally permissible, and not on any substantive claims concerning *when* such information gathering is morally permissible.

9. See, for example, Robert J. Araujo, "International Tribunals and Rules of Evidence: The Case for Respecting and Preserving the 'Priest-Penitent' Privilege Under International Law," *American University International Law Review* **15**(2000): 639–666.
10. See, for example, Jean V. McHale, "Medical Confidentiality and Legal Privilege," *Journal of Applied Philosophy* **11**, no. 2(1994): 241–242.
11. See, for example, Paul R. Rice, "Attorney-Client Privilege: The Eroding Concept of Confidentiality Should Be Abolished," *Duke Law Journal* **47** (1998): 853–898, and John R. Przypyszny, "Public Assault on the Attorney-Client Privilege: Ramifications of Bakes v. Doe," *Georgetown Journal of Legal Ethics* **3** (1989): 351.
12. See, for example, Alan Meisel, "Confidentiality and Rape Counseling—Privacy vs. the Right to a Fair Trial," *Hastings Center Report* **11** (1981): 5–7.
13. See, for example, both Mark R. Wicclair, "A Shield Privilege for Reporters vs. the Administration of Justice and the Right to a Fair Trial: Is There a Conflict?" *Business and Professional Ethics Journal* 4 (1985): 1–14, and Richard P. Cunningham, "Commentary on Wicclair's: A Shield Privilege for Reporters vs. the Administration of Justice and the Right to a Fair Trial," *Business and Professional Ethics Journal* 4 (1985): 15–17.
14. For a general discussion of this issue, see Bernard Baumrin, "Is There a Freedom Not to Speak?" *Metaphilosophy* 6 (1975): 25–34.
15. Thus, this argument should *not* be taken as an endorsement of the extended surveillance powers granted to law enforcement agencies by this Act.
16. The use of such technology was noted by Andrew J. Charlesworth, "Privacy, Personal Information, and Employment," *Surveillance and Society* 1, no. 2 (2003): 218.
17. Jeremy Bentham's Panopticon was originally designed to be a humane prison, in which the prisoners were reformed through subjecting them both to isolation and to the possibility of covert surveillance. Such conditions, Bentham thought, would lead the prisoners to modify their own behavior to conform to that which they believed their (possible) observers would endorse. The Panopticon was designed as a ring of cells, in the center of which was an observation tower equipped with special shutters, so that the guards could see out, but the prisoners could not see in—and so could not tell if they were being watched or not. See Jeremy Bentham, *Panopticon, or, The Inspection House*, originally published 1791, and Janet Semple, *Bentham's Prison: A Study of the Panopticon Penitentiary* (Oxford Clarendon Press, 1993).
18. That overt surveillance deters persons from committing crimes is well documented. J. Ditton and E. Short, for example, have shown that the use of CCTV surveillance in Airdne, Scotland, resulted in a significant reduction in crime in the immediate area, with no displacement of criminal activity to the adjoining areas without CCTV. They also noted that after the introduction of CCTV there was a reduction in the number of large-scale affrays. "Evaluating Scotland's first town center CCTV scheme," in C. Norns, J. Moran, and G. Armstrong, eds., *Surveillance, Closed Circuit Television and Social Control* (Aldershot, UK: Ashgate, 1998), 155–174.
19. In a survey on the effect that the presence of CCTV had on police behavior that was conducted by Benjamin J. Goold between June 1997 and March 2000 in six towns in the south of England over two-thirds of the fifty police officers interviewed said that "the introduction of cameras had forced them to be 'more careful' when out on patrol" to avoid being prosecuted for such breaches of duty as unlawful arrest or assault. See Benjamin J. Goold, "Public Area Surveillance and Police Work: The Impact of CCTV on Police Behavior and Autonomy," *Surveillance & Society* 1, no. 2 (2002) 192, 194.
20. Jay Stanley and Barry Steinhardt, *Bigger Monster, Weaker Chains: The Growth of an American Surveillance Society* (ACLU Technology and Liberty Program, 2003), 8.
21. Ibid., 9.
22. Benjamin J. Goold claims that 1% of the targets tracked by CCTV operators in Britain are for voyeuristic purposes. See his *CCTV and Policing Public Area Surveillance and Police Practices in Britain* (Oxford: Oxford University Press, 2004), 144. It must be stressed that the use of CCTV that Goold examined was not subject to the penalties that are proposed for misuse in this paper.
23. As such, then, it is highly unlikely that State surveillance of any but the most minimal kind would be justified in the contemporary United States, owing to the lack of judicial oversight of State action that Stanley and Steinhardt note.
24. Few rights theorists ascribe to this extreme libertarian position. Instead, the rights that they ascribe to persons such as privacy, or private property, are

frequently conditional on such persons not being situated in "emergency situations" such as this.

25. One might, of course, challenge the extreme libertarian to provide a defensible account of the strong property rights that she must invoke as a basis for her argument. But this would not provide a definitive rebuttal of the extreme libertarian position so much as it would merely shift the burden of proof to its proponents.
26. These two objections might also be expressed in terms of moral rights, namely, that such surveillance would violate the citizens' right to privacy, or their right to autonomy. If the following arguments are sound, then, they also show that such rights-based objections are mistaken. See also notes 31 and 36.
27. Stanley and Steinhardt, *Bigger Monster, Weaker Chains*, p. 1. Although Stanley and Steinhardt use the term "liberty" rather than "autonomy," they make it clear in their essay that they are concerned with the erosion of control that persons have over how they live their lives that could be engendered by subjecting them to surveillance, and to the increase in the possibility that persons might be subject to an increase in State coercion if they are placed under surveillance. As such, then, it would not be inappropriate to hold that their concern with liberty is also a concern with autonomy.
28. The account of privacy that is offered here is an account of what it is for something (e.g., an item of information) to *be* private, rather than an account of what it is for a person to be *in a condition* of privacy. (As Adam Moore puts it, the concern of the account of privacy outlined here "is what should be considered a 'private affair'—something that is no one else's business." "Intangible Property: Privacy, Power, and Information Control," *American Philosophical Quarterly*, Vol. 35, no. 4 [1998], 372.) The focus of this account of privacy is thus different from accounts of privacy such as that developed by William Parent or Ferdinand Schoeman, for whom, respectively, "Privacy is the condition of not having undocumented personal knowledge about one possessed by others," and "A person has privacy to the extent that others have limited access to information about him... the intimacies of his life, or...his thoughts or his body." W. A. Parent, "Privacy, Morality, and the Law," in D. Johnson and J. Snapper, *Ethical Issues in the Use of Computers* (Wadsworth, 1985), 203 (reprinted from *Philosophy and Public Affairs* [1983]: 269–288), and Ferdinand Schoeman, "Privacy Philosophical Dimensions of the Literature," in Schoeman, ed., *Philosophical Dimensions of Privacy*, 3. This difference in focus is important, for it explains why descriptive (rather than normative) accounts of privacy (such as Parent's and Schoeman's) do not compete with the normatively laden account that is offered here, and so there is no need to argue that this account is preferable to (e.g.) Parent's.
29. Thus, if persons did possess a moral right to privacy this pro-surveillance argument would not justify its violation. And this is true whether this right to privacy was purely a principle-based right, or one that was based on practical considerations (i.e., that such a right is needed to protect some more fundamental human good, such as autonomy or well-being).
30. It should be noted that, unlike the type of surveillance argued for here, that which the Party subjected the citizens of Oceania to frequently *did* violate their privacy.
31. For a discussion of the relationships that hold between privacy, autonomy, and the ceding of control, see Taylor, "Autonomy and Privacy," 460–473.
32. "There was of course no way of knowing whether you were being watched at any given moment.... You had to live—did live, from habit that became instinct—in the assumption that every sound you made was overheard, and, except in darkness, every movement scrutinized" Orwell, 1984, 4–5.
33. David Lyon offers evidence that shows that persons do not change their behavior when they are under surveillance once they realize that it is unlikely that their images will be accessed. See his discussion of the use of surveillance cameras in retail stores in *Surveillance Society: Monitoring Everyday Life* (Milton Keynes, UK: Open University Press), 51, 62.
34. Thus, if persons did possess a moral right to autonomy, this pro-surveillance argument would not justify its violation.
35. The claim that the proliferation of surveillance devices will lead to an "Orwellian nightmare" occurs frequently in the philosophical literature on this subject. See, for example, Adam Moore, "Employee Monitoring and Computer Technology: Evaluative Surveillance V. Privacy," *Business Ethics Quarterly*, Vol. 10, no. 3 (2000), 698. 36.
36. I thank an anonymous referee for *Public Affairs Quarterly* for his or her exceptionally generous

and helpful comments on an earlier version of this paper and the Editor of that journal for encouraging me to develop my arguments. I also thank Mort Winston for encouraging me to refine this paper further, and to acknowledge the concerns that would legitimately arise from the increase in State surveillance in the present-day United States.

2.3 ARTIFICIAL INTELLIGENCE, ROBOTICS, AND NANOTECHNOLOGY

2.3.1 Us and Them

RODNEY A. BROOKS

To the physical and emotional relief of many, technology has made it possible to incorporate various types of mechanical devices into our bodies in recent years. Although various scientific advances during that period suggested to some that far greater achievements were on the horizon, progress toward reaching those lofty goals has not been as rapid as earlier believed. Today, according to Rodney Brooks, the director of the Artificial Intelligence Laboratory at MIT since 2003, a new age is about to begin and such changes will have a major impact on our lives.

In both literature and film, robots have often been depicted as vying with humans for supremacy and posing serious threats to the continuation of life as we know it. In this article Brooks discusses ways in which humans in the future will incorporate many of the desirable characteristics of robots into their own bodies.

Most of his research at MIT was focused on designing and building intelligent robots capable of operating in unstructured environments. But his view of the future has shifted. The devices that he sees becoming part of us would go far beyond the artificial joints and other similar devices that benefit many today.

In addition to repairing damage to our bodies resulting from accidents, disease, or normal aging, Brooks asserts that we are on the verge of being able to enhance our natural capabilities in ways never before envisioned. The ability to move further into the realm of creating "designer" superbodies will bring with it new responsibilities and require a new form of ethics. From the mundane mechanical devices such as artificial hips or knees to the more esoteric such as cochlea and retinal implants using neural connections, Brooks is concerned with the broad ethical issues as well as the social acceptability of these new technologies.

Source: Rodney Brooks, "*Flesh and Machines: How Robots Will Change Us*," pp. 213–236. Copyright © 2002 Rodney A. Brooks. Reprinted by permission of Pantheon Books, a division of Random House, Inc.

FOCUS QUESTIONS

1. How does what Brooks foresees relate to the issue of "man's powers" discussed by Jonas? (Selection 1.3.2) What ethical dilemmas might arise if technology ultimately permits humans to be modified as described by Brooks?
2. In what ways is the era of "engineered biotechnology" going to alter how we think of cyborgs, and where does Brooks see this ultimately leading?
3. How does Brooks see computers and humans integrating in the future and what might our ability to exercise direct control over living cells mean in the not-too-distant future?
4. How do you believe you would feel if you could benefit from an available medical technology of the types discussed by Brooks but were denied such treatment on ethical or moral grounds?

KEYWORDS

actuators, body augmentation, cochlea, cyborg, electrical stimulation, engineered biotechnology, feedback, high bandwidth, implant, invasive technologies, Lamarckian theory, mental tapping, neural connection, remote-presence robot, social acceptability, social constraints, thought control

As director of the MIT Artificial Intelligence Laboratory, I have the pleasure of telling visitors about all the far-out fantastic work that is being done in our lab. Not only am I lucky enough to be at perhaps the world's premier technology institution, but I am able to represent a laboratory at that institution which is at the extreme of creativity and, in the information technology area, the hottest technology of our time. Now of course at MIT there is also a downside. There happen to be two other even bigger information technology laboratories at the same place, competing for attention with the same sponsors. In 1997, *U.S. News & World Report* ranked the MIT Laboratory for Computer Science, the MIT Media Laboratory, and the MIT AI Lab as three of the country's top-ten information technology laboratories. So the cloud in the silver lining is that I often have to share the innovation limelight with our sister laboratories. While feeling to us like just about one of the best labs in the world, there are two siblings on the same block to keep us humble about our own accomplishments.

The Media Lab had a big impact during the nineties with their wearable computers. A number of students, including Steve Mann and Thad Starner, started wearing computers permanently. They usually had a single-hand keyboard in one hand, and a video screen covering one eye, so that as they walked around campus, sat in classes or meetings, or went about their research, they were always connected and computing. They were integrating computers into their everyday life in a completely pervasive way. And they were doing it visibly. Before long they became known as the Cyborgs. Part human and part machine, they had an identity of their own on the MIT campus. Colin Angle and I had experimented with some of these ideas in late 1989, and we had even dressed Colin up in some mocked-up interfaces for a series of concept photos. I had taken the idea to a conference in Japan, where I was the last-minute replacement for Arthur C. Clarke when he was too ill to travel, and there I talked about all sorts of future work that might be done. But we had never done it, and the Media Lab had instead done their own take on the idea. The AI Lab did not have any cyborgs. I often wondered, what if I had pursued those ideas, what if…

One day late in 1999, I walked from my office on the ninth floor of the AI Lab building out to the elevator lobby. The freight elevator from the basement stopped and the doors slid open. Out walked a modified version of Hugh Herr.

Hugh has a half-time appointment as an assistant professor at the Harvard Medical School and a half-time appointment as a research scientist in the MIT AI Lab. As Hugh stepped from the elevator, a chill went up my spine. From the thighs up he was all human. From the thighs down he was all robot. And not an elegant robot. He was prototype robot. Metal rods instead of bones, computer boards where muscles would normally be, batteries hanging on by black electrical tape, and wires dangling everywhere. Now *this* was a cyborg!

Hugh is a double-leg amputee, and one can see how that has shaped his professional career. He completed a Ph.D. with the late Tom McMann at Harvard on animal locomotion. He worked with Gill Pratt in the AI Lab on legged robots, and then the two of them teamed up to develop a robotic prosthetic leg that is now in production for amputees everywhere to use. More recently he has started work on using cultured mammal muscle to actuate small robots and aims to eventually build artificial legs in this way—biological muscles rather than electric motors.

Hugh's motivations are plain for all to see, and already his work has helped many other people who are also amputees. His tenacity is admirable. The tenacity of others working to replace other sorts of lost human functionality is equally strong. With solid clinical credentials and motivations, they are developing a new set of technologies that will soon be adopted into human bodies wholesale, in ways the inventors did not originally imagine.

WE THE MACHINES

Today there are tens of thousands of people walking around with implants that connect electronics directly to their nervous systems. These people have accepted that they are better off becoming a hybrid, part human, part machine, than staying purely human. I am speaking here of people with cochlea implants that enable them to hear.

As with most of the technologies I am about to discuss, there are good, understandable clinical reasons why those with damage to the small hairs in their cochleas have chosen an artificial augmentation of their body. They have made the choice because it restores to them an ability that they have lost.

For people who grew up able to hear and who learned to hear and speak a language in the normal way, but later lost hearing because of damage to their cochlea, an implant is often able to successfully restore their ability to hear spoken language. The *implant* is an electronic device that separates multiple sound frequencies received by a microphone in the ear and outputs the strength of six or so frequencies on electrodes. The electrodes are implanted next to nerve cells that would normally receive signals from sensor cells that transduce the motion of the small cochlea hairs. They are lined up so that the frequencies measured by the artificial cochlea are inserted along the length of the real *cochlea* at the place that would normally be responding to approximately the same frequency.

With these implants people are able to hear well enough to understand speech better than less impaired people using a hearing aid only. The small number of frequency bands does not at this point let people hear music or other sounds very well, but that ability may come as more sophisticated implants are built over time—there are very active research programs in both the United States and Europe in building better implants.

The devices are surgically inserted into people's ears, and electrodes are permanently implanted, so that there is direct electrical connection between the electronics of the silicon device and the nervous system of the patient. They hear through a combination of flesh and machine.

Artificial cochleas are not the first machine components to be inserted in human bodies on a very large scale. For years people have used structural implants, ranging from plates and screws to support broken bones, to wholesale replacements of hip joints. Indeed, a hip-joint-replacement operation is hardly remarked upon today. Most people in the Western world have relatives or friends with artificial hips. There are also chips that are regularly implanted in animals in many parts of the world. In the United Kingdom all dogs have a chip implanted under their skin. This can be interrogated externally so that their identity can be established against a national registry—a dog that shows up at the pound can be returned to its owner whether they want it or not. Understandably there have been a handful of advocates and a bevy of opponents arguing about whether the same sort of thing should be done for all people at birth. In any case, these chips are not really part of the body of the dogs in which they are installed. They operate completely independently from the dog, without any interface with its neural system.

But artificial cochleas are not, in fact the first implants that introduce electrical activity into people's bodies. There have been heart pacemakers implanted under people's chests for over thirty years. A small periodic electrical signal stimulates heart muscle, and the heart entrains that stimulation, enabling it to beat regularly. Such an electrical connection somehow seems more mindless than that of the artificial cochleas. The cochleas process sensory information, partition it, and send it to multiple destinations in the nervous system. The artificial cochlea really becomes an integral part of the way in which a person with one implanted is able to sense the world.

Many people are working to improve the performance of the artificial cochleas. They are increasing the number of frequency channels handled, they are increasing the sophistication of the signal processing done on the sounds that are received, and they are looking at better ways to implant the electrodes into the patient's flesh. All these improvements are responses to the natural demands of the medical marketplace. There are many people who lose their hearing due to natural degeneration of their ears, through damage from sustained loud noise, or through infections. Providing such technology and administering it to people is just like any other form of clinical medicine. There really seems to be very little in the way of a moral argument that could say that using technology in this way is bad. As such, we can expect it to continue.

While improvements are being made in cochlea implants, work is progressing in many countries toward the first retinal implants. These are for previously sighted patients who have damaged retinas. The most common target is for people with macular degeneration. This is a progressive disease that attacks the foveal part of the retina and gradually takes away people's ability to see fine detail. Those affected lose the ability to read and recognize faces, and eventually they can do no more than get general contextual cues from their peripheral vision.

A retinal implant is a silicon retina, like the pixel array inside a video or digital camera. The idea is to collect light in the electronic pixels, then send that information to the spatially appropriate nerve cell, or neuron, in the optic nerve that would have received such information from the retina itself had it still been intact.

Retinal implants are much more complex than cochlea implants. Rather than just a handful of electrodes, it will be necessary to interface with the nervous system at tens of thousands of different nerves or neurons. This increases the complexity of both the device and the implantation technique.

The way in which sound is processed by an intact cochlea is well understood and reasonably straightforward to emulate in electronics. The processing the retina does is not so well understood at this time. Thus, although the spatial structure of how light falling onto a particular part of the retina should be mapped to which neurons is easy to understand, there is still a lot of research necessary to understand just what signals should be transmitted. These unknowns, along with the increased number of connections necessary, mean that artificial retinas are not as far along as artificial cochleas. There are no people walking around today with artificial retinas permanently implanted. They have been experimentally implanted in volunteers for daylong periods. The subjects report being able to distinguish light and dark and notice "differences" when looking at different things. They can hardly be said to *see* in the way that cochlea implant patients can hear, however. Nevertheless, progress is being made. It seems reasonable to expect that artificial retinas will become clinically expedient in the next decade or so. People who can be helped by them are a natural market, and helping blind people to see is a noble goal.

There are many other arenas where there is a clinical push to connect silicon circuits directly to nervous systems.

Many people have suggested making *neural connections* between nerves in the stump of an amputee to a prosthetic arm or leg. For legs this turns out to be not such an attractive option. People need their legs to adapt as they walk over rough ground, smooth ground, up stairs and down stairs, but their legs do not need to be really dexterous. The possible payoff from having direct neural connections to control their artificial legs is not great enough to compensate for the myriad inconveniences and problems that it brings. They want to simply strap their leg on in the morning and not need to be worried about plugging in connections, whether they be through a connector extruding from their flesh, with its associated infection problems, or a carefully placed receiver for skin galvanic currents, or a wireless connection from an implant within the leg stump. Gill Pratt and Hugh Herr have accommodated this desire by inventing an artificial leg that can tell what the person is doing and adjust its actions accordingly. While a doctoral student, Ari Wilkenfeld programmed the first prototype prosthetic leg to interpret sensors and decide whether the person was walking up stairs or down stairs, or across relatively flat terrain, and also to sense how fast the person was trying to walk. The intelligent leg mitigates the need for direct neural connection.

Artificial arms are another story, however. People want to be able to do many different things with their arms. They want to be able to grasp many different-sized and -shaped objects with different requirements of delicacy and force to be used. They want to be able to pick up and put down objects, but they also want to be able to turn the page of a book, or put the stopper in the kitchen sink, or turn a door handle, or pull the refrigerator door open, or open an envelope, or turn the ignition key in their car. They want to be able to blow their nose and wipe their bum.

For prosthetic arms there is a real need for *high bandwidth* connections between the wearer's nervous system and the artificial device. To this end there are many experiments with animals in developing ways to have permanent connections between electrical devices and neurons. The most promising way seems to be to implant *a silicon chip* with holes through it right in the path of a severed cluster of nerve cells. The nerves regrow through the holes, and the silicon circuits can both measure electrical activities in the nerves and inject their own signals into the nerves. The chip communicates wirelessly to an external monitor strapped to the skin. There are many research issues that still need a lot of work. What sort of material should be used so that it neither harms the body nor is rejected by the immune system? How should the signals on the nerves be interpreted? How can the brain to the person best be trained to interpret the signals, such as those that might come from force or touch sensors in the artificial arm?

This work is proceeding. There are clinical pushes for it to be made to work, and there are thousands of people who will be very grateful when it becomes practical. But there is not a total urgency for those with one missing arm. They are able to function in the world, though not as well as they would like, and deserve. For people who have damage to their spinal cords, especially high up on their spinal cords, the situation is much more immediate and dire. Their whole life is defined by their inability to move. Some people with really high-up damage are not able to breathe on their own even, and the only part of their bodies they can control is their eyes. They cannot talk, just look. They have immediate and pressing needs for new technologies that let them connect their brains to robots.

There are some things that can be done without direct neural connections. One of my graduate students, Holly Yanco, modified a wheelchair and put in a robot control system. The wheelchair is able to follow corridors and go through doorways on its own indoors. Outdoors, it is able to follow along a sidewalk, and avoid falling down stairs. Holly used a system developed by Jim Gips at Boston College that allows the profoundly impaired to give signals to a computer by moving their eyes. Small electrodes taped to the temples and forehead pick up the electrical signals that their brain sends to the eye muscles and the computer can infer which ways their eyes have moved. Holly hooked this up to her robot control system. A person riding in the wheelchair simply looks at an icon on a screen attached to the wheelchair's arms, such as GO FORWARD, and the robot wheelchair takes care of the second-to-second adjustments in speed and direction necessary for successful navigation.

While such aids can help the very disabled, they themselves clearly want something better. There have been some experiments with a handful of very disabled patients in making direct connections between their nervous systems and a computer. One patient is able to move a mouse pointer about on his computer screen just by thinking. There is an implant into his nervous system and wires coming out of his body that connect him to a computer interface card. With this small attachment the patient is able to have infinitely more control over his own life than he could before. He can type and send messages to people. He can read their messages as he chooses, and he can surf the Internet, bringing the information resources of the world into his service, displaying what he wants before his own eyes.

Experiments such as this are very limited. There are ethical questions about what sort of *invasive technologies* should be put inside a human patient when so little is known about how well it will work. So experiments proceed with animals, but often it is hard to know just what capabilities an implant gives them. As reported in November 2000, however, there was a recent experiment with monkeys that had a very clear outcome.

Miguel Nicolelis at Duke University implanted electrodes into the motor control region of the brains of small new-world owl monkeys. Over a period of two years they monitored the signals on these electrodes as the monkeys moved their arms about to reach for food. By putting the food in different locations relative to the monkeys, the researchers were able to get the monkey to do the same motion many times. The electrodes picked up signals from many hundreds of neurons. With some signal-processing techniques they were able to measure the electrical activity in these individual neurons and watch that activity during different arm reaches to different places. After collecting and analyzing enough data the researchers were able to predict the activity in individual neurons for any particular reaching task that they gave to the monkey.

Ordinarily such predictions followed by analysis of recorded data would have been enough to establish that the researchers had found a correlation between neural activity and particular motions of the monkey's arms. But Nicolelis and his colleagues came up with a much more vivid demonstration. They attached a real-time computer to the electrodes and programmed it to predict where the monkey's arm was about to move. Then they connected that computer to a robot arm and had it move in the direction and reach that it predicted the monkey was about to undertake. The monkey reaches for a piece of food, and the robot arm, unseen by the monkey, moves in the same direction and reaches out the same distance. As an encore, the research group at Duke teamed up with a group at MIT and had a robot arm in Massachusetts reaching simultaneously with the monkey in North Carolina. Monkey remote presence. Almost. The monkey never knew about the existence of the robot arm.

The follow-on set of experiments from this work are to give the monkey *feedback* from the robot arm, so that it can feel the forces and touches that the robot arm encounters in the world. This sort of force and haptic feedback has become routine in the robotics world, but the signals are usually reflected as forces on a person's arm. With the direct brain connection of the Duke monkeys the leap will be to send the forces directly into the monkey's brains. This work will not be simple. Figuring out how to represent the forces and touches electrically, and which nerve cells they should go to, will be a challenge. Since perceptual signals go through multiple processing stages in the brain, there will be multiple candidate sites. Which ones will give the monkeys a sense that the robot arm is really theirs will be a difficult question. The place that the signals are injected will have to be one where the adaptive mechanisms of the brain are able to operate, to map and learn the correlations between sensation and what is really happening in the world. We know from the *"phantom limb"* phenomenon—where someone who loses an arm both adapts to the loss and yet still can feel the nonexistent arm—that this is a complex issue. Thus we do not yet know how difficult it will be to really have the monkeys feel that the robot arm is their own.

Such work is critical to being able to attach prosthetic arms to human amputees and to let their brains control the arms directly, while feeling that the arm is an extension of themselves. Likewise, this work is necessary to give quadriplegics the ability to control robots as substitutes for their own bodies. At the moment there appear to be no insurmountable obstacles to making this work out. There is research to be done, and the details of what will be necessary are far from clear. But the current indications are encouraging that it will not be too many years before such work will be ready to tried on human patients.

The monkeys in these experiments live carefully circumscribed lives. They are treated well, but they are not subjected to the complications of a life in the wild, a life in a rough-and-tumble monkey society. These experimental animals have electrodes in their brains, sticking out through their skulls, so that computers can be hooked up to them directly. This will not be the way amputees and quadriplegics will wish to interface to their technologies. In the short term there will need to be extremely low-powered wireless connections implanted directly in their brains so that they can communicate through their skulls and skins with the devices that are external to their bodies. Later, when artificial arms are permanently attached to their bones and their own skin merges with the skin of the prostheses, it will be possible to route the wires from their brains down into the arms, and even the legs.

Routing of wires within people's nervous systems is another area that is an active area of research. *Electrical stimulation* of nerve cells in the thalamus has been used as an effective way to relieve the symptoms of Parkinson's disease. Sometimes the symptoms of this and other motor control diseases are so severe, making people shake so violently and consistently, that patients prefer to be surgically paralyzed in their affected limbs rather than live with the constant tiring motion. To make this happen it is necessary to cut major nerve fiber highways so that no signals can get through to muscles. Often the correct signals are present, but they are swamped by the other, spurious signals, caused by the disease, that are also present.

Some researchers are now looking into the possibility of bypassing diseased or damaged parts of the brain in cases of Parkinson's and other diseases, by routing nerve signals around those areas. By inserting wires into the brain and connecting them to nerve cells at either end, it is hoped that signals can be routed from motor control centers to muscles while the interfering natural pathways can be severed. This work is also in its early stages, but there are many suffering patients and good clinical reasons to pursue these possibilities.

Many of these technologies are going to come to fruition in the next ten years, and almost certainly they will all be perfected within twenty years.

THE FUTURE OF SURGERY

The nature of surgery is undergoing a rapid transformation. While human surgeons are still in charge, sometimes for good reason, and sometimes just for historical reasons, they are being augmented with computer vision and robotic aids.

Computer vision techniques that Eric Grimson and his students perfected at the MIT Artificial Intelligence Laboratory are used daily by surgeons at Brigham and Women's Hospital in Boston to remove brain tumors. The system measures the exact location of a patient and gives the surgeon X-ray vision inside the patient's head, overlaying MRI data that has been segmented and color-coded for the tumor and functionally different parts of the brain. The data is projected in such a way that as the surgeon looks at the patient through a special screen, or sometimes on a TV monitor on the side, he or she sees all this extra data exactly aligned with the patient. The surgeon can see things that were formerly not visible. The tools the surgeon uses are instrumented, and their exact three-dimensional position shows up in the displays too. Surgeries are now less invasive through smaller openings, and they take less time because the surgeons know more exactly what they are doing. These new "Nintendo" surgeons no longer watch their hands. They watch the TV screen as their nimble and skilled hands swiftly manipulate their tools.

The same techniques have been adapted for orthopedic and other surgeries. They allow for much less invasive surgeries than before because the surgeon does not have to directly see inside. He or she is given the virtual reality illusion of seeing inside, and that is enough to do the job well, even better than the limited view from just one set of eyes using the visual spectrum.

Robots themselves are also starting to be used for surgery, although again a human is in ultimate control. Intuitive Surgical of Mountain View, California, sells a remote-presence surgical system. The surgeon sits at a console with his fingers inserted into loops. As he moves his hands, a tiny robot with very different shape and form moves inside a human patient on the other side of the room. A camera inside the patient gives the surgeon a view of what is happening. As the surgeon twists his wrists and reorients his hands, the two small robot manipulators react accordingly. The surgical manipulators, developed at the MIT AI Lab by Ken Salisbury and Akhil Madhani, are able to cut and grasp. They are at the end of long rigid tubes less than half an inch in diameter that enter the patient through very small incisions. The tubes do not move at all during surgery, only the tiny manipulator at the end moves around inside the patient. The surgeon is able to elect to operate directly with 1 millimeter of their motion translating to 1 millimeter of robot motion, or at a five-to-one ratio, in which case the robot only moves a fifth of a millimeter. Intuitive Surgical's robots are being used throughout Europe and the United Sates for a variety of surgeries, including heart-valve replacements. So far, the surgeries have all been performed with the surgeon in the same location as the patient, but there is no reason that this could not change. Time lags across networks are ultimately determined by the speed of light, so it will not be possible to let the surgeons have effective control if they are too far from the patient, but distances of 100 kilometers or so should be possible in the not-too-distant future.

These sorts of surgical aids are just the tip of the iceberg. Many other robots are being developed for surgery throughout the world. For ethical reasons the work of all these robots is overseen by a human surgeon. But that may change in the future. For some of the systems the robot could carry out the motions themselves today. Humans are only in the loop to appease the fears of the patients and the overseeing hospital and regulatory boards. Just as we eventually gave up the demand that all automobiles be preceded by a human on foot waving a warning flag, we might eventually let these robots do more of the actual surgery. Twenty years from now it may be common to have surgeries overseen by medical technicians whose training will be years less than that of a surgeon. Surgery will become much more routine and common. Just as we now have laser eye surgery done in our shopping malls, correcting our vision permanently by changing the shape of our natural lenses, we will soon have other forms of elective surgery done in ways that are easily accessible to the masses.

ELECTIVE SURGERY

Within twenty years surgery will be vastly more convenient and available than today, and there will be many techniques for embedding silicon and steel inside human beings to compensate for lost capabilities.

Of course, things will not stop there. There will be a whole new class of enhancements for our human bodies. These will all start innocently enough, but there will be inexorable pressure to push the technologies into more elective realms. Just as cosmetic surgery has become commonplace, technological body enhancements will become socially acceptable. People who are nominally healthy will start introducing robotic technologies into their bodies.

How could this happen? Will we really overcome our fear, and even revulsion, at changing our bodies into machines? Let us look at one scenario for a gradual change that will lead to a wholesale reversal of attitudes.

Just as cochlea implants have become fairly routine, so too will retinal implants for people who have lost their sight through degeneration of their retinas. Initially people who have one good eye but one eye damaged through an accident will not be considered for implants. There will be sufficient demand from people with two bad eyes that it will be considered morally responsible to treat them first. But the demand from those patients will make the technology and operations more common and routine, and before too long people with one good eye will start to have the procedure on their bad eye.

But some people might opt for a little enhancement on their bad eye. Perhaps they would like a silicon retina that is enhanced for night vision. We already know how to build silicon arrays for digital cameras that are many times more sensitive than the human eye at night. So someone who has one good eye and has lived for many years blind in the other eye might decide that they can get around just fine during the day, but it would be great to be able to see at night—something that no ordinary person can do. *Why not upgrade their useless eye to give them* that capability? The silicon retina would need to have an electronic auto-iris so that it did not flood the person's optic nerve with signals during the day. In fact, in the early models it might have to simply shut down in daylight. But that is not something that might worry our hypothetical patient. Their bad eye is useless during both the day and night without the surgery.

Being able to see everything clearly at night is going to be an awfully interesting option for some people. Anyone who wants to operate clandestinely: soldiers, drug smugglers, terrorists.

Night vision enhancement will get to the point that some people with two perfectly good eyes may be willing to sacrifice one for it. In poorer countries people are already willing to sell some of their own organs for what appear to be pitiful amounts of money. In other parts of the world people are willing to become human bombs to support their causes. Modifying a good eye, to give superhuman performance, will not be too outrageous for lots of individuals, resistance movements, and governments.

People with extreme hobbies might also find eye modification useful and, when it becomes affordable, opt to do it. Mountain climbers, spelunkers, ultramarathoners, and Arctic trekkers and sledders might all be attracted by the idea of being able to see through the dark night. It would even help for driving a car at night. Our licensing authorities insist that we wear corrective lenses for driving if our eyes are not up to normal standards. Where does this slippery slope head, let alone end?

Night vision is not the only option, of course. *A shift in the portion of the spectrum in* which we can see might also be useful. More toward the infrared and we could become much more sensitive to seeing heat sources. This would be great for search-and-rescue teams, or even for firefighters. More toward the ultraviolet, and we could make all sorts of fine distinctions about the health of living plants—what farmer would not want to understand his crops better? And what if we could consciously change the sensitivities of our eyes, from night vision, to ultraviolet sensitivity, to infrared sensitive, back to normal? All we would need would be some connection between our neurons and the circuitry implanted in our previously normal eyes, and then the somewhat pesky detail of making sure that those neurons are under conscious control of the person in some intuitive way.

The clinical push on letting amputees and quadriplegics control external devices is not only the key to eventually being able to control our imagined modulatable eyes, but is also going to make us part of the Internet.

The current systems that let people control a computer mouse will let people control their eyes' spectral sensitivity. These techniques work by having the person imagine moving part of their body that they no longer have direct control over. Eventually that conscious effort becomes much more unconscious as the person's brain remaps their internal body image. We are all familiar with this phenomenon. When we first start driving an automobile, it is a thing that we are inside of and trying to control. Sometimes it feels like it has a will of its own and we need to concentrate to give the right control inputs to it. Before long, however, it becomes part of us. Initially as we drive into a parking spot, we are directing this box of steel to go to a particular place. After a while we are driving into the spot, and have a body awareness of the extent of our car *as an extension of our body*. It is no longer us and the car but just an extended us, with a car body.

There are other ways in which we extend ourselves too. Many of the technologies that have become indispensable parts of our lives are external to our bodies—they have become the new talismans that we carry with us everywhere we go. The most noticeable of these are our cellular telephones. We have become dependent on these to communicate with our families and our office. But now we are becoming dependent on them for all sorts of information services, ranging from weather predictions, train schedules, movie schedules, directions to places we are going, stock market prices, and purchasing objects both large and small. Many of us also carry a personal digital assistant and have all of our professional lives scheduled on these devices, along with all our business contacts and our notes, drawings, and plans. Then, of course, there is the Internet, that external information space that dominates many of our lives. We gather, and post, most of the information that we use, and send and receive tens to hundreds of e-mail messages per day. We are chained to our desk machine, or our portable is glued to our lap (except during takeoff and landing) almost permanently so that we have access to these information channels. What if we could make all these external devices internal, what if they were all just part of our minds, just as our ability to see and hear is just a part of our mind?

A person with a thought-controllable mouse can browse the Internet by thinking, but that browsing is mediated by their eyes. Now combine the mouse with an implanted retina chip. Instead of having the artificial retina be a camera, make it a display device, connected to the computer that the thought mouse controls. Now the person could wander the information ways of cyberspace within a mental cocoon. But this would require the sacrifice of an eye. What if instead of inserting the visual image of the screen at the retina it was done in the rear of the brain in one of the visual-processing areas that reside there? When the display was switched off, everything in the visual system would work as usual. With the display switched on, there would be an interruption to normal service, with the screen image replacing what would normally have been seen. Now, there are quite a few details to work through to make all this work out as I have suggested. It may well take a solid twenty years of research and experiments to get there. But there does not seem to be an in-principle reason why this could not be made to work. It may take quite some practice and training for a person to be able to adequately perceive the appropriate information, but it certainly seems quite possible, and even probable.

Of course, it may turn out that there are better ways to interface the Internet and the equivalent of our PDAs to the insides of our heads. Rather than mediate all this information through a visual representation, somewhere in one of our retinotopic maps, it may eventually be possible to have the information appear much more directly in our minds. Most of us are pretty good at retrieving our home phone number, but beyond a dozen or two frequently dialed numbers, we need to go to an external device. When we think of our own number, we do not conjure up a visual image of the digits. Instead, the "number," whatever that means, is just there. When we go to our external device, we do see the number as visual images of the digits. When our external devices are surgically implanted in our brains, perhaps we will find a way to bypass that visualization step, and get the information directly.

Working out how to do this will be a significant research undertaking. However, there will be market pull. Initially there will be research pressure for the blind, with useless eyes, to have direct Internet access. That will drive the development of direct mental access to the Internet. Then, because the sighted majority will not need to sacrifice a good eye to get it, there will be plenty of pressure to allow them to get hold of this technology.

Once we have figured out this *direct mental-tapping technology* there may be a whole new set of services that spring up. Just as standard HTML Web pages proliferated, and then specialized WAP (Wireless Application Protocol) services for mobile phones with tiny screens came along, there might well be, twenty years from now, a whole host of "mentalese" service providers. They will be packaging information in a form most easily browsable with direct neural connections rather than optimizing it for visual presentation.

Of course, once there are Internet connections, all the services of cell phones and PDAs will be easily layered on top of this infrastructure. We will be able to communicate by thought with anyone else with the same technology implanted, anywhere in the world. Whether this form of communication will feel more like text-based instant messaging, or more like some sort of Vulcan mind-meld will depend on the particular technologies that it is possible to develop.

Having such things implanted in our brains will make us tremendously more powerful. Just as the current external Web and cell phones enable us to do more, often, so too will our mental access to cyberspace. We will be able to think the lights off downstairs instead of having to stumble down in the dark to switch them off, and as an externally silent alarm goes off inside our head, leaving our spouse to sleep longer undisturbed, we will be able to think the coffee machine on, down in the kitchen.

Even face-to-face in a meeting, we might choose to open up a separate mental communication channel (perhaps ultimately transported by the cellphone network, after all) with a particular person in the room, so that we can have a private side discussion with them, strategizing about how to proceed publicly. These, and many other as yet unimaginable capabilities, will change the very ways in which human beings interact. We will be superhumans in many respects. And through our thought-mediated connections to cyberspace, we will have access to physical control of our universe, just with our thoughts. *Remote-presence robots* will be at our mental beck and call. While we may be physically present in one particular place, we will be able to mentally project ourselves to any remote-presence device and location for which we have authorization. Each of the have-nots will soon want to become one of the haves.

Initially the haves will be the weird ones. In our Olympic sports we do not let athletes who use performance-enhancing drugs compete. We might outlaw implanted Internet devices among students taking the SATs, as they will have an unfair advantage. But before long, just as with calculators, we might come to expect that everyone taking the SATs will have mental Internet access. What starts out as bizarre will probably become the norm.

ACCEPTABILITY

Some people will be repelled by the idea of incorporating technology into their bodies, while others will be curious and even eager to try these modifications. Initially the choice will certainly be much more complicated than a personal decision. There will be strong issues of social acceptability. These issues will probably vary from country to country and even in different regions within a single country.

The acceptability of food made from genetically engineered crops is very different in different Western countries at the start of the new millennium. In Germany it is a very intensely debated issue, while it hardly registers in the United States. Likewise, the current issues around body modification are subject to very different social mores in different countries.

Kidney, liver, lung, and heart transplants are a current-technology form of body augmentation. For people with diseased internal organs transplants from a donor person are a replacement methodology. We currently do not have steel and silicon versions of these organs that work as well as biological organs. And unlike an eye transplant, say, such organs are able to make all the necessary connections when implanted in someone else's body and to function normally.

But accepting such organs into one's body is not a morality-free issue. For kidneys there is often the possibility of taking one from a willing living relative, since we all start out with two but are able to survive well with only one. In this case, we are accepting the flesh of another living person into our own body. For lung and heart transplants we are relying on the death of someone else, and then we have part of that dead person in our body, giving us life. Since livers can grow, even in an adult, both possibilities are open—a living or a dead donor.

Kidney and heart transplants are common in the United States. Indeed kidney transplants are now so common as to be unremarkable. In Japan, however, there have been only a handful of such operations in total. It was only in February 1999 that the second heart transplant was carried out. The first such transplant thirty-one years before had ended in accusations of murder against the transplant surgeon Wada Juro for removing a beating heart from the donor. In the West the notion of brain death has been long accepted, but it was only enacted as law in 1997 in Japan. The 1999 transplant from someone who had signed a donor card became a media circus because of the moral implications of removing organs from someone who was not "dead" by the traditional Japanese measures. Lest one think that this implies a consistently different Japanese sensibility for all human life, one must remember that, unlike in the United States, abortion is completely acceptable in Japan. And deformed thalidomide babies had three times the infant mortality rate that they had in the United States, despite much better overall infant mortality rates in Japan.

The point here is not that one community or country has better or superior moral values. Rather, different countries and communities hold to different moral values on particular issues. These moral values impact the acceptability of medical procedures even when life may hang in the balance for the recipient. They will certainly impact the social acceptability of cosmetic medical procedures such as silicon (as distinct from silicone) implants.

Such social constraints are not immutable over time, and we do see them change in relatively short periods on the order of a decade or two. The Japanese are easing their restrictions on transplants. Likewise, they are changing notions of the sanctity of the body and just what bodily modifications are socially acceptable. Pierced ears for women were taboo in Japan well into the nineties, but now a sojourn on the Tokyo subway shows that the taboo seems to have completely disappeared. In the West pierced ears on males were reserved only for pirates well into the eighties. Now a man with a pierced ear is unremarkable through most of the professional ranks in the United States. It would still be unlikely for a president or a Supreme Court justice to have such a body modification, but that too will change over time. Just as the baby boomers with their history of drug experimentation have gotten there, eventually those offices will be occupied by today's kids from generation Y, and there is no real going back on a hole through your flesh or cartilage.

Today many of us might say, "I don't want any stinking microchips inside my head, no titanium extensions to my bones, no sensory augmentations." It would feel unnatural. It would not be me. Some of us may change. Our children may feel differently. And their children almost certainly will.

BEYOND CYBORGS

Our technology has been under development for thousands of years. It is just now getting to the point where we can incorporate it inside our bodies. And we will. We will change ourselves from being purely the product of our genetic heritage to a more Lamarckian sort of species wherein we will be the product also of our own technology.

For the moment that technology is based on silicon and steel. Before this new century is out, that technology will have long been surpassed, and our bodies by the middle of the century will reflect that next wave.

The robots of the mid twenty-first century will have silicon components, and steel components, and titanium, and maybe even some gallium arsenide, and certainly a bunch of other materials and superconductors, and polymers, and structures that we have hardly even imagined. Our bodies too will contain all these technologies. But we and our robots are going to be full of a new round of technologies too—engineered biotechnology.

For fifty years we have been developing technology that lets us understand biology at the molecular level. Recently people have started turning that technology from analysis to synthesis. This is the standard transition from science to engineering.

The first attempts at using molecular biology technology as an engineering substrate have been brutish and clumsy but nevertheless extraordinarily powerful. Now work is proceeding on newer, more refined techniques that will be even more powerful.

Much work has been done in culturing cells and controlling their growth so that now a replacement pinna, the cartilaginous portion of the external ear, can be grown in vitro and attached permanently to a person who has lost one of hers. Experimental work also proceeds on growing replacement organs in vitro.

Recently there has begun serious work on using these sorts of technologies in robotics. Hugh Herr, the cyborg in the opening of this chapter, is not satisfied with the electrically operated dampers in his new generation of artificial legs. He wants active muscles but knows that electric motors will not have the right characteristics, and they will take large batteries. Hugh and his students at our lab have started building robots that are actuated by mouse muscles—muscles that can be grown in vitro from a single cell. His first robots must be bathed in a weak sugar solution to work, but they are the marriage of silicon and steel with biological matter. A small microprocessor receives high-level commands such as "swim," "turn right," etc., and turns them into coordinated signals that travel out on wires that innervate the biological but artificial muscles. The robot swims and turns right.

There are many research issues remaining, of course: how to shape the muscles appropriately as they grow, how to feed them sugar without their needing to be floating in it, and how to keep them alive over long periods so that a useful replacement leg can last a reasonable amount of time.

Hugh's work uses cells as they currently exist. But there is also work that modifies what goes on inside cells. There has been a lot of work done on genetic modification of existing organisms. The technology for inserting and deleting genes was critical for understanding the role of genes and for the roles of the proteins for which those genes coded. These techniques are now being used to insert new characteristics into crops or to remove genes that cause disease.

But such approaches are in some sense rather crude. They rely on mixing and matching existing genes to get some hoped-for result out of the complex dynamics of the interactions of all the proteins that are coded for by those genes. It is a little like plug and play with peripheral devices in your stereo system or your home computer. You are not really inventing anything new, just capitalizing on the ways in which the manufacturers have enabled all the components to communicate with each other. A less crude thing to do would be to build new components yourself. A really masterful thing would be to completely redesign the central processing unit of your computer. In the case of engineering genes, some work is starting on the middle ground—the complete redesign is still beyond us.

Tom Knight and Ron Weiss at the MIT Artificial Intelligence Laboratory have started to turn genetically engineered living *E. coli* cells into little tiny robots. They use a menu of sensors and actuators that exist already in the *E. coli,* or which they can easily genetically engineer in using the crude techniques that are well known. They have built little tiny *E. coli* robots that sense molecules (homoserine lactones, to be precise) that can be absorbed through the cell wall. They are also considering using naturally occurring sensors for pH, light, electric, and magnetic fields, and for other simple molecules. The actuators for their cell robots have been the same sorts of lactone molecules diffused through the cell walls, which emitted light, using a gene stolen from *Monocentris japonicus,* the Japanese pine-cone fish. They are also looking into controlling flagellar motors, cell death, and the production of enzymes as actuators for these robots.

The most challenging part of Knight and Weiss's robots are the computations that they do in order to decide how to produce their outputs as a function of their current state and their inputs. They impose a digital discipline on these cells. They take simple digital circuits and compile them into a string of DNA that they insert in the genome of their population of *E. coli.* The molecular dynamics of the cells and the transcription mechanism of the cell is hijacked into doing the originally specified computations by this string of DNA. For instance, the compiler might choose to have protein A inhibit the transcription of protein B. By ensuring that there is the appropriate nonlinear transfer curve in this inhibition, the concentration of protein B in the cell can be seen as the logical inversion of the concentration of protein A. Thus the RNA transcription mechanism implements a logical NOT gate inside the cell, as determined by Knight and Weiss's compiler. More complex logic gates are easily built on top of this mechanism, and so complex computations can be forced to happen inside the living cell. With the right sensors and actuators a robot is born. Already Knight and Weiss have produced beakers full of robots, billions of robots of two different species, communicating with each other and switching on and off luminescence displays in response to messages from other robots and the concentration of signaling molecules in the solution. The computation speed of these robots is only impressive in that it is so slow—tens of minutes to make simple decisions. Such techniques will not replace silicon in our quest for ever more computation. What is important here is that computation ultimately controls some of the internal processes of a living cell.

In the not-too-distant future, people might achieve similar control over the molecular processes of living cells in more subtle ways, without going all the way to a digital process. But Knight and Weiss's work shows that it can be done. When we look ahead thirty years, we can imagine that we will be able to have programmed cells within living organisms, and even within ourselves. We will certainly have them in our robots, as they are very easy to manufacture. Living cells can already self-repair and self-reproduce. All you need to do is feed them simple sugars and you get more of them.

It is too early and the present too murky to see where all this leads, but it is clear that robotic technology will merge with biotechnology in the first half of this century. And so the robotic technology we are adopting into our bodies will ultimately become biotechnology: technology that will be programmed into our cells through modifications to our genes.

We are on a path to changing our genome in profound ways. Not simple improvements toward ideal humans as is often feared. In reality, we will have the power to manipulate our own bodies in the way we currently manipulate the design of machines. We will have the keys to our own existence. There is no need to worry about mere robots taking over from us. We will be taking over from ourselves with manipulatable body plans and capabilities easily able to match that of any robot.

The distinction between us and robots is going to disappear.

FURTHER READING

Knight, T. F., and R. Weiss 2000. "Engineered Communications for Microbial Robotics." From Proceedings of the 6th International Workshop on DNA-Based Computers, DNA 2000, Leiden, The Netherlands. Edited by A. Condon and G. Rozenberg. In *Lecture Notes in Computer Science.* Vol. **2054**, pp. 1–16 Berlin: Springer-Verlag.

Loeb, G. 2001. "Prosthetics, Neural." In *Handbook of Brain Theory and Neural Networks.* 2nd ed. Pp. 768–72. Edited by M. A. Arbib. Cambridge, Mass.: MIT Press.

Ramachandran, V. S., and S. Blakeslee. 1999. *Phantoms in the Brain: Probing the Mysteries of the Human Mind.* New York: Quill.

2.3.2 Artificial Intelligence and the Future

WILLIAM F. CLOCKSIN

The promise of artificial intelligence (AI) has long fascinated both scientists and the lay public. In this article, William Clocksin, professor of computing science at Oxford Brookes University (England), examines the history of artificial intelligence, analyzes impediments to progress in the field, and proposes that future progress in artificial intelligence will depend on adopting an alternative conceptual framework that understands context and social relationships as keys to intelligent behavior.

Early computer scientists tended to overestimate how quickly artificial intelligence would replicate lower-animal and even human thought processes. Despite the fact that many see the intelligent computer of the future having humanlike thought processes, the computer of today is structured much differently than the human or even lower-animal brain. Clocksin considers a number of reasons why progress in this area has not been nearly as rapid as originally thought but argues against skeptics who claim that artificial intelligence is not even possible. He describes some of those differences in relation to soft computing that attempts to mimic the ability of human brains to tolerate imprecision and uncertainty. There are presently some applications of this soft-computing technology in factory automation and manufacturing where subjective judgments and determinations are often needed.

Clocksin observes that it's relatively easy to program computers to perform expert tasks, such as playing chess, but it's very difficult to program them to do mundane tasks such as washing dishes. The fact that IBM researchers could design and build Deep Blue, the computer that defeated grand master and reigning world champion Gary Kasparov in 1997, does not, according to Clocksin, teach us much about the nature of human intelligence. Rather, the challenge of programming computers and robots to perform mundane skills requires a shift from the dominant "command and control" paradigm of conventional programming to a model of mind "based on persons, identity, and social context." This social constructionist approach would be a new "conceptual framework" for artificial intelligence that, according to the author, makes the possibility of designing "strong AI" systems more feasible.

FOCUS QUESTIONS

1. Discuss the four possible reasons presented by Clocksin for why AI progress has been slower than expected.
2. How does the view expressed by Brooks (Selection 2.3.1) of how technology will be integrated into future human beings compare with Clocksin's concept of "soft" computing?

Source: From "Artificial Intelligence and the Future," Philosophical Transitions Vol. 361, No. 1809, *Information, Knowledge and Technology*, August 15, 2003, pp. 1721–1748. Reprinted by permission.

3. Describe why Clocksin believes that "narratives" are significant and need to be considered when designing an AI system. In what ways is his view consistent with a social constructionist perspective or at variance with it?
4. What argument does the author present for refuting the belief of many that man is a "rational animal," and how does he believe this erroneous impression has impeded progress in the field of AI?

KEYWORDS

AI, automatic reasoning, connectionism, intelligent agent, learning, narratives, neural networks, problem solving, sensory-motor coordination, social constructionism, soft computing, strong AI, weak AI

We consider some of the ideas influencing current artificial-intelligence research and outline an alternative conceptual framework that gives priority to social relationships as a key component and constructor of intelligent behaviour. The framework starts from Weizenbaum's observation that intelligence manifests itself only relative to specific social and cultural contexts. This is in contrast to a prevailing view, which sees intelligence as an abstract capability of the individual mind based on a mechanism for rational thought. The new approach is not based on the conventional idea that the mind is a rational processor of symbolic information, nor does it require the idea that thought is a kind of abstract problem solving with a semantics that is independent of its embodiment. Instead, priority is given to affective and social responses that serve to engage the whole agent in the life of the communities in which it participates. Intelligence is seen not as the deployment of capabilities for problem solving, but as constructed by the continual, ever-changing and unfinished engagement with the social group within the environment. The construction of the identity of the intelligent agent involves the appropriation or "taking up" of positions within the conversations and narratives in which it participates. Thus, the new approach argues that the intelligent agent is shaped by the meaning ascribed to experience, by its situation in the social matrix, and by practices of self and of relationship into which intelligent life is recruited. This has implications for the technology of the future, as, for example, classic artificial intelligence models such as goal-directed problem solving are seen as special cases of narrative practices instead of as ontological foundations.

1. INTRODUCTION

Artificial intelligence (AI) is a branch of computer science with the objective of equipping machines with reasoning and perceptual abilities. This overall objective is pursued through two routes, which one might crudely divide into applied and theoretical.

a. Applied: to engineer systems capable of performing tasks which, if performed by a human, would be said to require intelligence.
b. Theoretical: to pursue a scientific understanding of the computational principles underlying intelligent behaviour, as manifested in humans and other animals.

Both routes need to propose and understand operational principles of thought and action in unambiguous (computational) terms. These principles may form the foundations of computer implementations of thought and action and, if suitably grounded in experimental method, may in some ways contribute to explanations of human thought and behaviour.

Few definitions of intelligence adequately capture the richness of human experience. AI research has tended to use fluid boundaries of definition. For example, one traditional focus has been on problem solving and with the sensory and symbol processing capabilities that support problem solving. Yet, the concern is not restricted to humans: AI researchers have long been intrigued by the behaviour of animals, which seems to show complex capabilities for sensory-motor coordination and action, even though reptiles and insects are not considered intelligent in the way in which humans are.

AI received its name at a workshop at Dartmouth College in New Hampshire in 1956. There, the founders of the field set the agenda for AI research for the next 40 years. From this workshop, goal-directed problem solving implemented by search algorithms and supported by methods of automatic logical inference became the dominant conceptual framework, and continues to be so for most of the AI research community.

From an engineering perspective, AI research has been applied in useful ways. Computer programs using methods derived from AI research play chess at the expert level, assess insurance and credit risks, schedule gates at airports, and search the contents of the Internet. From the scientific perspective, however, the aim of understanding intelligence from a computational point of view remains elusive. Current programs for automatic reasoning can prove useful theorems concerning the correctness of large-scale digital circuitry, but exhibit little or no common sense. Current language-processing programs can translate simple sentences into database queries, but the programs are misled by the kind of idioms, metaphors, conversational ploys or ungrammatical expressions that we take for granted. Current vision programs can recognize a simple set of human faces in standard poses, but are misled by changes of illumination, or natural changes in facial expression and pose, or changes in cosmetics, spectacles or hairstyle. Current knowledge-based medical-expert systems can diagnose an infectious disease and prescribe an antibiotic therapy but, if you describe your motor car to the system, it will tell you what kind of meningitis your car has: the system does not know that cars do not get diseases. Current learning systems based on neural networks can forecast financial trends, given historical data, but cannot predict the date of Easter nor prime numbers given a large set of examples.

Computer scientists have known for many years that it is relatively easy to program computers to accomplish skilled tasks that are difficult for people to do (such as to solve huge systems of equations), while at the same time we are unable to design a computer program to do things that people can do easily (such as to recognize friends' faces reliably under changing conditions). This distinction is unexpected, paradoxical, and a block to further progress in AI. Software based on AI methods can land a jumbo jet safely, but there are no convincing demonstrations of computers carrying out the range of perception and motor-control tasks that even a year-old infant can do easily. Yet, serious and informed thinkers had predicted that the problem of AI would be essentially solved by now. Turing (1950) predicted that, within 50 years, computers would be able to take part convincingly in human conversation. Minsky (1967) predicted that "within a generation, the problem of creating 'artificial intelligence' will be substantially solved." Several years later, the then Stanford Research Institute published the results of a study on the future of AI technology (Firschein *et al.* 1973). Using the Delphi technique of technological forecasting, they put a large and carefully designed battery of questions concerning future trends to an international panel of experts. The replies were analysed, and summaries fed back to the experts, each of whom was asked for comments on and revision of his earlier estimates. After the third iteration, an additional questionnaire was used to calibrate each individual's error in an unrelated numerical estimation task, and a self-rating scheme was employed to assess professional expertise over the various topics involved. A few of the results are listed in table 3.1: Michie (1974) gives a fuller account. In his commentary on this report, Michie was even more optimistic: "if the authors' survey results can be criticized, it is on the grounds of conservatism." Yet, although a few supporting

TABLE 3.1 A Selection of Delphi Study Results Taken from Firschein et al. (1973)

Product	Median Prototype Date	Commercial Median Date
voice-response order taker	1978	1983
insightful economic model	1984	1990
universal game player	1980	1985
automatic language translator	1987	1995
robot chauffeur	1992	2000
general factotum	2000	2010

components of the products listed are in the development stage, the state of the art is nowhere near the expected targets.

Why is it that AI research has become impeded or limited? And is this related to which tasks are relatively harder or easier to implement? I have previously (Clocksin 1998, p. 105) considered some possible reasons for impediments to AI research; Brooks (2001) has arrived at similar conclusions independently. The following is a selection of possible reasons why progress in AI has been much slower than expected.

Resource limitations. Our theories are right, but our computers do not have enough processing power or memory capacity to do the job properly. Chess playing is one example where it is important to have enough processing power. Current programs employ brute-force search of possible board positions to arrive at a good move, and more computing power and memory space means that more variations can be searched more thoroughly. However, we do not know precisely how people play chess, but it is clear that people do not play chess by brute-force search. It is not obvious that resource limitations are relevant if we do not have a theory that specifies the resource requirements.

Complexity limitations Perhaps intelligence is a property that emerges when the underlying process becomes sufficiently complex. The complexity might be so great that the process is not understandable. According to this reason, AI research is impeded because we are unable to arrange a sufficient degree of complexity. For example, complexity could take the form of a massive number of indiscernible connections between large numbers of processes, or a massive number of constraints that influence the solution to an ill-conditioned problem having a massive number of unknown parameters. Yet we have no reason to support a complexity argument if we do not possess a theory that explains precisely why the complexity is necessary, and why the operational principles of the problem in question cannot be discerned.

The impossibility of AI. Dreyfus (1972), Penrose (1990) and Searle (1990) argue that AI is impossible. Against this one has to face the fact that intelligent beings exist, at least one of them is reading this paper, and intelligent behaviour can be assumed to be based on physically realizable principles of operation that it is the task of science to understand and articulate in computational form. Understanding these principles—which we do not yet do—must come prior to attempts to implement them as computer programs, so I believe we are not yet in a position to pronounce on the impossibility of AI.

Conceptual limitations. That is, AI is not impossible, but we are not working within a suitable conceptual framework. Or we are not paying sufficient attention to investigations made in other fields where other potentially significant conceptual frameworks obtain.

There are several types of conceptual limitations, and several authors have attempted to explain such limitations by what Brooks calls a "new stuff" hypothesis: that there may be some extra form of "stuff" in intelligent systems outside our current scientific understanding. "New stuff" theories are prevalent in popular writings about the problem of consciousness and AI. For example, Penrose (1990) suggests that quantum effects in the microtubules of neurons might be the locus of consciousness. He has not worked out a theory of how this might work, but claims that it is an essential element. Another "new stuff" hypothesis has been advanced by Chalmers (1996, p. 127). Just as Maxwell's theory related electric fields with magnetic fields in a way inconceivable before Maxwell (to simplify the history), Chalmers suggests the possibility of yet undiscovered psychophysical laws that relate physical stimulation with psychological percepts. Such laws would not be additional physical laws, but would be supervenience laws, describing how experience arises from physical processes. I shall not consider "new stuff" hypotheses further in this paper.

One type of conceptual limitation can be described as "going against the grain" of physical reality. That is, AI is limited because we are not identifying and exploiting known properties of physical reality that mediate and facilitate intelligence in ways that are as yet unknown. It is felt among some in the AI research community that, when the problem of AI is finally "cracked", the solution will turn out to be much simpler that we might have guessed it to be, and this will be because we have found a solution that somehow "goes along the grain" of what is already known about physical reality. As naive as this hope may appear, AI practitioners might draw some inspiration from past situations where simple solutions have been found for difficult problems by going "along the grain" of nature. Two examples are making the perfect "French fry," and starting a gas turbine jet engine. French fries, known in the UK as chips, are made by cooking cut rods of potato (with approximately square cross-section) in a deep fat fryer. The problem is cooking the potato so that the finished product has a consistent appearance and texture, and this involves knowing the optimal cooking time. Once a rule determining the optimal cooking time is found, it can be automated. The difficulty is that potatoes vary widely in their water and sugar content, requiring significant variation in cooking time (although the sugar content can be regulated to an extent by storing the potatoes at a warm temperature for several weeks in order to convert sugars to starch, and water content can be regulated to an extent by pre-cooking at a certain temperature). The problem remains of how to control the cooking time when sugar and water content are known only to within a fairly wide range. The engineer is tempted to design a system that measures the water and sugar content of a batch of chips, then sets a timer based on the measurement. Two shortcomings of this approach are that measuring the water and sugar content of the potato pieces immediately before frying is not practicable, and the process is not controlled after the timer is set. The actual solution adopted is based on the observation that when a batch of cold raw potato pieces is dumped into a vat of hot cooking oil, the temperature of the oil will immediately drop and then slowly rise. Once the oil temperature has risen *ca.* 3°C from the lowest point, the chips are ready (Gladwell 2001). The solution requires only a temperature sensor and simple electrical circuitry; it turns out not to be necessary to control anything at all during the cooking process.

The second example is starting or re-starting a gas turbine jet engine. One type of simple jet engine consists of a compressor fan and a turbine wheel connected by an axial rotor. Atmospheric air is admitted and compressed by the compressor fan, and is then mixed with fuel. The fuel-air mixture ignites and expands rearwards through the blades of the turbine wheel, rotating it and therefore the compressor fan, which in turn sucks in more air to mix with the fuel to continue the cycle. A self-sustaining combustion can be produced under the right conditions. The problem is starting the engine, or possibly quickly restarting an engine that has lost combustion (or "flamed out") in flight. An electric starter motor is provided to spin the compressor to a given speed. Once combustion is self-sustaining, a centrifugal clutch disengages the starter motor. The difficulty is that combustion will only occur and self-sustain under the right conditions of ambient and internal temperatures, atmospheric and internal pressures, compressor speed and ratio of fuel-air mixture. The only variable that can be controlled is the rotational speed of the starter motor (fuel input is controllable, but can be set to a known value). The engineer is tempted to design a system that measures all these parameters and sets the optimum speed of the starter motor to spin the compressor. However, the solution that was adopted in early jet aircraft was simply to start the compressor to spin at maximum speed, then disengage the clutch and switch off the starter motor while starting the fuel feed. The compressor would gradually slow down, and when the optimum air pressure was achieved, self-sustaining combustion would occur, spinning the compressor up to operating levels. I hasten to reassure the reader that the modern jet engines used in commercial airliners have highly sophisticated engine-management systems that are far more reliable and robust than their predecessors. Both solutions involve arranging a naturally occurring optimization of a single variable by sequential "search": in the first case by a monotonic increase of cooking oil temperature after the potatoes are immersed, and in the second case by a monotonic decrease in compressor speed. It is no accident that these two problems were dealt with during the mid 1950s, a time during which technology was sufficiently advanced and user requirements were sufficiently demanding to engender the problems in the first place, but microcomputer and sensor technology were not sufficiently advanced to tempt the engineer to adopt more complicated solutions.

2. SOFT COMPUTING

Another type of conceptual limitation can be described as the "wrong technology": the idea that progress in AI will be blocked until it adopts a particular kind of software/hardware implementation technique. Since its beginning, most AI research has assumed that the principles of intelligence can be implemented by conventional means, in the form of suitably designed algorithms with associated data structures, and that sequential execution of the algorithm by a digital computer would suffice to implement the particular principle that is being programmed. If intelligence is based on principles of operation that are computable—and there is no convincing reason why this should be otherwise—then an algorithm executed on a sequential digital computer would at least demonstrate the principle of operation. However, a brief glance at the architecture of animal brains suggests an organization quite different from the digital computer: a densely interconnected network having comparatively low transmission rate exhibiting alarmingly high levels of stochasticity. Furthermore, human thought is quite different from algorithmic specifications in its tolerance of imprecision, uncertainty and facts that are known only partly. Many conventionally programmed systems are static, linear, brittle, inflexible and do not adapt to changes in the world. By contrast, intelligent systems need to perceive, reason, plan, negotiate, act and learn from previous experience.

The research area known as soft computing aspires to find methods that tolerate imprecision and uncertainty to achieve tractability and robustness. Furthermore, from a control-theory perspective, soft computing claims to offer model-free design approaches that have certain advantages over classical and modern control theory when dealing with systems exhibiting complicated nonlinear dynamics. A basic review of soft-computing technology is given by de Silva (2003) and by Jamshidi (2003). The ideas underlying soft computing can be traced back to fuzzy sets (Zadeh 1965), with subsequent developments in fuzzy logic and fuzzy control theory, together referred to as fuzzy systems. Now, soft computing is generally agreed to be a fusion of fuzzy systems, artificial neural network theory (Bishop 1995), evolutionary computing (Fogel 2000), and probabilistic reasoning (John & Birkenhead 2001). These distinct and yet interrelated methodologies have found a number of practical applications ranging from industrial process control, fault diagnosis and smart appliances to speech recognition and planning under uncertainty. The principal contribution of fuzzy logic is its provision of a foundation for approximate reasoning, while neural network theory provides an effective methodology for learning from examples. Evolutionary computing is based on an iterative generate-and-test approach, often referred to as genetic algorithms (Koza 1992), in which collections of approximate solutions to a problem are randomly improved to provide better solutions. Probabilistic reasoning systems furnish computationally effective techniques for representing and propagating probabilities and beliefs in complex inference networks.

A key application area of soft computing is in factory automation, where several computing systems must be integrated with sensors and effectors to process and inspect materials. In such environments it is essential to tolerate acceptable dimensional variation, the inaccuracy of sensors and effectors, the uncertainty of specification and the vagaries of production management. One example is given by de Silva (2003), who describes a prototype fish-cutting machine. Another system is a machine for inspecting ceramic tiles (Dalziel *et al.* 1996). Ceramic-tile factories offer interesting possibilities for soft computing because there is a mixture of continuous and discrete control, and information-processing technology in this industry is somewhat underdeveloped compared with, say, the automotive industry. This lack of theoretical and practical grasp stems partly from the need to deal with natural materials that are intrinsically difficult to model and handle: the ceramic particulates from which tiles are made, "gloopy" glaze materials and brittle workpieces. Ceramic tiles are made from "natural" materials, and there is a tradition of inspecting them according to subjective judgements and intuitions. These judgements and intuitions are difficult to understand, quantify and specify in algorithmic form. Furthermore, there is a large number of potential defects and quality categories, so any automated system must have comprehensive competence. In the Textone and Integrale ceramic-tile inspection systems... manufactured by Axiom (Cambridge) Ltd, soft-computing techniques are used for: calibration of the image sensors and illumination in the presence of changing environmental conditions; image-processing techniques whereby salient visual features are extracted from the images; and the classification process by which the tiles are graded. The Textone and Integrale are used in ceramic-tile factories in Italy and Spain, the world's two largest exporters of ceramic tiles.

Connectionism—the study of computer simulated neural networks—has been heralded as a fresh start to AI (Churchland 1996) by advocating a technology that is considered to be closer to natural neural systems than the sequential digital computer is. However, despite its significant and important advances in the theory and technology of pattern recognition, connectionism, like the other constituents of soft computing, does not propose a change in our ideas about what processing is for and what the goals of the intelligent computer should be. Connectionism has simply advocated different ways to do it: essentially, an implementation technique based on approximating an unknown input-output relationship with or without a training set of exemplars. Such approximation methods can also be implemented without neural nets; many methods in the end boil down to conventional curve fitting or parameter estimation of one sort or another. Whether a particular problem is being solved by a conventional algorithm or by a neural network, the computer is still carrying out an abstract task in isolation, defined and specified in a way judged appropriate by its author. Whether the computer is programmed by explicit specification of an algorithm or by iterative improvement of a matrix of numerical weights is not a sufficiently deep distinction upon which to claim a new approach to AI. Uptake of neural network and other soft-computing technology by industry has been slow, cautious and selective. The "black box" nature of neural networks makes it difficult to certify them for safety-critical applications. Also, there are concerns over the use of probability-based methods. The events of interest for reliability analysis (failures) are rare events and are associated with the tails of distributions, which are often badly characterized. In addition, the standard practice of representing each event as a deviation from an estimated sample mean (Duda *et al.* 2001) can be problematic even for non-failures. For example, in an optical character recognition problem, it is a routine implementation technique to estimate the letter shape *A* as having a conditional probability of say 0.89 given the mean shape A, with other positive probabilities available given other mean shapes. However, to put it bluntly, human readers will agree that the shape *A* is the first letter of the Roman alphabet with probability 1.0, and it is any other letter with probability 0.0. A new approach to AI will need to be concerned about this conceptual mismatch between implementation techniques and human behaviour.

The importance of soft-computing stems from its approach to problems that do not satisfy the assumptions often made by classical computational and statistical methods. In such problems, the data size or dimension is too large to be tractable, models or factors are unknown, and there are missing data and a high proportion of outliers. Soft computing can offer flexible and adaptive solutions for unpredictable real-time environments for which sound mathematical models are difficult or impossible to provide. In individual cases, soft-computing methods can work when other methods fail. For this reason one may agree to adopt implementation techniques based on results from soft computing, but at the same time one must remain unconvinced by "wrong technology" arguments that claim that the goals of AI can be achieved primarily though adopting particular implementation techniques.

3. FRAMEWORK AND METHOD

The type of conceptual limitation motivating the remainder of this paper is of the "wrong framework" variety. To prepare the ground, let us reconsider the paradox that it is relatively easy to program computers to accomplish skilled tasks that are difficult for people to do, while at the same time we are unable to design a computer program to do things that people can do easily. The root of this paradox lies in the distinction between mundane and expert tasks. People perform mundane tasks automatically, yet these seem to require complex reasoning. The principles of washing dishes, changing babies' diapers, hammering nails or installing car windscreens can be taught within minutes to people who have widely varying intellectual abilities, creativity and insight. These tasks involve the handling of imprecise quantities of intractable materials such as soap suds, cloth, slippery dishes and glass sheets, all difficult to model mathematically. In these tasks no precise measurement is called for ("squirt about this much soap into the sink"), specifications are incomplete ("then jiggle it round until it fits"; "then pin these two bits together") and circular ("you know it fits when it snaps into place"), yet dextrous perceptual–motor operations and sensitive judgements are employed. The fact that apparently easy tasks may conceal a large amount of unconscious sophisticated analysis and processing is not the point. Whether these tasks need "insight" or "representations" or "knowledge" or "problem solving" is also not the point. The point to make here is that these tasks are taught by "showing how" and learned "by doing," relying on social interaction, with performance parameters circumscribed by the embodiment of the participants in the social interaction.

By contrast, expert tasks require specialized skill and training, for example, medical diagnosis, playing expert chess, and financial decision making. Paradoxically, mundane tasks are the harder to automate, and expert tasks are the easier to automate. Why is it hard to program computers to do things people find easy to do? And why is it easy to program computers to do things that people find hard to do? The answer is that implementing expert tasks does not require theories of the person. It requires a theory of medical diagnosis, or chess, or financial markets, or whatever the task domain may be. We can formulate such theories, and the implemented system can function with reference to and perform relative to such theories, and this is often sufficient to perform the task. On the other hand, implementing the mundane tasks seems to involve knowing how the embodied person relates to things or other persons, and this is one of the theories we lack today.

Chess playing was once thought to be the paradigm of the application of intelligence, and chess-playing automata have been proposed through the centuries. Modern precursors to AI include Shannon's and Turing's proposals for chess-playing computer programs, and game playing has long been an interest of AI research. The claims of a game-playing approach to AI are that playing a game demonstrates intelligence, much intelligent behaviour can be represented as (or reduced to) a game, and various activities of interest to military funders of AI can be represented as a game. These claims were particularly prominent during the Cold War "think tank" years of the 1950s to the 1970s (Edwards 1996). Yet, though programs can now play expert chess, the process of developing these programs has taught us very little about intelligence. McCarthy (1997) remarks that

> in 1965 the Russian mathematician Alexander Kronrod said, "Chess is the *Drosophila* of artificial intelligence." However, computer chess has developed much as genetics might have if the geneticists had concentrated their efforts starting in 1910 on breeding racing *Drosophila*. We would have some science, but mainly we would have very fast fruit flies.

The substantial effort in game playing research has taught us only what a limited model it is for human intelligence. The simplifications and abstractions it offers can be misleading, but the technical effort devoted towards this aim has been useful for the development of new algorithms and data structures.

Artificial intelligence as a scientific enterprise is in a vulnerable position partly because there are no ready-made theories, and partly because it is not clear that what we *can* theorize and write computer programs about is relevant to the concern. If there were a reasonably complete theory of intelligence, current technology might put us in a position to implement at least parts of the theory in a productive way. Other scientific fields benefit from the existence of ready-made theories developed within the last 150 years. For example, a theory of electromagnetism offers a relationship between an electric field and a magnetic field, and can be used to simulate, design and analyse electrical circuits as well as to develop better theories of electromagnetism. A theory of aerodynamics offers a relationship between lift, thrust, drag and gravity. This helps to design aircraft, to understand natural flight, and to develop better theories of aerodynamics. By contrast, AI research has collected a body of theory about algorithms for problem solving, but these theories are not about intelligence nor are they about persons. Problem solving has been seen as an abstract capability independent from the needs and desires of the individual, and independent of the cultural and social context. Theories of mind and intelligence have been considered by philosophers and psychologists, but generally these are not phrased in terms that can be translated to effective algorithms.

I have argued elsewhere (Clocksin 1995, 1998) that AI is limited not by processing power nor in handling complexity, but by taken-for-granted concepts that form an implicit normative load. Historically, AI research has been freighted by a "command and control" paradigm (Edwards 1996) in which intelligent behaviour is seen as the application of decision processes, represented using formal reasoning, to abstract well-specified tasks. The emphasis on formal reasoning describes a "rationalist" approach, from the logician's definition of rationalism as a chain of deductive reasoning that does not result in a contradiction. Indeed, the effort to make progress in AI through one style of knowledge representation and automated reasoning, namely logic programming and the PROLOG programming language (e.g. Kowalski 1979; Clocksin & Mellish 1981; Baral & Gelfond 1994), culminating in Japan's Fifth Generation Programme of the 1980s (Feigenbaum & McCorduck 1983; Unger 1987), was one of the more ambitious manifestations of this approach.

It may be necessary to break away from the rationalist tradition in order to do justice to alternative models of minds—models based on persons, identity and social context—that may ultimately provide a practical foundation for AI. There are signs that this "re-framing" of AI is already underway to a limited extent. The remainder of this paper is concerned with a framework for AI informed by four strands of thought emerging from social and developmental psychology. First, there has been an increasing concern with person-hood: with persons, agency and action, rather than causes, behaviour and objects (Shotter & Gergen 1989). Second, there has been an increasing emphasis on the self as a social construct, that persons are the result of interactions with significant others, and that the nature of these interactions is in turn shaped by the settings in which these interactions occur (Levine 1992). Third, the self and identity are no longer considered to be prior givens (Luntley 1995). Though the self may lack an objective centre, the self engages in the performance of a centralized focus that can assert itself as a prior given. Fourth, logical reasoning is neither a good model for the functioning mind nor for human performance. We come to value logical reasoning not because it mirrors the operation of the mind (which it does not), but for the benefits it confers, such as accountability of discourse.

4. REFRAMING RATIONALITY

In the wake of the 1956 Dartmouth workshop, the conceptual framework for AI research and the rational problem solving approach to intelligence began to be mapped out (McCarthy 1959; Minsky 1961; Newell & Simon 1961). Almost 20 years passed before this framework became more clearly articulated. The "physical symbol system hypothesis" (Newell & Simon 1976) holds that the processes required to produce intelligent action can be simulated with a collection of physical symbols and a set of mechanisms that produce structures built from those symbols. According to this hypothesis, intelligence is realized through a representational system based on a physical symbol system, and that intelligent activity is goal-orientated, symbolic activity. McCarthy (1977) states that

> the epistemological part of AI studies what kind of *facts* about the world are available to an observer with given opportunities to observe, how these facts can be represented in the memory of a computer, and what *rules* permit legitimate conclusions to be drawn from these facts.

The two essential ingredients are representation—the idea that relevant aspects of the world need to be encoded in symbolic form in order to be usable—and the symbolic activity of inference, by which rational conclusions can be made by applying rules of inference to axioms. As Waltz (1999, p. 32) has expressed it,

> a substantial community within AI has long held the view that the human brain somehow implements a perfect logic machine and that all intelligence is built on top of this. A corollary to this view is that in order to create a fully intelligent system all we need to do is create a perfect logic machine and then build everything on top of it.

While AI's emphasis on logical symbol-processing as the basis of intelligence had been criticized by Weizenbaum (1976) and by Dreyfus (1972), Winograd & Flores (1985) were probably the first to call for a re-examination of the rationalistic tradition and its influence on AI research. According to Dreyfus & Dreyfus (1986), the failure of AI research will continue until intelligence ceases to be understood as abstract reason and computers cease to be used as reasoning machines.

Furthermore, McDermott (1987, p. 151) argues that

> the skimpy progress observed so far is no accident, and in fact it is going to be very difficult to do much better in the future. The reason is that the unspoken premise…, that a lot of reasoning can be analysed as deductive or approximately deductive, is erroneous.

Objections to AI's equation of commonsense reasoning with "approximately deductive" reasoning were anticipated from the start. In his response to McCarthy's (1959) paper, Oliver Selfridge replied

> I have never yet heard of someone drawing correct conclusions from correct premises. I mean this seriously.… Most women have never inferred it, but they get along pretty well, marrying happy husbands, raising happy children, without ever using deductive logic at all.

No doubt it is a mark of social progress that Selfridge's point would be phrased slightly differently were it to be expressed nowadays. Moving from the problems of deductive (or approximately deductive) reasoning to the problems of representation and problem solving, Brooks (1991*b*, p. 583) has given a powerful critique of traditional AI research. From AI's origins in the late 1950s,

> traditional AI has adopted a style of research where the agents that are built to test theories of intelligence are basically problem solvers that work in a symbolic abstract domain.

Brooks (1991a, *b)* argues that abstract knowledge representation and problem solving methods "cannot account for large aspects of what goes into intelligence" and that the field "concentrates much of its energies on anomalies within formal systems which are never used for any practical task."

AI's assumptions about rationality as the seat of intelligence come from a philosophical tradition that goes back more than 2000 years. However, is man, as Aristotle put it, really a "rational animal"? Rationality in the logician's terms is related to consistency: an argument is rational if it does not produce a contradiction. However, consistency of argument is difficult to achieve in the face of assumptions and rules that change over time. Beginning with Doyle (1979) and McCarthy (1980), much effort has been devoted to "truth maintenance": methods for automatic deductive reasoning that prevent the derivation of contradictions in the presence of changing assumptions. This is still an area of active research. And yet human performance in problem solving is marked by two characteristics that suggest that people sit rather more lightly to logical consistency: people can happily entertain contradictory views (even without being aware of it) and, when put to the test, human 'rationality' is frail and fallible. People do not rely on deductive inference in their everyday thinking. Human experience is marked by incompetence, blunders and acts of misjudgement. The average AI programmer (but not the average psychologist) might be surprised to learn that for normal people, irrational (in the technical sense) behaviour is the norm rather than the exception. The more accessible background literature on the "normality" of irrationality includes Sutherland (1992), Manktelow & Over (1990), Dixon (1976) and Piattelli-Palmarini (1994). Human reasoning thrives on the basis of actions and beliefs that cannot be justified nor supported logically. We often make profoundly irrational assumptions, then argue rationally to reach conclusions that are irrational but desirable. We sometimes proceed not by what we discover to be true, but by what we want to be true. Yet non-rationality works in everyday situations. Non-rationality has worked also in matters of historical and political significance. Judd (1999) describes the British constitution as

> that wonderfully various, flexible, colourful, moth-eaten brocade, at best only semi-rational, but the product of centuries of hard won wisdom in how to manage ourselves, more responsive to our inchoate desires and needs, and more adaptable to change...

One will not be able to find a copy of the British constitution: it has what one can call a "de-centred" identity Its identity is distributed, and subsists in collections of stories, cases, practices, assumptions and precedents, each with their own exceptions, each admitting plural and contested interpretations. In such an environment there is no point in truth maintenance or in trying to find consistent interpretations.

So is intelligence based on a capacity for rational thought? If so, then why does there seem to be a lack of connection between rationality and everyday behaviour? And, if a rational mind is based on a rational brain, then why should we have a rational brain at all, as it seems to find little employment as an engine of logic? It is important to stress that in drawing attention to the inadequacy of rationality as an explanation of intelligence, we are not advocating unreason, nor is this an attempt to doubt rationalism as a means of making scientific progress. There is no questioning the fact that humans are users of rational discourse to the extent possible under limiting circumstances, and that we value the benefits that such discourse brings. The question is concerned only with a foundational assumption of AI research: whether intelligence relies on a rational problem-solving capability based in the individual's brain. So which is the more likely hypothesis intelligence derives from a rational mind, operating according to rules of logic (with truth-maintenance and the rest), but can hardly ever be used in the way "intended," or the mind is not based on principles of rationality, but as people in society we have come to perform and to value a developed but imperfect rational discourse because it has tangible benefits. The benefits of rational discourse include mutual intelligibility and accountability.

The traditional conceptual framework for AI decomposes the problem of intelligence into a set of abstract, isolated, context-free problems that the brain is assumed to solve. Yet surely problems take this form simply because it is attractive (for theoretical and practical reasons) for researchers to specify and represent them in that way. By contrast, an alternative conceptual framework sees intelligence as a set of context-bound, situated, socially and historically contingent and provisional performances. It is not obvious that mechanized reasoning and problem solving are appropriate, effective and usable within such a framework. I have previously argued (Clocksin 1998) that logical reasoning is a normative product of, rather than a foundation for, such a framework. Waltz (1999, p. 32) has independently come to similar conclusions:

> my view is that logic is really the fruit of learning, one of the *last* things we learn, not the system on which everything is based.

5. CONSTRUCTIONISM

A new framework for AI can make use of a way of thinking about persons known as "social constructionism." To reduce confusion it is useful to make a distinction between *constructivism* and *constructionism.* Constructivism, a term coined probably by Nelson Goodman and also-called cognitive constructivism, describes the work of renowned psychologists Jean Piaget and Ulric Neisser. The main idea is that understanding is created through the operation of a variety of mental schemata and procedures for analysis and synthesis of schemata. This is the main assumption behind cognitive psychology, and it is safe to say this is closely related to the prime—if unexpressed—assumptions of most AI research. The interaction between cognitive science and AI has been fruitful (e.g. Johnson-Laird 1983). In this context, AI has been concerned with the design of data structures to implement mental schemata, and the design of algorithms to implement the analysis and synthesis procedures.

By contrast, constructionism describes the work of Gergen (1991, 1994), Potter (1996), Shotter (1993) and Harre (1992). It has also been called discursive constructivism, which is probably the source of the confusion of terminology. The main concern of social constructionism are the processes by which human abilities, experiences, common sense and scientific knowledge are both produced in, and reproduce, human communities (Shotter & Gergen 1994, p. i). The idea is that constructional processes are to be found in relationships, often discursive, between persons. These relationships embody situated reasoning: that is, a contextualized meaning-producing performance.

The AI pioneer Seymour Papert has been informed by the constructivist tradition, but has begun to address constructionist concerns (thus leading some commentators to confuse the terminology further). Papert has a special concern with the role of physical artifacts, or objects, in thinking. Papert (1993) writes that

> construction that takes place in the head often happens especially felicitously when it is supported by construction of a more public sort "in the world"... Part of what I mean by "in the world" is that the product can be shown, discussed, examined, probed and admired. It is out there.

Papert argues that we learn through interacting with artefacts: that we create an understanding of the world by creating artefacts, experimenting with them to see how they work and modifying them to work better. Since artefacts are in the world and can provide an anchor for understanding among a group of people, they can also address a problem that faces the constructivist cognitive scientists. Namely, if we construct knowledge as an individual act, how can understandings be shared?

By contrast, constructionist approaches stress the way mind and action are contingent on specific cultural forms. They see minds not as having fixed essences from which behaviour flows, but as being built from the symbolic resources of cultures by means of participation in human relationships. Discourse in narrative form—examples are conversations and stories—is seen as the central organizing principle of construction. Thus, understandings are never fully shared, but they are negotiated among conversants, and this process itself is the meaning-bearing act.

Constructionist approaches offer an alternative concept of the self. The tradition we have inherited from recent centuries places a central emphasis on the individual as autonomous agent. In this tradition,

> *individuals are the fundamental units of society; relationships are secondary or artificial, a byproduct or interacting individuals.*
>
> GERGEN (1991, P. 156)

This inherited tradition has acted to foster an area of AI research activity known variously as intelligent-agent or autonomous-agent research (e.g. Maes 1990; Wooldridge & Jennings 1995). However, constructionist approaches question these concepts

> *... of the individual as the centre of knowledge ("one who knows"), as possessor of rationality, as author of his or her own words; as one who creates, decides, manipulates or intends.*
>
> GERGEN (1991, P. 156)

Instead, one's own role becomes that of a participant in social processes. The constructionist concept of the self and identity is discussed further in the following section on narrative.

Constructionist approaches provide a different concept of language and communication. The tradition we have inherited assumes a "transmission theory" of communication, in which messages are transmitted from one person to another. These messages are encoded and decoded so that they represent either the world of objects that exists outside the communication process, or the internal world of meanings and emotions of those who communicate. By contrast, the constructionist view sees communication as

> *Patterns of social action that are co-constructed in sequences of evocative and responsive acts; these patterns comprise an ecology that is our social world.... [Communication] calls into being and reproduces the events and objects of our social worlds; it is a process of making and doing.*
>
> PEARCE (1994, P. 19)

> *... Instead of thinking of conversation as the exchange of messages between conversants, the social constructionist perspective sees conversants as within an interlocking matrix of conversations. Each conversant is the product of previous conversations and the producer of the present and future conversations.*
>
> PEARCE (1994, P. 23)

According to familiar AI models, the intelligent agent operates a perception-processing-action loop in order to solve problems that are presented to it. Meaning is constructed in the mind as a result of internal symbol-processing capability. By contrast, the constructionist approach privileges social interaction as the meaning-constructing process. Here the mind is for social development, engagement with persons and the institution and appropriation of personhood and identity.

> *In this way, meaning is born of interdependence. And because there is no self outside a system of meaning, it may be said that relation (ship)s precede and are more fundamental than self. Without relationship there is no language with which to conceptualize the emotions, thoughts, or intentions of the self.*
>
> GERGEN (1991, P. 157)

For the social constructionist, the reality of relationships is persons in conversation.

> *Instead of taking it for granted that we understand another person's speech simply by grasping the inner ideas they have supposedly put into words, that picture of how we understand each other is coming to be seen as the exception rather than the rule. Most of the time, we realize, we do not fully understand what another person says. Indeed, in practice, shared understandings occur only occasionally, if they occur at all. And when they do, it is by people testing and checking each other's talk, by them questioning and challenging it, reformulating and elaborating it and so on. For in practice, shared understandings are developed or negotiated over a period of time, in the course of an ongoing conversation.*
>
> GERGEN (1991, P. 157)

By contrast, AI research has concentrated on practical applications such as question answering and information retrieval, exemplified by the following dialogue (the human's part is introduced by H, and the computer's reply is introduced by C):

H: All cats are mammals. C: I understand.
H: There is a cat in the box. C: I understand.
H: Is there a mammal in the box? C: Yes.

Statements made by the human are treated as facts to be stored in a database. The response "I understand" is an acknowledgement that the statement has been converted to an internal representation and database storage has taken place. Questions posed by the human are treated as theorems that need to be proved from the information in the database together with basic rules of inference. Though this style of interaction was popularized by the impressive SHRDLU program of Winograd (1972), current state-of-the-art systems (e.g. Shapiro 2000) offer mainly technical improvements in the handling of linguistic and logical details. Such models of communication are far removed from the richness of the social constructionist approach, and much conceptual adjustment needs to be made in AI research before a constructionist model of communication can be accommodated.

6. EMOTIONS

Conventional models of AI do not include emotions. The separation of intelligence from emotions goes back at least as far as Plato, with the separation of the rational soul from the body with its skills, emotions and appetites. Aristotle continued this dichotomy when he defined man as the rational animal, and Descartes further refined this type of dualism. By now the separation of intelligence and emotion pervades our thinking about computers, with the computer representing pure intelligence unaffected by emotion. This view has been challenged more recently. Picard (1997) argues that AI has long ignored the importance of emotions, and that emotions are part of the essential foundation for intelligence.

An example of the way that emotions are marginalized by the conventional understanding of intelligence is illustrated by Mr. Data, the android character on the popular television programme *Star Trek: The Next Generation*. Mr. Data can function perfectly well as an intelligent being without emotions, but has an optional plug-in "emotion chip" that makes him more human. Most of the time he prefers to function without the emotion chip. With the chip at his disposal, Mr. Data is at least more versatile than Mr Spock of the original *Star Trek* series. Half-human, half-Vulcan (an alien humanoid species), Spock has been trained since infancy to repress emotion because the Vulcan culture prizes logic above all things. Much of the dramatic content of these programmes is concerned with how Data and Spock function in a human culture: there is plenty of scope for misunderstanding and the "comedy of manners." Given that these accounts are after all science fiction that is aimed at a particular audience, these characters will appeal to adolescent males who themselves can find difficulty coming to terms with their emotions and the complexities of the social realities in which they are beginning to find themselves. How much more comforting to retreat to a simplified world by identifying with heroes who succeed by applying pure logic and calculation.

By contrast, the constructionist finds such accounts incoherent. Not only are there glaring inconsistencies in the model—the Data and Spock characters actually behave in ways that use the affective skills they are reputed not to require—but also the "optionality" of affect is associated with individuals one sees only in the human population as profoundly disordered. It is probably intuitions of this type that led Picard and others to reject the optionality of affect, and instead to adopt a view that treats the world of affect as something prior to intelligence and problem solving. Developmentally, this could imply an early requirement for social relationship between the mother and newborn. This is borne out by studies (Sluckin 1999; Aitken & Trevarthen 1997) that demonstrate that humans are conversational from birth. The inescapable conclusion from this work is that mothers and neonates are able to coordinate their actions so as to take account of each other. Both act into what Wittgenstein (1963) would call emergent rule games.

There are good reasons to suppose that AI technology of the future will be emotional. Arguing that intelligence must be situated in the totality of human life and experience, Dreyfus (1992, p. 63) condemns the traditional separation of rationality from needs and desires:

> if one thinks of the importance of the sensory-motor skills in the development of our ability to recognize and cope with objects, or of the role of needs and desires in structuring all social situations, or finally of the whole cultural background of human self-interpretation in our simply knowing how to pick out and use chairs, the idea that we can simply ignore this know-how while formalizing our intellectual understanding as a complex system of facts and rules is highly implausible.

In contrast to the *Star Trek* stories about Spock and Data, two recent science-fiction films start from a perspective that sees intelligence as depending upon and formed by human relationships. The film *Bicentennial Man** was based on the short story of the same name (Asimov 1982) and the novel *The Positronic Man* (Asimov & Silverberg 1992). The theme is a robot's 200 year journey from household appliance to human being. The humanoid robot Andrew is designed as a simple domestic servant, but has been equipped with a sense of curiosity, creativity and enquiry. Put into the service of a suburban family, the friendships he forms within the family teach him what it is to be human. Andrew decides to buy his freedom using the proceeds of earnings from the sale of his original woodcarvings and strikes out on his own. Outliving his original owners, over a period of decades Andrew gradually replaces his robot parts with new organic technology. After 100 years he falls in love with a descendent of his original owners. He fights a lengthy legal battle for status as a human. Humanity also means death, so he gratefully dies known as the Bicentennial Man.

The film *AI: Artificial Intelligencey*† depicts a society largely dependent on humanoid robots who are highly skilled at various tasks but who are not considered truly intelligent because they lack human emotion. In a quest to develop the truly intelligent robot, Professor Hobby designs a small boy robot, David, to be placed with a family who will bring up the boy as their own. The chosen father is a colleague whose wife, Monica, has sunk into remorse because their natural son, Martin, has fallen into a coma and is not expected to live. Monica comes to appreciate David's virtues and presents him with Martin's old teddy bear, which becomes his faithful companion. Programmed to give and elicit love and affection, David is soon calling Monica "Mommy" and, bereft of her only natural child, she accepts and warms to the artificial boy. A medical advance heals Martin, who is resentful of David and teases him. Monica is persuaded to abandon David in a forest, where he must make his way in a harsh dystopia where vengeful humans destroy hapless robots for amusement in circuses. Eventually David makes his way home and pursues his dream not just to love a human but to be loved by one. Whatever one might think of the derivative and sentimental nature of these films, they portray a new idea of the intelligent robot. Instead of the robot as the emotionless supreme calculating engine such as Mr. Data, who will always work with human society but who will never be a true part of it, these films present the truly intelligent robot as one whose identity and capabilities are developed within the context of a social group, with all the propinquity of relationships this implies. Such an account coheres with Weizenbaum's (1976) observation, which is of profound significance for a new conceptual framework for AI:

> intelligence manifests itself only relative to specific social and cultural contexts.

A similar observation was expressed by Dreyfus (1972) and has been repeated since in thousands of undergraduate philosophy essays: "since intelligence must be situated, it cannot be separated from the rest of human life."

The two films offer another way to consider the "strong AI" versus "weak AI" controversy. Searle (1980) has distinguished "strong" and "weak" forms of AI in the following way. In

---

**Bicentennial Man*, film, directed by Chris Columbus. USA: Touchstone Pictures, 1999.

†*AI: Artificial Intelligence*, film, directed by Steven Spielberg. USA: Amblin Entertainment/Warner Brothers, 2001.

weak AI, the computer is considered to be simply a tool in the study of the mind that enables us to test psychological explanations. In strong AI, the appropriately programmed computer really is a mind, in the sense that computers given the right programs can be said to understand and have cognitive states. These two films depict robot protagonists that exhibit the "strong AI" model: they really do have minds. Many AI researchers are unwilling to adopt a "strong AI" position because they cannot imagine how a rational logic engine could be said to be or have a mind. The weak AI position on the other hand is a safe harbour that also offers the comfort of intellectual credibility. However, if one starts from another perspective, as these films do, of the computer as constructing its social reality by participation in human relationships, then the strong AI position may not seem so implausible. These films are of course pure fiction, but often our shared stories act as "thought experiments" that can change our expectations of future technology and can act to gradually replace outmoded normative assumptions with newer ones.

7. COORDINATION

The intelligent robot of the future will account for itself in negotiating the episodes that are occurring and for negotiating the meanings of particular acts within episodes. For example, within a conversation, conversants need to handle scripts that describe or prescribe how certain things should be done, and their own goals for which episodes they want to achieve or what to prevent. When understanding a story, the listener/reader needs to discern the scripts, plans and goals being enacted by the characters in the story. There has been some effort within AI research on formulating the principles of scripts and goals to address the problem of understanding simple stories and conversations.

The main elements are scripts, plans, goals and themes. Schank & Abelson (1977) start from the premise that knowledge of specific situations is stored in the human mind as scripts. A script is a structure that describes appropriate sequences of events in a particular context. Encountering a familiar situation such as entering a restaurant activates a stored script of this situation that might include sitting at a table, ordering a meal, paying for the meal and leaving the restaurant. When encountering a new situation not covered in the script, people resort to plans, the mechanisms that underlie scripts. A plan is a repository for general information that connects events that cannot be connected by the use of an available script or by standard rules of inference. The purpose of plan understanding is to find out the goals of the actors in a story. Goals (intentions underlying action) can be grouped into themes. Themes contain the background information upon which we base our predictions that an individual will have a certain goal. Themes can be categorized into role themes, interpersonal themes and life themes. Goals are needs like sleep or hunger, which in turn are explained by themes, such as success or love.

More recent work has focused on improving the knowledge structures that are extracted from the story. Dyer's (1983) thematic abstraction units are more abstract than the Schank-Abelson scripts and contain information for dealing with plans relating to the events at hand. They define abstract knowledge structures that aim to capture a deep level of understanding that can be used for story categorization. Story categorization is achieved through "cross-contextual remindings" and by recalling abstract story types, called adages. Adages provide planning information: given a particular situation, they determine which plan should be used, what its intended effect is, why the plan failed and a recovery strategy for the plan. Given a text in story form, Dyer's system constructs a knowledge dependency structure, characterizing the story in terms of plans, failed plans and attempted recovery of plans. It links common sense relationships between goals, plans and events, in order to organize and package the internal components of knowledge structures.

The computer programs implemented to test portions of these theories run into a number of problems. At the level of technical linguistics, the computer programs cannot handle quantification, anaphora and metaphor. They have been used in only very limited settings (a restaurant setting and a divorce story). No indication is given how scripts might be constructed apart from being programmed explicitly and there is no consideration given as to whether these ideas could be applied to longer narratives than the toy systems presented. But more serious concerns are to do with the implied conceptual framework. It is true that many of our everyday social activities are stereotyped, but no matter how stereotyped, going to the restaurant is not a self-contained context-free game. Most of the activity that goes on is a "background" of practices that do not relate specifically to restaurant-going, but that influence the particular sequence and detail of events. In fact, we understand going to a restaurant because it is a part of our many activities in which we interact with other people.

One telling point is that these systems are unable to deal with what Pearce (1994), in a textbook on human communication, refers to as coordination problems. Stories and conversations are located within a complex web of culturally defined intentions, anticipated responses and justifications which are constructed because participants experience emotions and feel empathy for one another. Fluent understanding of stories and taking part in a conversation call for the coordination of the participants' scripts and goals with their insight into other people's nature. Stories and conversations thereby have a "moral order," in which every culture and relationship develops sets of expectations for how our behaviours relate to the rights and responsibilities that we have as interlocutors (for example as authors, readers, conversants). When understanding a story, we place ourselves in the story and image how we would react, how particular episodes or characters would make us feel if we encountered them in our lives. Finding meaning in stories and conversations therefore requires empathy, not simply the representation of facts in a database. This point is relevant to the previous discussion on emotions, for in order to have empathy, one needs to be able to feel one's own emotions.

One possible way forward concerns the use of "accounts." An account is an explanation that attempts to change the meanings of an action. Human conversants use accounts to solve coordination problems. Empathy is essential for the account giver, because to offer an account requires an understanding that a coordination problem has occurred or is about to occur, and such problems are recognized and validated by insight into the conversant. Accounts can be variously volunteered, demanded and accepted. Following Buttney (1987) and Pearce (1994), we illustrate two types of accounts: disclaimers and excuses. Disclaimers (Hewitt & Stokes 1975), some examples of which are given in the following list, are offered before performing an action that might create a coordination problem.

(i) "Hedging" is an explicit statement that what follows is tentative. It is a signal that the actor may not be able to defend what follows, and gives an opening for an interlocutor to inform or disagree; for example, "you might think this is a crazy idea, but...."
(ii) A "sin licence" is a statement that acknowledges that what is about to be said violates the script for appropriate behaviour; for example, "you'll probably resent my saying so, but...."
(iii) An "appeal for suspended judgement" asks for an opportunity to explain the statement that is about to be made before being required to defend oneself or the statement from attack; for example, "no, let me finish my point...."

Excuses (Semin & Manstead 1983) are given after the action, for example:

(i) accidents, in which the actor denies the intention to threaten the coordinated episode, e.g. "I did not mean to do that";
(ii) evasion, in which an actor denies agency, e.g. "I cannot remember doing that";
(iii) appeals for sympathy, in which actors appeal to mitigating circumstances, e.g. "it seemed like a good idea at the time."

The point here is not whether accounts are convenient additional symbol-processing capabilities that need to be spoon-fed to AI systems. Instead, accounts need to be learned as a result of co-constructing the meaning of actions in conversation, based upon conversants who have emotional abilities and who thereby increase their competence by using forming and using accounts.

8. CONVERSATION AND NARRATIVES

The new framework for AI outlined here is built upon the social constructionist priority given to conversation and narrative. The narrative or story provides a framework that facilitates the interpretation of experience, for it is through the narratives people have about their own lives and the lives of others that they make sense of their experience. Narratives are not restricted to the form of a story with its initial complication followed by its denouement, although stories can be good examples of narratives. The idea of narrative is not restricted to written texts. Not only do narratives influence the meaning that people give to experience, they also influence which aspects of experience people select for articulation. Narratives provide not merely a reflection or mirror of life, but provide for the shaping and structure of life.

There is a social process involved in moving from the conversational use of language to the construction of the closed set of intralinguistic references that are typical of narratives. As Shotter (1993) expresses it, there is a transition from a reliance on particular meanings negotiated "on the spot" with reference to a immediate and shared context, to a reliance on a corpus of previously determined meanings—a body of interpretive resources into which the narrative user has been recruited.

It is possible that traditional AI research has misinterpreted the significance of narratives. It is an enormously difficult undertaking to write a computer program that can understand simple stories in a natural language, as such understanding seems to require a vast background knowledge. For example, the following alternatives of a simple two-sentence story

> Mary saw a dog in the window. She wanted it.

are given by Lenat & Feigenbaum (1991), and quoted by Dreyfus (1992). To understand the story we need to resolve the reference of the pronoun "it." Does "it" refer to the dog or the window? Most readers naturally assume that "it" refers to the dog. We need also to resolve the pronoun "she" which most readers refer to Mary, and not the dog, though binding "she" to "dog" would imply the extra information that the dog is female. However, consider two more alternative stories:

> Mary saw a dog in the window. She smashed it.

> Mary saw a dog in the window. She pressed her nose up against it.

In the second story, we understand that the window (not the dog) is being smashed by Mary (not the dog), perhaps in order to steal or liberate the dog. In the third story, both the dog and Mary are capable of pressing a nose against something. Most readers would conclude that Mary is pressing her own nose against the window in order to get a closer look at the dog, though it is possible that the (female) dog was eager to greet Mary and therefore pressed its nose against the window. It is unlikely that Mary has reached inside the window display and held the (female) dog's nose against the window. Yet all these interpretations are admissible by the syntax and semantics.

The standard AI approach to understanding stories like these relies on consulting facts and rules about dogs and windows and how a typical person would react. The analysis stops there, and stories like the above are usually presented as conundrums to inspire the developer of tomorrow's knowledge representation systems. Alternatively, a new conceptual framework would require the understander to imagine how it would feel in the situation, and thereby arrive at an understanding that is grounded in its experience. From an early age, children see dogs in windows and want the dog. Children understand the stories quoted above because they know what it is like to want a dog. This is related to the idea of reader-response criticism: the reading of texts is not an attempt to discover a meaning that is hidden until the necessary procedures are applied, but to construct a meaning from experience. Finding meaning in a text (story, conversation, narrative) thus requires empathy and insight into people's nature, not simply a collection of facts and rules. It is tempting to offer a traditional Schank-like solution based on thinking up a small set of facts and rules that are reckoned to determine empathy and insight into people's nature, but the lack of progress shown by this methodology does not inspire confidence that it is a productive way forward.

Another aspect of dialogue and story understanding is connected with the essential provisionality of discourse. Conventional AI treats text understanding as "finding the answer to a problem," whether the problem is resolution of pronoun anaphora or finding out who did what in a story. Real story understanding is more complex, and the so-called "hermeneutic circle" of critical theory may be relevant. Understanding and interpretation influence each other in a circular way. To understand a text (or take part in a conversation), we need to interpret it. But a certain understanding may lead us to consider a fresh interpretation. When the text is read in the light of the new interpretation, it may change our understanding of it. This may call for a revised interpretation, and so on. Such circles may occur several times during the reading and re-reading of a text, and may also account for the way in which conversations normally progress, not as an orderly sequence of question and answer, but as a tangle of starts and re-starts as both interlocutors negotiate respective hermeneutic circles to arrive at a co-constructed meaning.

Such circles might be better described as spirals, for one never visits the same locus in hermeneutic phase-space (as it were) twice. There is also no reason to restrict the number of trajectories through the space to one. AI research needs to be more attentive to the continual and developmental character of the hermeneutic circle. A system that is not committed to the hermeneutic circle cannot be said to understand. It is this capacity for continual co-evolution (in this example, of interpretation and understanding) or ontogenesis (Oyama 1985) that is characteristic of a sustaining system. Such a sustaining system is in turn characteristic of a functioning mind. The AI thought-world needs to reject "one shot" models such as finding the answer to a problem and maintaining consistency of beliefs. By contrast, ontogenesis of the type proposed here may proceed for a system in which problems and answers are not neatly defined, and consistency in a logical sense is never achievable. Thus, there needs to be an emphasis on the provisionality of thought, another hallmark of a social constructionist perspective.

Alasdair Maclntyre (1981) recognizes several diverse uses of narrative. He argues that human action is narrative in form, that human life has a fundamentally narrative shape, and that people are storytellers who position their lives and arguments within narrative histories. Communities and traditions are invested with continuity through narrative histories, and epistemological progress is marked by the construction and reconstruction of more adequate narratives. For Jerome Bruner (1986), narrative is one of the modes of cognitive functioning, a way of knowing that provides a distinctive way of ordering experience and constructing reality. The other mode is logical argument, and Bruner notes that while narrative deals with 'the vicissitudes of human intentions' and is built upon concern for the human condition, logical arguments are either conclusive or inconclusive.

The importance of narrative has also been stressed by the discursive psychology of Harré & Gillett (1994, pp. 25, 26), who are mainly concerned with higher cognitive functions and who see the mind as

> ...embedded in historical, political, cultural, social and interpersonal contexts. It is not definable in isolation. And to be a psychological being at all, one must be in possession of some minimal repertoire of the cluster of skills necessary to the management of the discourses into which one may from time to time enter.

A new conceptual framework for AI might depend on the use of narratives as a foundation for memory, learning and self-identity within the construction of meaning. The remaining points about narrative in this section are adapted from Clocksin (1998). The main difference between narratives and other structures such as knowledge representations as used in AI (Way 1991) is that narratives serve to engage the individual with the contingencies of identity and relationships with others. The individual develops or constructs identity by locating itself within the discourse—the conversations, stories, narratives—with which it engages. Thus, identity is not simply a matter of building up a store of knowledge or cognitive capabilities, but the taking up of positions within a set of discourses as they are negotiated. Therefore, behaviour involves a certain performance and production of a "self" which is the effect of a discourse, and which is always presented from a certain point of view. The fact that a developing self may claim to represent itself as a truth prior to the discourse must be seen as a phenomenon emerging from the engagement rather than as an ontological assumption.

This "taking up of a position" within a narrative may be identified at all levels: from the steady-state behavior of an electro-chemical process in tissues, to the habituation of a tissue in response to a pattern of conditioning stimuli, to the formation of a reflex, to learning a pattern of behaviour. At the highest social level it may involve the articulation, appropriation or commitment to a particular policy, a system of beliefs and values, a family group, a football team, ways of expressing one's role in society, and even beliefs about biological imperatives such as gender (Butler 1991, 1993). The ways in which one plays social games is the way in which the identity becomes, to use Butler's list of words "established, instituted, circulated and confirmed" (Butler 1991, p. 18).

Narrative serves as a memory, not only in a collective and institutional sense of telling stories to each other (memorial) but also as the foundation for the individual's memory (Middleton & Edwards 1990). Memory as narrative provides an alternative to the conventional idea of memory as a storehouse of knowledge and experience, and of remembering as a process of retrieval from the storehouse. Memory is understood not as the storage-and-retrieval manipulation of a network of entities, but rather as a particular practice within the context of a discourse. Memory is an active process in which experience can be emplotted (i.e. the lived experience is "recruited" by a prior narrative) and personified (i.e. attributed the status of a "character" in a prior narrative) in ways constrained by the usages and contexts of prior narratives. This "circular" definition is committed to the idea of memory not as storage and retrieval of facts, but as the continual remembering of our memories of our memories (sic). Memories cannot be decoupled from the narrative structure of remembering, for outside a narrative they have no meaning (Shotter 1990). Narratives can be edited, and this is particularly relevant to the question of memory and learning. As Platinga (1992, p. 45) puts it, "our memories are not inert, but undergo a process of editing, whereby they are regularized, rendered more retainable and reshaped with an eye to subsequent circumstances and events."

Learning can then be understood as means of editing or rewriting narratives. In this context, learning begins with the assumption that the stories of people's lives, as they or others have constructed them, do not sufficiently represent their lived experience. Learning then becomes a process of storying and re-storying the lives and experiences of people. In this way narrative comes to play a central role and points to the AI-related concepts of "belief revision" not as a method for guaranteeing a consistent deductive system, but as a description of what happens when re-storying takes place.

These points suggest a view of the mind that is an inversion of the conventional view taken by AI and cognitive science researchers. The conventional view assumes that behaviour arises from basic capabilities for cognition and problem solving. The emphasis seems to be on the individual mind that generates solutions to problems. The questions of emotion and interaction with others are considered as additional—possibly even unnecessary or irrelevant—complications or side-issues. By contrast, the "upside down" view sees problem solving as a practice or policy that has been constructed as a result of a basic capacity for social interaction within a cultural context, which itself is based on fundamental reciprocalities of need and desire. Therefore, further progress in AI research needs to be attentive to issues arising from the articulation of practices and policies that have been constructed though conversation and narrative.

CONCLUSION

This paper has outlined some elements of a new conceptual framework for AI that has been shaped by Weizenbaum's (1976) observation: intelligence manifests itself only relative to a matrix of social and cultural contexts. The framework has implications for how future investigations of AI will reconsider memory, reasoning, conversation, narrative and emotion.

A new conceptual framework for AI will not view intelligence as a kind of abstract puzzle solving applied by an individual to arbitrarily defined problems presented by an alien environment. It is true that certain isolated episodes of intelligent behaviour can be given an interpretation as puzzle solving, maximizing of utility, and so forth. However, these episodes gain their meaning not as the result of reasoning processes that solve various problems, but by being contextually bound within practices carried out by communities.

The fact that emotion needs to be treated in a framework for AI grows directly from the emphasis placed on conversation and narrative. Conversations and narratives construct forms of intelligibility that furnish accounts of events over several different time-scales. Individual actions gain their significance from they way in which they are found within the conversation or narrative. In the same way, emotional expressions find their meaning only when inserted into particular sequences of interaction. In effect, they are constituents of lived narratives (Gergen 1994).

There is a propinquity of participation in communities defined by historically individualized mutualities and reciprocalities of need and desire. The ways in which we participate with this matrix, and construct identities that take up positions within this matrix, are through policy, contract and institution. This participation and construction is made possible by a variety of means such as memorial, mimesis, ritual, education and therapy, all of which serve to expose and rewrite narratives. When a system is said to "understand," it is thus seen as an historical contingency constituted in part by policies articulated by the social group, rather than by the underlying cognitive nature of the individual brain.

One implication for future technology is the idea of narrative architectures, built upon a foundation which is attentive to the way that signals and symbols influence (and are influenced by) the way we as communities of individuals make sense of experience, construct our identities, and produce meaning in the world as conversants and narrative users. There is thus cause for optimism about the prospect for what John Searle (1980) called "strong AI." The characteristic of an AI system that really can be said to understand is that it can perform an account of the identity it has constructed within coordinated conversation using narratives it has appropriated from the culture and society that it shares with us. Such a system negotiates its positions to become instituted among the group, participating in the social consciousness it co-constructs with members of the group.

REFERENCES

Aitken, K. J. & Trevarthen, C. 1997 Self/other organization in human psychological development. *Dev. Psychopathol.* **9**, 653–677.

Asimov, I. 1982 The bicentennial man. In *The complete robot.* New York: Doubleday.

Asimov, I. & Silverberg, R. 1992 *The positronic man.* New York: Doubleday.

Baral, C. & Gelfond, M. 1994 Logic programming and knowledge representation. *J. Log. Program.* **19/20**, 73–148.

Bishop, C. 1995 *Neural networks for pattern recognition.* Oxford University Press.

Brooks, R. 1991*a* Intelligence without representation. *Artif. Intell.* **47**, 139–159.

Brooks, R. 1991*b* Intelligence without reason. In *Proc. 12th Int. Joint Conf. on Artificial Intelligence,* pp. 569–595. San Francisco, CA: Morgan Kaufmann.

Brooks, R. 2001 The relationship between matter and life. *Nature* 409, 409–411.

Bruner, J. 1986 *Actual minds, possible worlds.* Cambridge, MA: Harvard University Press.

Butler, J. 1991 Imitation and gender subordination. In *Inside/out: lesbian theories, gay theories* (ed. D. Fuss), pp. 13–31. New York: Routledge.

Butler, J. 1993 *Bodies that matter.* New York: Routledge.

Buttney, R. 1987 Blame-account sequences in therapy: the negotiation of relational meanings. *Semiotica* **78**, 219–247.

Chalmers, D. J. 1996 *The conscious mind.* Oxford University Press.

Churchland, P. M. 1996 *The engine of reason, the seat of the soul.* Cambridge, MA: MIT Press.

Clocksin, W. F. 1995 Knowledge representation and myth. In *Nature's imagination; the frontiers of scientific vision* (ed. J. Cornwell), pp. 190–199. Oxford University Press.

Clocksin, W. F. 1998 Artificial intelligence and human identity. In *Consciousness and human identity* (ed. J. Cornwell), pp. 101–121. Oxford University Press.

Clocksin, W. F. & Mellish, C. S. 1981 *Programming in Prolog*. Springer.

Dalziel, M. R., Wiseman, N. E., Oliver, M. A., Forrest, A. K., Clocksin, W. F. N., King, T. R., Wipfel, R. A., Warren, I., Phillips, D. J. & Chuang, P. D. 1996. Adaptive vision-based controller. US Patent 5579444.

de Silva, C. W. 2003 The role of soft computing in intelligent machines. *Phil. Trans. R. Soc. Land.* A **361**, 1749–1780.

Dixon, N. 1976 *On the psychology of military incompetence*. London: Futura.

Doyle, J. 1979 A truth maintenance system. *Artif. Intell.* **12**, 231–272.

Dreyfus, H. L. 1972 *What computers can't do*. Cambridge, MA: MIT Press.

Dreyfus, H. L. 1992 *What computers still can't do*. Cambridge, MA: MIT Press.

Dreyfus, H. L. & Dreyfus, S. E. 1986 *Mind over machine*. London: Macmillan.

Duda, R. O., Hart, P. E. & Stork, D. G. 2001 *Pattern classification*. Wiley.

Dyer, M. G. 1983 *In-depth understanding*. Cambridge, MA: MIT Press.

Edwards, P. N. 1996 *The closed world: computers and the politics of discourse in cold war America*. Cambridge, MA: MIT Press.

Feigenbaum, E. A. & McCorduck, P. 1983 *The fifth generation: artificial intelligence and Japan's computer challenge to the world*. Reading, MA: Addison-Wesley.

Firschein, O., Fischler, M. A., Coles, L. S. & Tenenbaum, J. M. 1973 Forecasting and assessing the impact of artificial intelligence on society. In *Proc. 3rd Int. Joint Conf. on Artificial Intelligence*, pp. 105–120. Stanford, CA: Stanford Research Institute.

Fogel, D. B. 2000 *Evolutionary computing: principles and practice for signal processing*. Bellingham, WA: SPIE Press.

Gergen, K. 1991 *The saturated self: dilemmas of identity in contemporary life*. New York: Basic Books.

Gergen, K. 1994 *Realities and relationships: soundings in social construction*. Cambridge, MA: Harvard University Press.

Gladwell, M. 2001 The trouble with fries. *The New Yorker*, 5 March 2001. (Available at http://www.gladwell.com/2001/2001_03_05_a_fries.htm).

Harré, R. 1992 *Social being: a theory for social psychology*. Oxford: Blackwell.

Harré, R. & Gillett, G. 1994 *The discursive mind*. London: Sage.

Hewitt, J. & Stokes, R. 1975 Disclaimers. *Am. Social. Rev.* **40**, 1–11.

Jamshidi, M. 2003 Tools for intelligent control: fuzzy controllers, neural networks and genetic algorithms. *Phil. Trans. R. Soc. Lond.* A **361**, 1781–1808.

John, R. & Birkenhead, R. 2001 *Developments in soft computing*. Heidelberg: Physica.

Johnson-Laird, P. N. 1983 *Mental models: towards a cognitive science of language, inference and consciousness*. Cambridge University Press.

Shotter, J. 1993 *Conversational realities: constructing life through language*. London: Sage.

Shotter, J. & Gergen, K. 1989 *Texts of identity*. London: Sage.

Shotter, J. & Gergen, K. 1994 Series preface. In *Constructing the social* (ed. T. R. Sarbin & J. I. Kitsuse). London: Sage.

Sluckin, A. 1999 Humans are conversational from birth: systemic therapy, developmental psychology and the artistic metaphor. *Human. Syst.* **10**, 11–23.

Sutherland, S. 1992 *Irrationality: the enemy within*. London: Penguin.

Turing, A. M. 1950 Computing machinery and intelligence. *Mind* **59**, 433–460.

Unger, J. M. 1987 *The fifth generation fallacy: why Japan is betting its future on artificial intelligence*. Oxford University Press.

Waltz, D. 1999 The importance of importance (AAAI-98 Presidential Address). *Artif. Intell.* **20**, 19–35.

Way, E. C. 1991 *Knowledge representation and metaphor*. London: Kluwer.

Weizenbaum, J. 1976 *Computer power and human reason*. London: Penguin.

Winograd, T. 1972 *Understanding natural language*. Academic.

Winograd, T. & Flores, F. 1985 *Understanding computers and cognition: a new foundation for design*. Addison-Wesley.

Wittgenstein, L. 1963 *Philosophical investigations* (transl. G. Anscombe). New York: Macmillan.

Wooldridge, M. & Jennings, N. R. 1995 Intelligent agents: theory and practice. *Knowl. Engng. Rev.* **10**, 115–152.

Zadeh, Z. 1965 Fuzzy sets. *Inform. Control* **8**, 338–353.

2.3.3 Why the Future Doesn't Need Us

BILL JOY

When this article by the chief scientist and cofounder of Sun Microsystems was published in *Wired Magazine* in April 2000, it created quite a buzz. Joy is clearly no Luddite, but in this reading, he issues a stern warning about the dangers that lie ahead for humanity if we continue down the current technological path toward creating superintelligent, self-replicating machines. The idea that our machines might one day destroy us has been a staple of science fiction books and movies, but the prospect of a race of superintelligent robots actually displacing human beings as the dominant life-form on the planet has long been dismissed as overheated fantasy.

In the autobiographical section of his discussion, Joy recounts how he became a technophile and how his own work and that of colleagues have opened up the realistic possibility of creating robots with human-level intelligence by the year 2030. When the potentials of contemporary biotechnology and nanotechnology are examined, Joy thinks we face the prospect of enabling the creation of weapons of mass destruction that could threaten the very existence of life on earth. While contemplating these dangers, Joy recommends that we approach these twenty-first-century technological possibilities with a degree of humility and that we learn from the experience of the twentieth century, particularly with respect to nuclear energy, how difficult it is to control the technological genie once it gets out of the bottle. In a personal and almost confessional style, Joy struggles with the question of what kind of future we humans want for ourselves. After having devoted a career to the pursuit of material progress through science and technology, he is now having second thoughts about whether this is the path that we should be taking.

FOCUS QUESTIONS

1. What is surprising about the long quote that Joy discusses at the beginning of this reading? Is this dystopian vision wholly unrealistic?
2. What is GNR? Why are these technologies different from the NBC technologies of the twentieth century? Explain.
3. What are the important ethical values and principles that Joy believes we need to remember as we contemplate the technological future? Does he believe that "ethical humans" will be able to control the forces that "technological humans" unleash?
4. Compare this selection with those by Hans Jonas (1.3.2), Leon Kass (2.4.2), and Michael Sandel (2.4.3). What are the common themes and issues running through these readings?

KEYWORDS

biotechnology, chaos theory, extinction, genetic engineering, Luddites, nanotechnology, nuclear weapons, relinquishment, robotics, self-replication, terrorism, weapons of mass destruction

---

Source: "Why the Future Doesn't Need Us." Copyright © August 4, 2000 by Bill Joy. This article originally appeared in *Wired Magazine*. Reprinted by permission of the author.

From the moment I became involved in the creation of new technologies, their ethical dimensions have concerned me, but it was only in the autumn of 1998 that I became anxiously aware of how great are the dangers facing us in the 21st century. I can date the onset of my unease to the day I met Ray Kurzweil, the deservedly famous inventor of the first reading machine for the blind and many other amazing things.

Ray and I were both speakers at George Gilder's Telecosm conference, and I encountered him by chance in the bar of the hotel after both our sessions were over. I was sitting with John Searle, a Berkeley philosopher who studies consciousness. While we were talking, Ray approached and a conversation began, the subject of which haunts me to this day.

I had missed Ray's talk and the subsequent panel that Ray and John had been on, and they now picked right up where they'd left off, with Ray saying that the rate of improvement of technology was going to accelerate and that we were going to become robots or fuse with robots or something like that, and John countering that this couldn't happen, because the robots couldn't be conscious.

While I had heard such talk before, I had always felt sentient robots were in the realm of science fiction. But now, from someone I respected, I was hearing a strong argument that they were a near-term possibility. I was taken aback, especially given Ray's proven ability to imagine and create the future. I already knew that new technologies like genetic engineering and nanotechnology were giving us the power to remake the world, but a realistic and imminent scenario for intelligent robots surprised me.

It's easy to get jaded about such breakthroughs. We hear in the news almost every day of some kind of technological or scientific advance. Yet this was no ordinary prediction. In the hotel bar, Ray gave me a partial preprint of his then-forthcoming book *The Age of Spiritual Machines,* which outlined a utopia he foresaw—one in which humans gained near immortality by becoming one with robotic technology. On reading it, my sense of unease only intensified; I felt sure he had to be understating the dangers, understating the probability of a bad outcome along this path.

I found myself most troubled by a passage detailing a dystopian scenario:

THE NEW LUDDITE CHALLENGE

> First let us postulate that the computer scientists succeed in developing intelligent machines that can do all things better than human beings can do them. In that case presumably all work will be done by vast, highly organized systems of machines and no human effort will be necessary. Either of two cases might occur. The machines might be permitted to make all of their own decisions without human oversight, or else human control over the machines might be retained.
>
> If the machines are permitted to make all their own decisions, we can't make any conjectures as to the results, because it is impossible to guess how such machines might behave. We only point out that the fate of the human race would be at the mercy of the machines. It might be argued that the human race would never be foolish enough to hand over all the power to the machines. But we are suggesting neither that the human race would voluntarily turn power over to the machines nor that the machines would willfully seize power. What we do suggest is that the human race might easily permit itself to drift into a position of such dependence on the machines that it would have no practical choice but to accept all of the machines' decisions. As society and the problems that face it become more and more complex and machines become more and more intelligent, people will let machines make more of their decisions for them, simply because machine-made decisions will bring better results than man-made ones. Eventually a stage may be reached at which the decisions necessary to keep the system running will be so complex that human beings will be incapable of making them intelligently. At that stage the machines will be in effective control. People won't be able to just turn the machines off, because they will be so dependent on them that turning them off would amount to suicide.
>
> On the other hand it is possible that human control over the machines may be retained. In that case the average man may have control over certain private machines of his own, such as his car or his personal computer, but control over large systems of

> machines will be in the hands of a tiny elite—just as it is today, but with two differences. Due to improved techniques the elite will have greater control over the masses; and because human work will no longer be necessary the masses will be superfluous, a useless burden on the system. If the elite is ruthless they may simply decide to exterminate the mass of humanity. If they are humane they may use propaganda or other psychological or biological techniques to reduce the birth rate until the mass of humanity becomes extinct, leaving the world to the elite. Or, if the elite consists of soft-hearted liberals, they may decide to play the role of good shepherds to the rest of the human race. They will see to it that everyone's physical needs are satisfied, that all children are raised under psychologically hygienic conditions, that everyone has a wholesome hobby to keep him busy, and that anyone who may become dissatisfied undergoes "treatment" to cure his "problem." Of course, life will be so purposeless that people will have to be biologically or psychologically engineered either to remove their need for the power process or make them "sublimate" their drive for power into some harmless hobby. These engineered human beings may be happy in such a society, but they will most certainly not be free. They will have been reduced to the status of domestic animals.[1]

In the book, you don't discover until you turn the page that the author of this passage is Theodore Kaczynski—the Unabomber. I am no apologist for Kaczynski. His bombs killed three people during a 17-year terror campaign and wounded many others. One of his bombs gravely injured my friend David Gelernter, one of the most brilliant and visionary computer scientists of our time. Like many of my colleagues, I felt that I could easily have been the Unabomber's next target.

Kaczynski's actions were murderous and, in my view, criminally insane. He is clearly a Luddite, but simply saying this does not dismiss his argument; as difficult as it is for me to acknowledge, I saw some merit in the reasoning in this single passage. I felt compelled to confront it.

Kaczynski's dystopian vision describes unintended consequences, a well-known problem with the design and use of technology, and one that is clearly related to Murphy's law—"Anything that can go wrong, will." (Actually, this is Finagle's law, which in itself shows that Finagle was right.) Our overuse of antibiotics has led to what may be the biggest such problem so far: the emergence of antibiotic-resistant and much more dangerous bacteria. Similar things happened when attempts to eliminate malarial mosquitoes using DDT caused them to acquire DDT resistance; malarial parasites likewise acquired multi-drug-resistant genes.[2]

The cause of many such surprises seems clear: The systems involved are complex, involving interaction among and feedback between many parts. Any changes to such a system will cascade in ways that are difficult to predict; this is especially true when human actions are involved.

I started showing friends the Kaczynski quote from *The Age of Spiritual Machines;* I would hand them Kurzweil's book, let them read the quote, and then watch their reaction as they discovered who had written it. At around the same time, I found Hans Moravec's book *Robot: Mere Machine to Transcendent Mind.* Moravec is one of the leaders in robotics research, and was a founder of the world's largest robotics research program, at Carnegie Mellon University. *Robot* gave me more material to try out on my friends—material surprisingly supportive of Kaczynski's argument. For example:

THE SHORT RUN (EARLY 2000s)

> Biological species almost never survive encounters with superior competitors. Ten million years ago, South and North America were separated by a sunken Panama isthmus. South America, like Australia today, was populated by marsupial mammals, including pouched equivalents of rats, deers, and tigers. When the isthmus connecting North and South America rose, it took only a few thousand years for the northern placental species, with slightly more effective metabolisms and reproductive and nervous systems, to displace and eliminate almost all the southern marsupials.
>
> In a completely free marketplace, superior robots would surely affect humans as North American placental affected South American marsupials (and as humans have affected countless species). Robotic industries would compete vigorously among themselves for matter, energy, and space, incidentally

> driving their price beyond human reach. Unable to afford the necessities of life, biological humans would be squeezed out of existence.
>
> There is probably some breathing room, because we do not live in a completely free marketplace. Government coerces nonmarket behavior, especially by collecting taxes. Judiciously applied, governmental coercion could support human populations in high style on the fruits of robot labor, perhaps for a long while.

A textbook dystopia—and Moravec is just getting wound up. He goes on to discuss how our main job in the 21st century will be "ensuring continued cooperation from the robot industries" by passing laws decreeing that they be "nice,"[3] and to describe how seriously dangerous a human can be "once transformed into an unbounded superintelligent robot." Moravec's view is that the robots will eventually succeed us—that humans clearly face extinction.

I decided it was time to talk to my friend Danny Hillis. Danny became famous as the cofounder of Thinking Machines Corporation, which built a very powerful parallel supercomputer. Despite my current job title of Chief Scientist at Sun Microsystems, I am more a computer architect than a scientist, and I respect Danny's knowledge of the information and physical sciences more than that of any other single person I know. Danny is also a highly regarded futurist who thinks long-term—four years ago he started the Long Now Foundation, which is building a clock designed to last 10,000 years, in an attempt to draw attention to the pitifully short attention span of our society....

So I flew to Los Angeles for the express purpose of having dinner with Danny and his wife, Pati. I went through my now-familiar routine, trotting out the ideas and passages that I found so disturbing. Danny's answer—directed specifically at Kurzweil's scenario of humans merging with robots—came swiftly, and quite surprised me. He said, simply, that the changes would come gradually, and that we would get used to them.

But I guess I wasn't totally surprised. I had seen a quote from Danny in Kurzweil's book in which he said, "I'm as fond of my body as anyone, but if I can be 200 with a body of silicon, I'll take it." It seemed that he was at peace with this process and its attendant risks, while I was not.

While talking and thinking about Kurzweil, Kaczynski, and Moravec, I suddenly remembered a novel I had read almost 20 years ago—*The White Plague,* by Frank Herbert—in which a molecular biologist is driven insane by the senseless murder of his family. To seek revenge he constructs and disseminates a new and highly contagious plague that kills widely but selectively. (We're lucky Kaczynski was a mathematician, not a molecular biologist.) I was also reminded of the Borg of *Star Trek,* a hive of partly biological, partly robotic creatures with a strong destructive streak. Borg-like disasters are a staple of science fiction, so why hadn't I been more concerned about such robotic dystopias earlier? Why weren't other people more concerned about these nightmarish scenarios?

Part of the answer certainly lies in our attitude toward the new—in our bias toward instant familiarity and unquestioning acceptance. Accustomed to living with almost routine scientific breakthroughs, we have yet to come to terms with the fact that the most compelling 21st-century technologies—robotics, genetic engineering, and nanotechnology—pose a different threat than the technologies that have come before. Specifically, robots, engineered organisms, and nanobots share a dangerous amplifying factor: They can self-replicate. A bomb is blown up only once—but one bot can become many, and quickly get out of control.

Much of my work over the past 25 years has been on computer networking, where the sending and receiving of messages creates the opportunity for out-of-control replication. But while replication in a computer or a computer network can be a nuisance, at worst it disables a machine or takes down a network or network service. Uncontrolled self-replication in these newer technologies runs a much greater risk: a risk of substantial damage in the physical world.

Each of these technologies also offers untold promise: The vision of near immortality that Kurzweil sees in his robot dreams drives us forward; genetic engineering may soon provide treatments, if not outright cures, for most diseases; and nanotechnology and nanomedicine can address yet more ills. Together they could significantly extend our average life span and improve the quality of our lives. Yet, with each of these technologies, a sequence of small, individually sensible advances leads to an accumulation of great power and, concomitantly, great danger.

What was different in the 20th century? Certainly, the technologies underlying the weapons of mass destruction (WMD)—nuclear, biological, and chemical (NBC)—were powerful, and the weapons an enormous threat. But building nuclear weapons required, at least for a time, access to both rare—indeed, effectively unavailable—raw materials and highly protected information; biological and chemical weapons programs also tended to require large-scale activities.

The 21st-century technologies—genetics, nanotechnology, and robotics (GNR)—are so powerful that they can spawn whole new classes of accidents and abuses. Most dangerously, for the first time, these accidents and abuses are widely within the reach of individuals or small groups. They will not require large facilities or rare raw materials. Knowledge alone will enable the use of them.

Thus we have the possibility not just of weapons of mass destruction but of knowledge-enabled mass destruction (KMD), this destructiveness hugely amplified by the power of self-replication.

I think it is no exaggeration to say we are on the cusp of the further perfection of extreme evil, an evil whose possibility spreads well beyond that which weapons of mass destruction bequeathed to the nation-states, on to a surprising and terrible empowerment of extreme individuals.

Nothing about the way I got involved with computers suggested to me that I was going to be facing these kinds of issues.

My life has been driven by a deep need to ask questions and find answers. When I was 3, I was already reading, so my father took me to the elementary school, where I sat on the principal's lap and read him a story. I started school early, later skipped a grade, and escaped into books—I was incredibly motivated to learn. I asked lots of questions, often driving adults to distraction.

As a teenager I was very interested in science and technology. I wanted to be a ham radio operator but didn't have the money to buy the equipment. Ham radio was the Internet of its time: very addictive, and quite solitary. Money issues aside, my mother put her foot down—I was not to be a ham; I was antisocial enough already.

I may not have had many close friends, but I was awash in ideas. By high school, I had discovered the great science fiction writers. I remember especially Heinlein's *Have Spacesuit Will Travel* and Asimov's *I, Robot,* with its Three Laws of Robotics. I was enchanted by the descriptions of space travel, and wanted to have a telescope to look at the stars; since I had no money to buy or make one, I checked books on telescope-making out of the library and read about making them instead. I soared in my imagination.

Thursday nights my parents went bowling, and we kids stayed home alone. It was the night of Gene Roddenberry's original *Star Trek,* and the program made a big impression on me. I came to accept its notion that humans had a future in space, Western-style, with big heroes and adventures. Roddenberry's vision of the centuries to come was one with strong moral values, embodied in codes like the Prime Directive: to not interfere in the development of less technologically advanced civilizations. This had an incredible appeal to me; ethical humans, not robots, dominated this future, and I took Roddenberry's dream as part of my own.

I excelled in mathematics in high school, and when I went to the University of Michigan as an undergraduate engineering student I took the advanced curriculum of the mathematics majors. Solving math problems was an exciting challenge, but when I discovered computers I found something much more interesting: a machine into which you could put a program that attempted to solve a problem, after which the machine quickly checked the solution. The computer had a clear notion of correct and incorrect, true and false. Were my ideas correct? The machine could tell me. This was very seductive.

I was lucky enough to get a job programming early supercomputers and discovered the amazing power of large machines to numerically simulate advanced designs. When I went to graduate school at UC Berkeley in the mid-1970s, I started staying up late, often all night, inventing new worlds inside the machines. Solving problems. Writing the code that argued so strongly to be written.

In *The Agony and the Ecstasy*, Irving Stone's biographical novel of Michelangelo, Stone described vividly how Michelangelo released the statues from the stone, "breaking the marble spell," carving from the images in his mind.[4] In my most ecstatic moments, the software in the computer emerged in the same way. Once I had imagined it in my mind I felt that it was already there in the machine, waiting to be released. Staying up all night seemed a small price to pay to free it—to give the ideas concrete form.

After a few years at Berkeley I started to send out some of the software I had written—an instructional Pascal system, Unix utilities, and a text editor called vi (which is still, to my surprise, widely used more than 20 years later)—to others who had similar small PDP-11 and VAX minicomputers. These adventures in software eventually turned into the Berkeley version of the Unix operating system, which became a personal "success disaster"—so many people wanted it that I never finished my PhD. Instead I got a job working for Darpa putting Berkeley Unix on the Internet and fixing it to be reliable and to run large research applications well. This was all great fun and very rewarding. And, frankly, I saw no robots here, or anywhere near.

Still, by the early 1980s, I was drowning. The Unix releases were very successful, and my little project of one soon had money and some staff, but the problem at Berkeley was always office space rather than money—there wasn't room for the help the project needed, so when the other founders of Sun Microsystems showed up I jumped at the chance to join them. At Sun, the long hours continued into the early days of workstations and personal computers, and I have enjoyed participating in the creation of advanced microprocessor technologies and Internet technologies such as Java and Jini.

From all this, I trust it is clear that I am not a Luddite. I have always, rather, had a strong belief in the value of the scientific search for truth and in the ability of great engineering to bring material progress. The Industrial Revolution has immeasurably improved everyone's life over the last couple hundred years, and I always expected my career to involve the building of worthwhile solutions to real problems, one problem at a time.

I have not been disappointed. My work has had more impact than I had ever hoped for and has been more widely used than I could have reasonably expected. I have spent the last 20 years still trying to figure out how to make computers as reliable as I want them to be (they are not nearly there yet) and how to make them simple to use (a goal that has met with even less relative success). Despite some progress, the problems that remain seem even more daunting.

But while I was aware of the moral dilemmas surrounding technology's consequences in fields like weapons research, I did not expect that I would confront such issues in my own field, or at least not so soon.

Perhaps it is always hard to see the bigger impact while you are in the vortex of a change. Failing to understand the consequences of our inventions while we are in the rapture of discovery and innovation seems to be a common fault of scientists and technologists; we have long been driven by the overarching desire to know that is the nature of science's quest, not stopping to notice that the progress to newer and more powerful technologies can take on a life of its own.

I have long realized that the big advances in information technology come not from the work of computer scientists, computer architects, or electrical engineers, but from that of physical scientists. The physicists Stephen Wolfram and Brosl Hasslacher introduced me, in the early 1980s, to chaos theory and nonlinear systems. In the 1990s, I learned about complex systems from conversations with Danny Hillis, the biologist Stuart Kauffman, the Nobel-laureate physicist Murray Gell-Mann, and others. Most recently, Hasslacher and the electrical engineer and device physicist Mark Reed have been giving me insight into the incredible possibilities of molecular electronics.

In my own work, as codesigner of three microprocessor architectures—SPARC, picoJava, and MAJC—and as the designer of several implementations thereof, I've been afforded a deep and firsthand acquaintance with Moore's law. For decades, Moore's law has correctly predicted the exponential rate of improvement of semiconductor technology. Until last year I believed that the rate of advances predicted by Moore's law might continue only until roughly 2010, when some physical limits would begin to be reached. It was not obvious to me that a new technology would arrive in time to keep performance advancing smoothly.

But because of the recent rapid and radical progress in molecular electronics—where individual atoms and molecules replace lithographically drawn transistors—and related nanoscale technologies, we should be able to meet or exceed the Moore's law rate of progress for another 30 years. By 2030, we are likely to be able to build machines, in quantity, a million times as powerful as the personal computers of today—sufficient to implement the dreams of Kurzweil and Moravec.

As this enormous computing power is combined with the manipulative advances of the physical sciences and the new, deep understandings in genetics, enormous transformative power is being unleashed. These combinations open up the opportunity to completely redesign the world, for better or worse: The replicating and evolving processes that have been confined to the natural world are about to become realms of human endeavor.

In designing software and microprocessors, I have never had the feeling that I was designing an intelligent machine. The software and hardware is so fragile and the capabilities of the machine to "think" so clearly absent that, even as a possibility, this has always seemed very far in the future.

But now, with the prospect of human-level computing power in about 30 years, a new idea suggests itself: that I may be working to create tools which will enable the construction of the technology that may replace our species. How do I feel about this? Very uncomfortable. Having struggled my entire career to build reliable software systems, it seems to me more than likely that this future will not work out as well as some people may imagine. My personal experience suggests we tend to overestimate our design abilities.

Given the incredible power of these new technologies, shouldn't we be asking how we can best coexist with them? And if our own extinction is a likely, or even possible, outcome of our technological development, shouldn't we proceed with great caution?

The dream of robotics is, first, that intelligent machines can do our work for us, allowing us lives of leisure, restoring us to Eden. Yet in his history of such ideas, *Darwin Among the Machines,* George Dyson warns: "In the game of life and evolution there are three players at the table: human beings, nature, and machines. I am firmly on the side of nature. But nature, I suspect, is on the side of the machines." As we have seen, Moravec agrees, believing we may well not survive the encounter with the superior robot species.

How soon could such an intelligent robot be built? The coming advances in computing power seem to make it possible by 2030. And once an intelligent robot exists, it is only a small step to a robot species—to an intelligent robot that can make evolved copies of itself.

A second dream of robotics is that we will gradually replace ourselves with our robotic technology, achieving near immortality by downloading our consciousnesses; it is this process that Danny Hillis thinks we will gradually get used to and that Ray Kurzweil elegantly details in *The Age of Spiritual Machines*....

But if we are downloaded into our technology, what are the chances that we will thereafter be ourselves or even human? It seems to me far more likely that a robotic existence would not be like a human one in any sense that we understand, that the robots would in no sense be our children, that on this path our humanity may well be lost.

Genetic engineering promises to revolutionize agriculture by increasing crop yields while reducing the use of pesticides; to create tens of thousands of novel species of bacteria, plants, viruses, and animals; to replace reproduction, or supplement it, with cloning; to create cures for many diseases, increasing our life span and our quality of life; and much, much more. We now know with certainty that these profound changes in the biological sciences are imminent and will challenge all our notions of what life is.

Technologies such as human cloning have in particular raised our awareness of the profound ethical and moral issues we face. If, for example, we were to reengineer ourselves into several separate and unequal species using the power of genetic engineering, then we would threaten the notion of equality that is the very cornerstone of our democracy.

Given the incredible power of genetic engineering, it's no surprise that there are significant safety issues in its use. My friend Amory Lovins recently cowrote, along with Hunter Lovins, an editorial that provides an ecological view of some of these dangers. Among their concerns: that "the new botany aligns the development of plants with their economic, not evolutionary, success."... Amory's long career has been focused on energy and resource efficiency by taking a whole-system view of human-made systems; such a whole-system view often finds simple, smart solutions to otherwise seemingly difficult problems, and is usefully applied here as well.

After reading the Lovins' editorial, I saw an op-ed by Gregg Easterbrook in *The New York Times* (November 19, 1999) about genetically engineered crops, under the headline: "Food for the Future: Someday, rice will have built-in vitamin A. Unless the Luddites win."

Are Amory and Hunter Lovins Luddites? Certainly not. I believe we all would agree that golden rice, with its built-in vitamin A, is probably a good thing, if developed with proper care and respect for the likely dangers in moving genes across species boundaries.

Awareness of the dangers inherent in genetic engineering is beginning to grow, as reflected in the Lovins' editorial. The general public is aware of, and uneasy about, genetically modified foods, and seems to be rejecting the notion that such foods should be permitted to be unlabeled.

But genetic engineering technology is already very far along. As the Lovins note, the USDA has already approved about 50 genetically engineered crops for unlimited release; more than half of the world's soybeans and a third of its corn now contain genes spliced in from other forms of life.

While there are many important issues here, my own major concern with genetic engineering is narrower: that it gives the power—whether militarily, accidentally, or in a deliberate terrorist act—to create a White Plague.

The many wonders of nanotechnology were first imagined by the Nobel-laureate physicist Richard Feynman in a speech he gave in 1959, subsequently published under the title "There's Plenty of Room at the Bottom." The book that made a big impression on me, in the mid-'80s, was Eric Drexler's *Engines of Creation,* in which he described beautifully how manipulation of matter at the atomic level could create a Utopian future of abundance, where just about everything could be made cheaply, and almost any imaginable disease or physical problem could be solved using nanotechnology and artificial intelligences.

A subsequent book, *Unbounding the Future: The Nanotechnology Revolution,* which Drexler cowrote, imagines some of the changes that might take place in a world where we had molecular-level "assemblers." Assemblers could make possible incredibly low-cost solar power, cures for cancer and the common cold by augmentation of the human immune system, essentially complete cleanup of the environment, incredibly inexpensive pocket supercomputers—in fact, any product would be manufacturable by assemblers at a cost no greater than that of wood—spaceflight more accessible than transoceanic travel today, and restoration of extinct species.

I remember feeling good about nanotechnology after reading *Engines of Creation.* As a technologist, it gave me a sense of calm—that is, nanotechnology showed us that incredible progress was possible, and indeed perhaps inevitable. If nanotechnology was our future, then I didn't feel pressed to solve so many problems in the present. I would get to Drexler's Utopian future in due time; I might as well enjoy life more in the here and now. It didn't make sense, given his vision, to stay up all night, all the time.

Drexler's vision also led to a lot of good fun. I would occasionally get to describe the wonders of nanotechnology to others who had not heard of it. After teasing them with all the things Drexler described I would give a homework assignment of my own: "Use nanotechnology to create a vampire; for extra credit create an antidote."

With these wonders came clear dangers, of which I was acutely aware. As I said at a nanotechnology conference in 1989, "We can't simply do our science and not worry about these ethical issues."[5] But my subsequent conversations with physicists convinced me that nanotechnology might not even work—or, at least, it wouldn't work anytime soon. Shortly thereafter I moved to Colorado, to a skunk works I had set up, and the focus of my work shifted to software for the Internet, specifically on ideas that became Java and Jini.

Then, last summer, Brosl Hasslacher told me that nanoscale molecular electronics was now practical. This was *new* news, at least to me, and I think to many people—and it radically changed my opinion about nanotechnology. It sent me back to *Engines of Creation*. Rereading Drexler's work after more than 10 years, I was dismayed to realize how little I had remembered of its lengthy section called "Dangers and Hopes," including a discussion of how nanotechnologies can become "engines of destruction." Indeed, in my rereading of this cautionary material today, I am struck by how naive some of Drexler's safeguard proposals seem, and how much greater I judge the dangers to be now than even he seemed to then. (Having anticipated and described many technical and political problems with nanotechnology, Drexler started the Foresight Institute in the late 1980s "to help prepare society for anticipated advanced technologies"—most important, nanotechnology.)

The enabling breakthrough to assemblers seems quite likely within the next 20 years. Molecular electronics—the new subfield of nanotechnology where individual molecules are circuit elements—should mature quickly and become enormously lucrative within this decade, causing a large incremental investment in all nanotechnologies.

Unfortunately, as with nuclear technology, it is far easier to create destructive uses for nanotechnology than constructive ones. Nanotechnology has clear military and terrorist uses, and you need not be suicidal to release a massively destructive nanotechnological device—such devices can be built to be selectively destructive, affecting, for example, only a certain geographical area or a group of people who are genetically distinct.

An immediate consequence of the Faustian bargain in obtaining the great power of nanotechnology is that we run a grave risk—the risk that we might destroy the biosphere on which all life depends.

As Drexler explained:

> "Plants" with "leaves" no more efficient than today's solar cells could out-compete real plants, crowding the biosphere with an inedible foliage. Tough omnivorous "bacteria" could out-compete real bacteria. They could spread like blowing pollen, replicate swiftly, and reduce the biosphere to dust in a matter of days. Dangerous replicators could easily be too tough, small, and rapidly spreading to stop—at least if we make no preparation. We have trouble enough controlling viruses and fruit flies.
>
> Among the cognoscenti of nanotechnology, this threat has become known as the "gray goo problem." Though masses of uncontrolled replicators need not be gray or gooey, the term "gray goo" emphasizes that replicators able to obliterate life might be less inspiring than a single species of crabgrass. They might be superior in an evolutionary sense, but this need not make them valuable.
>
> The gray goo threat makes one thing perfectly clear: We cannot afford certain kinds of accidents with replicating assemblers.

Gray goo would surely be a depressing ending to our human adventure on Earth, far worse than mere fire or ice, and one that could stem from a simple laboratory accident.[6] Oops.

It is most of all the power of destructive self-replication in genetics, nanotechnology, and robotics (GNR) that should give us pause. Self-replication is the modus operandi of genetic engineering, which uses the machinery of the cell to replicate its designs, and the prime danger underlying gray goo in nanotechnology. Stories of run-amok robots like the Borg, replicating or mutating to escape from the ethical constraints imposed on them by their creators, are well established in our science fiction books and movies. It is even possible that self-replication may be more fundamental than we thought, and hence harder—or even impossible—to control. A recent article by Stuart Kauffman in *Nature* titled "Self-Replication: Even Peptides

Do It" discusses the discovery that a 32-amino-acid peptide can "autocatalyse its own synthesis." We don't know how widespread this ability is, but Kauffman notes that it may hint at "a route to self-reproducing molecular systems on a basis far wider than Watson-Crick base-pairing."[7]

In truth, we have had in hand for years clear warnings of the dangers inherent in widespread knowledge of GNR technologies—of the possibility of knowledge alone enabling mass destruction. But these warnings haven't been widely publicized; the public discussions have been clearly inadequate. There is no profit in publicizing the dangers.

The nuclear, biological, and chemical (NBC) technologies used in 20th-century weapons of mass destruction were and are largely military, developed in government laboratories. In sharp contrast, the 21st-century GNR technologies have clear commercial uses and are being developed almost exclusively by corporate enterprises. In this age of triumphant commercialism, technology—with science as its handmaiden—is delivering a series of almost magical inventions that are the most phenomenally lucrative ever seen. We are aggressively pursuing the promises of these new technologies within the now-unchallenged system of global capitalism and its manifold financial incentives and competitive pressures.

This is the first moment in the history of our planet when any species, by its own voluntary actions, has become a danger to itself—as well as to vast numbers of others.

> It might be a familiar progression, transpiring on many worlds—a planet, newly formed, placidly revolves around its star; life slowly forms; a kaleidoscopic procession of creatures evolves; intelligence emerges which, at least up to a point, confers enormous survival value; and then technology is invented. It dawns on them that there are such things as laws of Nature, that these laws can be revealed by experiment, and that knowledge of these laws can be made both to save and to take lives, both on unprecedented scales. Science, they recognize, grants immense powers. In a flash, they create world-altering contrivances. Some planetary civilizations see their way through, place limits on what may and what must not be done, and safely pass through the time of perils. Others, not so lucky or so prudent, perish.

That is Carl Sagan, writing in 1994, in *Pale Blue Dot,* a book describing his vision of the human future in space. I am only now realizing how deep his insight was, and how sorely I miss, and will miss, his voice. For all its eloquence, Sagan's contribution was not least that of simple common sense—an attribute that, along with humility, many of the leading advocates of the 21st-century technologies seem to lack.

I remember from my childhood that my grandmother was strongly against the overuse of antibiotics. She had worked since before the first World War as a nurse and had a common-sense attitude that taking antibiotics, unless they were absolutely necessary, was bad for you.

It is not that she was an enemy of progress. She saw much progress in an almost 70-year nursing career; my grandfather, a diabetic, benefited greatly from the improved treatments that became available in his lifetime. But she, like many level-headed people, would probably think it greatly arrogant for us, now, to be designing a robotic "replacement species," when we obviously have so much trouble making relatively simple things work, and so much trouble managing—or even understanding—ourselves.

I realize now that she had an awareness of the nature of the order of life, and of the necessity of living with and respecting that order. With this respect comes a necessary humility that we, with our early-21st-century chutzpah, lack at our peril. The commonsense view, grounded in this respect, is often right, in advance of the scientific evidence. The clear fragility and inefficiencies of the human-made systems we have built should give us all pause; the fragility of the systems I have worked on certainly humbles me.

We should have learned a lesson from the making of the first atomic bomb and the resulting arms race. We didn't do well then, and the parallels to our current situation are troubling.

The effort to build the first atomic bomb was led by the brilliant physicist J. Robert Oppenheimer. Oppenheimer was not naturally interested in politics but became painfully aware of what he perceived as the grave threat to Western civilization from the Third Reich, a threat surely grave because of the possibility that Hitler might obtain nuclear weapons. Energized by this concern, he brought his strong intellect, passion for physics, and charismatic leadership skills to Los Alamos and led a rapid and successful effort by an incredible collection of great minds to quickly invent the bomb.

What is striking is how this effort continued so naturally after the initial impetus was removed. In a meeting shortly after V-E Day with some physicists who felt that perhaps the effort should stop, Oppenheimer argued to continue. His stated reason seems a bit strange: not because of the fear of large casualties from an invasion of Japan, but because the United Nations, which was soon to be formed, should have foreknowledge of atomic weapons. A more likely reason the project continued is the momentum that had built up—the first atomic test, Trinity, was nearly at hand.

We know that in preparing this first atomic test the physicists proceeded despite a large number of possible dangers. They were initially worried, based on a calculation by Edward Teller, that an atomic explosion might set fire to the atmosphere. A revised calculation reduced the danger of destroying the world to a three-in-a-million chance. (Teller says he was later able to dismiss the prospect of atmospheric ignition entirely.) Oppenheimer, though, was sufficiently concerned about the result of Trinity that he arranged for a possible evacuation of the southwest part of the state of New Mexico. And, of course, there was the clear danger of starting a nuclear arms race.

Within a month of that first, successful test, two atomic bombs destroyed Hiroshima and Nagasaki. Some scientists had suggested that the bomb simply be demonstrated, rather than dropped on Japanese cities—saying that this would greatly improve the chances for arms control after the war—but to no avail. With the tragedy of Pearl Harbor still fresh in Americans' minds, it would have been very difficult for President Truman to order a demonstration of the weapons rather than use them as he did—the desire to quickly end the war and save the lives that would have been lost in any invasion of Japan was very strong. Yet the overriding truth was probably very simple: As the physicist Freeman Dyson later said, "The reason that it was dropped was just that nobody had the courage or the foresight to say no."

It's important to realize how shocked the physicists were in the aftermath of the bombing of Hiroshima, on August 6, 1945. They describe a series of waves of emotion: first, a sense of fulfillment that the bomb worked, then horror at all the people that had been killed, and then a convincing feeling that on no account should another bomb be dropped. Yet of course another bomb was dropped, on Nagasaki, only three days after the bombing of Hiroshima.

In November 1945, three months after the atomic bombings, Oppenheimer stood firmly behind the scientific attitude, saying, "It is not possible to be a scientist unless you believe that the knowledge of the world, and the power which this gives, is a thing which is of intrinsic value to humanity, and that you are using it to help in the spread of knowledge and are willing to take the consequences."

Oppenheimer went on to work, with others, on the Acheson-Lilienthal report, which, as Richard Rhodes says in his recent book *Visions of Technology,* "found a way to prevent a clandestine nuclear arms race without resorting to armed world government"; their suggestion was a form of relinquishment of nuclear weapons work by nation-states to an international agency.

This proposal led to the Baruch Plan, which was submitted to the United Nations in June 1946 but never adopted (perhaps because, as Rhodes suggests, Bernard Baruch had "insisted on burdening the plan with conventional sanctions," thereby inevitably dooming it, even though it would "almost certainly have been rejected by Stalinist Russia anyway"). Other efforts to promote sensible steps toward internationalizing nuclear power to prevent an arms race ran afoul either of US politics and internal distrust, or distrust by the Soviets. The opportunity to avoid the arms race was lost, and very quickly.

Two years later, in 1948, Oppenheimer seemed to have reached another stage in his thinking, saying, "In some sort of crude sense which no vulgarity, no humor, no overstatement can quite extinguish, the physicists have known sin; and this is a knowledge they cannot lose."

In 1949, the Soviets exploded an atom bomb. By 1955, both the US and the Soviet Union had tested hydrogen bombs suitable for delivery by aircraft. And so the nuclear arms race began.

Nearly 20 years ago, in the documentary *The Day After Trinity,* Freeman Dyson summarized the scientific attitudes that brought us to the nuclear precipice:

> "I have felt it myself. The glitter of nuclear weapons. It is irresistible if you come to them as a scientist. To feel it's there in your hands, to release this energy that fuels the stars, to let it do your bidding. To perform these miracles, to lift a million tons of rock into the sky. It is something that gives people an illusion of illimitable power, and it is, in some ways, responsible for all our troubles—this, what you might call technical arrogance, that overcomes people when they see what they can do with their minds."[8]

Now, as then, we are creators of new technologies and stars of the imagined future, driven—this time by great financial rewards and global competition—despite the clear dangers, hardly evaluating what it may be like to try to live in a world that is the realistic outcome of what we are creating and imagining.

In 1947, *The Bulletin of the Atomic Scientists* began putting a Doomsday Clock on its cover. For more than 50 years, it has shown an estimate of the relative nuclear danger we have faced, reflecting the changing international conditions. The hands on the clock have moved 15 times and today, standing at nine minutes to midnight, reflect continuing and real danger from nuclear weapons. The recent addition of India and Pakistan to the list of nuclear powers has increased the threat of failure of the nonproliferation goal, and this danger was reflected by moving the hands closer to midnight in 1998.

In our time, how much danger do we face, not just from nuclear weapons, but from all of these technologies? How high are the extinction risks?

The philosopher John Leslie has studied this question and concluded that the risk of human extinction is at least 30 percent,[9] while Ray Kurzweil believes we have "a better than even chance of making it through," with the caveat that he has "always been accused of being an optimist." Not only are these estimates not encouraging, but they do not include the probability of many horrid outcomes that lie short of extinction.

Faced with such assessments, some serious people are already suggesting that we simply move beyond Earth as quickly as possible. We would colonize the galaxy using von Neumann probes, which hop from star system to star system, replicating as they go. This step will almost certainly be necessary 5 billion years from now (or sooner if our solar system is disastrously impacted by the impending collision of our galaxy with the Andromeda galaxy within the next 3 billion years), but if we take Kurzweil and Moravec at their word it might be necessary by the middle of this century.

What are the moral implications here? If we must move beyond Earth this quickly in order for the species to survive, who accepts the responsibility for the fate of those (most of us, after all) who are left behind? And even if we scatter to the stars, isn't it likely that we may take our problems with us or find, later, that they have followed us? The fate of our species on Earth and our fate in the galaxy seem inextricably linked.

Another idea is to erect a series of shields to defend against each of the dangerous technologies. The Strategic Defense Initiative, proposed by the Reagan administration, was an attempt to design such a shield against the threat of a nuclear attack from the Soviet Union. But as Arthur C. Clarke, who was privy to discussions about the project, observed: "Though it might be possible, at vast expense, to construct local defense systems that would 'only' let through a few percent of ballistic missiles, the much touted idea of a national umbrella was nonsense. Luis Alvarez, perhaps the greatest experimental physicist of this century, remarked to me that the advocates of such schemes were 'very bright guys with no common sense.' "

Clarke continued: "Looking into my often cloudy crystal ball, I suspect that a total defense might indeed be possible in a century or so. But the technology involved would produce, as a byproduct, weapons so terrible that no one would bother with anything as primitive as ballistic missiles."[10]

In *Engines of Creation,* Eric Drexler proposed that we build an active nanotechnological shield—a form of immune system for the biosphere—to defend against dangerous replicators of all kinds that might escape from laboratories or otherwise be maliciously created. But the shield he proposed would itself be extremely dangerous—nothing could prevent it from developing autoimmune problems and attacking the biosphere itself.[11]

Similar difficulties apply to the construction of shields against robotics and genetic engineering. These technologies are too powerful to be shielded against in the time frame of interest; even if it were possible to implement defensive shields, the side effects of their development would be at least as dangerous as the technologies we are trying to protect against.

These possibilities are all thus either undesirable or unachievable or both. The only realistic alternative I see is relinquishment: to limit development of the technologies that are too dangerous, by limiting our pursuit of certain kinds of knowledge.

Yes, I know, knowledge is good, as is the search for new truths. We have been seeking knowledge since ancient times. Aristotle opened his Metaphysics with the simple statement: "All men by nature desire to know." We have, as a bedrock value in our society, long agreed on the value of open access to information, and recognize the problems that arise with attempts to restrict access to and development of knowledge. In recent times, we have come to revere scientific knowledge.

But despite the strong historical precedents, if open access to and unlimited development of knowledge henceforth puts us all in clear danger of extinction, then common sense demands that we reexamine even these basic, long-held beliefs.

It was Nietzsche who warned us, at the end of the 19th century, not only that God is dead but that "faith in science, which after all exists undeniably, cannot owe its origin to a calculus of utility; it must have originated *in spite* of the fact that the disutility and dangerousness of the 'will to truth,' of 'truth at any price' is proved to it constantly." It is this further danger that we now fully face—the consequences of our truth-seeking. The truth that science seeks can certainly be considered a dangerous substitute for God if it is likely to lead to our extinction.

If we could agree, as a species, what we wanted, where we were headed, and why, then we would make our future much less dangerous—then we might understand what we can and should relinquish. Otherwise, we can easily imagine an arms race developing over GNR technologies, as it did with the NBC technologies in the 20th century. This is perhaps the greatest risk, for once such a race begins, it's very hard to end it. This time—unlike during the Manhattan Project—we aren't in a war, facing an implacable enemy that is threatening our civilization; we are driven, instead, by our habits, our desires, our economic system, and our competitive need to know.

I believe that we all wish our course could be determined by our collective values, ethics, and morals. If we had gained more collective wisdom over the past few thousand years, then a dialogue to this end would be more practical, and the incredible powers we are about to unleash would not be nearly so troubling.

One would think we might be driven to such a dialogue by our instinct for self-preservation. Individuals clearly have this desire, yet as a species our behavior seems to be not in our favor. In dealing with the nuclear threat, we often spoke dishonestly to ourselves and to each other, thereby greatly increasing the risks. Whether this was politically motivated, or because we chose not to think ahead, or because when faced with such grave threats we acted irrationally out of fear, I do not know, but it does not bode well.

The new Pandora's boxes of genetics, nanotechnology, and robotics are almost open, yet we seem hardly to have noticed. Ideas can't be put back in a box; unlike uranium or plutonium, they don't need to be mined and refined, and they can be freely copied. Once they are out, they are out. Churchill remarked, in a famous left-handed compliment, that the American people and their leaders "invariably do the right thing, after they have examined every other alternative." In this case, however, we must act more presciently, as to do the right thing only at last may be to lose the chance to do it at all.

As Thoreau said, "We do not ride on the railroad; it rides upon us"; and this is what we must fight, in our time. The question is, indeed, Which is to be master? Will we survive our technologies?

We are being propelled into this new century with no plan, no control, no brakes. Have we already gone too far down the path to alter course? I don't believe so, but we aren't trying yet, and the last chance to assert control—the fail-safe point—is rapidly approaching. We have our first pet robots, as well as commercially available genetic engineering techniques, and our nanoscale techniques are advancing rapidly. While the development of these technologies proceeds through a number of steps, it isn't necessarily the case—as happened in the Manhattan Project and the Trinity test—that the last step in proving a technology is large and hard. The breakthrough to wild self-replication in robotics, genetic engineering, or nanotechnology could come suddenly, reprising the surprise we felt when we learned of the cloning of a mammal.

And yet I believe we do have a strong and solid basis for hope. Our attempts to deal with weapons of mass destruction in the last century provide a shining example of relinquishment for us to consider: the unilateral US abandonment, without preconditions, of the development of biological weapons. This relinquishment stemmed from the realization that while it would take an enormous effort to create these terrible weapons, they could from then on easily be duplicated and fall into the hands of rogue nations or terrorist groups.

The clear conclusion was that we would create additional threats to ourselves by pursuing these weapons, and that we would be more secure if we did not pursue them. We have embodied our relinquishment of biological and chemical weapons in the 1972 Biological Weapons Convention (BWC) and the 1993 Chemical Weapons Convention (CWC).[12]

As for the continuing sizable threat from nuclear weapons, which we have lived with now for more than 50 years, the US Senate's recent rejection of the Comprehensive Test Ban Treaty makes it clear relinquishing nuclear weapons will not be politically easy. But we have a unique opportunity, with the end of the Cold War, to avert a multipolar arms race. Building on the BWC and CWC relinquishments, successful abolition of nuclear weapons could help us build toward a habit of relinquishing dangerous technologies. (Actually, by getting rid of all but 100 nuclear weapons worldwide—roughly the total destructive power of World War II and a considerably easier task—we could eliminate this extinction threat.[13])

Verifying relinquishment will be a difficult problem, but not an unsolvable one. We are fortunate to have already done a lot of relevant work in the context of the BWC and other treaties. Our major task will be to apply this to technologies that are naturally much more commercial than military. The substantial need here is for transparency, as difficulty of verification is directly proportional to the difficulty of distinguishing relinquished from legitimate activities.

I frankly believe that the situation in 1945 was simpler than the one we now face: The nuclear technologies were reasonably separable into commercial and military uses, and monitoring was aided by the nature of atomic tests and the ease with which radioactivity could be measured. Research on military applications could be performed at national laboratories such as Los Alamos, with the results kept secret as long as possible.

The GNR technologies do not divide clearly into commercial and military uses; given their potential in the market, it's hard to imagine pursuing them only in national laboratories. With their widespread commercial pursuit, enforcing relinquishment will require a verification regime similar to that for biological weapons, but on an unprecedented scale. This, inevitably, will raise tensions between our individual privacy and desire for proprietary information, and the need for verification to protect us all. We will undoubtedly encounter strong resistance to this loss of privacy and freedom of action.

Verifying the relinquishment of certain GNR technologies will have to occur in cyberspace as well as at physical facilities. The critical issue will be to make the necessary transparency acceptable in a world of proprietary information, presumably by providing new forms of protection for intellectual property.

Verifying compliance will also require that scientists and engineers adopt a strong code of ethical conduct, resembling the Hippocratic oath, and that they have the courage to whistleblow as necessary, even at high personal cost. This would answer the call—50 years after Hiroshima—by the Nobel laureate Hans Bethe, one of the most senior of the surviving members of the Manhattan Project, that all scientists "cease and desist from work creating, developing, improving, and manufacturing nuclear weapons and other weapons of potential mass destruction."[14] In the 21st century, this requires vigilance and personal responsibility by those who would work on both NBC and GNR technologies to avoid implementing weapons of mass destruction and knowledge-enabled mass destruction.

Thoreau also said that we will be "rich in proportion to the number of things which we can afford to let alone." We each seek to be happy, but it would seem worthwhile to question whether we need to take such a high risk of total destruction to gain yet more knowledge and yet more things; common sense says that there is a limit to our material needs—and that certain knowledge is too dangerous and is best forgone.

Neither should we pursue near immortality without considering the costs, without considering the commensurate increase in the risk of extinction. Immortality, while perhaps the original, is certainly not the only possible utopian dream.

I recently had the good fortune to meet the distinguished author and scholar Jacques Attali, whose book *Lignes d'horizons* (*Millennium,* in the English translation) helped inspire the Java and Jini approach to the coming age of pervasive computing.... In his new book *Fraternite's,* Attali describes how our dreams of utopia have changed over time:

> At the dawn of societies, men saw their passage on Earth as nothing more than a labyrinth of pain, at the end of which stood a door leading, via their death, to the company of gods and to *Eternity.* With the Hebrews and then the Greeks, some men dared free themselves from theological demands and dream of an ideal City where *Liberty* would flourish. Others, noting the evolution of the market society, understood that the liberty of some would entail the alienation of others, and they sought *Equality.*

Jacques helped me understand how these three different utopian goals exist in tension in our society today. He goes on to describe a fourth utopia, *Fraternity,* whose foundation is altruism. Fraternity alone associates individual happiness with the happiness of others, affording the promise of self-sustainment.

This crystallized for me my problem with Kurzweil's dream. A technological approach to Eternity—near immortality through robotics—may not be the most desirable utopia, and its pursuit brings clear dangers. Maybe we should rethink our utopian choices.

Where can we look for a new ethical basis to set our course? I have found the ideas in the book *Ethics for the New Millennium,* by the Dalai Lama, to be very helpful. As is perhaps well known but little heeded, the Dalai Lama argues that the most important thing is for us to conduct our lives with love and compassion for others, and that our societies need to develop a stronger notion of universal responsibility and of our interdependency; he proposes a standard of positive ethical conduct for individuals and societies that seems consonant with Attali's Fraternity utopia.

The Dalai Lama further argues that we must understand what it is that makes people happy, and acknowledge the strong evidence that neither material progress nor the pursuit of the power of knowledge is the key—that there are limits to what science and the scientific pursuit alone can do.

Our Western notion of happiness seems to come from the Greeks, who defined it as "the exercise of vital powers along lines of excellence in a life affording them scope."[15]

Clearly, we need to find meaningful challenges and sufficient scope in our lives if we are to be happy in whatever is to come. But I believe we must find alternative outlets for our creative forces, beyond the culture of perpetual economic growth; this growth has largely been a blessing for several hundred years, but it has not brought us unalloyed happiness, and we must now choose between the pursuit of unrestricted and undirected growth through science and technology and the clear accompanying dangers.

It is now more than a year since my first encounter with Ray Kurzweil and John Searle. I see around me cause for hope in the voices for caution and relinquishment and in those people I have discovered who are as concerned as I am about our current predicament. I feel, too, a deepened sense of personal responsibility—not for the work I have already done, but for the work that I might yet do, at the confluence of the sciences.

But many other people who know about the dangers still seem strangely silent. When pressed, they trot out the "this is nothing new" riposte—as if awareness of what could happen is response enough. They tell me, There are universities filled with bioethicists who study this stuff all day long. They say, All this has been written about before, and by experts. They complain, Your worries and your arguments are already old hat.

I don't know where these people hide their fear. As an architect of complex systems I enter this arena as a generalist. But should this diminish my concerns? I am aware of how much has been written about, talked about, and lectured about so authoritatively. But does this mean it has reached people? Does this mean we can discount the dangers before us?

Knowing is not a rationale for not acting. Can we doubt that knowledge has become a weapon we wield against ourselves?

The experiences of the atomic scientists clearly show the need to take personal responsibility, the danger that things will move too fast, and the way in which a process can take on a life of its own. We can, as they did, create insurmountable problems in almost no time flat. We must do more thinking up front if we are not to be similarly surprised and shocked by the consequences of our inventions.

My continuing professional work is on improving the reliability of software. Software is a tool, and as a toolbuilder I must struggle with the uses to which the tools I make are put. I have always believed that making software more reliable, given its many uses, will make the world a safer and better place; if I were to come to believe the opposite, then I would be morally obligated to stop this work. I can now imagine such a day may come.

This all leaves me not angry but at least a bit melancholic. Henceforth, for me, progress will be somewhat bittersweet.

NOTES

1. The passage Kurzweil quotes is from Kaczynski's Unabomber Manifesto, which was published jointly, under duress, by *The New York Times* and *The Washington Post* to attempt to bring his campaign of terror to an end. I agree with David Gelernter, who said about their decision:

   "It was a tough call for the newspapers. To say yes would be giving in to terrorism, and for all they knew he was lying anyway. On the other hand, to say yes might stop the killing. There was also a chance that someone would read the tract and get a hunch about the author, and that is exactly what happened. The suspect's brother read it, and it rang a bell.

   "I would have told them not to publish. I'm glad they didn't ask me. I guess."

   (*Drawing Life: Surviving the Unabomber.* Free Press, 1997: 120.)

2. Garrett, Laurie. *The Coming Plague: Newly Emerging Diseases in a World Out of Balance.* Penguin, 1994: 47–52, 414, 419, 452.
3. Isaac Asimov described what became the most famous view of ethical rules for robot behavior in his book *I, Robot* in 1950, in his Three Laws of Robotics: 1. A robot may not injure a human being, or, through inaction, allow a human being to come to harm. 2. A robot must obey the orders given it by human beings, except where such orders would conflict with the First Law. 3. A robot must protect its own existence, as long as such protection does not conflict with the First or Second Law.
4. Michelangelo wrote a sonnet that begins:

   Non ha l' ottimo artista alcun concetto
   Ch' un marmo solo in sè non circonscriva
   Col suo soverchio; e solo a quello arriva
   La man che ubbidisce all' intelleto.

   Stone translates this as

   The best of artists hath no thought to show
   which the rough stone in its superfluous shell
   doth not include; to break the marble spell is
   all the hand that serves the brain can do.

   Stone describes the process: "He was not working from his drawings or clay models; they had all been put away. He was carving from the images in his mind. His eyes and hands knew where every line, curve, mass must emerge, and at what depth in the heart of the stone to create the low relief."

(*The Agony and the Ecstasy.* Doubleday, 1961: 6, 144.)

5. First Foresight Conference on Nanotechnology in October 1989, a talk titled "The Future of Computation." Published in Crandall, B. C. and James Lewis, editors. *Nanotechnology: Research and Perspectives.* MIT Press, 1992: 269. See also *www.foresight.org/Conferences/MNT01/Nano1.html.*
6. In his 1963 novel *Cat's Cradle*, Kurt Vonnegut imagined a gray-goo-like accident where a form of ice called ice-nine, which becomes solid at a much higher temperature, freezes the oceans.
7. Kauffman, Stuart. "Self-replication: Even Peptides Do It." *Nature*, **382**, August 8, 1996: **496**. See *www.santafe.edu/sfi/People/kauffman/sak-peptides.html.*
8. Else, Jon. *The Day After Trinity: J. Robert Oppenheimer and the Atomic Bomb* (available at *www.pyramiddirect.com*).
9. This estimate is in Leslie's book *The End of the World: The Science and Ethics of Human Extinction*, where he notes that the probability of extinction is substantially higher if we accept Brandon Carter's Doomsday Argument, which is, briefly, that "we ought to have some reluctance to believe that we are very exceptionally early, for instance in the earliest 0.001 percent, among all humans who will ever have lived. This would be some reason for thinking that humankind will not survive for many more centuries, let alone colonize the galaxy. Carter's doomsday argument doesn't generate any risk estimates just by itself. It is an argument for *revising* the estimates which we generate when we consider various possible dangers." (Routledge, 1996: 1, 3, 145.)
10. Clarke, Arthur C. "Presidents, Experts, and Asteroids." *Science*, June 5, 1998. Reprinted as "Science and Society" in *Greetings, Carbon-Based Bipeds! Collected Essays, 1934–1998.* St. Martin's Press, 1999: 526.
11. And, as David Forrest suggests in his paper "Regulating Nanotechnology Development," available at *www.foresight.org/NanoRev/Forrest1989.html*, "If we used strict liability as an alternative to regulation it would be impossible for any developer to internalize the cost of the risk (destruction of the biosphere), so theoretically the activity of developing nanotechnology should never be undertaken." Forrest's analysis leaves us with only government regulation to protect us—not a comforting thought.
12. Meselson, Matthew. "The Problem of Biological Weapons." Presentation to the 1,818th Stated Meeting of the American Academy of Arts and Sciences, January 13, 1999. (*minerva.amacad.org/archive/bulletin4.htm*)
13. Doty, Paul. "The Forgotten Menace: Nuclear Weapons Stockpiles Still Represent the Biggest Threat to Civilization." *Nature*, **402**, December 9, 1999: 583.
14. See also Hans Bethe's 1997 letter to President Clinton, at *www.fas.org/bethecr.htm.*
15. Hamilton, Edith. *The Greek Way.* W. W. Norton & Co., 1942: 35.

2.3.4 Nanoscience, Nanotechnology, and Ethics: Promise and Peril

RAY KURZWEIL

Inventor of the first music synthesizer in 1982, entrepreneur, author, and futurist Ray Kurzweil is one of the leading thinkers about contemporary and future technology and its impact on society. In this reading, he argues that the pace of technological change is exponential rather than linear, as many people implicitly believe, and that the twenty-first century will witness a major technological revolution springing from the convergence of the science of genetics, nanotechnology, and robotics (GNR) and artificial intelligence. However, like all new technologies, GNR is a "double-edged sword" that holds great promise and great peril for human civilization. One worry, expressed by Bill Joy (Selection 2.3.3) is that self-replicating nanobots will escape into the environment and cause severe and irreparable damage to the natural world. Although he takes such threats seriously, Kurzweil believes that the development and introduction of GNR is inevitable and that broad relinquishment of these technologies is not feasible, but that it is also possible to develop ethical guidelines for "fine-grained" relinquishment of certain kinds of particularly dangerous GNR applications. While continuing to be optimistic about the promise of these technologies, he believes that it is possible for society to control them so as to enjoy their benefits while avoiding the dangers they pose.

FOCUS QUESTIONS

1. What are the three features of technological evolution that lead Kurzweil to conclude that the rate of technological change is exponential rather than linear?
2. Kurzweil suggests that the introduction of some kinds of nanotechnology devices is inevitable. What reasons does he adduce that support this conclusion?
3. At one point, Kurzweil refers to the views of Ted Kaczynski (aka the Unabomber) and, perhaps surprisingly, seems to endorse some aspects of his view of technology. What part of Kaczynski's view does he share? What part does he disagree with?
4. Why is Kurzweil opposed to the relinquishment of broad areas of technology? What kinds of "fine-grained" relinquishment does he think are feasible?
5. Do you agree with Kurzweil that it is possible for society to enjoy the benefits of twenty-first century GNR technologies while mitigating and controlling the risks? Explain.

KEYWORDS

defensive technologies, ELSI, GNR, Moore's law, molecular assemblers, nanobots, nanotechnology, paradigm shift, relinquishment, unified system

Our rapidly growing scientific and technological ability to manipulate matter and energy at ever smaller scales promises to transform virtually every sector of society, a phenomenon that presents manifest ethical responsibilities. There will be increasing overlap between nanotechnology and other technologies, such as biotechnology and artificial intelligence. And as with these previous scientific and technological transformations, we will be faced with deeply intertwined promise and peril.

THE NANO-FRONTIER

Nanoscience and nanotechnology today have been expanded to include essentially any science or technology where the key features are measured in a modest number of nanometers (under 100 by some definitions). By this standard, contemporary electronics has already passed this threshold. Eric Drexler has further developed the concept of building molecule-scale devices using molecular assemblers that would precisely guide chemical reactions by means of information. Moreover, just as technologies related to information develop at an exponential pace, generally doubling in capability and price-performance every year, so the size of technology is itself inexorably shrinking, and most of technology will be "nanotechnology" by the 2020s.

This era will bring us the ability to essentially convert software, that is, information, directly into physical products. We will be able to produce

Source: From the *Encyclopedia of Science, Technology, and Ethics*, Vol. a–c, 2006, Macmillan Reference, pp. xli–xlvii, Gale, a part of Cengage Learning.

virtually any product for pennies per pound. Computers will have greater computational capacity than the human brain, and we will be completing the reverse engineering of the human brain to reveal the software design of human intelligence. We are already placing devices with narrow intelligence in our bodies for diagnostic and therapeutic purposes. With the advent of nanotechnology, we will be able to keep our bodies and brains in a healthy, optimal state indefinitely. Nanotechnology and related advanced technologies will bring us the opportunity to overcome age-old problems, including pollution, poverty, disease, and aging.

Many object to the intermingling of the so-called natural world with the products of our technology. However, the increasing intimacy of our human lives with our technology is not a new story. Human life expectancy was thirty-seven years in 1800. Most humans at that time lived lives dominated by poverty, intense labor, disease, and misfortune. We are immeasurably better off as a result of technology, but there is still a lot of suffering in the world to overcome. We have a moral imperative, therefore, to continue the pursuit of knowledge and of advanced technologies that can continue to overcome human affliction. There is also an economic imperative to continue.

Nanotechnology is advancing on hundreds of fronts. We cannot relinquish its pursuit without essentially relinquishing all of technology, which would require acts of totalitarianism inconsistent with the values of our society. Technology has always been a double-edged sword, and that is certainly true of nanotechnology. However, we will have no choice but to confront the challenge of guiding nanotechnology in a constructive direction. Any broad attempt to relinquish nanotechnology will only push it underground, which would interfere with the benefits while actually making the dangers worse.

With the human genome project, three to five percent of the budgets were devoted to the ethical, legal, and social implications (ELSI) of the technology. A similar commitment for nanotechnology would be appropriate and constructive. Near-term applications of nanotechnology are more limited in their benefits and more benign in their potential dangers. We cannot say a priori that all nanoengineered particles are safe, nor would it be appropriate to deem them necessarily unsafe. Environmental tests thus far have not shown reasons for undue concern.

I believe that existing regulatory mechanisms are sufficient to handle near-term applications of nanotechnology. As for the long term, we need to appreciate that a myriad of nanoscale technologies are inevitable. The current examinations and dialogues on achieving the promise while ameliorating the peril are appropriate and will deserve increased attention as we get closer to realizing these revolutionary technologies.

THE NANO-BACKGROUND: MODELS OF TECHNOLOGY TRENDS

Models of technology trends show that nanotechnology and related advanced technologies are inevitable. They are deeply integrated into our society and are advancing on many diverse fronts, comprised of hundreds of small steps, each benign in itself.

Intuitive Linear and Historical Exponential Views Although exponential trends did exist a thousand years ago, they were at that very early stage where it is so flat and so slow that it looks like no trend at all. Today, everyone expects continuous technological progress and the social repercussions that follow. But the future will nonetheless be far more surprising than most observers realize because few have internalized the fact that the rate of change itself is accelerating.

Most long-range forecasts of technical feasibility underestimate the power of future developments because they are based on the "intuitive linear" view of history rather than the "historical exponential" view. We will not experience a hundred years of progress in the twenty-first century; rather we will witness on the order of twenty thousand years of progress (at today's rate of progress). An unexamined intuition provides the impression that progress changes at the rate that we have recently experienced because an exponential curve approximates a straight line when viewed for a brief duration.

But an assessment of the history of technology shows that technological change is exponential. Indeed, we find "double" exponential growth, meaning that the rate of exponential growth is itself growing exponentially. These observations are based on a rich model of diverse technological processes.

The Law of Accelerating Returns The ongoing acceleration of technology is the inevitable result of the "law of accelerating returns," which describes the acceleration of the pace and the exponential growth of the products of an evolutionary process, including technology, particularly information technologies.

The law of accelerating returns has three key features. First, evolution applies positive feedback as the more capable methods resulting from one stage of evolutionary progress are used to create the next stage. As a result, the rate progress of an evolutionary process increases exponentially over time, as the "returns" of that process (e.g., speed or cost-effectiveness) increase exponentially. As an evolutionary process becomes more effective, greater resources are invested in it, resulting in a second level of exponential growth (i.e., the rate of exponential growth itself grows exponentially).

A second feature is "technological paradigm shifts." A specific paradigm (a method or approach to solving a problem) provides exponential growth until the method exhausts its potential. When this happens, a paradigm shift (a fundamental change in the approach) occurs, which enables exponential growth to continue. Each paradigm follows an "S-curve," which consists of slow growth, followed by rapid growth, followed by a leveling off as the particular paradigm matures. During this third phase in the life cycle of a paradigm, pressure builds for the next paradigm shift. The acceleration of the overall evolutionary process proceeds as a sequence of S-curves, and the overall exponential growth consists of this cascade of S-curves.

A third key feature is that the resources underlying the exponential growth of an evolutionary process are relatively unbounded. One resource is the order of the evolutionary process itself. Each stage of evolution provides more powerful tools for the next. The other required resource is the "chaos" of the environment in which the evolutionary process takes place and which provides the options for further diversity. In technological evolution, human ingenuity and the ever-changing market sustain innovation.

The evolution of life forms and technologies constantly accelerates. With the advent of a technology-creating species, the exponential pace became too fast for evolution through DNA-guided protein synthesis and moved on to human-created technology. Technology goes beyond mere tool making; it is a process of creating ever more powerful technology using the tools from the previous round of innovation. The first technological steps took tens of thousands of years. For people living in this era, there was little noticeable technological change. By 1000 C.E., progress was much faster and a paradigm shift required only a century or two. The nineteenth century saw more technological change than in the nine centuries preceding it. Then in the first twenty years of the twentieth century, we saw more advancement than in all of the nineteenth century. Now, paradigm shifts occur in only a few years. The paradigm shift rate is currently doubling every decade. So the twenty-first century will see about a thousand times greater technological change than its predecessor.

Moore's Law and Beyond The exponential trend that has gained the greatest public recognition has become known as "Moore's Law." Gordon Moore, one of the inventors of integrated circuits, noted in the mid-1970s that we could squeeze twice as many transistors on an integrated circuit every twenty-four months. Given that the electrons have less distance to travel, the circuits also run twice as fast, providing an overall quadrupling of computational power.

However, the exponential growth of computing is much broader than Moore's Law. If we plot the speed per price of forty-nine famous calculators and computers spanning the twentieth century, we note that there were four paradigms that provided exponential growth in the price-performance of computing before integrated circuits. Therefore, Moore's Law was the fifth paradigm to exponentially grow the power of computation. When Moore's Law reaches the end of its S-curve, the exponential growth will continue with three-dimensional molecular computing, constituting the sixth paradigm.

Moore's Law narrowly refers to the number of transistors on an integrated circuit of fixed size. But the most appropriate measure to track is computational speed per unit cost. This takes into account many levels of innovation in computer design. For example, there are many nascent technologies that build circuitry in three dimensions in a way that mimics the parallel organization of the human brain. One cubic inch of nanotube circuitry would be a million times more powerful than the human brain. There are more than enough new computing technologies now being researched to sustain the law of accelerating returns as applied to computation.

Specific paradigms do ultimately reach levels at which exponential growth is no longer feasible. That is why Moore's Law is an S-curve. But the growth of computation will continue exponentially. Paradigm shift, or innovation, turns the S-curve of any specific paradigm into a continuing exponential. A new paradigm takes over when the old paradigm approaches its natural limit.

Other Technologies There are many examples of the exponential growth implied by the law of accelerating returns in technologies as varied as DNA sequencing, communication speeds, brain scanning, electronics of all kinds, and even in the rapidly shrinking size of technology. Exponential growth in communications technology has been even more explosive than in computation. Miniaturization is a trend that will have profound implications for the twenty-first century. The salient implementation sizes of technologies, both electronic and mechanical, are shrinking at a double-exponential rate.

The future nanotechnology age will result not from the exponential explosion of computation alone, but rather from the synergies that will result from intertwined technological revolutions. Every point on the exponential growth curves represents an intense human drama of innovation and competition. It is remarkable that these chaotic processes result in such smooth and predictable exponential trends.

EXAMPLES OF TRUE NANOSCIENCE AND NANOTECHNOLOGY

Ubiquitous nanoscience and nanotechnology is two to three decades away. One forthcoming achievement will be "nanobots," small robots the size of human blood cells that can travel inside the human bloodstream. There have already been successful animal experiments using this concept.

In addition to human brain reverse engineering, these nanobots will be able to perform a broad variety of diagnostic and therapeutic functions inside the human body. Robert Freitas, for example, has designed robotic replacements for human blood cells that perform thousands of times more effectively than their biological counterparts. His "respirocytes" (robotic red blood cells) could allow one to sprint for fifteen minutes without taking a breath. His robotic macrophages will be far more effective than our white blood cells at combating pathogens. His DNA repair robot would be able to repair DNA transcription errors, and even implement needed DNA changes. Although Freitas' conceptual designs are two or three decades away, there has already been progress on bloodstream-based devices.

Nanobot technology has profound military applications, and any expectation that such uses will be relinquished is highly unrealistic. Already, the U.S. Department of Defense (DOD) is developing "smart dust," or tiny robots to be used for surveillance. Billions of invisible spies could monitor every square inch of enemy territory and carry out missions to destroy enemy targets. The only way for an enemy to counteract such a force is with their own nanotechnology. Nanotechnology-based weapons will obsolete weapons of larger size.

In addition, nanobots will be able to expand our experiences and our capabilities. Nanobot technology will provide fully immersive virtual reality by taking up positions in close proximity to every interneuronal connection related to the senses. If we want to enter virtual reality, the nanobots suppress all of the inputs coming from the real senses, and replace them with the signals that would be appropriate for the virtual environment.

Scientists at the Max Planck Institute have developed "neuron transistors" that can detect the firing of a nearby neuron, or alternatively, can cause a nearby neuron to fire, or suppress it from firing. This amounts to two-way communication between neurons and the electronic-based neuron transistors. The scientists demonstrated their invention by controlling the movement of a living leech from their computer.

The Internet will provide many virtual environments to explore. We will be able to "go" to these virtual environments and meet others there, both real and simulated people. Of course, ultimately there will not be a clear distinction between the two. By 2030, going to a web site will mean entering a full-immersion virtual-reality environment, encompassing all of the senses and triggering the neurological correlates of emotions and sexual experiences.

"Experience beamers" circa 2030 will beam a person's entire flow of sensory experiences and emotions. We'll be able to go to a web site and experience other people's lives. Full-immersion visual-auditory environments will be available by 2010, with images written directly onto our retinas by our eyeglasses and contact lenses. The electronics will be embedded in our glasses and woven into our clothing, so computers as distinct objects will disappear.

The most significant implication of nanotechnology and related advanced technologies of the twenty-first century will be the merger of biological and nonbiological intelligence. Nonbiological intelligence is growing at a double-exponential rate and will vastly exceed biological intelligence well before the middle of this century. However, in my view, this nonbiological intelligence should still be considered human, as it is fully derivative of the human-machine civilization.

Our brains are relatively fixed in design, but brain implants based on massively distributed intelligent nanobots will ultimately expand our memories a trillion fold and improve all of our cognitive abilities. Since the nanobots are communicating with each other over a wireless network, they can create any set of new neural connections, break existing connections, create new hybrid biological-nonbiological networks, and add new nonbiological networks.

Using nanobots as brain extenders is a significant improvement over surgically installed neural implants. Nanobots will be introduced without surgery and can be directed to leave, so the process is easily reversible. They can change their configuration and alter their software. Perhaps most importantly, they are massively distributed and can take up billions or trillions of positions throughout the brain, whereas a surgically introduced neural implant can only be placed in a few locations.

THE ECONOMIC IMPERATIVES OF THE LAW OF ACCELERATING RETURNS

The economic imperative of a competitive marketplace is driving science and technology forward and fueling the law of accelerating returns, which, in turn, is transforming economic relationships. We are moving toward nanoscale, more intelligent machines as the result of many small advances, each with their own particular economic justification.

There is a vital economic imperative to create smaller and more intelligent technology. Machines that can more precisely carry out their missions have enormous value. There are tens of thousands of projects that are advancing the various aspects of the law of accelerating returns in diverse incremental ways. Regardless of near-term business cycles, the support for "high tech" in the business community has grown enormously. We would have to repeal capitalism and every visage of economic competition to stop this progression.

The economy has been growing exponentially throughout this century. Even the Great Depression of the 1930s represented only a minor blip compared to the underlying pattern of growth. Recessions, including the Depression, represent only temporary deviations from the underlying curve. Statistics in fact greatly understate productivity growth (economic output per worker), which has also been exponential.

Inflationary factors are offset by the double-exponential trends in the price-performance of all information-based technologies, which deeply affect all industries. We are also undergoing massive disintermediation in the channels of distribution through the Internet and other new communication technologies and escalating efficiencies in operations and administration. Current economic policy is based on outdated theories that do not adequately model the size of technology, bandwidth, megabytes, intellectual property, knowledge, and other increasingly vital constituents that are driving the economy.

Cycles of recession will not disappear immediately. However, the rapid dissemination of information, sophisticated forms of online procurement, and increasingly transparent markets in all industries have diminished the impact of these cycles. The underlying long-term growth rate will continue at a double-exponential rate. The rate of paradigm shift is not noticeably affected by the minor deviations caused by economic cycles. The overall growth of the economy reflects completely new forms of wealth and value that did not previously exist: nanoparticle-based materials, genetic information, intellectual property, communication portals, web sites, bandwidth, software, data bases, and many other new technology-based categories.

Another implication of the law of accelerating returns is exponential growth in human knowledge, including intellectual property, education, and learning. Over the course of the long twentieth century we increased investment in K-12 education by a factor of ten. We have a one hundred fold increase in the number of college students. Automation has been eliminating jobs at the bottom of the skill ladder while creating new and better paying jobs at the top. So, the ladder has been moving up, and we have been exponentially increasing investments in education at all levels.

PROMISE AND PERIL

Science and technology have always been double-edged swords, bringing us longer and healthier life spans, freedom from physical and mental drudgery, and many new creative possibilities, while at the same time introducing new and salient dangers. We will need to adopt strategies to encourage the benefits while ameliorating the risks. Relinquishing broad areas of technology, as some critics have proposed, is not feasible, and attempts to do so will only drive technology development underground, which will exacerbate the dangers.

As technology accelerates toward the full realization of biotechnology, nanotechnology and "strong" AI (artificial intelligence at or above human levels), we will see the same intertwined potentials: a feast of creativity resulting from greater human intelligence combined with many new dangers. Nanobot technology requires billions or trillions of such intelligent devices to be useful. The most cost-effective way to scale up to such levels is through self-replication. A defect in the mechanism curtailing nanobot self-replication could be disastrous. There are steps available now to mitigate this risk, but we cannot have complete assurance in any strategy that we devise today.

Other primary concerns include "Who is controlling the nanobots?" and "Who are the nanobots talking to?" Organizations or individuals could put undetectable nanobots in water or food supplies. These "spies" could monitor and even control thoughts and actions. Existing nanobots could be influenced through software viruses and other software "hacking" techniques. My own expectation is that the creative and constructive applications of this technology will dominate, as they do today. But we need to invest more heavily in developing specific defensive technologies.

There are usually three stages in examining the impact of future technology: awe at its potential to overcome problems; then a sense of dread at a new set of dangers; followed by the realization that the only viable and responsible path is to set a careful course that can realize the promise while managing the peril.

Bill Joy, cofounder of Sun Microsystems, has warned of the impending dangers from the emergence of self-replicating technologies in the fields of genetics, nanotechnology, and robotics, or "GNR." His concerns include genetically altered designer pathogens, self-replicating entities created through nanotechnology, and robots whose intelligence will rival and ultimately exceed our own. Who's to say we will be able to count on such robots to remain friendly to humans? Although I am often cast as the technology optimist who counters Joy's pessimism, I do share his concerns regarding self-replicating technologies. Many people have interpreted Joy's article as an advocacy of broad relinquishment, not of all technology, but of the "dangerous ones" like nanotechnology. Joy, who is now working as a venture capitalist with the legendary silicon valley firm of Kleiner, Perkins, Caufield & Byers investing in technologies such as nanotechnology applied to renewable energy and other natural resources, says that broad relinquishment is a misinterpretation of his position and was never his intent. He has recently said that the emphasis should be to "limit development of the technologies that are too dangerous," not on complete prohibition. He suggests, for example, a prohibition against self-replicating nanotechnology, which is similar to the guidelines advocated by the Foresight Institute.

Others, such as Bill McKibben, the environmentalist who was one of the first to warn against global warming, have advocated relinquishment of broad areas such as biotechnology and nanotechnology, or even of all technology. However, relinquishing broad fields would be impossible to achieve without essentially relinquishing all technical development.

There are real dangers associated with new self-replicating technologies. But technological advances, such as antibiotics and improved sanitation, have freed us from the prevalence of such plagues in the past. We may romanticize the past, but until fairly recently, most of humanity lived extremely fragile lives. Many people still live in this precarious way, which is one reason to continue technological progress and the economic enhancement that accompanies it. Should we tell the millions of people afflicted with devastating conditions that we are canceling the development of all bioengineered treatments because there is a risk that these same technologies may someday be used for malevolent purposes? Most people would agree that such broad-based relinquishment is not the answer.

The Relinquishment Issue Relinquishment at the right level is part of a responsible and constructive response to these genuine perils. The issue, however, is: At what level are we to relinquish technology? Ted Kaczynski (the Unabomber) would have us renounce all of it. This is neither desirable nor feasible. McKibben takes the position that many people now have enough wealth and technological capability and should not pursue more. This ignores the suffering that remains in the human world, which continued technological progress could alleviate.

Another level would be to forego certain fields (such as nanotechnology) that might be regarded as too dangerous. But such sweeping strokes of relinquishment are untenable. Nanotechnology is the inevitable result of the persistent trend toward miniaturization that pervades all of technology. It is not a single centralized effort, but is being pursued by a myriad of projects with many goals.

Kaczynski argued that modern industrial society cannot be reformed because technology is a unified system in which all parts are dependent on one another. It is not possible to get rid of the "bad" parts of technology and retain only the "good" parts. He cited modern medicine as an example, arguing that progress depends on several scientific fields and advancements in high-tech equipment. Kaczynski was correct on the deeply entangled nature of the benefits and risks, but his overall assessment of the relative balance between the two was way off. Joy and I both believe that technology will and should progress, and that we need to be actively concerned with the dark side. Our dialogue concerns the granularity of relinquishment that is feasible and desirable. Abandonment of broad areas of technology will only push them underground where development would continue unimpeded by ethics and regulation. In such a situation, it would be the less-stable, less-responsible practitioners who would have all the expertise.

One example of relinquishment at the right level is the proposed ethical guideline by the Foresight Institute that nanotechnologists agree to relinquish the development of physical entities that can self-replicate in a natural environment. Another is a ban on self-replicating physical entities that contain their own codes for self-replication. Such entities should be designed to obtain codes from a centralized secure server, which would guard against undesirable replication. This "broadcast architecture" is impossible in the biological world, which represents one way in which nanotechnology can be made safer than biotechnology. Such "finegrained" relinquishment should be linked to professional ethical guidelines, oversight by regulatory bodies, the development of technology-specific "immune" responses, as well as computer assisted surveillance by law enforcement agencies. Balancing privacy rights with security will be one of many challenges raised by some new nanotechnologies.

Computer viruses serve as a reassuring test case in our ability to regulate nonbiological self-replication. At first, concerns were voiced that as they became more sophisticated, software pathogens had the potential to destroy computer networks. Yet the "immune system" that has evolved in response to this challenge has been largely effective. Although self-replicating software entities do cause damage from time to time, no one would suggest we do away with computers and the Internet because of software viruses. This success is in a highly productive industry in which there is no regulation, and no certification for practitioners.

Defensive Technologies and The Impact of Regulation. Arguments such as McKibben's for relinquishment have been influential because they paint a picture of future dangers as if they were released into an unprepared world. But the sophistication and power of our defensive technologies and knowledge will grow along with the dangers. When we have "gray goo" (unrestrained nanobot replication), we will also have "blue goo" ("police nanobots"). We cannot say with assurance that we will successfully avoid all misuse. We have been able to largely control harmful software virus replication because the requisite knowledge is widely available to responsible practitioners. Attempts to restrict this knowledge would have created a far less stable situation.

The present challenge is self-replicating biotechnology. By reprogramming the information processes that lead to and encourage disease and aging, we will have the ability to overcome these afflictions. However, the same knowledge can also empower a terrorist to create a bioengineered pathogen.

Unlike biotechnology, the software industry is almost completely unregulated. Although bioterrorists do not need to put their "innovations" through the FDA, scientists developing defensive technologies are required to follow regulations that slow innovation. It is impossible under existing regulations and ethical standards to test defenses to bioterrorist agents on humans. Animal models and simulations will be necessary in lieu of infeasible human trials, but we will need to go beyond these steps to accelerate the development of defensive technologies.

We need to create ethical and legal standards and defensive technologies. It is quite clearly a race. In the software field the defensive technologies have remained ahead of the offensive ones. With extensive regulation in the medical field slowing down innovation, this may not happen with biotechnology.

There is a legitimate need to make biomedical research as safe as possible, but our balancing of risks is skewed. The millions of people who need biotechnology advances seem to carry little political weight against a few well-publicized casualties from the inevitable risks of progress. This equation will become even starker with the emerging dangers of bioengineered pathogens. We need a change in public attitude in terms of tolerance for necessary risk.

Hastening defensive technologies is vital to our security. We need to streamline regulatory procedures to achieve this. However, we also need to greatly increase our investment explicitly in defensive technologies. In the biotechnology field, this means the rapid development of antiviral medications.

The comparable situation will exist for nanotechnology once replication of nano-engineered entities has been achieved. We will soon need to invest in defensive technologies, including the creation of a nanotechnology-based immune system. Such an immune system may itself become a danger, but no one would argue that humans would be better off without an immune system because of the possibility of autoimmune diseases. The development of a technological immune system for nanotechnology will happen even without explicit efforts to create one.

It is premature to develop specific defensive nanotechnologies as long as we have only a general idea of the threat. However, there is a dialogue on this issue, and expanded investment in these efforts should be encouraged. The Foresight Institute, for example, has devised a set of ethical standards and strategies for assuring the development of safe nanotechnology. They are likely to be effective with regard to preventing accidental release of dangerous self-replicating nanotechnology entities. But the intentional design and release of such entities is more challenging.

CONCLUSION

Protection is not impossible, but we need to realize that any level of protection will only work to a certain level of sophistication. We will need to continue to advance the defensive technologies and keep them ahead of the destructive technologies. The challenge of self-replication in nanotechnology impels us to continue the type of study that the Foresight Institute has initiated. With the human genome project, three to five percent of the budget was devoted to the ethical, legal and social implications (ELSI) of the technology. A similar commitment for nanotechnology would be appropriate and constructive. Science and technology will remain double-edged swords, and the story of the twenty-first century has not yet been written. We have no choice but to work hard to apply these quickening technologies to advance our human values, despite what often appears to be a lack of consensus on what those values should be.

BIBLIOGRAPHY

Drexler, Erik K. (1986). *Engines of Creation*. Garden City, NY: Doubleday.

Drexler, Erik K. (1992). *Nanosystems: Molecular Machinery, Manufacturing, and Computation*. New York: Wiley.

Freitas, Robert, Jr. (1999). *Nanomedicine*. Vol. **1**: *Basic Capabilities*. Georgetown, TX: Landes Bioscience.

Joy, Bill. (2000). "Why the Future Doesn't Need Us." *Wired* **262**.

Kurzweil, Ray. (1999). *The Age of Spiritual Machines: When Computers Exceed Human Intelligence*. New York: Viking.

Kurzweil, Ray. (2005). *The Singularity Is Near: When Humans Transcend Biology*. New York: Viking.

McKibben, Bill. (2003). *Enough: Staying Human in an Engineered Age*. New York: Henry Holt.

2.4 BIOTECHNOLOGY AND GENETIC ENGINEERING

2.4.1 A Glimpse of Things to Come

LEE M. SILVER

Princeton University molecular biologist Lee Silver opened his 1997 book *Remaking Eden: Cloning and Beyond in a Brave New World* with this provocative discussion of what human reproduction might look like in 2010, 2050, and 2350. He predicts that reproductive genetic engineering technology will make it possible for lesbian couples to have children that are genetically related to both "parents," that genetic resistance to diseases such as AIDS will be woven into an embryo's DNA, that human cloning will become widely accepted, and that, in the further future, the human race will divide into two classes: the Naturals and the Gene-enriched, or GenRich. The Naturals and the GenRich will grow up in separate worlds, and eventually, the genetic gulf between them will become so wide that they will become separate species. But Silver's vision differs from the dystopia imagined by Aldous Huxley in his 1932 novel *Brave New World*. In Silver's vision, it is not a totalitarian government that controls people's personal reproductive decisions; rather, it is the free market. Affluent parents will choose to give their children genetic advantages that science and biotechnology make available, just as they now choose to pay for private schools and tutors to prepare them to get into the elite colleges. Such a "free-market eugenics" is consistent with the American values of individual liberty and free markets, and if parentally selected genetic enhancement does not cause harm to the child being enhanced, what reason can there be not to embrace this libertarian version of a brave new world?

FOCUS QUESTIONS

1. What arguments does Silver give for thinking that human genetic enhancement should be regarded as morally permissible? What are the arguments used by opponents of genetic enhancement?
2. Compare Silver's position with that in the reading by Leon Kass (Selection 2.4.2). How does Kass attempt to argue against Silver's position regarding human reproductive cloning? Which of these arguments do you find more persuasive?
3. In the reading by Michael Sandel (Selection 2.4.3), several arguments against the prospect of genetic enhancement are discussed. How do Sandel's arguments stack up against Silver's? Which of these authors does a better job dealing with the "unfairness" objection?
4. Compare the debate over human reproductive genetic engineering with the debate over robotics and artificial intelligence and the possibility of creating transhuman cyborgs. What similarities are there between these two debates? Is your personal position on these issues the same or is it different? Explain.

KEYWORDS

cloning, genetic enhancement, individual freedom, reproductive technology, reprogenetics

DATELINE BOSTON: JUNE 1, 2010

Sometime in the not-so-distant future, you may visit the maternity ward at a major university hospital to see the newborn child or grandchild of a close friend. The new mother, let's call her Barbara, seems very much at peace with the world, sitting in a chair quietly nursing her baby, Max. Her labor was—in the parlance of her doctor—"uneventful," and she is looking forward to raising her first child. You decide to make pleasant conversation by asking Barbara whether she knew in advance that her baby was going to be a boy. In your mind, it seems like a perfectly reasonable question since doctors have long given prospective parents the option of learning the sex of their child-to-be many months before the predicted date of birth. But Barbara seems taken aback by the question. "Of course I knew that Max would be a boy," she tells you. "My husband Dan and I chose him from our embryo pool. And when I'm ready to go through this again, I'll choose a girl to be my

---

Source: From *Remaking Eden: Cloning and Beyond in a Brave New World* by Lee M. Silver, pp. 1–11. Copyright © 1998 by Lee M. Silver. Reprinted by permission of HarperCollins Publishers, Inc.

second child. An older son and a younger daughter—a perfect family."

Now, it's your turn to be taken aback. "You made a conscious choice to have a boy rather than a girl?" you ask.

"Absolutely!" Barbara answers. "And while I was at it, I made sure that Max wouldn't turn out to be fat like my brother Tom or addicted to alcohol like Dan's sister Karen. It's not that I'm personally biased or anything," Barbara continues defensively. "I just wanted to make sure that Max would have the greatest chance for achieving success. Being overweight or alcoholic would clearly be a handicap."

You look down in wonderment at the little baby boy destined to be moderate in both size and drinking habits.

Max has fallen asleep in Barbara's arms, and she places him gently in his bassinet. He wears a contented smile, which evokes a similar smile from his mother. Barbara feels the urge to stretch her legs and asks whether you'd like to meet some of the new friends she's made during her brief stay at the hospital. You nod, and the two of you walk into the room next door where a thirty-five-year old woman named Cheryl is resting after giving birth to a nine-pound baby girl named Rebecca.

Barbara introduces you to Cheryl as well as a second woman named Madelaine, who stands by the bed holding Cheryl's hand. Little Rebecca is lying under the gaze of both Cheryl and Madelaine. "She really does look like both of her mothers, doesn't she?" Barbara asks you.

Now you're really confused. You glance at Barbara and whisper, "Both mothers?"

Barbara takes you aside to explain. "Yes. You see Cheryl and Madelaine have been living together for eight years. They got married in Hawaii soon after it became legal there, and like most married couples, they wanted to bring a child into the world with a combination of both of their bloodlines. With the reproductive technologies available today, they were able to fulfill their dreams."

You look across the room at the happy little nuclear family—Cheryl, Madelaine, and baby Rebecca—and wonder how the hospital plans to fill out the birth certificate.

DATELINE SEATTLE: MARCH 15, 2050

You are now forty years older and much wiser to the ways of the modern world. Once again, you journey forth to the maternity ward. This time, it's your own granddaughter Melissa who is in labor. Melissa is determined to experience natural childbirth and has refused all offers of anesthetics or painkillers. But she needs something to lift her spirits so that she can continue on through the waves of pain. "Let me see her pictures again," she implores her husband Curtis as the latest contraction sweeps through her body. Curtis picks the photo album off the table and opens it to face his wife. She looks up at the computer-generated picture of a five-year-old girl with wavy brown hair, hazel eyes, and a round face. Curtis turns the page, and Melissa gazes at an older version of the same child: a smiling sixteen-year-old who is 5 feet, 5 inches tall with a pretty face. Melissa smiles back at the future picture of her yet-to-be-born child and braces for another contraction.

There is something unseen in the picture of their child-to-be that provides even greater comfort to Melissa and Curtis. It is the submicroscopic piece of DNA—an extra gene—that will be present in every cell of her body. This special gene will provide her with lifelong resistance to infection by the virus that causes AIDS, a virus that has evolved to be ever more virulent since its explosion across the landscape of humanity seventy years earlier. After years of research by thousands of scientists, no cure for the awful disease has been found, and the only absolute protection comes from the insertion of a resistance gene into the single-cell embryo within twenty-four hours after conception. Ensconced in its chromosomal home, the AIDS resistance gene will be copied over and over again into every one of the trillions of cells that make up the human body, each of which will have its own personal barrier to infection by the AIDS-causing virus HIV. Melissa and Curtis feel lucky indeed to have the financial wherewithal needed to endow all of their children with this protective agent. Other, less well-off American families cannot afford this luxury.

Outside Melissa's room, Jennifer, another expectant mother, is anxiously pacing the hall. She has just arrived at the hospital and her contractions are still far apart. But, unlike Melissa, Jennifer has no need for a computer printout to show her what her child-to-be will look like as a young girl or teenager. She already has thousands of pictures that show her future daughter's likeness, and they're all real, not virtual. For the fetus inside Jennifer is her identical twin sister—her clone—who will be born thirty-six years after she and Jennifer were both conceived within the same single-cell embryo. As Jennifer's daughter grows up, she will constantly behold a glimpse of the future simply by looking at her mother's photo album and her mother.

DATELINE U.S.A.: MAY 15, 2350

It is now three hundred years later and although you are long since gone, a number of your great-great-great-great-great-great-great-great-great-great-grandchildren are now alive, mostly unbeknownst to one another. The United States of America still exists, but it is a different place from the one familiar to you. The most striking difference is that the extreme polarization of society that began during the 1980s has now reached its logical conclusion, with all people belonging to one of two classes. The people of one class are referred to as *Naturals,* while those in the second class are called the *Gene-enriched* or simply the *GenRich.*

These new classes of society cut across what used to be traditional racial and ethnic lines. In fact, so much mixing has occurred during the last three hundred years that sharp divisions according to race—black versus white versus Asian—no longer exist. Instead, the American populace has finally become the racial melting pot that earlier leaders had long hoped for. The skin color of Americans comes in all shades from African brown to Scandinavian pink, and traditional Asian facial features are present to a greater or lesser extent in a large percentage of Americans as well.

But while racial differences have mostly disappeared, another difference has emerged that is sharp and easily defined. It is the difference between those who are genetically enhanced and those who are not. The GenRich—who account for 10 percent of the American population—all carry synthetic genes. Genes that were created in the laboratory and did not exist within the human species until twenty-first century reproductive geneticists began to put them there. The GenRich are a modern-day hereditary class of genetic aristocrats.

Some of the synthetic genes carried by present-day members of the GenRich class were already carried by their parents. These genes were transmitted to today's GenRich the old-fashioned way, from parent to child through sperm or egg. But other synthetic genes are new to the present generation. These were placed into GenRich embryos through the application of genetic engineering techniques shortly after conception.

The GenRich class is anything but homogeneous. There are many types of GenRich families, and many subtypes within each type. For example, there are GenRich athletes who can trace their descent back to professional sports players from the twenty-first century. One subtype of GenRich athlete is the GenRich football player, and a sub-subtype is the GenRich running back. Embryo selection techniques have been used to make sure that a GenRich running back has received all of the natural genes that made his unenhanced foundation ancestor excel at the position. But in addition, at each generation beyond the foundation ancestor, sophisticated genetic enhancements have accumulated so that the modern-day GenRich running back can perform in a way not conceivable for any unenhanced Natural. Of course, all professional baseball, football, and basketball players are special GenRich subtypes. After three hundred years of selection and enhancement, these GenRich individuals all have athletic skills that are clearly "nonhuman" in the traditional sense. It would be impossible for any Natural to compete.

Another GenRich type is the GenRich scientist. Many of the synthetic genes carried by the GenRich scientist are the same as those carried by all other members of the GenRich class, including some that enhance a variety of physical and mental attributes, as well as others that provide resistance to all known forms of human disease. But in addition, the present-day GenRich scientist has accumulated a set of particular synthetic genes that work together with his "natural" heritage to produce an enhanced scientific mind. Although the GenRich scientist may appear to be different from the GenRich athlete, both GenRich types have evolved by a similar process. The foundation ancestor for the modern GenRich scientist was a bright twenty-first-century scientist whose children were the first to be selected and enhanced to increase their chances of becoming even brighter scientists who could produce even more brilliant children. There are numerous other GenRich types including GenRich businessmen, GenRich musicians, GenRich artists, and even GenRich intellectual generalists who all evolved in the same way.

Not all present-day GenRich individuals can trace their foundation ancestors back to the twenty-first century, when genetic enhancement was first perfected. During the twenty-second and even the twenty-third centuries, some Natural families garnered the financial wherewithal required to place their children into the GenRich class. But with the passage of time, the genetic distance between Naturals and the GenRich has become greater and greater, and now there is little movement up from the Natural to GenRich class. It seems fair to say that society is on the verge of reaching the final point of complete polarization.

All aspects of the economy, the media, the entertainment industry, and the knowledge industry are controlled by members of the GenRich class. GenRich parents can afford to send their children to private schools rich in the resources required for them to take advantage of their enhanced genetic potential. In contrast, Naturals work as low-paid service providers or as laborers, and their children go to public schools. But twenty-fourth-century public schools have little in common with their predecessors from the twentieth century. Funds for public education have declined steadily since the beginning of the twenty-first century, and now Natural children are only taught the basic skills they need to perform the kinds of tasks they'll encounter in the jobs available to members of their class.

There is still some intermarriage as well as sexual intermingling between a few GenRich individuals and Naturals. But, as one might imagine, GenRich parents put intense pressure on their children not to dilute their expensive genetic endowment in this way. And as time passes, the mixing of the classes will become less and less frequent for reasons of both environment and genetics.

The environmental reason is clear enough: GenRich and Natural children grow up and live in segregated social worlds where there is little chance for contact between them. The genetic reason, however, was unanticipated.

It is obvious to everyone that with each generation of enhancement, the genetic distance separating the GenRich and Naturals is growing larger and larger. But a startling consequence of the expanding genetic distance has just come to light. In a nationwide survey of the few interclass GenRich-Natural couples that could be identified, sociologists have discovered an astounding 90 percent level of infertility. Reproductive geneticists have examined these couples and come to the conclusion that the infertility is caused primarily by an incompatibility between the genetic makeup of each member.

Evolutionary biologists have long observed instances in which otherwise fertile individuals taken from two separate populations prove infertile when mated to each other. And they tell the sociologists and the reproductive geneticists what is going on: the process of species separation between the GenRich and Naturals has already begun. Together, the sociologists, the reproductive geneticists, and the evolutionary biologists are willing to make the following prediction: If the accumulation of genetic knowledge and advances in genetic enhancement technology continue at the present rate, then by the end of the third millennium, the GenRich class and the Natural class will become the GenRich humans and the Natural humans—entirely separate species with no ability to cross-breed, and with as much romantic interest in each other as a current human would have for a chimpanzee.

DATELINE PRINCETON, NEW JERSEY: THE PRESENT

Are these outrageous scenarios the stuff of science fiction? Did they spring from the minds of Hollywood screenwriters hoping to create blockbuster movies without regard to real world constraints? No. The scenarios described under the first two datelines emerge directly from scientific understanding and technologies that are already available today. The scientific framework for the last scenario is based on straightforward extrapolations from our current knowledge base. Furthermore, if biomedical advances continue to occur at the same rate as they do now, the practices described are likely to be feasible long before we reach my conservatively chosen datelines.

It's time to take stock of the current state of science and technology in the fields of reproduction and genetics and to ask, in the broadest terms possible, what the future may hold. Most people are aware of the impact that reproductive technology has already had in the area of fertility treatment. The first "test tube baby"—Louise Brown—is already eighteen years old, and the acronym for in vitro fertilization—IVF—is commonly used by laypeople. The cloning of human beings has become a real possibility as well, although many are still confused about what the technology can and cannot do. Advances in genetic research have also been in the limelight, with the almost weekly identification of new genes implicated in diseases like cystic fibrosis and breast cancer, or personality traits like novelty-seeking and anxiety.

What has yet to catch the attention of the public at large, however, is the incredible power that emerges when current technologies in reproductive biology and genetics are brought together in the form of *reprogenetics.* With reprogenetics, parents can gain complete control over their genetic destiny, with the ability to guide and enhance the characteristics of their children, and their children's children as well. But even as reprogenetics makes dreams come true, like all of the most powerful technologies invented by humankind, it may also generate nightmares of a kind not previously imagined.

Of course, just because a technology becomes feasible does not mean that it will be used. Or does it? Society, acting through government intervention, could outlaw any one or all of the reprogenetic practices that I have described. Isn't the *non*use of nuclear weapons for the purpose of mass destruction over the last half century an example of how governments can control technology?

There are two big differences between the use of nuclear technology and reprogenetic technology. These differences lie in the resources and money needed to practice each. The most crucial resources required to build a nuclear weapon—large reactors and enriched sources of uranium or plutonium—are tightly controlled by the government itself. The resources required to practice reprogenetics—precision medical tools, small laboratory equipment, and simple chemicals—are all available for sale, without restriction, to anyone with the money to pay for them. The cost of developing a nuclear weapon is billions of dollars. In contrast, a reprogenetics clinic could easily be run on the scale of a small business anywhere in the world. Thus, even if restrictions on the use of reprogenetics are imposed in one country or another, those intent on delivering and receiving these services will not be restrained. But on what grounds can we argue that they should be restrained?

In response to this question, many people point to the chilling novel *Brave New World* written by Aldous Huxley in 1932. It is the story of a future worldwide political state that exerts complete control over human reproduction and human nature as well. In this brave new world, the state uses fetal hatcheries to breed each child into a predetermined intellectual class that ranges from alpha at the top to epsilon at the bottom. Individual members of each class are predestined to fit into specific roles in a soulless utopia where marriage and parenthood are prevented and promiscuous sexual activity is strongly encouraged, where universal immunity to diseases has been achieved, and where an all-enveloping state propaganda machine and mood-altering drugs make all content with their positions in life.

While Huxley guessed right about the power we would gain over the process of reproduction, I think he was dead wrong when it came to predicting *who* would use the power and for what purposes. What Huxley failed to understand, or refused to accept, was the driving force behind babymaking. It is individuals and couples who want to reproduce themselves in their own images. It is individuals and couples who want their children to be happy and successful. And it is individuals and couples—like Barbara and Dan and Cheryl and Madelaine and Melissa and Curtis and Jennifer, *not governments*—who will seize control of these new technologies. They will use some to reach otherwise unattainable reproductive goals and others to help their children achieve health, happiness, and success. And it is in pursuit of this last goal that the combined actions of many individuals, operating over many generations, could perhaps give rise to a polarized humanity more horrific than Huxley's imagined Brave New World.

There are those who will argue that parents don't have the right to control the characteristics of their children-to-be in the way I describe. But American society, in particular, accepts the rights of parents to control every other aspect of their children's lives from the time they are born until they reach adulthood. If one accepts the parental prerogative after birth, it is hard to argue against it before birth, if no harm is caused to the children who emerge.

Many think that it is inherently unfair for some people to have access to technologies that can provide advantages while others, less well-off, are forced to depend on chance alone. I would agree. It is inherently unfair. But once again, American society adheres to the principle that personal liberty and personal fortune are the primary determinants of what individuals are allowed and able to do. Anyone who accepts the right of affluent parents to provide their children with an expensive private school education cannot use "unfairness" as a reason for rejecting the use of reprogenetic technologies.

Indeed, in a society that values individual freedom above all else, it is hard to find any legitimate basis for restricting the use of reprogenetics. And therein lies the dilemma. For while each individual use of the technology can be viewed in the light of personal reproductive choice—with no ability to change society at large—together they could have dramatic, unintended, long-term consequences.

As the technologies of reproduction and genetics have become ever more powerful over the last decade, most practicing scientists and physicians have been loathe to speculate about where it may all lead. One reason for reluctance is the fear of getting it wrong. It really is impossible to predict with certainty which future technological advances will proceed on time and which will encounter unexpected roadblocks. This means that like Huxley's vision of a fetal hatchery, some of the ideas proposed here may ultimately be technically impossible or exceedingly difficult to implement. On the other hand, there are sure to be technological breakthroughs that no one can imagine now, just as Huxley was unable to imagine genetic engineering, or cloning from adult cells, in 1932.

There is a second reason why fertility specialists, in particular, are reluctant to speculate about the kinds of future scenarios that I describe here. It's called politics. In a climate where abortion clinics are on the alert for terrorist attacks, and where the religious right rails against any interference with the "natural process" of conception, IVF providers see no reason to call attention to themselves through descriptions of reproductive and genetic manipulations that are sure to provoke outrage.

The British journal *Nature* is one of the two most important science journals in the world (the other being the American journal *Science*). It is published weekly and is read by all types of scientists from biologists to physicists to medical researchers. No one would ever consider it to be radical or sensationalist in any way. On March 7, 1996, *Nature* published an article that described a method for cloning unlimited numbers of sheep from a single fertilized egg, with further implications for improving methods of genetic engineering. It took another week before the ramifications of this isolated breakthrough sank in for the editors. On March 14, 1996, they wrote an impassioned editorial saying in part: "That the growing power of molecular genetics confronts us with future prospects of being able to *change the nature of our species* [my emphasis] is a fact that seldom appears to be addressed in depth. Scientific knowledge may not yet permit detailed understanding, but the possibilities are clear enough. This gives rise to issues that in the end will have to be related to people within the social and ethical environments in which they live. And the agenda is set by mankind as a whole, not by the subset involved in the science."

They are right that the agenda will not be set by scientists. But they are wrong to think that "mankind as a whole"—unable to reach consensus on so many other societal issues—will have any effect whatsoever. The agenda is sure to be set by individuals and couples who will act on behalf of themselves and their children. ... The use of reprogenetic technologies is inevitable. It will not be controlled by governments or societies or even the scientists who create it.

There is no doubt about it. For better *and* worse, a new age is upon us. And whether we like it or not, the global marketplace will reign supreme.

2.4.2 Preventing a Brave New World

LEON R. KASS

In this article, Leon Kass, Addie Clark Harding Professor at the Committee on Social Thought at the University of Chicago and member of the President's Commission on Bioethics, argues that modern medical science is poised to cross an ethical boundary that will have momentous consequences for the future of humanity. Harking back to the dystopian vision of Aldous Huxley's classic *Brave New World* (1932), Kass argues that "the technological imperative, liberal democratic society, compassionate humanitarianism, moral pluralism, and free markets" are leading us down a path that places us at risk of losing our humanity. Kass argues that we should enact a worldwide ban on human cloning as a means of deterring "renegade scientists" from engaging in the practice. His proposed ban would apply to both reproductive and therapeutic cloning of human embryos because he believes that banning only reproductive cloning would prove impossible to enforce. Kass believes that we have the power to exercise control over the technological project but can only do so if we muster the political will to just say "no" to human cloning.

FOCUS QUESTIONS

1. What are the three main factors that Kass identifies as limiting our ability to control the onward march of the biomedical project? What other factors contribute to our inability to avoid the dangers Kass is concerned about?
2. What reasons does Kass give for "drawing the line" at human reproductive cloning by prohibiting the practice? Are these reasons convincing? Do the same arguments apply with equal force to therapeutic cloning? Explain.
3. Why does Kass believe that employing cloning or genetic engineering techniques to produce human children is "profoundly dehumanizing, no matter how good the product"? Explain.
4. Compare Kass's arguments to those offered by Claire Hope Cummings (selection 2.4.4). Is there a moral difference between applying genetic engineering techniques to humans and to plants and nonhuman animals? Explain.

KEYWORDS

dehumanization, genetic determinism, infertility, reproductive cloning, reproductive freedom, somatic cell nuclear transfer

---

Source: "Preventing a Brave New World," by Leon R. Kass, M.D., *The New Republic*, May 21, 2001.
Copyright © 2001 by Leon R. Kass. Reprinted by permission of the author.

I.

The urgency of the great political struggles of the twentieth century, successfully waged against totalitarianisms first right and then left, seems to have blinded many people to a deeper and ultimately darker truth about the present age: all contemporary societies are travelling briskly in the same utopian direction. All are wedded to the modern technological project; all march eagerly to the drums of progress and fly proudly the banner of modern science; all sing loudly the Baconian anthem, "Conquer nature, relieve man's estate." Leading the triumphal procession is modern medicine, which is daily becoming ever more powerful in its battle against disease, decay, and death, thanks especially to astonishing achievements in biomedical science and technology—achievements for which we must surely be grateful.

Yet contemplating present and projected advances in genetic and reproductive technologies, in neuroscience and psychopharmacology, and in the development of artificial organs and computer-chip implants for human brains, we now clearly recognize new uses for biotechnical power that soar beyond the traditional medical goals of healing disease and relieving suffering. Human nature itself lies on the operating table, ready for alteration, for eugenic and psychic "enhancement," for wholesale re-design. In leading laboratories, academic and industrial, new creators are confidently amassing their powers and quietly honing their skills, while on the street their evangelists are zealously prophesying a post-human future. For anyone who cares about preserving our humanity, the time has come to pay attention.

Some transforming powers are already here. The Pill. In vitro fertilization. Bottled embryos. Surrogate wombs. Cloning. Genetic screening. Genetic manipulation. Organ harvesting. Mechanical spare parts. Chimeras. Brain implants. Ritalin for the young, Viagra for the old, Prozac for everyone. And, to leave this vale of tears, a little extra morphine accompanied by Muzak.

Years ago Aldous Huxley saw it coming. In his charming but disturbing novel, *Brave New World* (it appeared in 1932 and is more powerful on each re-reading), he made its meaning strikingly visible for all to see. Unlike other frightening futuristic novels of the past century, such as Orwell's already dated *Nineteen Eighty-Four,* Huxley shows us a dystopia that goes with, rather than against, the human grain. Indeed, it is animated by our own most humane and progressive aspirations. Following those aspirations to their ultimate realization, Huxley enables us to recognize those less obvious but often more pernicious evils that are inextricably linked to the successful attainment of partial goods.

Huxley depicts human life seven centuries hence, living under the gentle hand of humanitarianism rendered fully competent by genetic manipulation, psychoactive drugs, hypnopaedia, and high-tech amusements. At long last, mankind has succeeded in eliminating disease, aggression, war, anxiety, suffering, guilt, envy, and grief. But this victory comes at the heavy price of homogenization, mediocrity, trivial pursuits, shallow attachments, debased tastes, spurious contentment, and souls without loves or longings. The Brave New World has achieved prosperity, community, stability, and nigh-universal contentment, only to be peopled by creatures of human shape but stunted humanity. They consume, fornicate, take "soma," enjoy "centrifugal bumble-puppy," and operate the machinery that makes it all possible. They do not read, write, think, love, or govern themselves. Art and science, virtue and religion, family and friendship are all passe. What matters most is bodily health and immediate gratification: "Never put off till tomorrow the fun you can have today." Brave New Man is so dehumanized that he does not even recognize what has been lost.

Huxley's novel, of course, is science fiction. Prozac is not yet Huxley's "soma"; cloning by nuclear transfer or splitting embryos is not exactly "Bokanovskification"; MTV and virtual-reality parlors are not quite the "feelies"; and our current safe and consequenceless sexual practices are not universally as loveless or as empty as those in the novel. But the kinships are disquieting, all the more so since our technologies of bio-psycho-engineering are still in their infancy, and in ways that make all too clear what they might look like in their full maturity. Moreover, the cultural changes that technology has already wrought among us should make us even more worried than Huxley would have us be.

In Huxley's novel, everything proceeds under the direction of an omnipotent—albeit benevolent—world state. Yet the dehumanization that he portrays does not really require despotism or external control. To the contrary, precisely because the society of the future will deliver exactly what we most want—health, safety, comfort, plenty, pleasure, peace of mind and length of days—we can reach the same humanly debased condition solely on the basis of free human choice. No need for World Controllers. Just give us the technological imperative, liberal democratic society, compassionate humanitarianism, moral pluralism, and free markets, and we can take ourselves to a Brave New World all by ourselves—and without even deliberately deciding to go. In case you had not noticed, the train has already left the station and is gathering speed, but no one seems to be in charge.

Some among us are delighted, of course, by this state of affairs: some scientists and biotechnologists, their entrepreneurial backers, and a cheering claque of sci-fi enthusiasts, futurologists, and libertarians. There are dreams to be realized, powers to be exercised, honors to be won, and money—big money—to be made. But many of us are worried, and not, as the proponents of the revolution self-servingly claim, because we are either ignorant of science or afraid of the unknown. To the contrary, we can see all too clearly where the train is headed, and we do not like the destination. We can distinguish cleverness about means from wisdom about ends, and we are loath to entrust the future of the race to those who cannot tell the difference. No friend of humanity cheers for a post-human future.

Yet for all our disquiet, we have until now done nothing to prevent it. We hide our heads in the sand because we enjoy the blessings that medicine keeps supplying, or we rationalize our inaction by declaring that human engineering is inevitable and we can do nothing about it. In either case, we are complicit in preparing for our own degradation, in some respects more to blame than the bio-zealots who, however misguided, are putting their money where their mouth is. Denial and despair, unattractive outlooks in any situation, become morally reprehensible when circumstances summon us to keep the world safe for human flourishing.

Our immediate ancestors, taking up the challenge of their time, rose to the occasion and rescued the human future from the cruel dehumanizations of Nazi and Soviet tyranny. It is our more difficult task to find ways to preserve it from the soft dehumanizations of well-meaning but hubristic biotechnical "re-creationism"—and to do it without undermining biomedical science or rejecting its genuine contributions to human welfare.

Truth be told, it will not be easy for us to do so, and we know it. But rising to the challenge requires recognizing the difficulties. For there are indeed many features of modern life that will conspire to frustrate efforts aimed at the human control of the biomedical project. First, we Americans believe in technological automatism: where we do not foolishly believe that all innovation is progress, we fatalistically believe that it is inevitable ("If it can be done, it will be done, like it or not"). Second, we believe in freedom: the freedom of scientists to inquire, the freedom of technologists to develop, the freedom of entrepreneurs to invest and to profit, the freedom of private citizens to make use of existing technologies to satisfy any and all personal desires, including the desire to reproduce by whatever means. Third, the biomedical enterprise occupies the moral high ground of compassionate humanitarianism, upholding the supreme values of modern life—cure disease, prolong life, relieve suffering—in competition with which other moral goods rarely stand a chance. ("What the public wants is not to be sick," says James Watson, "and if we help them not to be sick, they'll be on our side.")

There are still other obstacles. Our cultural pluralism and easygoing relativism make it difficult to reach consensus on what we should embrace and what we should oppose; and moral objections to this or that biomedical practice are often facilely dismissed as religious or sectarian. Many people are unwilling to pronounce judgments about what is good or bad, right and wrong, even in matters of great importance, even for themselves—never mind for others or for society as a whole. It does not help that the biomedical project is now deeply entangled with commerce: there are increasingly powerful economic interests in favor of going full steam ahead, and no economic interests in favor of going slow. Since we live in a democracy, moreover, we face political difficulties in gaining a consensus to direct our future, and we have almost no political experience in trying to curtail the development of any new biomedical technology. Finally, and perhaps most troubling, our views of the meaning of our humanity have been so transformed by the scientific-technological approach to the world that we are in danger of forgetting what we have to lose, humanly speaking.

But though the difficulties are real, our situation is far from hopeless. Regarding each of the aforementioned impediments, there is another side to the story. Though we love our gadgets and believe in progress, we have lost our innocence regarding technology. The environmental movement especially has alerted us to the unintended damage caused by unregulated technological advance, and has taught us how certain dangerous practices can be curbed. Though we favor freedom of inquiry, we recognize that experiments are deeds and not speeches, and we prohibit experimentation on human subjects without their consent, even when cures from disease might be had by unfettered research; and we limit so-called reproductive freedom by proscribing incest, polygamy, and the buying and selling of babies.

Although we esteem medical progress, biomedical institutions have ethics committees that judge research proposals on moral grounds, and, when necessary, uphold the primacy of human freedom and human dignity even over scientific discovery. Our moral pluralism notwithstanding, national commissions and review bodies have sometimes reached moral consensus to recommend limits on permissible scientific research and technological application. On the economic front, the patenting of genes and life forms and the rapid rise of genomic commerce have elicited strong concerns and criticisms, leading even former enthusiasts of the new biology to recoil from the impending commodification of human life. Though we lack political institutions experienced in setting limits on biomedical innovation, federal agencies years ago rejected the development of the plutonium-powered artificial heart, and we have nationally prohibited commercial traffic in organs for transplantation, even though a market would increase the needed supply. In recent years, several American states and many foreign countries have successfully taken political action, making certain practices illegal and placing others under moratoriums (the creation of human embryos solely for research; human germ-line genetic alteration). Most importantly, the majority of Americans are not yet so degraded or so cynical as to fail to be revolted by the society depicted in Huxley's novel. Though the obstacles to effective action are significant, they offer no excuse for resignation. Besides, it would be disgraceful to concede defeat even before we enter the fray.

Not the least of our difficulties in trying to exercise control over where biology is taking us is the fact that we do not get to decide, once and for all, for or against the destination of a post-human world. The scientific discoveries and the technical powers that will take us there come to us piecemeal, one at a time and seemingly independent from one another, each often attractively introduced as a measure that will "help [us] not to be sick." But sometimes we come to a clear fork in the road where decision is possible, and where we know that our decision will make a world of difference—indeed, it will make a permanently different world. Fortunately, we stand now at the point of such a momentous decision. Events have conspired to provide us with a perfect opportunity to seize the initiative and to gain some control of the bio technical project. I refer to the prospect of human cloning, a practice absolutely central to Huxley's fictional world. Indeed, creating and manipulating life in the laboratory is the gateway to a Brave New World, not only in fiction but also in fact.

"To clone or not to clone a human being" is no longer a fanciful question. Success in cloning sheep, and also cows, mice, pigs, and goats, makes it perfectly clear that a fateful decision is now at hand: whether we should welcome or even tolerate the cloning of human beings. If recent newspaper reports are to be believed, reputable scientists and physicians have announced their intention to produce the first human clone in the coming year. Their efforts may already be under way.

The media, gawking and titillating as is their wont, have been softening us up for this possibility by turning the bizarre into the familiar. In the four years since the birth of Dolly the cloned sheep, the tone of discussing the prospect of human cloning has gone from "Yuck" to "Oh?" to "Gee whiz" to "Why not?" The sentimentalizers, aided by leading bioethicists, have downplayed talk about eugenically cloning the beautiful and the brawny or the best and the brightest. They have taken instead to defending clonal reproduction for humanitarian or compassionate reasons: to treat infertility in people who are said to "have no other choice," to avoid the risk of severe genetic disease, to "replace" a child who has died. For the sake of these rare benefits, they would have us countenance the entire practice of human cloning, the consequences be damned.

But we dare not be complacent about what is at issue, for the stakes are very high. Human cloning, though partly continuous with previous reproductive technologies, is also something radically new in itself and in its easily foreseeable consequences—especially when coupled with powers for genetic "enhancement" and germline genetic modification that may soon become available, owing to the recently completed Human Genome Project. I exaggerate somewhat, but in the direction of the truth: we are compelled to decide nothing less than whether human procreation is going to remain human, whether children are going to be made to order rather than begotten, and whether we wish to say yes in principle to the road that leads to the dehumanized hell of *Brave New World*.

...

For we have here a golden opportunity to exercise some control over where biology is taking us. The technology of cloning is discrete and well defined, and it requires considerable technical know-how and dexterity; we can therefore know by name many of the likely practitioners. The public demand for cloning is extremely low, and most people are decidedly against it. Nothing scientifically or medically important would be lost by banning clonal reproduction; alternative and non-objectionable means are available to obtain some of the most important medical benefits claimed for (nonreproductive) human cloning. The commercial interests in human cloning are, for now, quite limited; and the nations of the world are actively seeking to prevent it. Now may be as good a chance as we will ever have to get our hands on the wheel of the runaway train now headed for a post-human world and to steer it toward a more dignified human future.

II.

What is cloning? Cloning, or asexual reproduction, is the production of individuals who are genetically identical to an already existing individual. The procedure's name is fancy—"somatic cell nuclear transfer"—but its concept is simple. Take a mature but unfertilized egg; remove or deactivate its nucleus; introduce a nucleus obtained from a specialized (somatic) cell of an adult organism. Once the egg begins to divide, transfer the little embryo to a woman's uterus to initiate a pregnancy. Since almost all the hereditary material of a cell is contained within its nucleus, the renucleated egg and the individual into which it develops are genetically identical to the organism that was the source of the transferred nucleus.

An unlimited number of genetically identical individuals—the group, as well as each of its members, is called "a clone"—could be produced by nuclear transfer. In principle, any person, male or female, newborn or adult, could be cloned, and in any quantity; and because stored cells can outlive their sources, one may even clone the dead. Since cloning requires no personal involvement on the part of the person whose genetic material is used, it could easily be used to reproduce living or deceased persons without their consent—a threat to reproductive freedom that has received relatively little attention.

Some possible misconceptions need to be avoided. Cloning is not Xeroxing: the clone of Bill Clinton, though his genetic double, would enter the world hairless, toothless, and peeing in his diapers, like any other human infant. But neither is cloning just like natural twinning: the cloned twin will be identical to an older, existing adult; and it will arise not by chance but by deliberate design; and its entire genetic makeup will be preselected by its parents and/or scientists.

Moreover, the success rate of cloning, at least at first, will probably not be very high: the Scots transferred two hundred seventy-seven adult nuclei into sheep eggs, implanted twenty-nine clonal embryos, and achieved the birth of only one live lamb clone.

For this reason, among others, it is unlikely that, at least for now, the practice would be very popular; and there is little immediate worry of mass-scale production of multicopies. Still, for the tens of thousands of people who sustain more than three hundred assisted-reproduction clinics in the United States and already avail themselves of in vitro fertilization and other techniques, cloning would be an option with virtually no added fuss. Panos Zavos, the Kentucky reproduction specialist who has announced his plans to clone a child, claims that he has already received thousands of e-mailed requests from people eager to clone, despite the known risks of failure and damaged offspring. Should commercial interests develop in "nucleus-banking," as they have in sperm-banking and egg-harvesting; should famous athletes or other celebrities decide to market their DNA the way they now market their autographs and nearly everything else; should techniques of embryo and germline genetic testing and manipulation arrive as anticipated, increasing the use of laboratory assistance in order to obtain "better" babies—should all this come to pass, cloning, if it is permitted, could become more than a marginal practice simply on the basis of free reproductive choice.

What are we to think about this prospect? Nothing good. Indeed, most people are repelled by nearly all aspects of human cloning: the possibility of mass production of human beings, with large clones of look-alikes, compromised in their individuality; the idea of father-son or mother-daughter "twins"; the bizarre prospect of a woman bearing and rearing a genetic copy of herself, her spouse, or even her deceased father or mother; the grotesqueness of conceiving a child as an exact "replacement" for another who has died; the utilitarian creation of embryonic duplicates of oneself, to be frozen away or created when needed to provide homologous tissues or organs for transplantation; the narcissism of those who would clone themselves, and the arrogance of others who think they know who deserves to be cloned; the Frankensteinian hubris to create a human life and increasingly to control its destiny; men playing at being God. Almost no one finds any of the suggested reasons for human cloning compelling, and almost everyone anticipates its possible misuses and abuses. And the popular belief that human cloning cannot be prevented makes the prospect all the more revolting.

Revulsion is not an argument; and some of yesterday's repugnances are today calmly accepted—not always for the better. In some crucial cases, however, repugnance is the emotional expression of deep wisdom, beyond reason's power completely to articulate it. Can anyone really give an argument fully adequate to the horror that is father-daughter incest (even with consent), or bestiality, or the mutilation of a corpse, or the eating of human flesh, or the rape or murder of another human being? Would anybody's failure to give full rational justification for his revulsion at those practices make that revulsion ethically suspect?

I suggest that our repugnance at human cloning belongs in this category. We are repelled by the prospect of cloning human beings not because of the strangeness or the novelty of the undertaking, but because we intuit and we feel, immediately and without argument, the violation of things that we rightfully hold dear. We sense that cloning represents a profound defilement of our given nature as procreative beings, and of the social relations built on this natural ground. We also sense that cloning is a radical form of child abuse. In this age in which everything is held to be permissible so long as it is freely done, and in which our bodies are regarded as mere instruments of our autonomous rational will, repugnance may be the only voice left that speaks up to defend the central core of our humanity. Shallow are the souls that have forgotten how to shudder.

III.

Yet repugnance need not stand naked before the bar of reason. The wisdom of our horror at human cloning can be at least partially articulated, even if this is finally one of those instances about which the heart has its reasons that reason cannot entirely know. I offer four objections to human cloning: that it constitutes unethical experimentation; that it threatens identity and individuality; that it turns procreation into manufacture (especially when understood as the harbinger of manipulations to come); and that it means despotism over children and perversion of parenthood. Please note: I speak only about so-called reproductive cloning, not about the creation of cloned embryos for research. The objections that may be raised against creating (or using) embryos for research are entirely independent of whether the research embryos are produced by cloning. What is radically distinct and radically new is reproductive cloning.

Any attempt to clone a human being would constitute an unethical experiment upon the resulting child-to-be. In all the animal experiments, fewer than two to three percent of all cloning attempts succeeded. Not only are there fetal deaths and stillborn infants, but many of the so-called "successes" are in fact failures. As has only recently become clear, there is a very high incidence of major disabilities and deformities in cloned animals that attain live birth. Cloned cows often have heart and lung problems; cloned mice later develop pathological obesity; other live-born cloned animals fail to reach normal developmental milestones.

The problem, scientists suggest, may lie in the fact that an egg with a new somatic nucleus must re-program itself in a matter of minutes or hours (whereas the nucleus of an unaltered egg has been prepared over months and years). There is thus a greatly increased likelihood of error in translating the genetic instructions, leading to developmental defects some of which will show themselves only much later. (Note also that these induced abnormalities may also affect the stem cells that scientists hope to harvest from cloned embryos. Lousy embryos, lousy stem cells.) Nearly all scientists now agree that attempts to clone human beings carry massive risks of producing unhealthy, abnormal, and malformed children. What are we to do with them? Shall we just discard the ones that fall short of expectations? Considered opinion is today nearly unanimous, even among scientists: attempts at human cloning are irresponsible and unethical. We cannot ethically even get to know whether or not human cloning is feasible.

If it were successful, cloning would create serious issues of identity and individuality. The clone may experience concerns about his distinctive identity not only because he will be, in genotype and in appearance, identical to another human being, but because he may also be twin to the person who is his "father" or his "mother"—if one can still call them that. Unaccountably, people treat as innocent the homey case of intra-familial cloning—the cloning of husband or wife (or single mother). They forget about the unique dangers of mixing the twin relation with the parent-child relation. (For this situation, the relation of contemporaneous twins is no precedent; yet even this less problematic situation teaches us how difficult it is to wrest independence from the being for whom one has the most powerful affinity.) Virtually no parent is going to be able to treat a clone of himself or herself as one treats a child generated by the lottery of sex. What will happen when the adolescent clone of Mommy becomes the spitting image of the woman with whom Daddy once fell in love? In case of divorce, will Mommy still love the clone of Daddy, even though she can no longer stand the sight of Daddy himself?

Most people think about cloning from the point of view of adults choosing to clone. Almost nobody thinks about what it would be like to be the cloned child. Surely his or her new life would constantly be scrutinized in relation to that of the older version. Even in the absence of unusual parental expectations for the clone—say, to live the same life, only without its errors—the child is likely to be ever a curiosity, ever a potential source of déjà vu. Unlike "normal" identical twins, a cloned individual—copied from whomever—will be saddled with a genotype that has already lived. He will not be fully a surprise to the world: people are likely always to compare his doings in life with those of his alter ego, especially if he is a clone of someone gifted or famous. True, his nurture and his circumstance will be different; genotype is not exactly destiny. But one must also expect parental efforts to shape this new life after the original—or at least to view the child with the original version always firmly in mind. For why else did they clone from the star basketball player, the mathematician, or the beauty queen—or even dear old Dad—in the first place?

Human cloning would also represent a giant step toward the transformation of begetting into making, of procreation into manufacture (literally, "handmade"), a process that has already begun with in vitro fertilization and genetic testing of embryos. With cloning, not only is the process in hand, but the total genetic blueprint of the cloned individual is selected and determined by the human artisans. To be sure, subsequent development is still according to natural processes; and the resulting children will be recognizably human. But we would be taking a major step into making man himself simply another one of the man-made things.

How does begetting differ from making? In natural procreation, human beings come together to give existence to another being that is formed exactly as we were, by what we are—living, hence perishable, hence aspiringly erotic, hence procreative human beings. But in clonal reproduction, and in the more advanced forms of manufacture to which it will lead, we give existence to a being not by what we are but by what we intend and design.

Let me be clear. The problem is not the mere intervention of technique, and the point is not that "nature knows best." The problem is that any child whose being, character, and capacities exist owing to human design does not stand on the same plane as its makers. As with any product of our making, no matter how excellent, the artificer stands above it, not as an equal but as a superior, transcending it by his will and creative prowess. In human cloning, scientists and prospective "parents" adopt a technocratic attitude toward human children: human children become their artifacts. Such an arrangement is profoundly dehumanizing, no matter how good the product.

Procreation dehumanized into manufacture is further degraded by commodification, a virtually inescapable result of allowing baby-making to proceed under the banner of commerce. Genetic and reproductive biotechnology companies are already growth industries, but they will soon go into commercial orbit now that the Human Genome Project has been completed. "Human eggs for sale" is already a big business, masquerading under the pretense of "donation." Newspaper advertisements on elite college campuses offer up to $50,000 for an egg "donor" tall enough to play women's basketball and with SAT scores high enough for admission to Stanford; and to nobody's surprise, at such prices there are many young coeds eager to help shoppers obtain the finest babies money can buy. (The egg and womb-renting entrepreneurs shamelessly proceed on the ancient, disgusting, misogynist premise that most women will give you access to their bodies, if the price is right.) Even before the capacity for human cloning is perfected, established companies will have invested in the harvesting of eggs from ovaries obtained at autopsy or through ovarian surgery, practiced embryonic genetic alteration, and initiated the stockpiling of prospective donor tissues. Through the rental of surrogate-womb services, and through the buying and selling of tissues and embryos priced according to the merit of the donor, the commodification of nascent human life will be unstoppable.

Finally, the practice of human cloning by nuclear transfer—like other anticipated forms of genetically engineering the next generation—would enshrine and aggravate a profound misunderstanding of the meaning of having children and of the parent-child relationship. When a couple normally chooses to procreate, the partners are saying yes to the emergence of new life in its novelty—are saying yes not only to having a child, but also to having whatever child this child turns out to be. In accepting our finitude, in opening ourselves to our replacement, we tacitly confess the limits of our control.

Embracing the future by procreating means precisely that we are relinquishing our grip in the very activity of taking up our own share in what we hope will be the immortality of human life and the human species. This means that our children are not our children: they are not our property, they are not our possessions. Neither are they supposed to live our lives for us, or to live anyone's life but their own. Their genetic distinctiveness and independence are the natural foreshadowing of the deep truth that they have their own, never-before-enacted life to live. Though sprung from a past, they take an uncharted course into the future.

Much mischief is already done by parents who try to live vicariously through their children. Children are sometimes compelled to fulfill the broken dreams of unhappy parents. But whereas most parents normally have hopes for their children, cloning parents will have expectations. In cloning, such overbearing parents will have taken at the start a decisive step that contradicts the entire meaning of the open and forward-looking nature of parent-child relations. The child is given a genotype that has already lived, with full expectation that this blueprint of a past life ought to be controlling the life that is to come. A wanted child now means a child who exists precisely to fulfill parental wants. Like all the more precise eugenic manipulations that will follow in its wake, cloning is thus inherently despotic, for it seeks to make one's children after one's own image (or an image of one's choosing) and their future according to one's will.

Is this hyperbolic? Consider concretely the new realities of responsibility and guilt in the households of the cloned. No longer only the sins of the parents, but also the genetic choices of the parents, will be visited on the children—and beyond the third and fourth generation; and everyone will know who is responsible. No parent will be able to blame nature or the lottery of sex for an unhappy adolescent's big nose, dull wit, musical ineptitude, nervous disposition, or anything else that he hates about himself. Fairly or not, children will hold their cloners responsible for everything, for nature as well as for nurture. And parents, especially the better ones, will be limitlessly liable to guilt. Only the truly despotic souls will sleep the sleep of the innocent.

IV.

The defenders of cloning are not wittingly friends of despotism. Quite the contrary. Deaf to most other considerations, they regard themselves mainly as friends of freedom: the freedom of individuals to reproduce, the freedom of scientists and inventors to discover and to devise and to foster "progress" in genetic knowledge and technique, the freedom of entrepreneurs to profit in the market. They want large-scale cloning only for animals, but they wish to preserve cloning as a human option for exercising our "right to reproduce"—our right to have children, and children with "desirable genes." As some point out, under our "right to reproduce" we already practice early forms of unnatural, artificial, and extramarital reproduction, and we already practice early forms of eugenic choice. For that reason, they argue, cloning is no big deal.

We have here a perfect example of the logic of the slippery slope. The principle of reproductive freedom currently enunciated by the proponents of cloning logically embraces the ethical acceptability of sliding all the way down: to producing children wholly in the laboratory from sperm to term (should it become feasible), and to producing children whose entire genetic makeup will be the product of parental eugenic planning and choice. If reproductive freedom means the right to have a child of one's own choosing by whatever means, then reproductive freedom knows and accepts no limits.

Proponents want us to believe that there are legitimate uses of cloning that can be distinguished from illegitimate uses, but by their own principles no such limits can be found. (Nor could any such limits be enforced in practice: once cloning is permitted, no one ever need discover whom one is cloning and why.) Reproductive freedom, as they understand it, is governed solely by the subjective wishes of the parents-to-be. The sentimentally appealing case of the childless married couple is, on these grounds, indistinguishable from the case of an individual (married or not) who would like to clone someone famous or talented, living or dead. And the principle here endorsed justifies not only cloning but also all future artificial attempts to create (manufacture) "better" or "perfect" babies.

The "perfect baby," of course, is the project not of the infertility doctors, but of the eugenic scientists and their supporters, who, for the time being, are content to hide behind the skirts of the partisans of reproductive freedom and compassion for the infertile. For them, the paramount right is not the so-called right to reproduce, it is what the biologist Bentley Glass called, a quarter of a century ago, "the right of every child to be born with a sound physical and mental constitution, based on a sound genotype ... the inalienable right to a sound heritage." But to secure this right, and to achieve the requisite quality control over new human life, human conception and gestation will need to be brought fully into the bright light of the laboratory, beneath which the child-to-be can be fertilized, nourished, pruned, weeded, watched, inspected, prodded, pinched, cajoled, injected, tested, rated, graded, approved, stamped, wrapped, sealed, and delivered. There is no other way to produce the perfect baby.

If you think that such scenarios require outside coercion or governmental tyranny, you are mistaken. Once it becomes possible, with the aid of human genomics, to produce or to select for what some regard as "better babies"—smarter, prettier, healthier, more athletic—parents will leap at the opportunity to "improve" their offspring. Indeed, not to do so will be socially regarded as a form of child neglect. Those who would ordinarily be opposed to such tinkering will be under enormous pressure to compete on behalf of their as yet unborn children—just as some now plan almost from their children's birth how to get them into Harvard. Never mind that, lacking a standard of "good" or "better," no one can really know whether any such changes will truly be improvements.

Proponents of cloning urge us to forget about the science-fiction scenarios of laboratory manufacture or multiple-copy clones, and to focus only on the sympathetic cases of infertile couples exercising their reproductive rights. But why, if the single cases are so innocent, should multiplying their performance be so off-putting? (Similarly, why do others object to people's making money from that practice if the practice itself is perfectly acceptable?) The so-called science-fiction cases—say, Brave New World—make vivid the meaning of what looks to us, mistakenly, to be benign. They reveal that what looks like compassionate humanitarianism is, in the end, crushing dehumanization.

V.

Whether or not they share my reasons, most people, I think, share my conclusion: that human cloning is unethical in itself and dangerous in its likely consequences, which include the precedent that it will establish for designing our children. Some reach this conclusion for their own good reasons, different from my own: concerns about distributive justice in access to eugenic cloning; worries about the genetic effects of asexual "inbreeding"; aversion to the implicit premise of genetic determinism; objections to the embryonic and fetal wastage that must necessarily accompany the efforts; religious opposition to "man playing God." But never mind why: the overwhelming majority of our fellow Americans remain firmly opposed to cloning human beings.

For us, then, the real questions are: What should we do about it? How can we best succeed? These questions should concern everyone eager to secure deliberate human control over the powers that could re-design our humanity, even if cloning is not the issue over which they would choose to make their stand. And the answer to the first question seems pretty plain. What we should do is work to prevent human cloning by making it illegal.

We should aim for a global legal ban, if possible, and for a unilateral national ban at a minimum—and soon, before the fact is upon us. To be sure, legal bans can be violated; but we certainly curtail much mischief by outlawing incest, voluntary servitude, and the buying and selling of organs and babies. To be sure, renegade scientists may secretly undertake to violate such a law, but we can deter them by both criminal sanctions and monetary penalties, as well as by removing any incentive they have to proudly claim credit for their technological bravado.

Such a ban on clonal baby-making will not harm the progress of basic genetic science and technology. On the contrary, it will reassure the public that scientists are happy to proceed without violating the deep ethical norms and intuitions of the human community. It will also protect honorable scientists from a public backlash against the brazen misconduct of the rogues. As many scientists have publicly confessed, free and worthy science probably has much more to fear from a strong public reaction to a cloning fiasco than it does from a cloning ban, provided that the ban is judiciously crafted and vigorously enforced against those who would violate it.

...

... I now believe that what we need is an all-out ban on human cloning, including the creation of embryonic clones. I am convinced that all halfway measures will prove to be morally, legally, and strategically flawed, and—most important—that they will not be effective in obtaining the desired result. Anyone truly serious about preventing human reproductive cloning must seek to stop the process from the beginning. Our changed circumstances, and the now evident defects of the less restrictive alternatives, make an all-out ban by far the most attractive and effective option.

Here's why. Creating cloned human children ("reproductive cloning") necessarily begins by producing cloned human embryos. Preventing the latter would prevent the former, and prudence alone might counsel building such a "fence around the law." Yet some scientists favor embryo cloning as a way of obtaining embryos for research or as sources of cells and tissues for the possible benefit of others. (This practice they misleadingly call "therapeutic cloning" rather than the more accurate "cloning for research" or "experimental cloning," so as to obscure the fact that the clone will be "treated" only to exploitation and destruction, and that any potential future beneficiaries and any future "therapies" are at this point purely hypothetical.)

The prospect of creating new human life solely to be exploited in this way has been condemned on moral grounds by many people—including *The Washington Post,* President Clinton, and many other supporters of a woman's right to abortion—as displaying a profound disrespect for life. Even those who are willing to scavenge so-called "spare embryos"—those products of in vitro fertilization made in excess of people's reproductive needs, and otherwise likely to be discarded—draw back from creating human embryos explicitly and solely for research purposes. They reject outright what they regard as the exploitation and the instrumentalization of nascent human life. In addition, others who are agnostic about the moral status of the embryo see the wisdom of not needlessly offending the sensibilities of their fellow citizens who are opposed to such practices.

But even setting aside these obvious moral first impressions, a few moments of reflection show why an anti-cloning law that permitted the cloning of embryos but criminalized their transfer to produce a child would be a moral blunder. This would be a law that was not merely permissively "pro-choice" but emphatically and prescriptively "anti-life." While permitting the creation of an embryonic life, it would make it a federal offense to try to keep it alive and bring it to birth. Whatever one thinks of the moral status or the ontological status of the human embryo, moral sense and practical wisdom recoil from having the government of the United States on record as requiring the destruction of nascent life and, what is worse, demanding the punishment of those who would act to preserve it by (feloniously!) giving it birth.

But the problem with the approach that targets only reproductive cloning (that is, the transfer of the embryo to a woman's uterus) is not only moral but also legal and strategic. A ban only on reproductive cloning would turn out to be unenforceable. Once cloned embryos were produced and available in laboratories and assisted-reproduction centers, it would be virtually impossible to control what was done with them. Biotechnical experiments take place in laboratories, hidden from public view, and, given the rise of high-stakes commerce in biotechnology, these experiments are concealed from the competition. Huge stockpiles of cloned human embryos could thus be produced and bought and sold without anyone knowing it. As we have seen with in vitro embryos created to treat infertility, embryos produced for one reason can be used for another reason: today "spare embryos" once created to begin a pregnancy are now used in research, and tomorrow clones created for research will be used to begin a pregnancy.

Assisted reproduction takes place within the privacy of the doctor-patient relationship, making outside scrutiny extremely difficult. Many infertility experts probably would obey the law, but others could and would defy it with impunity, their doings covered by the veil of secrecy that is the principle of medical confidentiality. Moreover, the transfer of embryos to begin a pregnancy is a simple procedure (especially compared with manufacturing the embryo in the first place), simple enough that its final steps could be self-administered by the woman, who would thus absolve the doctor of blame for having "caused" the illegal transfer. (I have in mind something analogous to Kevorkian's suicide machine, which was designed to enable the patient to push the plunger and the good "doctor" to evade criminal liability.)

Even should the deed become known, governmental attempts to enforce the reproductive ban would run into a swarm of moral and legal challenges, both to efforts aimed at preventing transfer to a woman and—even worse—to efforts seeking to prevent birth after transfer has occurred. A woman who wished to receive the embryo clone would no doubt seek a judicial restraining order, suing to have the law overturned in the name of a constitutionally protected interest in her own reproductive choice to clone. (The cloned child would be born before the legal proceedings were complete.) And should an "illicit clonal pregnancy" be discovered, no governmental agency would compel a woman to abort the clone, and there would be an understandable storm of protest should she be fined or jailed after she gives birth. Once the baby is born, there would even be sentimental opposition to punishing the doctor for violating the law—unless, of course, the clone turned out to be severely abnormal.

For all these reasons, the only practically effective and legally sound approach is to block human cloning at the start, at the production of the embryo clone. Such a ban can be rightly characterized not as interference with reproductive freedom, nor even as interference with scientific inquiry, but as an attempt to prevent the unhealthy, unsavory, and unwelcome manufacture of and traffic in human clones.

...

I appreciate that a federal legislative ban on human cloning is without American precedent, at least in matters technological. Perhaps such a ban will prove ineffective; perhaps it will eventually be shown to have been a mistake. (If so, it could later be reversed.) If enacted, however, it will have achieved one overwhelmingly important result, in addition to its contribution to thwarting cloning: it will place the burden of practical proof where it belongs. It will require the proponents to show very clearly what great social or medical good can be had only by the cloning of human beings. Surely it is only for such a compelling case, yet to be made or even imagined, that we should wish to risk this major departure—or any other major departure—in human procreation.

Americans have lived by and prospered under a rosy optimism about scientific and technological progress. The technological imperative has probably served us well, though we should admit that there is no accurate method for weighing benefits and harms. And even when we recognize the unwelcome outcomes of technological advance, we remain confident in our ability to fix all the "bad" consequences—by regulation or by means of still newer and better technologies. Yet there is very good reason for shifting the American paradigm, at least regarding those technological interventions into the human body and mind that would surely effect fundamental (and likely irreversible) changes in human nature, basic human relationships, and what it means to be a human being. Here we should not be willing to risk everything in the naive hope that, should things go wrong, we can later set them right again.

Some have argued that cloning is almost certainly going to remain a marginal practice, and that we should therefore permit people to practice it. Such a view is shortsighted. Even if cloning is rarely undertaken, a society in which it is tolerated is no longer the same society—any more than is a society that permits (even small-scale) incest or cannibalism or slavery. A society that allows cloning, whether it knows it or not, has tacitly assented to the conversion of procreation into manufacture and to the treatment of children as purely the projects of our will. Willy-nilly, it has acquiesced in the eugenic re-design of future generations. The humanitarian superhighway to a Brave New World lies open before this society.

But the present danger posed by human cloning is, paradoxically, also a golden opportunity. In a truly unprecedented way, we can strike a blow for the human control of the technological project, for wisdom, for prudence, for human dignity. The prospect of human cloning, so repulsive to contemplate, is the occasion for deciding whether we shall be slaves of unregulated innovation, and ultimately its artifacts, or whether we shall remain free human beings who guide our powers toward the enhancement of human dignity. The humanity of the human future is now in our hands.

2.4.3 The Case against Perfection

MICHAEL J. SANDEL

In this reading, Michael Sandel, professor of political philosophy at Harvard University and also a member of the President's Council on Bioethics, develops an answer to some of the hardest ethical questions raised by genetic engineering, particularly the use of this technology for human genetic enhancement. It is one thing, he argues, to employ genetic technologies to prevent or cure diseases or repair injuries but quite another to use them to produce children who are genetically advantaged by parental choice. Many people have moral qualms about performance-enhancing drugs in sports, but it is difficult to isolate exactly the ethical basis of these intuitions. Sandel examines and dismisses several plausible explanations for such qualms but finds each of these arguments insufficient. Instead, he argues that what is problematic about drug or genetic enhancement is that it represents "a Promethean aspiration to remake nature, including human nature, to serve our purposes and satisfy our desires." This desire to remake ourselves coexists with a countervailing value in the "giftedness of life"—that is, the appreciation that "our talents and powers are not wholly our own doing." The "ethic of giftedness" provides a moral basis for rejecting the vision of "free-market eugenics" that has been advocated by many bioethicists. Instead, Sandel argues for constraining our drive to mastery with a humility born of the recognition that our individual genetic endowments should remain "gifts" rather than become products of deliberate design.

FOCUS QUESTIONS

1. Why does Sandel think that the objection to human cloning from autonomy or the value of an "open future" is unconvincing? What about the argument from unfairness? How can these objections be answered?
2. What does Sandel mean by the "ethic of willfulness"? How is this ethic manifest, for instance, in the use of performance-enhancing drugs by athletes?
3. What three key features of the moral landscape would be undermined, in Sandel's view, by the use of genetic enhancement technologies? Do you agree that these values should be protected and preserved? Explain.
4. Compare Sandel's view to those of Lee Silver (Selection 2.4.1). Is there any way to reconcile or balance their respective positions? Explain.

Source: From "The Case Against Perfection" by Michael J. Sandel, *The Atlantic Monthly*, April 2004, pp. 51–62. Copyright © 2004 Michael J. Sandel as first published in The Atlantic Monthly. Reprinted by permission.

KEYWORDS

chromosomal lottery, eugenics, gene therapy, genetic enhancement, human growth hormone, performance-enhancing drugs, sex selection

Breakthroughs in genetics present us with a promise and a predicament. The promise is that we may soon be able to treat and prevent a host of debilitating diseases. The predicament is that our newfound genetic knowledge may also enable us to manipulate our own nature—to enhance our muscles, memories, and moods; to choose the sex, height, and other genetic traits of our children; to make ourselves "better than well." When science moves faster than moral understanding, as it does today, men and women struggle to articulate their unease. In liberal societies they reach first for the language of autonomy, fairness, and individual rights. But this part of our moral vocabulary is ill equipped to address the hardest questions posed by genetic engineering. The genomic revolution has induced a kind of moral vertigo.

Consider cloning. The birth of Dolly the cloned sheep, in 1997, brought a torrent of concern about the prospect of cloned human beings. There are good medical reasons to worry. Most scientists agree that cloning is unsafe, likely to produce offspring with serious abnormalities. (Dolly recently died a premature death.) But suppose technology improved to the point where clones were at no greater risk than naturally conceived offspring. Would human cloning still be objectionable? Should our hesitation be moral as well as medical? What, exactly, is wrong with creating a child who is a genetic twin of one parent, or of an older sibling who has tragically died—or, for that matter, of an admired scientist, sports star, or celebrity?

Some say cloning is wrong because it violates the right to autonomy: by choosing a child's genetic makeup in advance, parents deny the child's right to an open future. A similar objection can be raised against any form of bioengineering that allows parents to select or reject genetic characteristics. According to this argument, genetic enhancements for musical talent, say, or athletic prowess, would point children toward particular choices, and so designer children would never be fully free.

At first glance the autonomy argument seems to capture what is troubling about human cloning and other forms of genetic engineering. It is not persuasive, for two reasons. First, it wrongly implies that absent a designing parent, children are free to choose their characteristics for themselves. But none of us chooses his genetic inheritance. The alternative to a cloned or genetically enhanced child is not one whose future is unbound by particular talents but one at the mercy of the genetic lottery.

Second, even if a concern for autonomy explains some of our worries about made-to-order children, it cannot explain our moral hesitation about people who seek genetic remedies or enhancements for themselves. Gene therapy on somatic (that is, nonreproductive) cells, such as muscle cells and brain cells, repairs or replaces defective genes. The moral quandary arises when people use such therapy not to cure a disease but to reach beyond health, to enhance their physical or cognitive capacities, to lift themselves above the norm.

Like cosmetic surgery, genetic enhancement employs medical means for nonmedical ends—ends unrelated to curing or preventing disease or repairing injury. But unlike cosmetic surgery, genetic enhancement is more than skin-deep. If we are ambivalent about surgery or Botox injections for sagging chins and furrowed brows, we are all the more troubled by genetic engineering for stronger bodies, sharper memories, greater intelligence, and happier moods. The question is whether we are right to be troubled, and if so, on what grounds.

In order to grapple with the ethics of enhancement, we need to confront questions largely lost from view—questions about the moral status of nature, and about the proper stance of human beings toward the given world. Since these questions verge on theology, modern philosophers and political theorists tend to shrink from them. But our new powers of biotechnology make them unavoidable. To see why this is so, consider four examples already on the horizon: muscle enhancement, memory enhancement, growth-hormone treatment, and reproductive technologies that enable parents to choose the sex and some genetic traits of their children. In each case what began as an attempt to treat a disease or prevent a genetic disorder now beckons as an instrument of improvement and consumer choice.

MUSCLES

Everyone would welcome a gene therapy to alleviate muscular dystrophy and to reverse the debilitating muscle loss that comes with old age. But what if the same therapy were used to improve athletic performance? Researchers have developed a synthetic gene that, when injected into the muscle cells of mice, prevents and even reverses natural muscle deterioration. The gene not only repairs wasted or injured muscles but also strengthens healthy ones. This success bodes well for human applications. H. Lee Sweeney, of the University of Pennsylvania, who leads the research, hopes his discovery will cure the immobility that afflicts the elderly. But Sweeney's bulked-up mice have already attracted the attention of athletes seeking a competitive edge. Although the therapy is not yet approved for human use, the prospect of genetically enhanced weight lifters, home-run sluggers, linebackers, and sprinters is easy to imagine. The widespread use of steroids and other performance-improving drugs in professional sports suggests that many athletes will be eager to avail themselves of genetic enhancement.

Suppose for the sake of argument that muscle-enhancing gene therapy, unlike steroids, turned out to be safe—or at least no riskier than a rigorous weight-training regimen. Would there be a reason to ban its use in sports? There is something unsettling about the image of genetically altered athletes lifting SUVs or hitting 650-foot home runs or running a three-minute mile. But what, exactly, is troubling about it? Is it simply that we find such superhuman spectacles too bizarre to contemplate? Or does our unease point to something of ethical significance?

It might be argued that a genetically enhanced athlete, like a drug-enhanced athlete, would have an unfair advantage over his unenhanced competitors. But the fairness argument against enhancement has a fatal flaw: it has always been the case that some athletes are better endowed genetically than others, and yet we do not consider this to undermine the fairness of competitive sports. From the standpoint of fairness, enhanced genetic differences would be no worse than natural ones, assuming they were safe and made available to all. If genetic enhancement in sports is morally objectionable, it must be for reasons other than fairness.

MEMORY

Genetic enhancement is possible for brains as well as brawn. In the mid-1990s scientists managed to manipulate a memory-linked gene in fruit flies, creating flies with photographic memories. More recently researchers have produced smart mice by inserting extra copies of a memory-related gene into mouse embryos. The altered mice learn more quickly and remember things longer than normal mice. The extra copies were programmed to remain active even in old age, and the improvement was passed on to offspring. Human memory is more complicated, but biotech companies, including Memory Pharmaceuticals, are in hot pursuit of memory-enhancing drugs, or "cognition enhancers," for human beings. The obvious market for such drugs consists of those who suffer from Alzheimer's and other serious memory disorders. The companies also have their sights on a bigger market: the 81 million Americans over fifty who are beginning to encounter the memory loss that comes naturally with age. A drug that reversed age-related memory loss would be a bonanza for the pharmaceutical industry: a Viagra for the brain. Such use would straddle the line between remedy and enhancement. Unlike a treatment for Alzheimer's, it would cure no disease; but insofar as it restored capacities a person once possessed, it would have a remedial aspect. It could also have purely nonmedical uses: for example, by a lawyer cramming to memorize facts for an upcoming trial, or by a business executive eager to learn Mandarin on the eve of his departure for Shanghai.

Some who worry about the ethics of cognitive enhancement point to the danger of creating two classes of human beings: those with access to enhancement technologies, and those who must make do with their natural capacities. And if the enhancements could be passed down the generations, the two classes might eventually become subspecies—the enhanced and the merely natural. But worry about access ignores the moral status of enhancement itself. Is the scenario troubling because the unenhanced poor would be denied the benefits of bioengineering, or because the enhanced affluent would somehow be dehumanized? As with muscles, so with memory: the fundamental question is not how to ensure equal access to enhancement but whether we should aspire to it in the first place.

HEIGHT

Pediatricians already struggle with the ethics of enhancement when confronted by parents who want to make their children taller. Since the 1980s human growth hormone has been approved for children with a hormone deficiency that makes them much shorter than average. But the treatment also increases the height of healthy children. Some parents of healthy children who are unhappy with their stature (typically boys) ask why it should make a difference whether a child is short because of a hormone deficiency or because his parents happen to be short. Whatever the cause, the social consequences are the same.

In the face of this argument some doctors began prescribing hormone treatments for children whose short stature was unrelated to any medical problem. By 1996 such "off-label" use accounted for 40 percent of human-growth-hormone prescriptions. Although it is legal to prescribe drugs for purposes not approved by the Food and Drug Administration, pharmaceutical companies cannot promote such use. Seeking to expand its market, Eli Lilly & Co. recently persuaded the FDA to approve its human growth hormone for healthy children whose projected adult height is in the bottom one percentile—under five feet three inches for boys and four feet eleven inches for girls. This concession raises a large question about the ethics of enhancement: If hormone treatments need not be limited to those with hormone deficiencies, why should they be available only to very short children? Why shouldn't all shorter-than-average children be able to seek treatment? And what about a child of average height who wants to be taller so that he can make the basketball team?

Some oppose height enhancement on the grounds that it is collectively self-defeating; as some become taller, others become shorter relative to the norm. Except in Lake Wobegon, not every child can be above average. As the unenhanced began to feel shorter, they, too, might seek treatment, leading to a hormonal arms race that left everyone worse off, especially those who couldn't afford to buy their way up from shortness.

But the arms-race objection is not decisive on its own. Like the fairness objection to bioengineered muscles and memory, it leaves unexamined the attitudes and dispositions that prompt the drive for enhancement. If we were bothered only by the injustice of adding shortness to the problems of the poor, we could remedy that unfairness by publicly subsidizing height enhancements. As for the relative height deprivation suffered by innocent bystanders, we could compensate them by taxing those who buy their way to greater height. The real question is whether we want to live in a society where parents feel compelled to spend a fortune to make perfectly healthy kids a few inches taller.

SEX SELECTION

Perhaps the most inevitable nonmedical use of bioengineering is sex selection. For centuries parents have been trying to choose the sex of their children. Today biotech succeeds where folk remedies failed.

One technique for sex selection arose with prenatal tests using amniocentesis and ultrasound. These medical technologies were developed to detect genetic abnormalities such as spina bifida and Down syndrome. But they can also reveal the sex of the fetus—allowing for the abortion of a fetus of an undesired sex. Even among those who favor abortion rights, few advocate abortion simply because the parents do not want a girl. Nevertheless, in traditional societies with a powerful cultural preference for boys, this practice has become widespread.

Sex selection need not involve abortion, however. For couples undergoing *in vitro* fertilization (IVF), it is possible to choose the sex of the child before the fertilized egg is implanted in the womb. One method makes use of preimplantation genetic diagnosis (PGD), a procedure developed to screen for genetic diseases. Several eggs are fertilized in a petri dish and grown to the eight-cell stage (about three days). At that point the embryos are tested to determine their sex. Those of the desired sex are implanted: the others are typically discarded. Although few couples are likely to undergo the difficulty and expense of IVF simply to choose the sex of their child, embryo screening is a highly reliable means of sex selection. And as our genetic knowledge increases, it may be possible to use PGD to cull embryos carrying undesired genes, such as those associated with obesity, height, and skin color. The science-fiction movie *Gattaca* depicts a future in which parents routinely screen embryos for sex, height, immunity to disease, and even IQ. There is something troubling about the *Gattaca* scenario, but it is not easy to identify what exactly is wrong with screening embryos to choose the sex of our children.

One line of objection draws on arguments familiar from the abortion debate. Those who believe that an embryo is a person reject embryo screening for the same reasons they reject abortion. If an eight-cell embryo growing in a petri dish is morally equivalent to a fully developed human being, then discarding it is no better than aborting a fetus, and both practices are equivalent to infanticide. Whatever its merits, however, this "pro-life" objection is not an argument against sex selection as such.

The latest technology poses the question of sex selection unclouded by the matter of an embryo's moral status. The Genetics & IVF Institute, a for-profit infertility clinic in Fairfax, Virginia, now offers a sperm-sorting technique that makes it possible to choose the sex of one's child before it is conceived. X-bearing sperm, which produce girls, carry more DNA than Y-bearing sperm, which produce boys; a device called a flow cytometer can separate them. The process, called MicroSort, has a high rate of success.

If sex selection by sperm sorting is objectionable, it must be for reasons that go beyond the debate about the moral status of the embryo. One such reason is that sex selection is an instrument of sex discrimination—typically against girls, as illustrated by the chilling sex ratios in India and China. Some speculate that societies with substantially more men than women will be less stable, more violent, and more prone to crime or war. These are legitimate worries—but the sperm-sorting company has a clever way of addressing them. It offers MicroSort only to couples who want to choose the sex of a child for purposes of "family balancing." Those with more sons than daughters may choose a girl, and vice versa. But customers may not use the technology to stock up on children of the same sex, or even to choose the sex of their firstborn child. (So far the majority of MicroSort clients have chosen girls.) Under restrictions of this kind, do any ethical issues remain that should give us pause?

The case of MicroSort helps us isolate the moral objections that would persist if muscle-enhancement, memory-enhancement, and height-enhancement technologies were safe and available to all.

It is commonly said that genetic enhancements undermine our humanity by threatening our capacity to act freely, to succeed by our own efforts, and to consider ourselves responsible—worthy of praise or blame—for the things we do and for the way we are. It is one thing to hit seventy home runs as the result of disciplined training and effort, and something else, something less, to hit them with the help of steroids or genetically enhanced muscles. Of course, the roles of effort and enhancement will be a matter of degree. But as the role of enhancement increases, our admiration for the achievement fades—or, rather, our admiration for the achievements shifts from the player to his pharmacist. This suggests that our moral response to enhancement is a response to the diminished agency of the person whose achievement is enhanced.

Though there is much to be said for this argument, I do not think the main problem with enhancement and genetic engineering is that they undermine effort and erode human agency. The deeper danger is that they represent a kind of hyperagency—a Promethean aspiration to remake nature, including human nature, to serve our purposes and satisfy our desires. The problem is not the drift to mechanism but the drive to mastery. And what the drive to mastery misses and may even destroy is an appreciation of the gifted character of human powers and achievements.

To acknowledge the giftedness of life is to recognize that our talents and powers are not wholly our own doing, despite the effort we expend to develop and to exercise them. It is also to recognize that not everything in the world is open to whatever use we may desire or devise. Appreciating the gifted quality of life constrains the Promethean project and conduces to a certain humility. It is in part a religious sensibility. But its resonance reaches beyond religion.

It is difficult to account for what we admire about human activity and achievement without drawing upon some version of this idea. Consider two types of athletic achievement. We appreciate players like Pete Rose, who are not blessed with great natural gifts but who manage, through striving, grit, and determination, to excel in their sport. But we also admire players like Joe DiMaggio, who display natural gifts with grace and effortlessness. Now, suppose we learned that both players took performance-enhancing drugs. Whose turn to drugs would we find more deeply disillusioning? Which aspect of the athletic ideal—effort or gift—would be more deeply offended?

Some might say effort: the problem with drugs is that they provide a shortcut, a way to win without striving. But striving is not the point of sports; excellence is. And excellence consists at least partly in the display of natural talents and gifts that are no doing of the athlete who possesses them. This is an uncomfortable fact for democratic societies. We want to believe that success, in sports and in life, is something we earn, not something we inherit. Natural gifts, and the admiration they inspire, embarrass the meritocratic faith; they cast doubt on the conviction that praise and rewards flow from effort alone. In the face of this embarrassment we inflate the moral significance of striving, and depreciate giftedness. This distortion can be seen, for example, in network-television coverage of the Olympics, which focuses less on the feats the athletes perform than on heartrending stories of the hardships they have overcome and the struggles they have waged to triumph over an injury or a difficult upbringing or political turmoil in their native land.

But effort isn't everything. No one believes that a mediocre basketball player who works and trains even harder than Michael Jordan deserves greater acclaim or a bigger contract. The real problem with genetically altered athletes is that they corrupt athletic competition as a human activity that honors the cultivation and display of natural talents. From this standpoint, enhancement can be seen as the ultimate expression of the ethic of effort and willfulness—a kind of high-tech striving. The ethic of willfulness and the biotechnological powers it now enlists are arrayed against the claims of giftedness.

The ethic of giftedness, under siege in sports, persists in the practice of parenting. But here, too, bioengineering and genetic enhancement threaten to dislodge it. To appreciate children as gifts is to accept them as they come, not as objects of our design or products of our will or instruments of our ambition. Parental love is not contingent on the talents and attributes a child happens to have. We choose our friends and spouses at least partly on the basis of qualities we find attractive. But we do not choose our children. Their qualities are unpredictable, and even the most conscientious parents cannot be held wholly responsible for the kind of children they have. That is why parenthood, more than other human relationships, teaches what the theologian William F. May calls an "openness to the unbidden."

May's resonant phrase helps us see that the deepest moral objection to enhancement lies less in the perfection it seeks than in the human disposition it expresses and promotes. The problem is not that parents usurp the autonomy of a child they design. The problem lies in the hubris of the designing parents, in their drive to master the mystery of birth. Even if this disposition did not make parents tyrants to their children, it would disfigure the relation between parent and child, and deprive the parent of the humility and enlarged human sympathies that an openness to the unbidden can cultivate.

To appreciate children as gifts or blessings is not, of course, to be passive in the face of illness or disease. Medical intervention to cure or prevent illness or restore the injured to health does not desecrate nature but honors it. Healing sickness or injury does not override a child's natural capacities but permits them to flourish.

Nor does the sense of life as a gift mean that parents must shrink from shaping and directing the development of their child. Just as athletes and artists have an obligation to cultivate their talents, so parents have an obligation to cultivate their children, to help them discover and develop their talents and gifts. As May points out, parents give their children two kinds of love: accepting love and transforming love. Accepting love affirms the being of the child, whereas transforming love seeks the well-being of the child. Each aspect corrects the excesses of the other, he writes: "Attachment becomes too quietistic if it slackens into mere acceptance of the child as he is." Parents have a duty to promote their children's excellence.

These days, however, overly ambitious parents are prone to get carried away with transforming love—promoting and demanding all manner of accomplishments from their children, seeking perfection. "Parents find it difficult to maintain an equilibrium between the two sides of love," May observes. "Accepting love, without transforming love, slides into indulgence and finally neglect. Transforming love, without accepting love, badgers and finally rejects." May finds in these competing impulses a parallel with modern science: it, too, engages us in beholding the given world, studying and savoring it, and also in molding the world, transforming and perfecting it.

The mandate to mold our children, to cultivate and improve them, complicates the case against enhancement. We usually admire parents who seek the best for their children, who spare no effort to help them achieve happiness and success. Some parents confer advantages on their children by enrolling them in expensive schools, hiring private tutors, sending them to tennis camp, providing them with piano lessons, ballet lessons, swimming lessons, SAT-prep courses, and so on. If it is permissible and even admirable for parents to help their children in these ways, why isn't it equally admirable for parents to use whatever genetic technologies may emerge (provided they are safe) to enhance their children's intelligence, musical ability, or athletic prowess?

The defenders of enhancement are right to this extent: improving children through genetic engineering is similar in spirit to the heavily managed, high-pressure child-rearing that is now common. But this similarity does not vindicate genetic enhancement. On the contrary, it highlights a problem with the trend toward hyperparenting. One conspicuous example of this trend is sports-crazed parents bent on making champions of their children. Another is the frenzied drive of overbearing parents to mold and manage their children's academic careers.

As the pressure for performance increases, so does the need to help distractible children concentrate on the task at hand. This may be why diagnoses of attention deficit and hyperactivity disorder have increased so sharply. Lawrence Diller, a pediatrician and the author of *Running on Ritalin,* estimates that five to six percent of American children under eighteen (a total of four to five million kids) are currently prescribed Ritalin, Adderall, and other stimulants, the treatment of choice for ADHD. (Stimulants counteract hyperactivity by making it easier to focus and sustain attention.) The number of Ritalin prescriptions for children and adolescents has tripled over the past decade, but not all users suffer from attention disorders or hyperactivity. High school and college students have learned that prescription stimulants improve concentration for those with normal attention spans, and some buy or borrow their classmates' drugs to enhance their performance on the SAT or other exams. Since stimulants work for both medical and nonmedical purposes, they raise the same moral questions posed by other technologies of enhancement.

However those questions are resolved, the debate reveals the cultural distance we have traveled since the debate over marijuana, LSD, and other drugs a generation ago. Unlike the drugs of the 1960s and 1970s Ritalin and Adderall are not for checking out but for buckling down, not for beholding the world and taking it in but for molding the world and fitting in. We used to speak of nonmedical drug use as "recreational." That term no longer applies. The steroids and stimulants that figure in the enhancement debate are not a source of recreation but a bid for compliance—a way of answering a competitive society's demand to improve our performance and perfect our nature. This demand for performance and perfection animates the impulse to rail against the given. It is the deepest source of the moral trouble with enhancement.

Some see a clear line between genetic enhancement and other ways that people seek improvement in their children and themselves. Genetic manipulation seems somehow worse—more intrusive, more sinister—than other ways of enhancing performance and seeking success. But morally speaking, the difference is less significant than it seems. Bioengineering gives us reason to question the low-tech, high-pressure child-rearing practices we commonly accept. The hyper-parenting familiar in our time represents an anxious excess of mastery and dominion that misses the sense of life as a gift. This draws it disturbingly close to eugenics.

The shadow of eugenics hangs over today's debates about genetic engineering and enhancement. Critics of genetic engineering argue that human cloning, enhancement, and the quest for designer children are nothing more than "privatized" or "free-market" eugenics. Defenders of enhancement reply that genetic choices freely made are not really eugenic—at least not in the pejorative sense. To remove the coercion, they argue, is to remove the very thing that makes eugenic policies repugnant.

Sorting out the lesson of eugenics is another way of wrestling with the ethics of enhancement. The Nazis gave eugenics a bad name. But what, precisely, was wrong with it? Was the old eugenics objectionable only insofar as it was coercive? Or is there something inherently wrong with the resolve to deliberately design our progeny's traits?

James Watson, the biologist who, with Francis Crick, discovered the structure of DNA, sees nothing wrong with genetic engineering and enhancement, provided they are freely chosen rather than state-imposed. And yet Watson's language contains more than a whiff of the old eugenic sensibility. "If you really are stupid, I would call that a disease," he recently told *The Times of London.* "The lower 10 percent who really have difficulty, even in elementary school, what's the cause of it? A lot of people would like to say, "Well, poverty, things like that." It probably isn't. So I'd like to get rid of that, to help the lower 10 percent." A few years ago Watson stirred controversy by saying that if a gene for homosexuality were discovered, a woman should be free to abort a fetus that carried it. When his remark provoked an uproar, he replied that he was not singling out gays but asserting a principle: women should be free to abort fetuses for any reason of genetic preference—for example, if the child would be dyslexic, or lacking musical talent, or too short to play basketball.

Watson's scenarios are clearly objectionable to those for whom all abortion is an unspeakable crime. But for those who do not subscribe to the pro-life position, these scenarios raise a hard question: If it is morally troubling to contemplate abortion to avoid a gay child or a dyslexic one, doesn't this suggest that something is wrong with acting on any eugenic preference, even when no state coercion is involved?

Consider the market in eggs and sperm. The advent of artificial insemination allows prospective parents to shop for gametes with the genetic traits they desire in their off-spring. It is a less predictable way to design children than cloning or pre-implantation genetic screening, but it offers a good example of a procreative practice in which the old eugenics meets the new consumerism. A few years ago some Ivy League newspapers ran an ad seeking an egg from a woman who was at least five feet ten inches tall and athletic, had no major family medical problems, and had a combined SAT score of 1400 or above. The ad offered

$50,000 for an egg from a donor with these traits. More recently a Web site was launched claiming to auction eggs from fashion models whose photos appeared on the site, at starting bids of $15,000 to $150,000.

On what grounds, if any, is the egg market morally objectionable? Since no one is forced to buy or sell, it cannot be wrong for reasons of coercion. Some might worry that hefty prices would exploit poor women by presenting them with an offer they couldn't refuse. But the designer eggs that fetch the highest prices are likely to be sought from the privileged, not the poor. If the market for premium eggs gives us moral qualms, this, too, shows that concerns about eugenics are not put to rest by freedom of choice.

A tale of two sperm banks helps explain why. The Repository for Germinal Choice, one of America's first sperm banks, was not a commercial enterprise. It was opened in 1980 by Robert Graham, a philanthropist dedicated to improving the world's "germ plasm" and counteracting the rise of "retrograde humans." His plan was to collect the sperm of Nobel Prize-winning scientists and make it available to women of high intelligence, in hopes of breeding super-smart babies. But Graham had trouble persuading Nobel laureates to donate their sperm for his bizarre scheme, and so settled for sperm from young scientists of high promise. His sperm bank closed in 1999.

In contrast, California Cryobank, one of the world's leading sperm banks, is a for-profit company with no overt eugenic mission. Cappy Rothman, M.D., a co-founder of the firm, has nothing but disdain for Graham's eugenics, although the standards Cryobank imposes on the sperm it recruits are exacting. Cryobank has offices in Cambridge, Massachusetts, between Harvard and MIT, and in Palo Alto, California, near Stanford. It advertises for donors in campus newspapers (compensation up to $900 a month), and accepts less than five percent of the men who apply. Cryo-bank's marketing materials play up the prestigious source of its sperm. Its catalogue provides detailed information about the physical characteristics of each donor, along with his ethnic origin and college major. For an extra fee prospective customers can buy the results of a test that assesses the donor's temperament and character type. Rothman reports that Cryobank's ideal sperm donor is six feet tall, with brown eyes, blond hair, and dimples, and has a college degree—not because the company wants to propagate those traits, but because those are the traits his customers want: "If our customers wanted high school dropouts, we would give them high school dropouts."

Not everyone objects to marketing sperm. But anyone who is troubled by the eugenic aspect of the Nobel Prize sperm bank should be equally troubled by Cryobank, consumer-driven though it be. What, after all, is the moral difference between designing children according to an explicit eugenic purpose and designing children according to the dictates of the market? Whether the aim is to improve humanity's "germ plasm" or to cater to consumer preferences, both practices are eugenic insofar as both make children into products of deliberate design.

A number of political philosophers call for a new "liberal eugenics." They argue that a moral distinction can be drawn between the old eugenic policies and genetic enhancements that do not restrict the autonomy of the child. "While old-fashioned authoritarian eugenicists sought to produce citizens out of a single centrally designed mould," writes Nicholas Agar, "the distinguishing mark of the new liberal eugenics is state neutrality." Government may not tell parents what sort of children to design, and parents may engineer in their children only those traits that improve their capacities without biasing their choice of life plans. A recent text on genetics and justice, written by the bioethicists Allen Buchanan, Dan W. Brock, Norman Daniels, and Daniel Wilder, offers a similar view. The "bad reputation of eugenics," they write, is due to practices that "might be avoidable in a future eugenic program." The problem with the old eugenics was that its burdens fell disproportionately on the weak and the poor, who were unjustly sterilized and segregated. But provided that the benefits and burdens of genetic improvement are fairly distributed, these bioethicists argue, eugenic measures are unobjectionable and may even be morally required.

The libertarian philosopher Robert Nozick proposed a "genetic supermarket" that would enable parents to order children by design without imposing a single design on the society as a whole: "This supermarket system has the great virtue that it involves no centralized decision fixing the future human type(s)."

Even the leading philosopher of American liberalism, John Rawls, in his classic *A Theory of Justice* (1971), offered a brief endorsement of noncoercive eugenics. Even in a society that agrees to share the benefits and burdens of the genetic lottery, it is "in the interest of each to have greater natural assets," Rawls wrote. "This enables him to pursue a preferred plan of life." The parties to the social contract "want to insure for their descendants the best genetic endowment (assuming their own to be fixed)." Eugenic policies are therefore not only permissible but required as a matter of justice. "Thus over time a society is to take steps at least to preserve the general level of natural abilities and to prevent the diffusion of serious defects."

But removing the coercion does not vindicate eugenics. The problem with eugenics and genetic engineering is that they represent the one-sided triumph of willfulness over giftedness, of dominion over reverence, of molding over beholding. Why, we may wonder, should we worry about this triumph? Why not shake off our unease about genetic enhancement as so much superstition? What would be lost if biotechnology dissolved our sense of giftedness?

From a religious standpoint the answer is clear. To believe that our talents and powers are wholly our own doing is to misunderstand our place in creation, to confuse our role with God's. Religion is not the only source of reasons to care about giftedness, however. The moral stakes can also be described in secular terms. If bioengineering made the myth of the "self-made man" come true, it would be difficult to view our talents as gifts for which we are indebted, rather than as achievements for which we are responsible. This would transform three key features of our moral landscape: humility, responsibility, and solidarity.

In a social world that prizes mastery and control, parenthood is a school for humility. That we care deeply about our children and yet cannot choose the kind we want teaches parents to be open to the unbidden. Such openness is a disposition worth affirming, not only within families but in the wider world as well. It invites us to abide the unexpected, to live with dissonance, to rein in the impulse to control. A *Gattaca*-like world in which parents became accustomed to specifying the sex and genetic traits of their children would be a world inhospitable to the unbidden, a gated community writ large. The awareness that our talents and abilities are not wholly our own doing restrains our tendency toward hubris.

Though some maintain that genetic enhancement erodes human agency by overriding effort, the real problem is the explosion, not the erosion, of responsibility. As humility gives way, responsibility expands to daunting proportions. We attribute less to chance and more to choice. Parents become responsible for choosing, or failing to choose, the right traits for their children. Athletes become responsible for acquiring, or failing to acquire, the talents that will help their teams win.

One of the blessings of seeing ourselves as creatures of nature, God, or fortune is that we are not wholly responsible for the way we are. The more we become masters of our genetic endowments, the greater the burden we bear for the talents we have and the way we perform. Today when a basketball player misses a rebound, his coach can blame him for being out of position. Tomorrow the coach may blame him for being too short. Even now the use of performance-enhancing drugs in professional sports is subtly transforming the expectations players have for one another; on some teams players who take the field free from amphetamines or other stimulants are criticized for "playing naked."

The more alive we are to the chanced nature of our lot, the more reason we have to share our fate with others. Consider insurance. Since people do not know whether or when various ills will befall them, they pool their risk by buying health insurance and life insurance. As life plays itself out, the healthy wind up subsidizing the unhealthy, and those who live to a ripe old age wind up subsidizing the families of those who die before their time. Even without a sense of mutual obligation, people pool their risks and resources and share one another's fate.

But insurance markets mimic solidarity only insofar as people do not know or control their own risk factors. Suppose genetic testing advanced to the point where it could reliably predict each person's medical future and life expectancy. Those confident of good health and long life would opt out of the pool, causing other people's premiums to skyrocket. The solidarity of insurance would disappear as those with good genes fled the actuarial company of those with bad ones.

The fear that insurance companies would use genetic data to assess risks and set premiums recently led the Senate to vote to prohibit genetic discrimination in health insurance. But the bigger danger, admittedly more speculative, is that genetic enhancement, if routinely practiced, would make it harder to foster the moral sentiments that social solidarity requires.

Why, after all, do the successful owe anything to the least-advantaged members of society? The best answer to this question leans heavily on the notion of giftedness. The natural talents that enable the successful to flourish are not their own doing but, rather, their good fortune—a result of the genetic lottery. If our genetic endowments are gifts, rather than achievements for which we can claim credit, it is a mistake and a conceit to assume that we are entitled to the full measure of the bounty they reap in a market economy. We therefore have an obligation to share this bounty with those who, through no fault of their own, lack comparable gifts.

A lively sense of the contingency of our gifts—a consciousness that none of us is wholly responsible for his or her success—saves a meritocratic society from sliding into the smug assumption that the rich are rich because they are more deserving than the poor. Without this, the successful would become even more likely than they are now to view themselves as self-made and self-sufficient, and hence wholly responsible for their success. Those at the bottom of society would be viewed not as disadvantaged, and thus worthy of a measure of compensation, but as simply unfit, and thus worthy of eugenic repair. The meritocracy, less chastened by chance, would become harder, less forgiving. As perfect genetic knowledge would end the simulacrum of solidarity in insurance markets, so perfect genetic control would erode the actual solidarity that arises when men and women reflect on the contingency of their talents and fortunes.

Thirty-five years ago Robert L. Sinsheimer, a molecular biologist at the California Institute of Technology, glimpsed the shape of things to come. In an article titled "The Prospect of Designed Genetic Change" he argued that freedom of choice would vindicate the new genetics, and set it apart from the discredited eugenics of old.

> To implement the older eugenics would have required a massive social programme carried out over many generations. Such a programme could not have been initiated without the consent and co-operation of a major fraction of the population, and would have been continuously subject to social control. In contrast, the new eugenics could, at least in principle, he implemented on a quite individual basis, in one generation, and subject to no existing restrictions.

According to Sinsheimer, the new eugenics would be voluntary rather than coerced, and also more humane. Rather than segregating and eliminating the unfit, it would improve them. "The old eugenics would have required a continual selection for breeding of the fit, and a culling of the unfit," he wrote. "The new eugenics would permit in principle the conversion of all the unfit to the highest genetic level."

Sinsheimer's paean to genetic engineering caught the heady, Promethean self-image of the age. He wrote hopefully of rescuing "the losers in that chromosomal lottery that so firmly channels our human destinies," including not only those born with genetic defects but also "the 50,000,000 'normal' Americans with an IQ of less than 90." But he also saw that something bigger than improving on nature's "mindless, age-old throw of dice" was at stake. Implicit in technologies of genetic intervention was a more exalted place for human beings in the cosmos. "As we enlarge man's freedom, we diminish his constraints and that which he must accept as given," he wrote, Copernicus and Darwin had "demoted man from his bright glory at the focal point of the universe," but the new biology would restore his central role. In the mirror of our genetic knowledge we would see ourselves as more than a link in the chain of evolution: "We can be the agent of transition to a whole new pitch of evolution. This is a cosmic event."

There is something appealing, even intoxicating, about a vision of human freedom unfettered by the given. It may even be the case that the allure of that vision played a part in summoning the genomic age into being. It is often assumed that the powers of enhancement we now possess arose as an inadvertent by-product of biomedical progress—the genetic revolution came, so to speak, to cure disease, and stayed to tempt us with the prospect of enhancing our performance, designing our children, and perfecting our nature. That may have the story backwards. It is more plausible to view genetic engineering as the ultimate expression of our resolve to see ourselves astride the world, the masters of our nature. But that promise of mastery is flawed. It threatens to banish our appreciation of life as a gift, and to leave us with nothing to affirm or behold outside our own will.

2.4.4 Trespass

CLAIRE HOPE CUMMINGS

A great deal of attention has been given to the prospect of human genetic engineering, but comparatively little notice has been paid to the growing use of genetic engineering technologies on plants and animals. For more than a decade, food products made from genetically modified organisms (GMOs) have been on American supermarket shelves, and millions of people have eaten them with no apparent ill effects. So what is the fuss about when environmentalists and some others warn the public about the dangers of so-called Frankenfoods? Are these fears merely the concerns of overwrought Luddites, or might there be some good reasons to be concerned about the genetic manipulation of nonhuman organisms? Lawyer and environmental journalist Claire Hope Cummings describes the history of the development of genetically modified foods, paying particular attention to the lack of regulatory oversight by the U.S. government prior to their release into the general food supply. The rapid introduction into the market of GMOs was made possible by "regulatory capture" of the government by agribusiness interests coupled with the increasing trend toward privately funded research at our nation's leading universities. In the process, scant attention was paid to the risk of genetic contamination of non-GMO plant species by genetic materials from their bioengineered cousins. Cummings thinks that GMO foods have been literally forced down our throats by big business, with little or no way for the public to opt out of this uncontrolled experiment whose ultimate effects on human health and the environment remain unknown.

FOCUS QUESTIONS

1. What does Cummings describe as "the central dogma" of modern molecular biology? Is there evidence to suggest that this belief might turn out to be false? Explain.

Source: "Trespass" by Claire Hope Cummings, *World Watch* magazine, January/February 2005. Copyright © 2004 Worldwatch Institute. Reprinted by permission.

2. What is the significance of the "revolving door" between government and agribusiness? How does this help explain why the federal government decided not to require labels on food products containing GMOs?
3. Does the fact that private corporations fund much of the academic research concerning the safety of GMOs concern you? Why or why not?
4. Evaluate Cummings's thesis that genetic contamination represents a "trespass" on the commons in light of the view of the commons articulated by the International Forum on Globalization (Selection 2.1.4). Are you troubled by the trend toward privatizing what was formerly regarded as the common inheritance of all humans? Explain why or why not.

KEYWORDS

academic freedom, agribusiness, genetically modified organisms (GMOs), molecular biology, regulatory oversight, substantial equivalence, transgenic instability

Hidden inside Hilgard Hall, one of the oldest buildings on the campus of the University of California at Berkeley, is a photograph that no one is supposed to see. It's a picture of a crippled and contorted corncob that was not created by nature, or even by agriculture, but by genetic engineering.[1] The cob is kept in a plastic bin called "the monster box," a collection of biological curiosities put together by someone who works in a secure biotechnology research facility.

What the photo shows is a cob that apparently started growing normally, then turned into another part of the corn plant, then returned to forming kernels, then went back to another form—twisting back and forth as if it could not make up its mind about what it was. It was produced by the same recombinant DNA technology that is used to create the genetically modified organisms (GMOs) that are in our everyday foods. When I saw this photo, I knew it was saying something very important about genetic engineering. I thought it should be published. But the person who owns it is frankly afraid of how the biotechnology industry might react, and would not agree. In order to get permission even to describe the photo for this article, I had to promise not to reveal its owner's identity.

What the distorted corncob represents is a mute challenge to the industry's claim that this technology is precise, predictable, and safe. But that this challenge should be kept hidden, and that a scientist who works at a public university should feel too intimidated to discuss it openly, told me that something more than just a scientific question was being raised. After all, if the new agricultural biotech were really safe and effective, why would the industry work so hard—as indeed it does—to keep its critics cowed and the public uninformed? Was there something about the way genetic engineering was developed, about how it works, that was inviting a closer look—a look that the industry would rather we not take? I had gone to Berkeley to see for myself what was going on behind biotechnology.

The University of California at Berkeley ("Cal") is the stage on which much of the story of genetic engineering has played out over the last 25 years. The biotechnology industry was born here in the San Francisco Bay area, and nurtured by scientists who worked at Berkeley and nearby universities. Critical controversies over the role genetic engineering and related research should have in society have erupted here. Even the architecture of the campus reflects the major scientific and policy divisions that plague this technology. Two buildings, in particular, mirror the two very different versions of biology that emerged in the last half of the twentieth century, and reflect two very different visions for agriculture in the future.

Hilgard Hall was built in 1918, at a time when mastering the classical form and celebrating beauty were important, perhaps even integral, to the accepted function of a building. Hilgard's façade is exquisitely decorated with friezes depicting sheaves of wheat, beehives, bunches of grapes, cornucopias, and bas relief sculptures of cow heads surrounded with wreaths of fruit. Above the entrance, carved in huge capital letters are the words, "TO RESCUE FOR HUMAN SOCIETY THE NATIVE VALUES OF RURAL LIFE." The massive front door opens to a grand two-story hall graced with granite, marble, and carved brass. But behind that elegant entrance is a building left in disrepair. Getting around inside Hilgard means navigating worn marble staircases and dark corridors laced with exposed pipes and heating ducts. The room where the monster box photograph is kept is small and dank. This building is home to the "old" biology—the careful observation of life, living systems, and their complex interactions. Being inside Hilgard is a visceral lesson in how Cal is neglecting the classic study of the intimate interrelationships among agriculture, the environment, and human society.

Nearby, and standing in stark contrast to Hilgard's faded splendor, is a newer, modern office building, Koshland Hall. Koshland is not unattractive, with its pitched blue tile roof lines and bright white walls lined with blue steel windows, but it was built in the mid-1990s in a functional style that, like most new campus buildings, has all the charm and poetry of an ice cube. The interior is clean and well lit. Next to office doors hang plaques that name the corporations or foundations that fund the activities inside. This is the home of the "new biology"—the utilitarian view that life is centered in DNA and molecules can be manipulated at will. Molecular biology is clearly doing well at Cal.

Koshland Hall was named after a distinguished member of the faculty, Daniel Koshland, former editor of the journal *Science* and chair of Berkeley's Department of Biochemistry, now a professor emeritus. He has the unique distinction of having been present at the two most important scientific revolutions of our time: he participated both in the Manhattan Project, which developed nuclear weapons, and in the early development of molecular biology. He is credited with "transforming" the biological sciences at Berkeley.

THE NEW BIOLOGY

One hundred years ago, no one had heard of a "gene." The word was not recognized until 1909, and even after that it remained an abstraction for decades. At the time, scientists and others were making an effort to find a material basis for life, particularly heritability, the fundamental function of life. The story of genetic engineering in the United States begins with the decision to identify genes as the basis of life. But the ideological roots of this story go even deeper, into the nation's earlier history and attachment to the ideas of manifest destiny, eugenics, and social engineering.

Early in the twentieth century, the new "science" of sociology made its appearance—along with the highly appealing belief that social problems were amenable to scientific solutions. In time, sociology began to combine with genetic science, giving strong impetus to technocratic forms of social control, and particularly to eugenics—the belief that the human race could be improved by selective breeding. Until the 1930s, the science of genetics had not developed much beyond Mendelian principles of heredity, but eugenics was already being promoted as the solution to social problems. As the idea that genes determined traits in people took hold, eugenics twisted it to foster the concept that there were "good" genes and "bad" genes, good and bad traits. Eugenics eventually gained a powerful foothold both in the popular imagination and in the U.S. government, as well as in Nazi Germany. Even today, these notions underlie the decisions biotechnologists make about what genes and traits are beneficial, what organisms are engineered, and who gets to decide how this technology will be used.

According to Lily Kay, an assistant professor of the history of science at Massachusetts Institute of Technology, genetic engineering came about as the result of the concerted effort of a few scientists, who, along with their academic and philanthropic sponsors, had a shared vision about how they could use genetics to reshape science and society. In her book *The Molecular Vision of Life: Caltech, the Rockefeller Foundation, and the Rise of the New Biology,* Kay writes that this vision was not so much about underlying biological principles as it was about social values. The new biology that evolved from this thinking was founded on a strong belief in "industrial capitalism" and its perceived mandate for "science-based social intervention." The potential for this idea, and the intentional strategy to use it for social purposes was clearly understood from the outset, says Kay. The developers of "molecular biology" (a term coined by the Rockefeller Foundation) were confident that it would offer them a previously unimagined power and control over both nature and society.

Science was molded to this agenda in 1945, when Vannevar Bush, the head of President Franklin D. Roosevelt's wartime Office of Scientific Research and Development, wrote "Science, The Endless Frontier"—a landmark report that outlined how science could better serve the private sector. As Kay tells the story, at that point the search for a science-based social agenda began in earnest. It was funded and directed by business corporations and foundations acting together as "quasi-public entities" using both private and public funds to harness "the expertise of the human sciences to stem what was perceived as the nation's social and biological decay and help realize the vision of America's destiny." Eventually, the combined efforts of corporate, academic, and government interests began to bear fruit and "the boundary between individual and corporate self-interest, between private and public control, would be increasingly blurred."[2]

The story of how James Watson and Francis Crick described the structure of the DNA helix in 1953 is well known. Less known, but of considerable consequence, is what followed. With little hesitation, they announced that DNA is "the secret of life"—and began to promote what was to become known as "the central dogma"—the notion that genetic information flows in only one direction, from DNA to RNA to a protein, and that this process directly determines an organism's characteristics. This dogma was, as described by geneticist Mae-Wan Ho, author of *Living with the Fluid Genome,* "just another way of saying that organisms are hardwired in their genetic makeup and the environment has little influence on the structure and function of the genes." In her book, Dr. Ho argues that the central dogma is too simplistic. She observes that not all DNA "codes for proteins" and that the genome is fluid and interactive. Similarly, in a 1992 *Harper's Magazine* article, "Unraveling the DNA Myth: The Spurious Foundation of Genetic Engineering," Queens College biologist Barry Commoner writes that "the central dogma is the premise that an organism's genome—its total complement of DNA genes—should fully account for its characteristic assemblage of inherited traits. The premise, unhappily, is false."

Still, the singular view of "life as DNA" dominated biology in the late twentieth century, in part because its very simplicity provided the biological rationale for engineering DNA. Technological advances in other fields—the study of enzymes that cut DNA, and bacteria that recombine it—were teamed up with high speed computers that provided the computational muscle needed. And yet, even as the old biology became the "new and improved" molecular biology, it was promoted with a social pedigree about how it would serve the public. Its mandate was the same one that was used to colonize the "new world" and to settle the Wild West—the promise that *this* progress would provide everyone a better life.

Judging by his comments, if James Watson had had his way, research would have proceeded undeterred by any concerns over the hazards that genetic engineering posed. He said he'd always felt that the "certain promise" of this revolutionary new technology far outweighed its "uncertain peril." But others, such as Paul Berg of Stanford University, were calling for a more measured approach. In 1975 Berg joined other scientists concerned about the risks of genetic engineering in a meeting held at the Asilomar conference center, near Monterey, California. It was a rare collective action, with participants coming from a spectrum of universities, government agencies, and research institutes.

In his introductory remarks, David Baltimore of MIT noted that the participants were there to discuss "a new technique of molecular biology," one that "appears to allow us to outdo the standard events of evolution by making combinations of genes which could be unique in natural history." He went on to say that they should design a strategy to go forward that would "maximize the benefits and minimize the hazards." They produced a 35-page report that detailed their concerns about creating new pathogens and toxins, the emergence of allergens and disease vectors that could cause cancer or immune disorders, as well as "unpredictable adverse consequences" and the specter of "wide ecological damages."

Then, in the last hours of the meeting, on the very last night, a couple of the participants pointed out that the public had the right to assess and limit this technology. What happened next was pivotal. These scientists believed they were entitled to benefit from the extraordinary potential of genetic engineering and they argued that they could find technological fixes for any problems that might emerge. Susan Wright, author of *Molecular Politics,* a history of biotech regulatory policy, recalls that there was virtual unanimity for the idea that scientists would create a central role for themselves in policymaking—to the exclusion of society in general. From then on, Wright says, this "reductionist discourse" became doctrine. Asilomar defined the boundaries of public discourse, and the questions about potential hazards that were raised there went unanswered.

PUBLIC POLICY: THE ENDLESS FRONTIER

The inoculation that Asilomar gave biotechnology against the ravages of government control was given a booster shot a few years later when executives from the Monsanto Corporation visited the Reagan White House. The industry sought and obtained assurance that they would not be blindsided by regulation. After all, these early developers of GMOs were agrochemical companies like Dow Chemical, DuPont, Novartis, and Monsanto, who were the sources of pervasive chemical pollution that resulted in the environmental laws that were passed in the 1960s. This time, they were intent on getting to the lawmakers before the public did.

The resulting "regulatory reform" was announced in 1992, by then Vice President Dan Quayle, at a press conference in the Indian Treaty Room near his office. It was custom-made for the industry. The new policy left just enough oversight in place to give the industry political cover, so that they could offer assurances to the public that the government was watching out for the public interest when in fact it was not. The regulatory system that was adopted, which is essentially what is still in place today, is basically voluntary and passive. It's a "don't look, don't tell" arrangement whereby the industry doesn't tell the government about problems with its products and the government doesn't look for them.

Quayle said that government "will ensure that biotech products will receive the same oversight as other products, instead of being hampered by unnecessary regulation." The rationale for this policy was a concept called "substantial equivalence," which means that GMOs are not substantially different than conventional crops and foods. The science journal *Nature* dubbed substantial equivalence a "pseudo-scientific concept… created primarily to provide an excuse for not requiring biochemical and toxicological tests." Nevertheless, it was adopted by all three agencies responsible for food and agriculture—the United States Department of Agriculture, the Environmental Protection Agency, and the Food and Drug Administration—and it is the reason there have been no safety studies of GMO foods, no post-market monitoring, no labels, no new laws, no agency coordination, and no independent review.

Henry Miller, head of biotechnology at FDA from 1979 to 1994, told the *New York Times* in 2001 that government agencies did "exactly what big agribusiness had asked them to do and told them to do." During Miller's tenure at the FDA, staff scientists were writing memos that called for further testing and warning that there were concerns about food safety. But the man in charge of policy development at FDA was Michael Taylor, a former lawyer for Monsanto. And, according to Steven Druker, a public-interest lawyer who obtained three of these internal FDA memos, under Taylor "references to the unintended negative effects of bioengineering were progressively deleted from drafts of the policy statement." Taylor went on to become an administrator at the USDA in charge of food safety and biotechnology, and then became a vice-president at Monsanto. All three agencies continue to employ people who are either associated with biotech companies or who formerly worked for them. At least 22 cases of this "revolving door" between government and industry have been documented. Biotech lawyers and lobbyists serve in policy-making positions, leave government for high paying jobs with industry, and in some cases return to government to defend industry interests again. Still, dismantling regulatory oversight was only part of industry's overall strategy to commercialize GMOs.

BREAKING THE BIOLOGICAL BARRIERS

All the big agrichemical seed companies—DuPont, Monsanto, Pioneer Hi-Bred, and Dekalb—were betting the farm on genetic technologies in the 1980s. But just one crop, corn, stood in their way. Corn was becoming the "Holy Grail" of agricultural biotechnology because these companies knew that if this idea was ever going to be commercially viable, it had to work with corn—which is of central importance to American agriculture. As they raced to find a way to genetically engineer corn, they perfected the complicated steps required to transform plants into transgenic crops. It all came together in June 1988, when Pioneer Hi-Bred patented the first viable and replicable transgenic corn plant.

In the end, the secret of recombining DNA was found not so much through a process of tedious, repetitive experimentation as of that traditional, Wild-West way of getting what you want—using stealth and brute force. The primary problem genetic engineers faced was how to get engineered DNA into target cells without destroying them. For some plants, like tobacco and soybeans, the problem was solved by the use of stealth. A soil microbe that produces cancer-like growths in plants was recruited to "infect" cells with new modified DNA. This *agrobacterium* formed a non-lethal hole in the wall of a plant cell that allowed the new DNA to sneak in. But that method did not work with corn. For corn, a more forceful cell invasion technique was called for, one that resulted in the invention of the gene gun.

One day in December 1983, during the Christmas break at Cornell University, three men put on booties, gowns, and hair coverings, picked up a gun, and entered the university's National Submicron Facility. John Sanford, a plant breeder at Cornell, and his colleagues, the head of the facility and a member of his staff, were about to shoot a bunch of onions to smithereens. For years, they had been looking for ways to speed up the conventional plant breeding process using genetic transformation techniques. Like other researchers, they had had difficulty forcing DNA fragments through the relatively thick walls of plant cells. They'd tried using lasers to drill mini-holes in cell walls and everything from ion beams to microscopic needles to electric shocks, but these methods either failed to deliver the payload or destroyed the cells in the process.

Then one day, while waging a backyard battle with some pesky squirrels, Sanford got the idea of using a gun. He figured out how to load the gun with specially coated microscopic beads, and then he and his friends tried the idea out on the onions. Soon, pieces of onion were splattered everywhere and the smell of onions and gun powder permeated the air. They kept up this odorous massacre until they figured out how to make it work. It seemed implausible, even laughable, at the time. But the gene gun, which uses .22-caliber ballistics to shoot DNA into cells, is now found in biotechnology laboratories all over the world.

Although it is clearly a "hit or miss" technique, transferring DNA is actually straightforward. The tricky part is getting the target plant to accept the new genes. That requires overcoming billions of years of evolutionary resistance that was specifically designed to keep foreign DNA out. You simply can't get a fish and a strawberry to mate, no matter how hard you try—or at least you couldn't until now. Genetic engineers are now able to take a gene that produces a natural anti-freeze from an arctic flounder and put it into a strawberry plant so that its fruit is frost resistant. But this feat can only be accomplished through the use of specially designed genes that facilitate the process. Along with the trait gene, every GMO also contains genetically engineered vectors and markers, antibiotic resistance genes, viral promoters made from the cauliflower mosaic virus, genetic switches and other constructs that enable the "transformation" process. Once all these genes are inserted, where they end up and what they may do are unknown. The only precise part of this technique is the identification and extraction of the trait DNA from the donor organism. After that, it's a biological free-for-all. In genetic engineering, failure is the rule. The way you get GMO crops to look and act like normal crops is to do thousands and thousands of insertions, grow the ones that survive out, and then see what you get. What you finally select for further testing and release are those "happy accidents" that appear to work. The rest of the millions of plants, animals and other organisms that are subjected to this process are sacrificed or thrown out—or end up in some lab technician's monster box.

PROCESS, NOT PRODUCT

The public controversy over GMOs has focused largely on the products, on how they are marketed, and on what is planted where. But it now appears that the process used to make them, and the novel genetic constructs used in the process, may constitute greater threats to human and environmental health than the products themselves. There are documented reports of allergenic reactions to GMO foods. According to a report in *Nature Biotechnology*, for example, the commonly used cauliflower mosaic virus contains a "recombination hotspot" that makes it unstable and prone to causing mutations, cancer, and new pathogens. The British Medical Association and the U.S. Consumer's Union have both warned about new allergies and/or adverse impacts on the immune system from GMO foods. And public health officials in Europe are concerned that anti-bacterial resistance marker genes in GMOs could render antibiotics ineffective. There have been only about 10 studies done on human health and GMOs, and half of them indicate reasons for concern, including malformed organs, tumors, and early death in rats.

There are also increasing reports of a phenomenon previously thought to be rare, "horizontal gene transfer," which happens when genes travel not just "vertically" through the normal processes of digestion and reproduction, but laterally, between organs in the body or between organisms—sort of like Casper the Ghost floating through a wall. Geneticist Mae-Wan Ho, who has been documenting this phenomenon, says it's happening because the new technology "breaks all the rules of evolution; it short-circuits evolution altogether. It bypasses reproduction, creates new genes and gene combinations that have never existed, and is not restricted by the usual barriers between species."

In 2001, the world's most widely grown GMO, Monsanto's Round-up Ready soybean, was found to contain some mysterious DNA. Monsanto claimed it was native to the plant. When it was shown instead to be the result of the transformation process, Monsanto couldn't explain how it got there. And it has been shown that the nutritional profile of the transgenic soybean is different than that of the conventional variety.

A new report, based on peer-reviewed scientific literature and USDA documents,[3] has found that significant genetic damage to the integrity of a plant occurs when it is modified, including rearrangement of genes at the site of the insertion and thousands of mutations and random modifications throughout the transgenic plant. Another study, by David Schubert of the Salk Institute for Biological Studies in La Jolla, California, found that just one transgenic insertion can disrupt 5 percent of the genes in a single-cell bacterium. Translated into plant terms, that means 15,000 to 300,000 genes get scrambled. Industry was given a blank check by government allowing it to commercialize the technology prematurely, before science could validate the techniques being used to evaluate the safety of the products being developed.

STRATEGIC CONTAMINATION

Even before GMOs were released in the mid-1990s, they were thought by some scientists to be promiscuous. Now that GMO contamination is running rampant, it's hard to believe that the biotech industry wasn't aware of that risk. The industry would have had to ignore early warnings such as a study done at the University of Chicago which found one transgenic plant that was 20 times more likely to interbreed with related plants than its natural variety. But now, because herbicide-tolerant genes are getting into all sorts of plants, farmers have to contend with "super-weeds" that cannot be controlled with common chemicals, and American agriculture is riddled with fragments of transgenic material. The Union of Concerned Scientists recently reported that the seeds of conventional crops—traditional varieties of corn, soybeans, and canola—are now "pervasively contaminated with low levels of DNA originating from engineered varieties of these crops." One laboratory found transgenic DNA in 83 percent of the corn, soy, and canola varieties tested.

GMO contamination is causing mounting economic losses, as farmers lose their markets, organic producers lose their certification, and processors have to recall food products. The contamination is even beginning to affect property values. Consumers are eating GMOs, whether they know it or not, and even GMOs not approved for human consumption have shown up in our taco shells. New "biopharmaceutical" crops used to grow drugs have leaked into the human food supply. And across the nation, hundreds of open field plots are growing transgenic corn, rice, and soybeans that contain drugs, human genes, animal vaccines, and industrial chemicals, without sufficient safeguards to protect nearby food crops.

It's not only food and farming that are affected. Part of what makes GMOs such an environmental threat is that, unlike chemical contamination, GMOs are living organisms, capable of reproducing and recombining, and once they get out, they can't be recalled. Now that there are genetically engineered fish, trees, insects, and other organisms, there's no limit to the kind of environmental surprises that can occur. The widespread ecological damage discussed at Asilomar is now a reality. In just one example of what can happen, a study found that when just 60 transgenic fish were released into a wild population of tens of thousands of fish, all the wild fish were wiped out in just 40 generations. And what will happen when there are plantations of transgenic trees, which can disperse GMO pollen for up to 40 miles and over several decades? Without physical or regulatory restraints, GMOs pose a very real threat to the biological integrity of the planet. As GMO activists say, it gives "pollution a life of its own."

The unasked question that lingers behind all the stories of GMO contamination is: what is the role of industry? How do the manufacturers of GMOs benefit from gene pollution? The fact is, the industry has never lifted a ringer to prevent it and the biological and political system they have designed for it encourage its spread. The industry calls contamination an "adventitious presence," as if it were a benign but unavoidable consequence of modern life, like background radiation from nuclear testing.

In the United States, there are no legal safeguards in place to protect the public—not even labels. Labels would at least provide the consumer with a means for tracing the source of any problems that occur. Plus, without liability laws, the industry avoids accountability for any health or environmental damage it causes. It opposes independent testing and then takes advantage of the lack of data to make false assurances about its products' safety. The *Wall Street Journal* reported in 2003 that "makers of genetically modified crops have avoided answering questions and submitted erroneous data" on the safety of their products to the federal government. They have spent hundreds of millions of dollars on massive public relations campaigns that use sophisticated "perception management" techniques all aimed at falsely assuring the public, and government agencies, that their products are useful and safe.

Beyond their not having to label and segregate GMOs, biotech companies can manufacture, sell, and distribute them without having to take expensive precautions against contamination. They do not have to monitor field practices or do any post-market studies. When farms or factories are contaminated with GMOs, the industry is not held responsible for clean-up costs, as would be the case with chemical contamination. Instead, massive GMO food and crop recalls have been subsidized by taxpayers. Industry not only doesn't pay for a farmer's losses; it often sues the farmer for patent infringement and makes money on the deal. Monsanto, in particular, has profited richly by extorting patent infringement fines from farmers whose crops were inadvertently contaminated.

In September 2004, a study reported that herbicide-resistant genes from Monsanto's new bioengineered creeping bentgrass were found as far away as measurements were made—13 miles downwind. Monsanto's response was that there was nothing to worry about; it had proprietary herbicides that could take care of the problem, assuring more the sale of its products than a limit to the contamination. By assiduously avoiding any responsibility for the proliferation of GMOs, and by defeating attempts by the public to contain them, the agricultural biotechnology industry has thus virtually ensured that GMO contamination will continue unabated. A biotech industry consultant with Promar International, Don Westfall, put it this way: "the hope of industry is that over time the market is so flooded that there's nothing you can do about it. You just sort of surrender."

The most alarming case of GMO contamination is the discovery of transgenes in corn at the center of the origin of corn in Mexico. From the time GMO corn was first planted in the U.S. Midwest, it took only six years to make its way back home in the remote mountainous regions of Puebla and Oaxaca, Mexico. Ignacio Chapela, a Mexican-born microbial biologist, was the scientist who first reported this contamination in 2001. Early in 2002, I visited the area with Dr. Chapela to investigate the cultural and economic implications of his findings. While I was there I got a first-hand look at the complicity of government and industry in the spread of GMO contamination.

The genetic diversity of corn, the world's most important food crop after rice, has been fostered for thousands of years by Zapotec and hundreds of other indigenous farming communities who have lived in these mountainous areas since before the Spanish arrived. Now their traditional land-based ways of life, the sacred center of their culture, and the source of their economic livelihood, corn, has been imperiled by this new form of colonization. The farmers I talked to there were well informed, but worried about their cultural and economic survival. What they did not understand was how transgenic corn got into their fields.[4]

Early press reports blamed the farmers themselves, based on the observation that in order to help support their families and communities, some of them travel to the U.S. to work as migrant workers. But in fact, it turned out that the cause of the contamination was the Mexican government and "free trade" rules. Although Mexico had banned the commercial planting of transgenic corn, under pressure of NAFTA and the biotech industry it was importing corn from the U.S. that it knew was contaminated. It then distributed this whole-kernel corn to poor communities as food aid, without labels or warnings to rural farmers that it should not be used for seed. This highly subsidized corn, which is being dumped on third world farmers at prices that are lower than the cost of production, undermines local corn markets. But instead of taking steps to stop the spread of this contamination, or to protect its farming communities, or even to guard its fragile biodiversity, the Mexican government, the international seed banks, and the biotech industry all deflected public and media attention to a convenient scapegoat —Dr. Chapela.

THE SUPPRESSION OF SCIENCE

Chapela and his graduate student, David Quist, had published their findings in the peer-reviewed journal *Nature*.[5] They had actually made two findings: first, that GMOs had contaminated Mexico's local varieties of corn—in technical terms, that "introgression" had occurred. And second, they found that once transgenes had introgressed into other plants, the genes did not behave as expected. This is evidence of transgenic instability, which scientists now regard with growing concern. But allegations of such instability can be dangerous to make because they undermine the central dogma's basic article of faith: that transgenes are stable and behave predictably. Not surprisingly, the industry attacked the first finding, but was foiled when the Mexican government's own studies found even higher levels and more widespread GMO contamination than the *Nature* article had reported. The industry then focused its attack to the finding of transgenic instability.

For over a year, the industry relentlessly assailed Quist and Chapela's work, both in the press and on the Internet. As the debate raged on, scientists argued both sides, fueled, Chapela says, by a well developed and generously funded industry public relations strategy that did not hesitate to make the attacks personal. Monsanto even retained a public relations firm to have employees pose as independent critics. The outcome was unprecedented. The editor of *Nature* published a letter saying that "in light of the criticisms ... the evidence available is not sufficient to justify" the publication of the original paper. This "retraction" made reference to the work of two relatively unknown biologists, Matthew Metz and Nick Kaplinsky. At the time, Kaplinsky was still a graduate student in the Department of Plant and Microbial Biology at UC Berkeley. Metz had finished his work at Berkeley and was a post-doctoral fellow at the University of Washington. What few knew was that their role in the *Nature* controversy was linked to another dispute that they, Quist, and Chapela, had been involved in. That earlier dispute, too, was about the integrity of science. And in that case, Chapela had led the faculty opposition—and Quist had been a part of the student opposition—to private funding of biotechnology research at UC Berkeley.

THE PIE ON THE WALL

The University of California at Berkeley is a "land grant" institution, meaning that it was created to support California's rich agricultural productivity. But by the late 1990s, Cal had all but abandoned its original mission. Berkeley had become the national leader in collecting royalty payments on its patents, many of which related to the development of genetic engineering. This development was facilitated by the passage of the Bayh-Dole Act of 1980, which allowed universities to patent their research, even if it was publicly funded. By the fall of 1998, the private funding of research at Berkeley was in its full glory. That year, the dean of the College of Natural Resources, Gordon Rausser, announced that he had brokered an unprecedented research deal with the Novartis Corporation, then a multinational Swiss agrochemical and pharmaceutical giant.

Novartis was giving just one department of the College, the Department of Plant and Microbial Biology, $25 million over a 5-year period. The deal was fraught with conflicts of interest, not the least of which was that Novartis employees served on academic committees and got first license rights to the Department's research products. Novartis proudly announced that "the ultimate goal" of the agreement was "to achieve commercialization of products." This took private intrusion into the public sector to a new level, allowing private investors to profit directly from public investment in research, and arousing concerns about the increasing privatization of public research institutions across the country.

In true Berkeley fashion, the controversy erupted into protests. When the deal was announced in November 1998, I covered the press conference. It was held in a packed room upstairs in Koshland Hall, home of the Department of Plant and Microbial Biology. Novartis executives stood shoulder to shoulder with UC Berkeley administrators and leading faculty. They all looked on benevolently while the agreement was formally signed. Then the speeches started. Steven Briggs, president of Novartis Agricultural Discovery Institute, the foundation that funnels corporate money to the university and gets government research and tax credits for Novartis, signed the deal on behalf of Novartis. Briggs, who is an expert on the corn genome, called the agreement—without the least suggestion of irony—"the final statement in academic freedom."

The person most responsible for the Novartis deal, Dean Rausser, was proud of his considerable connections in the private sector. While he was dean, he built a consulting company worth millions. During the press conference, he stood at the front of the room with the other key participants. The press and other guests were seated in folding chairs facing them, and students sat on the floor along the walls. Hefty security men in blue blazers with wires dangling from their ears were lined up along the back wall. I was in the front row. Suddenly I felt a commotion erupting behind me. Something rushed past my head, missed its intended target, and splattered on the wall behind the front table. Then another object followed, grazed Dean Rausser, and landed on the floor at his feet. It all happened fast, but I soon realized that I was in the middle of a pie-throwing protest. In their hallmark style, which is humorous political theater, the "Biotic Baking Brigade" had tossed two vegan pumpkin pies (it was Thanksgiving week, after all) at the signers of the Novartis agreement.

As campus security guards wrestled the protesters to the floor and then pulled them out of the room, the AP reporter who was sitting next to me jumped up and ran out to call in her story. I stayed and watched Dean Rausser, who had been speaking at the time. He just looked down, brushed some pie off his suit, then smiled and shrugged. I got the distinct feeling he was enjoying the moment. He went on with his presentation, and for the rest of the time he was speaking, pie filling drooled down the wall behind him.

As a child of the '60s and a member of the UC Berkeley class of 1965, I was reminded of the winter of 1964, when Mario Savio gave his famous "rage against the machine" speech[6] on the steps of the campus administration building. When it began, the Free Speech Movement was about academic freedom but it enlarged into demonstrations against the war in Vietnam and support for the civil rights and women's movements. A lot was achieved, especially in terms of environmental protection. But it was always about who controls the levers of "the machine," as Savio called it. By 1998, however, the conservative backlash that was provoked by these protests was in full bloom. Private interests had successfully dismantled the regulatory system, invaded the ivy tower, and taken over the intellectual commons. The corporate executives and their academic beneficiaries who were there to celebrate the Novartis agreement clearly had nothing to fear—a fact that was neatly affirmed by Dean Rausser's shrug.

The Novartis funding ended in 2003. By then, faculty and graduate students who were on both sides of the debate had gone their separate ways. Dr. Chapela stayed, and continued to teach at Berkeley. As 2003 drew to a close, he was up for a tenure appointment. Even though he'd garnered extraordinary support from faculty, students, and the public, his role in opposing corporate funding on campus apparently cost him his teaching career. After an unusually protracted process, the University denied him tenure. In 2004, a 10-person team at Michigan State University that had spent two years evaluating the Novartis-Berkeley agreement concluded that the deal was indeed "outside the mainstream for research contracts with industry" and that Berkeley's relationship with Novartis created a conflict of interest in the administration that affected their tenure decision against Dr. Chapela.

Instead of applauding the bravery of scientists who question biotechnology, or at least encouraging further scientific inquiry, the industry and its cronies in the academic world denounce their critics. Dr. Chapela has now joined a growing number of scientists who have paid a high price for their integrity. Others have lost jobs, been discredited in the press, told to change research results or to repudiate their findings.[7] And for each victim whose story is told publicly, there are others who have been silenced and cannot come forward. The implications of the trend toward the privatization of research and the repression of academic freedom go far beyond the question of where the funds come from and who decides what gets studied. It's a trend that deeply undermines the public's faith in science, and the result is that society will lose the means to adequately evaluate new technologies. It may also mean that we adopt a view of the natural world so mechanistic that we will not even recognize the threats we face.

If science were free to operate in the public interest, it could provide the intellectual framework for innovations that work with nature, instead of against it. There already are technologists that use natural solutions to heal the wounds of the industrial age, formulate sustainable food production and energy solutions, create new economic opportunities through the imaginative use of ecological design, and build local self-reliant communities that foster both cultural and biological survival. So we do have a choice of technologies, and nature remains abundantly generous with us. What we do not have, given the perilous environmental state of the planet, is a lot of time left to sort this out. And as long as the critics are silenced, we can be lulled by the "certain promises" of genetic engineering, that it will provide magic answers to those age old problems of hunger and disease, and in doing so, be diverted from attending to its "uncertain perils."

THE NATURE OF TRESPASS

Trespass, in legal parlance, means "an unlawful act that causes injury to person or property." It connotes an act of intrusion, usually by means of stealth, force, or violence. It also implies the right to allow or to refuse an intrusion. A trespass occurs when that right has been violated. Genetic engineering technology is a trespass on the public commons. This is because of the way transgenics are designed and the way "the molecular vision" has been pursued. This vision required that science be compromised to the point where it would overlook the complex boundary conditions that form the very foundation of life. It had to have the hubris to break the species barriers and place itself directly in the path of evolution, severing organisms from their hereditary lineage. And it requires the use of stealth and violence to invade the cell wall, and the implanting of transgenic life forms into an involuntary participant with organisms that are especially designed to overcome all resistance to this rude intrusion.

This trespass continues when ownership is forced on the newly created organisms in the form of a patent. The patenting of a life form was widely considered immoral, and until the U.S. Supreme Court approved the patenting of life in 1980, it was illegal. With that one decision, private interests were given the right to own every non-human life form on earth. We clearly are, as President Bush recently declared, "the ownership society." Now, when GMOs enter the borderless world of free trade and permeate every part of the web of life, they carry within them their owner's mark and effectively privatize every organism they infiltrate. This is made all the more unacceptable because this expensive technology is so unnecessary. Most of what agricultural biotechnology sells, such as insect-resistant plants and weed-control strategies, is already available by other means. Traditional plant breeding can produce all these advances and more—including increased yield, drought or salt resistance, and even nutritional enhancements. The whole point of the commercial use of the genetic engineering technology is the patents, and the social control they facilitate. The reason GMOs were inserted into crops is so that agbiochemical companies could own the seed supply and control the means and methods of food production, and profit at each link in the food chain.

Genetic engineering is a manifestation—perhaps the ultimate manifestation—of the term "full spectrum dominance." In this case, the dominance is achieved on multiple levels, first by exerting biological control over the organism itself, then by achieving economic control over the marketplace and then through "perceptual" control over public opinion. GMOs are disguised to look just like their natural counterparts, and then are released into the environment and the human food chain through a matrix of control that identifies and disables every political, legal, educational, and economic barrier that could thwart their owners' purpose. Arguably, this description suggests a more sinister level of intention than really exists. But the fact remains that denial of choice has been accomplished and it is crucial to this strategy's success. As a Canadian GMO seed industry spokesperson, Dale Adolphe, put it: "It's a hell of a thing to say that the way we win is don't give the consumer a choice, but that might be it."

Agricultural genetic engineering is dismantling our once deeply held common vision about how we feed ourselves, how we care for the land, water, and seeds that support us, and how we participate in decisions that affect us on the most intimate personal and most essential community level. The ultimate irony of our ecological crisis, says David Loy, a professor and author of works on modern Western thought, is that "our collective project to secure ourselves is what threatens to destroy us." But still, there are problems with making moral arguments like these. One is that we lack a practical system of public ethics—some set of common standards we can turn to for guidance. Another is that it does not address the most serious threat to our security, which is that no amount of science, fact, or even moral suasion is of any consequence when we are left with no options.

At the end of my inquiry I came to the conclusion that genetic engineering, at least as it is being used in agriculture is, by design, inherently invasive and unstable. It has been imposed on the American public in a way that has left us with no choice and no way to opt out, biologically or socially. Thus, the reality is that the evolutionary legacy of our lives, whether as human beings, bees, fish, or trees, has been disrupted. We are in danger of being severed from our own ancestral lines and diverted into another world altogether, the physical and social dimensions of which are still unknown and yet to be described.

NOTES

1. Although I use the terms "biotechnology" and "genetic engineering" interchangeably, along with references to "transgenes" and "genetically modified organisms," I am, in all cases, referring to recombinant DNA technology used to cross species boundaries. I am not using the term "biotechnology" in its general sense, which can include natural processes. This analysis of genetic engineering will focus *only* on its agricultural applications. It does not address issues that might apply to medical or other uses.
2. Kay, Lily E. *The Molecular Vision of Life. Caltech, the Rockefeller Foundation, and the Rise of the New Biology*, Oxford University Press, 1993, p. 23.
3. "Genome Scrambling—Myth or Reality? Transformation-induced Mutations in Transgenic Crop Plants" by Drs. Wilson, Latham, and Steinbrecher is available at www.econexus.info.
4. The full story of how GMOs got into native corn in Mexico is told in "Risking Corn, Risking Culture," by this author, Claire Hope Cummings, *World Watch*, November/December 2002.
5. Quist, D. and Chapela, I., "Transgenic DNA Introgressed into Traditional Maize Landraces in Oaxaca. Mexico." *Nature*, **414**: 541–543, November 29, 2001.
6. In that speech Savio said that there comes a time when "the operation of the machine becomes so odious, makes you so sick at heart, that you can't take part. You can't even passively take part and you've got to put your bodies upon the gears and upon the wheels, upon the levers, upon all the apparatus, and you got to make it stop"
7. The stories of four such scientists and their reflections on their experiences can be heard on a recording of a remarkable conversation among them called "The Pulse of Scientific Freedom in the Age of the Biotech Industry" held on the UC Berkeley campus in December, 2003.

2.5 POPULATION, ENERGY, AND CLIMATE CHANGE

2.5.1 The Tragedy of the Commons

GARRETT HARDIN

This article addresses the question of how to deal with the expected growth of the human population in the twenty-first century. Garrett Hardin argues that the problem of controlling human population growth has no technical solution. This is true, he argues, because of a general class of problems that arise from allowing individuals the freedom to act so as to

Source: *Managing the Commons* by Garrett Hardin and John Baden. Copyright © 1977 by W. H. Freeman and Company. Used with permission.

maximize their individual self-interests by exploiting resources held in common. Problems of this kind can produce tragic results because they have the paradoxical effect of eventually bringing ruin to all those who are seeking to maximize their own interests in the belief that doing so will produce "the greatest happiness for the greatest number." The solution to such problems, he suggests, can only be one that sets limits on the individual pursuit of self-interest or on the freedom of the commons.

FOCUS QUESTIONS

1. What does Hardin mean by "the tragedy of the commons"? How does this problem arise?
2. What are some examples of how "Freedom in a commons brings ruin to all"? Can you think of other examples of this general phenomenon?
3. How does the perspective of this reading relate to those developed by the International Forum on Globalization (Selection 2.1.4) and Robert Kates (Selection 2.5.4)? If the population problem has no technical solution, what kind of solutions, if any, does it have?

KEYWORDS

commons, ethical egoism, game theory, National Parks, overfishing, population control, rational self-interest, utilitarianism

At the end of a thoughtful article on the future of nuclear war, J. B. Wiesner and H. F. York concluded that "both sides in the arms race are … confronted by the dilemma of steadily increasing military power and steadily decreasing national security. *It is our considered professional judgment that this dilemma has no technical solution.* If the great powers continue to look for solutions in the area of science and technology only, the result will be to worsen the situation."[1]

I would like to focus your attention not on the subject of the article (national security in a nuclear world) but on the kind of conclusion they reached, namely that there is no technical solution to the problem. An implicit and almost universal assumption of discussions published in professional and semi-popular scientific journals is that the problem under discussion has a technical solution. A technical solution may be defined as one that requires a change only in the techniques of the natural sciences, demanding little or nothing in the way of change in human values or ideas of morality.

In our day (though not in earlier times) technical solutions are always welcome. Because of previous failures in prophecy, it takes courage to assert that a desired technical solution is not possible. Wiesner and York exhibited this courage; publishing in a science journal, they insisted that the solution to the problem was not to be found in the natural sciences. They cautiously qualified their statement with the phrase, "It is our considered professional judgment…." Whether they were right or not is not the concern of the present article. Rather, the concern here is with the important concept of a class of human problems which can be called "no technical solution problems," and more specifically, with the identification and discussion of one of these.

It is easy to show that the class is not a null class. Recall the game of tick-tack-toe. Consider the problem, "How can I win the game of tick-tack-toe?" It is well known that I cannot, if I assume (in keeping with the conventions of game theory) that my opponent understands the game perfectly. Put another way, there is no "technical solution" to the problem. I can win only by giving a radical meaning to the word "win"; I can hit my opponent over the head; or I can falsify the records. Every way in which I "win" involves, in some sense, an abandonment of the game, as we intuitively understand it. (I can also, of course, openly abandon the game and refuse to play it. This is what most adults do.) The class of "no technical solution problems" has members. My thesis is that the "population problem," as conventionally conceived, is a member of this class. How it is conventionally conceived needs some comment. It is fair to say that most people who anguish over the population problem are trying to find a way to avoid the evils of overpopulation without relinquishing any of the privileges they now enjoy. They think that farming the seas or developing new strains of wheat will solve the problem—technologically. I try to show here that the solution they seek cannot be found. The population problem cannot be solved in a technical way, any more than can the problem of winning the game of tick-tack-toe.

WHAT SHALL WE MAXIMIZE?

Population, as Malthus said, naturally tends to grow "geometrically," or, as we would now say, exponentially. In a finite world this means that the per-capita share of the world's goods must decrease. Is ours a finite world?

A fair defense can be put forward for the view that the world is infinite; or that we do not know that it is not. But, in terms of the practical problems that we must face in the next few generations with the foreseeable technology, it is clear that we will greatly increase human misery if we do not, during the immediate future, assume that the world available to the terrestrial human population is finite. "Space" is no escape.[2]

A finite world can support only a finite population; therefore, population growth must eventually equal zero. (The case of perpetual wide fluctuations above and below zero is a trivial variant that need not be discussed.) When this condition is met, what will be the situation of mankind? Specifically, can Bentham's goal of "the greatest good for the greatest number" be realized?

No—for two reasons, each sufficient by itself. The first is a theoretical one. It is not mathematically possible to maximize for two (or more) variables at the same time. This was clearly stated by von Neumann and Morgenstern,[3] but the principle is implicit in the theory of partial differential equations, dating back at least to D'Alembert (1717–1783).

The second reason springs directly from biological facts. To live, any organism must have a source of energy (for example, food). This energy is utilized for two purposes: mere maintenance and work. For man, maintenance of life requires about 1600 kilocalories a day ("maintenance calories"). Anything that he does over and above merely staying alive will be defined as work, and is supported by "work calories" which he takes in. Work calories are used not only for what we call work in common speech; they are also required for all forms of enjoyment, from swimming and automobile racing to playing music and writing poetry. If our goal is to maximize population it is obvious what we must do: We must make the work calories per person approach as close to zero as possible. No gourmet meals, no vacations, no sports, no music, no literature, no art.

... I think that everyone will grant, without argument or proof, that maximizing population does not maximize goods. Bentham's goal is impossible.

In reaching this conclusion I have made the usual assumption that it is the acquisition of energy that is the problem. The appearance of atomic energy has led some to question this assumption. However, given an infinite source of energy, population growth still produces an inescapable problem. The problem of the acquisition of energy is replaced by the problem of its dissipation, as J. H. Fremlin has so wittily shown.[4] The arithmetic signs in the analysis are, as it were, reversed; but Bentham's goal is unobtainable.

The optimum population is, then, less than the maximum. The difficulty of defining the optimum is enormous; so far as I know, no one has seriously tackled this problem. Reaching an acceptable and stable solution will surely require more than one generation of hard analytical work—and much persuasion.

We want the maximum good per person; but what is good? To one person it is wilderness, to another it is ski lodges for thousands. To one it is estuaries to nourish ducks for hunters to shoot; to another it is factory land. Comparing one good with another is, we usually say, impossible because goods are incommensurable. Incommensurables cannot be compared.

Theoretically this may be true; but in real life incommensurables are commensurable. Only a criterion of judgment and a system of weighting are needed. In nature the criterion is survival. Is it better for a species to be small and hideable, or large and powerful? Natural selection commensurates the incommensurables. The compromise achieved depends on a natural weighting of the values of the variables.

Man must imitate this process. There is no doubt that in fact he already does, but unconsciously. It is when the hidden decisions are made explicit that the arguments begin. The problem for the years ahead is to work out an acceptable theory of weighting. Synergistic effects, nonlinear variation, and difficulties in discounting the future make the intellectual problem difficult, but not (in principle) insoluble.

Has any cultural group solved this practical problem at the present time, even on an intuitive level? One simple fact proves that none has: there is no prosperous population in the world today that has, and has had for some time, a growth rate of zero. Any people that has intuitively identified its optimum point will soon reach it, after which its growth rate becomes and remains zero.

Of course, a positive growth rate might be taken as evidence that a population is below its optimum. However, by any reasonable standards, the most rapidly growing populations on earth today are (in general) the most miserable. This association (which need not be invariable) casts doubt on the optimistic assumption that the positive growth rate of a population is evidence that it has yet to reach its optimum.

We can make little progress in working toward optimum population size until we explicitly exorcise the spirit of Adam Smith in the field of practical demography. In economic affairs, *The Wealth of Nations* (1776) popularized the "invisible hand," the idea that an individual who "intends only his own gain," is, as it were, "led by an invisible hand to promote...the public interest."[5] Adam Smith did not assert that this was invariably true, and perhaps neither did any of his followers. But he contributed to a dominant tendency of thought that has ever since interfered with positive action based on rational analysis, namely, the tendency to assume that decisions reached individually will, in fact, be the best decisions for an entire society. If this assumption is correct it justifies the continuance of our present policy of laissez faire in reproduction. If it is correct we can assume that men will control their individual fecundity so as to produce the optimum population. If the assumption is not correct, we need to reexamine our individual freedoms to see which ones are defensible.

TRAGEDY OF FREEDOM IN A COMMONS

The rebuttal to the "invisible hand" in population control is to be found in a scenario first sketched in a little-known pamphlet in 1833 by a mathematical amateur named William Forster Lloyd (1794–1852).[6] We may well call it "the tragedy of the commons," using the word "tragedy" as the philosopher Whitehead[7] used it. "The essence of dramatic tragedy is not unhappiness. It resides in the solemnity of the remorseless working of things." He then goes on to say, "This inevitableness of destiny can only be illustrated in terms of human life by incidents which in fact involve unhappiness. For it is only by them that the futility of escape can be made evident in the drama."

The tragedy of the commons develops in this way. Picture a pasture open to all. It is to be expected that each herdsman will try to keep as many cattle as possible on the commons. Such an arrangement may work reasonably satisfactorily for centuries because tribal wars, poaching, and disease keep the numbers of both man and beast well below the carrying capacity of the land. Finally, however, comes the day of reckoning, that is, the day when the long-desired goal of social stability becomes a reality. At this point, the inherent logic of the commons remorselessly generates tragedy.

As a rational being, each herdsman seeks to maximize his gain. Explicitly or implicitly, more or less consciously, he asks, "What is the utility to me of adding one more animal to my herd?"

This utility has one negative and one positive component.

1. The positive component is a function of the increment of one animal. Since the herdsman receives all the proceeds from the sale of the additional animal, the positive utility is nearly +1.
2. The negative component is a function of the additional overgrazing created by one more animal. Since, however, the effects of overgrazing are shared by all the herdsmen, the negative utility for any particular decision-making herdsman is only a fraction of –1.

Adding together the component partial utilities, the rational herdsman concludes that the only sensible course for him to pursue is to add another animal to his herd. And another.... But this is the conclusion reached by each and every rational herdsman sharing a commons. Therein is the tragedy. Each man is locked into a system that compels him to increase his herd without limit in a world that is limited. Ruin is the destination toward which all men rush, each pursuing his own best interest in a society that believes in the freedom of the commons. Freedom in a commons brings ruin to all.

Some would say that this is a platitude. Would that it were! In a sense, it was learned thousands of years ago, but natural selection favors the forces of psychological denial.[8] The individual benefits as an individual from his ability to deny the truth even though society as a whole, of which he is a part, suffers. Education can counteract the natural tendency to do the wrong thing, but the inexorable succession of generations requires that the basis for this knowledge be constantly refreshed.

A simple incident that occurred a few years ago in Leominster, Massachusetts, shows how perishable the knowledge is. During the Christmas shopping season the parking meters downtown were covered with plastic bags that bore tags reading: "Do not open until after Christmas. Free parking courtesy of the mayor and city council." In other words, facing the prospect of an increased demand for already scarce space, the city fathers reinstituted the system of the commons. (Cynically, we suspect that they gained more votes than they lost by this retrogressive act.)

In an approximate way, the logic of the commons has been understood for a long time, perhaps since the discovery of agriculture or the invention of private property in real estate. But it is understood mostly only in special cases which are not sufficiently generalized. Even at this late date, cattlemen leasing national land on the Western ranges demonstrate no more than an ambivalent understanding, in constantly pressuring federal authorities to increase the head count to the point where overgrazing produces erosion and weed-dominance. Likewise, the oceans of the world continue to suffer from the survival of the philosophy of the commons. Maritime nations still respond automatically to the shibboleth of the "freedom of the seas." Professing to believe in the "inexhaustible resources of the oceans," they bring species after species of fish and whales closer to extinction.[9]

The National Parks present another instance of the working out of the tragedy of the commons. At present, they are open to all, without limit. The parks themselves are limited in extent—there is only one Yosemite Valley—whereas population seems to grow without limit. The values that visitors seek in the parks are steadily eroded. Plainly, we must soon cease to treat the parks as commons or they will be of no value to anyone.

What shall we do? We have several options. We might sell them off as private property. We might keep them as public property, but allocate the right to enter them. The allocation might be on the basis of wealth, by the use of an auction system. It might be on the basis of merit, as defined by some agreed-upon standards. It might be by lottery. Or it might be on a first-come, first-served basis, administered to long queues. These, I think, are all objectionable. But we must choose—or acquiesce in the destruction of the commons that we call our National Parks.

POLLUTION

In a reverse way, the tragedy of the commons reappears in problems of pollution. Here it is not a question of taking something out of the commons, but of putting something in—sewage, or chemical, radioactive, and heat wastes into water; noxious and dangerous fumes into the air; and distracting and unpleasant advertising signs into the line of sight. The calculations of utility are much the same as before. The rational man finds that his share of the cost of the wastes he discharges into the commons is less than the cost of purifying his wastes before releasing them. Since this is true for everyone, we are locked into a system of "fouling our own nest," so long as we behave as independent, rational, free-enterprisers.

The tragedy of the commons as a food basket is averted by private property, or something formally like it. But the air and waters surrounding us cannot readily be fenced, and so the tragedy of the commons as a cesspool must be prevented by different means, by coercive laws or taxing devices that make it cheaper for the polluter to treat his pollutants than to discharge them untreated. We have not progressed as far with the solution of this problem as we have with the first. Indeed, our particular concept of private property, which deters us from exhausting the positive resources of the earth, favors pollution. The owner of a factory on the bank of a stream—whose property extends to the middle of the stream—often has difficulty seeing why it is not his natural right to muddy the waters flowing past his door. The law, always behind the times, requires elaborate stitching and fitting to adapt it to this newly perceived aspect of the commons.

The pollution problem is a consequence of population. It did not much matter how a lonely American frontiersman disposed of his waste. "Flowing water purifies itself every ten miles," my grandfather used to say, and the myth was near enough to the truth when he was a boy, for there were not too many people. But as population became denser, the natural chemical and biological recycling processes became overloaded, calling for a redefinition of property rights.

HOW TO LEGISLATE TEMPERANCE

Analysis of the pollution problem as a function of population density uncovers a not generally recognized principle of morality, namely: *the morality of an act is a function of the state of the system at the time it is performed.*[10] Using the commons as a cesspool does not harm the general public under frontier conditions, because there is no public; the same behavior in a metropolis is unbearable. One hundred fifty years ago a plainsman could kill an American bison, cut out only the tongue for his dinner, and discard the rest of the animal. He was not in any important sense being wasteful. Today, with only a few thousand bison left, we would be appalled at such behavior.

In passing, it is worth noting that the morality of an act cannot be determined from a photograph. One does not know whether a man killing an elephant or setting fire to the grassland is harming others until one knows the total system in which his act appears. "One picture is worth a thousand words," said an ancient Chinese, but it may take ten thousand words to validate it. It is as tempting to ecologists as it is to reformers in general to try to persuade others by way of the photographic shortcut. But the essence of an argument cannot be photographed: it must be presented rationally—in words.

That morality is system-sensitive escaped the attention of most codifiers of ethics in the past. "Thou shaft not..." is the form of traditional ethical directives which make no allowance for particular circumstances. The laws of our society follow the pattern of ancient ethics, and therefore are poorly suited to governing a complex, crowded, changeable world. Our epicyclic solution is to augment statutory law with administrative law. Since it is practically impossible to spell out all the conditions under which it is safe to burn trash in the backyard or to run an automobile without smog-control, by law we delegate the details to bureaus. The result is administrative law, which is rightly feared for an ancient reason—*Quis custodiet ipsos custodes?*—Who shall watch the watchers themselves? John Adams said that we must have a "government of laws and not men." Bureau administrators, trying to evaluate the morality of acts in the total system, are singularly liable to corruption, producing a government by men, not laws.

Prohibition is easy to legislate (though not necessarily easy to enforce); but how do we legislate temperance? Experience indicates that it can be accomplished best through the mediation of administrative law. We limit possibilities unnecessarily if we suppose that the sentiment of *Quis custodiet* denies us the use of administrative law. We should rather retain the phrase as a perpetual reminder of fearful dangers we cannot avoid. The great challenge facing us now is to invent the corrective feedbacks that are needed to keep custodians honest. We must find ways to legitimate the needed authority of both the custodians and the corrective feedbacks.

FREEDOM TO BREED IS INTOLERABLE

The tragedy of the commons is involved in population problems in another way. In a world governed solely by the principle "dog eat dog"—if indeed there ever was such a world—how many children a family had would not be a matter of public concern. Parents who bred too exuberantly would leave fewer descendants, not more, because they would be unable to care adequately for their children. David Lack and others have found that such a negative feedback demonstrably controls the fecundity of birds.[11] But men are not birds, and have not acted like them for millenniums, at least.

If each human family were dependent only on its own resources; *if the* children of improvident parents starved to death; *if*, thus, overbreeding brought its own "punishment" to the germ line—*then* there would be no public interest in controlling the breeding of families. But our society is deeply committed to the welfare state,[12] and hence is confronted with another aspect of the tragedy of the commons.

In a welfare state, how shall we deal with the family, the religion, the race, or the class (of indeed any distinguishable and cohesive group) that adopts overbreeding as a policy to secure its own aggrandizement?[13] To couple the concept of freedom to breed with the belief that everyone born has an equal right to the commons is to lock the world into a tragic course of action.

Unfortunately this is just the course of action that is being pursued by the United Nations. In late 1967, some thirty nations agreed to the following: "The Universal Declaration of Human Rights describes the family as the natural and fundamental unit of society. It follows that any choice and decision with regard to the size of the family must irrevocably rest with the family itself, and cannot be made by anyone else."[14]

It is painful to have to deny categorically the validity of this right; denying it, one feels as uncomfortable as a resident of Salem, Massachusetts, who denied the reality of witches in the seventeenth century. At the present time, in liberal quarters, something like a taboo acts to inhibit criticism of the United Nations. There is a feeling that the United Nations is "our last and best hope," that we shouldn't find fault with it; we shouldn't play into the hands of the arch conservatives. However, let us not forget what Robert Louis Stevenson said: "The truth that is suppressed by friends is the readiest weapon of the enemy." If we love the truth we must openly deny the validity of the Universal Declaration of Human Rights, even though it is promoted by the United Nations. We should also join with Kingsley Davis[15] in attempting to get Planned Parenthood-World Population to see the error of its ways in embracing the same tragic ideal.

CONSCIENCE IS SELF-ELIMINATING

It is a mistake to think that we can control the breeding of mankind in the long run by an appeal to conscience. Charles Galton Darwin made this point when he spoke on the centennial of the publication of his grandfather's great book. The argument is straightforward and Darwinian.

People vary. Confronted with appeals to limit breeding, some people will undoubtedly respond to the plea more than others. Those who have more children will produce a larger fraction of the next generation than those with more susceptible consciences. The differences will be accentuated, generation by generation.

In C. G. Darwin's words: "It may well be that it would take hundreds of generations for the progenitive instinct to develop in this way, but if it should do so, nature would have taken her revenge, and the variety *Homo contracipiens* would become extinct and would be replaced by the variety *Homo progenitivus*."[16]

The argument assumes that conscience or the desire for children (no matter which) is hereditary —but hereditary only in the most general formal sense. The result will be the same whether the attitude is transmitted through germ cells, or exosomatically, to use A. J. Lotka's term. (If one denies the latter possibility as well as the former, then what's the point of education?) The argument has here been stated in the context of the population problem, but it applies equally well to any instance in which society appeals to an individual exploiting a commons to restrain himself for the general good—by means of his conscience. To make such an appeal is to set up a selective system that works toward the elimination of conscience from the race.

PATHOGENIC EFFECTS OF CONSCIENCE

The long-term disadvantage of an appeal to conscience should be enough to condemn it; but it has serious short-term disadvantages as well. If we ask a man who is exploiting a commons to desist "in the name of conscience," what are we saying to him? What does he hear?—not only at the moment but also in the wee small hours of the night when, half asleep, he remembers not merely the words we used but also the nonverbal communication cues we gave him unawares? Sooner or later, consciously or subconsciously, he senses that he has received two communications, and that they are contradictory: 1. (intended communication) "If you don't do as we ask, we will openly condemn you for not acting like a responsible citizen"; 2. (unintended communication) "If you *do* behave as we ask, we will secretly condemn you for a simpleton who can be shamed into standing aside while the rest of us exploit the commons."

Every man then is caught in what Bateson has called a "double bind." Bateson and his coworkers have made a plausible case for viewing the double bind as an important causative factor in the genesis of schizophrenia.[17] The double bind may not always be so damaging, but it always endangers the mental health of anyone to whom it is applied. "A bad conscience," said Nietzsche, "is a kind of illness."

To conjure up a conscience in others is tempting to anyone who wishes to extend his control beyond the legal limits. Leaders at the highest level succumb to this temptation. Has any president during the past generation failed to call on labor unions to moderate voluntarily their demands for higher wages, or to steel companies to honor voluntary guidelines on prices? I can recall none. The rhetoric used on such occasions is designed to produce feelings of guilt in noncooperators.

For centuries it was assumed without proof that guilt was a valuable, perhaps even an indispensable, ingredient of the civilized life. Now, in this post-Freudian world, we doubt it.

Paul Goodman speaks from the modern point of view when he says: "No good has ever come from feeling guilty, neither intelligence, policy, nor compassion. The guilty do not pay attention to the object but only to themselves, and not even to their own interests, which might make sense, but to their anxieties."[18]

One does not have to be a professional psychiatrist to see the consequences of anxiety. We in the Western world are just emerging from a dreadful two-centuries-long Dark Ages of Eros that was sustained partly by prohibition laws, but perhaps more effectively by the anxiety-generating mechanisms of education. Alex Comfort has told the story well in *The Anxiety Makers*;[19] it is not a pretty one.

Since proof is difficult, we may even concede that the results of anxiety may sometimes, from certain points of view, be desirable. The larger question we should ask is whether, as a matter of policy, we should ever encourage the use of a technique, the tendency (if not the intention) of which, is psychologically pathogenic. We hear much talk these days of responsible parenthood; the coupled words are incorporated into the titles of some organizations devoted to birth control. Some people have proposed massive propaganda campaigns to instill responsibility into the nation's (or the world's) breeders. But what is the meaning of the word conscience? When we use the word *responsibility* in the absence of substantial sanctions are we not trying to browbeat a free man in a commons into acting against his own interest? Responsibility is a verbal counterfeit for a substantial quid pro quo. It is an attempt to get something for nothing.

If the word responsibility is to be used at all, I suggest that it be in the sense Charles Frankel uses it.[20] "Responsibility," says this philosopher, "is the product of definite social arrangements." Notice that Frankel calls for social arrangements—not propaganda.

MUTUAL COERCION MUTUALLY AGREED UPON

The social arrangements that.produce responsibility are arrangements that create coercion, of some sort. Consider bank robbing. The man who takes money from a bank acts as if the bank were a commons. How do we prevent such action? Certainly not by trying to control his behavior solely by a verbal appeal to his sense of responsibility. Rather than rely on propaganda we follow Frankel's lead and insist that a bank is not a commons; we seek the definite social arrangements that will keep it from becoming a commons. That we thereby infringe on the freedom of would-be robbers we neither deny nor regret.

The morality of bank robbing is particularly easy to understand because we accept complete prohibition of this activity. We are willing to say "Thou shalt not rob banks," without providing for exceptions. But temperance also can be created by coercion. Taxing is a good coercive device. To keep downtown shoppers temperate in their use of parking spaces we introduce parking meters for short periods, and traffic fines for longer ones. We need not actually forbid a citizen to park as long as he wants to; we need merely make it increasingly expensive for him to do so. Not prohibition, but carefully biased options are what we offer him. A Madison Avenue man might call this persuasion; I prefer the greater candor of the word *coercion*.

Coercion is a dirty word to most liberals now, but it need not forever be so. As with the four-letter words, its dirtiness can be cleansed away by exposure to the light, by saying it over and over without apology or embarrassment. To many, the word *coercion* implies arbitrary decisions of distant and irresponsible bureaucrats; but this is not a necessary part of its meaning. The only kind of coercion I recommend is mutual coercion, mutually agreed upon by the majority of the people affected.

To say that we mutually agree to coercion is not to say that we are required to enjoy it, or even to pretend we enjoy it. Who enjoys taxes? We all grumble about them. But we accept compulsory taxes because we recognize that voluntary taxes would favor the conscienceless. We institute and (grumblingly) support taxes and other coercive devices to escape the horror of the commons.

An alternative to the commons need not be perfectly just to be preferable. With real estate and other material goods, the alternative we have chosen is the institution of private property coupled with legal inheritance. Is this system perfectly just? As a genetically trained biologist I deny that it is. It seems to me that, if there are to be differences in individual inheritance, legal possession should be perfectly correlated with biological inheritance—that those who are biologically more fit to be the custodians of property and power should legally inherit more. But genetic recombination continually makes a mockery of the doctrine "like father, like son" implicit in our laws of legal inheritance. An idiot can inherit millions, and a trust fund can keep his estate intact. We must admit that our legal system of private property plus inheritance is unjust—but we put up with it because we are not convinced, at the moment, that anyone has invented a better system. The alternative of the commons is too horrifying to contemplate. Injustice is preferable to total ruin.

It is one of the peculiarities of the warfare between reform and the status quo that is thoughtlessly governed by a double standard. Whenever a reform measure is proposed it is often defeated when its opponents triumphantly discover a flaw in it. As Kingsley Davis has pointed out,[21] worshipers of the staus quo sometimes imply that no reform is possible without unanimous agreement, an implication contrary to historical fact. As nearly as I can make out, automatic rejection of proposed reforms is based on one of two unconscious assumptions: (1) that the status quo is perfect; or (2) that the choice we face is between reform and no action; if the proposed reform is imperfect, we presumably should take no action at all, while we wait for a perfect proposal.

But we can never do nothing. That which we have done for thousands of years is also action. It also produces evils. Once we are aware that the status quo is action, we can then compare its discoverable advantages and disadvantages with the predicted advantages and disadvantages of the proposed reform, discounting as best we can for our lack of experience. On the basis of such a comparison, we can make a rational decision which will not involve the unworkable assumption that only perfect systems are tolerable.

RECOGNITION OF NECESSITY

Perhaps the simplest summary of this analysis of man's population problems is this: the commons, if justifiable at all, is justifiable only under conditions of low-population density. As the human population has increased, the commons has had to be abandoned in one aspect after another.

First we abandoned the commons in food gathering, enclosing farm land and restricting pastures and hunting and fishing areas. These restrictions are still not complete throughout the world.

Somewhat later we saw that the commons as a place for waste disposal would also have to be abandoned. Restrictions on the disposal of domestic sewage are widely accepted in the Western world; we are still struggling to close the commons to pollution by automobiles, factories, insecticide sprayers, fertilizing operations, and atomic energy installations.

In a still more embryonic state is our recognition of the evils of the commons in matters of pleasure. There is almost no restriction on the propagation of sound waves in the public medium. The shopping public is assaulted with mindless music, without its consent. Our government has paid out billions of dollars to create a supersonic transport which would disturb 50,000 people for every one person whisked from coast to coast 3 hours faster. Advertisers muddy the airwaves of radio and television and pollute the view of travelers. We are a long way from outlawing the commons in matters of pleasure. Is this because our Puritan inheritance makes us view pleasure as something of a sin, and pain (that is, the pollution of advertising) as the sign of virtue?

Every new enclosure of the commons involves the infringement of somebody's personal liberty. Infringements made in the distant past are accepted because no contemporary complains of a loss. It is the newly proposed infringements that we vigorously oppose; cries of "rights" and "freedom" fill the air. But what does "freedom" mean? When men mutually agreed to pass laws against robbing, mankind became more free, not less so. Individuals locked into the logic of the commons are free only to bring on universal ruin; once they see the necessity of mutual coercion, they become free to pursue other goals. I believe it was Hegel who said, "Freedom is the recognition of necessity."

The most important aspect of necessity that we must now recognize is the necessity of abandoning the commons in breeding. No technical solution can rescue us from the misery of overpopulation. Freedom to breed will bring ruin to all. At the moment, to avoid hard decisions many of us are tempted to propagandize for conscience and responsible parenthood. The temptation must be resisted, because an appeal to independently acting consciences selects for the disappearance of all conscience in the long run, and an increase in anxiety in the short.

The only way we can preserve and nurture other and more precious freedoms is by relinquishing the freedom to breed, and that very soon. "Freedom is the recognition of necessity"—and it is the role of education to reveal to all the necessity of abandoning the freedom to breed. Only so can we put an end to this aspect of the tragedy of the commons.

NOTES

1. J. B. Wiesner and H. F. York, *Scientific American* **211** (No. 4), 27 (1964).
2. G. Hardin, *Journal of Heredity* **50**, 68 (1959); S. von Hoernor, *Science* **137**, 18 (1962).
3. J. von Neumann and O. Morgenstern, *Theory of Games and Economic Behavior* (Princeton University Press, Princeton, N. J., 1947), p. 11.

4. J. H. Fremlin, *New Scientist*, No. 415 (1964), p. 285.
5. A. Smith, *The Wealth of Nations* (Modern Library, New York, 1937), p. 423.
6. W. F. Lloyd, *Two Lectures on the Checks to Population* (Oxford University Press, Oxford, England, 1833).
7. A. N. Whitehead, *Science and the Modern World* (Mentor, New York, 1948), p. 17.
8. G. Hardin, Ed., *Population, Evolution, and Birth Control* (Freeman, San Francisco, 1964), p. 56.
9. S. McVay, *Scientific American* **216** (No. 8), **13** (1966).
10. J. Fletcher, *Situation Ethics* (Westminster, Philadelphia, 1966).
11. D. Lack, *The Natural Regulation of Animal Numbers* (Clarendon Press, Oxford, England, 1954).
12. H. Girvetz, *From Wealth to Welfare* (Stanford University Press, Stanford, Calif., 1950).
13. G. Hardin, *Perspectives in Biology and Medicine* **6**, 366 (1963).
14. U. Thant, *International Planned Parenthood News*, No. 168 (February 1968), p. 3.
15. K. Davis, *Science* **158**, 730 (1967).
16. S. Tax, Ed., *Evolution After Darwin* (University of Chicago Press, Chicago, 1960), vol. **2**, p. 469.
17. G. Bateson, D. D. Jackson, J. Haley, J. Weakland, *Behavioral Science* **1**, 251 (1956).
18. P. Goodman, *New York Review of Books* **10** (8), **22** (23 May 1968).
19. A. Comfort, *The Anxiety Makers* (Nelson, London, 1967).
20. C. Frankel, *The Case for Modern Man* (Harper & Row, New York, 1955), p. 203.
21. J. D. Roslansky, *Genetics and the Future of Man* (Appleton-Century-Crofts, New York, 1966), p. 177.

2.5.2 Ethics and Global Climate Change

STEPHEN M. GARDINER

On April 6, 2007, the Intergovernmental Panel on Climate Change (IPCC) issued its Working Group II Fourth Assessment Report, entitled "Climate Change 2007: Climate Change Impacts, Adaptation and Vulnerability" (available online at www.ipcc.ch), in which it concluded "with high confidence" that "anthropogenic warming over the past three decades has had a discernible influence on many physical and biological systems" (p. 4). Among the observed impacts of global climate change thus far are the melting of glaciers; ground instability in permafrost regions; changes in Arctic ecosystems; the warming of many lakes and rivers; earlier timing of spring events; poleward shifts in the ranges of plant and animal species; changes in algae, plankton, and fish abundance; effects on agriculture and forestry; changes in infectious disease vectors; sea-level rise and coastal flooding in some areas; warmer and drier conditions in the Sahelian region in Africa; and other such observed changes. The report also concludes that, although different regions will be affected differently by climate change, "poor communities can be especially vulnerable" because they "tend to have more limited adaptive capacities, and are more dependent on climate-sensitive resources such as local water and food supplies" (p. 12). Several weeks later, on May 4, 2007, the report of Working Group III entitled "Mitigation of Climate Change" recommended that the nations of the world take immediate steps to reduce the growth of greenhouse gas emissions into Earth's atmosphere in order to stabilize the climate.

Many people have by now seen Al Gore's Oscar-winning documentary film about global climate change, *An Inconvenient Truth,* in which he declares, "It is not a political issue, it is a

Source: From "Ethics and Global Climate Change," from *ETHICS* 114 (April 2004), pp. 555–600.
Copyright © 2004 University of Chicago Press. Reprinted by permission.

moral issue." But rarely has this claim been subject to a close analysis by a moral philosopher. Although the article by University of Washington philosopher Stephen M. Gardiner reprinted here was published before the most recent IPCC reports, it contains a wealth of information about the science of climate change, as well as thought-provoking arguments about the ethics of the two leading strategies for dealing with it: mitigation and adaptation.

Mitigation strategies, such as those discussed in the most recent IPCC Working Group III report involve changing our technological practices, particularly those involving the use of fossil fuels that emit the main greenhouse gas, carbon dioxide—for instance by moving to more fuel-efficient vehicles and constructing more energy-efficient buildings (see Selection 2.5.3 from Janet Sawin and Kristen Hughes). Adaptation strategies, on the other hand, assume that significant changes in the world's climate will take place during the twenty-first century in any case and that the best strategy for coping with these changes is to prepare to adapt ourselves to them, particularly by helping poor countries to develop economically.

But who should bear the burdens and costs of these strategies? Is there any sound ethical basis for assuming that people presently living in the richer developed countries have strong moral responsibilities to make sacrifices to protect the interests of future persons living in poor countries? What is the moral basis for these obligations? Does coping with the global threat of climate change require a fundamental paradigm shift in our ethics?

FOCUS QUESTIONS

1. What reasons are there to think that the current forecasts about the likely effects of increasing percentages of greenhouse gases in Earth's atmosphere are too pessimistic? What reasons are there to think they might be too optimistic?
2. What is the difference between uncertainty and risk? How does this distinction relate to the debate about whether we need to do something now to address global climate change?
3. Which of the two main strategies, mitigation or adaptation, is likely to be less costly? Would it really be less costly in the long run to do nothing? Or is it possible, and necessary, for us to begin now to pursue both strategies?
4. Why have many moral philosophers concluded that the developed countries should take the lead role in bearing the costs of climate change? Which of these reasons do you find persuasive? Which don't you find persuasive?
5. Why is the Kyoto Treaty such a failure in Gardiner's view? What is needed for there to be an effective global regime to manage climate change?

KEYWORDS

climate change, greenhouse gas emissions, the precautionary principle, social discount rate, Kyoto Treaty

Very few moral philosophers have written on climate change. This is puzzling, for several reasons. First, many politicians and policy makers claim that climate change is not only the most serious environmental problem currently facing the world, but also one of the most important international problems per se. Second, many of those working in other disciplines describe climate change as fundamentally an ethical issue.

Third, the problem is theoretically challenging, both in itself and in virtue of the wider issues it raises. Indeed, some have even gone so far as to suggest that successfully addressing climate change will require a fundamental paradigm shift in ethics (Jamieson 1992, p. 292).

Arguably, then, there is a strong presumption that moral philosophers should be taking climate change seriously. So, why the neglect? In my view, the most plausible explanation is that study of climate change is necessarily interdisciplinary, crossing boundaries between (at least) science, economics, law, and international relations.

This fact not only creates an obstacle to philosophical work (since amassing the relevant information is both time-consuming and intellectually demanding) but also makes it tempting to assume that climate change is essentially an issue for others to resolve. Both factors contribute to the current malaise—and not just within philosophy, but in the wider community too.

My aims in this survey, then, will be twofold. First, I will try to overcome the interdisciplinary obstacle to some extent, by making the climate change issue more accessible to both philosophers and non-philosophers alike. Second, by drawing attention to the ethical dimensions of the climate change problem, I will make the case that the temptation to defer to experts in other disciplines should be resisted. Climate change is fundamentally an ethical issue. As such, it should be of serious concern to both moral philosophers and humanity at large.

The interdisciplinary nature of the climate change problem once prompted John Broome to imply that a truly comprehensive survey of the relevant literature would be impossible (Broome 1992, p. viii). I shall not attempt the impossible. Instead, I shall present an overview of the most major and recent work relevant to philosophical discussion. Inevitably, this overview will be to some extent selective and opinionated. Still, I hope that it will help to reduce the interdisciplinary obstacles to philosophical work on climate change, by giving both philosophers and the public more generally some sense of what has been said so far and what might be at stake. In my view, the ethics of global climate change is still very much in its infancy. Hopefully, this small contribution will encourage its development.

I. TERMINOLOGY

> *While global warming has catastrophic communications attached to it, climate change sounds a more controllable and less emotional challenge.*
>
> FRANK LUNTZ

Potential confusion about the climate change problem begins even with the terms used to describe it: from "greenhouse effect" to "global warming" to the more recently favored "climate change." To begin with, many people spoke of "the greenhouse effect." This refers to the basic physical mechanism behind projected changes in the climate system. Some atmospheric gases (called "greenhouse gases" [GHG]) have asymmetric interactions with radiation of different frequencies: just like glass in a conventional greenhouse, they allow shortwave incoming solar radiation through but reflect some of the Earth's outgoing long-wave radiation back to the surface. This creates "a partial blanketing effect," which causes the temperature at the surface to be higher than would otherwise be the case (Houghton 1997, pp. 11–12). Humans are increasing the atmospheric concentrations of these gases through industrialization. This would, other things being equal, be expected to result in an overall warming effect.

The basic greenhouse mechanism is both well understood and uncontroversial. Still, the term "greenhouse effect" remains unsatisfactory to describe the problem at hand. There are two reasons. First, there is a purely natural greenhouse effect, without which the earth would be much colder than it is now. Hence, it is not accurate to say that "the greenhouse effect" as such is a problem; in fact, the reverse is true: without some greenhouse effect, the Earth would be much less hospitable for life as we know it. The real problem is the enhanced, human-induced, greenhouse effect. Second, it is not the greenhouse effect in isolation which causes the climate problem. Whether an increase in the concentration of greenhouse gases does in fact cause the warming we would otherwise expect depends on how the immediate effects of an increase in low frequency radiation play out in the overall climate system. But that system is complex, and its details are not very well understood.

For a while, then, the term "global warming" was favored. This term captures the point that it is the effects of increased levels of greenhouse gases which are of concern. However, it also has its limitations. In particular, it highlights a specific effect, higher temperatures, and thus suggests a one-dimensional problem. But while it is true that rising temperature has been a locus for concern about increasing human emissions of greenhouse gases, it is not true that temperature as such defines either the core problem or even (arguably) its most important aspects. Consider, for example, the following. First, a higher global temperature does not in itself constitute the most important impact of climate change. Indeed, considered in isolation, there might be no particular reason to prefer the world as it is now to one several degrees warmer. However, second, this thought is liable to be misleading. For presumably if one is imagining a warmer world and thinking that it may be appealing, one is envisioning the planet as it might be in a stable, equilibrium state at the higher level, where humans, animals, and plants have harmoniously adapted to higher temperatures. But the problem posed by current human behavior is not of this kind. The primary concern of many scientists is that an enhanced greenhouse effect puts extra energy into the earth's climate system and so creates an imbalance. Hence, most of the concern about present climate change has been brought about because it seems that change is occurring at an unprecedented rate, that any equilibrium position is likely to be thousands, perhaps tens or hundreds of thousands, of years off, and that existing species are unlikely to be able to adapt quickly and easily under such conditions. Third, though it is at present unlikely, it is still possible that temperature might go down as a result of the increase in atmospheric greenhouse gas concentrations. But this does not cast any doubt on the serious nature of the problem. This is partly because a rapid and unprecedented lowering of temperature would have similar kinds of adverse effects on human and nonhuman life and health as a rapid warming, and partly because the effects most likely to cause cooling (such as a shutdown of the thermohaline circulation [THC] which supports the Gulf Stream current to Northern Europe [discussed in the next section]) may well be catastrophic even in relation to the other projected effects of global warming.

For all these reasons, current discussion tends to be carried out under the heading "climate change." This term captures the fact that it is interference in the climate system itself which is the crucial issue, not what the particular effects of that interference turn out to be. The fundamental problem is that it is now possible for humans to alter the underlying dynamics of the planet's climate and so the basic life-support system both for themselves and all other forms of life on Earth. Whether the alteration of these dynamics is most conveniently tracked in terms of increasing, declining, or even stable temperatures is of subsidiary interest in comparison to the actual changes in the climate itself and their consequences for human, and nonhuman, life.

II. CLIMATE SCIENCE

> *Almost no one would deny that in principle our actions and policies should be informed by our best scientific judgments, and it is hard to deny that our best scientific judgments about climate change are expressed in the IPCC reports.*
>
> JAMIESON, 1998, P. 116

> *Recent scientific evidence shows that major and widespread climate changes have occurred with startling speed.... Climate models typically underestimate the size, speed, and extent of those changes.... Climate surprise to be expected.*
>
> U.S. National Research Council, 2002, P. 1

What do we know about climate change? In 1988, the Intergovernmental Panel on Climate Change (IPCC) was jointly established by the World Meteorological Association and the United Nations Environment Program to provide member governments with state of the art assessments of "the science, the impacts, and the economics of—and the options for mitigating and/or adapting to—climate change" (IPCC 2001*c*, p. vii). The IPCC has, accordingly, submitted three comprehensive reports, in 1990, 1995, and 2001. The results have remained fairly consistent across all three reports, though the level of confidence in those results has increased. The main findings of the most recent are as follows.

The IPCC begins with an account of patterns of climate change observed so far. On temperature, they report: "The global average surface temperature has increased over the 20th century by about 0.6°C"; "Globally, it is very likely that the 1990s was the warmest decade and 1998 the warmest year in the instrumental record, since 1861"; and "The increase in temperature in the 20th century is likely to have been the largest of any century during the past 1,000 years" (IPCC 2001*c*, p. 152). For other phenomena, they say that snow cover and ice extent have decreased, global average sea level has risen, and ocean heat content has increased. They also cite evidence for increases in the amount of precipitation in some regions; the frequency of heavy precipitation events; cloud cover in some latitudes; and the frequency, persistence, and intensity of El Niño phenomenon.

The IPCC also surveys the literature on relevant human activities. They conclude that since preindustrial times (1750 is the usual benchmark), humans have altered "the atmosphere in ways that are expected to affect the climate" by markedly increasing the concentrations of greenhouse gases (IPCC 2001*c*, p. 154). The main culprit is carbon dioxide, for which "the concentration has increased by 31% since 1750"; "the present CO_2 concentration has not been exceeded during the past 420,000 years and likely not during the past 20 million years"; and "the current rate of increase is unprecedented during at least the past 20,000 years ... at about 1.5 ppm [parts per million] (0.4%) per year" (IPCC 2001*c*, p. 155). The main anthropogenic sources of CO_2 are the burning of fossil fuels (about 75 percent) and changes in land-use patterns (principally, deforestation). Of secondary importance is methane, where the present atmospheric concentration "has increased by ... 151% since 1750; and has not been exceeded during the past 420,000 years," and "slightly more than half of current ... emissions are anthropogenic (e.g., use of fossil fuels, cattle, rice agriculture and landfills)" (IPCC 2001*c*, pp. 156–57). Molecule for molecule, methane is a more potent greenhouse gas than carbon dioxide. Still, because CO_2 lasts much longer in the atmosphere (about 5–200 years, as opposed to methane's 12 years), it is the more important anthropogenic greenhouse gas.

The IPCC also tries to predict future climate. To do so, it uses computer models to simulate a variety of different possible future scenarios, incorporating different assumptions about economic growth, world population, and technological change. The basic results are as follows. First, carbon dioxide emissions due to the burning of fossil fuels are "virtually certain to be the dominant influence on the trends in atmospheric CO_2 concentration during the 21st century," and by 2100, that concentration should be 90–250 percent above preindustrial levels (of 280 parts per million), at 540–970 parts per million (IPCC 2001*c*, pp. 158–59). Second, if this occurs, the full range of model scenarios predict that surface temperature will increase by 1.4–5.8°C over the century. The IPCC states that this is not only a much larger projected rate of warming than that observed during the twentieth century but one "very likely...without precedent during at least the last 10,000 years." Third, models indicate that "stabilisation of atmospheric CO_2 concentrations at 450, 650 or 1,000 ppm would require global anthropogenic CO_2 emissions to drop below 1990 levels, within a few decades, about a century, or about two centuries, respectively, and continue to decrease steadily thereafter. Eventually CO_2 emissions would need to decline to *a very small fraction* of current emissions" (IPCC 2001*c*, p. 160; emphasis added).

Alarming as the IPCC predictions are, we should also pay attention to the fact that they might be overly optimistic. For some authors argue that the current climate models typically underestimate the potential for nonlinear threshold effects (U.S. National Research Council 2002; Gagosian 2003). One well-known threat of this sort is the potential collapse of the West Antarctic Ice Sheet (WAIS), which would eventually raise global sea levels by 4–6 meters. But the recent literature registers even greater concern about a lesser-known issue: the possibility of a weakening or shutdown of the deep circulation system which drives the world's ocean currents. This system, known as "the Ocean Conveyor," distributes "vast quantities of heat around our planet, and thus plays a fundamental role in governing Earth's climate ... [and] in the distribution of life-sustaining water" (Gagosian 2003, p. 4).

The Ocean Conveyor has been called the climate's Achilles Heel (Broecker 1997), because it appears to be a major threshold phenomenon. There are two grounds for concern. First, there is strong evidence that in the past the conveyor has slowed, and slowed very quickly, with significant climatic consequences. One such event, 12,700 years ago, saw a drop in temperatures in the North Atlantic region of around 5 degrees Celsius in a single decade. This apparently caused icebergs to spread as far south as the coast of Portugal and has been linked to widespread global drought. Second, the operation of the conveyor is governed by factors that can be affected by climate change. In particular, the world's currents are driven by the sinking of a large volume of salty water in the North Atlantic region. But this process can be disrupted by an influx of fresh water, which both dilutes the salty water and can also create a lid over it, restricting heat flow to the atmosphere.

The possibility of dramatic climate shifts of this sort complicates the picture of a global warming world in several ways. First, it suggests that gradual warming at the global level could cause, and coexist with, dramatic cooling in some regions. (Among other things, this has serious ramifications for our ability to plan for future changes.) Second, it envisages that the major losers from climate change may not be the usual suspects, the less developed countries (LDCs), for it is the rich countries bordering the North Atlantic that are particularly vulnerable to Conveyor shifts. Climate models predict that "the North Atlantic region would cool 3 to 5 degrees Celsius if conveyor circulation were totally disrupted," producing winters "twice as cold as the worst winters on record in the eastern United States in the past century" for a period of up to a century (Gagosian 2003, p. 7).

The IPCC does not emphasize the problem of the Ocean Conveyor. For one thing, though it acknowledges that most models predict a weakening of the conveyor during the twenty-first century, it emphasizes that such changes are projected to be offset by the more general warming; for another, it suggests that a complete shutdown is unlikely during the twenty-first century (though increasingly likely thereafter) (IPCC 2001*c*, p. 16). Hence, the IPCC's attitude is relatively complacent. Still, it is not clear what justifies such complacency. On the one hand, even if the threshold will not be reached for 100 years, this is still a matter of serious concern for future generations, since once the underlying processes which will breach it are in motion, it will be difficult, if not impossible, to reverse them. On the other hand, the current models of thermohaline circulation are not very robust, primarily because scientists simply do not know where the threshold is. And some models do predict complete shutdown within a range which overlaps with IPCC projections for the twenty-first century (IPCC 2001*c*, p. 440).

III. SCIENTIFIC UNCERTAINTY

Scientists aren't any time soon going to give politicians some magic answer. Policy makers for a long, long time are going to have to deal with a situation where it's not clear what the costs and benefits are, where lots of people disagree about them, and they can't wait until everything is resolved.

ROBERT J. LAMPERT

Should the public come to believe that the scientific issues are settled, their views about global warming will change accordingly. Therefore, you need to continue to make the lack of scientific certainty a primary issue.

FRANK LUNTZ, IN LEE 2003

It is sometimes argued that the uncertainty of the scientist's predictions is a reason for not acting at present, and that we should wait

> *until some further research has been concluded. This argument is poor economics.*
>
> BROOME, 1992, P. 17

Politically, the most common objection raised to action on climate change is that of scientific uncertainty. In this section, I will explain why most writers on the subject believe this objection to be a red herring.

The first thing to note is that, at least in economics, uncertainty is a technical term, to be distinguished from risk. In the technical sense, a risk involves a known, or reliably estimable, probability, whereas an uncertainty arises when such probabilities are not available. So to say that there is scientific uncertainty surrounding global warming is to claim that we do not know, and cannot reliably estimate, the probability that climate change will occur, nor its extent if it does occur.

This distinction is useful, because the first problem with the objection from scientific uncertainty is that the IPCC does not seem to view global warming as uncertain in the technical sense. As we have seen, the 2001 Scientific Assessment explicitly assigns probabilities to its main climate predictions, making the situation one of risk, rather than uncertainty. Furthermore, these probabilities are of considerable magnitude. (For example, the IPCC says that it is "very likely" that in the twenty-first century there will be "higher maximum temperatures and more hot days over nearly all land areas" [IPCC 2001*c*, p. 162], by which they mean a probability of 90–99 percent [IPCC 2001*c*, p. 152, n. 7].) Given that many of the effects assigned high probabilities are associated with significant costs, they would seem to justify some kinds of action.

But perhaps the idea is that the IPCC's probability statements are not reliable, so that we should ignore them, treat the situation as genuinely uncertain, and hence refuse to act. Still, there is a difficulty. For, to an important extent, some kind of uncertainty "is an inherent part of the problem" (Broome 1992, p. 18). Arguably, if we knew exactly what was going to happen, to whom, and whose emissions would cause it, the problem might be more easily addressed; at the very least, it would have a very different shape. Hence, to refuse to act because of uncertainty is either to refuse to accept the global warming problem as it is (insisting that it be turned into a more respectable form of problem before one will address it) or else to endorse the principle that to "do nothing" is the appropriate response to uncertainty. The former is a head-in-the-sand approach and clearly unacceptable, but the latter is also dubious and does not fit our usual practice.

The third, and perhaps most crucial, point to make about the problem of uncertainty is that it is important not to overplay it. For one thing, many decisions we have to make in life, including many important decisions, are also subject to considerable uncertainties. For another, all uncertainties are not created equal. On the one hand, the reason I am unable to assign probabilities may be that I know absolutely nothing about the situation, or else that I have only one past instance to go on. But I may also be uncertain in circumstances where I have considerable information.

Now it seems clear that uncertainty in the first kind of case is worse than uncertainty in the second, and potentially more paralyzing. Furthermore, and this is the crucial point, it seems reasonably clear that scientific uncertainty about global warming is of the second kind. As Donald Brown argues: "A lot of climate change science has never been in question, ... many of the elements of global warming are not seriously challenged even by the scientific skeptics, and ... the issues of scientific certainty most discussed by climate skeptics usually deal with the magnitude and timing of climate change, not with whether global warming is a real threat" (Brown 2002, p. 102). To see this, let us briefly examine a number of sources of uncertainty about global warming.

The first concerns the direct empirical evidence for anthropogenic warming itself. This has two main aspects. First, systematic global temperature records, based on measurements of air temperature on land and surface-water temperature measurements at sea, exist only from 1860, and satellite-based measurements are available only from 1979. The direct evidence for recent warming comes from the former. But skeptics suggest that the satellite measurements do not match the surface readings and do not provide evidence for warming. Second, there is no well-defined baseline from which to measure change. While it is true that the last couple of decades have been the warmest in human history, it is also true that the long-term climate record displays significant short-term variability and that, even accounting for this, climate seems to have been remarkably stable since the end of the last Ice Age 10,000 years ago, as compared with the preceding 100,000 years. Hence, global temperatures have fluctuated considerably over the long-term record, and it is clear that these fluctuations have been naturally caused.

The skeptics are right, then, when they assert that the observational temperature record is a weak data set and that the long-term history of the climate is such that even if the data were more robust, we would be rash to conclude that humans are causing it solely on this basis. Still, it would be a mistake to infer too much from the truth of these claims. For it would be equally rash to dismiss the possibility of warming on these grounds. For, even though it might be true that the empirical evidence is consistent with there being no anthropogenic warming, it is also true that it provides just the kind of record we would expect if there were a real global warming problem.

This paradox is caused by the fact that our epistemological position with respect to climate change is intrinsically very difficult: it may simply be impossible to confirm climate change empirically from this position. This is because our basic situation may be a bit like that of a coach who is asked whether the current performance of a fifteen-year-old athlete shows that she will reach the highest level of her sport. Suppose the coach has the best evidence that she can have. It will still only be evidence for a fifteen-year-old. It will be at most consistent with reaching the highest level. It cannot be taken as a certain prediction. But that does not mean it is no prediction at all, or worthless. It is simply the best prediction she is currently in a position to make.

Fortunately, for the climate change problem, the concern with the empirical record is not the end of the matter. For the temperature record is far from our only evidence for warming. Instead, we also have strong theoretical grounds for concern. First, the basic physical and chemical mechanisms which give rise to a potential global warming effect are well understood. In particular, there is no scientific controversy over the claims (*a*) that in itself a higher concentration of greenhouse gas molecules in the upper atmosphere would cause more heat to be retained by the earth and less radiated out into the solar system, so that other things being equal, such an increase would cause global temperatures to rise; and (*b*) that human activities since the industrial revolution have significantly increased the atmospheric concentration of greenhouse gases. Hence, everyone agrees that the basic circumstances are such that a greenhouse effect is to be expected.

Second, the scientific dispute, insofar as there is one, concerns the high level of complexity of the global climate system, given which there are the other mechanisms that might be in play to moderate such an effect. The contentious issue here is whether there might be negative feedbacks that either sharply reduce or negate the effects of higher levels of greenhouse gases, or even reduce the amount of them present in the atmosphere. However, current climate models suggest that most related factors will likely exhibit positive feedbacks (water vapor, snow, and ice), while others have both positive and negative feedbacks whose net effect is unclear (e.g., clouds, ocean currents). Hence, there is genuine scientific uncertainty. But this does not by itself justify a skeptical position about action on climate change. For there may be no more reason to assume that we will be saved by unexpectedly large negative feedbacks than that the warming effect will be much worse than we would otherwise anticipate, due to unexpectedly large positive feedbacks.

This is the basic scientific situation. However, three further aspects of uncertainty are worth mentioning. First, the conclusions about feedback are also open to doubt because considerable uncertainties remain about the performance of the models. In particular, they are not completely reliable against past data. This is to be expected because the climate is a highly complex system which is not very well understood. Still, it clouds the overall picture. Second, as mentioned earlier, the current models tend to assume that atmospheric feedbacks scale linearly with surface warming, and they do not adequately account for possible threshold effects, such as the possible collapse of the West Antarctic Ice Sheet. Hence, they may underestimate the potential risks from global warming. Finally, there is a great deal of uncertainty about the distribution of climate change. Though global rises may seem small, they disguise considerable variation within years and across regions. Furthermore, though it is very difficult to predict which regions will suffer most, and in what ways, such evidence as there is suggests that, at least in the medium term, the impact will be heaviest in the tropical and subtropical regions (where most of the LDCs are), and lighter in the temperate regions (where most of the richer countries are).

In conclusion, there are substantial uncertainties surrounding both the direct empirical evidence for warming and our theoretical understanding of the overall climate system. But these uncertainties cut both ways. In particular, while it is certainly conceivable (though, at present, unlikely) that the climate change problem will turn out to be chimerical, it is also possible that global warming will turn out to be much worse than anyone has yet anticipated. More importantly, the really vital issue does not concern the presence of scientific uncertainty, but rather how we decide what to do under such circumstances. To this issue we now turn.

IV. ECONOMICS

> *Economic analyses clearly show that it will be far more expensive to cut CO_2 emissions radically than to pay the costs of adaptation to the increased temperatures.*
>
> LOMBORG, 2001, P. 318

> *Cost-benefit analysis, when faced with uncertainties as big as these, would simply be self-deception. And in any case, it could not be a successful exercise, because the issue is too poorly understood, and too little accommodated in the current economic theory.*
>
> BROOME, 1992, P. 19

As it turns out, many recent skeptics no longer cite scientific uncertainty as their reason for resisting action on climate change. Instead, they claim to accept the reality of human-induced climate change but argue that there is a strong economic rationale for refusing to act. Prevention, they insist, is more expensive than adaptation; hence, both present and future generations would be better off if we simply accepted that there will be climate change and tried to live with it. Furthermore, they assert, money that might be spent on prevention would be better spent helping the world's poor. I will consider the first of these arguments in this section and the second later on.

Several attempts have been made to model the economic implications of climate change. Politically prominent among these is the DICE model proposed by the Yale economist William Nordhaus. The DICE model is an integrated assessment model. Integrated assessment (IA) models combine the essential elements of biophysical and economic systems in an attempt to understand the impact of climate and economic policies on one another. Typically, such models aim to find a climate policy which will maximize the social welfare function. And many give the surprising result that only limited abatement should occur in the next twenty to thirty years, since the costs of current reductions are too high in comparison to the benefits. Hence, proponents of these models argue that, based on economic costs, the developed world (and the United States in particular) should pursue adaptation rather than abatement. This is the argument embraced by Lomborg, who cites Nordhaus's work as his inspiration.

1. The Cost Argument

A full response to Lomborg's proposal requires addressing both the argument about costs and the more general argument for an adaptation, rather than mitigation, strategy. Let us begin with the cost argument.

The first point to make is that, even if Nordhaus's calculations were reliable, the costs of climate change mitigation do not seem unmanageable. As Thomas Schelling puts it:

> The costs in reduced productivity are estimated at two percent of GNP forever. Two percent of GNP seems politically unmanageable in many countries. Still, if one plots the curve of US per capita GNP over the coming century with and without the two percent permanent loss, the difference is about the thickness of a line drawn with a number two pencil, and the doubled per capita income that would have been achieved by 2060 is reached in 2062. If someone could wave a wand and phase in, over a few years, a climate-mitigation program that depressed our GNP by two percent in perpetuity, no one would notice the difference. (Schelling 1997)

Even Lomborg agrees with this. For he not only cites the 2 percent figure with approval but adds, "there is no way that the cost [of stabilizing abatement measures] will send us to the poor-house" (Lomborg 2001, p. 323).

The second point is that Nordhaus's work is extremely controversial. For one thing, some claim that his model is simplistic, both in itself and, especially, relative to the climate models. Indeed, one commentator goes so far as to say that "the model is extremely simple—so simple that I once, during a debate, dubbed it a toy model" (Gundermann 2002, p. 150). For another others offer rival models which endorse the exact opposite to Nodhaus's conclusion: that action now (in the form of carbon taxes, etc.) would be more beneficial in the long term than waiting, even perhaps if global warming does not actually transpire (e.g., Costanza 1996; De Leo et al. 2001; Woodward and Bishop 1997).

Part of the reason that such disputes arise is because the models embody some very questionable assumptions. Some are specific to Nordhaus (e.g., Gundermann 2002, p. 154). But others are the result of two more general kinds of difficulty.

The first is practical. There are severe informational problems involved in any reliable cost-benefit analysis for climate change. In particular, over the timescale relevant for climate change, "society is bound to be radically transformed in ways which are utterly unpredictable to us now," and these changes will themselves be affected by climate (Broome 1992, p. 10; see also Jamieson 1992, pp. 288–89). Hence, Broome, for example, argues that fine-grained cost-benefit analyses are simply not possible for climate change.

The second kind of difficulty, of more interest to ethicists perhaps, is that there are some basic philosophical problems inherent in the methods of conventional economic analysis. Here let me mention just two prominent examples.

One concerns the standard economic treatments of intergenerational issues. Economists typically employ a social discount rate (SDR) of 2–10 percent for future costs (Lomborg uses 5 percent; Nordhaus 3–6 percent). But this raises two serious concerns. The first is that, for the short- to medium-term effects of climate change (say, over ten to fifty years), model results can be extremely sensitive to the rate chosen. For example, Shultz and Kasting claim that the choice of SDR makes the rest of the climate change model largely irrelevant in Nordhaus's model, and variations in the SDR make a huge difference to model results more generally (Schultz and Kasting 1997, cited by Gundermann 2002, p. 147). The other concern is that, when the SDR is positive, all but the most catastrophic costs disappear after a number of decades, and even these become minimal over very long time periods. This has serious consequences for the intergenerational ethics of climate change. As John Broome puts it: "It is people who are now children and people who are not yet born who will reap most of the benefits of any project that mitigates the effects of global warming. Most of the benefits of such a project will therefore be ignored by the consumer-price method of project evaluation. It follows that this method is quite useless for assessing such long-term projects. This is my main reason for rejecting it [for climate change]" (Broome 1992, p. 72).

The second philosophical problem inherent in conventional economic analysis is that it cannot adequately capture all of the relevant costs and benefits. The obvious cases here are costs to nonhumans (such as animals, plants, species, and ecosystems) and noneconomic costs to humans, such as aesthetic costs (Sagoff 1998; Schmidtz 2001). But there is also concern that conventional economic analysis cannot adequately take into account costs with special features, such as irreversible and nonsubstitutable damages, that are especially associated with climate change (Shogren and Toman 2000; Costanza 1996).

We can conclude, then, that there are strong reasons to be skeptical about Lomborg's cost argument in particular and about the reliability of fine-grained economic analyses of climate change more generally. Still, John Broome argues that two things can be said with some confidence: first, the specific effects of climate change "are very uncertain," where (as argued in the previous section) "this by itself has important consequences for the work that needs to be done," and, second, these effects "will certainly be long lived, almost certainly large, probably bad, and possibly disastrous" (Broome 1992, p. 12). To these claims we might add that at 2 percent of world production, the estimated costs of stabilizing emissions do not seem obviously prohibitive.

2. The Adaptation Argument

We can now turn to the more general argument that, instead of reducing emissions, we should pursue a policy of trying to adapt to the effects of climate change. The first thing to note about this argument is that adaptation measures will clearly need to be part of any sensible climate policy, because we are already committed to some warming due to past emissions, and almost all of the proposed abatement strategies envisage that overall global emissions will continue to rise for at least the next few decades, committing us to even more. Hence, the choice cannot be seen as being one between abatement and adaptation, since advocates of abatement generally support a combination of strategies. The real issue is rather whether adaptation should be our only strategy, so that abatement is ignored.

If this is the proposal, several points can be made about it. First, we should beware of making the case for adaptation a self-fulfilling prophesy. For example, it is true that the existing capital stock in the United States made it difficult for America to meet its original Kyoto target for 2008–12. But it is also true that a significant amount of this capital was invested after the United States committed itself to stabilizing emissions at the Rio Earth Summit of 1992. Furthermore, matters will only get worse. The Bush administration's current energy plan calls for the building of 1,300 new power plants in the next twenty years, boosting supply (and thereby emissions) by more than 30 percent.

Second, the comparison between abatement and adaptation costs looks straightforward but is not. In particular, we have to bear in mind the different kinds of economic costs at stake in each case. On the one hand, suppose we allow global warming to continue unchecked. What will we be adapting to? Chances are, we will experience both a range of general gradual climatic changes and an increase in severe weather and climate events. On the other hand, if we go for abatement, we will also be adapting, but this time to increases in tax rates on (or decreases in permits for) carbon emissions. But there is a world of difference between these kinds of adaptation: in the first case, we would be dealing with sudden, unpredictable, large-scale impacts which descend at random on particular individuals, communities, regions, and industries and visit them with pure, unrecoverable costs, whereas, in the second, we would be addressing gradual, predictable, incremental impacts, phased in so as to make adaptation easier. Surely, adaptation in the second kind of case is, other things being equal, preferable to the first.

Third, any reasonable abatement strategy would need to be phased in gradually, and it is well documented that many economically beneficial energy savings could be introduced immediately, using existing technologies. These facts suggest that the adaptation argument is largely irrelevant to what to do now. For the first steps that need to be taken would be economically beneficial, not costly. Yet opponents of action on climate change do not want to do even this much.

V. RISK MANAGEMENT AND THE PRECAUTIONARY PRINCIPLE

The risk assessment process … is as much policy and politics as it is science. A typical risk assessment relies on at least 50 different assumptions about exposure, dose-response, and relationships between animals and humans. The modeling of uncertainty also depends on assumptions. Two risk assessments conducted on the same problem can vary widely in results.

RAFFENSBERGER and TICKNER, 1999, P. 2

Serious as they are, these largely technical worries about conventional economic analysis are not the only reasons to be wary of any economic solution to the climate change problem. For some writers suggest that exclusive reliance on economic analysis would be problematic even if all of the numbers were in, since the climate problem is ultimately one of values, not efficiency: as Dale Jamieson puts it, its "fundamental questions" concern "how we ought to live, what kinds of societies we want, and how we should relate to nature and other forms of life" (Jamieson 1992, p. 290).

But the problem may not be just that climate change raises issues of value. It may also show that our existing values are insufficient to the task. Jamieson, for example, offers the following argument. First, he asserts that our present values evolved relatively recently, in "low-population-density and low-technology societies, with seemingly unlimited access to land and other resources." Then he claims that these values include as a central component an account of responsibility which "presupposes that harms and their causes are individual, that they can be readily identified, and that they are local in time and space." Third, he argues that problems such as climate change fit none of these criteria. Hence, he concludes, a new value system is needed (Jamieson 1992, pp. 291–92).

How then should we proceed? Some authors advocate a rethinking of our basic moral practices. For example, Jamieson claims that we must switch our focus away from approaches (such as those of contemporary economics) which concentrate on "calculating probable outcomes" and instead foster and develop a set of "twenty-first century virtues," including "humility, courage, ... moderation," "simplicity and conservatism" (Jamieson 1992, p. 294).

Other climate change theorists, however, are less radical. For example, Henry Shue employs the traditional notions of a "No Harm Principle" and rights to physical security (Shue 1999*a*, p. 43). He points out that even in the absence of certainty about the exact impacts of climate change, there is a real moral problem posed by subjecting future generations to the risk of severe harm. This implies a motive for action in spite of the scientific and economic uncertainties. Similarly, many policy makers appeal to the "precautionary principle," which is now popular in international law and politics and receives one of its canonical statements in the 1992 United Nations Framework Convention on Climate Change (1992). The exact formulation of the precautionary principle is controversial; but one standard version is the Wingspread Statement, which reads: "When an activity raises threats of harm to human health or the environment, precautionary measures should be taken even if some cause and effect relationships are not fully established scientifically" (Wingspread Statement 1998).

Both no harm principles and the precautionary principle are, however, controversial. No harm principles are often criticized for being either obscure or else overly conservative when taken literally; and the precautionary principle generates similar objections: its critics say that it is vacuous, extreme, and irrational. Still, I would argue that, at least in the case of the precautionary principle, many of these initial objections can be overcome (Gardiner 2004*a*). In particular, a core use of the precautionary principle can be captured by restricting its application to those situations which satisfy John Rawls's criteria for the application of a maximum principle: the parties lack, or have good reason to doubt, relevant probability information; they care little for potential gains; and they face unacceptable outcomes (Rawls 1999, p. 134). And this core use escapes the initial, standard objections.

More importantly for current purposes, I would also claim that a reasonable case can be made that climate change satisfies the conditions for the core precautionary principle (Gardiner 2004*a*). First, many of the predicted outcomes from climate change seem severe, and some are catastrophic. Hence, there are grounds for saying there are unacceptable outcomes. Second, as we have seen, for gradual change, either the probabilities of significant damage from climate change are high or else we do not know the probabilities;

and for abrupt change the probabilities are unknown. Finally, given widespread endorsement of the view that stabilizing emissions would impose a cost of "only" 2 percent of world production, one might claim that we care little about the potential gains—at least relative to the possibly catastrophic costs.

There is reason to believe, then, that the endorsement by many policy makers of some form of precautionary or no harm approach is reasonable for climate change. But exactly which "precautionary measures" should be taken? One obvious first step is that those changes in present energy consumption which would have short-term, as well as long-term, economic benefits should be made immediately. In addition, we should begin acting on low-cost emissions-saving measures as soon as possible. Beyond that, it is difficult to say exactly how we should strike a balance between the needs of the present and those of the future. Clearly, this is an area where further thought is urgently needed.

Still, it is perhaps worthwhile closing this section with one, speculative, opinion about how we should direct our efforts. By focusing on the possibility of extreme events, and considering the available science, Brian O'Neill and Michael Oppenheimer suggest in a recent article in *Science* that "taking a precautionary approach because of the very large uncertainties, a limit of 2 C above 1990 global average temperature is justified to protect [the West Antarctic Ice Sheet]. To avert shutdown of the [Thermohaline circulation], we define a limit of 3 C warming over 100 years" (O'Neill and Oppenheimer 2002). It is not clear how robust these assertions are. Still, they suggest a reasonable starting point for discussion. For, on the assumption that these outcomes are unacceptable, and given the IPCC projections of a warming of between 1.4 and 5.8°C over the century, both claims appear to justify significant immediate action on greenhouse gas stabilization.

VI. RESPONSIBILITY FOR THE PAST

> *I'll tell you one thing I'm not going to do is I'm not going to let the United States carry the burden for cleaning up the world's air, like the Kyoto Treaty would have done. China and India were exempted from that treaty. I think we need to be more even-handed.*
>
> GEORGE W. BUSH, Quoted By Singer 2002, P. 30

> *Even in an emergency one pawns the jewellery before selling the blankets.... Whatever justice may positively require, it does not permit that poor nations be told to sell their blankets [compromise their development strategies] in order that the rich nations keep their jewellery [continue their unsustainable lifestyles].*
>
> SHUE, 1992, P. 397; Quoted By Grubb 1995, P. 478

> *To demand that [the developing countries] act first is patently unfair and would not even warrant serious debate were it not the position of a superpower.*
>
> HARRIS, 2003

Suppose, then, that action on climate change is morally required. Whose responsibility is it? The core ethical issue concerning global warming is that of how to allocate the costs and benefits of greenhouse gas emissions and abatement. On this issue, there is a surprising convergence of philosophical writers on the subject: they are virtually unanimous in their conclusion that the developed countries should take the lead role in bearing the costs of climate change, while the less developed countries should be allowed to increase emissions for the foreseeable future.

Still, agreement on the fact of responsibility masks some notable differences about its justification, form, and extent; so it is worth assessing the competing accounts in more detail. The first issue to be considered is that of "backward-looking considerations." The facts are that developed countries are responsible for a very large percentage of historical emissions, whereas the costs likely to be imposed by those emissions are expected to be disproportionately visited on the poorer countries (IPCC 1995, p. 94). This suggests two approaches. First, one might invoke historical principles of justice that require that one "clean up one's own mess." This suggests that the industrialized countries should bear the costs imposed by their past emissions. Second, one might characterize the earth's capacity to absorb man-made emissions of carbon dioxide as a common resource, or sink (Traxler 2002, p. 120), and claim that, since this capacity is limited, a question of justice arises in how its use should be allocated (Singer 2002, pp. 31–32). On this approach, the obvious argument to be made is that the developed countries have largely exhausted the capacity in the process of industrializing and so have, in effect, denied other countries the opportunity to use "their shares." On this view, justice seems to require that the developed countries compensate the less developed for this overuse.

It is worth observing two facts about these two approaches. First, they are distinct. On the one hand, the historical principle requires compensation for damage inflicted by one party on another and does not presume that there is a common resource; on the other, the sink consideration crucially relies on the presence of a common resource and does not presume that any (further) damage is caused to the disenfranchised beyond their being deprived of an opportunity for use. Second, they are compatible. One could maintain that a party deprived of its share of a common resource ought to be compensated both for that and for the fact that material harm has been inflicted upon it as a direct result of the deprivation.

Offhand, the backward-looking considerations seem weighty. However, many writers suggest that in practice they should be ignored. One justification that is offered is that, until comparatively recently, the developed countries were ignorant of the effects of their emissions on the climate and so should not be held accountable for past emissions (or at least those prior to 1990, when the IPCC issued its first report). This consideration seems to me far from decisive, because it is not clear how far the ignorance defense extends. On the one hand, in the case of the historical principle, if the harm inflicted on the world's poor is severe, and if they lack the means to defend themselves against it, it seems odd to say that the rich nations have no obligation to assist, especially when they could do so relatively easily and are in such a position largely because of their previous causal role. On the other hand, in the case of the sink consideration, if you deprive me of my share of an important resource, perhaps one necessary to my very survival, it seems odd to say that you have no obligation to assist because you were ignorant of what you were doing at the time. This is especially so if your overuse both effectively denies me the means of extricating myself from the problem you have created and also further reduces the likelihood of fair outcomes on this and other issues (Shue 1992).

A second justification for ignoring past emissions is that taking the past into account is impractical. For example, Martino Traxler claims that any agreement which incorporates backward-looking considerations would require "a prior international agreement on what constitutes international distributive justice and then an agreement on how to translate these considerations into practical allocations" and that, given that "such an agreement is [un]likely in our lifetime," insisting on it "would amount to putting off any implementation concerning climate change indefinitely" (Traxler 2002, p. 128). Furthermore, he asserts that climate change takes the form of a commons problem and so poses a significant problem of defection: "Each nation is (let us hope) genuinely concerned with this problem, but each nation is also aware that it is in its interest not to contribute or do its share, regardless of what other countries do.... In short, in the absence of the appropriate international coercive muscle, defection, however unjust it may be, is just too tempting" (Traxler 2002, p. 122).

Though rarely spelled out, such pragmatic concerns seem to influence a number of writers. Still, I am not convinced—at least by Traxler's arguments. For one thing, I do not see why a complete background understanding of international justice is required, especially just to get started. For another, I am not sure that defection is quite the problem, or at least has the implications, that Traxler suggests. In particular, Traxler's argument seems to go something like this: since there is no external coercive body, countries must be motivated not to defect from an agreement; but (rich) countries will be motivated to defect if they are asked to carry the costs of their past (mis) behavior; therefore, past behavior cannot be considered, otherwise (rich) countries will defect. But this reasoning is questionable, on several grounds. First, it seems likely that if past behavior is not considered, then the poor countries will defect. Since, in the long run, their cooperation is required, this would suggest that Traxler's proposal is at least as impractical as anyone else's. Second, it is not clear that no external coercive instruments exist. Trade and travel sanctions, for example, are a possibility and have precedents. Third, the need for such sanctions (and indeed, the problem of defection in general) is not brought on purely by including the issue of backward-looking considerations in negotiation, nor is it removed by their absence. So it seems arbitrary to disallow such considerations on this basis. Finally, Traxler's argument seems to assume (first) that the only truly urgent issue that needs to be addressed with respect to climate change is that of future emissions growth, and (second) that this issue is important enough that concerns about (i) the costs of climate change to which we are already committed, and (ii) the problem of inequity in the proceeds from those emissions (e.g., that the rich countries may have, in effect, stolen rights to develop from the poorer countries) can be completely ignored. But such claims seem controversial.

The arguments in favor of ignoring past emissions are then, unconvincing. Hence, contrary to many writers on this subject, I conclude that we should not ignore the presumption that past emissions pose an issue of justice which is both practically and theoretically important. Since this has the effect of increasing the obligations of the developed nations, it strengthens the case for saying that these countries bear a special responsibility for dealing with the climate change problem.

VII. ALLOCATING FUTURE EMISSIONS

> *The central argument for equal per capita rights is that the atmosphere is a global commons, whose use and preservation are essential to human well being.*
>
> BAER, 2002, P. 401

> *Much like self-defense may excuse the commission of an injury or even a murder, so their necessity for our subsistence may excuse our indispensable current emissions and the resulting future infliction of harm they cause.*
>
> TRAXLER, 2002, P. 107

Let us now turn to the issue of how to allocate future emissions. Here I cannot survey all the proposals that have been made; but I will consider four prominent suggestions.

1. Equal Per Capita Entitlements

The most obvious initial proposal is that some acceptable overall level of anthropogenic greenhouse emissions should be determined..., and then that this should be divided equally among the world's population, to produce equal per capita entitlements to emissions. This proposal seems intuitive but would have a radical redistributive effect. Consider the following illustration. Singer points out that stabilizing carbon emissions at current levels would give a per capita rate of roughly one tonne per year. But actual emissions in the rich countries are substantially in excess of this: the United States is at more than 5 tonnes per capita (and rising); and Japan, Australia, and Western Europe are all in a range from 1.6 to 4.2 tonnes per capita (with most below 3). India and China, on the other hand, are significantly below their per capita allocation (at 0.29 and 0.76, respectively). Thus, Singer suggests (against the present President Bush's claim at the beginning of the previous section), an "even-handed approach" implies that India and China should be allowed increases in emissions, while the United States should take a massive cut (Singer 2002, pp. 39–40).

Two main concerns have been raised about the per capita proposal. The first is that it might encourage population growth, through giving countries an incentive to maximize their population in order to receive more emissions credits (Jamieson 2001, p. 301). But this concern is easily addressed: most proponents of a per capita entitlement propose indexing population figures for each country to a certain time. For example, Jamieson proposes a 1990 baseline (relevant due to the initial IPCC report), whereas Singer proposes 2050 (to avoid punishing countries with younger populations at present). The second concern is more serious. The per capita proposal does not take into account the fact that emissions may play very different roles in people's lives. In particular, some emissions are used to produce luxury items, whereas others are necessary for most people's survival.

2. Rights to Subsistence Emissions

This concern is the basis for the second proposal on how to allocate emissions rights. Henry Shue argues that people should have inalienable rights to the minimum emissions necessary to their survival or to some minimal quality of life. This proposal has several implications. First, it suggests that there might be moral constraints on the limitation of emissions, so that establishing a global emissions ceiling will not be simply a matter for climatologists or even economists. If some emissions are deemed morally essential then they may have to be guaranteed even if this leads to an overall allocation above the scientific optimum. Traxler is explicit as to why this is the case. Even if subsistence emissions cause harm, they can be morally excusable because "they present their potential emitters with such a hard choice between avoiding a harm today or avoiding a harm in the future" that they are morally akin to self-defense. Second, the proposal suggests that actual emissions entitlements may not be equal for all individuals and may vary over time. For the benefits that can actually be drawn from a given quantity of greenhouse gas emissions vary with the existing technology, and the necessity of them depends on the available alternatives. But both vary by region, and will no doubt evolve in the future, partly in response to emissions regulation. Third, as Shue says, the guaranteed minimum principle does not imply that allocation of any remaining emissions rights above those necessary for subsistence must be made on a per capita basis. The guaranteed minimum view is distinct from a more robust egalitarian position which demands equality of a good at all levels of its consumption (Shue 1995*a*, pp. 387–88); hence, above the minimum some other criterion might be adopted.

The guaranteed minimum approach has considerable theoretical appeal. However, there are [two] reasons to be cautious about it. First, determining what counts as a "subsistence emission" is a difficult matter, both in theory and in practice. For example, Traxler defines subsistence emissions in terms of physiologically and socially necessary emissions but characterizes social necessity as "what a society needs or finds indispensable in order to survive" (Traxler 2002, p. 106). But this is problematic. For one thing, much depends on how societies define what they find "indispensable." (It is hard not to recall the first President Bush's comment, back in 1992, that "the American way of life is not up for negotiation.") For another, and perhaps more importantly, there is something procedurally odd about the proposal. For it appears to envisage that the climate change problem can be resolved by appealing to some notion of social necessity that is independent of, and not open to, moral assessment. But this seems somehow backwards. After all, several influential writers argue that part of the challenge of climate change is the deep questions it raises about how we should live and what kinds of societies we ought to have (Jamieson 1992, p. 290; and IPCC 2001*a* 1.4; questioned by Lomborg 2001, pp. 318–22).

Second, in practice, the guaranteed approach may not differ from the per capita principle, and yet may lack the practical advantages of that approach. On the first issue, given the foregoing point, it is hard to see individuals agreeing on an equal division of basic emissions entitlements that does anything less than exhaust the maximum permissible on other (climatological and intergenerational) grounds; and easy to see them being tempted to overshoot it. Furthermore, determining an adequate minimum may turn out to be almost the same task as (*a*) deciding what an appropriate ceiling would be and then (*b*) assigning per capita rights to the emissions it allows. For *a* would also require a view about what constitutes an acceptable form of life and how many emissions are necessary to sustain it. On the second issue, the subsistence emissions proposal carries political risks that the per capita proposal does not, or at least not to the same extent. For one thing, the claim that subsistence emissions are nonnegotiable seems problematic given the first point (above) that there is nothing to stop some people claiming that almost any emission is essential to their way of life. For another, the claim that nonsubsistence emissions need not be distributed equally may lead some in developed countries to argue that what is required to satisfy the subsistence constraint is extremely minimal and that emissions above that level should be either grandfathered or else distributed on other terms favorable to those with existing fossil-fuel intensive economies. But this would mean that developing countries might be denied the opportunity to develop, without any compensation.

3. Priority to the Least Well-Off

The third proposal I wish to consider offers a different justification for departing from the per capita principle: namely, that such a departure might maximally (or at least disproportionately) benefit the least well-off. The obvious version of this argument suggests, again, that the rich countries should carry the costs of dealing with global warming, and the LDCs should be offered generous economic assistance. But there are also less obvious versions, some of which may be attributable to some global warming skeptics.

The first is offered by Bjorn Lomborg. Lomborg claims that the climate change problem ultimately reduces to the question of whether to help poor inhabitants of the poor countries now or their richer descendents later. And he argues that the right answer is to help now, since the present poor are both poorer and more easily helped. Kyoto, he says, "will likely cost at least $150 billion a year, and possibly much more," whereas "just $70-80 billion a year could give all Third World inhabitants access to the basics like health, education, water and sanitation" (Lomborg 2001, p. 322).

But this argument is far from compelling. For one thing, it seems falsely to assume that helping the poor now and acting on climate change are mutually exclusive alternatives (Grubb 1995, p. 473, n. 25). For another, it seems to show a giant leap of political optimism. If their past record is anything to go by, the rich countries are even less likely to contribute large sums of money to help the world's poor directly than they are to do so to combat climate change (Singer 2002, pp. 26–27).

A second kind of priority argument may underlie the present President Bush's proposal of a "greenhouse gas intensity approach," which seeks to index emissions to economic activity. Bush has suggested reducing the amount of greenhouse gas per unit of U.S. GDP by 18 percent in ten years, saying "economic growth is the solution, not the problem" and "the United States wants to foster economic growth in the developing world, including the world's poorest nations" (Singer 2002, p. 43). Hence, he seems to appeal to a Rawlsian principle.

Peter Singer, however, claims that there are two serious problems with this argument. First, it faces a considerable burden of proof: it must show that U.S. economic activity not only makes the poor better off, but maximally so. Second, this burden cannot be met: not only do CIA figures show the United States "well above average in emissions per head it produces in proportion to per capita GDP," but "the vast majority of the goods and services that the US produces—89 percent of them—are consumed in the US" (Singer 2002, pp. 44–45). This, Singer argues, strongly suggests that the world's poor would be better off if the majority of the economic activity the United States undertakes (with its current share of world emissions) occurred elsewhere.

4. Equalizing Marginal Costs

A final proposal superficially resembles the equal intensity principle but is advocated for very different reasons. Martino Traxler proposes a "fair chore division" which equalizes the marginal costs of those aiming to prevent climate change. Such a proposal, he claims, is politically expedient, in that it (*a*) provides each nation in the global commons with "no stronger reasons to defect from doing its (fair) share than it gives any other nation" and so (*b*) places "the most moral pressure possible on each nation to do its part" (Traxler 2002, p. 129).

Unfortunately, it is not clear that Traxler's proposal achieves the ends he sets for it. First, by itself, *a* does not seem a promising way to escape a traditional commons or prisoner's dilemma situation. What is crucial in such situations is the magnitude of the benefits of defecting relative to those of cooperating; whether the relative benefits are equally large for all players is of much less importance. Second, this implies that *b* must be the crucial claim, but *b* is also dubious in this context. For Traxler explicitly rules out backward-looking considerations on practical grounds. But this means ignoring the previous emissions of the rich countries, the extent to which those emissions have effectively denied the LDCs "their share" of fossil-fuel-based development in the future, and the damages which will be disproportionately visited on the LDCs because of those emissions. So, it is hard to see why the LDCs will experience "maximum moral pressure" to comply. Third, equal marginal costs approaches are puzzling for a more theoretical reason. In general, equality of marginal welfare approaches suffer from the intuitive defect that they take no account of the overall level of welfare of each individual. Hence, under certain conditions, they might license taking large amounts from the poor (if they are so badly off anyway that changes for the worse make little difference), while leaving the rich relatively untouched (if they are so used to a life of luxury that they suffer greatly from even small losses). Now, Traxler's own approach does not fall into this trap, but this is because he advocates that costs should be measured not in terms of preferences or economic performance but, rather, in terms of subsistence, near subsistence, and luxury emissions. Thus, his view is that the rich countries should have to give up all of their luxury emissions before anyone else need consider giving up subsistence and near-subsistence emissions. But this raises a new concern. For in practice this means that Traxler's equal burdens proposal actually demands massive action from the rich countries before the poor countries are required to do anything at all (if indeed they ever are). And however laudable, or indeed morally right, such a course of action might be, it is hard to see it as securing the politically stable agreement that Traxler craves, or, at least, it is hard to see it as more likely to do so than the alternatives. So, the equal marginal costs approach seems to undercut its own rationale.

VIII. WHAT HAS THE WORLD DONE? THE KYOTO DEAL

> *This has been a disgraceful performance. It is the single worst failure of political leadership that I have seen in my lifetime.*
>
> AL GORE, Quoted By Hopgood 1998, P. 199

> *The system is made in America, and the Americans aren't part of it.*
>
> DAVID DONIGER

We have seen that there is a great deal of convergence on the issue of who has primary responsibility to act on climate change. The most defensible accounts of fairness and climate change suggest that the rich countries should bear the brunt, and perhaps even the entirety, of the costs. What, then, has the world done?

The current international effort to combat climate change has come in three main phases. The first came to fruition at the Rio Earth Summit of 1992. There, the countries of the world committed themselves to the Framework Convention on Climate Change (FCCC), which required "stabilization of greenhouse gas concentrations in the atmosphere at a level that would prevent dangerous anthropogenic interference with the climate system" and endorsed a principle of "common but differentiated responsibilities," according to which the richer, industrialized nations (listed under "Annex I" in the agreement) would take the lead in cutting emissions, while the less developed countries would pursue their own development and take significant action only in the future. In line with the FCCC, many of the rich countries (including the United States, European Union, Japan, Canada, Australia, New Zealand, and Norway) announced that they would voluntarily stabilize their emissions at 1990 levels by 2000.

Unfortunately, it soon became clear that merely voluntary measures were ineffective. For, as it turned out, most of those who had made declarations did nothing meaningful to try to live up to them, and their emissions continued to rise without constraint. Thus, a second phase ensued.

Meeting in Berlin in 1995, it was agreed that the parties should accept binding constraints on their emissions, and this was subsequently achieved in Japan in 1997, with the negotiation of the Kyoto Protocol. This agreement initially appeared to be a notable success, in that it required the Annex I countries to reduce emissions to roughly 5 percent below 1990 levels between 2008 and 2012. But it also contained two major compromises on the goal of limiting overall emissions, in that it allowed countries to count forests as sinks and to meet their commitments through buying unused capacity from others, through permit trading.

The promise of Kyoto turned out to be short lived. First, it proved so difficult to thrash out the details that a subsequent meeting, in the Hague in November 2000, broke down amid angry recriminations. Second, in March 2001, the Bush administration withdrew U.S. support, effectively killing the Kyoto agreement. Or so most people thought. For, as it turned out, the U.S. withdrawal did not cause immediate collapse. Instead, during the remainder of 2001, in meetings in Bonn and Marrakesh, a third phase began in which a full agreement was negotiated, with the European Union, Russia, and Japan playing prominent roles, and sent to participating governments for ratification. Many nations swiftly ratified, including the European Union, Japan, and Canada, so that, at the time of writing, the Kyoto Treaty needs only ratification by Russia to pass into international law.

On the surface, then, the effort to combat global climate change looks a little bruised, but still on track. But this appearance may be deceptive. For there is good reason to think that the Kyoto Treaty is deeply flawed, both in its substance and its background assumptions (Barrett 2003; Gardiner 2004*b*). Let us begin with *two* substantive criticisms.

The first is that Kyoto currently does very little to limit emissions. Initial projections suggested that the Bonn-Marrakesh agreement would reduce emissions for participants by roughly 2 percent on 1990 levels, down from the 5 percent initially envisaged by the original Kyoto agreement (Ott 2001). But recent research suggests that such large concessions were made in the period from Kyoto to Marrakesh that (*a*) even full compliance by its signatories would result in an overall increase in their emissions of 9 percent above 2000 levels by the end of the first commitment period; and (*b*) if present slow economic growth persists, this would actually match or exceed projected business-as-usual emissions (Babiker et al. 2002). Coupled with emissions growth in the LDCs, this means that there will be another substantial global increase by 2012. This is nothing short of astounding, given that by then we will be "celebrating" twenty years since the Earth Summit (Gardiner 2004*b*).

It is worth pausing to consider potential objections to this criticism. Some would argue that, even if it achieves very little, the current agreement is to be valued either procedurally (as a necessary first step), symbolically (for showing that some kind of agreement is possible), geopolitically (for showing that the rest of the world can act without the United States), or as simply the best that is possible under current conditions (Athanasiou and Baer 2001, 2002, p. 24). There is something to be said for these views. For the current Kyoto Protocol sets targets only for 2008–12, and these targets are intended as only the first of many rounds of abatement measures. Kyoto's enthusiasts anticipate that the level of cuts will be deepened and their coverage expanded (to include the developing countries) as subsequent targets for new periods are negotiated.

Nevertheless, I remain skeptical. This is partly due to the history of climate negotiations in general, and the current U.S. energy policy in particular; and partly because I do not think future generations will see reason to thank us for symbolism rather than action. But the main reason is that there are clear ways in which the world could have done better (Gardiner 2004*b*).

This leads us to the second substantive criticism of Kyoto: that it contains no effective compliance mechanism. This criticism arises because, although the Bonn-Marrakesh agreement allows for reasonably serious punishments for those who fail to reach their targets, these punishments cannot be enforced. For the envisioned treaty has been set up so that countries have several ways to avoid being penalized. On the one hand, enforcement is not binding on any country that fails to ratify the amendment necessary to punish it (Barrett 2003, p. 386). On the other, the penalties take the form of more demanding targets in the next decade's commitment period—but parties can take this into account when negotiating their targets for that commitment period, and in any case a country is free to exit the treaty with one year's notice, three years after the treaty has entered into force for it (FCCC, article 25).

The compliance mechanisms for Kyoto are thus weak. Some would object to this, saying that they are as strong as is possible under current institutions. But I argue that this is both misleading and, to some extent, irrelevant. It is misleading because other agreements have more serious, external sanctions (e.g., the Montreal Protocol on ozone depletion allows for trade sanctions), and also because matters of compliance are notoriously difficult in international relations, leading some to suggest that it is only the easy, and comparatively trivial, agreements that get made. It is somewhat irrelevant because part of what is at stake with climate change is whether we have institutions capable of responding to such global and long-term threats (Gardiner 2004*b*).

Kyoto is also flawed in its background assumptions. Consider the following three examples. First, the agreement assumes a "two track" approach, whereby an acceptable deal on climate can be made without addressing the wider issue of international justice. But this, Shue argues, represents a compound injustice to the poor nations, whose bargaining power on climate change is reduced by existing injustice (Shue 1992, p. 373). Furthermore, this injustice appears to be manifest, in that the treaty directly addresses only the costs of preventing future climate change and only indirectly (and minimally) addresses the costs of coping with climate change to which we are already committed (Shue 1992, p. 384). Second, the Bonn-Marrakesh deal eschews enforcement mechanisms external to the climate change issue, such as trade sanctions. Given the apparent fragility of such a commitment on the part of the participant countries, this is probably disastrous. Third, Kyoto takes as its priority the issue of cost-effectiveness. As several authors point out, this tends to shift the focus of negotiations away from the important ethical issues and (paradoxically) to tend to make the agreement less, rather than more, practical.

Why is Kyoto such a failure? The reasons are no doubt complex and include the political role of energy interests, confusion about scientific uncertainties and economic costs, and the inadequacies of the international system. But two further factors have also been emphasized in the literature. So, I will just mention them in closing. The first is the role of the United States, which, with 4 percent of the world's population, emits roughly 25 percent of global greenhouse gases. From the early stages, and on the most important issues, the United States effectively molded the agreement to its will, persistently objecting when other countries tried to make it stronger. But then it abandoned the treaty, seemingly repudiating even those parts on which it had previously agreed. This behavior has been heavily criticized for being seriously unethical (e.g., Brown 2002; Harris 2000*a*). Indeed, Singer even goes so far as to suggest that it is so unethical that the moral case for economic sanctions against the United States (and other countries which have refused to act on climate change) is stronger than it was for apartheid South Africa, since the South African regime, horrible as it was, harmed only its own citizens, whereas the United States harms citizens of other countries.

The second reason behind Kyoto's failure is its intergenerational aspect. Most analyses describe the climate change problem in intragenerational, game theoretic terms, as a prisoner's dilemma (Barrett 2003, p. 368; Danielson 1993, pp. 95–96; Soroos 1997, pp. 260–61) or battle-of-the-sexes problem (Waldron 1990). But I have argued that the more important dimension of climate change may be its intergenerational aspect (Gardiner 2001). Roughly speaking, the point is this. Climate change is caused primarily by fossil fuel use. Burning fossil fuels has two main consequences: on the one hand, it produces substantial benefits through the production of energy; on the other, it exposes humanity to the risk of large, and perhaps catastrophic, costs from climate change. But these costs and benefits accrue to different groups: the benefits arise primarily in the short to medium term and so are received by the present generation, but the costs fall largely in the long term, on future generations. This suggests a worrying scenario. For one thing, so long as high energy use is (or is perceived to be) strongly connected to self-interest, the present generation will have strong egoistic reasons to ignore the worst aspects of climate change. For another, this problem is iterated: it arises anew for each subsequent generation as it gains the power to decide whether or not to act. This suggests that the global warming problem has a seriously tragic structure. I have argued that it is this background fact that most readily explains the Kyoto debacle (Gardiner 2004*b*).

IX. CONCLUSION

This article has been intended as something of a primer. Its aim is to encourage and facilitate wider engagement by ethicists with the issue of global climate change. At the outset, I offered some general reasons why philosophers should be more interested in climate change. In closing, I would like to offer one more. I have suggested that climate change poses some difficult ethical and philosophical problems. Partly as a consequence of this, the public and political debate surrounding climate change is often simplistic, misleading, and awash with conceptual confusion. Moral philosophers should see this as a call to arms. Philosophical clarity is urgently needed. Given the importance of the problem, let us hope that the call is answered quickly.

REFERENCES

Athanasiou, Tom, and Baer, Paul. 2001. Climate Change after Marrakesh: Should Environmentalists Still Support Kyoto? Earthscape Update, December, http://www.earthscape.org/p1/att02/att02.html.

Athanasiou, Tom, and Baer, Paul. 2002. *Dead Heat: Global Justice and Global Warming.* New York: Seven Stories Press.

Babiker, Mustapha H., Jacoby, Henry D., Reilly, John M., and Reiner, David M. 2002. The Evolution of a Climate Regime: Kyoto to Marrakesh and Beyond *Environmental Science and Policy* **5**:195–206.

Baer, Paul. 2002. Equity, Greenhouse Gas Emissions, and Global Common Resources. In *Climate Change Policy: A Survey*, ed. Stephen H. Schneider, Armin Rosencranz, and John O. Niles, pp. 393–408. Washington, D.C.: Island Press.

Barrett, Scott. 2003. *Environment and Statecraft.* Oxford: Oxford University Press.

Broecker, Wallace S. 1997. Thermohaline Circulation, the Achilles' Heel of Our Climate System: Will Man-Made CO_2, Upset the Current Balance? *Science* **278** (November 28):1582–88.

Broome, John. 1992. *Counting the Cost of Global Warming.* Isle of Harris, UK: White Horse Press.

Brown, Donald. 2002. *American Heat: Ethical Problems with the United States' Response to Global Warming.* Lanham, Md: Rowman & Littlefield.

Costanza, Robert. 1996. Review of *Managing the Commons: The Economics of Climate Change*, by William D. Nordhaus. *Environment and Development Economics* **1**:381–84.

Danielson, Peter. 1993. Personal Responsibility. In Coward and Hurka 1993, pp. 81–98.

De Leo, Giulio; Rizzi, L.; Caizzi, A.; and Gatto, M. 2001. The Economic Benefits of the Kyoto Protocol. *Nature* **413**:478–79.

Gagosian, Robert. 2003. Abrupt Climate Change: Should We Be Worried? Woods Hole Oceanographic Institute. Available at http://www.whoi.edu/institutes/occi/hottopics_climatechange.html.

Gardiner, Stephen M. 2001. The Real Tragedy of the Commons. *Philosophy & Public Affairs* **30**:387–416.

Gardiner, Stephen M. 2004*a*. A Core Precautionary Principle. *International Journal of Global Environmental Problems: Special Issue on the Precautionary Principle*, vol. **5**, no. 2 (in press).

Gardiner, Stephen M. 2004*b*. The Global Warming Tragedy and the Dangerous Illusion of the Kyoto Protocol. *Ethics and International Affairs* **18**:23–39.

Grubb, Michael. 1995. Seeking Fair Weather: Ethics and the International Debate on Climate Change. *International Affairs* **71**:463–96.

Gundermann, Jesper. 2002. Discourse in the Greenhouse. In *Sceptical Questions and Sustainable Answers*, by Danish Ecological Council, pp. 139–64. Copenhagen: Danish Ecological Council.

Harris, Paul, ed. 2000*a*. *Climate Change and American Foreign Policy.* New York: St. Martin's.

Harris, Paul. 2003. Fairness, Responsibility, and Climate Change. *Ethics and International Affairs* **17**:149–56.

Hopgood, Stephen. 1998. *American Foreign Policy and the Power of the State.* Oxford: Oxford University Press.

Houghton, John. 1997. *Global Warming: The Complete Briefing.* 2d ed. Cambridge: Cambridge University Press.

IPCC (Intergovernmental Panel on Climate Change). 1995. *Climate Change 1995: Economic and Social Dimensions of Climate Change.* Cambridge: Cambridge University Press.

IPCC. 2001*a*. *Climate Change 2001: Mitigation.* Cambridge: Cambridge University Press. Available at http://www.ipcc.ch.

IPCC. 2001*b*. *Climate Change 2001: The Science of Climate Change.* Cambridge: Cambridge University Press. Available at http://www.ipcc.ch.

IPCC. 2001c. *Climate Change 2001: Synthesis Report.* Cambridge: University Press Cambridge. Available at http://www.ipcc.ch.

Jamieson, Dale. 1992. Ethics, Public Policy and Global Warming. *Science, Technology and Human Values* **17**:139–53. Reprinted in Dale Jamieson, *Morality's Progress.* Oxford: Oxford University Press, 2003. References are to the later version.

Jamieson, Dale. 1998. Global Responsibilities: Ethics, Public Health and Global Environmental Change. *Indiana Journal of Global Legal Studies* **5**:99–119.

Lee, Jennifer. 2003. GOP Changes Environmental Message. *Seattle Times*, March 2.

Lomborg, Bjorn. 2001. Global Warming. In *The Sceptical Environmentalist*, by Bjorn Lomborg, pp. 258–324. Cambridge: Cambridge University Press.

O'Neill, Brian, C., and Oppenheimer, Michael. 2002. Dangerous Climate Impacts and the Kyoto Protocol. *Science* **296** (June 14):1971–72.

Ott, Hermann. 2001. Climate Policy after the Marrakesh Accords From Legislation to Implementation. Available at http://www.upperinst.org-/download/Ott-after-marrakesh.pdf. Published as *Global Climate: Yearbook of International Law.* Oxford: Oxford University Press.

Raffensberger, Carolyn, and Tickner, Joel, eds. 1999. Protecting Public Health and the Environment: Implementing the Precautionary Principle. Washington, D.C.: Island Press.

Rawls, John. 1999. *A Theory of Justice.* Rev. ed. Cambridge, Mass.: Harvard University Press.

Sagoff, Mark. 1988. *The Economy of the Earth.* Cambridge: Cambridge University Press.

Schelling, Thomas. 1997. The Cost of Combating Global Warming: Facing the Tradeoffs. *Foreign Affairs* **76**:8–14.

Schmidtz, David. 2001. A Place for Cost-Benefit Analysis. *Noûs* **11**, suppl.: 148–71.

Schultz, Peter, and Kasting, James. 1997. Optimal Reductions in CO_2 Emissions. *Energy Policy* **25**:491–500.

Sen, Amartya. 1980. Equality of What? In *Tanner Lectures on Human Values*, ed. S. M. McMurrin, pp. 195–220. Salt Lake City: University of Utah Press.

Shogren, Jason, and Toman, Michael. 2000. Climate Change Policy. Discussion Paper 00–22, Resources for the Future, Washington, D.C., May 14–25, available at http://www.rff.org.

Shue, Henry. 1992. The Unavoidability of Justice. In *The International Politics of the Environment*, ed. Andrew Hurrell and Benedict Kingsbury, pp. 97–397. Oxford: Oxford University Press.

Shue, Henry, 1995*a*. Avoidable Necessity: Global Warming, International Fairness and Alternative Energy. In *Theory and Practice, NOMOS XXXVII*, ed. Ian Shapiro and Judith Wagner DeCew, pp. 239–642. New York: New York University Press.

Shue, Henry. 1999*a*. Bequeathing Hazards: Security Rights and Property Rights of Future Humans. In *Global Environmental Economics: Equity and the Limits to Markets*, ed. M. Dore and T. Mount, pp. 38–53. Oxford: Blackwell.

Singer, Peter. 2002. One Atmosphere. In *One World: The Ethics of Globalization*, by Peter Singer, chap. 2. New Haven, Conn.: Yale University Press.

Soroos, Marvin S. 1997. *The Endangered Atmosphere: Preserving a Global Commons.* Columbia: University of South Carolina Press.

Traxler, Martino. 2002. Fair Chore Division for Climate Change. *Social Theory and Practice* **28**:101–34.

United Nations Environment Program. 1999. *Climate Change Information Kit.* Available at http://www.unep.ch.iuc.

United Nations Framework Convention on Climate Change. 1992. *Framework Convention on Climate Change.* Available at http://www.unfccc.int.

U.S. National Research Council, Committee on Abrupt Climate Change. 2002. *Abrupt Climate Change: Inevitable Surprise.* Washington, D.C.: National Academies Press.

Waldron, Jeremy. 1990. Who Is to Stop Polluting? Different Kinds of Free-Rider Problem. In *Ethical Guidelines for Global Bargains.* Program on Ethics and Public Life. Ithaca, N.Y.: Cornell University.

Wingspread Statement. 1998. Available at http://www.gdrc.org/u-gov/precaution-3.html.

Woodward, Richard, and Bishop, Richard. 1997. How to Decide When Experts Disagree: Uncertainty-Based Choice Rules in Environmental Policy. *Land Economics* 73:492–507.

FURTHER READING

Gore, Al. *An Inconvenient Truth: The Planetary Emergency of Global Warming and What We Can Do About It.* Rodale Press, 2006.

Intergovernmental Panel on Climate Change (IPCC), http://www.ipcc.ch/.

Michaels, Patrick J. *Meltdown: The Predictable Distortion of Global Warming by Scientists, Politicians, and the Media.* Cato Institute (November 25, 2004).

Pew Center on Global Climate Change, http://www.pewclimate.org/.

Pittock, A. Barrie. *Climate Change: Turning Up the Heat.* Earthscan Press, 2006.

Weart, Spencer. *The Discovery of Global Warming.* Harvard University Press, 2003.

2.5.3 Energizing Cities

JANET L. SAWIN AND KRISTEN HUGHES

Janet L. Sawin is a senior researcher and director of the Energy and Climate Change Program, at the Worldwatch Institute. Kristen Hughes is a research associate and doctoral candidate of the Center for Energy and Environmental Policy, University of Delaware. This article considers the phenomenon of rapid urbanization of many areas in the world, especially in less-developed countries and the concomitant increased energy demands in the emerging megacities. Globalization (see Section 2.1) accounts for much of the change taking place in our world, including raising expectations by many in traditionally poor, less-developed countries (LDCs) for the "good life." Contemporary China and India, with enormous and growing populations, are developing quickly. What will be the consequences of this economic development on Earth's ecosystem? More people enjoying higher standards of living will consume more food, water, and energy, thereby creating more waste and pollution if sustainable forms of energy production and consumption are not adopted.

Janet Sawin and Kristen Hughes begin their article by describing some of the results of the shift to an urban population that actually began with the Industrial Revolution in England during the late eighteenth century as industries lured workers from the farm to the factory. This trend has continued to the present day around the world to the point where the UNHABITAT 2006 Annual Report estimated that by the middle of 2007 the majority of the world's population would be living in towns or cities. Unfortunately the Worldwatch Institute estimates that 1 billion of those urbanites will lack adequate shelter, clean water, toilets, or electricity. If the economic and social goals of LCDs are realized, the demands for energy in those regions of the world will increase dramatically. How we confront those needs will, to a large extent, determine whether pollution resulting from energy production and distribution is reduced to an sustainable level or allowed to grow with few or no restrictions.

Source: From "Energizing Cities," in *State of the World* 2007, pp. 90–111. Copyright © 2007 Worldwatch Institute. Reprinted by permission. www.worldwatch.org.

There is no doubt that both technological and political solutions to this problem are required. The economic benefits that might be realized from the numerous energy-related technologies described in this article are widely acknowledged, but as might be expected, there are reasons why they are not being widely adopted. This article describes a number of technological solutions to problems related to how we produce and consume energy. What is required to resolve these dilemmas is the will power of not only the citizens of the world but also our leaders.

FOCUS QUESTIONS

1. Discuss the three major obstacles that the authors see to installing proven renewable energy systems throughout the world.
2. What are some of the sustainable energy technologies described in this article, and how might they address issues of increased urbanization in the world?
3. The per-person consumption levels of energy are far higher in more developed countries (MDCs) than in LDCs such as India and China. What are some of the issues to be dealt with related to this fact as LDCs increase their standard of living as well as their energy demands?
4. What accounts for the "cheap" energy available in many parts of the world, and how does this condition impact progress toward a sustainable energy future?
5. To what extent do you believe citizens in MDCs might be willing to adopt a more ethical position toward the less fortunate in regard to energy consumption and worldwide pollution?

KEYWORDS

anaerobic digester, biofuel, biomass, deforestation, distributed generation (DG), eco-city, ecological footprint, fuel cell, geothermal heat pumps, green buildings, greenhouse gas (GHG), heat gain, infrastructure, Kyoto Protocol, LCD, LED, microturbine, MDC, NGO, photovoltaics (PV), solar thermal system, sustainability, waste heat

At night, Earth's cities are visible from space as stars or chains of light in a sea of blackness. Many appear to be vibrant and to exude energy. People are drawn to the "lights on Broadway," for example. But a closer examination reveals complex webs of streets, enormous buildings, vehicles, and burgeoning populations—all of which need energy to build, use, and sustain. To meet these needs, cities draw energy from the world around them, providing local benefits—but with health, security, and environmental consequences for all.

The portrait of urban energy use today contains real differences in consumption and resulting ecological footprints among the world's cities—differences that reflect the vast financial wealth separating the world's most industrialized, rich urban areas from the poorer cities just now experiencing rapid economic growth. Indeed, millions of people who live in or around the world's poorest cities do not have access to modern energy services.

Even as industrializing and poor nations seek to expand their economies to levels nearer those of rich nations, Earth's atmosphere and ecosystems are demonstrating real limits to our ever-increasing consumption of resources. Partly in recognition of this, hundreds of cities around the world are working to reduce their ecological footprints.[1]

The re-visioning of urban life reflects a critical moment in the history of cities, as many unfavorable factors have converged to make present trends insupportable. Over the past 150 years, cities have become increasingly reliant on dirty and distant energy sources, leaving them vulnerable to supply disruptions and destroying community-based notions of environmental protection. In the next few decades, the vast majority of expanded energy supply will be to meet the needs—direct and indirect—of cities. Increasingly, cities will need to play a more active role in planning and building their own energy futures.

Cities in the future will bear the brunt of many challenges related to today's unsustainable energy systems—from air and water pollution to climate change—particularly as growing populations put increasing pressure on resources. As cities continue to expand, the enormity of their contributions to major social and environmental problems is only expected to rise. Yet this same enormity of scale offers cities the potential to make beneficial changes with significant local and global impacts. As this chapter describes, cities hold the key to mitigating problems through urban planning, building design, and choice of end-use products and energy resources and technologies. Around the world, numerous cities are already improving their efficiency and producing more of their energy locally and sustainably, and many of these efforts can be replicated elsewhere to reduce environmental impacts and improve the quality of life for urban and rural dwellers alike.

URBAN ENERGY NEEDS AND CONSTRAINTS

It took millennia to make the transition from human muscle power to draft animals and then to primitive machines that tapped renewable energy flows from wind and water. In contrast, the Industrial Revolution came along in the mere blink of an eye. In the span of a few generations, cities were transformed from dense areas of narrow streets with small, low dwellings to skyscrapers and sprawling suburbs. Over time, urbanites traded horses for streetcars and, eventually, private vehicles. Rarely very large before the advent of steam engines, urban populations began to soar as opportunity drew waves of immigrants to cities and as cleaner streets reduced death rates. Energy use surged as well, and the advent of the fossil fuel age—which provided power for elevators, electric lights, and motor vehicles—enabled cities to become what they are today.[2]

Direct energy consumption per person in industrial-country cities is often lower than in rural areas due to the greater density of living and commuting spaces. Urban residents in Japan, for example, use less energy per capita than rural residents do. In older cities, designed before the widespread use of private cars, energy use per person is lower than in sprawling modern cities. The dense environment of Manhattan more than compensates for its massive, often old and inefficient buildings, making New York City one of the most resource- and energy-efficient places in the United States.[3]

In developing countries, where many rural people lack access to modern energy services, the reverse is often true. The one third of India's population who live in cities consumes 87 percent of the nation's electricity. And in China, urban residents typically use 40 percent more commercial energy than their rural counterparts. (People in rural China actually use more total primary energy, mainly in the form of biomass, but most of this is lost during inefficient combustion.)[4]

Cities require energy to build infrastructure, to light, heat and cool buildings, to cook, to manufacture goods, and to transport people. The infrastructure itself, including streets, buildings, bridges, and other urban features, represents large quantities of embodied energy—the energy invested in these structures during their lifetimes from the cradle of raw materials, to city block, to eventual grave.... Urban residents also consume large amounts of energy indirectly in the food and other goods they import.[5]

Most if not all of the energy used directly in cities must be imported as well, raising a host of significant costs and challenges. Pipes carrying gas, for example, pose serious safety and environmental threats in urban areas, where leaks or explosions can cause injuries and deaths. Electricity generally comes from large, central power plants via transmission and distribution (T & D) systems that are often inefficient and unreliable. The centralized grid permits blackouts to cascade throughout entire regions. The August 2003 blackout in the northeastern United States and

Canada, for example, which was caused initially by a fallen tree, affected 50 million people and cost the region $4.5–10 billion. A month later, another tree hit a high-voltage transmission line in Italy, leaving 57 million people in the dark.[6]

Transmission bottlenecks are particularly pronounced in large metropolitan areas, which require vast amounts of power to traverse great distances through a limited number of lines. The share of electricity lost along the way ranges from 4 to 7 percent in industrial countries to more than 50 percent in parts of the developing world, where much of the loss is due to people tapping lines illegally. In parts of New Delhi, electric cables are caught in a tangle of hooks and wires as slum dwellers, small factories, Hindu temples, and even wealthy businessmen siphon off 36 percent of the city's power.[7]

One of the greatest challenges of the current system is getting energy services to all urban residents. Nearly one fifth of the estimated 1.6 billion people worldwide who lack access to electricity and other modern energy services live in the world's cities. Because access is defined as areas with grid extensions, the actual number truly without access could be higher. About one third of Africans live in urban areas, and at least one quarter of city dwellers on the continent do not have access to electricity.[8]

Too many of the world's people thus must struggle daily to afford or find energy resources—most often wood, charcoal, dung, or other biomass. Indoor air pollution caused by burning these inferior fuels results in millions of deaths annually. Heavy reliance on biomass has also increased the destruction of forests around cities, exacerbating local air pollution and soil erosion. In India, Sri Lanka, and Thailand, wood harvesting by the urban poor has produced a halo of deforestation around cities, towns, and roads. And a radius of some 400 kilometers has been cleared around Khartoum in Sudan.[9]

For those with access to modern energy services, the predominant fuel used for non-transport energy is coal, which accounted for nearly one fourth of total global energy use in 2003; the International Energy Agency (IEA) projects that coal consumption will continue to rise significantly through at least 2030. Energy from coal and other conventional sources comes with high costs, including soil and water pollution resulting from resource extraction and use, air pollution from burning, and associated health problems. In China alone, coal use causes the death of 100 miners weekly on average, significant urban air pollution, and acid rain damage to more than a third of the country.[10]

Furthermore, heavy reliance on fossil fuels, particularly in cities, is the primary driver of global climate change. Cities now house just shy of half the world's population, but they are responsible for the vast majority of greenhouse gas emissions from human activities.[11]

REDUCING DEMAND WITHOUT DIMMING THE LIGHTS

Much of the energy that people pipe, wire, and truck into cities is used by and in buildings—constructing and operating them as well as making their occupants comfortable. Globally, buildings account for more than 40 percent of total energy use. When the energy required for materials, transportation, and construction is included, buildings devour more than half the energy used in the United States each year.[12]

As cities become more populated, more and more of the world's buildings are found in urban areas. In 2005, Shanghai constructed more building space than exists in all the office buildings of New York City. Every month, China adds urban infrastructure equal to that found in Houston, Texas, simply to keep up with the masses of people migrating from rural areas to cities.[13]

The advent of cheap and readily available energy let the modern building work in spite of nature rather than with it. Yet around the world there is a small but rapidly growing movement to make buildings "green"—lowering their energy needs, for example, through efficiency improvements, embodied energy reductions, and the use of on-site energy resources. Green buildings incorporate designs and technologies often considered new and innovative; in reality, many of these ideas have been around for centuries. Today, architects, planners, and others are rediscovering traditional ways to light, heat, and cool indoor spaces and adapting them for modern uses.

Lighting accounts for nearly 20 percent of total electricity consumption worldwide. Much of this occurs when the sun is shining. Thus energy use could be reduced dramatically with simple design techniques such as natural daylighting, mirrors and reflective paints, and light shelves-horizontal fins at windows that act as shading devices, reduce glare, and allow daylight to penetrate deep into buildings. Technology has improved to the point where glass transmits light while reflecting unwanted heat. These techniques and materials not only offset some of the lighting load, they also lower the significant heat gains associated with lighting, reducing air conditioning needs.[14]

Once design changes have lowered the need for artificial light, energy demand can be reduced further with modern technologies like motion sensors—which turn lights, appliances, or machinery off when they are not needed—and energy-efficient bulbs and lamps. Conventional incandescent bulbs convert about 10 percent of energy to light and the remainder to heat. In contrast, compact fluorescent bulbs and light-emitting diodes (LEDs) use far less energy to produce a comparable amount of light while producing a fraction of the heat. These alternatives cost more upfront, but they save energy and money over their lifetimes.[15]

Heating water and space also requires significant amounts of energy. Better insulation, proper building orientation, and the use of solar heating and other techniques can dramatically lower energy demand and associated costs, as can reducing the scale of buildings. In developing countries, one of the most cost-effective ways to increase thermal comfort for the urban poor is to install ceilings beneath their roofs in order to reduce heat loss; energy savings from such programs in South Africa have exceeded 50 percent.[16]

"Waste" heat that is vented in conventional large-scale power plants or in small systems like microturbines or fuel cells can be captured for heating, cooling, or additional power generation. Such combined heat and power systems improve overall efficiency levels dramatically. The Verdesian, a new building in New York City's Battery Park, captures heat from a natural gas microturbine to produce hot water, increasing overall energy efficiency to 80 percent or higher, compared with the 25–35 percent efficiency of a typical fossil fuel power plant.[17]

The means used to distribute such heat can also improve efficiency. Radiant floor heating, for example, is generally more energy-efficient than conventional alternatives, and today's systems can operate with fossil or renewable fuels. Rediscovered early in the twentieth century and now commonplace in much of Europe and the United States, radiant heating was devised by the Romans, who placed terra cotta pipes beneath stone floors to heat villas with flue gases from wood fires. A more modern technique is used in the Hewlett Foundation building in Menlo Park, California, where air is circulated through a raised floor, heating and cooling workers rather than the space above them and allowing individuals to control temperatures.[18]

During hot months, space cooling is becoming increasingly important to keep cities running. The concrete and asphalt jungles that replace natural life absorb heat and raise urban temperatures further, creating what is known as the "heat island effect." In China's major cities, air conditioning accounts for 40 percent of the public's summer energy demand and is the primary cause of power shortages that began in 2003. And in Tokyo, a modeling study found that waste heat emissions from air conditioning are responsible for 1 degree Celsius of warming during the summer, exacerbating the heat island effect. A similar study of Houston, Texas, found that total waste heat emissions were responsible for warming of up to a half-degree Celsius in daytime and 2.5 degrees at night.[19]

For at least 2,000 years, people in the Mediterranean region have passively cooled buildings with a variety of techniques. These include cross ventilation over the surface of a pool of water, open buildings, tree shading, careful placement and sizing of windows, and the use of massive, thick walls and floors as insulation from summer heat. Some of these techniques are being revitalized today, along with options not available two millennia ago.[20]

Natural ventilation—the use of outdoor air to cool buildings—reduces the need for air conditioning in some climates. Studies show that effective night ventilation, adapted to local conditions, could reduce the cooling load in office buildings by 55 percent or more. And the U.S. Environmental Protection Agency (EPA) estimates that careful placement of trees can reduce the energy required for cooling by 7–40 percent, depending on the extent of tree canopy.[21]

Another way to reduce energy demand for cooling is to top buildings with reflective surfaces—such as white paint or metal shingles that act as radiant barriers. An EPA-funded study that considered both cooling benefits and heating penalties of such "cool roofs" found significant net savings in energy use for 11 major U.S. cities.[22]

Green roofs and walls reduce heat gain in summer and they also insulate building from cold in winter. Temperatures on conventional roofs can be 50 degrees Celsius (90 degrees Fahrenheit) higher than the ambient temperature; atop a "green roof," the temperature on a hot day can actually be below ambient. A study of an eight-story residential building in Madrid, Spain, found that adding a green roof cut annual energy use by 1 percent, while reducing the peak cooling load on upper floors by 25 percent. With enough "cool" or green rooftops throughout a city, substantial reductions in the urban heat island effect are possible, with the added benefit of less urban smog. Green roofs also filter and retain storm water, reducing urban runoff problems, and they create habitat for birds and recreational space for people.[23]

Each of these features alone provides significant savings. The integration of intelligent design with several efficiency measures can reduce energy use to half or less that in a comparable conventional building. Some experts believe savings of up to 80 percent are possible. As peak loads for lighting, heating, and cooling decline, the required size of boilers, fans, and other machinery does also, providing greater savings in energy and construction costs. The Accord 21 Building, opened in 2000, was the first internationally certified green project in China. It uses 70 percent less energy than standard buildings, causing astonished inspectors to return repeatedly to check that energy meters are functioning propertly.[24]

There are good economic reasons for constructing more-efficient buildings: they generally have healthier and more-comfortable occupants, higher worker productivity, reduced tenant turnover, and better performing students in schools. The Internationale Nederlanden Bank headquarters in Amsterdam uses about 10 percent of the energy of its predecessor and reduces worker absenteeism by 15 percent, for a total savings of $3.4 million annually. In the United States, the average premium for a "green" building is 2–5 percent, but studies find that the associated financial benefits over 20 years are more than 10 times the initial investment. And the costs of green buildings are falling with design and construction experience.[25]

Although the marginal cost of improving efficiency is lowest when buildings are constructed, retrofits can be highly cost-effective as well. Simple strategies like daylighting, efficient lighting, and glazing can pay for themselves in as little as one year. More than 300 retrofit projects—from insulation to water system improvements—undertaken in China in recent years had an average payback period of 1.3 years.[26]

Such advances can also provide important benefits for the world's poor. In industrial nations, maximizing efficiency through design and cost-effective end-use technologies can ensure that poor residents are not forced from their homes by rising energy costs. In the developing world, efficiency advances can bring dramatic quality-of-life improvements by making energy services more affordable to the poor. LEDs, for example, provide an estimated 200 times more useful light than kerosene lamps. At $55 each, solar-powered lamps with LEDs could brighten the nights of the poor. In Tembisa, a shantytown of Johannesburg, South Africa, a survey found that almost 10,000 households spend more than $60 each for candles and paraffin every year; with access to microcredit…, such families could afford cleaner, better lighting freely powered by the sun.[27]

In ancient Greece, many cities were planned in grids so that every home had access to the sun for warmth and light in winter; the ancient

Romans went so far as to pass "sun-right laws," forbidding builders from blocking access to the winter sun. Green roofs date back thousands of years, the most famous being the Hanging Gardens of Babylon, constructed around 500 BC. The lessons of these ancient practices, combined with state-of-the-art technologies and materials, provide today's cities with powerful tools to achieve dramatic efficiency improvements.[28]

POWERING CITIES LOCALLY

When Thomas Edison installed his first electric systems in the late nineteenth century, he envisioned an industry with dozens of companies generating power close to the point of use. Such a system would be particularly suited to densely populated urban areas. Initially, the industry evolved along these lines, with many companies producing power on site and capturing the waste heat. But by the mid-1930s most industrial countries had established monopoly industries, driven greatly by the economic benefits of ever-larger generating stations matched with transmission and distribution systems. It was not until the 1980s that efficiency limits were met—which, combined with a variety of economic and environmental challenges, led many experts to realize that bigger is not always better when it comes to energy production.[29]

Small-scale, locally installed power equipment, also called distributed generation (DG), could enable cities to meet much of their own energy needs once again. Today, DG remains more expensive per unit of energy output than conventional, centralized generation, but costs continue to fall and associated benefits are significant. Distributed generation reduces the need for expensive transmission and distribution infrastructure while lowering grid losses. By bypassing the T&D system, DG also improves reliability and reduces vulnerability to accident or sabotage. Because they are modular and can be installed rapidly, distributed small-scale generators can expand to keep pace with demand as a city grows, deferring or preventing the need for new central power plants. This is particularly important in developing countries, where migration is rapidly raising urban numbers as well as energy demand. And distributed systems provide local control and ownership of energy resources, encouraging community-level economic development....

Most DG today comes from inefficient diesel generators or natural gas turbines. But several new options are emerging, with technological progress on a variety of fronts. For example, advanced technologies such as high-performance microturbines and fuel cells promise reliable, efficient alternatives. Fuel cells require minimal maintenance and can be sited in crowded urban centers because they are clean, quiet, and highly flexible. Several fuel cell technologies are under development, with many already producing power for modern office buildings and hotels; advanced fuel cells could soon generate enough energy to supply a large proportion of the electricity and heat needed to power a city and warm its buildings.[30]

Today fuel cells or advanced microturbines must rely primarily on natural gas that has to be piped into cities. But alternatives already exist: methane from a local landfill will soon drive a fuel cell in the city of Vaasa, Finland, supplying heat and power for 50 homes. Eventually, fuel cells can use hydrogen produced from a variety of renewable sources.[31]

Far beyond feeding turbines and fuel cells, renewable resources can provide energy for cooking, lighting, heating, cooling, and even transportation in the world's cities and beyond. Renewables already meet the energy needs of millions of people around the globe, and renewable energy markets are experiencing exponential growth. Wind and solar power are the fastest-growing electricity sources, and biofuels are the world's fastest-growing fuels; all are experiencing double-digit annual growth rates.[32]

Wherever the sun shines, buildings—whether shacks or skyscrapers—can become mini-power or heating stations. Solar photo-voltaics (PVs) generate electricity directly from sunlight, often at precisely the time when power demand is greatest and electricity is most costly. PV technology has advanced to the point where it can literally be integrated into structures—in roofing tiles and shingles, outer walls, and glass windows—generating not only electricity but also shade and insulation.

When used for building facades, PVs can be cheaper than granite or marble. Building-integrated PV (BIPV) is now widely used in Europe and is spreading to other regions as well. The IEA estimates that BIPVs could meet nearly one fifth of annual electricity demand in Finland, more than 40 percent in Australia, and about half of the total in the United States.[33]

Solar thermal systems, which use the sun's warmth to heat water and space, adorn rooftops from Freiburg in Germany to Jerusalem in Israel and can pay for themselves in just a few years through fuel savings. Shanghai and other Chinese cities are becoming hotbeds for solar energy, driven by the need to reduce coal and oil consumption. China now leads the world in the manufacture and use of solar thermal systems. Solar power and heating offer enormous potential in other developing-country cities as well, where they could provide electricity, heat, and hot water for families and communities in informal settlements that currently have no access to the electric grid or other modern energy services—and for far less than it would cost to extend the grid.[34]

Cities can also tap the insulating properties of the ground beneath them. Heat pumps use the near-constant temperatures of Earth or groundwater as a heat source in winter and a heat sink in summer to heat and cool water and space. The U.S. military replaced individual space heating, cooling, and water heating systems with ground-source (also called geothermal) heat pumps in more than 4,000 housing units in Fort Polk, Louisiana, eliminating nearly one third of the community's electricity use and 100 percent of the natural gas previously required for heating and cooling. In the world's largest residential application of this technology to date, the Beijing Linked Hybrid Project will use heat pumps to heat and cool almost 140,000 square meters (1.5 million square feet) of new apartments.[35]

There is evidence that high-temperature geothermal water was used to heat buildings in ancient Pompeii. Today, such sources are tapped for district heating systems in cities in France, Iceland, the United States, Turkey, and elsewhere. Paris has the largest such system in the European Union.[36]

Although cities have little land available for energy crops, they have an enormous potential resource for biomass energy: urban waste. New York City, for example, produces 12,000 tons of garbage per day. The waste must be shipped as far away as Ohio, and disposal costs the city more than $1 billion annually. In industrial- and developing-country cities alike, per person generation of municipal waste is increasing with population and lifestyle changes. Due primarily to a lack of resources and disposal sites, as much as 90 percent of the waste in some developing-country cities is not collected; instead, it is burned or left to rot in the streets, creating heavy smoke and fumes, water pollution, and disease.[37]

But one person's trash is another's black gold, and urban waste can be used to produce everything from cooking fuel for individual households to grid-based electricity for office buildings and homes or biofuels for modern vehicles. Where waste does make it to landfill sites, methane can be extracted to generate electricity, reducing release into the atmosphere of a greenhouse gas (GHG) that is 21 times more potent than carbon dioxide. Landfill gas produces electricity in many U.S. cities, in São Paulo in Brazil, and in Riga in Latvia, and it meets nearly two thirds of power demand for lighting in Monterrey, Mexico.[38]

Waste can also be treated in anaerobic digesters, which break down almost any organic material—from paper and yard waste to garbage and municipal sewage—into compostable solids, liquid fertilizer, and a gaseous fuel that can be carried or piped to stoves, heaters, electric turbines, and any device fueled by natural gas. Most poor people in the developing world spend at least 20 percent of their monthly incomes on fuel for cooking. But low-cost, household-sized digesters fed with feedstock readily available in urban areas can displace dung or firewood, reducing pressure on local forests while providing families with a smoke-free and healthier environment. And a Tanzanian study found that biogas could save five hours of household labor daily, giving women and children more time for productive activities.[39]

On a larger scale, many industrial-country cities—including Frankfurt, Vienna, and Zurich—are converting waste to gas for energy. In early

2006, San Francisco launched a pilot project to produce power from dog waste after finding that it accounted for nearly 4 percent of the residential garbage collected. Oslo, Norway, has perhaps the largest system in the world that uses raw sewage to produce space and water heating. Heat is drawn from the sewer and transferred to a network of water pipes that feed thousands of radiators and faucets throughout the city. And the Swedish coastal city of Helsingborg runs its buses on biogas made from local organic wastes. New technologies can convert even inorganic materials—from hospital and industrial wastes to car tires—into electricity and transport fuels.[40]

Although the potential is limited in urban areas, even wind and water can provide some cities with much-needed energy. Wind energy, in particular, faces visual and resource siting constraints, but these challenges have not always discouraged its use. Tokyo has installed 2.5 megawatts of wind turbines along its waterfront, and in May 2005 an electricians' union installed the first commercial wind turbine in Boston, which will provide electricity for its regional training center. Cities along coastlines or large water bodies can tap local resources from new directions, helping to alleviate transmission constraints. The Middelgrunden Windfarm off the coast of Copenhagen meets 4 percent of the city's electricity needs and is the world's largest cooperatively owned wind power project.[41]

Both New York and San Francisco have proposed projects to use marine energy for power. And some cities are literally tapping local water sources for cooling. Paris pumps water from the Seine River to run air-conditioning systems, and Toronto uses the deep, frigid waters of Lake Ontario for district cooling. Toronto's system has enough capacity to cool 3.2 million square meters of office space, or the equivalent of 100 office towers.[42]

Although few cities will meet all their energy needs with distributed renewable resources in the foreseeable future, some urban areas are already doing so. A new district with 1,000 dwellings in Malmö, Sweden, meets 100 percent of its electricity needs with solar and wind power, gets its heat from sea and rock strata and from the sun, and fuels its vehicles with biogas from local refuse and sewage. The planned Chinese eco-city on Dongtan Island will tap similar resources for an expected population of 500,000 by 2040.[43]

Energy efficiency improvements in building design, proper orientation and materials, and more-efficient end-use technologies facilitate the use of renewable energy for two reasons. First, because the scale becomes more manageable, renewables can meet a city's energy needs more easily; second, as a city reduces its demand for energy, it is in a better position to bear the higher costs per unit of output that come with many renewable technologies today.[44]

While renewable energy technologies are capital-intensive, they have low to zero fuel costs, reducing exposure to fluctuations in fossil fuel prices. They have far lower impacts on air, soil, and water and, as a result, on human health than conventional fuels and technologies. And they can provide a reliable and secure supply of power. An analysis of the 2003 blackout in the U.S. Northeast found that a few hundred megawatts of PV generation strategically placed in and around the major cities involved would have reduced the risk of the power outages dramatically.[45]

Renewables also provide local control over energy supply and generate valuable tax revenue and local jobs—one of the most pressing concerns of city mayors, according to a 1997 U.N. Development Programme survey. Approximately 170,000 new jobs in Germany are attributed to the renewable energy industry. About 250,000 Chinese are employed in the solar heating industry, and the biogas industry has created more than 200,000 jobs in India. Further, renewables can provide energy services where many conventional technologies do not or cannot go—into the homes and communities of the very poorest people.[46]

PIONEERING CITIES

While cities face formidable challenges in reforming energy generation and use, many are taking bold steps in this direction—ranging from daily municipal operations to special events and gatherings.... Their actions demonstrate at practical levels which policies have proved most effective in a variety of conditions of economic wealth, natural resource endowment, and cultural and political heritage. They also indicate the vital role that cities can play in reducing greenhouse gas emissions and averting climate change.[47]

In Barcelona, Spain, after the Green Party won in city council elections it introduced strong policies to support renewable energy and reduce reliance on nuclear power. The primary focus has been on developing the city's solar energy potential—which is 10 times as large as its total energy demand. From 1995 to 1999, demonstration projects and stakeholder consultations took place to develop policy and a realistic timeline for industry compliance.[48]

In 2000, the Barcelona city council mandated that solar water heating provide 60 percent of hot water in new and substantially refurbished buildings. Less than four years after enactment of the Solar Ordinance, installed solar capacity in Barcelona had grown nearly twelvefold; by April 2004, the city's solar water heating systems saved the equivalent of almost 16 megawatt-hours of energy a year, reducing CO_2 emissions by 2.8 tons annually. The city has since extended the requirements to even more buildings. By early 2006, more than 70 Spanish cities and municipalities had adopted solar water heating ordinances; following their lead, the national government has enacted a similar policy.[49]

In other cities where governments encourage increased local reliance on green power, one popular mechanism is quota systems, which require that a growing amount of municipal or community energy be obtained from renewable resources, with market forces competing to identify the most economical projects. Often referred to as renewable portfolio standards, these policies can apply to public or private energy utilities. The publicly owned Sacramento Municipal Utility District in California—building on its long-running commitment to green energy—aims to derive 23 percent of its electricity supply from renewable resources by 2011. And to encourage local PV installations by residential, commercial, and industrial customers, the utility offers incentive payments for every watt installed.[50]

Cities served by privately owned utilities or other actors over which the municipality has little control must often follow other strategies. In 1995 and 1999, Chicago sweltered under serious heat waves that brought rolling blackouts and hundreds of local deaths. Following a $100-million settlement with the private utility ComEd due to the outages, the city chose to apply the funds it received toward greater sustainability in local energy use in order to reduce the likelihood and impact of future blackouts. In 2001, Chicago negotiated a new power purchase agreement with ComEd, requiring the utility to provide 20 percent of the city government's electricity from renewable sources by 2006 (although that was later changed to 2010).[51]

Through these and other initiatives, Chicago has started a campaign to become "the most environmentally friendly city in America." As of 2004, new or substantially refurbished public buildings must meet Leadership in Energy and Environmental Design (LEED) certification as defined by the U.S. Green Building Council. Retrofits of municipal buildings totaling 1.4 million square meters (15 million square feet) could save the city $6 million in energy costs annually.[52]

Chicago's vision for change is not only bearing economic fruit, it is also altering the very texture of the urban environment. Green roofs have sprouted to life atop City Hall and on more than 232,000 square meters (2.5 million square feet) of residential and commercial structures. Some 250,000 trees planted over the last decade offer shade and beauty to local neighborhoods. In effect, a city long known for its industrial heritage is preparing to seize the next wave of global economic opportunity—one linked explicitly to "green" and "clean" development.[53]

Another option for cities with private utilities is evident in the growing movement for governments to help a collection of communities meet their energy needs. In the United States, for example, cities and towns in California, Massachusetts, New Jersey, Ohio, and Rhode Island are now authorized to do this for local government, area homes, and businesses, thanks to recent regulatory changes. In turn, localities may shop among a range of energy options. This community aggregation may allow cities to set more-stringent rules for energy efficiency and renewables than federal or state standards as a condition of utility contracts.[54]

Beyond the issue of municipal control and local utility ownership, some cities seek clean local power as a way to keep pace with the demands of an industrializing society. Since 2000, Daegu in South Korea has pursued increasingly comprehensive urban planning that links renewable energy with local economic development. During the 1997–98 Asian economic crises, the devaluation of South Korea's currency contributed to a doubling of energy prices due to the nation's large reliance on imported energy. Against the backdrop of high population density and rapid urbanization, this focused attention on Daegu's need to alter its energy model.[55]

Daegu has established a goal of local renewables meeting 5 percent of its total energy demand by 2010, with long-term targets set through 2050. In addition, the Center for Solar City Daegu, a joint effort of the municipality and Kyungpook National University, is working to disseminate green technologies. These include PV and solar water heating installations at schools, on the university campus, and at sewage and water treatment facilities. To help homeowners install solar roof systems, the city and national government are funding up to 80 percent of installation costs. Strong citizen participation has been reinforced by municipal leadership in Daegu.[56]

The need to address environmental threats while widening social access to critical energy services is driving efforts in Mexico City—home to 20 million people in the metro area—where a cloud of haze relentlessly shrouds views of surrounding mountains. In 1998, the World Resources Institute named Mexico City "the most dangerous city in the world for children" because of its poor air quality, and the city remains among the world's most polluted urban areas.[57]

In 2002, officials finally addressed this situation when they enacted a range of policies that are now organized under Mexico City's Proaire initiative for climate protection. Energy efficiency improvements are being achieved through the installation of advanced light bulbs in 30,000 new residential units and 45,000 existing homes. Solar heating systems are due to be installed in some 50,000 residences. Financial supporters of Proaire include local electric and water utilities, the World Bank, corporate foundations, the Chicago Climate Exchange, and nonprofit organizations.[58]

Since 2003, Cape Town in South Africa has sought to advance energy efficiency and renewable energy as a way to bring basic electricity service to poor, underserved neighborhoods and to reduce the impact of a national power shortage that is expected to begin in 2007. The municipal government aims for 10 percent of its energy to come from renewables by 2020 and has begun energy audits and efficiency retrofits at public facilities. In the Kuyasa region of the city, a pilot project under the Clean Development Mechanism (CDM) of the Kyoto Protocol, which aims to reduce GHG emissions in developing countries, has insulated ceilings and provided residents with solar water heaters and compact fluorescent bulbs. The GHG reductions earned Kuyasa Gold Standard CDM recognition in 2005 for exceptional standards in sustainable design.[59]

Numerous other cities are adopting goals and programs that support sustainable energy systems. (See Table 5.1.) And many cities have united to form larger networks that can pursue green energy development for both climate protection and urban quality of life. In many ways their collaboration—as well as the actions of regional and state governments—reflects an effort to act in place of national governments and the international community, which to date have largely failed to resolve major problems associated with conventional energy use.[60]

Examples of these networks include the U.S. Mayors' Climate Protection Agreement, which encourages cities to lobby the federal government for a national climate change policy, and the Cities for Climate Protection Campaign of ICLEI-Local Governments for Sustainability, which focuses on the design and use of climate-related policies among some 650 participating local governments. Through such partnerships, city officials are able to share best practices and encourage ongoing municipal leadership. And a few governments are now stepping forward to reinforce these efforts. For example, the Australian government has

TABLE 5.1 Selected Municipal Energy Targets

City	Target
Beijing, China	Reduce energy intensity of the city's economic output by 32 percent between 2004 and 2010
Berlin, Germany	Reduce energy use in public buildings 30 percent by 2010; incorporate solar water heating into 75 percent of new buildings annually
Copenhagen, Denmark	Energy audits required for buildings exceeding 1,500 square meters; all new buildings must rely on district heating (electric heating banned)
Freiburg, Germany	10 percent of all public and private electricity must come from renewable sources by 2010
Leicester, United Kingdom	Reduce municipal building energy use 50 percent from 1990 level by 2025
Melbourne, Australia	Increase municipal use of renewable energy by 50 percent from 1996 levels and private use by 22 percent by 2010
Oxford, United Kingdom	10 percent of homes must use solar hot water or PV by 2010
Portland, Oregon, United States	100 percent green power for municipal government by 2010; all new city-owned construction to meet LEED Gold certification
Tokyo, Japan	Minimum 5-percent renewable energy use in large municipal facilities starting in 2004; renewables proposed to supply 20 percent of total energy by 2020

See endnote 60.

funded a national independent ICLEI office, which involves 216 councils representing 87 percent of Australia's population.[61]

The International Solar Cities Initiative, created to address climate change through effective actions in cities, has devised an explicit target to guide "pathfinder" cities toward major GHG emissions reductions. The target was established by estimating how much greenhouse gas each person on Earth can emit annually without overwhelming the ability of the atmosphere and biosphere to absorb it. The target for 2050 is about 3.3 tons CO_2-equivalent per person. This is about as much as the average person in China or Argentina emits today.[62]

LIGHTING THE WAY

Cities have great potential to influence change. This power comes not only from the more manageable scale of local population and energy use but also from their role as national and regional seats of political power. Cities also frequently represent centers of political and technological innovation, where constituents are closer to these seats of power and thus retain more influence over policy-makers. And because powerful industries do not wield the same influence at the local level as at national or regional levels, cities can provide a more even playing field for all. Under such conditions, supporters of clean power and related alternatives may find it easier to introduce groundbreaking changes in cities.

Given that local renewable energy development can yield significant benefits, what is standing in the way of change? One major obstacle is the limited resources available to pursue local initiatives. As noted, there are numerous options for minimizing energy use and increasing reliance on clean power, but cities need financial, technical, and administrative support to pursue these strategies. Although this is more commonly a problem in the developing world, it is also a constraint among municipalities in industrial countries.

Investment priorities deserve particular attention in the world's poorest urban areas. To help achieve more balanced, sustainable economic development that simultaneously meets people's needs, nongovernmental organizations (NGOs) and community groups can encourage governments to link clean energy access to poverty alleviation. Bilateral and multilateral program funding must also move more quickly from fossil fuels toward renewables. Initiatives under the CDM and related global programs could be used more frequently for energy projects that reduce GHG emissions.[63]

The second fundamental challenge is posed by national and international politics. For decades, conventional fuels and technologies have received the lion's share of global investment in energy infrastructure. In 2002, the World Council for Renewable Energy noted that the $300 billion of energy subsidies spent every year on nuclear power and fossil fuels is four times as much as has been spent promoting renewable energies in the last two decades. This trend is all too evident, for example, in the Bush administration's push for next-generation nuclear and "clean" coal technologies, in efforts to boost nuclear power in India and China, and in subsidies used by some developing countries to support fuels like kerosene and diesel, which make renewable energy less competitive. Countering these developments is going to require a political commitment to clear, mandatory targets for renewable energy use and for technology research and development.[64]

A third barrier is market pressures that ignore environmental and social costs and benefits in energy prices. As a result, development of green energy remains at a disadvantage beyond the most immediately profitable niches, such as wind generation as a hedge against volatile natural gas prices. This is particularly clear in areas where the electricity sector has been privatized over the last decade, where governments have often found it necessary to impose firm renewable energy goals for retail electric providers in order to ensure green power's continued advance. Such actions highlight national governments' crucial role in correcting for prices and market structures that fail to signal the true costs of conventional fuels.[65]

The effect of market pressure is also apparent in the priorities of most electric utilities, which focus on expanding supply rather than conservation to meet customers' needs. "Negawatts"—electricity that is never actually produced or sold—would be a viable energy service to consumers if more governments introduced regulations that encouraged utilities to pursue conservation.[66]

The issue of pricing and costs also plagues the building sector. Although developers in cities like Chicago now have trouble finding the requisite "anchor" tenants if a new building does not meet certain voluntary green standards, this is rarely the case in other municipalities. Energy costs often represent only a small share of overall business or household expenses, and cost savings from efficiency measures are not always reflected in conventional accounting. As a result, price signals fail to drive change.[67]

Another fundamental challenge involves altering the common skepticism that even a large number of small-scale, local renewable systems combined with conservation and efficiency will ever be able to produce enough energy to meet the demands of a large city. To some extent, such mindsets are starting to change, as evident in the growing movement toward more sustainable cities and in recent efforts by former President Bill Clinton to encourage climate protection in some of the world's largest urban centers.[68]

Yet a great deal remains to be done in cities. As one example, despite some policy efforts to encourage or require green construction, the typical new U.S. home still remains highly energy-inefficient, requiring 30–70 percent more energy than new "advanced" green homes. This gap points to the need for larger awareness of the long-term gains, both ecological and economic, that can be achieved through more ambitious mandates for sustainable practices. In effect, a paradigm shift is needed—one that embraces radical improvements in energy efficiency, with the remaining demand met primarily by renewable energy.[69]

Relevant actors and institutions—from all levels of government to the finance sector—must consider new ways of evaluating the life-cycle costs and benefits of renewable energy and of building design that considers local conditions and uses local knowledge. This will mean involving the authorities that have the most power to mandate new requirements and monitor enforcement. It can also ensure the institutional capacity —in the form of financing for "green" home improvements, for example—to assist people who participate in efficiency and renewable energy programs.[70]

Contrary to some people's perceptions, many sustainability goals can be pursued through policies that do not increase taxpayers' costs, as in Chicago, where green buildings receive expedited permitting. City planners can incorporate the "new urbanism"—which involves building for people rather than cars—and related planning approaches for mixed-use communities that combine residential and commercial space. This can minimize energy use and suburban sprawl while making city life more sustainable and enhancing the overall quality of life.[71]

In addition to education and public awareness campaigns, political pressure must be brought to bear against powerful forces that favor the status quo. Positive changes in the energy sector, particularly in the world's poorest urban areas, will require action from not only municipal authorities but also regional, provincial, and national governments as well as NGOs and aid and lending institutions. (See Table 5.2.)[72]

TABLE 5.2 Roadmaps for Powering Cities Locally

Obstacle	Strategic Response
Lack of control over energy sector	Municipal government can set targets for its own green energy use, procure goods and services made with local green power, aggregate customer demand, and form power purchase agreements with utilities. Municipal government can target energy efficiency and conservation in public and private buildings by requiring energy audits and mandating use of specific technologies and construction practices, through city planning and permitting. Citizens can form cooperatives for local energy development or purchase green power.
Lack of widespread access to energy service (particularly common in low-income cities)	Governments can support pricing reform and commit to replanting trees to ensure wider availability of fuelwood and other biomass resources. Legalized secondary power arrangements can give urban dwellers access to power sources "owned" by other individuals, thereby avoiding or reducing otherwise prohibitive upfront fees (the utility can set basic technical standards to enhance safety of energy delivery, while the de facto electricity distributor determines rates). Reduced lifeline electricity tariffs (available to low-income users for lower levels of use) can spread out upfront fees (such as grid connection charges) into future payments over time.
Lack of funds or expertise to identify and undertake projects	Local actors (public or private) can partner with energy service companies or, in low- to moderate-income cities, bundle projects to leverage microfinance or multi- or bilateral assistance for the lease or purchase of solar water heaters, PV systems, and safer and more efficient stoves and smoke hoods.
Lack of awareness or understanding of benefits of local green energy or how to use technologies	Municipal government can work with local trade organizations, private-sector champions, and citizens' groups on information campaigns, product labeling, professional training, and school curricula. NGOs and community groups can sponsor demonstration projects.
Lack of utility involvement or of regional, national, or international emphasis on renewable energy development, energy efficiency, conservation, and GHG reductions	Municipal or grassroots efforts can coordinate lobbying across locales for changes in political priorities (toward regional or national targets and commitments) to include mandates for both public and private utilities. States and cities can develop and implement their own policies and band together in multi-state or multi-city agreements to set "de facto" policy.

Source: See endnote 72.

The challenge lies in moving beyond local voluntary partnerships toward strong intergovernmental and societal commitments for change. Wider civil society involvement will be critical and has already figured prominently in many recent movements for more-sustainable energy use in cities. Citizens' groups can do more by calling for national and international changes in investment priorities and can work with private financial institutions favoring clean energy as a profitable strategy for minimizing business risks from climate change.[73]

Today cities have an unprecedented opportunity to change the way they supply and use energy. New eco-cities such as Dongtan in China may show the way, even as existing cities turn to technologies rooted in the past—from adobe architecture to passive solar heating. When complemented by conservation, more-efficient technologies, and new decentralized, small-scale energy services, these efforts can help cities confidently navigate the forthcoming peak of cheap oil and natural gas production while reducing the impact of climate change. Energy transformation in cities can be the doorway to security and vitality in urban life.

NOTES

1. Real limits from John Byrne et al., "An Equity- and Sustainability-Based Policy Response to Global Climate Change," *Energy Policy*, March 1998, pp. 335–43.
2. Bridging to the Future, "How Have Energy Systems Shaped Cities Through History? Human Food Cities; Wood and Hay Cities; Coal Cities," at www.bridgingtothefuture.org, viewed 8 August 2006.
3. Tetsunari Iida, Institute for Sustainable Energy Policies, Tokyo, e-mail to Janet Sawin, 29 August 2006; New York most efficient from GreenHomeNYC, "For Tenants," 2003, at www.greenhomenyc.org/page/tenants.
4. India from "Underpowering," *The Economist*, 22 September 2005; China from Arno Rosemarin, United Nations Development Programme (UNDP), *China Human Development Report 2002: Making Green Development a Choice* (New York: Oxford University Press, 2002), p. 57.
5. Box 5-1 from the following: Emissions and 40 percent from U.N. Environment Programme (UNEP), International Environmental Technology Centre, *Energy and Cities: Sustainable Building and Construction* (Osaka, Japan: 2003); embodied energy of concrete from Alex Wilson, "Cement and Concrete: Environmental Considerations," *Environmental Building News*, March 1993, embodied energy of steel from Center for Building Performance Research, University of Wellington, "Table of Embodied Energy Coefficients," 7 July 2004, at www.vuw.ac.nz/cbpr/resources/index.aspx; San Francisco home based on 66.6 million Btus per household in Pacific region for space and water heating, cooling, refrigerators, lighting, and appliances, from U.S. Department of Energy (DOE), Energy Information Administration (EIA), "Total Energy Consumption in U.S. Households by West Census Region, 2001," updated 18 November 2004, at www.eia.doe.gov/emeu/recs/recs2001/ce_pdf/enduse/cel-12c-westregion2001.pdf; embodied energy of cement from Wilson, op. cit. this note; emissions from cement industry from Nadav Malin, "The Fly Ash Revolution: Making Better Concrete with Less Cement," *Environmental Building News*, June 1999; emissions in Japan from Carbon Dioxide Information Analysis Center, cited in UNDP, "Human Development Reports 2005—Indicators: Carbon Dioxide Emissions, Share of World Total," at hdr.undp.org/statistics/data/indicators.cfm?x=212&y=1&z=1; 15 percent from U.S. Environmental Protection Agency, "Cement and Concrete," updated 15 August 2006, at www.epa.gov/cpg/products/cement.htm; potential savings from Malin, op. cit. this note; Germany from World Resources Institute (WRI), *Climate Analysis Indicators Tool* (Washington, DC: 2003); lighter, stronger bricks from "Superior Building Products," University of New South Wales, New South Innovations (Sydney, Australia: June 2006); completely replacing cement from Doug Cross, Jerry Stephens, and Jason Vollmer, *Structural Applications of 100 Percent Fly Ash Concrete* (Billings, MT: Montana State University, 2005); benefits of local materials from Montana State Ibrahim Togola, Mali Folkecentre, "Sustainable Building of Local Materials in Sahel Countries of West Africa" (draft paper), sent to Janet Sawin, 4 August 2006; transportation share of embodied energy from Wilson, op. cit. this note; Big Dig waste from Raphael Lewis, "End Nears for Elevated Artery," *Boston Globe*, 14 April 2002;

"Man Builds Home From Big Dig Scrap Materials," *Associated Press*, 30 July 2006.

6. Effect on 50 million people and blackout in Italy from Alan Katz, "Maintaining Facility Power in the Age of the Blackout," *Electrical Construction and Maintenance*, 1 June 2004; cause and costs of August blackout from Electricity Consumers Resource Council, *The Economic Impacts of the August 2003 Blackouts* (Washington, DC: 2004).
7. Line losses from World Bank, *World Development Report 1997* (New York: Oxford University Press, 1997), from M. S. Bhalla, "Transmission and Distribution Losses (Power)," in *Proceedings of the National Conference on Regulation in Infrastructure Services: Progress and Way Forward* (New Delhi: The Energy and Resources Institute, 2000), and from Seth Dunn, *Micropower: The Next Electrical Era*, Worldwatch Paper 151 (Washington, DC: Worldwatch Institute, 2000), p. 46; New Delhi from John Lancaster, "Sniffing Out the Freeloaders Who Stress the Grid," *Washington Post*, 12 June 2006.
8. One fifth from World Bank, *Energy Poverty Issues and G8 Actions*, Discussion Paper (Washington, DC: 2 February 2006), p. 1; number could be higher from "Power to the Poor," *The Economist*, 8 February 2001; Africans from Bereket Kebede and Ikhupuleng Dube, "Chapter 1: Introduction," in Bereket Kebede and Ikhupuleng Dube, eds., *Energy Services for the Urban Poor in Africa: Issues and Policy Implications* (London: Zed Books in Association with the African Energy Policy Research Network, 2004), p. 1.
9. Millions of deaths from "Power to the Poor," op. cit. note 8; India, Sri Lanka, and Thailand from Emily Matthews et al., *The Pilot Analysis of Global Ecosystems: Forest Ecosystems* (WRI Washington, DC: 2000), Khartoum from Business in Africa, "Energy in Africa: Is There Energy for All?" 4 November 2005, p. 1.
10. Coal use from "Chapter 5: World Coal Markets," in EIA, *International Energy Outlook 2006* (Washington, DC: DOE, 2006); coal projections from International Energy Agency (IEA), *Key World Energy Statistics 2006* (Paris: 2006), p. 46; impact in China from Bill McKibben, "The Great Leap: Scenes from China's Industrial Revolution," *Harper's Magazine*, December 2005.
11. Cities account for 75 percent of world's fossil fuel consumption (and hence about 75 percent of energy-related emissions); see World Council for Renewable Energy (WCRE), "Renewable Energy and the City," discussion paper for World Renewable Energy Policy and Strategy Forum, Berlin, Germany, 13–15 June 2005.
12. Buildings more than 40 percent from UNEP, International Environmental Technology Centre, *Energy and Cities: Sustainable Building and Construction* (Osaka, Japan: 2003), p. 1; U.S. buildings from Greg Franta, "High-Performance Buildings Through Integrated Design," *RMI Solutions*, summer 2006, p. 6, and from Greg Franta, Rocky Mountain Institute, e-mail to Stephanie Kung, Worldwatch Institute, 20 September 2006.
13. Shanghai from David Barboza, "China Builds Its Dreams, and Some Fear a Bubble," *New York Times*, 18 October 2005; China urban infrastructure from McKibben, op. cit. note 10.
14. Lighting from IEA, "Light's Labour's Lost—Policies for Energy-Efficient Lighting," press release (Paris: 29 June 2006); Eric Corey Freed, "Ask the Green Architect: Mirrors for Lighting; Radiant Heating for Floors; Efficient Exit Signs," Green-Biz.com, undated; Jonathan Rider, *Light Shelves*, Advanced Buildings, Technologies and Practices (Ottawa, ON: Natural Resources Canada and Public Works and Government Services Canada); glass from Rick Cook, Partner, Cook + Fox Architects, interview on "The Green Apple," *Design* E^2, U.S. Public Broadcasting System series, summer 2006.
15. Incandescent bulbs and compact fluorescents from DOE, Office of Energy Efficiency and Renewable Energy (EERE), "Technology Fact Sheet: Improved Lighting," GHG Management Workshop, 25–26 February 2003, pp. 1–2; DOE, EERE, "Energy Efficient Lighting and Light Emitting Diodes," fact sheet (Richland, WA: May 2006); DOE, EERE, "LED Traffic Lights Save Energy in Idaho," *Conservation Update*, May–June 2004.
16. Ceilings in South Africa from Randall Spalding-Fecher et al., "The Economics of Energy Efficiency for the Poor—A South Africa Case Study," *Energy*, December 2002, pp. 1099–117.
17. Combined heat and power efficiency from DOE, EERE, "Distributed Energy Resources: Combined Heat & Power Program for Buildings, Industry and District Energy," at www.eere.energy.gov/de/pdfs/chp_buildings_industry_district.pdf, viewed 15 July 2006; Verdesian, 80 percent or higher, and typical fossil fuel plant from Robin Pogrebin, "Putting Environmentalism on the

Urban Map," *New York Times*, 17 May 2006; typical plant efficiency also from DOE, Office of Fossil Energy, "DOE Launches Project to Improve Materials for Supercritical Coal Plants," press release (Pittsburgh, PA: 16 October 2001).

18. Radiant heating from DOE, EERE, Office of Energy Efficiency and Renewable Energy, "Radiant Heating," updated 12 September 2005; Romans from Freed, op. cit. note 14; Hewlett building from The William and Flora Hewlett Foundation, "The Hewlett Foundation Building: Energy Efficiency," (Menlo Park, CA: updated 23 August 2005), and from Stephanie Kung, Worldwatch Institute, personal observations.
19. Cooling in China from National Renewable Energy Laboratory, *Renewable Energy in China: Development of the Geothermal Heat Pump Market in China* (Golden, CO: 2006); Tokyo and Houston from David J. Sailor and Chittaranjan Vasireddy, "Correcting Aggregate Energy Consumption Data to Account for Variability in Local Weather," *Environmental Modelling & Software*, May 2006, p. 733.
20. Susan Roaf and Mary Hancock, "Future-Proofing Buildings Against Climate Change Using Traditional Building Technologies in the Mediterranean Region," *EuroSun 98*, II.1.13, pp. 1–7.
21. M Santamouris, "Special Issue of the Solar Energy Program Devoted to Natural Ventilation in Urban Areas" (editorial), *Solar Energy*, April 2006, pp. 369–70; EPA, "Heat Island Effect—What Can Be Done—Trees & Vegetation," fact sheet (Washington, DC: 9 June 2006).
22. Cool roof savings from Hashem Akbari, "Estimating Energy Saving Potentials of Heat Island Mitigation Measures," Heat Island Group, Lawrence Berkeley National Laboratory, Power-Point presentation, updated 16 June 1999.
23. EPA, op. cit. note 21; Madrid study and heat island reductions from Susana Saiz et al., "Comparative Life Cycle Assessment of Standard and Green Roofs," *Environmental Science & Technology*, 1 July 2006, pp. 4312–16; heat island and smog reductions from Akbari, op. cit. note 22.
24. Less than half from DOE, EERE, "Technology Fact Sheet: Resources for Whole Building Design," GHG Management Workshop, 25–26 February 2003, p. 11; savings up to 80 percent from James Read, associate director, Arup Communications, on "Deeper Shades of Green," *Design E*^{2}, op. cit. note 14; savings in energy and construction costs from Franta, "High-Performance Buildings," op. cit. note 12, p. 7; Accord 21 Building from Robert Watson, senior scientist, Natural Resources Defense Council, on "China: From Red to Green?" *Design E*^{2}, op. cit. note 14.
25. Healthier, more comfortable occupants and greater worker productivity from Gregory H. Kats, "Green Budding Costs and Financial Benefits," Massachusetts Technology Collaborative, 2003, p. 6, from Judith Heerwagen, "Sustainable Design Can Be an Asset to the Bottom Line," *Environmental Design + Construction*, 15 July 2002, and from DOE, op. cit. note 24, p. 11; reduced turnover from "Study: Environmentally Friendly Buildings Also Most Market Friendly," Greenbiz.com, 31 October 2005; Heschong Mahone Group, "Day-lighting in Schools: An Investigation into the Relationship Between Daylighting and Human Performance," prepared for the California Board for Energy Efficiency (Fair Oaks, CA: 20 August 1999); Warren E. Hathaway et al., *A Study into the Effects of Light on Children of Elementary School Age—A Case Study of Daylight Robbery* (Edmonton, AB: Policy and Planning Branch, Planning and Information Services Division, Alberta Education, 1992); bank building from Nicholas Lenssen and David Roodman, *A Building Revolution*, Worldwatch Paper 124 (Washington, DC: Worldwatch Institute, 1994), p. 45; more than 10 times the benefits from Kats, op. cit. this note, p. 8; and from U.S. Green Building Council, "Green Buildings by the Numbers," 2006, at www.usgbc.org/DisplayPage.aspx? CMS PageID=1442; costs falling from Kats, op. cit. this note, p. 3.
26. One year payback from Franta, "High-Performance Buildings," op. cit. note 12, p. 7; retrofit projects from Jiang Lin et al., *Developing an Energy Efficiency Service Industry in Shanghai* (Berkeley, CA: Lawrence Berkeley National Laboratory, 2004), pp. 2, 17.
27. Anuj Chopra, "Low-cost Lamps Brighten the Future of Rural India," *Christian Science Monitor*, 3 January 2006.
28. John Perlin, "Solar Evolution: The History of Solar Energy," California Solar Center, 2005, at www.californiasolarcenter.org/history_passive.html; Babylon from The Garland Company, "History of Green Roofs," at www.garlandco.com/green-roof-history.html, viewed 9 August 2006.
29. Edison and evolution of industry from Dunn, op. cit. note 7, pp. 6, 11, 13–14.
30. For microturbines, see, for example, Wilson TurboPower, Inc., "The Wilson Microturbine," at www.wilsonturbopower.com; fuel cells already

producing power from Joel N. Swisher, *Cleaner Energy, Greener Profits: Fuel Cells as Cost-Effective Distributed Energy Resources* (Snowmass, CO: Rocky Mountain Institute, 2002), p. 12; Susan Nasr, "More Powerful Fuel Cells Get Closer to Market," *Technology Review*, 13 June 2006.

31. Energy & Enviro Finland, "Utilizing Biogas as a Fuel: Wartsila Fuel Cell Unit to Power the City of Vaasa," 15 June 2006.
32. Renewables from REN21 Renewable Energy Policy Network, *Executive Summary: Renewables Global Status Report 2006 Update* (Washington, DC: Worldwatch Institute, 2006), wind, solar, and biofuels from Worldwatch Institute, *Vital Signs 2006–2007* (New York: W. W. Norton & Company, 2006), pp. 36–41.
33. Cheaper for budding facades from Steven Strong, "Solar Electric Buildings: PV as a Distributed Resource," *Renewable Energy World*, July–August 2002, p. 171; Europe from "BIPV Technology," Wisconsin Public Service, University of Wisconsin, at www.buildingsolar.com/technology.asp; use elsewhere from Natural Resources Canada, *Technologies and Applications—Photovoltaic: Integrating Photovoltaic Arrays in Buildings* (Ottawa, ON: updated 26 July 2006); potential in Finland, Australia, and United States (adjusted for the fact that it was based on 1998 electricity consumption data and conservative estimates for available rooftops and facades and for solar resources) from IEA, *Summary: Potential for Building Integrated Photovoltaics* (Paris: 2002), p. 8.
34. UNDP, Equator Initiative, "Solar City—Germany," August 2000, at www.tve.org/ho/doc.cfm?aid=657, viewed 23 September 2006; David Faiman, "Solar Energy in Israel," Ben-Gurion University of the Negev, Sde Boker, Israel, 26 November 2002; fuel savings from Environmental and Energy Study Institute, "Renewable Energy Fact Sheet: Solar Water Heating—Using the Sun's Energy to Heat Water" (Washington, DC: May 2006); China solar energy from REN21, *Renewables Global Status Report 2006 Update* (Paris and Washington, DC: REN21 Secretariat and Worldwatch Institute, 2006); China's driver from Zijun Li, "Solar Energy Booming in China," *China Watch*, 23 September 2005.
35. P. J. Hughes and J. A. Shonder, *The Evaluation of a 4000 Home Geothermal Heat Pump Retrofit at Fort Polk, Louisiana: Final Report* (*Oak Ridge*, TN: Oak Ridge National Laboratory, March 1998), p. 2; Beijing Linked Hybrid Project from Li Hu, Partner, Steven Holl Architects, on "China: From Red to Green?" *Design* E^2, op. cit. note 14.
36. Pompeii and list of countries from Geothermal Education Office, "Geothermal Energy," slideshow, funded by DOE, undated; Paris from European Renewable Energy Council, "Joint Declaration for a European Directive to Promote Renewable Heating and Cooling," Brussels, undated, p. 8.
37. New York waste and shipped to Ohio from Timothy Gardner, "Hot Trash-to-Fuel Technology Gathering Steam," *Reuters*, 27 February 2004; disposal costs as of 2002 from Steven Cohen, "Putting Garbage to Good Use," *New York Times*, 15 August 2002; increasing waste in industrial countries from Euiyoung Yoon and Sunghan Jo, "Municipal Solid Waste Management in Tokyo and Seoul," Proceedings of Workshop of IGES/APN Mega-City Project, Kitakyushu, Japan, 23–25 January 2002, p. 1; developing countries, garbage burned or left to rot, and impacts from "Hazardous Waste: Special Reference to Municipal Solid Waste Management," in The Energy and Resources Institute, *India: State of the Environment 2001* (Delhi: 2001), pp. 133–41; 90 percent not collected from UNEP, "At a Glance: Waste," *Our Planet*, 1999.
38. Methane potency from EPA, "Global Warming—Emissions," at Yosemite.epa.gov/OAR/globalwarming.nsf/content/Emissions.html; U.S. cities from Daniela Chen, "Converting Trash Gas into Energy Gold," CNN.com, 17 July 2006; Sao Paulo and Riga from Carl R. Bartone, Horacio Terraza, and Francisco Grajales-Cravioto, "Opportunities for LFGTE Projects in LAC Utilizing International Carbon Financing," World Bank, presentation at LMOP 8th Annual Conference, Baltimore, MD, 10–11 January 2005; Cheryl Smith, "Monterrey Plans to Turn Rotting Garbage into Electricity," *Christian Science Monitor*, 21 March 2002.
39. Incomes spent on cooking fuel from Christopher Flavin and Molly Hull Aeck, *Energy for Development: The Potential Role of Renewable Energy in Meeting the Millennium Development Goals* (Washington, DC: Worldwatch Institute, 2005), p. 17; Innocent Rutamu, "Low Cost Biodigesters for Zero Grazing Smallholder Diary Farmers in Tanzania," *Livestock Research for Rural Development*, July 1999.
40. European cities and San Francisco from "San Francisco to Test Turning Dog Waste into Power," *Reuters*, 23 February 2006; Alister Doyle, "Oslo's Sewage Heats Its Homes," *Reuters*, 10 April

2006; Helsingborg from Michael D. Lemonick, "Cleaner Air Over Scandinavia," *Time*, 3 April 2006, p. 47; hospital and industrial wastes to electricity from Timothy Gardner, "Hot Trash-to-Fuel Technology Gathering Steam," *Reuters*, 27 February 2006, "$84 Million for the First Tires-to-Ethanol Facility," RenewableEnergy Accesscom, 23 March 2006.

41. "Tokyo Embraces Renewable Energy," *Environment News Service*, 6 April 2006; "Boston's First Wind Turbine Serves as Example," Renewable EnergyAccess.com, 18 May 2005; Middelgrunden Wind Turbine Cooperative, "The Middelgrunden Offshore Wind Farm—A Popular Initiative," un dated, at www.middelgrunden.dk/MG_UK/project_info/mg_pjece.htm.

42. New York and San Francisco from Jeff Johnson, "Power from Moving Water," *Chemical and Engineering News*, 4 October 2004, and from Adam Aston, "Here Comes Lunar Power," *Business Week*, 6 March 2006; Paris from Doyle, op. cit. note 40; "Deep Lake Water Cooling: Chilled Water for Cooling Toronto's Buildings," at www.enwave.com/enwave/view.asp?/dlwc/energy, viewed 6 August 2006.

43. Environment Department, City of Malmo, "100 Percent Locally Renewable Energy in the Western Harbour of Malmo in Sweden," *ICLEI in Europe: Cities in Action—Good Practice Examples*, at www.iclei-europe.org; Dongtan from Fred Pearce, "Eco-cities Special: A Shanghai Surprise," *New Scientist*, 21 June 2006; expected population from Jean-Pierre Langellier and Brice Pedroletti, "China to Build First Eco-city," *The Guardian Weekly*, 2006.

44. Janet L. Sawin, "National Policy Instruments: Policy Lessons for the Advancement & Diffusion of Renewable Energy Technologies Around the World," background paper prepared for Secretariat of the International Conference of Renewable Energies, Bonn, Germany, January 2004, p. 24.

45. Blackout from Richard Perez et al., "Solution to the Summer Blackouts? How Dispersed Solar Power-Generating Systems Can Help Prevent the Next Major Outage," *Solar Today*, July/August 2005, and from Richard Perez, Atmospheric Sciences Research Center, State University of New York at Albany, e-mail to Janet Sawin, 3 October 2006.

46. UNDP survey from Molly O'Meara, *Reinventing Cities for People and the Planet*, Worldwatch Paper 147 (Washington, DC: 1999), p. 57; Germany from Preben Maegaard, "Wind, Not Nuclear!—Why Does the UK Not Take This Opportunity?" WCRE, July 2006: China's solar heating industry from REN21 Renewable Energy Policy Network. *Renewables 2005 Global Status Report* (Washington, DC: Worldwatch Institute, 2005), pp. 24–25; India's biogas industry from Institute of Science in Society, "Biogas Bonanza for Third World Development," press release (London: 20 June 2005).

47. Box 5-2 from the following: event statistics and Olympics overview from The Hon. Tom Roper, "The Environmental Challenge of Major Events," presented at the Eighth World Congress Metropolis, Berlin, Germany, 2005, pp. 1–2, 6, and from Tom Roper, "Producing Environmentally Sustainable Olympic Games and Greening Major Public Events," *Global Urban Development Magazine*, March 2006; additional Beijing data from Environment News Service, "Beijing Enlists U.S. Help to Green the 2008 Olympic Games," 18 April 2005, p. 1; World Cup data from Federation Internationale de Football Association (FIFA), "Green Goal™: Environmental Protection Targets," Zurich, 2005; renewable sources from FIFA, "Sunny Days Ahead in Kaiserslautern," Zurich, 26 May 2006.

48. Forum Barcelona, "Imma Mayol: The Closure of Nuclear Power Stations in Catalonia is One of the Prime Objectives to Be Carried Out in the Next 15 Years, in Terms of Defining a New Energy Model," 2004; Ajuntament de Barcelona, *Plan for Energy Improvement in Barcelona* (Barcelona: 2002); elections, sunlight and energy equivalent, demonstration, and timeline from Pamela Stirzaker, "Spain's Chain Reaction: Municipal Obligations Spur on Solar Thermal Growth," *Renewable Energy World*, September–October 2004, pp. 2–3, and from Josep Puig i Boix, "The Barcelona Solar Ordinance: A Case Study About How the Impossible Became Reality," presented at the International Sustainable Energy Organization Special Session, World Summit for Sustainable Development, Johannesburg, South Africa, 28 August 2002.

49. Toni Pujol, Barcelona Energy Agency, "The Barcelona Solar Thermal Ordinance: Evaluation and Results," presented at the 9th Annual Conference of Energie-Cités, Martigny, 22–23 April 2004; expanded requirements from REN21, op. cit. note 34, p. 10; more than 70 cities and national government from European Solar Thermal Industry Federation, "Spain Approves National

Solar Thermal Obligation," at www.estif.org, viewed 7 July 2006, and from REN21, op. cit. note 34.

50. Sacramento Municipal Utility District (SMUD), "EBSS Solicitations-Solicitation Detail," at www.bids.smud.org/sDsp/sDsp004.asp?solicitation_id=2195, viewed 19 September 2006; SMUD, "Solar for Your Home: PV Pioneers," at www.smud.org/green/solar/index.html, viewed 21 September 2006; from SMUD, "Solar Power for Your Business," at www.smud.org/green/solar/compv.html, viewed 21 September 2006.
51. Heat wave and ComEd settlement from Ken Regelson, *Sustainable Cities: Best Practices for Renewable Energy & Energy Efficiency* (Sierra Club-Rocky Mountain Chapter Denver, CO: 2005), pp. 10–15; 20 percent agreement from City of Chicago, Office of the Mayor and Department of Environment, *Energy Plan* (Chicago, IL: 2001); target year moved to 2010, for budgetary and contractual reasons, from Mike Johnson, project coordinator, City of Chicago Department of Energy, Environment and Air Quality, discussion with Kristen Hughes, 4 October 2006, and from SustainLane, "#4 Chicago: The Wind at its Back," at www.sustainlane.com/article/846, viewed 7 October 2006.
52. "Most environmentally friendly" from City of Chicago, "A Message from the Mayor," at www.cityofchicago.org/Transportation/bikemap, viewed 26 September 2006; Regelson, op. cit. note 51.
53. Kevin McCarthy, "Chicago Approves Big Grants for Green Roof Retrofits," Construction.com, 19 July 2006; trees from J. Slama, "Chicago Will Be America's Greenest City," *Conscious Choice*, April 2002.
54. David Engle, "With the Power at Hand: Examining the Merits of Distributed Energy," *Planning Magazine* (American Planning Association), July 2006; community aggregation impacts from Donald Aitken, Donald Aitken Associates, e-mail to Kristen Hughes, 4 September 2006.
55. Jong-dall Kim, Dong-hi Han, and Jung-gyu Na, "The Solar City Daegu 2050 Project: Visions for a Sustainable City," *Bulletin of Science, Technology & Society*, April 2006, pp. 99–100; financial crisis from EIA, "South Korea: Environmental Issues," at www.eia.doe.gov/emeu/cabs/skoren.html, viewed 9 August 2006.
56. Renewables goal from REN21, op. cit. note 46, p. 28; 2050 planning from Eric Martinot, "Solar City Case Study: Daegu, Korea," Renewable Energy Information on Markets, Policy, Investment, and Future Pathways, 2004, p. 1; Kim, Han, and Na, op. cit. note 55, pp. 98–99.
57. Population from Dejan Sudjic, "Making Cities Work: Mexico City," *BBC News*, 21 June 2006; haze from Michelle Hibler, "Taking Control of Air Pollution in Mexico City," *IDRC Reports*, 12 August 2003; "most dangerous" title from "New Center a Breath of Fresh Air for Mexico City," *Environment News Service*, 3 June 2002; remains among most polluted from EIA, "Mexico: Environmental Issues," at www.eia.doe.gov/emeu/cabs/mexenv.html, viewed 8 August 2006.
58. Proaire campaign and installation figures from The Climate Group, *Less Is More: 14 Pioneers in Reducing Greenhouse Gas Emissions* (Woking, Surrey, U.K.: 2004), p. 29; supporting organizations from The Climate Group, "Mexico City-Municipal Government," at www.theclimategroup.org/index.php?pid=427, viewed 5 August 2006.
59. The Climate Group, *Cape Town-Municipal Government* (Woking, Surrey, U.K.: undated), pp. 1–3; Gold Standard from Renewable Energy and Energy Efficiency Partnership (REEEP), "CDM Housing Project to Become Replicable Energy Savings Model for South Africa," at www.reeep.org/index.cfm?articleid=1198&ros=l, viewed 6 September 2006.
60. Table 5-1 from the following: "China's Capital Launches Plan to Save Sparse Energy for Sustainable Development," *People's Daily Online*, 7 June 2005; Berlin, Copenhagen, Melbourne, and Tokyo from The Climate Group, *Low Carbon Leader: Cities Oct. 2005* (Woking, Surrey, U.K.: 2005); Freiburg, Oxford, and Portland from Eric Martinot, "Index of Solar Cities," at www.martinot.info/solarcities, viewed 19 July 2006; Leicester from ICLEI, "Profiting from Energy Efficiency: 7.0 Best Municipal Practices for Energy Efficiency," at www.iclei.org/index.php?id=1677&0, viewed 11 July 2006; City of Portland, Resolution Adopted 27 April 2005, at www.portlandonline.com/osd/index.cfm?a=112681&c=41701, viewed 7 August 2006; Toronto Environmental Alliance, *Getting Green Power On-line in Toronto* (Toronto, ON: 2005); Tokyo Metropolitan Government Bureau of Environment, "Tokyo Renewable Energy Strategy," 3 April 2006, at www.isep.or.jp/e/Eng_project/TokyoREstrategy060526.pdf, viewed 20 July 2006.

61. U.S. Mayors' agreement and ICLEI from Wilson Rickerson and Kristen Hughes, "The Policy Framework for Greenhouse Gas Reductions in New York City," presented at the 2006 International Solar Cities Congress, Oxford, U.K., 4 April 2006; ICLEI, "About CCP," at www.iclei.org/index/php?id=811, viewed 19 September 2006; Office of the Mayor, *U.S. Mayors Climate Protection Agreement* (Seattle, WA: 2005); Australia ICLEI from Tom Roper, Project Leader, Global Sustainable Energy Islands Initiative, discussion with Kristen Hughes, 17 August 2006, and from Cities for Climate Protection® Australia, "About CCP Australia," at www.iclei.org/index.php?id=about, viewed 19 September 2006.
62. Target for pathfinders from International Solar Cities Initiative, "International Solar Cities Congress 2006," at www.solarcities.org.uk, viewed 19 July 2006; 3.3 tons from Byrne et al., op. cit. note 1; Argentina and China from United Nations Statistics Division, "Millennium Development Goals Indicators: Data Availability by Country," at millenniumindicators.un.org/unsd/mdg/default.aspx, viewed 19 September 2006.
63. Investment priorities from WCRE and Asia Pacific & Renewable Energy Foundation Limited, *Asia Pacific Renewable Energy and Sustainable Development Agenda 2004* (Bonn, Germany: 2004), pp. 4–6; initiatives in global programs from Practical Action, *Power to the People: Sustainable Energy Solutions for the World's Poor* (Rugby, U.K.: 2002), p. 8.
64. Subsidies from WCRE, *Action Plan for the Global Proliferation of Renewable Energy* (Bonn, Germany: 2002), p. 8, and from WCRE, "First World Renewable Energy Policy and Strategy Forum Successfully Carried Out," press release (Bonn, Germany: 18 June 2002); The White House, *Department of Energy—Overview: The Budget for Fiscal Tear 2005* (Washington, DC: 2005); India and China from Jon Gertner, "Atomic Balm?" *New Tork Times*, 16 July 2005; leadership from WCRE and Asia Pacific & Renewable Energy Foundation Limited, op. cit. note 63; Janet Sawin, "Charting a New Energy Future," in Worldwatch Institute, *State of the World 2003* (W. W. Norton & Company New York: 2003), p. 105.
65. Lori Bird et al., "Policies and Market Factors Driving Wind Power Development in the United States," *Energy Policy*, July 2005, p. 1405; electricity privatization from Kirsty Hamilton, "Finance and Investment: A Challenge of Scale," *Renewable Energy World*, September–October 2002.
66. Negawatts from Amory Lovins, "The Negawatt Revolution—Solving the CO_2 Problem," presented at Green Energy Conference, Montreal, 14–17 September 1989.
67. Anchor tenants from David Roeder, "Eco-Friendly Builders Starting to Grow," *Chicago Sun Times*, 20 February 2006; energy costs small share of expenses from Board of Governors of the Federal Reserve System, *Monetary Policy Report to the Congress* (Washington, DC: 19 July 2006), p. 20; savings not reflected in conventional accounting from Massachusetts Public Interest Research Group, "Testimony on Senate Bill 360: 'An Act To Promote An Energy Efficient Massachusetts,' Cost-Effective Solutions to Protect Consumers, Reduce Pollution, and Boost Our Economy," submitted 27 March 2001.
68. Juliet Eilperin, "22 Cities Join Clinton Anti-Warming Effort," *Washington Post*, 2 August 2006.
69. DOE, "Energy Savers: Homeowners," at www.energysavers.gov/homeowners.html, viewed 6 September 2006, and "Building Energy Efficient New Homes," at www.eere.energy.gov/buildings/info/homes/newconstruction.html, viewed 6 September 2006.
70. Local conditions and expertise from UNEP, op. cit. note 12, pp. 1, 3, 8–9; institutional capacity from Tom Roper, "5 Star Housing—Victoria, Australia: Performance Based Building Regulation Delivers Major Sustainability Outcomes," presented to Greenbuild 2005, Atlanta, GA, 9–11 November 2005, pp. 1, 5–7.
71. Chicago from Tom Roper, Project Leader, Global Sustainable Energy Islands Initiative, e-mail to Kristen Hughes, 21 August 2006, and from Chicago Department of Construction and Permits, *Green Permit Program* (Chicago: date unknown), p. 3; "New Urbanism: Creating Livable Sustainable Communities," at www.newurbanism.org, viewed 5 September 2006.
72. Table 5-2 from the following: Cooperatives from Paul Gipe, *Community Wind: The Third Way* (Toronto: Ontario Sustainable Energy Association, 2004); fuelwood pricing and replanting from Practical Action, *Energy: Working with Communities to Provide Appropriate Solutions* (Rugby, U.K.: 2006), p. 5; secondary power and lifeline tariffs from Kebede and Dube, op. cit. note 8, pp. 1,4, 6–8; energy service companies from Lin et al.,

op. cit. note 26, p. 2; microfinance and loans from Abhishek Lal and Betty Meyer, "An Overview of Microfinance and Environmental Management," Global Development Research Center, at www.gdrc.org/icm/environ/abhishek.html, viewed 19 April 2006, p. 9; bundling from Hamilton, op. cit. note 65, pp. 5–6; solar water heaters from REEEP, "Innovative Financing for Solar Water Heating Increases Affordability," press release (Vienna, Austria: April 2006); importance of champions and utility involvement from Roper, op. cit. note 71; demonstration projects and awareness from Practical Action, op. cit. note 63, pp. 3–4; state and city de facto policy from Aitken, op. cit. note 54.

73. Partnerships and commitments from Practical Action, op. cit. note 63, p. 1; importance of private-sector allies from Innovest Strategic Value Advisors, *Climate Change & The Financial Services Industry: Module 1—Threats and Opportunities*, prepared for the UNEP Finance Initiatives Climate Change Working Group (Toronto, ON: 2002).

2.5.4 The Nexus and the Neem Tree

ROBERT W. KATES

In this reading, Robert W. Kates, university professor emeritus at Brown University and coconvener of the Initiative on Science and Technology for Sustainability, examines the concept of sustainable development in light of what he regards as the failures of the contemporary pattern of globalization. Kates characterizes sustainable development as an oxymoron that "seeks to finesse the real conflicts between economy and environment and between the present and the future." Finding the correct balance between these ends requires that we examine the current system of globalization to determine whether or not it is enabling us to meet the goals of reducing the numbers of chronically hungry people while preserving Earth's life-support system for future generations. On both of these counts, Kates believes that the current form of globalization is failing to meet these goals overall, even though there are important and hopeful signs of progress in some areas. Instead of being opposed to globalization, the challenge, as he sees it, is to "humanize" it by changing the way in which the current system of globalization is governed in the direction of greater local control and democracy at the grass-roots level. Only by "civilizing" globalization in this way can we ensure that the benefits of economic development will be fairly distributed and used to address human needs.

FOCUS QUESTIONS

1. How does the U.S. National Academy of Sciences—National Research Council define the concept of sustainable development? To what extent are the basic human needs identified in this concept adequately satisfied for the approximately 6 billion humans living today? Discuss.
2. In what respects does the Neem tree stand as a metaphor for globalization? What are the defining characteristics of globalization? Has globalization as it has been developed thus far helped to reduce the number of chronically hungry people in the world? Why or why not?

Source: Robert Kates, "The Nexus and the Neem Tree," in *Worlds Apart: Globalization and the Environment*, ed. by James Gustave Speth, pp. 85–107. Copyright © 2003 Island Press. Reprinted by permission of Island Press, Washington, D.C.

3. What does the IPAT formula tell us about the causes of environmental degradation? Why does the author believe that this formula is only partially accurate? What factors need to be added to improve it? Explain.
4. Compare Kates's view of globalization with those of Jagdish Bhagwati (Selection 2.1.2) and the International Forum on Globalization (Selection 2.1.4). Which of these authors presents the most balanced and informed assessment of globalization's benefits, risks, and costs?

KEYWORDS

consumption, globalization, governance, population, risk assessment, sustainable development

The world of this new century is in transition—becoming more crowded and more consuming, warmer and more stressed, more interconnected, yet diverse and divided. Can this transition also be a transition for sustainability, in which the more than 9 billion people of the next half century meet their wants and needs in ways that do not further degrade the planet's life-support systems? In this chapter, I explore this transition to sustainability, the context in which it will take place, and the ways in which the new–old phenomenon of globalization affects it. My title is a play on the title of what may be the best-known book on globalization—Tom Friedman's *The Lexus and the Olive Tree.*

Friedman describes his title as follows:

> So there I was speeding along at 180 miles an hour on the most modern train in the world, reading this story about the oldest corner of the world. And the thought occurred to me that these Japanese, whose Lexus factory I had just visited and whose train I was riding, were building the greatest luxury car in the world with robots. And over here, on the top of page 3 of the *Herald Tribune,* the people with whom I had lived for so many years in Beirut and Jerusalem, whom I knew so well, were still fighting over who owned which olive tree. It struck me then that the Lexus and the olive tree were pretty good symbols of this post-Cold War era: half the world seemed to be emerging from the Cold War intent on building a better Lexus, dedicated to modernizing, streamlining and privatizing their economies in order to thrive in the system of globalization. And half the world—sometimes half the same country, sometimes half the same person—was still caught up in the fight over who owns which olive tree (p. 31).

But unlike this Lexus, which stands for all that is modern and different in globalization, and the olive tree for all that resists it, the nexus I explore is that of environment and development and the context in which it will play out over the coming two generations. And the Neem tree symbolizes the globalizing world where the elements of both the Lexus and the olive tree coexist in an uneasy tension of mutual attraction and repulsion.

I use three critical goals required for a successful sustainability transition—meeting human needs, reducing hunger and poverty, and preserving the life-support systems of the planet—to ask how globalization might help or hinder achieving these. For globalization to help more than hinder, it will need to be "civilized," and I conclude with an analog of how that might take place.

SUSTAINABLE DEVELOPMENT: THE NEXUS OF ENVIRONMENT AND DEVELOPMENT

The nexus of society's developmental goals with its environmental limits over the long term comes together in "sustainable development," which is only the most recent effort to link together the collective aspirations of the peoples of the world. Over my adult life, four aspirations emerged: first, for peace in the postwar world of 1945; then for freedom, in the struggles in the late 1940s and 1950s to end imperialism; followed by development for the poorest three-fourths of the world; and last, in the final quarter of the century, a concern for a healthy environment for humankind, the earth itself, and its complex systems that support life. As global aspirations develop, good people try to bring them together in a characteristic pattern of international high-level commissions (Brandt, Palme, Brundtland), followed by great international conferences. Such was the 1987 report of the World Commission on Environment and Development (WCED, also known as the Brundtland Commission) widely disseminated as *Our Common Future* (WCED, 1987), followed by the United Nations Conference on Environment and Development (UNCED) in Rio de Janeiro in 1992, and now a decade later in South Africa as the World Summit for Sustainable Development.

"Sustainable development" is now central to the mission of countless international organizations, national institutions, "sustainable cities" and locales, transnational corporations, and nongovernmental organizations. The genius of the oxymoron of sustainable development lies in its essential ambiguity that seeks to finesse the real conflicts between economy and environment and between the present and the future. While sharing a common concern for the fate of the earth, proponents of sustainable development differ in their emphases on what is to be sustained, what is to be developed, how to link environment and development, and for how long a time (see Figure 5.1). Thus, proponents differ on what is to be sustained: Is it nature itself, or nature in the utilitarian life support of humankind, and does it include sustaining the community of the olive tree, as Friedman (2000) describes it: "everything that roots us ... family, a community, a tribe, a nation, a religion or, most of all, a place called home" (p. 31)? Proponents differ on what is to be developed: Is it the economy, some broader notion of society, or is it people themselves? And how shall we link the two: sustain only, develop mostly, develop only but sustain somewhat, sustain or develop?—these and many more permutations are found.

Finally, over what time horizon will this occur? The Brundtland report employs the usefully ambiguous and widely accepted time horizon as "now and in the future." But in a future of a single generation, twenty-five years, almost any development appears sustainable. Over an infinite forever, none does, as even the smallest growth extended indefinitely creates situations that seem surely unsustainable. And over the century, now encompassed in many assessments such as that of climate change, the large and the long future is both remote and uncertain.

While a major political success, sustainable development has not been a significant scientific

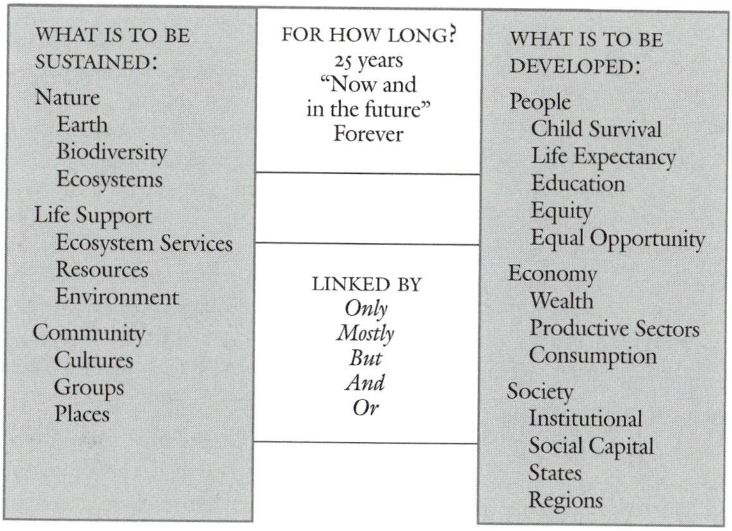
WHAT IS TO BE SUSTAINED:
Nature
Earth
Biodiversity
Ecosystems
Life Support
Ecosystem Services
Resources
Environment
Community
Cultures
Groups
Places
FOR HOW LONG?
25 years
"Now and in the future"
Forever
LINKED BY
Only
Mostly
But
And
Or
WHAT IS TO BE DEVELOPED:
People
Child Survival
Life Expectancy
Education
Equity
Equal Opportunity
Economy
Wealth
Productive Sectors
Consumption
Society
Institutional
Social Capital
States
Regions

FIGURE 5.1 Sustainable Development: Common Concerns, Differing Emphases.

focus beyond the earliest days of its conceptualization. While originating in the scientific activities of the early 1980s, particularly the work of the International Union for the Conservation of Nature (IUCN), as sustainable development gained greater political adherence, organized science found less to address. This has now changed, and a focus on a transition toward sustainability has made sustainable development scientifically manageable, and measurable for the world academies of science (IAP, 2000), for the international organizations of science (ICSU/WFEO, 2002), and increasingly for an emergent sustainability science (Kates et al., 2001).

In 1995, the Board on Sustainable Development of the U.S. National Academy of Sciences-National Research Council (NAS-NRC) sought to resolve some of the ambiguity I have described by focusing on a transition to sustainability over the next fifty years. By focusing on a transition, we took as our starting point the best understood of future trends—the demographic transition from a world with a population that grew by many births and many deaths to one that stabilized with few births and few deaths. With such a transition well under way, we can with some confidence project a declining or steady state population by the end of this century, with the bulk of that population born by 2050 (perhaps 9 billion of an eventual 10 billion). Thus, the human development needs of that population will surely increase, compared to the more than 6 billion alive today, but probably not more than by half again as much as that of today. The board defined a sustainability transition as one that would meet the human needs for food, nurture, housing, education, and employment of that larger but finite population, significantly reducing hunger and poverty, while still maintaining the essential life-support systems of the planet (NRC-BSD, 1999). These human needs are unmet today; for example, in 1995, 16 percent of the world population was hungry, 24 percent had unsafe water to drink, and 24 percent were illiterate (Raskin et al., 1998).

For these three normative goals, we found ample consensual support and measurable targets in the deliberations and subsequent treaties of international conferences and summits of leaders. For example, for the amount of reduction in hunger and poverty we used international consensus statements that call for reducing hunger and poverty by half within one to two decades (IMF et al., 2000) and suggested a target of reducing hunger by half in each of the next two generations.

Compared to meeting human needs, quantitative targets for preserving life-support systems are fewer, more modest, and more contested. Global targets now exist for reducing ozone-depleting substances, greenhouse gases, and, regionally, for some air pollutants. Absolute prohibitions (zero targets) exist for ocean dumping of radioactive wastes and some toxics (persistent organic pesticides), for the taking and/or sale of a few large mammals (whales, elephants, seals), migratory birds when breeding or endangered, and certain regional fishing stocks. International standards exist for many toxic materials, organic pollutants, and heavy metals that threaten human health, but not for ecosystem health. Water, land, and vegetative resources, such as arid lands or forests, have at best qualitative aspirations for sustainable management or restoration.

THE NEEM TREE: THE NEW AND OLD GLOBALIZATION

The 1992 NAS-NRC report *Neem: A Tree for Solving Global Problems* begins:

> Neem is a fascinating tree. On the one hand, it seems to be one of the most promising of all plants, and may eventually benefit every person on the planet. Probably no other yields as many strange and varied products or has as many exploitable by-products. Indeed, as foreseen by some scientists, this plant may usher in [a] new era in pest control, provide millions with inexpensive medicines, cut down the rate of human population growth, and perhaps even reduce erosion, deforestation, and the excessive temperature of an overheated globe.

The Neem tree, *Azadirachta indica,* is an attractive broad-leafed evergreen that grows tall and broad and can live for a century or more. Native to South Asia, it has been carried over the last century to the rest of tropical and semitropical Asia, Africa, and increasingly to the Caribbean and Central America and is now well established in thirty countries and has been introduced to many more. Everywhere it grows, it is prized for its ability to grow in marginal soils, to provide shade, firewood, oil for lamps, cosmetics, soaps, lubrication, and medicinals that date back several millennia, twig toothbrushes that prevent gum disease, and as a natural insecticide. Even where it does not grow, word of its wonders [is] carried on numerous Web sites, many dedicated to the Neem itself.

But it is for its pesticidal qualities—as a safer alternative to dangerous neurotoxins, effective across a large range of insects, fungi, nematodes, and the like, and seemingly safe for humans, birds, and animals—that Neem has attracted considerable scientific and commercial interest. More than seventy patents for uses or processes related to Neem products exist, and in May 2000 in an important decision, the European Patent Office revoked the patent given to W. R. Grace company for a fungicidal product, a decision hailed by Vandana Shiva, who had challenged the original patent, as "a great day for all who have been fighting to take back control of their resources and knowledge-systems from the patent regimes of the North" (Anon., 2000).

Thus, the Neem shares three major characteristics of globalization. It is not new, but quite ancient, as is globalization. In ancient Sanskrit it is known as *aristha,* or reliever of sickness. As with previous globalizations, it spread with religion and with empire. Part of traditional ayurvedic medicine, the Neem is found wherever Hinduism is found and often where the British Empire ruled. But as with globalization, there is much that is new in its dispersal and product development, as Neem seeds are now an international commodity. Modern science is close to synthesizing its major insecticidal properties, international nongovernmental organizations encourage its usage for impoverished rural peoples, and Web sites huckster its cosmetic and medicinal values. Finally, as with globalization, it is full of unrealized promise and currently realized discord. For except as a source of shade, firewood, toothbrushes, oil, or home remedies, it is not widely used beyond its South Asian home; and its most promising commercial products—refined or synthesized and standardized pesticides, medicinals, or contraceptives—are either underdeveloped or contested as to their efficacy and safety, as well as ethically in relation to the commercialization of an ancient legacy of nature and humankind.

CONTEMPORARY GLOBALIZATION

As to globalization in general, I prefer the simplified definition by Held, McGrew, Goldblatt, and Perraton (1999) in *Global Transformations: Politics, Economics, and Culture,* a study that some think is currently the best academic book on the subject. Held et al. say that "in its simplest sense globalization refers to the widening, deepening and speeding up of global inter-connectedness..." (p. 14). But, of course, as good academics they are not content with such simplicity and go on to describe a set of technical terms and criteria to mirror these items as extensiveness, intensiveness, velocity, and the impacts of interconnections.

Globalization, as noted, is not new, and Held et al. recognize four major periods of globalization: the premodern period of early empires and world religions, the early modern period of Western expansion, the modern industrial era, and the contemporary period from 1945 to the present. I would add two others: the earliest prehistoric period in which humans spread out of Africa around the world, and the future, especially that of the first half of the twenty-first century.

Reviewing the contemporary period and projecting to the future, our academy study (NRC-BSD, 1999) identified some major dimensions of contemporary globalization. The first is global interconnectedness with the much larger population of the future more closely connected by ties of economic production and consumption, migration, communication, and interlinked technologies. Since 1950, trade between nations has grown at more than twice the rate of the economy, and now some 20 percent of the world's goods and services pass over a border. Trade in money and capital—a hundred times the volume of world trade—now moves at a dizzying pace with electronic movement of funds, worldwide currency markets, and twenty-four-hour financial markets.

Words, images, and ideas also outpace the flow of products. New information technologies and mass communication techniques will continue to penetrate many different linguistic, cultural, and political barriers. Flows of people—temporary, permanent, and forced—have also increased, although most movements are poorly measured. The rate of increase in refugees is more rapid than that of world trade.

The rapid movement of peoples and products also makes possible the rapid transmission of infectious diseases of people, crops, and livestock and the biological invasions so destructive of native biota. Environmental harms are exported to countries with weak environmental standards. Most feared of all may be the rapid increases in consumption fueled by aggressive marketing and rapid cultural change. But as communication carries a culture of consumption, it also carries a culture of universal concern with the fate of the earth and links to common international efforts, shared information, and growing numbers of environmental groups.

But the academy study also considered the persistence of diversity, how connectedness, while increasing the similarity of places, can also increase diversity, particularly in urban areas that attract migrants. Places of wealth or opportunity toward which people and products are drawn actually become more diverse. There are also strong countercurrents to global culture that emphasize ethnic, national, and religious distinctiveness.

Finally, connectedness and diversity are also reflected in institutional innovation and power shifts (Mathews, 1997). At a global level, new institutions of governance have emerged, transnational corporate and financial institutions grow and consolidate, and networks of nongovernmental institutions collaborate and expand. At the subnational level, government has devolved, privatization is common, and civic society in many places has been strengthened. Power has shifted from the national state—upward to the global level and downward to the local level—and at all levels from the public to the private.

How does globalization affect a transition toward sustainability in meeting human needs, reducing hunger and poverty, and preserving life-support systems? It helps in some ways, hinders in others, and for many important characteristics, it does both. In this exploration of a highly complex subject, I present two illustrative examples using qualitative, but ordered, judgments. For one, I combine the first two human needs, feeding and nurturing, with the related goal of reducing hunger. In the second, I explore the determinants of threats to the life-support systems.

FEEDING, NURTURING, AND REDUCING HUNGER

There are three major types of hunger: chronic household hunger, episodic hunger, and special-needs hunger. Each responds somewhat differently to globalization.

Globalization and Reducing Chronic Hunger

Current estimates find some 800–900 million people who are chronically hungry—living in households with insufficient income or its equivalent to provide for health, children's growth, and ability to work. The numbers of hungry people differ greatly between regions of the world, with the largest numbers in Asia and the greatest proportion in Africa (Table 5.1).

TABLE 5.1 Numbers and Proportion of Chronically Hungry Population, 1996–1998

Regions	% Total Population	Hungry Population (millions)
Sub-Saharan Africa	34	186
Near East/North Africa	10	36
Latin America and the Caribbean	11	55
China and India	16	348
Other Asia	19	166
Developing countries: Total	18	791

FAO, 2000.

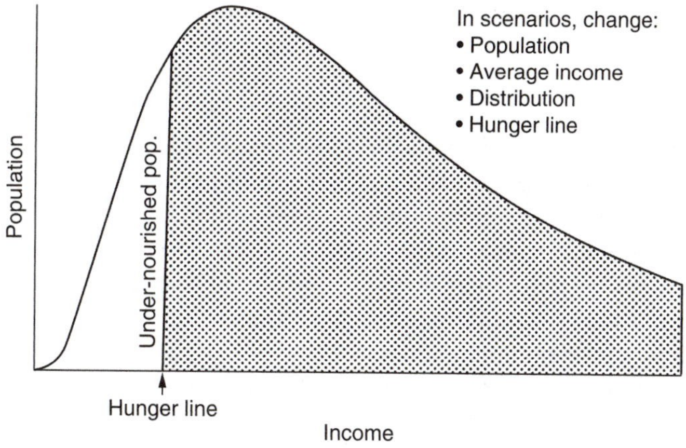

FIGURE 5.2 Hunger and Income.

The number of chronically hungry people can be approximately estimated by using four variables: the size of the population, the average income per person, the distribution of income across the population, and the definition of a hunger line of income, or its equivalent, below which the population is thought to be hungry (see Figure 5.2).

It is useful to examine some differences in these major determinants over the period of contemporary globalization beginning in 1950. World *population* grew over a half century from 2.5 billion to 6 billion, but the peak growth rate was in the 1960s and has been slowing ever since. Nonetheless, about 80 million people are added each year, increasing the numbers of chronically hungry even as the proportion of hungry people diminishes. Examining trends in *income* (Table 5.2) in this period, per capita gross domestic product (GDP) grew in all world regions between 1950 and 1973, but between 1973 and 1992, GDP in Eastern Europe declined, and it stagnated in Africa and Latin America.

Inequality in the *distribution of income* occurs both between countries and regions and within countries and regions. Between regions, Africa, Eastern Europe, and Latin America (Table 5.2) show growing inequality with the United States (ratio of U.S. GDP per capita to regional GDP per capita), even as the rest of Europe converged with the United States and the ratio of U.S. per capita GDP to Asia declines from sevenfold in

TABLE 5.2 Trends in Regional GDP Per Capita, 1950, 1973, and 1992

		GDP/Capita/1950 GDP/Capita		U.S. GDP/Capita/REGIONAL GDP/Capita		
World Regions	**1950 GDP/Capita (in 1990 $)**	**1973**	**1992**	**1950**	**1973**	**1992**
United States	9573	1.7	2.3	1.0	1.0	1.0
Western Europe	5513	2.1	3.2	1.7	1.4	1.2
East Europe	2235	2.4	2.0	4.3	3.1	4.7
Latin America	3478	1.4	1.7	2.8	3.3	3.6
Asia	863	2.8	6.1	11.1	6.8	4.1
Africa	893	1.5	1.5	10.7	12.5	16.2

Madison, 1995.

1973 to fourfold in the course of two decades. Using a different data set (Deininger and Squire, 1996), within-region inequality of income (as measured by the Gini coefficient, a standard measure of inequality) differs almost twofold with the greatest inequality found in Latin America and the least found among the former socialist countries of Eastern Europe. Over time, for most regions, within-region inequality has been generally diminishing except in Africa and in Eastern Europe with the end of socialism. Finally, the *hunger line* grows over time as income increases, access to informal sources of food declines, food purchases increase, and diets change.

The NAS-NRC Board on Sustainable Development commissioned a study on the feasibility of reducing hunger by half in each of the two generations before 2050 using these variables and contrasting two different scenarios. The reference scenario projected major current trends, institutional continuity, economic globalization, and the slow convergence of developing countries toward the socioeconomic norms of developed countries. In this scenario, the number of hungry actually increased by 2050, although the proportion of hungry people declined. The "policy reform" scenario assumed that a proactive set of initiatives is instituted to achieve sustainability goals. In this scenario, hunger is cut in half with a small change in the speed of the demographic transition leading to less population, with growth in income at the higher end of plausible income growth rates, and most important, a convergence of equity to the current levels of Europe. The contrasting scenarios are shown in Figure 5.3 for the world as a whole and by region.

For these contrasting scenarios and the four major causal elements that underlie them, what are the impacts of globalization? In Table 5.3, I set out my qualitative judgments (using a scale of one plus sign [+] for small impact and four plus signs [++++] for very large impacts) as to how globalization helps or hinders the causal elements linked to chronic hunger. For *population*, globalization probably helps through a population growth rate decline by influencing all three important determinants for reducing fertility: making contraception more accessible; providing opportunities for education and work for women; and encouraging postponement of marriage through such opportunities for education and work, as well as through diffused Western lifestyle concepts.

For *income*, globalization helps increase per capita income in some parts of the world, but practices not-so-benign neglect in others. The development of an export-oriented industry in Southeast Asia, accompanied by significant public sector actions, led to major reductions in hunger in that region until the recent financial crisis slowed and even reversed some of those gains. But in

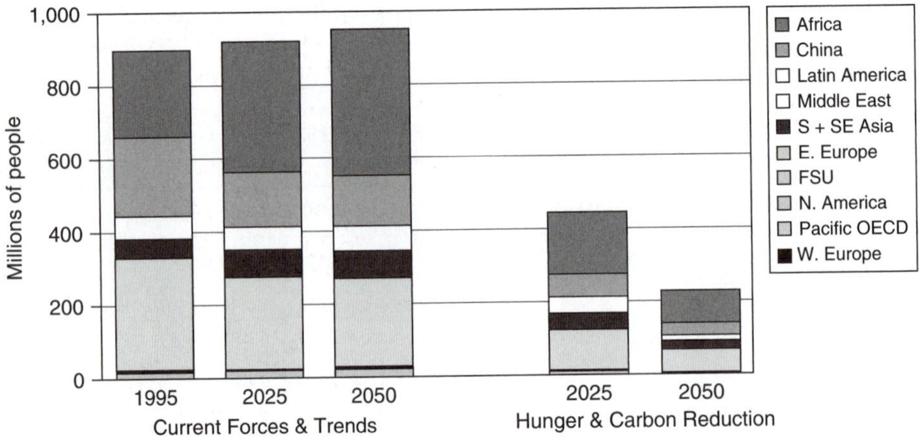

FIGURE 5.3 Reducing Chronic Hunger by Halves.

TABLE 5.3 Globalization's Impacts on Reducing Chronic Hunger

Causal Element	HELP	HINDER
Population Growth Decrease	++	
Increase in Income per capita	++	++ In Africa
Decrease In Inequity	+ Between Nations	+++ Within Nations
Decrease in Hunger Line		+

Africa, where hunger will increase most, globalization has exacerbated some of the region's problems, its export trade in such products of affluence as oil or diamonds fueling corruption and conflict, while development aid has diminished without an equivalent growth in private investment. But most of all, it has suffered not-so-benign neglect and has been marginalized from the globalized world system.

While globalization will probably decrease *inequity* overall between countries, globalization will, for some time at least, increase inequity within countries, particularly affecting the poorest of the poor. This is so because rapid export-oriented growth in developing countries reduces somewhat the differences in income with developed countries, but within countries opportunities vary greatly. Thus, for example, China, which had made enormous gains in reducing hunger, might well suffer an increase in hunger as the income gap between regions increases, as employment opportunities expand in export manufacturing and services but decline in local manufacturing and agriculture, and overall, the safety net system diminishes. Finally, the hunger line shifts relatively as diets expand (by preferences for both animal products and imported products or brands), more and more basic food enters the market, and the income requirement to meet these new needs increases.

Globalization and Reducing Episodic Hunger

Applying similar judgments to episodic hunger (Table 5.4), the reduction of famine-determined hunger from natural hazards is a great recent success story of a globalized emergency food aid system that relies on both public and private efforts. Today, famine-inspired hunger exists only where war and violent conflict persist. Globalization, however, increases famine vulnerability in the sense of entitlement shifts, as Sen (1981) has shown, especially in cases where the availability of food and purchasing power of rural landless workers can be diminished by far-off events. Globalization has increased the incidence of war and civil conflict both by making weapons easily available (the ubiquitous Kalashnikov) and by diminishing the impacts of war by providing emergency food aid. Recent financial crises often triggered by globalized movements of capital have created sudden episodic hunger in countries where such episodes were rare—as in Southeast Asia, which had made marked progress in reducing hunger prior to the crises. Finally, structural adjustment efforts initiated either internally or at the behest of the IMF almost always lead to an increase in hunger from a decrease in social services and programs, despite some counterefforts.

TABLE 5.4 Globalization's Impacts on Reducing

Causal Element	HELP	HINDER
Famine	+++	+
War	+	+
Financial Crisis		+++
Structural Adjustment		++

Globalization and Reducing Special-Needs Hunger

Concerning special-needs hunger (Table 5.5), global efforts to address some major causes of child undernutrition, especially from sickness and disease, by addressing immunization, treatment of diarrhea, and breast-feeding have helped to reduce the rate of

TABLE 5.5 Globalization's Impacts on Reducing Special-Needs Hunger

Hunger Type	HELP	HINDER
Mothers and Children	+++	+
Iron, Iodine, Vitamin A	+++	+

wasting and stunting of children (although the actual numbers have increased as a result of population growth centered in the youngest ages). Similarly, the major micronutrient deficiencies of iodine, vitamin A, and iron have been reduced by international programs to encourage iodizing salt, to increase intakes of vitamin A through vitamin A-rich foods and through vitamin A supplementation, and to a much lesser extent, to reduce anemia by iron supplements. In some cases the diversification of diets has helped as well—for example, by providing greater access to iodized salt.

The major countercurrent related to globalization is similar to the previous case: Structural adjustment and diminished development aid have severely constrained many programs directed at addressing these special needs.

PRESERVING LIFE-SUPPORT SYSTEMS

The life-support systems of the planet are often factored into major media: atmosphere, freshwater, oceans, and the biota as biomes, ecosystems, and species. The major threats to atmosphere, freshwater, oceans, and the biota are threefold: (1) the large-scale introduction of pollutants, such as acid rain and chlorofluorocarbons in the atmosphere, heavy metals in the soil, or chemicals in groundwater; (2) the massive assault on biota, such as deforestation in the tropics and the mountains, desertification in dry lands, overfishing of marine resources, and species extinction everywhere; and (3) human-induced climate change.

These threats are incredibly recent. In nine of twelve indicators of global environmental change, half of all the change that took place over the last ten thousand years occurred in our lifetime (Table 5.6).

DRIVING FORCES OF ENVIRONMENTAL CHANGE

These changes coincide but are not necessarily caused by the most recent wave of globalization.

A general consensus among scientists posits that growth in population, in affluence, and in technology are jointly major driving forces for such change and related environmental problems. This has become enshrined in a useful, albeit overly simplified, identity known as IPAT, first published in 1972 by Ehrlich and Holdren in *Environment* magazine in response to a more limited version by Commoner et al. (1971). In this identity, various forms of environmental or resource impacts (I) equals population (P) times affluence (A), usually income per capita, times the impacts per unit of income as determined by technology (T) and the institutions that use it. Academic debate has now shifted from the greater or lesser importance of each of these driving forces of environmental degradation or resource depletion, to debate about their interaction and the ultimate forces that drive them.

Let me introduce a variant of the IPAT identity (Figure 5.4)—which might be called the PC version—and restating that identity in terms of population and consumption, it would be $I = P*C/P*I/C$. I equals environmental

TABLE 5.6 10,000 Years of Environmental Change: Selected Indicators

	Selected Indicators	
10,000 Years of Environmental Change	**Rate of Change Still Accelerating**	**Rate of Change Now Decelerating**
Half occurred before our lifetimes	Deforested area Soil area loss	Terrestrial vertebrate diversity
Half occurred during our Lifetimes	Carbon releases Nitrogen releases Floral diversity Sediment flows Water withdrawals	Carbon tetrachloride releases Lead releases Marine mammal diversity Sulphur releases

Turner et al., 1990

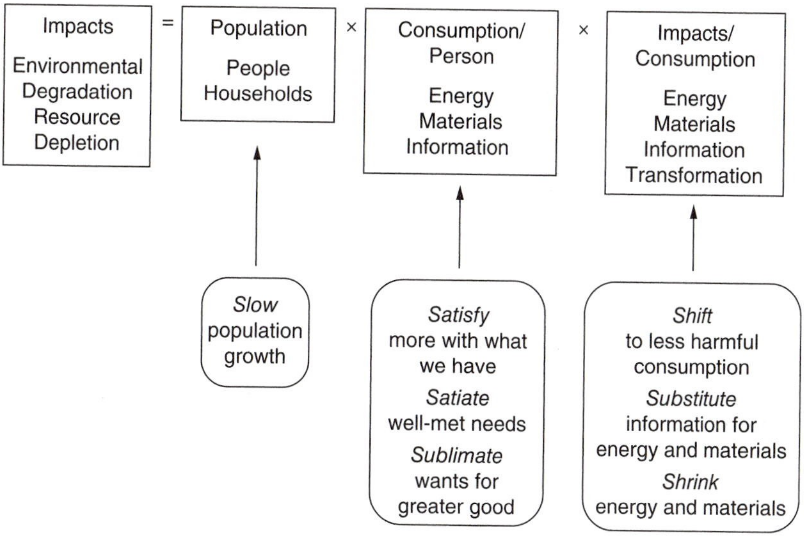

FIGURE 5.4 Variant of IPAT Identity.

degradation and/or resource depletion; P equals the number of people or households; and C equals the consumption per person of energy, materials, and information.

With such an identity as a template and with the goal of reducing environmentally degrading and resource-depleting influences, there are at least seven major directions for research and policy. To reduce the level of impacts per unit of consumption, separate more damaging consumption from less harmful forms and *shift* to these, *shrink* the amounts of environmentally damaging energy and materials per unit of consumption, and *substitute* information for energy and materials. To reduce consumption per person or household, *satisfy* more with what is already had, *satiate* well-met consumption needs, and *sublimate* wants for a greater good. Finally, *slow* population growth and then stabilize population numbers as indicated earlier.

Before using these proximate determinants of the identity, a bit of caution is in order. IPAT is very useful, but is more complex than a simple identity. The PAT terms are only proximate; each in turn is driven by diverse underlying processes. Nor are the PAT terms independent of each other; for example, income (or affluence) influences the rate of population growth and consumption, as well as the technologies used to produce it. Indeed, the supposed technology term is really a catch-all of all the diverse items that determine a different set of impacts per unit of consumption—including technology, but also all kinds of ideas and institutions. Nor do I think the PAT terms are sufficient to examine the impact of globalization on Earth's life-support systems.

To add to the classic determinants, let me borrow from an analysis by Clark (2000) of environmental globalization, one that includes not only the globalization of environmental "stuff"—the energy, materials, biota transformed by production and consumption—but also the globalization of environmental ideas and governance. Specifically, Clark notes three major ideas: planetary management, risk assessment, and sustainable development; along with three forms of governance: by governments; by nongovernmental organizations, both profit and nonprofit; and by coalitions and networks that bring them together.

GLOBALIZATION AND PRESERVING LIFE-SUPPORT SYSTEMS

Thus, there are five causal elements related to globalization's impact on preserving the life-support systems of the planet: population, consumption,

TABLE 5.7 Globalization's Impacts on Preserving Life-Support Systems

Causal Element	HELP	HINDER
Population	++	
Consumption		++++
Technology	+++	+
Ideas	+++	++
Governance	++	++

technology, ideas, and governance. Examining these five causal elements (Table 5.7), beginning with *population,* globalization, as noted, will encourage a decline in the population growth rate, thus lessening future human impacts on the environment. But globalization also accelerates *consumption* in three ways. Insofar as globalization increases income and to a degree inequity, it encourages greater production and consumption. Insofar as it extends the reach of trade and transport, it makes possible consumption of distant resources that would not be consumed locally and the import of goods not available locally. With the spread of ideas and images of "Western material standards of living," it further encourages consumption. Much of this enhanced consumption is desperately needed and desired by the poorer peoples of the world, but much of it will be in the form of material and energy transformations that are environmentally degrading and resource-depleting.

At the same time, globalization facilitates both the creation and the diffusion of *technologies* that lessen the need for energy and materials per unit of production or consumption, that create fewer toxics and pollutants, or that substitute information for energy and material use. Countering these helpful technologies are trickle-down technologies that export secondhand or second-rate technologies, buildings, and toxic or polluting processes to regions heretofore relatively free of degrading or depleting activities.

In the realm of *ideas,* there are also dual impacts. Development is seen as a good to be pursued, with environmental concerns a luxury that developing countries cannot readily afford. Countering this has been the rapid spread of the major environmental ideas of planetary and risk management and sustainable development, to the extent that while rhetoric persists as to differences between the North and the South, international surveys show little difference in the high environmental aspirations among the people of both North and South.

As to *governance,* while there are some 180 international environmental treaties in force to date, they are insufficient to counter the major threats to the atmosphere, oceans, and biota, with the possible exception of the Montreal protocol on ozone depletion. But as Clark notes, governance is greater than governments, and the governance activities of advocacy coalitions and the discourses between transnational corporations and international environmental groups can be very substantial in helping to maintain the planet's life-support system. Indeed, it is often the ability to draw global attention to some local threat that leads to mitigative or preventive actions. All of these forms of governance will grow with globalization. Substantially countering these forms are the notions of free trade unhindered by environmental constraint or regulation currently ensconced in the operation of the World Trade Organization and in various regional trade treaties.

GLOBALIZATION AND TWO-ARMED SCIENTISTS

The Maine version of a well-known story has Senator Edmund Muskie listening to testimony on the need for clean-air legislation. After a series of cautious scientific testimonies by scientists, he asks whether anyone in the room is a "one-armed scientist" who can testify without the endless academic qualifications of "on the one hand … then on the other hand…"

It is obvious that I must plead guilty to being a two-armed scientist. But it is difficult for anyone thoughtfully confronting globalization not to be. Indeed, whether you sing paeans to globalization as Tom Friedman (2000) does or fear "the manic logic of global capitalism" as Bill Grieder (1997) does, the other hand, whichever it might be, is always present. What may separate the two more is that Friedman thinks that globalization itself will in time deal with its many harms, whereas Grieder believes in the need for radical revision and strong local to international action.

So, what can the two-armed scientist conclude from this first, tentative attempt to assess the impact of globalization on a sustainability transition: meeting human needs, reducing hunger and poverty, preserving the life-support systems of the planet? In this brief assessment I have focused on how globalization has affected the reduction of hunger and meeting the human needs for food and nurture and on the driving forces of global environmental change.

In sum, globalization to date has not helped reduce the numbers of chronically hungry in the world, although the proportion decreases as population grows. The shifts in investment, income, and job opportunities in some parts of the world are matched by the growth of hunger elsewhere. Episodic and special-needs hunger have benefited more as globalized public and private programs have expanded to respond rapidly to famine, to the special needs of children, and to two of the three major micronutrient diseases. Finally, the increase in hunger from globalized financial crises and policy decisions argues for new sources of instability for the fragile existence of the poorest of the poor. Short-run and long-run simulations of halving hunger argue for these trends to persist.

In preserving the life-support systems, the crucial issue is globalization's impact on current and projected production and consumption of energy and materials that are environmentally degrading and resource depleting. To date, despite major gains in technologies that reduce the use of energy and materials per unit of production, the absolute growth in consumption overwhelms the steady global technological progress. The globalization of environmental ideas has been truly remarkable, and these, along with feminism and human rights, constitute the major ideological revolutions of the contemporary period of globalization. The spread of these ideas has been well facilitated by global interconnections. Similarly, the rise of environmental governance writ large to include corporate behavior and local and international popular initiatives is facilitated by the interconnectedness of globalization and is a great portent for the future. But to date, these have all been insufficient to counter the major threats to the life-support systems, and when projected to address the extraordinary increases in the consumption of the future, such helpful developments may fail as well.

CIVILIZING GLOBALIZATION

If the goods of globalization are to be realized for most of the world's peoples, and if its ills are to be reduced for those people and natural systems most vulnerable, then globalization itself must change in significant ways. Gerry Helleiner (2000), the Canadian economist, as well as Held et al. (1999), call this process "civilizing" globalization. All of them focus on changing governance. Helleiner asks, "Can the global economy be civilized?" "Globalized markets," he argues, "operate within politically defined rules and governance institutions. The current global rules and economic governance institutions are in need of repair, updating and relegitimization," and he goes on to suggest some of those initiatives.

Held et al. (1999) focus not on economy but on politics and three major approaches to civilizing and democratizing contemporary globalization: a liberal-internationalism approach to reform global governance; a cosmopolitan, democratic approach to reconstruct global governance; and a radical republican approach to create alternative structures of governance. Exploring these issues is well beyond the scope of this chapter, but I conclude with my own thoughts on the efforts to "civilize" globalization.

CIVILIZING U.S. CAPITALISM: 100 YEARS

As I contemplate the varied efforts to understand globalization and how to reform or reconstruct it, I am struck by the similarity of contemporary globalization to an earlier period of American history. I perceive an analog to the current global situation in the U.S. economic history of the post-Civil War era. At the time, a truly integrated and nationalized industrial capitalism was created, spurred by the growth of interconnections of railroad and telegraph. Reading of this age of "robber-baron" capitalism, I am struck by the parallels with current globalization, for example, the great uncertainty at the time, even by the major participants, in understanding the new and different systems that had emerged.

Whatever emerged from the fierce competition and growing monopolization of economic power was initially marred by an absence of law and regulation. Much early regulatory effort was needed around what today are called "rule of law" and "transparency" issues, such as those that make contracts enforceable or stock certificates verifiable. These initial efforts were followed by numerous attempts to control monopoly power and maintain genuine competitiveness.

Almost parallel to these efforts, but much slower, were those that recognized the victims, harms, inequities, and externalities generated by the new integrated industrial system. The initial focus, as it is currently, was on child labor, followed by other working conditions, and then the essentials of a social safety net including disability insurance, unemployment insurance, pensions, and the like. Efforts to gain workers' rights began early and were repeatedly rebuffed, and it was not until 1935 that they were basically recognized. Finally, environmental issues were not really recognized until Earth Day 1970, thus capping a century of effort to civilize U.S. capitalism. Throughout this whole period the individual states of the United States served as the focus for innovative leadership and the testing ground for appropriate regulation that only later was emulated or taken over by the federal government.

The challenge for civilizing globalization is to reduce these century-long efforts to, at most, two decades. The good news is that this effort is well under way, again with a push for "humanizing globalization" or "globalization from the bottom." I illustrate with Bangor, Maine, population 35,000.

CIVILIZING GLOBALIZATION: IN BANGOR, MAINE

Beginning in 1991, Bangor became a sister-city to Carasque, a small village in the highlands of El Salvador, as part of a group of twenty-nine such sister-cities all trying to support returned populations who had been refugees from the civil war. From Bangor, Carasque has received a rebuilt truck, pedal sewing machines, school and health materials, and, when needed, support for human and economic rights in the form of communications expressed to both the U.S. and El Salvador governments. From Carasque, Bangor has received an opportunity to learn of the realities of poor people in the developing world, a model of how young people can exercise leadership in their own communities, and instructive experience as to what alternative schooling might provide.

Trying to find an issue in common to both communities, people in Bangor identified sweatshop- or *maquiladora*-made clothes, the making of which takes jobs from Mainers and exploits Salvadorans. Today, there are a thousand consumers and thirty businesses in Bangor displaying the "clean clothes" sweatshop-free logo, and four Maine communities are now committed to selective sweatshop-free city purchasing. This has led to a statewide selective purchasing act for textiles and footwear that is now being implemented. The "clean clothes" criteria for such selective purchasing—protecting children and workers, providing a living wage, and giving workers rights to bargain—is an agenda for civilizing globalization. Finally, many of the same Mainers recently took a five-hour trip to Quebec City, Canada, for the so-called Americas Summit to protest a free trade area until it incorporates children's, workers', and environmental concerns.

GLOBALIZATION AND A TRANSITION TOWARD SUSTAINABILITY

The very notion of a transition toward sustainability and the concept of sustainable development from which it derives are products of the widening, deepening, and speeding up of the interconnectedness that characterizes globalization. To think of humankind as a whole, to see its links to the fate of the blue planet, has been an essential part of the globalization process. Thus, those of us who aspire to a transition toward sustainability, to meet human needs while preserving the life support of the planet, cannot be "against globalization." But what we can say (and are saying) is that for globalization to continue to encourage such a transition, it will need to redouble those aspects of this complex movement in our collective lives that help a sustainability transition and to dampen those that hinder such a transition. It is this nexus that will make real the promise of the Neem tree.

REFERENCES

Anon. 2000. "Neem tree free," *The Ecologist*, 30/4:8.

Clark, William C. 2000. "Environmental globalization." In Joseph S. Nye Jr. and John D. Donahue, eds., *Governance in a Globalizing World*. Washington, D.C.: Brookings Press.

Commoner, B., M. Corr, and P. Stamler. 1971. "The causes of pollution," *Environment*, April, pp. 2–19.

Deininger, Klaus, and Lyn Squire. 1996. "A new data set measuring income inequality," *World Bank Economic Review* 10(3):565–591.

Ehrlich, Paul, and John Holdren. 1972. "Review of *The Closing Circle*," *Environment* 14(3):24–39.

Food and Agriculture Organization of the United Nations (FAO). 2000. *Agriculture: Towards 2015/30*. Technical Interim Report. Rome: FAO.

Friedman, Thomas L. 2000. *The Lexus and the Olive Tree*. New York: Anchor Books.

Grieder, William. 1997. *One World Ready or Not: The Manic Logic of Global Capitalism*. New York: Simon and Schuster.

Held, David, Anthony McGrew, David Goldblatt, and Jonathan Perraton. 1999. *Global Transformations: Politics, Economics, and Culture*. Stanford, Calif.: Stanford University Press.

Helleiner, Gerald K. 2000. "Markets, politics and globalization: Can the global economy be civilized?" The Tenth Raúl Prebisch Lecture, Geneva, 11 December.

InterAcademy Panel (IAP) on International Issues. 2000. *Transition to Sustainability in the 21st Century*. Conference of the World's Scientific Academies. 15–18 May 2000, Tokyo, Japan, http://interacademies.net/intracad/tokyo2000.nsf/all/home.

International Council for Science (ICSU) and the World Federation of Engineering Organizations (WFEO). 2002. *Role and Contributions of the Scientific and Technological Community (S&TC) to Sustainable Development*. World Summit on Sustainable Development Secretary-General's Note for the Multi-Stake Holder Dialogue Segment of the Second Preparatory Committee. Addendum No. 8: Dialogue Paper by Scientific and Technological Communities. United Nations Economic and Social Council E/CN.17/2002/PC.2/6. Add.8. Advance Copy, 28 January 2002.

International Monetary Fund (IMF), Organisation for Economic Cooperation and Development (OECD), United Nations (UN), and World Bank Group (WB). 2000. *A Better World for All: Progress towards the International Development Goals*. Washington, D.C.: IMF, OECD, UN, WB.

Kates, Robert W., William C. Clark, Robert Corell, J. Michael Hall, Carlo C. Jaeger, Ian Lowe, James J. McCarthy, Hans Joachim Schellnhuber, Bert Bolin, Nancy M. Dickson, Sylvie Faucheux, Gilberto C. Gallopin, Arnulf Gruebler, Brian Huntley, Jill Jäger, Narpat S. Jodha, Roger E. Kasperson, Akin Mabogunje, Pamela Matson, Harold Mooney, Berrien Moore III, Timothy O'Riordan, and Uno Svedin. 2001. "Sustainability science." *Science* 292:641–642, April 27. http://sustainabilityscience.org/keydocs/fulltext/wssd_stc_020128.pdf.

Madison, Angus. 1995. *Monitoring the World Economy 1820–1992*. Paris: Organization for Economic Cooperation and Development.

Mathews, Jessica. 1997. "Power shift," *Foreign Affairs* 76(1):50–66.

National Research Council, Board on Science and Technology for International Development (BOSTID). 1992. *Neem: A Tree for Solving Global Problems*. Washington, D.C.: National Academy Press.

National Research Council, Board on Sustainable Development (NRC-BSD). 1999. *Our Common Journey: A Transition Toward Sustainability*. Washington, D.C.: National Academy Press.

Raskin, Paul, Gilberto Gallopin, Pablo Gutman, Alan Hammond, and Rob Swart. 1998. *Bending the Curve: Toward Global Sustainability, a Report of the Global Scenario Group*. Polestar Series, Report No. 8. Boston: Stockholm Environmental Institute.

Sen, Amartya. 1981. *Poverty and Famines: An Essay on Entitlement and Deprivation*. New York: Oxford University Press.

Turner, B. L. II, William C. Clark, Robert W. Kates, John F. Richards, Jessica T. Mathews, and William B. Meyer, eds. 1990. *The Earth as Transformed by Human Action: Global and Regional Changes in the Biosphere over the Past 300 Years.* Cambridge: Cambridge University Press.

World Commission on Environment and Development (WCED). 1987. *Our Common Future.* New York: Oxford University Press. (Brundtland Report).

BIBLIOGRAPHY

Aiken, W. E. (1977). *Technocracy and the American Dream: The Technocratic Movement 1900–1941.* Berkeley: University of California Press.

Appleyard, B. (1998). *Brave New Worlds: Staying Human in the Genetic Future.* New York: Viking Press.

Baden, J. A., Noonan, D. S., and Ruckelshaus, W. D. (Eds.). (1998). *Managing the Commons,* 2nd ed. Bloomington: Indiana University Press.

Barnet, R. J., and Cavanagh, J. (1994). *Global Dreams: Imperial Corporations and the New World Order.* New York: Touchstone.

Beniger, J. (1986). *The Control Revolution: Technological and Economic Origins of the Information Society.* Cambridge, MA: Harvard University Press.

Bijker, W. E., Hughes, T. P., and Pinch, T. (1990). *The Social Construction of Technological Systems.* Cambridge, MA: MIT Press.

Bolter, J. D. (1984). *Turing's Man.* Chapel Hill: University of North Carolina Press.

Boorstin, D. J. (1978). *The Republic of Technology.* New York: Harper & Row.

Boot, M. (2006). *War Made New: Technology, Warfare, and the Course of History—1500 to Today.* New York: Gotham Books.

Borgrnann, A. (1984). *Technology and the Character of Contemporary Life: A Philosophical Inquiry.* Chicago: University of Chicago Press.

Bright, C. (1998). *Life Out of Bounds: Bioinvasion in a Borderless World.* New York: Norton.

Brook, J., and Boal, I. A. (Eds.). (1995). *Resisting the Virtual Life: The Culture and Politics of Information.* San Francisco: City Lights Books.

Budinger, T., and Budinger, F. (2006). *Ethics of Emerging Technologies: Scientific Facts and Moral Challenges.* New York: Wiley.

Burke, J., and Ornstein, R. (1997). *The Axmaker's Gift: Technology's Capture and Control of Our Minds and Culture.* New York: Putnam Group.

Bush, C. G. (1983). *Machina Ex Dea.* New York: Teachers College Press.

Carnegie Commission on Science, Technology, and Government. (1992). *Enabling the Future: Linking Science and Technology to Societal Goals.* New York: Carnegie Commission on Science, Technology, and Government.

Carson, R. (1962). *Silent Spring.* Boston: Houghton Mifflin.

Cavanagh, J., and Mander, J. (2004). *Alternatives to Economic Globalization: A Better World Is Possible,* 2nd ed. San Francisco: Berrett-Koehler.

Chanda, N. (2007). Bound Together: How Traders, Preachers, Adventurers, and Warriors Shaped Globalization. New Haven, CT: Yale University Press.

Chandler, A. D., Jr. (1977). *The Visible Hand: The Management Revolution in American Business.* Cambridge, MA: Belknap Press.

Clark, A. (2004). *Natural-Born Cyborgs: Minds, Technologies, and the Future of Human Intelligence.* New York: Oxford University Press.

Clark, G. (2007). *A Farewell to Alms: A Brief History of the Economic World.* Princeton, NJ: Princeton University Press.

Commoner, B. (1971). *The Closing Circle: Nature, Man and Technology.* New York: Knopf.

Corn, J. (Ed.). (1986). *Imagining Tomorrow: History, Technology, and the American Future.* Cambridge, MA: MIT Press.

Cothran, H. (Ed.). (2002). *Energy Alternatives: Opposing Viewpoints.* San Diego, CA: Greenhaven Press.

Cowan, R. S. (1983). *More Work for Mother: The Ironies of Household Technology from the Open Hearth to the Microwave.* New York: Basic Books.

Cowan, R. S. (1996). *A Social History of American Technology.* New York: Oxford University Press.

Cross, G. (1993). *Time and Money: The Making of Consumer Culture.* New York: Routledge.

Daly, H. E., and Cobb, J. B., Jr. (1994). *For the Common Good: Redirecting the Economy toward Community, the Environment, and a Sustainable Future.* New York: Beacon Press.

Davies, P. (2004). *What's This India Business? Offshoring, Outsourcing, and the Global Services Revolution.* London: Nicholas Brealey International.

Dawkins, R. (1990). *The Selfish Gene.* Oxford: Oxford University Press.

Desmond, K. (1986). *The Harwin Chronology of Inventions, Innovations, Discoveries.* London: Constable.

Diamond, J. (1999). *Guns, Germs, and Steel: The Fates of Human Societies.* New York: Norton.

Diamond, J. (2005). *Collapse: How Societies Choose to Fail or Succeed.* New York: Penguin.

Douglas, M., and Wildavsky, A. (1982). *Risk and Culture: The Selection of Technical and Environmental Dangers.* Berkeley: University of California Press.

Dreyfus, H. (1979). *What Computers Can't Do: The Limits of Artificial Intelligence*, 2nd ed. New York: Basic Books.

Dreyfus, H. (1992). *What Computers Still Can't Do: A Critique of Artificial Reason.* Cambridge, MA: MIT Press.

Drucker, P. (1993). *Post-Capitalist Society.* New York: HarperCollins.

Dunn, L. (1965). *A Short History of Genetics.* New York: Plenum.

Dyson, F. (1999). *The Sun, the Genome, and the Internet: Tools of Scientific Revolutions.* New York: Oxford University Press.

Dyson, G. B. (1997). *Darwin among the Machines: The Evolution of Global Intelligence.* New York: Perseus.

Easton, T. (2007). *Taking Sides: Clashing Views in Science, Technology, and Society.* New York: McGraw-Hill/Dushkin.

Edgar, S. (1997). *Morals and Machines: Perspectives in Computer Ethics.* New York: Jones and Bartlett.

Edgerton, D. (2006). *The Shock of the Old: Technology and Global History since 1900.* New York: Oxford University Press.

Ellul, J. (1964). *The Technological Society*, trans J. Wilkenson. New York: Knopf.

Elsterd, J. (1983). *Explaining Technical Change.* Cambridge: Cambridge University Press.

Ermann, M. D., Williams, M., and Shauf, M. (Eds.). (1997). *Computers, Ethics, and Society*, 2nd ed. New York: Oxford University Press.

Feenberg, A. (1999). *Questioning Technology.* New York: Routledge.

Feenberg, A., and Hannay, A. (Eds.). (1995). *Technology and the Politics of Knowledge.* Bloomington: Indiana University Press.

Feeré, F. (1995). *Philosophy of Technology.* Athens, GA: University of Georgia Press.

Fishman, T. (2005). *China, Inc.: How the Rise of the Next Superpower Challenges America and the World.* New York: Scribner.

Fox, M. (1992). *Superpigs and Wondercorn: The Brave New World of Biotechnology and Where It May Lead.* New York: Lyons and Burford.

Frenkel, S. (Ed.). (1999). *On the Front Line: Organization of Work in the Information Age.* Ithaca, NY: Cornell University Press.

Friedman, T. L. (1999). *The Lexus and the Olive Tree.* New York: Farrar, Straus & Giroux.

Friedman, T. L. (2005). *The World Is Flat: A Brief History of the Twenty-First Century.* New York: Farrar, Straus & Giroux.

Gimpel, J. (1977). *The Medieval Machine: The Industrial Revolution of the Middle Ages.* New York: Penguin.

Gordon, J. (2004). *An Empire of Wealth: The Epic History of American Economic Power.* New York: HarperCollins.

Gutkind, L. (2007). *Almost Human: Making Robots Think.* New York: Norton.

Hardin, G. (1993). *Living within Limits: Ecology, Economics, and Population Taboos.* New York: Oxford University Press.

Hardison, O. B., Jr. (1989). *Disappearing through the Skylight: Culture and Technology in the Twentieth Century.* New York: Viking Press.

Heidegger, M. (1977). *The Question Concerning Technology and Other Essays*, Trans W. Lovitt, New York: Harper & Row.

Heinberg, R. (2005). *The Party's Over: Oil, War and the Fate of Industrial Societies.* British Columbia: New Society.

Henry, D. (1989). *From Foraging to Agriculture.* Philadelphia: University of Pennsylvania Press.

Hofstetter, R. (1997). *Mobius.* New York: Vantage Press.

Hughes, T. P. (1989). *American Genesis: A Century of Invention and Technological Enthusiasm.* New York: Viking Press.

Ihde, D. (1990). *Technology and the Lifeworld: From Garden to Earth.* Bloomington: Indiana University Press.

Jonas, H. (1974). *Philosophical Essays: From Ancient Creed to Technological Man.* Englewood Cliffs, NJ: Prentice Hall.

Jonas, H. (1984). *The Imperative of Responsibility: In Search of an Ethics for the Technological Age.* Chicago: University of Chicago Press.

Karliner, J. (1997). *The Corporate Planet: Ecology and Politics in the Age of Globalization.* San Francisco: Sierra Club Books.

Kevles, D. (1995). *In the Name of Eugenics: Genetics and the Uses of Human Heredity.* Cambridge, MA: Harvard University Press.

Keynes, J. (1989). *General Theory of Employment, Interest and Money.* New York: Harcourt Brace.

Kidder, T. (1982). *The Soul of a New Machine.* London: Allen Lane.

Kitcher, P. (1996). *The Lives to Come: The Genetic Revolution and Human Possibilities.* New York: Touchstone.

Koestler, A. (1964). *The Act of Creation*. New York: Macmillan.

Korten, D. C. (1995). *When Corporations Rule the World*. West Hartford, CT: Kumarian Press.

Kraybill, D. (2001). *The Riddle of Amish Culture*. Baltimore: Johns Hopkins University Press.

Kuhn, R. (2000). *Made in China*. New York: TV Books.

Kuhn, T. (1970). *The Structure of Scientific Revolutions*, 2nd ed. Chicago, IL: University of Chicago Press.

Kurzweil, R. (1990). *The Age of Intelligent Machines*. Cambridge, MA: MIT Press.

Kurzweil, R. (1999). *The Age of Spiritual Machines: When Computers Exceed Human Intelligence*. New York: Viking Press.

Kurzweil, R. (2006). *The Singularity Is Near*. New York: Penguin.

Landes, D. (1983). *Revolution in Time: Clocks and the Making of the Modern World*. Cambridge, MA: Harvard University Press.

Latour, B. (1987). *Science in Action*. Cambridge, MA: Harvard University Press.

Longman, P. (2004). *The Empty Cradle: How Falling Birthrates Threaten World Prosperity and What to Do about It*. New York: Basic Books.

Lovins, A. B. (1977). *Soft Energy Paths: Towards a Durable Peace*. Cambridge, MA: Ballinger.

Lyons, J., and Corner, P. (1966). *Altered Fates: Gene Therapy and the Retooling of Human Life*. New York: Norton.

Mackenzie, D., and Wajcman, J. (Eds.). (1999). *The Social Shaping of Technology*. Philadelphia: Open University Press.

Maisels, C. (1990). *The Emergence of Civilization: From Hunting and Gathering to Agriculture, Cities, and the State in the Near East*. London: Routledge & Kegan Paul.

Marx, L. (1964). *The Machine in the Garden: Technology and the Pastoral Ideal in America*. New York: Oxford University Press.

McGee, G. (1997). *The Perfect Baby: A Pragmatic Approach to Genetics*. Lanham, MD: Rowman & Littlefield.

McLuhan, M. (1964). *Understanding Media: The Extensions of Man*. New York: McGraw-Hill.

McPhee, J. (1989). *The Control of Nature*. New York: Farrar, Straus & Giroux.

Meredith, R. (2007). *The Elephant and the Dragon: The Rise of India and China and What It Means for All of Us*. New York: Norton.

Mesthene, E. (1970). *Technological Change: Its Impact on Man and Society*. New York: New American Library.

Meyerowitz, J. (1985). *No Sense of Place: The Impact of Electronic Media on Sociable Behavior*. New York: Oxford University Press.

Mills, S. (Ed.). (1997). *Turning Away from Technology: A New Vision for the 21st Century*. San Francisco: Sierra Club Books.

Mitcham, C. (1994). *Thinking through Technology: The Path between Engineering and Philosophy*. Chicago: University of Chicago Press.

Mitcham, C. (Ed.). (2006). *Encyclopedia of Science, Technology, and Ethics*. Macmillan Reference. New York: Thomson/Gale.

Mitcham, C., and Mackey, R. (Eds.). (1983). *Philosophy and Technology: Readings in Philosophical Problems of Technology*. New York: Free Press.

Moravec, H. (1989). *MindChildren: The Future of Robot and Human Intelligence*. Cambridge, MA: Harvard University Press.

Moravec, H. (1999). *Robot: Mere Machine to Transcendent Mind*. New York: Oxford University Press.

Mulhall, D. (2002). *Our Molecular Future: How Nanotechnology, Robotics, Genetics, and Artificial Intelligence Will Transform Our World*. Amherst, NY: Prometheus Books.

Mumford, L. (1934). *Technics and Civilization*. New York: Harcourt, Brace, and World.

Mumford, L. (1966). *Technics and Human Development*. New York: Harcourt Brace Jovanovich.

Naisbitt, J. (1984). *Megatrends: Ten New Directions Transforming Our Lives*. New York: Warner Books.

Negroponte, N. (1995). *Being Digital*. New York: Vintage Books.

Noble, D. F. (1979). *America by Design: Science, Technology, and the Rise of Corporate Capitalism*. New York: Oxford University Press.

Noble, D. F. (1984). *Forces of Production: A Social History of Industrial Automation*. New York: Knopf.

Noble, D. F. (1997). *The Religion of Technology: The Divinity of Man and the Spirit of Invention*. New York: Knopf.

Nye, D. E. (1994). *American Technological Sublime*. Cambridge, MA: MIT Press.

Oakley, A. (1984). *The Captured Womb: A History of the Medical Care of Pregnant Women*. Oxford: Blackwell.

Oldenziel, R. (2004). *Making Technology Masculine: Men, Women, and Modern Machines in America*. Netherlands: Amsterdam University Press.

Pacey, A. (1983). *The Culture of Technology.* Cambridge, MA: MIT Press.

Perrin, N. (1979). *Giving Up the Gun: Japan's Reversion to the Sword, 1543–1879.* Boston: David R. Godine.

Petersen, J. (2007). *Understanding Surveillance Technologies: Spy Devices, Privacy, History, and Applications.* Boca Raton, FL: Auerbach Publications.

Petrovski, H. (1985). *The Engineer Is Human: The Role of Failure in Successful Design.* New York: St. Martin's Press.

Petrovski, H. (1996). *Invention by Design: How Engineers Get from Thought to Thing.* Cambridge, MA: Harvard University Press.

Pitt, J. C. (2000). *Thinking about Technology: Foundations of the Philosophy of Technology.* New York: Seven Bridges Press.

Pool, R. (1997). *Beyond Engineering: How Society Shapes Technology.* New York: Oxford University Press.

Postman, N. (1985). *Amusing Ourselves to Death: Public Discourse in the Age of Show Business.* New York: Viking Press.

Postman, N. (1992). *Technopoly: The Surrender of Culture to Technology.* New York: Knopf.

Postrel, V. (1998). *The Future and Its Enemies: The Growing Conflict over Creativity, Enterprise, and Progress.* New York: Free Press.

Pursell, C. (2007). *The Machine in America: A Social History of Technology.* Baltimore, MD: Johns Hopkins University Press.

Reich, R. (1992). *The Work of Nations: Preparing Ourselves for 21st Century Capitalism.* New York: Random House.

Rheingold, H. (1991). *Virtual Reality.* New York: Summit Books.

Rifkin, J. (1995). *The End of Work: The Decline of the Global Labor Force and the Dawn of the Post-Market Era.* New York: Putnam.

Rifkin, J. (2002). *The Hydrogen Economy: The Creation of the World-Wide Energy Web and the Redistribution of Power on Earth.* New York: Jeremy P. Tarcher.

Roberts, J. M. (1993). *A Short History of the World.* New York: Oxford University Press.

Roberts, P. (2004). *The End of Oil: On the Edge of a Perilous New World.* Boston, MA: Houghton Miffin.

Rodrik, D. (2007). *One Economics, Many Recipes: Globalization, Institutions, and Economic Growth.* Princeton, NJ: Princeton University Press.

Rosenberg, N. (1982). *Inside the Black Box: Technology and Economics.* Cambridge, MA: Cambridge University Press.

Roszak, T. (1994). *The Cult of Information: A Neo-Luddite Treatise on High Tech, Artificial Intelligence, and the True Art of Thinking,* 2nd ed. Berkeley: University of California Press.

Russo, E., and Cove, D. (1995). *Genetic Engineering: Dreams and Nightmares.* New York: Viking Press.

Rybczynski, W. (1985). *Taming the Tiger: The Struggle to Control Technology.* New York: Freeman.

Sachs, J. (2006). *The End of Poverty: Economic Possibilities for Our Time.* New York: Penguin.

Sahal, D. (1981). *Patterns of Technological Innovation.* Cambridge, MA: Cambridge University Press.

Schick, K. D., and Toth, N. (1993). *Making Silent Stones Speak: Human Evolution and the Dawn of Technology.* New York: Simon & Schuster.

Schor, J. (1991). *The Overworked American: The Unexpected Decline of Leisure.* New York: Basic Books.

Schumacher, E. F. (1973). *Small Is Beautiful: Economics as if People Mattered.* New York: Harper & Row.

Sclove, R. E. (1995). *Democracy and Technology.* New York: Guilford Press.

Shaiken, H. (1985). *Work Transformed: Automation and Labor in the Computer Age.* New York: Holt, Rinehart & Winston.

Shrader-Frechette, K., and Westra, L. (Eds.). (1997). *Technology and Values.* Totowa, NJ: Rowman & Littlefield.

Silver, L. (1997). *Remaking Eden: Cloning and Beyond in a Brave New World.* New York: Avon Books.

Singer, P. (2002). *One World: The Ethics of Globalization.* New Haven, CT: Yale University Press.

Smith, A. (1937). *An Inquiry into the Nature and Causes of the Wealth of Nations.* New York: Modern Library.

Speth, J. (2004). *Red Sky at Morning: America and the Crisis of the Global Environment.* New Haven, CT: Yale University Press.

Stiglitz, J. (2006). *Making Globalization Work.* New York: Norton.

Strasser, S. (1989). *Satisfaction Guaranteed: The Making of the American Mass Market.* New York: Pantheon.

Strobel, F. (1993). *Upward Dreams, Downward Mobility: The Economic Decline of the American Middle Class.* Lanham, MD: Rowman & Littlefield.

Strong, D. (1995). *Crazy Mountains: Learning from Wilderness to Weigh Technology.* Albany: State University of New York Press.

Sunstein, C. (2006). *Infotopia: How Many Minds Produce Knowledge.* New York: Oxford University Press.

Teich, A. H. (1997). *Technology and the Future,* 7th ed. New York: St. Martin's Press.

Tenner, E. (1997). *Why Things Bite Back: Technology and the Revenge of Unintended Consequences.* Cambridge, MA: Harvard University Press.

Thurow, L. C. (1996). *The Future of Capitalism: How Today's Economic Forces Shape Tomorrow's World.* New York: Morrow.

Tiles, M., and Oberdiek, H. (1995). *Living in a Technological Culture: Human Tools and Human Values.* New York: Routledge.

Toffler, A., and Toffler, H. (1990). *Powershift.* New York: Bantam Books.

Turkle, S. (1982). *The Second Self: The Human Spirit in a Computer Culture.* New York: Simon & Schuster.

Turney, J. (1998). *Frankenstein's Footsteps: Science, Genetics and Popular Culture.* New Haven, CT: Yale University Press.

Uchitelle, L. (2007). *The Disposable American: Layoffs and Their Consequences.* New York: Vintage Press.

Van Creveld, M. (1989). *Technology and War: From 2000 BC to the Present.* New York: Free Press.

Vandermeer, J., and Goldberg, D. (2003). *Population Ecology: First Principles.* Princeton, NJ: Princeton University Press.

Volti, R. (1992). *Society and Technological Change,* 2nd ed. New York: St. Martin's Press.

Wajcman, J. (1991). *Feminism Confronts Technology.* University Park, PA: Pennsylvania State University Press.

White, L., Jr. (1966). *Medieval Technology and Social Change.* New York: Oxford University Press.

Wilson, D. (2005). *How to Survive a Robot Uprising: Tips on Defending Yourself against the Coming Rebellion.* London: Bloomsbury.

Wilson, E. O. (1998). *Consilience: The Unity of Knowledge.* New York: Knopf.

Winner, L. (1977). *Autonomous Technology: Technics-Out-of-Control as a Theme in Political Thought.* Cambridge, MA: MIT Press.

Winner, L. (1986). *The Whale and the Reactor: A Search for Limits in an Age of High Technology.* Chicago: University of Chicago Press.

Wosk, J. (2003). *Women and the Machine: Representations from the Spinning Wheel to the Electronic Age.* Baltimore, MD: Johns Hopkins University Press.

Wresch, W. (1996). *Disconnected: Haves and Have-Nots in the Information Age.* New Brunswick, NJ: Rutgers University Press.

Wright, L. (1964). *Home Fires Burning: The History of Domestic Heating and Cooking.* London: Routledge & Kegan Paul.

Yergin, D. (1991). *The Prize: The Epic Quest for Oil, Money, and Power.* New York: Simon & Schuster.

Young, S. (2005). *Designer Evolution: A Transhumanist Manifesto.* Amherst, NY: Prometheus Books.

Zuboff, S. (1988). *In the Age of the Smart Machine: The Future of Work and Power.* New York: Basic Books.

APPENDIX A

Technology and Ethics in the News

The following news items were selected to illustrate the ethical issues that can arise with scientific and technological innovation. Each news item has been selected to ensure that there is no obviously correct ethical response to the innovation in question, allowing students the opportunity to defend competing ethical approaches to them. Given this, it is recommended that instructors use the suggested discussion questions as guidelines for stimulating debate, rather than for directing students towards a particular ethical solution to the issues at hand.

In addition to using these items as a basis for discussion it would also be a good idea to assign students to search for similar news stories that highlight the ethical and social issues related to technology. To aid this suggested keywords and search terms have been offered at the end of each news item, as well as suggestions for further reading. Some of the articles linked to have sections for the online posting of comments. It could be a useful teaching exercise to require students to find an article that allows such posting, read it, and then post a comment of their own.

1) GLOBALIZATION AND ECONOMICS

Labor disputes increasing in China

Labor disputes are becoming more common in China, as workers are becoming encouraged to protect their rights and demand higher wages as a result of government policies from 2008 aimed at closing the income gap between its citizens and protecting its workers. In 2008, for example, there was almost double the number of factory shutdowns as a result of labor disputes than there were in 2007, according to the Ministry of Human Resources and Social Security. In many parts of China there is a backlog of labor dispute cases awaiting arbitration, with many workers having to wait up to a year for their complaints to be addressed.

However, if the Chinese currency is revaluated, making Chinese exports less competitive on the world market, to remain competitive on the global stage Chinese companies and local officials might collude to prevent these new laws being enforced.

The Chinese workers are in a weak position to defend themselves, for they still do not have the right to form unions independent of those controlled by the government, while many details of the laws designed to protect workers—such as the 2008 Labor Contract law—are vague. And companies often avoid paying the minimum legal wage and overtime pay.

Western experts hold that Chinese workers would be better protected were they allowed to form unions independent of those sanctioned by the Chinese government, although the government-sanctioned union has a major presence in state-owned companies and is reaching out to foreign-owned companies. In 2006, for example, it unionized Wal-Mart stores in China, while, in the United States, no Wal-Mart store employees have been organized by a union.

Further Readings

"As China Aids Labor, Unrest is Still Rising": http://www.nytimes.com/2010/06/21/world/asia/21chinalabor.html?_r=1&hp

"What does China labour unrest mean for firms?": http://in.reuters.com/article/idINIndia-50139920100715

"How sincere is Wal-Mart's demand that Chinese suppliers meet labor and environmental standards?": http://www.nakedcapitalism.com/2010/02/how-sincere-is-wal-marts-demand-that-chinese-suppliers-meet-labor-and-environmental-standards.html

KEYWORDS

ACTFU, Chinese labor unrest, International Labor Organization, Universal Declaration of Human Rights, Wal-Mart unionization

Questions:

1. Do you believe that Chinese workers should be allowed to form unions that are independent of Government control, as is the case in the United States, or not? Does a government prohibition on such unions violate any human rights of workers? What is the basis and origin of these rights, if they exist?
2. Do you believe that multinational corporations like Wal-Mart should be required to provide equitable working conditions to all of their employees, regardless of the country in which they work?
3. Should governments require companies to provide a living wage and decent working conditions to their employees? Or should companies be permitted to offer the lowest wages for which workers will settle, in order to increase profits?
4. Do the western brand-name retail companies who source their products from factories in China and other low-wage countries have any responsibility to help to improve working conditions for these workers? Explain your point of view.

2) GLOBALIZATION AND PRODUCTION TRANSPARENCY

Who really makes what you buy?

Consumers currently have significant access to marketplace information, but it can still be hard to know which companies made the goods that we purchase. For example, it is hard to determine whether Foxconn—a company which employs around 400,000 workers in its factories in China, and which recently was in the news owing to a rash of worker suicides—made devices, equipment, or components for particular gadgets, even though it supplies parts for items made by a diverse set of major manufacturers.

But what if it was possible to find out where items were made just as easily as it is now simple to find consumer reviews or the cheapest price on something? Would such increased consumer access to information have any effect on the global economy?

There are some efforts already in place to secure such transparency. At ProjectLabel.org it is possible to discover a company's scores in such categories as waste management and worker treatment, while GoodGuide.com offers health, environment, and safety scores for 65,000 products. Moreover, some companies, such as The Gap, offer their own information summaries, but it is often difficult to translate these into information about the specific product you are considering buying. And there's the rub: knowing something about a specific product is likely to mean more to consumers than a big-picture summary of a company's practices. But if this could be done and if the production of every product was made truly transparent it is likely to change the way that companies operate.

Further Readings

"Where do gadgets really come from?" http://www.nytimes.com/2010/06/27/magazine/27FOB-consumed-t.html?ref=magazine

"Rob Walker strikes again ... Where do gadgets really come from?": http://jules.dailygrommet.com/2010/06/28/rob-walker-strikes-again-where-do-gadgets-really-come-from/

"True gadget transparency: in the works!": http://www.murketing.com/journal/?p=5728

KEYWORDS

Business and human rights, global production, supply chain transparency

Questions:

1. Would it alter your purchasing habits if you could tell where items you purchase were made, and how the companies that made their components and distributed them treated their workers and affected the environment? In what ways would your purchasing habits change, if they would at all?
2. Do you think that companies would have commercial reasons for wishing to avoid such transparency? Would they, for example, wish their competitors to know of their supply chains? If so, do you think that this is ethically relevant?
3. Have you ever read corporate social and environmental responsibility reports and summaries that companies like The Gap issue? Do you trust them? If so, why? If not, why not?
4. Do you believe that you have an ethical responsibility to make purchasing decisions based on how companies treat their workers or how their business activities affect the environment either in your own or other countries? Explain.

5. Would you be willing to pay more for products that you were sure were ethically manufactured if you were certain the extra money would directly benefit workers and help protect the environment? Why or why not?

3) ETHICAL ISSUES IN MEDICAL TECHNOLOGY

Extending life—but at what cost?

Many Americans are the victims of financial incentives that encourage medical providers to provide them with the maximum amount of treatment possible. Such treatment can save the lives of persons who might have otherwise died, but it could leave them unable to care for themselves. This has resulted in as many millions of people in America, mainly women, caring for older family members. Nearly a third of Americans over 85, for example, need to be cared for as they suffer from dementia. The number of such caregivers grows each day, as medical technology saves and prolongs the lives of people who would previously have been killed by the health crises that they experienced.

Yet although new medical technology is saving more lives, many of those who are saved would have preferred to have died. Indeed, patients are more likely than physicians to reject aggressive life-saving treatment when fully informed of its costs and benefits. Unfortunately, however, patients are sometimes not in a position to make their treatment decisions themselves, and their relatives opt for aggressive treatment, believing this to be in their best interests. Moreover, doctors have financial incentives to pursue aggressive treatment, for no one makes money when medical interventions are declined. By contrast, the profit margins for manufacturers of cardiac devices, for example, are close to 30%. And it is not irrelevant to note that the research that shows the most positive benefits of such devices has strong financial ties, either directly or indirectly, to the companies that produce them.

In addition to the effects on the life-spans of the patients themselves, life-extending technology has an effect on those of their caregivers. An Ohio State University study showed that the DNA of the caregivers of Alzheimer's patients suffer from the degradation of their chromosomes that reduces their life-span by four to eight years. And, finally, for persons who serve as caregivers trust in physicians as healers can be lost.

Further Readings

"What broke my father's heart": http://www.nytimes.com/2010/06/20/magazine/20pacemaker-t.html?ref=magazine&pagewanted=print

"Oregon medical board, death with dignity safeguards protect patients" http://compassionandchoices.org/blog/?m=201006

"Medical technology prolongs lives—but is that a good thing?" http://www.medcitynews.com/2010/06/medical-technology-prolongs-lives-but-is-that-a-good-thing/

KEYWORDS

Caregiver lifespan, death with dignity, life extension, medical technology, QALY

Questions:

1. In discussing the effects of life-extending technology on caregivers one might infer that caregivers trade off some of their (good) years of life to keep those

they are caring for alive in a diminished state, and that it would have been better had this trade-off not occurred. Do you believe that persons' years of life can be traded off in this way? If so, should we make such trade-offs between other groups of people? For example, should we reallocate medical care from the elderly to younger persons, on the grounds that the latter could benefit more from our investment in them?

2. Could the financial incentives that encourage physicians to pursue aggressive treatment be rectified? If so, how? Could a market system do this itself, or would it require government intervention?
3. Should we be more concerned with the length of our lives, or with their quality? Who should be able to make this kind of judgment? Explain your answer.
4. Do you think that it is ethical for a family member serving as a caregiver to request that the life-extending technology, such as a pacemaker, that is keeping those they are caring for alive be turned off? Is there a conflict of interest between the caregiver and the cared for that is problematic? Explain.
5. Is there any moral difference between a physician letting patients die by withdrawing a life-sustaining treatment and assisting them in dying (e.g., through injecting them with overdoses of morphine), at their request?

4) BUSINESS ETHICS

Virtue, ethics codes, and the Gulf oil spill

In June 2010 the House Energy and Commerce Committee detailed its findings about the BP Gulf Oil spill, which at that time was still spewing thousands of barrels of oil each day into the Gulf of Mexico. The disaster, which killed 11 workers, was the worst oil spill in U.S. history. The committee noted that BP repeatedly made decisions that increased the risk of a blowout in order to cut costs, in part because the project was already late and costing at least $500,000 a day in overruns. For example, even though engineers recognized the risks of proceeding with only 6 instead of the recommended 21 centralizers, devices that would have reduced the risk of a blowout, they proceeded to save installation time. One engineer commented that it would "probably be fine" and asked "who cares?"

This attitude indicates an absence of ethics similar to that which was the part cause of the sub-prime mortgage crisis.

In response to the perceived prevalence of this attitude, faculty and students at Harvard Business School have launched an initiative to promote ethical behavior in MBA graduates. The MBA Oath is based on the Hippocratic Oath, and is a pledge that can be taken voluntarily, committing those who take it to high standards of ethical and professional behavior.

However, in addition to this Oath persons need practice in living ethically—both those engaged in business and those who are supposed to oversee and regulate their conduct. For example, it has been learned that members of the federal agency charged with overseeing oil and gas drilling, the Minerals Management Service, have accepted gifts from oil and gas companies.

Businesses do have to take risks, but the risks that they take should be weighed in comparison with the common good. And, as such, they need to be weighed by persons with solid ethical values and the experience of living in accord with them.

Further Readings

"BP: Creaky ethics in the Gulf oil spill" http://www.speroforum.com/a/35142/site/privacy.asp

"Gulf oil spill": http://www.huffingtonpost.com/news/bp-oil-spill

KEYWORDS

Gulf oil spill, professional ethics, virtue ethics

Questions:

1. The writer of this article and the students and faculty of Harvard Business School write of ethics and of responsibility. Is such talk sufficient to provide moral guidance, or should codes of ethics be more substantial than this? If they should be more substantial, who or what determines their content? (Please refer to Appendix B for some examples of ethics codes.)
2. Do you believe that businesses should be concerned with the common good? Why, or why not? If so, what is the common good, and how are we to assess it? If not, do you believe that business should operate as though their actions have no effects on others at all, and just blindly pursue profits?
3. Should authors of codes of ethics seek to outline a rule-based approach to morality, or is it enough to rely on persons being good persons in the light of their own moral codes? If we do rely on ethics codes, how do they supplement the virtuous life?
4. Do you believe that industries or professions should adopt their own codes of ethics, or should there simply be a uniform code of ethics that can guide a good human life in any situation, regardless of persons' occupations or professions? How does you answer to this question relate to the sample ethics codes found in Appendix B?

5) CONSUMER PROTECTION: NANOFOOD RISKS

Nanofood, risk, and choices

An increasing amount of food products across the world is becoming nanofood—food in which nanotechnology is used in its cultivation, processing, or packaging. The food industry favors nanofood as it sees it as a way to increase its profits; the business is already worth $200 billion a year, and is growing rapidly.

Nanotechnology can be used in smart food, such as a drink whose color, flavor, and nutritional value customers can customize after purchase through placing it in a specially tuned microwave that activates nanocapsules containing the chemicals necessary to satisfy the choices made. Nanotechnology is already being deployed in food production; a European company, for example, produces a nanoscale version of a class of food additives called carotenoids, which it sells to major food and beverage companies.

Nanorobots—robots that are at or close to the microscopic scale of a nanometer—could also be used in food production. But there are other possible uses for them, too, such as injecting them into humans to alter neurological or biological processes. Yet, since this is an emerging technology there is little current understanding of how to control these devices once they have been injected.

The large corporations insist that nanofood is natural, uses no new substances, and are just smaller versions of old ones. But others disagree as matter behaves differently at the nanoscale displaying, for example, quantum effects leading to different risks being associated with it. For example, while aluminum is typically stable, it is explosive at the nanoscale, and carbon nanostructures used in electronics are highly toxic when released into the environment.

Proponents of nanofood hold that nanotechnology promises to increase productivity and cost-effectiveness, help in the design of healthier and tastier products, and provide better food safety. However, we still do not know what the risks of nanofood are and, in the view of some, the new regulations on nanofood do not address these risks adequately. We should also make nanofood transparent, providing the public with information about the use of this new technology through clear information and labeling.

Further Readings

"Nanofood, Nanotech and Nanites: Quantum Effects and Fundamental Choices?" http://www.huffingtonpost.com/dk-matai/nanofood-nanotech-and-nan_b_536768.html

"Nanofood": http://innovationwatch-archive.com/choiceisyours/choiceisyours.2006.07.31.htm

"Are nanofoods sustainable?": http://food.change.org/blog/view/are_nanofoods_sustainable

KEYWORDS

Nanofood, nanotechnology, sustainability

Questions:

1. Do you believe that businesses should follow the precautionary principle and allow nanofoods to be marketed only when all of the risks of them are known and a determination has been made that they are outweighed by the benefits of the foods in question? Who should make such a determination? Can we ever know all of the risks of a product in advance? If the answer to the last question is no, how confident do we need to be in our assessment to allow a product to be marketed?
2. Given that nanotechnology could potentially impose risks on everyone, should companies be allowed to determine for themselves when a product can come to market—or should this be subject to government regulation or some kind of independent review? How should such decisions be made and by whom?
3. Since people are willing to tolerate different levels of risk, is it fair to require people to accept risks that they would not choose to accept were the decision up to them? If so, why? If not, should marketing decisions be guided according to the preferences of the most risk-averse or the least risk-averse members of our society?
4. Do consumers have a right to know if they are consuming products made with nanotechnology? Why, or why not? How does your answer to this question influence your view of the question of whether there should be transparency in the production of consumer goods, addressed in "Who Really Makes What You Buy?" on page 426?

6) ETHICS AND THE ENVIRONMENT

Are electric cars bad for the environment?

The production and use of electric cars is not necessarily good for the environment if it leads to our reliance on oil turning into a greater reliance on coal, which is burned to generate electricity—especially since many believe both the mining and burning of coal as a fuel is even more destructive to the environment than the use of oil.

According to the U.S. Environmental Protection Agency's data from 1999, burning coal in power plants releases 48 tons of mercury into the air and water of America every year, as well as contributing 40% of U.S. carbon dioxide emissions. As well as the health effects of such coal-burning emissions, the National Academy of Sciences estimates that coal mining and burning cause $62 billion worth of environmental damage each year in the United States alone.

Currently, electricity is mainly produced by burning coal; over half of the electricity in the United States is produced in this way, while the figure is estimated to be around 70% in China. Given the increase in demand for electricity that will be generated to meet the increase in use of electric and plug-in hybrid cars, coal-fired electricity plants will increase output unless renewable sources of electric power (such as solar- and wind-based power plants) are increased.

Further Readings

"Will more electric cars increase reliance on coal?": http://business-ethics.com/2010/03/13/1438-will-electric-cars-increase-reliance-on-coal/

"Who killed my electric car?": http://www.cnn.com/2006/US/07/25/paul.commentary/

"So, what's the deal with electric cars?": http://www.oregonlive.com/environment/index.ssf/2009/04/so_whats_the_deal_with_electri.html

KEYWORDS

coal and electricity, Electric/hybrid cars, global warming.

Questions:

1. In what way does the demand for electric and hybrid cars generate unintended and counterproductive side effects? Can you think of other examples in which ethically motivated demands for products lead to such unintended consequences? Could such problems be solved by increased education? Who should be responsible for providing this education? What are some other means by which such problems might be solved?
2. Who bears the costs of the various types of pollution and environmental degradation resulting from producing most of our electricity by burning coal? Should we require coal-burning plants to bear all the costs of their pollution? Do the consumers of their products benefit from their failing to do so? If so, should the consumers be responsible for some of the costs of the pollution these plants produce? Do they already bear these costs? If so, how?
3. Do we have an ethical duty to be environmentally responsible consumers? What are some examples of environmentally responsible consumption? What are some examples of consumption that is not environmentally responsible? Explain your answers.

4. Do you believe that people should demand that their utility producers bring more green power online? How might persons be motivated to do this? Do you see any practical obstacles to individuals being motivated to demand such change? Explain your answers.
5. Should the United States make its commitment to reduce the use of coal-fired electric energy generation contingent upon a similar reduction being made by other countries? If yes, the how might such an agreement be monitored and enforced?

7) WATER SCARCITY AND NUCLEAR ENERGY

Nuclear power, the water crisis, and climate change

Experts warn that the United States is entering a time of water scarcity. This has widespread implications, including for the nation's nuclear power plants.

Generating electricity from nuclear power is extremely water intensive, as nuclear power plants use hundreds of millions of gallons of water a day in cooling and condensing steam after it has been produced by the heat generated through nuclear fusion, spinning turbines which in turn drive electric generators. Increasing water scarcity raises concerns that the water levels of the rivers and lakes on which nuclear power plants are often located could drop below the plants' intake pipes, or that the shallow water could become too warm for use in cooling.

It is worth noting that the owners of nuclear plants have often argued that they should be allowed to operate their plants beyond their 40-year permits on the basis of climate change and clean energy. But owing to the vulnerability of some plants to drought and higher water temperatures doubts have been raised about their role in confronting climate changes. If too much of our climate change mitigation strategy relies on nuclear power, we risk our ability to slow the rate of climate change. So, we must solve the climate and water crises together to meet energy needs in an environmentally sustainable manner.

Further Readings

"Water Scarcity: Nuclear Power's Achilles' Heel" http://www.huffingtonpost.com/kyle-rabin/water-scarcity-nuclear-po_b_628294.html

"Waste not: Mohave Sun Power's solution for water scarcity" http://social.csptoday.com/qa/waste-not-mohave-sun-powers-solution-water-scarcity

KEYWORDS

Climate change, nuclear power, water scarcity

Questions:

1. In what way is nuclear power a cleaner form of energy than that produced by burning coal? In what ways might it be considered to be less clean? Which form of energy do you think is environmentally preferable, and why?
2. How does the water crisis affect nuclear power plants? How does this undermine their owners' claims to be of use in addressing climate change? How might the owners of these plants respond to it?

3. If water is becoming increasingly scarce, should it be rationed by the government? If so, what principles should determine how water is allocated and for what uses? Or should we just allow the market to set a price for water? Explain your answer.
4. How should we respond to the water scarcity crisis on (a) an individual level, (b) a national level? Explain your answer.

8) ARTIFICIAL INTELLIGENCE AND EMPLOYMENT

Does technological innovation threaten our jobs?

Microsoft's medical avatar project is one of several projects intended to show people how they and computers might soon be communicating. Progress in moving toward the development of artificial intelligence has been increasing rapidly, which is leading to transformations not only in how people and machines can communicate and collaborate but which could also lead to significant changes in the workplace, eliminating millions of jobs, creating others, and altering the nature and routines or the workplace.

Some developments are striking, such as Microsoft's creation of a medical avatar—a face on a screen—which can talk to patients and offer preliminary diagnoses of their medical issues. Others are more mundane, such as persons talking to their cell phones instead of typing into them, and drivers talking to their cars to find directions or play music. Doctors are increasingly using speech-recognition software to transcribe patient visits, while the military uses it for in-field translation between languages. So good is this technology becoming that it is now useful in many ways. It allows many calls-to-call centers to be automated entirely, and can even detect emotion in a person's voice and route their call accordingly.

Given this, such technology might soon replace the estimated four million workers in American call centers, as well as other workers—such as medical transcriptionists—whose jobs it will soon be able to do. However, just as it will serve to eliminate jobs, so too will this technology create new ones, just as the Internet has led to new jobs at new businesses like Google.

Some people worry, however, that smart machines capable of artificial intelligence, at some time, could be sued to insulate corporations, governments, and the wealthy from the rest of society. Rather than having to listen to customer complaints, for example, companies might use machines to do this for them. But, even in the face of these worries, the growing usefulness of this technology means that it will spread, and it will be up to humans to determine its applications and risks.

Further Readings

"Computers Learn to Listen, and Some Talk Back": http://www.nytimes.com/2010/06/25/science/25voice.html?pagewanted=1&sq=virtual%20reality&st=cse&scp=27

"Scientists, not artists, will solve the world's big problems": http://www.theaustralian.com.au/higher-education/opinion-analysis/fruits-of-the-poetry-of-discovery/story-e6frgcko-1225888653726

KEYWORDS

Artificial intelligence and jobs, automation, avatar, expert systems, Luddites

Questions:

1. Are any moral duties owed to persons whose jobs are lost as a result of the introduction of new technologies? Do you believe, for example, that there should be government programs that discourage companies from replacing workers with artificially intelligent robots? Why, or why not?
2. Since this sort of technology is best suited to performing the sorts of tasks that could be performed by workers with little education, do you believe that its introduction raises issues of distributive justice insofar as those who are likely to be adversely affected by it being among some of the most economically vulnerable in society?
3. In what ways could this technology be used to isolate business, social, and government elites from others in society? What forces do you think might be at work to counteract the possibility of this happening? Of these three categories of elites, which do you think might be the least amenable to being isolated in this way, and why? Which of these elites do you think might be the most likely to use this technology to distance itself?
4. Do you think that new communication technologies serve to distance persons from each other, or do you think that they help persons to stay connected? What are the ethical implications of the effects of such technologies? Explain your point of view.
5. Do you believe that the introduction of these new communication technologies is making society more unequal? Explain your answer.

9) ETHICS AND GENETIC ENGINEERING

Do gourmets dream of modified fish?

The Food and Drug Administration is considering whether to approve for human consumption of genetically engineered salmon that can grow at twice the rate of normal salmon, reaching market size in 16 to 18 months rather than three years. The salmon will not be bigger than normal salmon.

The developer of the salmon has been trying to secure FDA approval for a decade, but as of June 2010 seems to have submitted most or all of the data needed to secure approval, including that which shows that the salmon are safe to eat, safe for the environment, and nutritionally equivalent to other salmon.

The approval of the salmon would pave the way for the approval of other genetically engineered animals, such as pigs that could supply healthier bacon, or whose manure is less toxic to the environment.

Critics of the FDA's approval process charge that it does not allow a full assessment of the environmental effects of the procedure under review.

It is not clear how consumers will react to the genetically altered salmon, and there is an ongoing discussion as to whether or not they should be labeled as such. It is also not clear there the legal authority exists to require such labeling, but it could be a voluntary matter on the part of the companies who produce genetically altered animals for consumption.

Further Readings

"FDA nears approval of genetically engineered salmon": http://www.kansascity.com/2010/07/11/2075775/fda-nears-approval-of-genetically.html

"Genetically Altered Salmon Get Closer to the Table": http://www.nytimes.com/2010/06/26/business/26salmon.html?pagewanted=1&_r=2&hp

"FDA Close to Approving Genetically Engineered Salmon?" http://www.politicsdaily.com/2010/07/12/fda-close-to-approving-genetically-engineered-salmon/

KEYWORDS

FDA, genetic engineering, genetically engineered salmon

Questions:

1. In what ways could the production of genetically altered life forms pose a danger to the environment? Could such dangers be mitigated or eliminated in all cases? Explain your reasoning here. How does genetic engineering differ morally from altering animals through selective breeding—if it differs at all? Explain your answer.
2. Do consumers have a right to know if the food they eat has been genetically engineered? Why, or why not? Should there be a labeling requirement in the United States such as exists in European Union countries, or should we continue to rely on a voluntary labeling scheme?
3. Do you think the Food and Drug Administration should require that its approval be secured before genetically engineered foods and drugs be put into the marketplace? What ethical arguments could be used to support and to criticize this requirement?

10) GENETICALLY MODIFIED ORGANISMS

Genetically modified insects: benefit or bane?

Many scientists believe that genetically modified (GM) insects could be used to prevent human deaths through reducing death and incapacitation due to insect-borne diseases as well as through reducing insect damage to crops and livestock. In addition to agricultural uses, insects are being genetically modified to produce pharmaceutical proteins, while honeybees are being modified so that they are resistant to diseases and parasites.

However, there are concerns about releasing genetically modified insects into the wild. A few years ago, in Arizona, genetically modified pink bollworms were released into the wild under netting. If the experiment was a success they would be further modified and then released into the wild to breed but produce no offspring that survive. This would lessen the need for expensive pesticides; in other insect species it could reduce the risk of insect-borne diseases. GM crop companies that sell GM crops designed to combat insects are also concerned that modified insects could reduce the demand for their products.

There is still uncertainty about the effects that GM insects could have. It is possible, for example, that transgenic traits could be transmitted into the wild population of insects, creating new challenges—which might include the more effective transmission of disease, or the transmission of new diseases. It is also possible that modifying the genetic composition of food-producing insects like honeybees could result in modifications to the food they produce. These uncertainties need to be addressed by regulators who must weigh and balance the costs and benefits of GM insects to manage their risks. There is also a question of whether the regulators would stand up to the producers if they needed to, and whether the pace of new GM research would outpace regulatory preparedness, which would require cross-disciplinary cooperation.

It should also be noted that insects can migrate between countries relatively easily. This poses international regulatory challenges that GM crops have not given rise to, and so international regulatory bodies could be needed.

Further Readings

"Genetically Modified Insects: What Next?": http://www.huffingtonpost.com/dk-matai/genetically-modified-inse_b_618190.html

"New Report Finds Genetically Modified Insects May Offer Public Health and Agricultural Benefits, but Clear Regulatory Oversight Is Lacking": http://www.pewtrusts.org/news_room_detail.aspx?id=17958

"Worm Turns For US Cotton Farmers": http://www.geneticengineering.net/first-gminsectstobereleased.htm

KEYWORDS

Genetically modified crops, genetically modified insects, genetically modified organisms

Questions:

1. Should the fact that GM insects could pose economic problems to companies that sell GM crops be of ethical concern? What are the similarities and differences between this issue and that of worker displacement by new technologies of the sort discussed in the article "Does Technological Innovation Threaten Our Jobs" on page 434?
2. In what ways are the ethical problems posed by GM insects similar to those posed by GM salmon, as discussed in the article "Do Gourmets Dream of Modified Fish" on page 435? In what ways are they different? Do genetically altered salmon raise the same international ethical concerns as do GM insects? Why, or why not? Could they?
3. The author of "Genetically Modified Insects: What Next?" holds that the uncertainties associated with GM insects should be addressed by regulators. Do you agree with this, or do you think that the use of GM insects should be unchecked? Would it make a difference to you if companies would be required to pay for any damages that they caused? Would this be a suitable approach to take for GM organisms? Why, or why not?
4. Do you think that it is unethical to eradicate a species of insect, even if it is harmful? Why, or why not? Do you think that it is unethical to kill individual insects? Do you believe that a species has a higher moral status in itself than the individuals within it? Why, or why not?

11) THE GLOBALIZATION OF TECHNOLOGY

The Butterfly Effect and the Gulf Oil Crisis

According to the Butterfly Effect, the smallest change in one part of the world can set in motion a chain of events that lead to a significant change in another part of it.

The oil that is currently polluting the world means that major Butterfly Effects are imminent, especially as the Great Ocean Conveyor Belt circulates some of these effects to all of the oceans. Moreover, since the oil spills are much more significant than the flapping of a butterfly's wings, they are likely to lead to major changes. In this context the findings of "The Father of Chaos Theory"—Edward Lorenz—are worth noting. Lorenz held that complexity will arise out of simplicity, step by step—a claim that is an illustration of the Butterfly Effect. However, chaotic behavior can lead not only to destruction but also to creativity and to life. Chaos theory is relevant to all branches of science; the human heartbeat is chaotic, as is the solar system, the weather, and the stock market.

Since the effects of the oil spill in the Gulf are likely to have worldwide effects, it seems that other countries and international organizations should be involved.

Further Readings

"Butterfly Effect, Oil Gusher & Edge of Chaos: World Wide Summit?": http://beforeitsnews.com/story/104/053/Butterfly_Effect,_Oil_Gusher_Edge_of_Chaos:_World_Wide_Summit.html

"Too Complex Not to Fail: UT Professors Analyze the Gulf Oil Spill": http://blogs.mccombs.utexas.edu/energy/2010/06/24/too-complex-not-to-fail-ut-professors-analyze-the-gulf-oil-spill/

"Oil spill initiates butterfly effect": http://www.voiceccc.com/local/oil-spill-initiates-butterfly-effect-1.2276837#5

KEYWORDS

Butterfly effect, chaos theory, Gulf oil spill

Questions:

1. Given that the Butterfly Effect can lead to both good and bad consequences, should we be less concerned about the Gulf oil spill, on the grounds that it might have overall positive benefits in the long run? Or can we assume that we know which large-scale actions will have adverse consequences and which will have beneficial ones?
2. If even small actions could have large-scale effects, is it also true that our omissions—the things that we choose not to do—could similarly have large-scale effects? Does this mean that we should think just as carefully about our omissions as our actions? Why, or why not?
3. If we cannot accurately predict the effects of some of our actions, how can we be held morally responsible for them? Could we be held responsible for some of the effects of our actions, but not others? Which ones?
4. Do you believe that the international community should have a say in how the United States responds to the oil spill? If so, do you believe that it should have a say in any major event that could potentially affect the world? Why, or why not?
5. How is the Butterfly Effect relevant to concerns about nanofoods, as expressed in the article "Nanofood, Risk, and Choices" on page 430?

12) TECHNOLOGY AND PERSONAL IDENTITY

How cognitively connected are we becoming?

Many writers are commenting on whether technology and its capacity for social networking is changing the way our minds work. Nicholas Carr, a blogger for the New York Times, fears that being digitally distracted will diminish a person's capacity for concentration and contemplation. However, maybe discussing whether technology is good or bad for us misses the point. Perhaps we should instead try to understand where technological evolution is headed.

Kevin Kelly, founding editor of Wired magazine, believes that technology is increasingly like a complex being that follows its own urges. It is certainly true that humans are being linked technologically into electronic webs that resemble large brains. Technology is also creating new social bonds, and can also make people more efficient; even though they might lack focus on any one particular task, we can add value to lots of different social endeavors. This is not a new phenomenon; the telephone achieved similar effects. Indeed, in the 1950 David Reisman and two colleagues noted that the inner-directed American who was guided by values shared with a small and stable group was giving way to the outer-directed American, who had more and shallower social contacts. This, too, was a form of loss of coherence at the level of the individual, which was—and is—being replaced by increasing social coherence.

Perhaps the point of evolution is to create such social brains. If we accept this scenario, is it bad news that humans might be subsumed by a social brain? At least the superorganism that seems to be emerging is decentralized, and so seems to be reconcilable with liberty. Moreover, we should welcome some increased coherence because a divided human cannot flourish, owing to the destructive power that technology affords us.

Further Readings

"Building one big brain": http://opinionator.blogs.nytimes.com/2010/07/06/the-web-we-weave/

"The Lonely Crowd": http://www.robertfulford.com/LonelyCrowd.html

"Internet use increases social connectivity": http://www.informationweek.com/news/internet/social_network/showArticle.jhtml?articleID=221600719

KEYWORDS

Internet use, social connectivity, technological alienation, the lonely crowd

Questions:

1. Do you think it is true that Americans are becoming increasingly outer-directed? If so, do you think that this should be a cause for ethical concern, whether this concern is positive or negative?
2. Do you believe it is possible that a decentralized superorganism would be more conducive to liberty than one which has a centralized structure? Why, or why not?
3. Are there any benefits to persons becoming more connected? What might they be?

4. In what ways do you think technological advances of the sort discussed here could affect the identity of persons? Do you think that people will remain fundamentally the same despite such technological advances, or not? Explain your answer.
5. Do you agree that a concern with whether or not technology is good or bad for us misses the point, as the author claims? Why, or why not?

13) GLOBALIZATION, CENSORSHIP, AND THE INTERNET

Google and China reach a compromise

In 2010 Google decided to stop censoring search results in China after discovering an attempt by someone based in China to hack into the e-mail accounts of human rights activists. Google was also prepared to close its business in China, if issues surrounding its decision to stop censoring search results could not be resolved with the Chinese government.

However, Google will now be running Google.cn into 2011, after the company places another click between Chinese citizens and unfiltered search results by placing a picture of a search box on its main site, which when clicked on takes Chinese citizens to Google.hk.com. That Google can get away with this is a testament to its power.

Google does not want to test its power just by shutting down Google.cn as the Chinese market is the largest in the world, and because Google is loved by the growing middle and upper classes in China the Chinese government is willing to make some concessions, so long as it is not seen to be kowtowing to a powerful U.S. corporation.

This compromise is either a good thing for net freedom or a capitulation by Google.

Further Readings

"Google to Stop Censoring Search Results in China After Hack Attack": http://www.wired.com/threatlevel/2010/01/google-censorship-china/

"Google and China agree on a fiction": http://www.cnn.com/2010/TECH/web/07/09/analysis.google.china/

KEYWORDS

Google censorship, Google hack attack, Google in China, Internet freedom.

Questions:

1. Do you think that Google should have agreed to this compromise? Why, or why not?
2. In this controversy, Google negotiated with a government almost as equals—as if the corporation had governmental-like power. Is this a good thing for a corporation to have, or a bad thing? Are corporations more or less accountable to the public for their actions than citizens? Why, or why not?
3. Do you believe that Google has an ethical responsibility to try to use its power to diminish the Chinese government's use of censorship? Or do you think that corporations should not interfere in Government affairs? Would it make a difference to your answer if China was a democracy? Why, or why not?

4. How do the Chinese government's concerns with Google illustrate one of the ways in which technological advances can enhance human well-being? Do you believe that all technological advances would have this effect? Indeed, do you think that this should even be the focus of ethical concern with information technology? Or should our concerns be focused elsewhere, as suggested in the article "How Cognitively Connected Are We Becoming?" on page 439?
5. Even though China is not a democracy, this story illustrates that its government must still be responsible to its citizens' desires in certain ways. How does it show this? Which portion of its citizenry is the Chinese government most concerned with? What does this tell you about one of the ethical implications of China's economic success?

14) PRIVACY AND SURVEILLANCE

Surveillance cameras: Crime prevention or privacy invasion?

Whether you are in a mall, a hotel, a public park, or a street, there is a good chance that a surveillance camera is close by. Surveillance cameras have played an important role into the investigation of the murder of Stephany Flores in Peru, as well as in the capture of the "Craigslist Killer," who was identified using hotel surveillance equipment, and the identification of persons thought to be responsible for the terrorist bombings in Mumbai and London.

Raymond Kelly, the police commissioner for New York City, believes that surveillance cameras act as a deterrent to crime, and could potentially provide information about crimes that occur.

But some people are critical of the use of surveillance. The legislative counsel for the American Civil Liberties Union, Chris Calabrese, notes that surveillance cameras are unregulated and are often installed without any public discussion. He also believes that they are changing the way that people behave in public.

However, surveys show that a majority of Americans support the increased use of surveillance cameras in public places. And no matter which side of the issue one supports, it seems that the cameras are not going to go away.

Further Readings

"Surveillance Camera Privacy Debate Widens": http://www.cbsnews.com/stories/2010/06/30/earlyshow/contributors/susankoeppen/main6633635.shtml

"CCTV in the sky: police plan to use military-style spy drones": http://www.guardian.co.uk/uk/2010/jan/23/cctv-sky-police-plan-drones

KEYWORDS

CCTV, privacy, surveillance, surveillance and crime

Questions:

1. What are the advantages and disadvantages of the use of surveillance cameras in public places? Do you believe that the advantages outweigh the disadvantages, or not? Explain your answer.

2. Do you think that there should be a public discussion about the installation of a surveillance camera before it is put in place? If so, do you think that such discussion should take place with respect to any method used to detect or deter crime, or not? If you do not think that there should be a public discussion about individual cameras, should there be one before a police department or other public agency is authorized to use them at all? Explain your answers.
3. How might cameras change how people behave in public? In what ways might such possible changes be beneficial to human well-being—and in what ways might they be detrimental?
4. Should we install cameras only in public areas, or should we install them also in (previously) private areas? Explain your answer.
5. Do you believe that the use of surveillance cameras should be regulated, and, if so, how?
6. Do you think that these regulations should be different for private users of surveillance as compared to its use by public bodies, such as police forces? If so, what should these regulatory differences be?

15) SUSTAINABILITY

Restaurants moving towards eco-friendly fishing

With reports that the oceans of the world are in danger of being emptied of fish, companies such as McDonald's Corp. and Yum Brands Inc., the owner of Long John Silver's, are moving towards more eco-friendly seafood buying.

Some experts note that their efforts are not coming too soon. A recent United Nations study predicts that without changes by the middle of this century commercial fisheries will produce less than 10% of what they were once capable of, while annual seafood demand will rise to at least 150 million metric tons by 2030. In illustration of this, Newfoundland cod-fishing grounds became so overfished that the fishery shut down in the early 1990s.

McDonald's used to purchase only North Atlantic cod, of the sort that had been caught in the Newfoundland fisheries. It now judges fisheries on how closely they are monitored, whether the fishing is sustainable, and the degree to which the type of fishing used affects the environment.

Since wild fisheries are unlikely to meet the world's growing seafood demand, aquaculture could be used to make up the shortfall. But this has its own challenges. Farm-raised fish need more pesticides and antibiotics, while some fish, such as salmon, have to be fed dye to give their flesh the color consumers expect. Farm-raised fish also consume feed that comes from the sea, which depletes that available for wild fish.

Greenpeace says some restaurants are still looking too narrowly at sustainability, noting that harvesting of Alaskan Pollock affects the food supply of Stella lions and fur seals.

Further Readings

"Restaurants Mobilize to Save Fisheries": http://online.barrons.com/article/SB10001424052748703389004575304353151872876.html?mod=fox_australian

"The Forecasted Collapse of a Fishery": http://blogs.discovermagazine.com/intersection/2010/07/11/the-forecasted-collapse-of-a-fishery-2/

KEYWORDS

Aquaculture, overfishing, sustainable fishing, tragedy of the commons

Questions:

1. Drawing from this article, what are the narrow and broad ways of understanding sustainability?
2. How does the problem of overfishing illustrate the tragedy of the commons? How could we try to avoid this tragedy?
3. What ethical issues arise with aquaculture? Do you believe that this is a good solution to the problem of sustainable fish stocks? Why, or why not?
4. Should we be concerned about the decline in fish stocks for our own sakes, for the sake of the fish that are declining, or for the sake of the ecosystems of which they are a part? Are these objects of concern mutually exclusive, or not? If not, should we be equally concerned about them? Explain.
5. What are some of the reasons described in this article for the concerns being expressed today about the sustainability of seafood? How do you think you would feel about the sustainability issue in this regard if you made your living from fishing?

APPENDIX B

Codes of Ethics

The products of technology typically have life cycles in which they pass through several distinct stages: the design stage, the dissemination stage, the usage stage, and finally disposal. At each of these stages ethical and legal issues can arise that should be considered carefully by those involved in these processes.

During the design stage those involved include engineers, technologists, and designers, most of whom are employed by corporations. The companies who employ engineers to design and develop new products are often the same ones that bring them to market. But the dissemination of new products is also often regulated and controlled by government agencies to ensure that these products are safe and will not harm public health. As consumers or end-users of technological products we all have a moral responsibility to use them in an appropriate manner and, when they have reached the end of their useful life, to dispose of them properly.

Many professional engineering organizations have recognized the importance of their members considering moral and ethical issues in relation to their professional roles and have developed and adopted codes of ethics to help guide individuals in making ethical decisions. Members of these professional organizations are expected to understand and abide by the principles detailed in the codes, and to participate in training sessions designed to ensure that they remain current on the ethical dimensions of their professional activities.

The Accreditation Board for Engineering and Technology (ABET) has specified that among the essential learning outcomes for engineering programs is that their graduates acquire "an ability to understand professional, ethical and social responsibilities," and that students develop "a respect for diversity and a knowledge of contemporary professional, societal, and global issues" (ABET 2007). One of the ways in which engineering students and others can develop their understanding of the professional, ethical, and social responsibilities associated with engineering and technology is through the study of professional ethical codes, charters, and international conventions that address many of the ethical and social issues discussed in this book.

A recent study of practices in ethics teaching in ABET engineering programs argued that "professional codes of ethics in engineering provide a useful framework for thinking about the goals of student learning in the area of ethics and professional responsibility" (Colby and Sullivan 2008, 327). These authors identify several key themes and values that are found in these codes. First, these codes emphasize the importance of protecting public safety, health and welfare, and the protection of the environment in the engineering profession. Second, they call upon professional engineers to be loyal to their employers and clients and to perform their professional responsibilities with their best interests in mind. Third, these codes call upon professional engineers to be fair and honest in their professional activities and to avoid conflicts of interest, discrimination, and unfair or unethical practices. In addition, many of the more recent codes also emphasize understanding the potential impacts of one's work in a global context and, in particular, to contribute to environmental sustainability. However, simply reading the provisions of a code of ethics or a convention does not by itself provide students with the ability to apply and interpret it in practice.

The ability to apply and interpret ethical guidelines in practice is something that requires ongoing professional development and life-long learning. One must gradually develop the habits of thought and reflection that enable one to be sensitive to potential risks and harms to the public, their employers, their profession, and themselves, both in the near and long term. They must learn to evaluate alternative solutions to ethical dilemmas, and also to deal with the inevitable trade-offs and conflicts that arise between one's personal, professional, and social responsibilities. In order to achieve these kinds of deeper understandings, undergraduate students should be encouraged to integrate their technical engineering education with other learning goals, often found in liberal arts courses, internship experiences, and service-learning programs that emphasize not only their professional ethical responsibilities but also the responsibilities of corporations and other institutional contexts within which engineers and designers work, as well as one's social responsibilities, broadly defined.

In this appendix, we present several documents that have been selected in order to provide a basis for beginning this process: (1) the National Society of Professional Engineers (NSPE) Code of Ethics for Engineers, (2) The United Nations Global Compact, (3) the Universal Declaration of Human Rights, and (4) The Earth Charter.

The NSPE Code is one of the most often cited professional ethics codes for engineering and its provisions capture many of the same principles and values found in some more specialized engineering codes, for instance, those for mechanical, electronic, and chemical engineers.

The United Nations Global Compact was launched in the year 2000 as an initiative of then UN Secretary General Kofi Annan. Over the past decade it has evolved into one of the most cited set of ethical principles for guiding the activities of multinational corporations in the global context. Its ten core principles dealing with human rights, labor rights, the environment, and corruption are touchstones for understanding the ethical ground rules for businesses of all kinds.

The Universal Declaration of Human Rights is the essential reference for understanding the term "human rights". Passed by the United Nations General Assembly on December 10, 1948, it is the foundation of all other contemporary human rights conventions, covenants, and declarations. Although it was developed in the shadow of the atrocities and horrors of World War II, it represents the first major statement of the rights that belong to every human being, and its principles and values have influenced many other ethical codes as well as the laws of many nations.

The fourth document, the Earth Charter, grew out of discussions among various civil society organizations following the 1987 World Commission on Environment and Development. In 1997, an independent Earth Charter Commission was formed which developed the current text of the Charter, which was released in March 2000. Since that time, thousands of individuals and organizations have endorsed the Earth Charter's goal of promoting "the transition to sustainable ways of living and a global society founded on a shared ethical framework that includes respect and care for the community of life, ecological integrity, universal human rights, respect for diversity, economic justice, democracy, and a culture of peace." The Earth Charter can be understood as a statement of social and environmental responsibilities for global citizens in the twenty-first century.

BIBLIOGRAPHY

ABET. *Criteria for Accrediting Engineering Technology Programs Effective for Evaluations during the 2007–2008 Accreditation Cycle.* Baltimore: Accreditation Board for Engineering and Technology, 2007.

Colby, Ann, and William M. Sullivan. "Ethics Teaching in Undergraduate Ethics Education." *Journal of Engineering Education* 97, no. 3 (July 2008): 327–338.

NSPE Code of Ethics for Engineers

PREAMBLE

Engineering is an important and learned profession. As members of this profession, engineers are expected to exhibit the highest standards of honesty and integrity. Engineering has a direct and vital impact on the quality of life for all people. Accordingly, the services provided by engineers require honesty, impartiality, fairness, and equity, and must be dedicated to the protection of the public health, safety, and welfare. Engineers must perform under a standard of professional behavior that requires adherence to the highest principles of ethical conduct.

I. Fundamental Canons

Engineers, in the fulfillment of their professional duties, shall:

1. Hold paramount the safety, health, and welfare of the public.
2. Perform services only in areas of their competence.
3. Issue public statements only in an objective and truthful manner.
4. Act for each employer or client as faithful agents or trustees.
5. Avoid deceptive acts.
6. Conduct themselves honorably, responsibly, ethically, and lawfully so as to enhance the honor, reputation, and usefulness of the profession.

II. Rules of Practice

1. Engineers shall hold paramount the safety, health, and welfare of the public.
   a. If engineers' judgment is overruled under circumstances that endanger life or property, they shall notify their employer or client and such other authority as may be appropriate.

   b. Engineers shall approve only those engineering documents that are in conformity with applicable standards.
   c. Engineers shall not reveal facts, data, or information without the prior consent of the client or employer except as authorized or required by law or this Code.
   d. Engineers shall not permit the use of their name or associate in business ventures with any person or firm that they believe is engaged in fraudulent or dishonest enterprise.
   e. Engineers shall not aid or abet the unlawful practice of engineering by a person or firm.
   f. Engineers having knowledge of any alleged violation of this Code shall report thereon to appropriate professional bodies and, when relevant, also to public authorities, and cooperate with the proper authorities in furnishing such information or assistance as may be required.
2. Engineers shall perform services only in the areas of their competence.
   a. Engineers shall undertake assignments only when qualified by education or experience in the specific technical fields involved.
   b. Engineers shall not affix their signatures to any plans or documents dealing with subject matter in which they lack competence, nor to any plan or document not prepared under their direction and control.
   c. Engineers may accept assignments and assume responsibility for coordination of an entire project and sign and seal the engineering documents for the entire project, provided that each technical segment is signed and sealed only by the qualified engineers who prepared the segment.
3. Engineers shall issue public statements only in an objective and truthful manner.
   a. Engineers shall be objective and truthful in professional reports, statements, or testimony. They shall include all relevant and pertinent information in such reports, statements, or testimony, which should bear the date indicating when it was current.
   b. Engineers may express publicly technical opinions that are founded upon knowledge of the facts and competence in the subject matter.
   c. Engineers shall issue no statements, criticisms, or arguments on technical matters that are inspired or paid for by interested parties, unless they have prefaced their comments by explicitly identifying the interested parties on whose behalf they are speaking, and by revealing the existence of any interest the engineers may have in the matters.
4. Engineers shall act for each employer or client as faithful agents or trustees.
   a. Engineers shall disclose all known or potential conflicts of interest that could influence or appear to influence their judgment or the quality of their services.
   b. Engineers shall not accept compensation, financial or otherwise, from more than one party for services on the same project, or for services pertaining to the same project, unless the circumstances are fully disclosed and agreed to by all interested parties.
   c. Engineers shall not solicit or accept financial or other valuable consideration, directly or indirectly, from outside agents in connection with the work for which they are responsible.

d. Engineers in public service as members, advisors, or employees of a governmental or quasi-governmental body or department shall not participate in decisions with respect to services solicited or provided by them or their organizations in private or public engineering practice.
e. Engineers shall not solicit or accept a contract from a governmental body on which a principal or officer of their organization serves as a member.

5. Engineers shall avoid deceptive acts.
   a. Engineers shall not falsify their qualifications or permit misrepresentation of their or their associates' qualifications. They shall not misrepresent or exaggerate their responsibility in or for the subject matter of prior assignments. Brochures or other presentations incident to the solicitation of employment shall not misrepresent pertinent facts concerning employers, employees, associates, joint venturers, or past accomplishments.
   b. Engineers shall not offer, give, solicit, or receive, either directly or indirectly, any contribution to influence the award of a contract by public authority, or which may be reasonably construed by the public as having the effect or intent of influencing the awarding of a contract. They shall not offer any gift or other valuable consideration in order to secure work. They shall not pay a commission, percentage, or brokerage fee in order to secure work, except to a bona fide employee or bona fide established commercial or marketing agencies retained by them.

III. Professional Obligations

1. Engineers shall be guided in all their relations by the highest standards of honesty and integrity.
   a. Engineers shall acknowledge their errors and shall not distort or alter the facts.
   b. Engineers shall advise their clients or employers when they believe a project will not be successful.
   c. Engineers shall not accept outside employment to the detriment of their regular work or interest. Before accepting any outside engineering employment, they will notify their employers.
   d. Engineers shall not attempt to attract an engineer from another employer by false or misleading pretenses.
   e. Engineers shall not promote their own interest at the expense of the dignity and integrity of the profession.
2. Engineers shall at all times strive to serve the public interest.
   a. Engineers are encouraged to participate in civic affairs; career guidance for youths; and work for the advancement of the safety, health, and well-being of their community.
   b. Engineers shall not complete, sign, or seal plans and/or specifications that are not in conformity with applicable engineering standards. If the client or employer insists on such unprofessional conduct, they shall notify the proper authorities and withdraw from further service on the project.
   c. Engineers are encouraged to extend public knowledge and appreciation of engineering and its achievements.
   d. Engineers are encouraged to adhere to the principles of sustainable development[1] in order to protect the environment for future generations.

3. Engineers shall avoid all conduct or practice that deceives the public.
   a. Engineers shall avoid the use of statements containing a material misrepresentation of fact or omitting a material fact.
   b. Consistent with the foregoing, engineers may advertise for recruitment of personnel.
   c. Consistent with the foregoing, engineers may prepare articles for the lay or technical press, but such articles shall not imply credit to the author for work performed by others.
4. Engineers shall not disclose, without consent, confidential information concerning the business affairs or technical processes of any present or former client or employer, or public body on which they serve.
   a. Engineers shall not, without the consent of all interested parties, promote or arrange for new employment or practice in connection with a specific project for which the engineer has gained particular and specialized knowledge.
   b. Engineers shall not, without the consent of all interested parties, participate in or represent an adversary interest in connection with a specific project or proceeding in which the engineer has gained particular specialized knowledge on behalf of a former client or employer.
5. Engineers shall not be influenced in their professional duties by conflicting interests.
   a. Engineers shall not accept financial or other considerations, including free engineering designs, from material or equipment suppliers for specifying their product.
   b. Engineers shall not accept commissions or allowances, directly or indirectly, from contractors or other parties dealing with clients or employers of the engineer in connection with work for which the engineer is responsible.
6. Engineers shall not attempt to obtain employment or advancement or professional engagements by untruthfully criticizing other engineers, or by other improper or questionable methods.
   a. Engineers shall not request, propose, or accept a commission on a contingent basis under circumstances in which their judgment may be compromised.
   b. Engineers in salaried positions shall accept part-time engineering work only to the extent consistent with policies of the employer and in accordance with ethical considerations.
   c. Engineers shall not, without consent, use equipment, supplies, laboratory, or office facilities of an employer to carry on outside private practice.
7. Engineers shall not attempt to injure, maliciously or falsely, directly or indirectly, the professional reputation, prospects, practice, or employment of other engineers. Engineers who believe others are guilty of unethical or illegal practice shall present such information to the proper authority for action.
   a. Engineers in private practice shall not review the work of another engineer for the same client, except with the knowledge of such engineer, or unless the connection of such engineer with the work has been terminated.
   b. Engineers in governmental, industrial, or educational employ are entitled to review and evaluate the work of other engineers when so required by their employment duties.

c. Engineers in sales or industrial employ are entitled to make engineering comparisons of represented products with products of other suppliers.

8. Engineers shall accept personal responsibility for their professional activities, provided, however, that engineers may seek indemnification for services arising out of their practice for other than gross negligence, where the engineer's interests cannot otherwise be protected.
   a. Engineers shall conform with state registration laws in the practice of engineering.
   b. Engineers shall not use association with a nonengineer, a corporation, or partnership as a "cloak" for unethical acts.
9. Engineers shall give credit for engineering work to those to whom credit is due, and will recognize the proprietary interests of others.
   a. Engineers shall, whenever possible, name the person or persons who may be individually responsible for designs, inventions, writings, or other accomplishments.
   b. Engineers using designs supplied by a client recognize that the designs remain the property of the client and may not be duplicated by the engineer for others without express permission.
   c. Engineers, before undertaking work for others in connection with which the engineer may make improvements, plans, designs, inventions, or other records that may justify copyrights or patents, should enter into a positive agreement regarding ownership.
   d. Engineers' designs, data, records, and notes referring exclusively to an employer's work are the employer's property. The employer should indemnify the engineer for use of the information for any purpose other than the original purpose.
   e. Engineers shall continue their professional development throughout their careers and should keep current in their specialty fields by engaging in professional practice, participating in continuing education courses, reading in the technical literature, and attending professional meetings and seminars.

Footnote 1 "Sustainable development" is the challenge of meeting human needs for natural resources, industrial products, energy, food, transportation, shelter, and effective waste management while conserving and protecting environmental quality and the natural resource base essential for future development.

—As Revised July 2007

For more information on the NSPE Code of Ethics see http://www.nspe.org/Ethics/CodeofEthics/index.html

---

The United Nations Global Compact

The UN Global Compact asks companies to embrace, support and enact, within their sphere of influence, a set of core values in the areas of human rights, labour standards, the environment, and anti-corruption:

THE TEN PRINCIPLES OF THE UNITED NATIONS GLOBAL COMPACT

Human rights

Principle 1	Businesses should support and respect the protection of internationally proclaimed human rights; and
Principle 2	make sure that they are not complicit in human rights abuses.

Labour

Principle 3	Businesses should uphold the freedom of association and the effective recognition of the right to collective bargaining;
Principle 4	the elimination of all forms of forced and compulsory labour;
Principle 5	the effective abolition of child labour; and
Principle 6	the elimination of discrimination in respect of employment and occupation.

Environment

Principle 7	Businesses should support a precautionary approach to environmental challenges;
Principle 8	undertake initiatives to promote greater environmental responsibility; and
Principle 9	encourage the development and diffusion of environmentally friendly technologies.

Anti-corruption

Principle 10	Businesses should work against corruption in all its forms, including extortion and bribery.

Published by the United Nations Global Compact Office, October 2008.

UN Global Compact Office. United Nations, DC2-612, New York City, NY 10017, USA.

For more information on the UN Global Compact see: www.unglobalcompact.org

Universal Declaration of Human Rights

PREAMBLE

Whereas recognition of the inherent dignity and of the equal and inalienable rights of all members of the human family is the foundation of freedom, justice and peace in the world,

Whereas disregard and contempt for human rights have resulted in barbarous acts which have outraged the conscience of mankind, and the advent of a world in which human beings shall enjoy freedom of speech and belief and freedom from fear and want has been proclaimed as the highest aspiration of the common people,

Whereas it is essential, if man is not to be compelled to have recourse, as a last resort, to rebellion against tyranny and oppression, that human rights should be protected by the rule of law,

Whereas it is essential to promote the development of friendly relations between nations,

Whereas the peoples of the United Nations have in the Charter reaffirmed their faith in fundamental human rights, in the dignity and worth of the human person and in the equal rights of men and women and have determined to promote social progress and better standards of life in larger freedom,

Whereas Member States have pledged themselves to achieve, in cooperation with the United Nations, the promotion of universal respect for and observance of human rights and fundamental freedoms,

Whereas a common understanding of these rights and freedoms is of the greatest importance for the full realization of this pledge,

Now, therefore The General Assembly proclaims this Universal Declaration of Human Rights as a common standard of achievement for all peoples and all nations, to the end that every individual and every organ of society, keeping this Declaration constantly in mind, shall strive by teaching and education to promote respect for these rights and freedoms and by progressive measures, national and international, to secure their universal and effective recognition and observance, both among the peoples of Member States themselves and among the peoples of territories under their jurisdiction.

Article 1

All human beings are born free and equal in dignity and rights. They are endowed with reason and conscience and should act towards one another in a spirit of brotherhood.

Article 2

Everyone is entitled to all the rights and freedoms set forth in this Declaration, without distinction of any kind, such as race, colour, sex, language, religion, political or other opinion, national or social origin, property, birth or other status.

Furthermore, no distinction shall be made on the basis of the political, jurisdictional or international status of the country or territory to which a person belongs, whether it be independent, trust, non-self-governing or under any other limitation of sovereignty.

Article 3

Everyone has the right to life, liberty and security of person.

Article 4

No one shall be held in slavery or servitude; slavery and the slave trade shall be prohibited in all their forms.

Article 5

No one shall be subjected to torture or to cruel, inhuman or degrading treatment or punishment.

Article 6

Everyone has the right to recognition everywhere as a person before the law.

Article 7

All are equal before the law and are entitled without any discrimination to equal protection of the law. All are entitled to equal protection against any discrimination in violation of this Declaration and against any incitement to such discrimination.

Article 8

Everyone has the right to an effective remedy by the competent national tribunals for acts violating the fundamental rights granted him by the constitution or by law.

Article 9

No one shall be subjected to arbitrary arrest, detention or exile.

Article 10

Everyone is entitled in full equality to a fair and public hearing by an independent and impartial tribunal, in the determination of his rights and obligations and of any criminal charge against him.

Article 11

1. Everyone charged with a penal offence has the right to be presumed innocent until proved guilty according to law in a public trial at which he has had all the guarantees necessary for his defence.
2. No one shall be held guilty of any penal offence on account of any act or omission which did not constitute a penal offence, under national or international law, at the time when it was committed. Nor shall a heavier penalty be imposed than the one that was applicable at the time the penal offence was committed.

Article 12

No one shall be subjected to arbitrary interference with his privacy, family, home or correspondence, nor to attacks upon his honour and reputation. Everyone has the right to the protection of the law against such interference or attacks.

Article 13

1. Everyone has the right to freedom of movement and residence within the borders of each State.
2. Everyone has the right to leave any country, including his own, and to return to his country.

Article 14

1. Everyone has the right to seek and to enjoy in other countries asylum from persecution.
2. This right may not be invoked in the case of prosecutions genuinely arising from non-political crimes or from acts contrary to the purposes and principles of the United Nations.

Article 15

1. Everyone has the right to a nationality.
2. No one shall be arbitrarily deprived of his nationality nor denied the right to change his nationality.

Article 16

1. Men and women of full age, without any limitation due to race, nationality or religion, have the right to marry and to found a family. They are entitled to equal rights as to marriage, during marriage and at its dissolution.
2. Marriage shall be entered into only with the free and full consent of the intending spouses.
3. The family is the natural and fundamental group unit of society and is entitled to protection by society and the State.

Article 17

1. Everyone has the right to own property alone as well as in association with others.
2. No one shall be arbitrarily deprived of his property.

Article 18

Everyone has the right to freedom of thought, conscience and religion; this right includes freedom to change his religion or belief, and freedom, either alone or in community with others and in public or private, to manifest his religion or belief in teaching, practice, worship and observance.

Article 19

Everyone has the right to freedom of opinion and expression; this right includes freedom to hold opinions without interference and to seek, receive and impart information and ideas through any media and regardless of frontiers.

Article 20

1. Everyone has the right to freedom of peaceful assembly and association.
2. No one may be compelled to belong to an association.

Article 21

1. Everyone has the right to take part in the government of his country, directly or through freely chosen representatives.
2. Everyone has the right to equal access to public service in his country.
3. The will of the people shall be the basis of the authority of government; this will shall be expressed in periodic and genuine elections which shall be by universal and equal suffrage and shall be held by secret vote or by equivalent free voting procedures.

Article 22

Everyone, as a member of society, has the right to social security and is entitled to realization, through national effort and international co-operation and in accordance with the organization and resources of each State, of the economic, social and cultural rights indispensable for his dignity and the free development of his personality.

Article 23

1. Everyone has the right to work, to free choice of employment, to just and favourable conditions of work and to protection against unemployment.
2. Everyone, without any discrimination, has the right to equal pay for equal work.
3. Everyone who works has the right to just and favourable remuneration ensuring for himself and his family an existence worthy of human dignity, and supplemented, if necessary, by other means of social protection.
4. Everyone has the right to form and to join trade unions for the protection of his interests.

Article 24

Everyone has the right to rest and leisure, including reasonable limitation of working hours and periodic holidays with pay.

Article 25

1. Everyone has the right to a standard of living adequate for the health and well-being of himself and of his family, including food, clothing, housing and medical care and necessary social services, and the right to security in the event of unemployment, sickness, disability, widowhood, old age or other lack of livelihood in circumstances beyond his control.
2. Motherhood and childhood are entitled to special care and assistance. All children, whether born in or out of wedlock, shall enjoy the same social protection.

Article 26

1. Everyone has the right to education. Education shall be free, at least in the elementary and fundamental stages. Elementary education shall be compulsory. Technical and professional education shall be made generally available and higher education shall be equally accessible to all on the basis of merit.
2. Education shall be directed to the full development of the human personality and to the strengthening of respect for human rights and fundamental freedoms. It shall promote understanding, tolerance and friendship among all nations, racial or religious groups, and shall further the activities of the United Nations for the maintenance of peace.
3. Parents have a prior right to choose the kind of education that shall be given to their children.

Article 27

1. Everyone has the right freely to participate in the cultural life of the community, to enjoy the arts and to share in scientific advancement and its benefits.
2. Everyone has the right to the protection of the moral and material interests resulting from any scientific, literary or artistic production of which he is the author.

Article 28

Everyone is entitled to a social and international order in which the rights and freedoms set forth in this Declaration can be fully realized.

Article 29

1. Everyone has duties to the community in which alone the free and full development of his personality is possible.
2. In the exercise of his rights and freedoms, everyone shall be subject only to such limitations as are determined by law solely for the purpose of securing due recognition and respect for the rights and freedoms of others and of meeting the just requirements of morality, public order and the general welfare in a democratic society.
3. These rights and freedoms may in no case be exercised contrary to the purposes and principles of the United Nations.

Article 30

Nothing in this Declaration may be interpreted as implying for any State, group or person any right to engage in any activity or to perform any act aimed at the destruction of any of the rights and freedoms set forth herein.

The United Nations, General Assembly, December 10, 1948.

For more information on the Universal Declaration of Human Rights see: http://www.ohchr.org/en/udhr/pages/introduction.aspx

---

The Earth Charter

PREAMBLE

We stand at a critical moment in Earth's history, a time when humanity must choose its future. As the world becomes increasingly interdependent and fragile, the future at once holds great peril and great promise. To move forward we must recognize that in the midst of a magnificent diversity of cultures and life forms we are one human family and one Earth community with a common destiny. We must join together to bring forth a sustainable global society founded on respect for nature, universal human rights, economic justice, and a culture of peace. Towards this end, it is imperative that we, the peoples of Earth, declare our responsibility to one another, to the greater community of life, and to future generations.

Earth, Our Home

Humanity is part of a vast evolving universe. Earth, our home, is alive with a unique community of life. The forces of nature make existence a demanding and uncertain adventure, but Earth has provided the conditions essential to life's evolution. The resilience of the community of life and the well-being of humanity depend upon preserving a healthy biosphere with all its ecological systems, a rich variety of plants and animals, fertile soils, pure waters, and clean air. The global environment with its finite resources is a common concern of all peoples. The protection of Earth's vitality, diversity, and beauty is a sacred trust.

The Global Situation

The dominant patterns of production and consumption are causing environmental devastation, the depletion of resources, and a massive extinction of species. Communities are being undermined. The benefits of development are not shared equitably and the gap between rich and poor is widening. Injustice, poverty, ignorance, and violent conflict are widespread and the cause of great suffering. An unprecedented rise in human population has overburdened ecological and social systems. The foundations of global security are threatened. These trends are perilous—but not inevitable.

The Challenges Ahead

The choice is ours: form a global partnership to care for Earth and one another or risk the destruction of ourselves and the diversity of life. Fundamental changes are needed in our values, institutions, and ways of living. We must realize that when basic needs have been met, human development is primarily about being more, not having more. We have the knowledge and technology to provide for all and to reduce our impacts on the environment. The emergence of a global civil society is creating new opportunities to build a democratic and humane world. Our environmental, economic, political, social, and spiritual challenges are interconnected, and together we can forge inclusive solutions.

Universal Responsibility

To realize these aspirations, we must decide to live with a sense of universal responsibility, identifying ourselves with the whole Earth community as well as our local communities. We are at once citizens of different nations and of one world in which the local and global are linked. Everyone shares responsibility for the present and future well-being of the human family and the larger living world. The spirit of human solidarity and kinship with all life is strengthened when we live with reverence for the mystery of being, gratitude for the gift of life, and humility regarding the human place in nature.

We urgently need a shared vision of basic values to provide an ethical foundation for the emerging world community. Therefore, together in hope we affirm the following interdependent principles for a sustainable way of life as a common standard by which the conduct of all individuals, organizations, businesses, governments, and transnational institutions is to be guided and assessed.

PRINCIPLES

I. Respect and Care for the Community of Life

1. **Respect Earth and life in all its diversity.**
   a. Recognize that all beings are interdependent and every form of life has value regardless of its worth to human beings.
   b. Affirm faith in the inherent dignity of all human beings and in the intellectual, artistic, ethical, and spiritual potential of humanity.
2. **Care for the community of life with understanding, compassion, and love.**
   a. Accept that with the right to own, manage, and use natural resources comes the duty to prevent environmental harm and to protect the rights of people.

b. Affirm that with increased freedom, knowledge, and power comes increased responsibility to promote the common good.

3. **Build democratic societies that are just, participatory, sustainable, and peaceful.**
   a. Ensure that communities at all levels guarantee human rights and fundamental freedoms and provide everyone an opportunity to realize his or her full potential.
   b. Promote social and economic justice, enabling all to achieve a secure and meaningful livelihood that is ecologically responsible.
4. **Secure Earth's bounty and beauty for present and future generations.**
   a. Recognize that the freedom of action of each generation is qualified by the needs of future generations.
   b. Transmit to future generations values, traditions, and institutions that support the long-term flourishing of Earth's human and ecological communities. In order to fulfill these four broad commitments, it is necessary to:

II. Ecological Integrity

5. **Protect and restore the integrity of Earth's ecological systems, with special concern for biological diversity and the natural processes that sustain life.**
   a. Adopt at all levels sustainable development plans and regulations that make environmental conservation and rehabilitation integral to all development initiatives.
   b. Establish and safeguard viable nature and biosphere reserves, including wild lands and marine areas, to protect Earth's life support systems, maintain biodiversity, and preserve our natural heritage.
   c. Promote the recovery of endangered species and ecosystems.
   d. Control and eradicate non-native or genetically modified organisms harmful to native species and the environment, and prevent introduction of such harmful organisms.
   e. Manage the use of renewable resources such as water, soil, forest products, and marine life in ways that do not exceed rates of regeneration and that protect the health of ecosystems.
   f. Manage the extraction and use of non-renewable resources such as minerals and fossil fuels in ways that minimize depletion and cause no serious environmental damage.
6. **Prevent harm as the best method of environmental protection and, when knowledge is limited, apply a precautionary approach.**
   a. Take action to avoid the possibility of serious or irreversible environmental harm even when scientific knowledge is incomplete or inconclusive.
   b. Place the burden of proof on those who argue that a proposed activity will not cause significant harm, and make the responsible parties liable for environmental harm.
   c. Ensure that decision making addresses the cumulative, long-term, indirect, long distance, and global consequences of human activities.
   d. Prevent pollution of any part of the environment and allow no build-up of radioactive, toxic, or other hazardous substances.
   e. Avoid military activities damaging to the environment.

7. **Adopt patterns of production, consumption, and reproduction that safeguard Earth's regenerative capacities, human rights, and community well-being.**
   a. Reduce, reuse, and recycle the materials used in production and consumption systems, and ensure that residual waste can be assimilated by ecological systems.
   b. Act with restraint and efficiency when using energy, and rely increasingly on renewable energy sources such as solar and wind.
   c. Promote the development, adoption, and equitable transfer of environmentally sound technologies
   d. Internalize the full environmental and social costs of goods and services in the selling price, and enable consumers to identify products that meet the highest social and environmental standards.
   e. Ensure universal access to health care that fosters reproductive health and responsible reproduction.
   f. Adopt lifestyles that emphasize the quality of life and material sufficiency in a finite world.
8. **Advance the study of ecological sustainability and promote the open exchange and wide application of the knowledge acquired.**
   a. Support international scientific and technical cooperation on sustainability, with special attention to the needs of developing nations.
   b. Recognize and preserve the traditional knowledge and spiritual wisdom in all cultures that contribute to environmental protection and human well-being.
   c. Ensure that information of vital importance to human health and environmental protection, including genetic information, remains available in the public domain.

III. Social and Economic Justice

9. **Eradicate poverty as an ethical, social, and environmental imperative.**
   a. Guarantee the right to potable water, clean air, food security, uncontaminated soil, shelter, and safe sanitation, allocating the national and international resources required.
   b. Empower every human being with the education and resources to secure a sustainable livelihood, and provide social security and safety nets for those who are unable to support themselves.
   c. Recognize the ignored, protect the vulnerable, serve those who suffer, and enable them to develop their capacities and to pursue their aspirations.
10. **Ensure that economic activities and institutions at all levels promote human development in an equitable and sustainable manner.**
   a. Promote the equitable distribution of wealth within nations and among nations.
   b. Enhance the intellectual, financial, technical, and social resources of developing nations, and relieve them of onerous international debt.
   c. Ensure that all trade supports sustainable resource use, environmental protection, and progressive labor standards.
   d. Require multinational corporations and international financial organizations to act transparently in the public good, and hold them accountable for the consequences of their activities.

11. **Affirm gender equality and equity as prerequisites to sustainable development and ensure universal access to education, health care, and economic opportunity.**
    a. Secure the human rights of women and girls and end all violence against them.
    b. Promote the active participation of women in all aspects of economic, political, civil, social, and cultural life as full and equal partners, decision makers, leaders, and beneficiaries.
    c. Strengthen families and ensure the safety and loving nurture of all family members.
12. **Uphold the right of all, without discrimination, to a natural and social environment supportive of human dignity, bodily health, and spiritual well-being, with special attention to the rights of indigenous peoples and minorities.**
    a. Eliminate discrimination in all its forms, such as that based on race, color, sex, sexual orientation, religion, language, and national, ethnic or social origin.
    b. Affirm the right of indigenous peoples to their spirituality, knowledge, lands and resources and to their related practice of sustainable livelihoods.
    c. Honor and support the young people of our communities, enabling them to fulfill their essential role in creating sustainable societies.
    d. Protect and restore outstanding places of cultural and spiritual significance.

IV. Democracy, Nonviolence, and Peace

13. **Strengthen democratic institutions at all levels, and provide transparency and accountability in governance, inclusive participation in decision making, and access to justice.**
    a. Uphold the right of everyone to receive clear and timely information on environmental matters and all development plans and activities which are likely to affect them or in which they have an interest.
    b. Support local, regional and global civil society, and promote the meaningful participation of all interested individuals and organizations in decision making.
    c. Protect the rights to freedom of opinion, expression, peaceful assembly, association, and dissent.
    d. Institute effective and efficient access to administrative and independent judicial procedures, including remedies and redress for environmental harm and the threat of such harm.
    e. Eliminate corruption in all public and private institutions.
    f. Strengthen local communities, enabling them to care for their environments, and assign environmental responsibilities to the levels of government where they can be carried out most effectively.
14. **Integrate into formal education and life-long learning the knowledge, values, and skills needed for a sustainable way of life.**
    a. Provide all, especially children and youth, with educational opportunities that empower them to contribute actively to sustainable development.
    b. Promote the contribution of the arts and humanities as well as the sciences in sustainability education.

   c. Enhance the role of the mass media in raising awareness of ecological and social challenges.
   d. Recognize the importance of moral and spiritual education for sustainable living.

15. **Treat all living beings with respect and consideration.**
   a. Prevent cruelty to animals kept in human societies and protect them from suffering.
   b. Protect wild animals from methods of hunting, trapping, and fishing that cause extreme, prolonged, or avoidable suffering.
   c. Avoid or eliminate to the full extent possible the taking or destruction of non-targeted species.

16. **Promote a culture of tolerance, nonviolence, and peace.**
   a. Encourage and support mutual understanding, solidarity, and cooperation among all peoples and within and among nations.
   b. Implement comprehensive strategies to prevent violent conflict and use collaborative problem solving to manage and resolve environmental conflicts and other disputes.
   c. Demilitarize national security systems to the level of a non-provocative defense posture, and convert military resources to peaceful purposes, including ecological restoration.
   d. Eliminate nuclear, biological, and toxic weapons and other weapons of mass destruction.
   e. Ensure that the use of orbital and outer space supports environmental protection and peace.
   f. Recognize that peace is the wholeness created by right relationships with oneself, other persons, other cultures, other life, Earth, and the larger whole of which all are a part.

THE WAY FORWARD

As never before in history, common destiny beckons us to seek a new beginning. Such renewal is the promise of these Earth Charter principles. To fulfill this promise, we must commit ourselves to adopt and promote the values and objectives of the Charter.

This requires a change of mind and heart. It requires a new sense of global interdependence and universal responsibility. We must imaginatively develop and apply the vision of a sustainable way of life locally, nationally, regionally, and globally. Our cultural diversity is a precious heritage and different cultures will find their own distinctive ways to realize the vision. We must deepen and expand the global dialogue that generated the Earth Charter, for we have much to learn from the ongoing collaborative search for truth and wisdom. Life often involves tensions between important values. This can mean difficult choices. However, we must find ways to harmonize diversity with unity, the exercise of freedom with the common good, short-term objectives with long-term goals. Every individual, family, organization, and community has a vital role to play. The arts, sciences, religions, educational institutions, media, businesses, nongovernmental organizations, and governments are all called to offer creative leadership. The partnership of government, civil society, and business is essential for effective governance.

In order to build a sustainable global community, the nations of the world must renew their commitment to the United Nations, fulfill their obligations under existing international agreements, and support the implementation of Earth Charter principles with an international legally binding instrument on environment and development.

Let ours be a time remembered for the awakening of a new reverence for life, the firm resolve to achieve sustainability, the quickening of the struggle for justice and peace, and the joyful celebration of life.

For more information on the Earth Charter see: http://www.earthcharterinaction.org/content/

BIBLIOGRAPHY

Aiken, W. E. (1977). *Technocracy and the American Dream: The Technocratic Movement 1900–1941.* Berkeley: University of California Press.

Appleyard, B. (1998). *Brave New Worlds: Staying Human in the Genetic Future.* New York: Viking Press.

Baden, J. A., Noonan, D. S., and Ruckelshaus, W. D. (Eds.). (1998). *Managing the Commons*, 2nd ed. Bloomington: Indiana University Press.

Barnet, R. J., and Cavanagh, J. (1994). *Global Dreams: Imperial Corporations and the New World Order.* New York: Touchstone.

Beniger, J. (1986). *The Control Revolution: Technological and Economic Origins of the Information Society.* Cambridge, MA: Harvard University Press.

Bijker, W. E., Hughes, T. P., and Pinch, T. (1990). *The Social Construction of Technological Systems.* Cambridge, MA: MIT Press.

Bolter, J. D. (1984). *Turing's Man.* Chapel Hill: University of North Carolina Press.

Boorstin, D. J. (1978). *The Republic of Technology.* New York: Harper & Row.

Boot, M. (2006). *War Made New: Technology, Warfare, and the Course of History—1500 to Today.* New York: Gotham Books.

Borgrnann, A. (1984). *Technology and the Character of Contemporary Life: A Philosophical Inquiry.* Chicago: University of Chicago Press.

Bright, C. (1998). *Life Out of Bounds: Bioinvasion in a Borderless World.* New York: Norton.

Brook, J., and Boal, I. A. (Eds.). (1995). *Resisting the Virtual Life: The Culture and Politics of Information.* San Francisco: City Lights Books.

Budinger, T., and Budinger, F. (2006). *Ethics of Emerging Technologies: Scientific Facts and Moral Challenges.* New York: Wiley.

Burke, J., and Ornstein, R. (1997). *The Axmaker's Gift: Technology's Capture and Control of Our Minds and Culture.* New York: Putnam Group.

Bush, C. G. (1983). *Machina Ex Dea.* New York: Teachers College Press.

Carnegie Commission on Science, Technology, and Government. (1992). *Enabling the Future: Linking Science and Technology to Societal Goals.* New York: Carnegie Commission on Science, Technology, and Government.

Carson, R. (1962). *Silent Spring.* Boston: Houghton Mifflin.

Cavanagh, J., and Mander, J. (2004). *Alternatives to Economic Globalization: A Better World Is Possible*, 2nd ed. San Francisco: Berrett-Koehler.

Chanda, N. (2007). *Bound Together: How Traders, Preachers, Adventurers, and Warriors Shaped Globalization.* New Haven, CT: Yale University Press.

Chandler, A. D., Jr. (1977). *The Visible Hand: The Management Revolution in American Business.* Cambridge, MA: Belknap Press.

Clark, A. (2004). *Natural-Born Cyborgs: Minds, Technologies, and the Future of Human Intelligence.* New York: Oxford University Press.

Clark, G. (2007). *A Farewell to Alms: A Brief History of the Economic World.* Princeton, NJ: Princeton University Press.

Commoner, B. (1971). *The Closing Circle: Nature, Man and Technology.* New York: Knopf.

Corn, J. (Ed.). (1986). *Imagining Tomorrow: History, Technology, and the American Future.* Cambridge, MA: MIT Press.

Cothran, H. (Ed.). (2002). *Energy Alternatives: Opposing Viewpoints.* San Diego, CA: Greenhaven Press.

Cowan, R. S. (1983). *More Work for Mother: The Ironies of Household Technology from the Open Hearth to the Microwave.* New York: Basic Books.

Cowan, R. S. (1996). *A Social History of American Technology.* New York: Oxford University Press.

Cross, G. (1993). *Time and Money: The Making of Consumer Culture.* New York: Roudedge.

Daly, H. E., and Cobb, J. B., Jr. (1994). *For the Common Good: Redirecting the Economy toward Community, the Environment, and a Sustainable Future.* New York: Beacon Press.

Davies, P. (2004). *What's This India Business? Offshoring, Outsourcing, and the Global Services Revolution.* London: Nicholas Brealey International.

Dawkins, R. (1990). *The Selfish Gene.* Oxford: Oxford University Press.

Desmond, K. (1986). *The Harwin Chronology of Inventions, Innovations, Discoveries.* London: Constable.

Diamond, J. (1999). *Guns, Germs, and Steel: The Fates of Human Societies.* New York: Norton.

Diamond, J. (2005). *Collapse: How Societies Choose to Fail or Succeed.* New York: Penguin.

Douglas, M., and Wildavsky, A. (1982). *Risk and Culture: The Selection of Technical and Environmental Dangers.* Berkeley: University of California Press.

Dreyfus, H. (1979). *What Computers Can't Do: The Limits of Artificial Intelligence*, 2nd ed. New York: Basic Books.

Dreyfus, H. (1992). *What Computers Still Can't Do: A Critique of Artificial Reason.* Cambridge, MA: MIT Press.

Drucker, P. (1993). *Post-Capitalist Society.* New York: HarperCollins.

Dunn, L. (1965). *A Short History of Genetics.* New York: Plenum.

Dyson, G. B. (1997). *Darwin among the Machines: The Evolution of Global Intelligence.* New York: Perseus.

Dyson, R. (1999). *The Sun, the Genome, and the Internet: Tools of Scientific Revolutions.* New York: Oxford University Press.

Easton, T. (2007). *Taking Sides: Clashing Views in Science, Technology, and Society.* New York: McGraw-Hill/Dushkin.

Edgar, S. (1997). *Morals and Machines: Perspectives in Computer Ethics.* New York: Jones and Bartlett.

Edgerton, D. (2006). *The Shock of the Old: Technology and Global History since 1900.* New York: Oxford University Press.

Ellul, J. (1964). *The Technological Society*, trans J. Wilkenson. New York: Knopf.

Elsterd, J. (1983). *Explaining Technical Change.* Cambridge: Cambridge University Press.

Ermann, M. D., Williams, M., and Shauf, M. (Eds.). (1997). *Computers, Ethics, and Society*, 2nd ed. New York: Oxford University Press.

Feenberg, A. (1999). *Questioning Technology.* New York: Roudedge.

Feenberg, A., and Hannay, A. (Eds.). (1995). *Technology and the Politics of Knowledge.* Bloomington: Indiana University Press.

Feere, F. (1995). *Philosophy of Technology.* Athens: University of Georgia Press.

Fishman, T. (2005). *China, Inc.: How the Rise of the Next Superpower Challenges America and the World.* New York: Scribner.

Fox, M. (1992). *Superpigs and Wondercorn: The Brave New World of Biotechnology and Where It May Lead.* New York: Lyons and Burford.

Frenkel, S. (Ed.). (1999). *On the Front Line: Organization of Work in the Information Age.* Ithaca, NY: Cornell University Press.

Friedman, T. L. (1999). *The Lexus and the Olive Tree.* New York: Farrar, Straus & Giroux.

Friedman, T. L. (2005). *The World Is Flat: A Brief History of the Twenty-First Century.* New York: Farrar, Straus & Giroux.

Gimpel, J. (1977). *The Medieval Machine: The Industrial Revolution of the Middle Ages.* New York: Penguin.

Gordon, J. (2004). *An Empire of Wealth: The Epic History of American Economic Power.* New York: HarperCollins.

Gutkind, L. (2007). *Almost Human: Making Robots Think.* New York: Norton.

Hardin, G. (1993). *Living within Limits: Ecology, Economics, and Population Taboos.* New York: Oxford University Press.

Hardison, O. B., Jr. (1989). *Disappearing through the Skylight: Culture and Technology in the Twentieth Century.* New York: Viking Press.

Heidegger, M. (1977). *The Question Concerning Technology and Other Essays*, Trans W. Lovitt. New York: Harper & Row.

Heinberg, R. (2005). *The Party's Over: Oil, War and the Fate of Industrial Societies.* British Columbia: New Society.

Henry, D. (1989). *From Foraging to Agriculture.* Philadelphia: University of Pennsylvania Press.

Hofstetter, R. (1997). *Mobius.* New York: Vantage Press.

Hughes, T. P. (1989). *American Genesis: A Century of Invention and Technological Enthusiasm.* New York: Viking Press.

Ihde, D. (1990). *Technology and the Lifeworld: From Garden to Earth.* Bloomington: Indiana University Press.

Jonas, H. (1974). *Philosophical Essays: From Ancient Creed to Technological Man.* Englewood Cliffs, NJ: Prentice Hall.

Jonas, H. (1984). *The Imperative of Responsibility: In Search of an Ethics for the Technological Age.* Chicago: University of Chicago Press.

Karliner, J. (1997). *The Corporate Planet: Ecology and Politics in the Age of Globalization.* San Francisco: Sierra Club Books.

Kevles, D. (1995). *In the Name of Eugenics: Genetics and the Uses of Human Heredity.* Cambridge, MA: Harvard University Press.

Keynes, J. (1989). *General Theory of Employment, Interest and Money.* New York: Harcourt Brace.

Kidder, T. (1982). *The Soul of a New Machine.* London: Allen Lane.

Kitcher, P. (1996). *The Lives to Come: The Genetic Revolution and Human Possibilities.* New York: Touchstone.

Koestler, A. (1964). *The Act of Creation.* New York: Macmillan.

Korten, D. C. (1995). *When Corporations Rule the World.* West Hartford, CT: Kumarian Press.

Kraybill, D. (2001). *The Riddle of Amish Culture.* Baltimore: Johns Hopkins University Press.

Kuhn, R. (2000). *Made in China.* New York: TV Books.

Kuhn, T. (1970). *The Structure of Scientific Revolutions,* 2nd ed. Chicago: University of Chicago Press.

Kurzweil, R. (1990). *The Age of Intelligent Machines.* Cambridge, MA: MIT Press.

Kurzweil, R. (1999). *The Age of Spiritual Machines: When Computers Exceed Human Intelligence.* New York: Viking Press.

Kurzweil, R. (2006). *The Singularity Is Near.* New York: Penguin.

Landes, D. (1983). *Revolution in Time: Clocks and the Making of the Modern World.* Cambridge, MA: Harvard University Press.

Latour, B. (1987). *Science in Action.* Cambridge, MA: Harvard University Press.

Longman, P. (2004). *The Empty Cradle: How Falling Birthrates Threaten World Prosperity and What to Do about It.* New York: Basic Books.

Lovins, A. B. (1977). *Soft Energy Paths: Towards a Durable Peace.* Cambridge, MA: Ballinger.

Lyons, J., and Corner, P. (1966). *Altered Fates: Gene Therapy and the Retooling of Human Life.* New York: Norton.

Mackenzie, D., and Wajcman, J. (Eds.). (1999). *The Social Shaping of Technology.* Philadelphia: Open University Press.

Maisels, C. (1990). *The Emergence of Civilization: From Hunting and Gathering to Agriculture, Cities, and the State in the Near East.* London: Routledge & Kegan Paul.

Marx, L. (1964). *The Machine in the Garden: Technology and the Pastoral Ideal in America.* New York: Oxford University Press.

McGee, G. (1997). *The Perfect Baby: A Pragmatic Approach to Genetics.* Lanham, MD: Rowman & Littlefield.

McLuhan, M. (1964). *Understanding Media: The Extensions of Man.* New York: McGraw-Hill.

McPhee, J. (1989). *The Control of Nature.* New York: Farrar, Straus & Giroux.

Meredith, R. (2007). *The Elephant and the Dragon: The Rise of India and China and What It Means for All of Us.* New York: Norton.

Mesthene, E. (1970). *Technological Change: Its Impact on Man and Society.* New York: New American Library.

Meyerowitz, J. (1985). *No Sense of Place: The Impact of Electronic Media on Sociable Behavior.* New York: Oxford University Press.

Mills, S. (Ed.). (1997). *Turning Away from Technology: A New Vision for the 21st Century.* San Francisco: Sierra Club Books.

Mitcham, C. (1994). *Thinking through Technology: The Path between Engineering and Philosophy.* Chicago: University of Chicago Press.

Mitcham, C. (Ed.). (2006). *Encyclopedia of Science, Technology, and Ethics.* Macmillan Reference. New York: Thomson/Gale.

Mitcham, C., and Mackey, R. (Eds.). (1983). *Philosophy and Technology: Readings in Philosophical Problems of Technology.* New York: Free Press.

Moravec, H. (1989). *MindChildren: The Future of Robot and Human Intelligence.* Cambridge, MA: Harvard University Press.

Moravec, H. (1999). *Robot: Mere Machine to Transcendent Mind.* New York: Oxford University Press.

Mulhall, D. (2002). *Our Molecular Future: How Nanotechnology, Robotics, Genetics, and Artificial*

Intelligence Will Transform Our World. Amherst, NY: Prometheus Books.

Mumford, L. (1934). *Technics and Civilization.* New York: Harcourt, Brace, and World.

Mumford, L. (1966). *Technics and Human Development.* New York: Harcourt Brace Jovanovich.

Naisbitt, J. (1984). *Megatrends: Ten New Directions Transforming Our Lives.* New York: Warner Books.

Negroponte, N. (1995). *Being Digital.* New York: Vintage Books.

Noble, D. F. (1979). *America by Design: Science, Technology, and the Rise of Corporate Capitalism.* New York: Oxford University Press.

Noble, D. F. (1984). *Forces of Production: A Social History of Industrial Automation.* New York: Knopf.

Noble, D. F. (1997). *The Religion of Technology: The Divinity of Man and the Spirit of Invention.* New York: Knopf.

Nye, D. E. (1994). *American Technological Sublime.* Cambridge, MA: MIT Press.

Oakley, A. (1984). *The Captured Womb: A History of the Medical Care of Pregnant Women.* Oxford: Blackwell.

Oldenziel, R. (2004). *Making Technology Masculine: Men, Women, and Modern Machines in America.* Netherlands: Amsterdam University Press.

Pacey, A. (1983). *The Culture of Technology.* Cambridge, MA: MIT Press.

Perrin, N. (1979). *Giving Up the Gun: Japan's Reversion to the Sword, 1543-1879.* Boston: David R. Godine.

Petersen, J. (2007). *Understanding Surveillance Technologies: Spy Devices, Privacy, History, and Applications.* Boca Raton, FL: Auerbach Publications.

Petrovski, H. (1985). *The Engineer Is Human: The Role of Failure in Successful Design.* New York: St. Martin's Press.

Petrovski, H. (1996). *Invention by Design: How Engineers Get from Thought to Thing.* Cambridge, MA: Harvard University Press.

Pitt, J. C. (2000). *Thinking about Technology: Foundations of the Philosophy of Technology.* New York: Seven Bridges Press.

Pool, R. (1997). *Beyond Engineering: How Society Shapes Technology.* New York: Oxford University Press.

Postman, N. (1985). *Amusing Ourselves to Death: Public Discourse in the Age of Show Business.* New York: Viking Press.

Postman, N. (1992). *Technopoly: The Surrender of Culture to Technology.* New York: Knopf.

Postrel, V. (1998). *The Future and Its Enemies: The Growing Conflict over Creativity, Enterprise, and Progress.* New York: Free Press.

Pursell, C. (2007). *The Machine in America: A Social History of Technology.* Baltimore, MD: Johns Hopkins University Press.

Reich, R. (1992). *The Work of Nations: Preparing Ourselves for 21st Century Capitalism.* New York: Random House.

Rheingold, H. (1991). *Virtual Reality.* New York: Summit Books.

Rifkin, J. (1995). *The End of Work: The Decline of the Global Labor Force and the Dawn of the Post-Market Era.* New York: Putnam.

Rifkin, J. (2002). *The Hydrogen Economy: The Creation of the World-Wide Energy Web and the Redistribution of Power on Earth.* New York: Jeremy P. Tarcher.

Roberts, J. M. (1993). *A Short History of the World.* New York: Oxford University Press.

Roberts, P. (2004). *The End of Oil: On the Edge of a Perilous New World.* Boston: Houghton Muffin.

Rodrik, D. (2007). *One Economics, Many Recipes: Globalization, Institutions, and Economic Growth.* Princeton, NJ: Princeton University Press.

Rosenberg, N. (1982). *Inside the Black Box: Technology and Economics.* Cambridge: Cambridge University Press.

Roszak, T. (1994). *The Cult of Information: A Neo-Luddite Treatise on High Tech, Artificial Intelligence, and the True Art of Thinking,* 2nd ed. Berkeley: University of California Press.

Russo, E., and Cove, D. (1995). *Genetic Engineering: Dreams and Nightmares.* New York: Viking Press.

Rybczynski, W. (1985). *Taming the Tiger: The Struggle to Control Technology.* New York: Freeman.

Sachs, J. (2006). *The End of Poverty: Economic Possibilities for Our Time.* New York: Penguin.

Sahal, D. (1981). *Patterns of Technological Innovation.* Cambridge: Cambridge University Press.

Schick, K. D., and Toth, N. (1993). *Making Silent Stones Speak: Human Evolution and the Dawn of Technology.* New York: Simon & Schuster.

Schor, J. (1991). *The Overworked American: The Unexpected Decline of Leisure.* New York: Basic Books.

Schumacher, E. F. (1973). *Small Is Beautiful: Economics as if People Mattered.* New York: Harper & Row.

Sclove, R E. (1995). *Democracy and Technology.* New York: Guilford Press.

Shaiken, H. (1985). *Work Transformed: Automation and Labor in the Computer Age.* New York: Holt, Rnehart & Winston.

Shrader-Frechette, K., and Westra, L. (Eds.). (1997). *Technology and Values.* Totowa, NJ: Rowman & Littlefield.

Silver, L. (1997). *Remaking Eden: Cloning and Beyond in a Brave New World.* New York: Avon Books.

Singer, P. (2002). *One World: The Ethics of Globalization.* New Haven, CT: Yale University Press.

Smith, A. (1937). *An Inquiry into the Nature and Causes of the Wealth of Nations.* New York: Modern Library.

Speth, J. (2004). *Red Sky at Morning: America and the Crisis of the Global Environment.* New Haven, CT: Yale University Press.

Stiglitz, J. (2006). *Making Globalization Work.* New York: Norton.

Strasser, S. (1989). *Satisfaction Guaranteed: The Making of the American Mass Market.* New York: Pantheon.

Strobel, F. (1993). *Upward Dreams, Downward Mobility: The Economic Decline of the American Middle Class.* Lanham, MD: Rowman & Littlefield.

Strong, D. (1995). *Crazy Mountains: Learning from Wilderness to Weigh Technology.* Albany: State University of New York Press.

Sunstein, C. (2006). *Infotopia: How Many Minds Produce Knowledge.* New York: Oxford University Press.

Teich, A. H. (1997). *Technology and the Future,* 7th ed. New York: St. Martin's Press.

Tenner, E. (1997). *Why Things Bite Back: Technology and the Revenge of Unintended Consequences.* Cambridge, MA: Harvard University Press.

Thurow, L. C. (1996). *The Future of Capitalism: How Today's Economic Forces Shape Tomorrow's World.* New York: Morrow.

Tiles, M., and Oberdiek, H. (1995). *Living in a Technological Culture: Human Tools and Human Values.* New York: Roudedge.

Toffler, A., and Toffler, H. (1990). *Powershift.* New York: Bantam Books.

Turkle, S. (1982). *The Second Self: The Human Spirit in a Computer Culture.* New York: Simon & Schuster.

Turney, J. (1998). *Frankenstein's Footsteps: Science, Genetics and Popular Culture.* New Haven, CT: Yale University Press.

Uchitelle, L. (2007). *The Disposable American: Layoffs and Their Consequences.* New York: Vintage Press.

Van Creveld, M. (1989). *Technology and War: From 2000 BC to the Present.* New York: Free Press.

Vandermeer, J., and Goldberg, D. (2003). *Population Ecology: First Principles.* Princeton, NJ: Princeton University Press.

Volti, R. (1992). *Society and Technological Change,* 2nd ed. New York: St. Martin's Press.

Wajcman, J. (1991). *Feminism Confronts Technology.* University Park: Pennsylvania State University Press.

White, L., Jr. (1966). *Medieval Technology and Social Change.* New York: Oxford University Press.

Wilson, D. (2005). *How to Survive a Robot Uprising: Tips on Defending Yourself against the Coming Rebellion.* London: Bloomsbury.

Wilson, E. O. (1998). *Consilience: The Unity of Knowledge.* New York: Knopf.

Winner, L. (1977). *Autonomous Technology: Technics-Out-of-Control as a Theme in Political Thought.* Cambridge, MA: MIT Press.

Winner, L. (1986). *The Whale and the Reactor: A Search for Limits in an Age of High Technology.* Chicago: University of Chicago Press.

Wosk, J. (2003). *Women and the Machine: Representations from the Spinning Wheel to the Electronic Age.* Baltimore, MD: Johns Hopkins University Press.

Wresch, W. (1996). *Disconnected: Haves and Have-Nots in the Information Age.* New Brunswick, NJ: Rutgers University Press.

Wright, L. (1964). *Home Fires Burning: The History of Domestic Heating and Cooking.* London: Routledge & Kegan Paul.

Yergin, D. (1991). *The Prize: The Epic Quest for Oil, Money, and Power.* New York: Simon & Schuster.

Young, S. (2005). *Designer Evolution: A Transhumanist Manifesto.* Amherst, NY: Prometheus Books.

Zuboff, S. (1988). *In the Age of the Smart Machine: The Future of Work and Power.* New York: Basic Books.

Timeline of Significant Technological Innovations

(continued from front of book)

Event	Date
Fuel cell	1839
Genetic engineering	1973
Germ theory (infection)	1850s
Glassblowing	100 BCE
Glasses (eye)	1286
GPS	1970
Gravity explained	1687
Great Wall of China	300 BCE
Guitar (electric)	1931
Gum (chewing/bubble)	1870/1928
Gun	1288
Gunpowder/fireworks	1280
Hair dryer (electric)	1902
Harness (horse)	300 BCE
Helicopter (theory)	1500
Helicopter (practical flight)	1939
Heliocentric theory	1543
Hieroglyphics	3300 BCE
Hole (donut)	1850
Homo erectus	2 MYA
Homo habilise	2.4 MYA
Homo sapiens	90,000 BCE
Horseshoe	900
Human flight	1783
Human Genome Project	1989
Humanoids	15 MYA
Inkjet printer	1976
Integrated electronic circuit	1959
Interchangeable parts	1430
Internal combustion engine	1877
iPod	2001
Irradiation (food)	1905
Irrigation	2400 BCE
Knife (electric)	1938
Lamp (incandescent/fluorescent)	1841/1938
Laser	1958
Lathe	1500
LEGO toys	1932
Lens (convex)	300 BCE
Life (bacteria)	2.75 BYA
Life (earliest forms)	1.5 BYA
Lighthouse (Pharos)	300 BCE

Event	Date
Linotype (typesetting)	1884
Lock/key	400 BCE
Loom (earliest)	2000 BCE
Loom (Vaucanson)	1745
LP record	1948
Mammals	65 MYA
Mammogram	1913
Map	2300 BCE
McDonald's (hamburgers)	1948
Measurement (foot)	2100 BCE
Microscope	1660
Microwave oven	1953
Mirror (metal)	2500 BCE
Motion pictures (silent/sound)	1888/1927
Mouse (computer)	1968
MRI (human)	1977
Mummification	2600 BCE
Musical instruments	30,000 BCE
Neanderthals	300,000 BCE
Needle	20,000 BCE
Newspaper (printed)	1590
Nuclear reaction	1942
Numerical controlled machines	1952
Nylon	1934
Oil lamp	250 BCE
Oil tanker (ship)	1872
Organ transplant (kidney/heart)	1953/1967
Oven	40,000 BCE
Pacemaker (external/internal)	1958/1959
Papyrus	3100 BCE
Pap test	1928
Papermaking (China/Europe)	140 BCE/1200 CE
Paperback book	1937
Parachute (demonstrated)	1783
Parchment	250 BCE
Pasteurization	1856
Patent system	1474
Paved roads	150 BCE
Photography (black and white/color)	1835/1907
Photovoltaic cell	1839
Plants (land based)	400 MYA